THE BIBLE AS READ AND PREACHED
IN THE OLD SYNAGOGUE

לא ישא גוי אל גוי חרב
ולא ילמדו עוד מלחמה

"Nation shall not lift up sword
against nation
Neither shall they learn war
any more"

THE BIBLE
AS READ AND PREACHED
IN THE OLD SYNAGOGUE

A STUDY IN THE CYCLES OF THE READINGS FROM
TORAH AND PROPHETS, AS WELL AS FROM PSALMS,
AND IN THE STRUCTURE OF THE MIDRASHIC HOMILIES

BY

JACOB MANN ז״ל M.A., D.Litt. (London)

AND

ISAIAH SONNE ז״ל Ph.D. (Zurich)

VOLUME II

The Palestinian Triennial Cycle:
Leviticus and Numbers to Seder 106

WITH A HEBREW SECTION CONTAINING MANUSCRIPT
MATERIAL OF MIDRASHIM TO THESE BOOKS

THE MANN-SONNE PUBLICATION COMMITTEE
HEBREW UNION COLLEGE - JEWISH INSTITUTE OF RELIGION
CINCINNATI, OHIO, 1966

PRINTED IN THE UNITED STATES OF AMERICA

PRESS OF *Maurice Jacobs*, INC.

1010 ARCH STREET, PHILADELPHIA, PA. 19107

DEDICATED

TO THE SACRED MEMORY OF

Lillie Goldsmith
Charles Goldsmith
Coleman Harris
Rose Fay Krieger
Benjamin Aronowitz

זכרונם לברכה

By

Frieda and Louis Goldsmith

CONTENTS

PROLEGOMENA

SECTION I (Concluded)

THE TRIENNIAL CYCLE

A DETAILED DESCRIPTION OF THE SEDARIM AND THEIR
CORRESPONDING HAFṬAROT AND AN ANALYSIS OF THE
STRUCTURE OF THE PERTINENT MIDRASHIC HOMILIES.

LEVITICUS

NUMBERS

FOREWORD TO VOLUME II

On page 554 of Volume I, The Bible as Read and Preached in The Old Synagogue, Jacob Mann concluded the English section of the Triennial Cycle, with these words:

"Herewith ends the discussion of the Sedarim of Exodus. The investigation of the remainder of TC (Triennial Cycle) to Leviticus, Numbers and Deuteronomy, as well as of the Palestinian readings from Torah and Prophets on special occasions, 'distinguished' Sabbaths and the Festivals, will be the subject of Volume II of this work."

Inscrutable Providence was to interfere with this design in its full dimension. Jacob Mann, in his Preface to Volume I, written Dec. 17, 1939, outlined the majestic scope of his entire scientific study. There were to have been three volumes, the last an historical study. Hopefully, some scholar will arise to do this necessary task.

Isaiah Sonne worked on the rich material that Jacob Mann left behind. Since the Almighty raises one star when another sets, it is our prayerful confidence that with the publication of Volume II, incomplete as it now appears, there will arise a disciple of the wise who will carry forward the dream of Jacob Mann.

It is a source of especial joy to express thanks to all those who shared in this labor of love for the cause of Hebrew letters in bringing this volume to birth:

Solomon B. Freehof, Co-Chairman; Ezra Spicehandler, Secretary; Abraham Cronbach ל״ז, Abba Hillel Silver ל״ז, Louis L. Mann ל״ז, Bernard J. Bamberger, William G. Braude, Frederic A. Doppelt, A. Stanley Dreyfus, Alvin I. Fine, Roland B. Gittelsohn, Nelson Glueck, Richard C. Hertz, Robert I. Kahn, Joseph Klein, Bertram W. Korn, Arthur J. Lelyveld, Julius Mark, Eugene Mihaly, Albert G. Minda, Joseph R. Narot, Levi A. Olan, Ely E. Pilchik, David Polish, Jacob M. Rothschild, Samuel Sandmel, David J. Seligson, Jacob K. Shankman, Daniel Jeremy Silver, Edgar E. Siskin, James A. Wax, Herbert Weiner, Jacob J. Weinstein, David H. Wice. All these distinguished rabbis constituted the Mann-Sonne Publication Committee of Volume II.

We are grateful to countless others: The H.U.C. - J.I.R. Alumni Association; generous rabbis of the Central Conference of American Rabbis, and the Rabbinical Assembly, and friends, whose advance orders and gifts helped.

We record with gratitude the help of THE ALEXANDER KOHUT MEMORIAL FOUNDATION, INC. and Professor SHALOM SPIEGEL, its Secretary. Our gratitude to Dr. Solomon B. Freehof for obtaining this initial grant.

We are under great obligation to THE LUCIUS N. LITTAUER FOUNDATION and its President, HARRY STARR, for indispensable support.

We express thanks to Mr. SIDNEY BRANT, of Cincinnati, for most generous assistance.

We are under great debt to FRIEDA AND LOUIS GOLDSMITH, of Cincinnati, for their princely gift in memory of their parents and uncle to whom this Volume is reverently dedicated.

We thank Mr. JACOB LICHTER for placing this book in twenty-five of the world's leading libraries.

Our debt to MAURICE JACOBS, for his patience and unwearying interest in bringing this manuscript to light.

And to the Klau Library, Hebrew Union College, Cincinnati for giving sanctuary to this manuscript these many years.

It need hardly be said that Margit Mann Sonne, widow of these two tremendous scholars, has shared in the effort to see that these literary remains did not forever lie neglected.

ברוך אתה יי אלהינו מלך העולם שהחינו
וקימנו והגיענו לזמן הזה:

We praise Thee, O Lord our God, King of the Universe, who has kept us alive, sustained us, and permitted us to see this day.

VICTOR E. REICHERT
IN THE CITY OF CINCINNATI
February 1, 1966 — Shebat 11, 5726

JACOB MANN*
1888–1940

By Victor E. Reichert

The death of Jacob Mann on Wednesday evening, October 23, 1940, in his fifty-third year, deprived America of a foremost Jewish savant and the Hebrew Union College of one of the greatest, most original and productive scholars in the history of that famed institution.

Jacob Mann was unquestionably one of the world's most renowned authorities of our time in the field of Jewish history. He salvaged from the Genizah a vast assortment of worm-eaten documents and pieced together dusty and illegible fragments that would have been the despair of a less assiduous researcher. His immense learning was recognized and appreciated in every civilized corner of the earth where Jewish lore is prized and pursued. His name was a passport and open sesame in every great repository of Jewish manuscripts and books, — in the British Museum, London; the Bodleian, Oxford; the Bibliothèque Nationale, Paris; the Library of the Vatican, Rome; the State Public Library, Leningrad; the Hebrew University, Jerusalem; the Library of the Jewish Theological Seminary, New York.

His scholarly range was prodigious and his original contributions to Jewish lore and letters in a vast array of articles, reviews, brochures, essays and enormous books containing hitherto undeciphered and undecipherable Hebrew documents, cover well-nigh every branch of Jewish studies.

R. Mahler, in a warm tribute to "Jacob Mann's Life and Works" in *Yivo Bleter*, the Journal of the Yiddish Scientific Institute, listed no less than sixty separate items from the indefatigable pen of the tireless scholar. (*Yivo Bleter*, Vol. XVI, no. 2, Nov.-Dec., 1940.) This list included five formidable volumes on the Jews in Egypt and in Palestine under the Fatimid Caliphs, I, Oxford, 1920; II, Oxford, 1922; Texts and Studies

* From *The American Jewish Year Book* 5702, New York, The American Jewish Committee, 1941.

in Jewish History and Literature, Vol. I, Cincinnati, 1931; II (Karaitica), Philadelphia, 1935; The Bible as Read and Preached in the Old Synagogue, Cincinnati, 1940; all containing material that had hitherto remained undeciphered in Genizoth or neglected in libraries.

As though that were not enough, Dr. Joshua Bloch, Librarian of the Jewish Division of the New York Public Library, gave an addendum to Jacob Mann's Bibliography in the subsequent issue of the *Yivo Bleter*, (Vol. XVII, No. 1, Jan.-Feb., 1941), adding fourteen more items that had escaped Mahler's eye, — a total of seventy-four. Further bibliographical investigations may show the list of Jacob Mann's contributions still to be incomplete!

The genius of Jacob Mann was not only that of an extra-ordinary scientific imagination that enabled him to piece together and make whole the dusty tattered shreds of a forgotten or neglected yesterday. It was the genius of indefatigable and herculean industry, of infinite painstaking care and patience, of heroic self-effacement and enormous singleness of purpose that made him put aside all frivolity or allurement of pleasure and follow the quest for wisdom and truth. To this martyr-like devotion to the Torah, Jacob Mann brought a spirit that was the embodiment of reverence, piety and humility.

Jacob Mann was an intellectual giant in whom knowledge and faith were completely and beautifully fused. His love of truth for its own sake was reflected in every line he wrote, in the almost naked exactness and freedom from fanciful specula-tion in his meticulously restrained sentences. He frowned upon all glittering generalizations and was impatient of all over-ingenious theorizing. Because he worshipped at the shrine of truth, he hated all sham and pretense. He could not endure the false parade of pompous conceit or vanity. He shunned bluff and hypocrisy as though they were a plague.

Jacob Mann has left us the clue to his own lofty standards of scholarship as well as a hint of the obstacles that stood in the way of the modest, consecrated student of research in these lines penned in the preface to "Texts and Studies in Jewish History and Literature" Vol. I, 1931:

"All these studies," he writes, "based as they are on raw material, which supplements and illumines the already known, will, it is to be hoped, be appreciated by scholars and students who, like the writer, are averse to fanciful theories spun out as a rule from a minimum of available data — a new type of 'making bricks without straw,' or of rearing castles in the air. Only by a cautious and laborious inductive method and by adding constantly to our knowledge of the actual realities of the Jewish past (as against the speculative imaginings of which we have enough and to spare) can we understand this past fully and truly and ultimately hope to obtain the synthesis that every research worker sets before himself as his ultimate goal. The more the material stored up in manuscripts is made accessible in a scientific manner, the better will the history of Jewish life and activities in the course of the past ages be reconstructed anew. With the widening of the horizon new perspectives are revealed and events, movements and personalities are placed in a different setting and proportion.

"As for those, who in their vaunted superiority condescend to look down pityingly on studies of this kind as consisting of dry minutiae culled from dusty and worn out writings and who either cannot or will not accompany in spirit the seeker for truth in his quest for the evidence of the realities of the past wherever it can be discovered — for such persons research studies of this nature are frankly never intended and their inherent lack of appeal is a foregone conclusion. In the true process of research experience has, however, shown over and over again how seemingly small data become missing links in whole chains of evidence which thereby obtain a significance never realized before."

As stupendous as was his learning, so deep was his religious devotion and personal faith. He revered the memory of his sainted father who had been his first teacher of Torah, and he loved to speak in gratitude and affectionate appreciation of Dr. Adolph Büchler, the late principal of Jews' College, to whom he was indebted for first guidance into the scientific method of scholarly research.

Jacob Mann was a modest and retiring scholar, — modest almost to a fault. He was one of the shyest men I have ever known. He shunned the glare and parade of cheap publicity and sedulously avoided all occasions for personal glorification. He never made the Torah a spade with which to dig. He was content to give himself to scholarly investigation so that study became for him a mode of prayer and worship.

Jacob Mann was born in Przemysl, Galicia, on the 26th of August, 1888, of humble parentage so far as worldly goods were concerned. His father, Nisan Mann, was a poor *shohet*. But he gave his son the infinitely more precious heritage of a love of Jewish learning and an intuitive piety and faith. Like his illustrious former kinsman, Solomon Judah Rapoport, whose pioneer work in Jewish history and Geonica he was destined to carry on, Jacob Mann was steeped, in his early boyhood and youth in an atmosphere of Jewish study and worship, uncontaminated by the secular heresies of the outer world.

Coming to England in 1908, from this boyhood, Hasidic home of piety and learning in Galicia, Jacob Mann, an un-prepossessing youth of twenty, prepared himself for the rabbinate at Jews' College while pursuing his secular studies at London University. Those were days of loneliness and of penury, but despite the handicaps of unfamiliarity with the language, strangeness in a strange land, and a natural diffidence and shyness with people, he soon gave evidence of the brilliant scholastic achievements that were to bring him international recognition as one of the foremost Jewish savants of the twentieth century.

In 1913, he passed his B.A. examination at London University with First Class Honors. The following year he qualified for the Jewish Ministry at Jews' College.

Jacob Mann rarely spoke of them and you had to pry it out of him, but somewhere in his study, packed to the ceiling with practically all the important and fundamental books of Judaism, there are M.A. (1915) and D.Litt. (London, 1920) parchments, conferred upon this modest, diffident student for academic achievements of the highest scholastic merit.

The Chief Rabbi of the British Empire, Dr. J. H. Hertz, soon discovered the rare ability of Jacob Mann and employed him as his Hebrew secretary. Dr. Hertz was also helpful in

making possible the publication of two volumes which established Jacob Mann's place in the galaxy of stars who have en-
riched what is known as "the Science (Wissenschaft) of Judaism."
These two tremendously important volumes, based upon hitherto
unexplored Genizah material, ("The Jews in Egypt and in
Palestine Under the Fatimid Caliphs") I, Oxford, 1920; II,
Oxford, 1922; were dedicated to Joseph H. Hertz, the Chief
Rabbi of the British Empire. It is not without interest to record
that Jacob Mann was, during those student days in England,
also the private tutor of Cecil Roth, one of the most able and
brilliant popularizers of Jewish history in the world today.

But even before the publication of "The Jews in Egypt and
in Palestine," the learned world had become aware that a new
genius had arisen to carry forward the scientific investigations
of men like Zunz, Krochmal, Schechter, and especially Solomon
Judah Rapoport. In 1917, the *Jewish Quarterly Review*, n. s.
beginning in Vol. VII and continuing through Vol. XI published
a prize essay that Jacob Mann had written at Jews' College on
the subject of "The Responsa of the Babylonian Geonim as a
Source of Jewish History." Mann explored these sources in a
spirit of broader historical investigation than the clues Rapoport had found in them for his biographical sketches.

"The responsa," Mann wrote, "furnish in particular ample
material for our knowledge of the internal life of the Jews: their
relations to the authorities and to their non-Jewish neighbors,
their economic position, their communal organization, and their
standard of culture and morality. All this material has not yet
been made use of sufficiently; the Jewish history of that period
was rather treated as a collection of biographies of the prominent
spiritual and communal leaders. Important as this aspect of historical treatment is, the life of the people as a whole is of sufficient
importance to be investigated and understood. Therefore the
latter course of historical investigation will be chiefly followed."

In 1920 Jacob Mann came to the United States. He was
engaged as instructor of Bible, Talmud and Jewish History at
Baltimore Hebrew College and Teachers' Training School during
1921–1922. Then he came to the Hebrew Union College to
occupy with distinction the chair of Jewish History which had

been left vacant by the death of Prof. Gotthard Deutsch. He
served the College faithfully, later adding to his duties the field
of Talmud when that place became vacant through the retire-
ment of Prof. Jacob Z. Lauterbach.

In 1927–1928 he was honored by the Hebrew University of
Jerusalem with an invitation to teach as a visiting Professor.
It was during that trip abroad that he gathered much new docu-
mentary material in the Government Public Library at Leningrad, in Cairo and elsewhere, which later flowered in his Texts
and Studies Vol. I and II (1931 and 1935) of new Geonic and
Karaitic investigations.

His few last remaining years were overcast for Jacob Mann
by heartbreaking anguish over the calamitous events affecting
European Jewry. Suddenly and without warning, his heart
gave way. There were long days of pain, lit by the devotion of
his remarkable wife, Margit, and by the presence of his two boys,
Alfred and Daniel. There was a slow, patient pull out of the
valley aided by the indomitable will to finish the great new
investigation on "The Bible as Read and Preached in the Old
Synagogue — a Study in the Cycles of the Readings from Torah
and Prophets, as well as from Psalms, and in the Structure of
the Midrashic Homilies."

Dr. Mann had amassed an enormous amount of new Midrashic material, and had made a discovery, hitherto unknown,
of the role played by the *Haftarot* of the Palestinian Triennial
Cycle in determining the structure and the trend of the Midrashic homilies.

One of the great joys that came to relieve his days at the
hospital and at his home after his first severe heart attack was
the knowledge that some of his students, as a small return for
the priceless boon that had been theirs to sit at his feet, were
raising the funds needed to publish Volume One of this mas-
sive work.

"*Lo aleha ha-m'lachah ligmor*"
"It is not incumbent upon thee to finish the work."

In the midst of these monumental labors on "The Bible as
Read and Preached in the Old Synagogue," Jacob Mann, who

brought glory and fame to the Hebrew Union College, and immeasurably added to its place as one of the world's most distinguished academies of Jewish learning, in the prime of his years, at the age of fifty-two, was fatally stricken. He had taught his class that morning, Wednesday, October 23, 1940. It was the last time that his students would have the visible presence and inspiration of his precise mind, his amazing memory and his deep love for Judaism. By nightfall Jacob Mann breathed his last. Like the patriarch Jacob's departure from Beer-Sheba, his passing took with it something of the glory and splendor that he had brought to Cincinnati and to the Hebrew Union College.

In seeking to find comfort and to measure Jacob Mann's prodigious achievements by some better yardstick than the barren dimension of time, we think of a noteworthy Midrash to the Book Ecclesiastes that is read by observant Jews during the week of Tabernacles in which he died. Recorded there is a beautiful parable spoken by Rabbi Zera upon the death of Rabbi Boon, the brilliant son of Rabbi Hiyya who died in his twenty-eighth year:

There was once a king who possessed a lovely vineyard. He had hired a number of workmen to take care of it for him. Among the laborers, there was a certain man who excelled all the others in his resourcefulness and ability. Seeing this, the king called the talented servant aside and walked about with him chatting for hours. When twilight came and the workmen gathered about for their pay, this laborer stood with the others and received the same reward as did the men who had toiled all the day. When the workmen saw this, they were indignant and complained bitterly, saying: "We worked from dawn till dusk and he only for two hours; and yet his majesty gives him the same reward!"

"Why do you complain?" replied the king. "This man accomplishes in two brief hours what you with all your effort cannot achieve in a whole day."

Al m'komo yovo v'shalom — May Jacob Mann, revered teacher and master, come to his place in peace!

ISAIAH SONNE

1887–1960*

When Isaiah Sonne died in his sleep in the early hours of Sunday, November 27, 1960, he carried away with him a mind amazingly stored with Jewish knowledge that had won him a place of highest eminence in the world of scholarship. Seemingly withdrawn from the world, the record of Isaiah Sonne's seventy-three years will show that he was a brave fighter in the stormy battlefield of life. The flaming sword he unsheathed from his scabbard he wielded with devastating skill because the delicate hand that held it was directed by a mind singularly clear in perception and filled with erudition so comprehensive and accurate in its factual detail as to thrill and delight his admirers and dismay his foes.

Among the papers that were found in his desk, there is a brief "Curriculum Vitae" that modestly sets forth the barest outline of Isaiah Sonne's life before he came to our Cincinnati Hebrew Union College. It reads:

"Schaje (ital. Isaia) Sonne, born on February 26th, 1887, in Mosciska (Galicia). Absolved theological studies in the Italian Rabbinical College (Collegio Rabbinico Italiano) in Florence in 1913. Graduated as Doctor of Philosophy from the Faculty of Philosophy at the University of Zürich, in 1919. Appointed professor of talmud and rabbinical literature at the above mentioned Rabbinical College in Florence in 1925. Appointed in 1936 by the Federation of Jewish Communities in Italy (Unione della Communità Israelitiche Italiane) and with the consent of the Governor of Rhodes (Egeo) Director (Direttore) of the Collegio Rabbinico there, and remained there up to the end of 1938.)"

* From Words spoken by Victor E. Reichert at the Memorial Service, Hebrew Union College Chapel, Cincinnati, Ohio, Wednesday, Jan. 11, 1961, 11:45 A.M.

The memorandum ends here abruptly. But another sheet, bearing the date of Nov. 5, 1947, has these four items that apparently Isaiah Sonne wanted someone to remember:

"1) Fellow of the American Academy for Jewish Research — since 1942.

2) Appointed member of the editorial council of *Jewish Social Studies* — June, 1947.

3) Hebrew paper on "The Walls of the Dura Synagogue" was read at the World Conference on Jewish Studies in Jerusalem — July, 1947.

4) Accepted invitation of the director of the Jewish Museum, New York, to participate in a round-table discussion (January 15, 1948) on the relation between early Christian art and Jewish art of late antiquity. The other participants are: Prof. Carl Kraeling and Dr. Meyer Schapiro."

The sheet ends with the date and the simple typed "I. Sonne." A modest, drab statement for a life that shines resplendent with the light of intellectual genius!

Isaiah Sonne loved Hebrew manuscripts and old books with a tremendous passion. His inner world was the world of ideas and thought of which manuscripts and books were the outward visible evidence of inward spiritual adventure. Isaiah Sonne knew more in accurate precision about Jewish paleography and the Science of Judaism than perhaps any other savant of our time. In this world he was the ardent, dedicated *Matmid*, who delighted literally to wear out his eyes in the loving labor of mastering these hallowed literary monuments of our past. Libraries were his true sanctuary and a light shone about him as he turned the lamp of his remarkably original and creative intelligence on these tattered bits of testimony of the vanished life to which they bore mute but indefeasible evidence.

Isaiah Sonne well knew that Literature is life in ink but that beyond the fleeting fingerprints of the written or printed word, there is a reality larger than any poet or more illusive than any historian can contain. And so, to the astonishingly varied linguistic skills and the immense treasures of learning that he had amassed through a life-time of painstaking study and retentive memory for intricate detail, he brought that rarest of gifts — a poetic imagination and a philosophic depth of insight. Few men of our time had Isaiah Sonne's brilliant powers of bringing together from scattered and unlikely crannies the hard factual data that fortified his new constructions of old, baffling texts or of suggesting illuminating interpretations for new finds, as in the Dura Synagogue murals or the Dead Sea Scrolls. He relished nothing more than tackling some thorny problem, like the controversial Kol Sakhal of Leon de Modena or the enigma of a textually corrupt poem, like Psalm 2.

In the catalogue of our College Library, are more than ninety cards that represent more than fifty pieces from his pen. Some of these studies are monographs of considerable length. This does not include his work, still in manuscript, of Volume 2, of the Genizah finds gathered by Jacob Mann and reconstructed as *The Bible as Read and Preached in the Old Synagogue.* His published writings reveal with astonishing certainty the spacious range of his interests and the amazing ease with which he could deal with Hebrew, Italian, English; Bible, Talmud, liturgy, philosophy, history, responsa, art, music.**

Though he is gone, his smiling presence will always remain in our Library where he worked and in our College whose tradition of high scientific scholarship he helped enrich with his own unique creative mind.

** Dr. Sonne was also much involved in the work of others through his membership on the Board of Editors of the *Hebrew Union College Annual* and *Studies in Bibliography and Booklore.*

Now, at last, Sonne's work on Mann's Genizah finds finally sees the light of publication.

ISAIAH SONNE'S PREFACE TO VOLUME II

Isaiah Sonne left behind, in fragmentary form, on sheets both typed and hand-written, often pencilled with annotations, what he evidently intended to be an Introduction to Jacob Mann's unfinished Volume II. I have tried to put this together as faithfully as possible. Bracketed passages ( ) indicate fuller references. Passages marked * indicate conjectural words added. V.E.R.

The first volume of Dr. Mann's planned monumental work, "The Bible as Read and Preached in The Old Synagogue" has rightly earned general admiration of the learned world. There also has been a consensus of opinion, in substance though not in form, among the few savants in a position to weigh the scientific value of the work. Generous recognition was paid to the Author by the late Prof. Elbogen who termed the work an "Opus Magnificum" and its findings "an inspiration to the scholar." (Cf. J.Q.R. N.S. Vol. XXXI: 1940–1941 — pp. 193–195. Prof. Elbogen is an authority in the field of liturgy, of which Reading of the Torah, etc. is an integral part. Elbogen's fuller comment is:

> "The author has investigated and collected an enormous amount of material for evidence of his thesis. He is a master in finding out in the Midrashim the tallying words of real or possible Haftarot. His findings give inspiration to the scholar, the biblical as well as to the haggadical and the liturgical. One cannot always agree with his theories which sometimes seem too bold — so daring, in fact, as to make the author hesitate (Cf. pp. 135, 145, 174, 440) — but there is no doubt that he establishes his main thesis and presents a new view in his treatment of the use of the Bible in the Synagogue and a new conception of the history of preaching."

But Elbogen did not fail to remark that "it contains theories sometimes too bold to make the author hesitate."

The work wrung qualified approval from a rival scholar in the field of Midrashic studies, Prof. Albeck. "It cannot be denied," he admits, "that there is a shred of truth in such suggestion, namely that the point of departure of many Petiḥot and Yelamdenu questions were the Haftarot." "But," he hastens to add, "we should not generalize and assert that all the Petiḥot are based on the Haftara." Albeck especially finds fault with the method. "Instead of the scientific method which requires that we prove the intrinsic or verbal link of all the given Haftarot with the respective Y and Petiḥot, Mann was often compelled to ignore transmitted Haftarot and to invent new ones which would fit his theory."

Prof. Saul Lieberman, in his equanimity, contrives to express a more balanced judgment. Following the Haftara-pattern of concluding with "consolation", in contrast to Albeck, he starts with the alleged weak spots of the work, by pointing out: a) "Scholars of the past century have already observed that the Y homilies were sometimes based on the H (see Rapoport, Erek Millin, s.v. Aphtara II; Friedmann PR, I, note 1); b) Dr. Mann's conclusions that the Y homilies are always based only on the H are undoubtedly exaggerated. There are many Yelamdenu-homilies where the Y Halakah is much better linked up with the Seder than with the H.

Despite all this, concludes Dr. Lieberman, "it should be recognized that never before has any scholar stressed with such emphasis the close connection between H and Y homilies as did Dr. Mann." He undoubtedly proved that the relationship between H and Y is of a much more intimate nature than that which scholars were inclined to assume. To have proclaimed this relationship and insisted upon it so forcefully is, according to Dr. Lieberman, the great merit of Dr. Mann.

All these authoritative voices, different as they may sound, concur in the affirmative of the important role played by the H in the structure of the homilies. But they also concur in certain limitations and qualification of the dependence of the homily upon the Haftara. These qualifications are termed "too bold theories", "exaggerated conclusions", or bluntly "unscientific generalizations."

It is clear that all these critics have accepted the Author's view that "the most important result of his study was the discovery of the role played by the Haftarot of the Triennial Cycle in determining the structure and the trend of the Midrashic homilies which has hitherto remained unknown." Judged from this angle, I would have no difficulty in agreeing with their qualifications. It is almost unavoidable that the importance of a discovery should assume larger dimensions in the eyes of the discoverer.

But as often happens in a work of such immense scope, the author is the last to grasp the mysterious imponderable which constitutes its real and enduring value. Indeed, Dr. Mann's vision was deflected by his "scientific" bent. A votary of the gravest of scientific procedure, he focused his attention on "the discovery of something hitherto unknown", the ultimate goal of all scientific research.

As a scientific discovery it inevitably assumed a causal character; the H became an indispensable factor, not only in the structure but also its creative principle, the producing of the homily; no negative instances could be admitted. Hence the herculean labor of removing all the apparent considerable number of negative instances, those bold theories to make the author hesitate.

From a strict "scientific" point of view*, measured with a strict "scientific yardstick", the objections of Albeck and Lieberman are justified. The discovery of the H as important factor in the structure development of the homily has been hinted at by Rapoport, though I could not find any reference to the Petihot or the Y in Erek Millin, and especially in the Pesiktas. Nor could the H influence prove to be an indispensable factor in the Petihot and Y. There are enough negative instances that could be produced to stigmatize the principle as "unscientific generalization", rather than a justified induction. Hence Mann's efforts to remove all the negative instances are not always convincing.

We must admit that measured with a strict "scientific" yardstick, the conclusions are rather disappointing. "The discovery" is not entirely new. Rapoport, Zunz, and Friedmann all of them sensed the influence of the H on the homily, although I could not find any references to the Petiḥot and Y's in the earlier studies. We also can hardly consider his demonstration to prove the "discovery"as following the strict "scientific, inductive" method.

The truth of the matter is that while Dr. Mann strove to reach, believed he had sailed towards a new scientific island, he inadvertently landed in the realm of art. The truth of the matter is that this is one of the merits of Dr. Mann, that though a votary of the gravest of scientific procedure, he inadvertently left the realm of science and landed in that of art. Without realizing it, his science is at fault. He does not scientifically explain the origin of the Petiḥot and Yelamdenus, but he rightly conceived the homilies as a complicated artistic composition whose style he analyzes penetratingly. He would be best described* as the Winckelman of the Midrash. And he achieved his most valuable results, not by some new discovery, but rather by the unique gift, the capacity of incorporating and absorbing all that might be retained of the disconnected, and sometimes only vague divinations of the insights of all the scholars who preceeded him, in definite, clearly discernible contours.

It is only in tracing the elements which were absorbed by the Author in the making of his work that enable us to see enormous development. And his work may be best appraised by paraphrasing Hegel's description* of Winckelman's work that "by contemplation of the *ideal*" the work of the ancient homily received a sort of inspiration, through which he opened a new sense for the study of the Midrash.

RAPOPORT AND MANN

There can be no doubt that these two greatest scholars in the field of "Wissenschaft des Judentums", the one ushering in the period, the other closing it, show a great deal of affinity in approach and temper. Their main contribution lies in disclosing hidden *treasures* (*Genizah*) of the Gaonic period, or better, of the dark ages which was made possible by a phenomenal erudition, combined with a special gift of piecing together various bits of seemingly unimportant data into a clear picture, rich, thrilling, mosaic, glittering. This becomes clear when one compares Rapoport's biographies of Kalir, Nathan of Rome, Saadiah Gaon, etc. with Mann's "The Jews in Egypt and in Palestine Under the Faṭimid Caliphs" (Oxford University Press, 1922). The pattern is the same. Mann's scope is of course much vaster, his method immensely refined. A whole century of intense scientific cultivation of this field is well reflected in Mann's work. And yet the affinity, not dependence, is still vividly recognizable.

No less affinity can be discovered in this present* monumental work where again their spheres of interest meet in the Midrashic and Liturgical field.

SEDARIM

Over a century ago (1842) Gabriel Pollack sent out certain questions to various scholars in order to publish their answers in a work* called *Halikot Kedem* (published 1846). Among the questions sent to Rapoport was one* about the division of the Pentateuch into *Sedarim*.

What are these Sedarim? What purpose does this division serve? Rapoport, observing in the Masorah that the number of the Sedarim of the Pentateuch amount to 154 made the startling suggestion that the number corresponds to the number of the Sabbaths which occur in three years. He then combined this finding with the report in the Talmud and later Rabbinic literature* that "in the West" (Palestine) they used to finish the reading of the Pentateuch in *three years.*" Consequently, he concluded, the Sedarim are but the pericopes or *Parshiyot* of those congregations which did not finish the Torah during one year (Annual Cycle), but during three years (Triennial Cycle).

Rapoport has already noted that some of the Sedarim are too short of the minimum 21 verses necessary for the Sabbatical reading, i. e. 3 verses for 7 persons. His answers are too ingenious. He again found a source saying that in "the West they used to split a verse into three." Consequently 7 verses could suffice for the Sabbatical reading of 7 persons each counting for 3. But Rapoport did recognize that the splitting of verses was not the right solution. It could hardly justify the existence of these short Sedarim at the time of the Massorites when the number of the verses was definitely established.

Rapoport therefore suggests another solution for the later period. He found that according to a rule in Tractate Soferim (11.4) it was permissible to *borrow* a certain number of verses from the subsequent Seder. In this way certain verses could be used to supplement the end of one Seder for the necessary 21 verses, and at the same time, these same verses would then form the beginning of the subsequent Seder. This, however, seems also hardly satisfactory because, although one may borrow from the second Seder, it is hardly probable that such borrowing has been fixed as a permanent feature.

A quarter of a century later, around 1870, the Yemenite Genizah was disclosed by the traveller Jacob Saphir who brought to Europe the well-known "Mahaberet Ha-Tigian", in which Rapoport's suggestion was confirmed, and the identification of the Sedarim with the Triennial Cycle scientifically approved and fixed by Derenbourg . . .

This new discovery, however, revealed certain discrepancies in the number of the Sedarim (the last containing 167 instead of 154) as well as the beginning of many Sedarim. The only conclusion to be drawn from such observation was that there existed different local customs with regard to the beginning of certain Sedarim. This, according to A. Epstein, would also explain the difference of number, because the M. ha-T. apparently introduced 13 Sedarim which represent another local custom and are but variants for the same.

This new gained fact, the local existence of different Sedarim lists, provided a new solution for the vexed problem of the Sedarim short of the minimum 21 verses. These, it was argued, are but alternates to the preceding Sedra according to another local custom (Friedmann, Bet Talmud, III), Theodor (1885), Büchler, Albeck (Hiluf Minhagim).

Almost at the same time a new source, or list, of the Triennial

Sedarim was discovered simultaneously by Friedmann, Derenbourg and Theodor, a source which in part has been within
the anticipated guessed focus of Rapoport's intuition, namely
the sections of certain Midrashim which correspond with the
division of the Sedarim. The chapters of certain Midrashim
follow the division of TC. Rapoport worked with numbers.
He only remarked that the number of the chapters of Deut. R.
correspond to the number of the Sedarim in Deuteronomy in the
Masoretic list. A detailed investigation of Lev. R., Num. R.,
and especially the Tanhumas yielded a new complete list of
the Triennial Sedarim, showing some more discrepancies with the
other two lists, another evidence of the existence of various
local lists.

With the studies of Theodor, the function of the Sedarim
TC was firmly established, also the existence of local varieties,
and the vast scope of this cycle made plausible. In order to
make some step further in this field it was necessary to proceed
from the accumulated fact to their order. Whether all these
local differences are simply the center of interest had to be
shifted from the periphery, external reflections of the Sedarim,
to the center, the Sedarim themselves.

And it is exactly here where Mann concentrated his mind.
He rightly refused to be satisfied with the findings that there
were different local customs, knowing that this would mean that
division of the Sedarim followed no principle, and that they
could be altered without any reason but a local caprice. He who
penetrated more than any one into the skill and structure of
this part of the liturgy could not perceive the Sedarim as ar-
bitrary, lacking inner order and purpose. As a work of art, it
should follow some pattern, and could not be simply altered
arbitrarily. There was no short cut, no external help. There
should be certain principles involved which could not always
agree, be harmonized, so that various local practices* followed
various principles until the one prevailed over the other. These
principles could only be extracted from the Sedarim themselves. These principles might even have been followed by
those who fixed the Sedarim without being formulated, without
knowing, being aware whether they are patterns, general pat-

terns governing the whole field of intellectual and artistic activity of the period.

Dr. Mann himself did not enumerate these principles, and rightly so, because he knew very well that there might be*, and surely were, so many other factors involved. He only applied certain principles which are generally recognized in most of the works, literary as well as artistic, of the period.

Besides the topical division, there is a tendency toward symmetry and balance. Balance is the numerical symmetry between two consecutive Sedarim; symmetry, inner symmetry, correspondence of the end of the Seder with the beginning . . . or the end of one Seder as transition to the subsequents. The one is a numerical factor; the other takes more into consideration, the content, the topic. The other principle determining the division is* to avoid, as far as possible, a bad ending or a bad beginning. This principle is taken over from the Haftara where, through the ruling that one can jump from one place to another, the happy ending could be easily achieved. In the Torah, this might have necessitated a Seder to be disproportioned long or short. Here we have a conflict of principles. There was room for two customs, the one following the numerical, external principle; the other the intrinsic.

One other principle is that of repetition. The Sedarim being conceived as topic for instruction, one would avoid the repetition of the same topic at the beginning of the Sedra even if it meant to upset the balance.

How far do we do justice to Mann in considering his theory as a consistent application of a principle first discovered by Rapoport and occasionally uttered by Friedmann? Is it the same principle which consistently applied leads to the same results?

A careful and *respectful* reading and comparison of the two theories will show that the only common element is the Haftara as factor in the development of the homily, but its real function is entirely different, yes to a certain extent, running in opposite directions. It will become clear when we quote Rapoport (Erek Millin, pp. 167 ff. s. v. *Aftara*):

"It seems to me," says Rapoport, speaking of the ספרי

אפטרתא "that 'aftarta books' contained also the *Targum*, Aramaic translation of the Haftarot . . . with additions of *aggadoth* and homilies," Aramaic version of the Prophetic portion. Speaking about the reason for the introduction of the Haftara, Rapoport continues, "The main reason was because they, the heads . . ., wanted to honor also the prophetic books on the Sabbath. The reading from them after the reading of the Torah was a kind of admonition, ethical instruction, exhortation-edification, for the people . . . They, the readers, searched in the prophetic writings for* a section related to the Torah portion of the day. This prophetic section was translated and commented upon profusely, and this comment constituted already a kind of homily." (p. 168)

The origin of the "Derashah" therefore is to be found in the *Targum*, Palestinian Targum or Targum on the Prophets. And Rapoport gathered his material from the Targum to prove his theory. (Zunz, 79) Envisaged by Zunz and rejected. This is still the case with regard to the Pesikta, containing mostly a comment on the Haftara of certain Sabbaths (#5).

How could this theory be applied to Midrashim, Y, R, T.? There is hardly any comment on the H. in these Midrashim. Their point of departure is usually taken from Hagiographa. By a very ingenious combination, Rapoport was able to *invent* the reading of Haftarot taken from Hagiographa at the *Minḥah* service on Sabbath. The Midrashim grew up as a result. They* are the *Targum* profused comments on these Haftarot. The *Haftara* factor is therefore considered as a natural outgrowth of the explanation, from which the homily gradually freed it.

What Rapoport was looking for was the *origin*, the beginning of the homily which was nothing else but an expanded explanation or translation of the Haftara. This factor was rather an external one which tended to disappear in the more developed homilies. It was not an immanent-formative principle that could be laid bare by a minute analysis of the well developed homily.

In other words, the Haftara served Rapoport to lead us back to the first stage of the homily, but not to reveal the structure of the homily in its highest degree of development. And this for the simple reason that there was no such structure.

Of the same character is the other quotation by Lieberman, that of Friedmann. Friedmann's merit on the exploration of the midrashic world is well known, and commands our admiration, but his remark has nothing to do with Dr. Mann's theory. That a great deal of the Pesikta are so-called "Midrash Aftarot", based on the Haftarot, or better contain an homiletical comment on the Haftarot of certain special Sabbaths has been pointed out by all scholars, beginning with Zunz, Buber . . . But again this is what Rapoport proposed was the case with all the other Midrashim. The Petiḥot, mostly from the Hagiographa, were the real Haftarot, and in connection with the explanation of the H. verse. All the Haftara did was to supply, so to speak, the material, or the starting point. This done, it disappeared, and only rarely some verse of it was used.

All this has been done simply by concentrating on the surface of the Midrash, but there is not the slightest attempt even to penetrate the inner structure. I should say the organic structure, and this for the simple reason that no such structure was ever thought of as existing in the old homily. Conceived as so many different comments on certain verses, no unity of purpose, nor unity of thought, nor any structural unity was considered possible.

Modern Midrash studies, beginning with Zunz, did pay attention to the structure, but mostly to the structure of the single elements.

Of these, the *Yelamdenu* element has especially attracted the attention of scholars, because by its very nature and strangeness to the main substance of the homily, it reveals that we have to do with a mere ornament artificiality, and as such has to be studied as a rhetoric form . . .

The second element is the *Petiḥot* which to a certain extent occupies the same place as the *Yelamdenu*, the starting point of the homily. The difference is that its artificiality at first sight is not as manifest as that of the *Yelamdenu*.

The third element which can be considered as a corollary to the second was the peroration, the conclusion. Inasmuch as the two last elements form the beginning and the end of the homily, they were considered as forming the frame, but only the external frame of the homily. No attempt was made to penetrate the inner structure of the homily as a whole, for the simple reason that no such structure was conceived extant at all. The general view predominant was that the Jewish homily, while containing a wealth of gems, lacks unity of purpose, unity of ideas, unity of intention . . . and so forth.

A step towards a more intrinsic investigation of the midrashic structure marks Bacher's study on the Petiḥa. While he still devotes most of his study to the external form, the various formulae, the appearance in the various Midrashim; the various authors of Petiḥas and their like, he clearly formulated the principle of the Petiḥa. The underlying idea was to stress the unity of the three parts of Scripture: that there is nothing in the Prophets and the Hagiographa that could not be found in the Pentateuch, that all three parts are but one and the same expressed in various forms, various modes of the same substance. This is a unifying principle which links the Torah reading, the Haftara (Prophetic reading) and the homily, beginning with a verse from Hagiographa, together. This principle, however, though clearly formulated, was not, and could not have been, shown in action, systematically, consistently, without a thorough study of the Sedarim, their respective *Haftaroth*, a study which was made possible by certain fragments of Haftarah lists. (Büchler, Abrahams) (* Genizah list of Triennial Cycle Hafṭarot published by Dr. A. Büchler, JQR, VI, 39–42. For Mann's comments on material gathered by Dr. Israel Abrahams, cf. Prolegomena, pp. 17–18 under III. *Taylor-Schechter Collection*, etc.)

This principle, so clearly defined by Bacher, remained a mere external frame as long as no principle of, no pattern of this unity, no scheme of unity was excogitated other than that one verse should be explainer or put in relation to another, insisting, as does Bacher on the absolute free play of the preacher's fancy. The various elements of the homily became pearls, without a string to hold them together. It was not considered necessary to search for a unity of plan, unity of composition, in the homily. (HUCA, Vol. XX — 1947 The Plan of the Dura Synagogue, 261 ff.)

It was only when some modern scholars became aware of the relationship between the Greek *diatribe* and midrashic homily that more attention was paid the homily as a literary work and consequently to its style. (A. Marmorstein, Th ackground of the Haggadah, HUCA, Vol. IV — 1929, 183   , its external form. "The Haggadah has a style of its own, worth studying. The preachers developed a homiletical style which is not much behind that of the masters of oratory in Latin and Greek. M. finds many rhetorical forms of the diatribe, like dialogue, etc. used by the homilists."

This, in itself, does not tackle the problem of the structure of the Midrash as a whole, its unity of composition, of plan. But in stressing the importance of the style and its similarity with diatribe, he made it clear that we have to do with an artistic work which cannot be considered as something capricious, haphazard, but as something following certain literary style, and consequently must have some kind of unity of plan and composition.

Parting from the same point, namely, the comparison with diatribe, led Menahem Stein somewhat nearer the main question: the structural unity of the sermon. Dealing with the peroration, mainly with the various forms, parallel to the peroration in the diatribe, Stein tackles also the question of the connection of the peroration with the main topic or the beginning of the homily. (HUCA, *VIII–IX (1931–32)

(* Cf. Vol. I, p. 14 — Prolegomena — J. Mann's comment in note 21: "The study of Stein on "Die Homiletische Peroratio im Midrasch" (HUCA, VIII–IX (1931–32), 353 ff.) again is defective on account of not realizing the dependence of the peroration on the H, as pointed out in the body of this work in connection with each item.)

SUPPLEMENTARY NOTES

Isaiah Sonne here elaborates on his earlier remarks. Some
of this is repetitious. But there is much that is new. I have
therefore decided to add it as a postscript to Sonne's Preface.

V.E.R.

Much more charitable is the judgment of Prof. Saul Lieberman, the other recognized authority in the field of Talmud and
Midrash.

In קובץ מדעי, in memory of Moses Schorr, 1945, pp. 183 ff.
תנא היכא קאי, especially pp. 186–188:

"Already the students (scholars) of the past generation said
that the Yelamdenu homilies were sometimes based on the
H of a given S. Rapoport אפטרהא II, Friedmann, beg. of PR.
note 1.) Five years ago J. Mann published a long study on this
subject, and concluded that the Y. homilies are always based
only on the H and not on the S itself.

"There is no doubt that Mann exaggerated in his conclusion.
So, for instance, when he makes an effort to find a connection
between the Y homily on circumcision and the H of S (Gen. 17)
p. 126. There is no need for any effort of this kind. The homily
is simply connected with the topic of the S and not with H.
Similarly there is no need for a link with the H in Gen. 39:7
(p. 305).

"The Y is well connected with the S. There are many more
Y homilies where the Y hal. is linked up with the S much better
than with the H. Nevertheless, and despite this, never had
anyone stressed the great affinity and the close connection which
runs between the homily and the Haftara as did Mann. The
relation between the Haftara and the homily is much greater
than the scholars ever surmised, and great is the merit of Mann
to have proved, stressed and proclaimed this relationship."

This statement from a scholar who could not be suspected
of being especially biased in favor of Dr. Mann is the best

proof* if any is needed of the great value of this work. And in my opinion, it is also the best objective evaluation of the work, for the reader, the most competent; although the real cannot be apprehended other than by trying to associate oneself and share the work. This I was compelled to do when charged with the edition of the unfinished second volume. Only then I could catch a glimpse of the enormous research labor in those little, seemingly unimportant notes and remarks, those subtle connections, gigantic of particulars to find his way in the labyrinth of Midrashim. One can appreciate all this, but at the same time one can understand and forgive some of the unavoidable exaggerations and tour de force in order to achieve absolute uniformity, to find the theory substantiated without any exception. It is human and sometimes even necessary to resist common sense.

However, Lieberman, as well as most of the scholars who are less charitable, less generous in their appraisal of Mann's work, (for instance, Albeck) did not quite realize the real contribution of Mann's work and I doubt whether Mann himself had a clear idea of the real and enduring work he was performing. The connection between the H and the homilies has been quite persistently stressed by Rapoport, as rightly pointed out by Lieberman, and it would be surprising* if Mann's should be nothing else but a revival of Rapoport's theory. The fact is that in some respect, Mann's theory is directed against Rapoport.

Indeed, according to Rapoport and Friedmann, the homilies developed as a natural explanation of the Haftara. They found such homilies in Targum Yonathan on the Prophets . . .

It is quite clear that in this case we should find in the homilies much more than simple allusions to the H, but should center on the H. Rapoport was compelled to assert that the Petiḥa homilies, which mostly have as starting point a verse in the Hagiographa, developed out of alleged readings of the Hagiographa at *Minḥa* prayer.

Albeck, who similarly seems to see in Mann's work only the special stress of connection between H and Yelamdenu, remarks:

"We cannot understand why, according to this theory, the

preacher should have contented himself with a mere allusion to the H, some verse of H, and did not insert them expressly into the homily, just as he connected the H with the Pet. Y in the Pes. Rabbati. Sometimes he did insert verses of the H into the Pet., so for instance, GR 24:1; 48:6."

It is in opposition to this concept of the homilies as mere exposition, aggadic exposition of the Haftara without any form* that Mann asserts that the homily has nothing to do with the exposition or explanation of the H, but is a *very* complicated artistic composition in which a theme is developed within a well defined frame, in which frame the Haftara plays the most important role.

In other words, the H does not determine the *theme* of the homily, does not penetrate the fabric of the homily. It is only the mainstay of, the center of gravitation of the external frame, the structure of the homily ... And in order to be able to accomplish this central function, ... it had to be separated from its content and used as cement welding together the various elements by artificial joints.

Here again, it would be idle to pretend as if Mann invented (discovered) something entirely new. Already the Old Master Zunz has pointed out the complicated, artistic structure of certain types of homilies (Chap. 20) especially the Y type; but no attempt has been made to *lay open*, trace a design of the supporting pillars and traves, giving consistency to the external frame of the homily. And not only this, but to discover the various elements in each of the homilies.

But in doing so, Mann ... with his scientific training and an eye always on the particular, failed to realize that his greatest achievement in this field is not a *scientific explanation* of the connection of the particular Y Pet. with H, but in recognizing and penetrating into the design* of the structure or into the secret* which makes up the style of the homilies.

But no historian of art would ever dream to find all the truth*, even the essential ones, of a certain style, in all the *structures* belonging to a certain style. They may try to explain why these deviations occur,* but are not bound to assert absolute uniformity. Had Mann realized that what he really did was to open our eyes to see the *style*, the components of this style which are quite visible in most of the homilies, he would not have been at pains in *explaining* at any cost or eliminating all the homilies which he could not "explain". True, sometimes Mann, almost unaware, admitted the preacher seems to have been unable to build* the more complicated structure, and therefore a simpler one, an easier one was chosen. (He might have purposely rejected the other style.)

But on the whole, Mann was too much of a scientific mind, thinking rather in terms of explanation than in terms of artistic insight. This he accomplished despite his scientific temper which might have dissuaded him from persisting in his effort to set the H as the central pillar carrying the weight of the entire structure.

Prof. Albeck's objection that he did not proceed scientifically to explain first all the single instances before jumping to conclusions is only a tribute* to Mann's vision that it was not entirely obfuscated by the insistent scientific demand. His creative imagination could not be suppressed by the mass of scientific explanation. He did not fail to see the forest for the trees.

In this he was most influenced* by Büchler who, dealing with the H, stressed likewise the artificial structure, or connection between the H and the S. According to Büchler, originally the H was connected with the S by a common topic. The topic determined the H. Later on, because of the great number of the Sedarim, the topic gave way to a more artificial, external method of linking H with S.

Transferring this principle to the Midrashim and stressing here the importance of the verbal link so much successfully employed by Büchler, Mann succeeded in laying open the necronature of the homily, its structure.

It may sometime sound fantastic, incredible, but who ever had occasion to deal with the early liturgical poetry, the Ḳerobah, which is, as is now thanks to the indefatigable labors of Dr. Zulay become known in all its complicated forms, and which is now generally recognized as the substitute for the homily, or better, the direct child of the homily, of the Y type — he will find the links of Mann natural, especially taking into consideration the later development of Kalir. They are completely justified whenever Mann used them to explain the links of a given H.

If we have to complain against the method, it is that Mann sometimes did not go far enough in detecting hidden links and led him to substitute new H's for those which are recorded. In this elasticity of linkage, as Mann calls it, it is, of course, difficult to define certain fixed types. However, there is one thing which might have saved Mann all his ingenuity in order to find some unrecorded H which could explain all the Pet. of a certainty*, and might instead have shown him that the recorded H can well be taken care of by a certain technique I found often employed in medieval poetry. It consists in a simple procedure*.

Scholars of medieval poetry are well acquainted with the realization* that the first thing to do in order to understand such poetry consists in the uncovering* of all the allusions to the Bible, sometimes also to post Biblical literature*. Indeed the references are the indispensable illumination* to any commentary on such poetry. However it is not generally known that the mere reference to the verse alluded to in the composition* not always is sufficient to give us a complete understanding of the passage.

It is often necessary to explore the context of the whole chapter, or a greater part of it, or the whole area, and only then the whole thing makes good sense.

I used to call the area as the magnetic field attracting the imagination of the poet. The single expression or word does not have to be placed in the very center of this area. It may also be, and often is, on the periphery. Whenever we are confronted with an H which seems entirely alien, unrelated to S, we should extend our exploration beyond the limits of the H proper and search* the adjacent area which may give us the clue to it. . . .

The other thing we should not forget is that the S was never supplanted by the H. The ideal type of a Pet. was a common link with S as well as with H, and possibly the same link which connected H with S was to serve also as a link with the Pet. as well as with the Y Hal. That all this was the ideal type but not always realizable does not diminish* its meaning as point of departure, as a goal to personify the perfect unity of the three parts of Scripture, as an indissoluble unity. Of course, the most urgent need for such proclamation was felt with regard to the Prophets who were sometimes thought* of* as opposed to the Pentateuch, the Law. On the other hand, the Hagiographa in themselves represented already a welding of the Pentateuch with the Prophets, with the latter prevalent.

All this complicated process must have given way to a number of variations in the structure of the homily, leaning mainly on S or on H. — (Lieberman) —

Our task will be to stress the weight of the S which was neglected by Mann, concentrating his investigation on the H. We frankly admit that we had no intention nor the time to do a thorough study to supplement that of Mann. We only did this in case Mann felt compelled to assume a different H from the one recorded. For such cases we were trying to see whether the two mentioned instruments could not guide us into the Midrashic structure retaining the recorded H. And even in those cases, we did not try to explain all the details, but rather to indicate how to work with the instruments.

The last point: *Dura Europas. Yannai*

The links to be looked for in the first place in the first two, mostly also third verse of S and first verse of H.

While we are inclined to extend links, material links, beyond the limits of the H proper and take into consideration the whole area, we would limit the verbal links to the first two, including occasionally also the third verse of S and the first, perhaps also the last, verse of H to lay bare the traves supporting that structure.

The motive that found its expression in art and its structure has many similar features with the Midrashic as outlined by Mann. It is of course not scientifically proven and it does not pretend to be a scientific structure, but one which one who has eyes for architecture may apprehend.

LIST OF ABBREVIATIONS

(Exclusive of those usual for Biblical books, tractates of Talmud
and Periodicals.)

A = Adler Collection of Manuscripts at the Library of the
Jewish Theological Seminary, New York, followed by the
number of the respective manuscript.

AB = *Agadath Bereshith* (אגדה מדרש תכיל ,ת י ש א ר ב ת ד ג א
על ספר בראשית, בתחלה פרשת תורה, ואח"כ פרשת נביאים, ואח"כ
פרשת כתובים), ed. Buber, Cracow 1902.

AC = Annual Cycle of readings from Torah and Prophets.

'Adat Deborim (עדת דבורים), by Joseph of Constantinople
(12th century), Massoretic and grammatical work (Ms.
Leningrad); see the description by Harkavy, חדשים גם ישנים,
No. 2, pp. 11–13.

Agg. = Aggadah.

B = Genizah list of Triennial Cycle Haftarot (Bodl. 2727³),
published by Dr. A. Büchler, *JQR*, VI, 39–42. Each item
is indicated by B followed by the respective page of in
JQR (see infra, p. 17).

Bar. = Baraita.

BHM = Bet Ha-Midrasch (בית המדרש), ed. Jellinek, 6 parts.

Bodl. = Genizah fragments at the Bodleian, Oxford, cited
according the numbers in Neubauer-Cowley, *Catalogue
of the Hebrew Manuscripts in the Bodleian Library*, Vol. II,
1906.

Buber, מבוא = Introduction to his edition of Midrash Tanḥuma
(see TB).

c., ch. = Chapter.

C = Lists of Triennial Cycle Haftarot in T.-S. Collection at
University Library, Cambridge (see infra, p. 17–18).

CL = Cambridge Library Collection, ibidem (ditto).

DR = Deuteronomy Rabba (cited according to Romm ed. of
מדרש רבא, Wilna).

ER = Exodus Rabba (ditto).

FS = Festskrift Simonsen, Copenhagen 1923 (see infra, p. 18)

Ginsburg, *Introd.* or *Introduction* = Chr. D. Ginsburg, *Intro-duction to the Massoretico-Critical Edition of the Hebrew Bible*, London, 1897.

GR = Genesis Rabba (cited according to ed. Theodor-Albeck, Berlin, 1912–1929).

GS = *Genizah Studies in Memory of Doctor Solomon Schechter.* (גנזי שעכטער), Vol. I: Midrash and Haggadah, by Louis Ginzberg, New York, 1928; Vol. III: Liturgical and Secular Poetry, by Israel Davidson, New York, 1928.

H = Hafṭarah.

H. pt. = Hebrew part.

HV = Haupt Volume, viz. *Paul Haupt Festschrift*, Leipzig, 1926 (see infra, p. 18).

J. T. S. = Jewish Theological Seminary Library.

JTS Ms. = Midrash Manuscript at Jewish Theological Seminary Library (edited infra, Hebrew part, p. 149 ff.).

Kahle, *M. d. W.* = R. Kahle, *Masoreten des Westens*, I, Stutt-gart 1927; II, 1930.

LR = Leviticus Rabba.

LT = המכונה פסיקתא זוטרתא ל ק ח ט ו ב, by R. Tobias b. Eliezer.

M. = Mishnah.

Mekh. = Mekhilta.

MHG = Midrash Ha-Gadol (מדרש הגדול), I, to Genesis, ed. Schechter, Cambridge 1902; II, to Exodus (up to the end of יתרו פ'), ed. Hoffmann, Berlin 1913–1921, for the remain-der a manuscript belonging to the Jew. Theolog. Semin. Library has been used; III, to Leviticus, ed. Rabinowitz, New York, 1932; IV, to Numbers, and V, to Deuteronomy, manuscripts in the above-mentioned library.

Midr. = Midrash.

Midr. Agg. = מדרש אגדה על חמשה חומשי תורה, ed. Buber, Vienna 1894.

Midr. Yel. = מדרש ילמדנו.

MY = מחזור יניי (see infra, p. 18–19).

NR = Numbers Rabba.

Pet. = Petiḥta (פתיחתא).

PR = Pesiḵta Rabbati (מדרש פסיקתא רבתי), ed. Friedmann, Vienna 1880.

PRE = Pirḵē R. Eli'ezer.

PRK = פסיקתא דרב כהנא, ed. Buber, Lyck 1868.

S = Seder of Triennial Cycle.

SH = Sheeltot of R. Aḥa of Shabḥa.

SHL = L. Grünhut, *Sefer Ha-Likkutim* (קובץ ,ספר הלקוטים מדרשים ישנים ומאמרים שונים), 6 parts.

T = Tanḥuma, ordinary version of מדרש תנחומא, cited according to Sidra of the week followed by the respective paragraph.

Tanh. = Tanḥuma.

TB = the version of מדרש תנחומא, edited by Buber, cited in same manner as T.

TC = Triennial Cycle.

Tos. = Tosephta.

v. = verse.

Y = ילמדנו.

Yel. = ditto.

Yer. = Yerushalmi.

YHM = ילקוט המכירי, by R. Makhir b. Abba Mari.

YSH = ילקוט שמעוני.

YTT = ילקוט תלמוד תורה (see infra, Hebrew part, p. 270 ff.).

Zulay's List = the indications of the Triennial Cycle Hafṭarot, found in the Piyyuṭim of Yannai, as listed by M. Zulay, מחקרי יניי (see infra, p. 18).

אהבת ציון וירושלים = אהצ"ו, by B. Ratner.

דקדוקי סופרים = ד"ס, Variae Lectiones, by R. Rabbinovicz.

Inc. = incomplete — projected by Mann but did not live to complete.

Unv. = Unverifiable. The Editors could not find the reference.

The Frontispiece Facsimile reproduced is from the Cambridge Library, England, The Taylor-Schechter Genizah. It is identified as T-S. Box C I (8).

THE BIBLE AS READ AND PREACHED
IN THE OLD SYNAGOGUE

PROLEGOMENA

The discussion here is intended to indicate in a preliminary manner the problems involved and the procedure pursued in their treatment. Only after the progressive attention to all the available data, many of which are presented here for the first time, will the subsequent summary enable us to reach back more safely into the obscure field of origin and evolution.

1. SCOPE OF INQUIRY

The reading from Torah and Prophets, forming a notable part of the services on Sabbaths and Festivals as well as on certain other occasions, was a significant and unique institution of the Synagogue. It provided, together with the accompanying sermons, continuous and sustained adult education in Judaism year in and year out. The young were taught and prepared to partake of this instruction as future members of the congregations.[1] The origin of this institution is shrouded

---

[1] Cp. M. Sabb. 1.3: באמת אמרו החזן רואה היכן תינוקות קוראים, אבל הוא לא יקרא.
From the remark of R. Simon b. Gamliel it is evident that the school children were preparing (or revising) on Sabbath eve the passages to be read from the Torah on the following morning (Babli 13a, top): רשב"ג אומר תינוקות של בית רבן מסדרין פרשיותיהן לאור הנר, according to the reading of Ms. Munich, ד"ס, p. 20; in Tos. 1.12, ed. Zuckermandel, p. 110, for: תינוקות ור ב מתקנין read also תינוקות של בית רבן וכו' פרשיותיהן לילי שבת לאור הנר; cp. also Yer. 3b, bottom: תני רשב"ג אומר התינוקות מתקנין להן ראשי פסוקיהן לאור הנר, and the correct comment in תני, בתוספתא שם רשב"ג אומר מתקנין פרשיותיהן לאור הנר, מכינין: פני משה לידע מקום הפרשה שיקראו למחר. In the Yer. wording ראשי פסוקיהן does not mean the beginnings of the verses (as Bacher, *Terminologie*, II, 160, note 3, seems to assume, and likewise Blau, *JQR*, IX, 129), but "of the *sections*" (cp. פְּסָקָא), divisions, within the portion read from the Torah. Thus Yer. remarks immediately before: מהו מתקן? ראשי פרקים, פסקין (in ed. Venice: פוסקין), showing that פסקין or פסוקין are the equivalent of פרקים; by the latter term are meant here the groups of verses recited in order from the Scroll by the people called upon to do so (cp. also M. Ber. 2.2 where the sections of Shema' are indicated by פרקים). Accordingly, פסוקין in Yer. is the same as פרשיות in Babli and Tos., and the procedure of supervising the school children on the part of the synagogue attendant (החזן) was to indicate to them the beginnings of the sections comprising the Torah lection for the following morning (ראשי פסוקין [ראשי] פרשיות = פרקים) and letting them read these by themselves without further aid so as not to become engrossed in reading himself and be led unwittingly to trim the wick of the lamp or candle.

3

in obscurity owing to its very antiquity. Attempts to connect it with the struggle against the Samaritans[2] do not seem to me to be well-founded. Altogether the "anti"-motive has been carried too far. Thus Leszynsky[3] would make the regular Torah readings on the Sabbaths to have been directed against the spread of Hellenism among the Jews. And Venetianer[4] has endeavored to find in the choice of the Hafṭarot polemical or apologetical tendencies against Christianity! Rather the positive aim and need of familiarizing the ordinary Jew on the leisure days of the Jewish calendar with a knowledge of his religion and tradition should be regarded as the main *raison d'être* of this institution. But this problem will be dealt with fully in vol. III of this work. We have first to examine inductively and comprehensively this feature of the synagogue service, its technique and its concomitants, and then draw conclusions as to its beginnings and development. Only in this manner are we likely to avoid the pitfalls inherent in haphazard theorizings.

It is well established that there was in vogue in Palestine a Triennial Cycle (= TC) of the Torah readings. There is no need to enter here into a detailed refutation of the arguments of Finfer, in his learned but diffuse and unsystematic work,[5] against the prevalence of TC in the Holy Land regarding the whole arrangement of the Sedarim as late and unofficial.[6]

---

[2] Thus Dr. Büchler, *JQR*, V, 424: "It seems to me that it was the Samaritans who gave the occasion for the first step", etc. Cp. also Elbogen, *Jüd. Gottesdienst*[2], 157, bottom, though hesitatingly: "Wenn es richtig ist, dass die ersten nach ihrem Inhalte festgelegten Vorlesungen u. Erläuterungen der Bibel infolge der abweichenden Auslegung der Festesvorschriften durch die *Samaritaner* eingeführt wurden", etc.

[3] *Die Sadduzäer*, Berlin 1912, 133 ff. Cp. also against him Elbogen, *l. c.*, 539.

[4] "Ursprung u. Bedeutung der Propheten-Lektionen" (reprint from *Z. D. M. G.*, LXIII, 1909), p. 8: "Das Ergebnis der Untersuchung wird ... auch zeigen, dass die Propheten-Lektionen den Mittelpunkt der Polemik gegen das im Entstehen begriffene Christentum gebildet haben".

[5] מסורת התורה והנביאים. Wilna 1906, pp. 39–45.

[6] Cp. his sharp remarks, p. 43, bottom: עלובה העיסה המבישה את הלש והאופה
... ובצדק נקראו (היינו: הסדרים) בלשון זכרים, כלשון המקרא צלמות ולא סדרים, אין לו
יחס במקרא ולא נזכר בקדמונים, ולדעתי הוא מעשה יחיד, הדיוט מאחד בעם וכו'.

Gaster has followed suit in a long-winded article on "the Biblical Lessons."[7] Our whole study in the structure of TC and in the Midrashic homilies based on it furnishes running evidence for the actual employment of this Cycle in the Pal. synagogue during the Talmudic period. Already R. Eli'ezer b. Hyrcanus at the beginning of his career as a brilliant student of R. Yoḥanan b. Zakkai in Jerusalem, several years before 70 C. E., preached on a theme connected with a TC Seder and its corresponding Hafṭarah (see Vol. I, p. 105). There is further evidence that R. Gamliel of Yabneh and his colleagues, who accompanied him on his mission to Rome in the fall of 95, preached there on a Sabbath when another such Seder and respective Hafṭarah were recited (Vol. I, p. 472–3). The crux of the difficulty raised against TC is the Bar. in Meg. 31b: תניא רשב"א אומר עזרא תיקן להן לישראל שיהו קורין קללות שבתו"כ קודם עצרת ושבמשנה תורה קודם ר"ה which supposed arrangement was only possible according to the Annual Cycle (=AC) as prevalent in Babylon and later on adopted all over the Diaspora.[8] But this Bar. occurs only in Babli and there is serious doubt whether it was ever regarded as authentic in Palestine (more will be said infra, vol. III). (Inc.)

Owing to the hegemony of the Babylonian Gaonate over the Jewries of the Diaspora, the Pal. ritual was discarded in preference to the Babyl. one, and consequently TC was ousted by AC, except in a few localities such as Fusṭāṭ where the former was adhered to in the local Pal. synagogue still in the 13th century.[9] The full significance of TC and its development were thus only dimly known. The Massorites have preserved bare lists of the Sedarim of the Pentateuch which, with all their variants, constituted already the final stage of the process

[7] *Jewish Review*, London 1912–13 = *Studies and Texts*, I, 503 ff.

[8] Cp. R. Z. H. Chajes in his Novellae, *a. l.*: לפי זה לא ידעתי לבני מערבא דמסקי אורייתא בתלת שנין, עיין לעיל כ"ט ע"ב, איך היו עושים בתקנת עזרא זאת שתבוא קריאת הקללות קודם עצרת בכל שנה. See also Rapoport in Polak's קדם הליכות, p. 13. The different interpretation of the Bar. by Friedmann, *Bēt Talmud*, III, 105, is rather forced.

[9] Cp. Mann, *Jews in Egypt*, I, 221–22, II, 378–79; *Texts and Studies*, I, 416–17.

of fixation of this Cycle. The Midrashic literature reveals the existence of many different Sedarim, showing that numerous shiftings have taken place.

That the main Midrashim to the Pent., such as the Rabbot and the Tanḥuma versions, were based on TC is a highly creditable result of Theodor's research.[10] But he only realized the external aspect of the matter, viz. that the Midrashic sections were arranged according to the Pal. Sedarim and not according to the Babyl. Sidras as in their present printed form. The internal and essential structure of these sections, viz. their dependence not only on the Sedarim of TC *but also on the respective Haftarot to the latter*, has hitherto remained obscure (see infra, sub 3).

What Prophetic lections there were in the Pal. ritual has become known only since the discovery of the Fusṭāṭ Genizah. Dr. Büchler was the first to utilize some of this Genizah material in his essay on "The Reading of the Law and the Prophets in a Triennial Cycle."[11] But he brilliantly became involved in an untenable theory of TC having started in Nisan, and not in Tishri, which theory resulted in equally unwarranted corollaries as to the origin and the evolution of the whole institution and its features. He, too, was unaware of the role played by the TC Haftarot in determining the structure and the trend of the Midrashic homilies. Now considerable additional material is available in the form of such lists of TC Haftarot (see infra, sub 4). Moreover, there is further the evidence for the latter in the indications contained in the Ḳerobot of Yannai which he composed for the Sabbaths according to this Cycle (Maḥzor Yannai = MY, see ibid.). Yannai lived before the Muhammedan conquest of Palestine, as can now be definitely stated, since his Piyyuṭim contain no reference whatever to Islām and its dominion over the Holy Land whereas there are numerous allusions

---

[10] "Die Midraschim zum Pentateuch u. der dreijährige pal. Cyclus" (*M. G. W. J.*, vols. 34–36, 1885–87).

[11] *JQR*, V, 420–68, VI, 1–73. The article of Joseph Jacobs in *J. E.*, XII, 254–57, is very inadequate, and especially misleading is the diagram there of TC Readings.

therein to Edom-Rome and Christianity (as rightly pointed out by M. Zulay, *Piyyute Yannai*, 1938, Introd., p. xvii). The Pal. Minhag obtaining in the period of this early Paiṭan (say at the end of the 6th century or the beginning of the 7th) corresponds on the whole to that evident from the Genizah lists, with regard to the identity of both the Sedarim and their respective Hafṭarot. However, just as in the case of the former the Midrashic literature reveals the existence of different commencements of the Torah lections, which go back to earlier times, so in the case of the latter the same literature presupposes many other Prophetical readings going back to times prior to the final fixing of TC. This latter discovery forms the crux of the novel investigation pursued here into the structure and the technique of the sermons that accompanied the readings from Torah and Prophets — an approach never yet attempted because of the very unawareness of *the whole underlying sermonic technique of drawing upon the Hafṭarah as the background of the homilies.* This technique applies to the Petiḥtot as well as to the items beginning with Halakhic themes, the so-called Yelammedenu (= Y) homilies. And the same is the case with the perorations forming the conclusions of certain Midrashic sections to the respective Sedarim (see infra, sub 3). The investigation has ultimately an important bearing on determining the respective age of the Midrashim. Thus, e. g., the Y homilies, so frequently assumed by scholars to have been a late innovation, often turn out upon close examination to be based on Hafṭarot older than those indicated by Yannai, who reflected the Pal. Minhag of his time, and by the compilers of the Genizah lists who may be regarded to have had in mind the practice obtaining in the Pal. synagogue in Fusṭāṭ. These earlier Hafṭarot, presupposed by the Y items, correspond as a rule to those forming the basis of the Petiḥtot of the leading Amoraic Aggadists (see also infra, p. 14). This problem of the literary history of the Midrashim based on the readings from Torah and Prophets will be discussed more fully in vol. III.

2. CHARACTERISTICS OF TC SEDARIM AND HAFṬAROT

According to the established rule requiring a person to recite from the Torah at least 3 verses (M. Meg. 4.4), the lection on the Sabbath morning, when seven people were called upon to do so in succession (ibid. 4.2), had to contain a minimum of 21 verses. This minimum is also reflected in the Bar. (Meg. 23a, bottom) regulating the Hafṭarah to consist, too, of 21 verses so as to correspond to the Torah lection.[12] If sometimes there occurs a Seder (= S) of less than this minimum, say of 20, 19 or 18 verses, recourse can be taken to the assumption that the 7th person repeated one or two verses from the portion recited by his predecessor, or even the entire one in case of the last instance. There is also another possibility that such Sedarim are relics of the custom that must have prevailed at some time to call up on the Sabbath only six persons (cp. the dispute between R. 'Aḳiba and R. Ishma'el in Babli Meg. 23a, top, but see Tos. 4(3).11, ed. Zuckerm., 226, where the dispute is about adding to the minimum and not about the latter itself). But it is inconceivable that a S comprised only 14 verses, such as Gen. 8.1–14, or even 9 verses, such as Num. 25.1–9. Such Sedarim are really to be explained in connection with the numerous shiftings of their respective commencements, viz. that in some localities the S began with Gen. 8.1 whereas in others the S *for the same Sabbath* commenced with 8.15, and the same applies to Num. 25.1 and 25.10 respectively (see Vol. I, pp. 76–77 and 122). The whole process of shifting becomes evident from the consideration of each item in the body of this work, and at the conclusion of the section on TC there will be given lists covering the whole Pentateuch as graphic illustration. We also notice that the Sidras of the Babyl. AC coincided with the points at which there commenced TC Sedarim, although there were divergences in this respect which the final fixation of TC failed to remove entirely (cp. e. g., Vol. I, p. 183, with regard to פ' חיי שרה, and p. 314 f., with regard to פ' ויחי). The Babyl. AC of Torah and Prophetic readings and its derivatives will be treated fully in vol. III.

---

12 המפטיר בנביא לא יפחות מכ"א פסוקין, כנגד שבעה שקראו בתורה.

As regards the length of the TC Hafṭarah (=H), according to the Bar. (see note 12) it should comprise 21 verses corresponding to the minimum of the Torah lection. However, the custom developed to shorten the former, whenever there was an official Meturgeman, who rendered it into Aramaic, or an accompanying sermon, in order not to weary the congregation by too prolonged a service. In Babli Meg. 23b, top, it is reported that R. Yoḥanan b. Nappaḥa would direct the shortening of H to 10 verses,[13] but in Yer. IV (75a, bottom) the minimum is reduced to even 3 verses.[14] The point of a sermon, as the cause of a shortened H, is not mentioned expressly, but is implied in the answer of R. Abbahu to R. Ḥelbo: "Shall not R. Yoḥ. be as a Meturgeman?", viz. because of the sermons this Rabbi used to deliver the H was shortened just as in the case of a Meturgeman. The Pal. custom in this respect is stated in 'ס ואם היה המעשים לבני ארץ ישראל (Tarbiz, I, pt. 3, p. 6) as follows: בשבת תורגמן או דרשה, המפטיר אומר שלשה פסוקין או חמשה או שבעה, אינו חושש לעשרים וארבעה פסוקין.[15] From the Genizah lists of TC Hafṭarot it is apparent that as a rule the Prophetic lection consisted of 10 verses, though sometimes 11 verses are given or 9 or 8. It would thus seem as if the version in Babli concerning R. Yoḥanan's practice, viz. 10 verses, is more genuine. Or should we say that these lists were drawn up at a time when already Babli prevailed over Yerushalmi? Be this as it may (and more will be said later on), the conclusion of Dr. Büchler from some of these lists that there were prevalent Hafṭarot of 2 verses or

[13] זמנין סגיאין הוה קאימנא קמיה דר' יוחנן, וכי הוה קרינן עשרה פסוקי אמר לן: אפסיקו.

[14] א"ר חלבו קומי ר' אבהו: קומי ר' יוחנן קראיי תלתה, א"ל: ולא יהא ר' יוחנן כתורגמן, a better reading is found in ס', p. 277: העתים (צ"ל: שיש) שאין כתב במקום ובירושלמי. Cp. also מתורגמן קורין ג'. א"ר חלבו קומי ר' אבהו: והא קמיה ר' יוחנן קרו תלת, א"ל וכו' Ratner, אהצ"ו, Meg., p. 89.

[15] Cp. also Mas. Soferim 12.6 and 13.15 (ed. Higger, 230 and 250). The number 24 here for the ordinary H, as against 21 in Bar., is due to the view of not including the Mafṭir among the 7 persons called upon to read from the Torah, hence the 24 Prophetic verses would correspond to the 24 Torah verses recited by these persons plus the Mafṭir. In Mas. Sof. 13.15 (p. 250) 22 verses are given, the last one corresponding to the חזון הכנסת. See my remarks in Tarbiz, l. c., note 14.

even one verse will be shown to be erroneous (see Vol. I, pp. 60, 85, 125, 161, 422–3, 459).

An interesting feature of TC H is that of *skipping*, viz. in order to conclude H with a 'happy ending' the 10th verse was added after leaving out the intervening Prophetic portion; sometimes the last 2 or 3 verses were added in the same manner. This procedure of skipping is already indicated in M. Meg. 4.4: מדלגין בנביא וכו' and in Tos. 4(3).18 (ed. Zuckermandel, 226 f.): מדלגין בנביא ואין מדלגין בתורה, ואין מדלגין מנביא לנביא, ובנביא של שנים עשר מדלגין (cp. Babli 24a and Yer. IV, 75b). The matter will be discussed farther on, but here attention is drawn to it because of the following observation. Very frequently the Bible codices contain the siglum סדר=ס' either at the verse where the H began or where it ended, and moreover the concluding verse of 'happy ending', added after the skipping, often coincides with the one having this siglum. Thus we have *the origin of the whole Massoretic division of the Prophets into Sedarim.* Just as with regard to the Torah the latter indicated the commencements of the lections according to TC, so with regard to the Prophets originally the siglum 'Seder' indicated where the TC Haftarot either began or concluded and also where the final verse occurred after the skipping. The siglum was thus first intended as an aid in the employment of the Prophetic books at the service of the Synagogue in the form of Haftarot *accompanying the Sedarim of the Torah.* Later on these sigla were extended all over the Prophets to provide so-called divisions of each book, and were even carried over to the Hagiographa although never recited as specific readings except for the Psalms and the 5 Megillot. This connection of the Sedarim in the Prophets with the TC Haftarot has to my knowledge not yet been realized.[16] It explains the placing of these sigla at points that hitherto were puzzling and seemed very strange, e. g. Josh. 4.24, 8.33, 14.15, 22.34, Judges 4.31, etc., etc. In the body of this work attention is drawn at each particular H to this

---

[16] Thus neither by Dr. Büchler nor by Ginsburg, *Introduction*, ch. IV: Sedarim (p. 32 ff.); the latter correctly termed the Pent. Sedarim as "the Triennial Pericopes", but did not offer any explanation for the Sedarim of Prophets and Hagiographa.

indication 'Seder' in the Bible codices. A fuller treatment will be given farther on in conjunction with lists as graphic illustration.

In the choice of a particular H to a given Torah lection the principle of *tallying* was predominant, viz. there had to be linguistic affinity between the initial verse or verses of S and H respectively. In addition there was frequently an intrinsic connection between the two, but more often the tallying was merely of the former character as long as the chosen H was one of consolation and encouragement of Israel (נחמת ישראל). The latter requirement was also the main reason for the skipping within the Prophetic lection in order to lead down to a conclusion that was heartening and foretelling the ultimate redemption of Israel. Sometimes a given H can be detected as already the result of an Aggadic homily that antedated it. Such a H as a rule is late and an earlier one can be ascertained by means of other data. This will be demonstrated in the course of the following investigation item by item.

3. The Midrashic Homilies as Based on TC Sedarim and Haftarot

The discovery of Theodor as to the Midrashic sections having been arranged according to the Pal. Cycle has been mentioned before (p. 6). But this discovery applies only to their external form. The inner structure has not yet been properly understood. Take the case of the *Petiḥta* (= Pet.) to which Bacher has devoted a valuable monograph.[17] According to him "the Pet. verse was left entirely to the free choice of the speaker; just in the selection of the Pet. verse and its interpretation, as well as in its coupling with the text of the (Torah) pericope, there were to become evident the esprit and the skill of the preacher" (p. 7). In the fact that the H, which would have been very suitable for Pet. texts, was not used at all for

---

[17] *Die Proömien in der alten jüd. Homilie*, Leipzig 1913. The previous literature on this theme is listed there on pp. 1–2. Cp. also Albeck, מבוא ומפתחות למדרש בראשית רבא, I, Berlin 1931, p. 11 ff.

that purpose, Bacher has found special proof for the above
freedom of choice on the part of the homilist.[18] By the latter
observation Bacher has missed the crux of the whole matter.
*The H was not used explicitly because it was tacitly employed
throughout!* In the following pages it will be demonstrated in
connection with each TC Seder how the verse chosen to introduce a particular Pet. *tallied linguistically with a verse found
within the compass of the H.* Often the whole trend of the Aggadah developed in the Pet. can be accounted for only by turning
to the H which gave the homilist his starting-point. He had
the H constantly in mind and utilized for his purpose even the
part skipped therein. In many cases the Pet. would tally with
the initial verses of both S and H, which in their turn were
connected in the same manner, but frequently the tally of the
Pet. verse can only be found in the H. The connection is either
positive or by way of contrast. Thus the H formed the bridge
that joined the Torah S with the Pet. verse which as a rule was
chosen from the Hagiographa (though occasionally the latter
emanated from the Prophets and even from the Pent.). In
this manner the preacher demonstrated to his audience *the
union of the three divisions of the Bible.*

This discovery of the role played by the H in determining
the structure and often the trend of the Aggadot dawned upon
me as a result of the investigation of the items beginning with
ילמדנו רבינו. What criterion was there to guide the selection of a
particular Halakhah with which to open these so-called Yel.
sermons? Often the Hal. has no bearing whatever on the Torah
reading.[19] There is indeed evident the consummate skill of the
preacher in proceeding from the Hal. to Aggadah in order to

---

[18] P. 7, bottom: "Die Freiheit in der Wahl des Prooemientextes zeigt
sich besonders deutlich in dem Umstande, dass die als Haphtara vorgelesenen
Prophetenabschnitte, die sich wie von selbst zur Wahl des Prooemientextes
darboten, keineswegs zu diesem Zwecke bevorzugt wurden".

[19] See Vol. I, p. 23–4, concerning the "classical proof for the dependence
of Y on Sheeltot" which Lerner thought to have discovered in the very first
Y item to Gen. 1.1. The latter in reality is due to the H to that S which
manifestly was its starting-point. The groping in the dark concerning the
real nature of the Y sermons is also evident from A. Epstein's remarks (see

lead down to the initial verse of S using the formula: מנין? ממה שקרינו בענין. We thus notice the end of the homiletic process, but what caused its starting-point, viz. what guiding principle aided the homilist to choose out of the mass of Halakhot the particular one for his purpose?[20] Then there are to several Sedarim 2 or 3 Y items. This fact also demanded an explanation. In turning to the TC Haftarot there was found the solution to the whole problem. *Within the given H the homilist always obtained a suggestion for the choice of the particular Hal. to begin with his sermon by means of the formula* ילמדנו רבינו. As there were frequently more than one H to a certain S, so there had to be more than one Y item in order to correspond to the former situation. Thus it became clear that the principle of *tallying*, which applied to the choice of a H to a given S, was also extended to the selection of the Hal. to be utilized. In this manner there was demonstrated *the union of the Written Law with the Oral*. The investigation of the Y items led to a close examination of the Petiḥtot to each S, with the result that the process of tallying with regard to the Pet. verses became manifest (as described above, p. 12). This whole procedure further showed that the TC Haftarot, as indicated in Yannai's Piyyuṭim and in the Genizah lists, frequently were late ones; the Midrashic homilies were based on quite different Haftarot, and thus it became a part of our task to ascertain from the underlying data the original Prophetic lections. The same task became incumbent when dealing with those Sedarim that had been eliminated as a result of the final fixation of TC; their respective

---

their summary in the Appendix to Bacher's *Ag. d. pal. Amor.*, III, 512–14). He speaks of rhetorical homilies under the influence of the Greek sophists. Thus "there was submitted to the preacher a question *pro forma* introduced by ילמדנו רבינו. The latter usually has either no connection or only a loose one with the text of the sermon". Therein Epstein finds a Sophist parallel as he does in the following Petiḥta (ibid., p. 512, Nos. 1–2). But *the originality of the Jewish sermon, based as it was on an ingenious employment of S and H,* will become evident throughout our following investigation.

[20] In the long essay on Yel. (GS, I, 449 ff.) this aspect is not considered at all. The attempt of Stein (see infra, p. 24, note 4) was bound to be unsuccessful because of his unawareness of the role of the Haftarot in determining the whole structure of the Y sermons.

Haftarot had to be deduced from the Midrashic material bearing on these erewhile Torah lections. The structure of the Y sermons and the great homiletic ingenuity of their authors appeared clearly out of the haze of obscurity. The role of the H became visible as a red thread running through the web and woof first of the portion beginning with ילמדנו רבינו, then of the following Petiḥta or Petiḥtot, and finally of the *peroration* that concluded such a sermon; the final verse of 'happy ending', usually cited therein, also tallied with the H.[21] The analysis of the very first Y unit to Gen. 1.1 (S 1), as found in T, Bereshit, §§4–5, will demonstrate clearly the structure that now stands revealed after pointing out the role played by the H (see Vol. I, pp. 23–28).

The dependence of a given Y homily on the respective H at once makes impossible the arbitrariness adopted by some scholars of transferring the former from its proper place to some other S, as will be shown frequently in the course of the discussion of each item separately. Moreover, the fact that numerous Y topics presuppose older Haftarot than those listed in Yannai's Ḳerobot and in the Genizah fragments — the same older Prophetic lections also underlying the Petiḥtot of the leading Amoraic Aggadists — tends to show that the Y homilies are not as late as usually assumed since otherwise they would have been based on the later Haftarot and not on the earlier ones. The procedure adopted in our investigation also throws new light on the structure of the other Midrashim. Thus, e. g., the analysis of Aggadat Bereshit (=AB), with its threefold sections to each S headed Torah, Nebiim and Ketubim respectively, reveals frequently that the first one is based on one H whereas the second one on a different one, while in the section called Ketubim there can be detected *the selection of specific Psalms to be recited on given Sabbaths* — these Psalms containing tallies with either the respective Sedarim or with their corresponding Haftarot. This structure of AB can also be traced in certain parts of

---

[21] The study of Stein on "Die Homiletische Peroratio im Midrasch" (*HUCA*, VIII-IX [1931–32], 353 ff.) again is defective on account of not realizing the dependence of the peroration on the H, as pointed out in the body of this work in connection with each item.

Exodus Rabba. In vol. III there will be given a summary of the literary composition of the various Midrashim on the basis of the results obtained from the investigation of TC and of the readings on special Sabbaths and Festivals. Likewise the use of the Psalms in connection with the readings from Torah and Prophets will be summed up. Also the whole technique of the art of preaching as developed in the Old Synagogue will be set forth.

4. Procedure and Sources Employed

The Sedarim are dealt with in numerical succession one after another, both the 'regular' ones and the 'irregular' ones (see Vol. I, p. 51, note 32). The process of *shifting* of the commencements of the Sedarim, as evident from the 'irregular' ones, is pointed out in each case and the probable reasons for the shifting are suggested. Then the respective H is indicated and its *tallying* with the corresponding S is discussed. As far as possible, all the available Genizah data concerning the H are added, in addition to the indications in the Piyyuṭim of Yannai and of others. Thereupon *the structure of the Midrashic homilies* to each S is analyzed. Wherever the material at hand permits, the analysis is devoted first to the *Y Sermon*, not because it is older than the other homilies such as the Petiḥtot so frequently woven into the former, but because the Halakhic topic introducing the Y sermon offers a concrete criterion for our process of ascertaining whether the underlying H was identical with the one listed in the Genizah data or a different H is to be presupposed in order to account for the topic chosen. Then the tallying of the Petiḥtot and the other homilies with the given H is investigated. All the available Midrashic material, including that contained in the manuscripts edited in the Hebrew section at the end of this volume, is reviewed in the course of this analysis. Thereby the composition of the various Midrashim is scrutinized and constantly laid bare. Numerous points become clear and erroneous notions are rectified. In the case of the 'irregular' Sedarim, to which no Genizah data supply the respective Haftarot, our procedure of obtaining from the Midrashic homilies the underlying Prophetic lections becomes complex, requiring great caution especially when no Y topics are available, but is for this very reason all the more important since the results obtained reveal the existence of numerous TC Haftarot hitherto unrecorded; and the same applies frequently even to the 'regular' Sedarim whenever the Genizah H differs with the one evident from the Midrashim. Parallel lists of all the Sedarim and Haftarot will be given at the conclusion of our detailed investigation of TC. The same procedure will be applied to the readings on special Sabbaths and on Festivals and their respective sermons.

The following Genizah fragments containing TC Haftarot have been utilized.

I. *Collection Adler* (=*A*).

1) Ms. 470:—a) One damaged leaf containing a list of Prophetic lections to the Sedarim from Ex. 1.1 to 30.1 (reproduced Vol. I in Appendix, No. II, pp. 572–74). b) Two leaves comprising H to S at Num. 17.16 and 18.25. c) Two leaves of H with Targum (lacuna between fols. 1 and 2); see the description in *JQR*, VIII, 528–529, which has to be rectified as indicated in the body of this work to each respective S.

2) Ms. 2103:—a) Two vellum leaves of H with Targum (lacuna between fols. 1 and 2). Fol. 1, recto, is blank; verso begins with אשלמ[חא דסדר בראשית,[22] thus to Gen. 1.1; fol. 2 contains part of H to S 6 (Gen. 8.1). b) Two vellum leaves of H with Targum (lacuna between fols. 1 and 2) to Sedarim 4–6 and 10–12 respectively.

3) Ms. 2105, originally part of a vellum scroll but now pasted on a cardboard. See facsimile in *Cat. Adler*, Plate 96. I have also consulted the original. The Haftarot are to Sedarim comprising Deut. 2.2–10.1.

Ms. Adler, Nos. 2020, 2021, and 2652, listed in *Cat. Adler*, p. 6, as containing TC Haftarot, unfortunately could not be located.

---

[22] About this term for H see Vol. I, pp. 555–59.

II. *Collection Bodleian*, Oxford (= Bodl.)

1) 2603^{19}		6) 2740^6
2) 2607^7		7) 2822^7
3) 2610^7		8) 2826^{36}
4) 2615^{18}		9) 2828^{27}
5) 2727^3		10) 2851^{14}

All these items, except No. 5, are described in Neubauer-Cowley, *Cat.*, II, which reliable description I have followed (here and there some obvious rectifications are necessary as pointed out infra to each respective S); No. 3 (Bodl. 2610^7) has not been recognized in *Cat.* as being TC Haftarot.

No. 5 (Bodl. 2727^3), containing a long list of H to Sedarim 4–77 (Gen. 5.1 — Lev. 6.12), has been published by Dr. Büchler, *JQR*, VI, 39–42. I have compared the printed text with the original by means of a photostat. This list is cited here to each item as B followed by the respective page in *JQR*. It also has been reproduced in Vol. I, Appendix, No. I (pp. 561–571).

III. *Taylor-Schechter Collection, Cambridge* (= C), *and University Library Collection* (= CL).

The late Dr. Israel Abrahams has examined the respective fragments containing TC Haftarot and described them in a Note-Book now belonging to the Library of Christ's College, Cambridge. There are also several rough notes of his in a separate bundle. Through the kind assistance of Mr. Herbert J. Loewe, this material has been loaned to me for use here. The original Genizah fragments I have been unable to consult. There are apparent a number of inaccuracies in the data collected by Abrahams, as pointed out in Vols. I–II in connection with each S discussed. These data are cited as C or CL followed by the respective number in the Note-Book. Those indicated as C emanate mostly from the fragments found in T.-S. B 17 and 18. A portion of his collected material Dr. Abrahams has published in *Festskrift David Simonsen* (= FS), Copenhagen, 1923, pp. 77–80: "A group of Genesis Haftaroth", and in *Oriental Studies dedicated to Paul Haupt* (= HV), 1926, pp. 1–2: "Some Triennial Haftaroth". Unfortunately these articles contain numerous typographical errors with regard to the respective verses comprising the Prophetic lections, as shown in Vols. I–II to each pertaining S. Also Abrahams' manner of referring to fragments Oxford is misleading since what he mentions as "No." so and so is really the page in Neubauer-Cowley, *Cat.*, II, and not the particular No. used by the authors. Thus in HV he refers to "Oxford fragment, No. 243", in reality Bodl. 2822[7] described on p. 243! The same applies to his "No. 324", viz. Bodl. 2851[14] described on p. 324 of *Cat.* One does not gather from his brief papers the impression of his having fully understood the characteristics of TC Haftarot (see above, pp. 9–11). However, the writer is grateful to him for the material he had collected the general results of which he was not granted to publish (cp. FS, p. 77).

IV. *The Haftarot indicated in Mahzor Yannai* (= *MY*).

M. Zulay was the first to observe in part III of the Ḳerobot a reference to the respective H of the Sabbath or the Festival to which these Piyyuṭim pertained (see his *Zur Liturgie der Babyl. Juden*, Bonner Orient. Studien, Heft 2, 1933, pp. 13–16, cp. also p. 84–5). In his valuable study on and survey of Yannai's compositions (מחקרי יניי, in ידיעות המכון לחקר השירה העברית, II [1936], pp. 213 ff.) he was thus able to indicate a goodly number of Haftarot pertaining to TC (ibid., pp. 271–273). This is cited infra to each S as *Zulay's List*. Yannai's Haftarot correspond almost entirely to those found in the above Genizah fragments, showing that at the time of this early Paiṭan TC had reached already its final phase of fixation. However, the Haftarot indicated in the Ḳerobot of the Paiṭan Simon Hakkohen b. Megas (Zulay, *l. c.*, p. 272, note 2, and cp. pp. 221–231) show some significant variants which go back to earlier times, as shown infra in connection with the discussion of each respective S.

Zulay's edition of MY is now available under the title: *Piyyute Yannai* (פיוטי יניי, מלוקטים מתוך כתבי הגניזה ומקורות אחרים), Berlin, 1938; it was thus just possible to insert in the body of this part the respective pagination of this new publication. In vol. III of our work more will be said about the use

made by Yannai and other Paiṭanim of the Petiḥtot and other
Midrashic homilies to each S. His use of a Y topic is evident
from ed. Davidson, מחזור יני, p. 21, top (=ed. Zulay, p. 156,
l. 34 ff.), as will be shown infra, Vol. II, to the S beginning with
Lev. 15.25. See also Vol. I, H. pt., 83–86, concerning a Midrashic section incorporated within his Ḳerobah to Seder 41.

In dealing with the Midrashic homilies, my endeavor was
to utilize, in addition to all available in printed form, as much
material as possible from manuscripts. Hence the substantial
Hebrew sections at the end of the present volume as well as of
Vol. II that is to follow. The introductions to each item therein
and the textual notes supply the necessary information. As
regards the still unpublished portions of Midrash Ha-Gadol
(=MHG), viz. to the second half of Exodus (from פ' משפטים)
and to Numbers and Deuteronomy, manuscripts belonging
to the Jew. Theological Seminary Library in New York were
consulted. As my aim was not to edit this work but to obtain
additional data bearing on the Aggadot to the respective Sedarim,
there was no attempt made to compare the several MSS. for
possible variants. Finally it should be added that for the text
of Leviticus Rabba (=LR) I was able to consult photostats[23]
of the valuable MSS. of Brit. Mus. Add. 27169, being the same
MS. as used for Genesis Rabba (=GR) in ed. Theodor-Albeck
(see מבוא ומפתחות למדרש בראשית רבא, I, 105–107), and of Vat.
Ebraico, No. 32 (cp. about No. 30 to GR, ibid. 107–8).

After the above Prolegomena, which should suffice as an
introduction, we turn to the detailed discussion of TC which
comprises Section I of this work.

---

[23] Kindly lent to me by Prof. Sol Finesinger, Hebrew Union College,
Cincinnati.

SECTION I (Concluded)

THE TRIENNIAL CYCLE

A detailed description of the Sedarim and their corresponding Haftarot and an analysis of the structure of the pertinent Midrashic Homilies.

CONCERNING THE MANN-SONNE POSTHUMOUS MANUSCRIPT

We wish to alert the serious reader to the fact that we have faithfully tried to reproduce the Mann-Sonne Manuscript as it was bequeathed to us.

1. Obvious errors in spelling, dittography, citation of source, so far as we were able, have been corrected.

2. Where marginal hand-written notations have been easily decipherable, we have included them.

3. The notes by Mann, supplemented by Sonne, are indicated as follows: (i. e. [1*]) an asterisk after the note number, indicating that both Mann and Sonne comment.

4. Where Sonne alone comments, this is indicated as follows: ([53s]) the letter "s" raised next to the numbered note to indicate Sonne.

5. The Mann notes appear at the bottom of each page. The Sonne notes are printed together. There are also "Additional" Sonne notes. These too are printed together, following the original Sonne comments.

6. THE ORIGINAL MANUSCRIPT IS BOUND IN LEATHER AND REPOSES IN THE DALSHEIMER RARE BOOK BUILDING OF THE HEBREW UNION COLLEGE LIBRARY IN CINCINNATI.

7. Wherever the author has mentioned italics in the Hebrew text, it means that the Hebrew is letter spaced; i. e., spread out.

LEVITICUS

SEDER 74 (1)[1]

ויקרא אל משה וידבר ה ' אליו מאהל מועד לאמר, Leviticus 1.1.

Haftarah: קול ה ' לעיר יקרא ותושיה יראה שמך שמעו מטה ומי יעדה,
Micah 6.9–7.8 (16 verses), so B 42 where the copyist erroneously cited the last verse (7.8) as אל תשמחי פלשת כלך instead of
אל תשמחי אויבתי לי, due to confusion with Is. 14.29.[2] No doubt
there was skipping, thus Mic. 6.9–16+7.7–8 (hence 10 verses).
Yannai in his Ḳerobah also seems to indicate Mic. 6.9 as the
initial v. of H (see *Piyyute Yannai*, ed. Zulay, p. 121 <l. 13:
יקרא קול לעיר>.).

H tallies with S merely by means of the expression 'calling'
by God. There is no reference to sacrifices which are the topic
of the S.[1s] This Prophetic lection is really one of denunciation
and not of 'consolation of Israel'; only the last two verses (7.7–8),
added after the skipping, contain a 'happy ending' (cp. infra,
p. 4). See further infra, p. 19, concerning the H to S 76.

STRUCTURE OF HOMILIES

1. *Y Sermon.* T, Wayyikra, #2, TB, #3:

ויקרא אל משה. ילמדנו רבינו: העובר לפני התיבה וטעה ולא הזכיר ברכת
המינין, מנין שמחזירין אותו (בת"ב: ולא אמר ברכת קללת המינין, מהו שמחזירין
אותו). כך שנו רבותינו: העובר לפני התיבה וטעה, בכל הברכות כולן אין
מחזירין אותו, בברכת המינין מחזירין אותו ואומרה בעל כרחו, ומפני מה
מחזירין אותו, חיישינן שמא מין הוא, שאם יהא בו צד מינות קלל עצמו ועונין
הקהל אמן (בת"ב: מחזירין אותו בעל כרחו, חיישינן שמא מין הוא, ולכך
מחזירין אותו שאם היה בו צד מינות יהיה מקלל את עצמו והקהל עונין אמן).
וכן מי שלא אמר בונה ירושלים מחזירין אותו, חיישינן שמא כותי הוא וכו'.
The above Halakhah is based upon a Baraita cited in Yer.

---

[1] The figure in parenthesis denotes the respective number of the S in Leviticus proper. See above, vol. I, p. 358, note 380, with regard to Exodus.

[2] See ibid., p. 571, note 155.

Ber. V, 9c (see note 5). The Mishnaic rule was that a reader
who erred in his recital of the Amidah should be substituted by
another one.[3] But this rule was not rigidly adhered to, and
recourse was taken to the alternative of making the former repeat
the portion wherein he had erred.[4] R. Joshua b. Levi was very
lenient and even permitted a reader, who had skipped two or
three benedictions (evidently inside the Amidah), to proceed
uninterruptedly. But another view was to make an exception
with regard to three specific benedictions, the second, twelfth,
and fourteenth respectively, because they involved points at
issue with Sadducees, Minim (Judaeo-Christians, Gnostics and
other non-conformists) and Samaritans — these items the erring
or forgetful reader had to repeat nolens volens.[5]

Here in the Yel. passage the item pertaining to the second
benediction (מחיה המתים) is omitted; probably because it belonged
to the first 3 benedictions of the Amidah, an erroneous recital or
omission of which resulted anyhow in a repetition of the whole
commencement of the prayer.[6]*

[3] Ber. 5.3: העובר לפני התיבה וטעה יעבור אחר תחתיו.
[4] See Yer. a. l. 9c., and cp. Babli 34a.
[5] Yer. a. l.: רבי אחא ורבי יודה בן פזי יתבין בחד כנישתא, אתי עבר חד קומי תיבותא
ואשגר חד ברכה, אתון ושיילון לרבי סימון, אמר לו (צ"ל לו') —לון) רבי סימון בשם רבי
יהושע בן לוי ש"צ שהשגיר שתים שלש ברכות אין מחזירין אותו. אשכח תני ופליג לכל אין
מחזירין אותו חוץ ממי שלא אמר מחיה המתים ומכניע זדים ובונה ירושלם, אני אומר מין הוא.
The last Bar. is the basis of the Hal. in the Y passage here (as has been
rightly pointed out by Ginzberg, cp. GS, I, 473, No. 55). This provision
to make the reader repeat ברכת המינים, and not to remove him, is contradictory to the tradition in Babli 29a, top, in the name of Rab, that the former
was superseded by another one: טעה בכל הברכות כולן אין מעלין אותו, בברכת
(אין מחזירין . . . מחזירין) המינין מעלין אותו, חיישינן שמא מין הוא (ed. Bomberg has
On account of this discrepancy, an attempt is made in תוספות רבי יהודה החסיד
אין מחזירין אותו (see ברכה משולשת, Warsaw, 1863, 17a) to explain the phrase
in Yer. as the equivalent of אין מעלין אותו in Babli: פירושו דאין מחזירין אותו היינו
למקומם (צ"ל: למקומו), כלומר אין מעלין אותו וכו' שמא מין הוא, ולא מיירי הירושלמי מידי
בחזרה לתחילת ברכות. But this is of course forced, and the whole Yer. passage
plainly proves the contrary.[1]*

[6] חוזר בתחילה in Yer., חוזר לראש in Babli. — The reason for this omission,
as given in GS, l. c., is unacceptable since it is based on the assumption that
"the whole homily here is to teach us that the Samaritans were regarded as
untrue proselytes" (שכל הדרשה כאן היא ללמדנו שהכותים אינם גרי אמת וכו') — to
which there is no indication either in TB or in T.[2]*

From the above Hal., which aimed at excluding a mas-
querading heretic from the service of the Synagogue, the homilist
proceeds to cite a similar rule concerning a would-be proselyte
who is to be rejected as such, if he failed to accept all the in-
junctions of Biblical and Rabbinic Judaism. On the other hand,
a genuine conforming neophyte is precious in the eyes of God for
forsaking idolatry and joining Judaism. In this manner there is
built up a contrast between a Jewish heretic, whom God rejects
notwithstanding his Jewish origin, and a newcomer whom He
cherishes despite his gentilic ancestry. This contrast leads down
to the conclusion of the Y homily which is truncated both in
TB and in T. However, it can be restored by means of the
comments on Lev. 1.2 in Sifra (ed. Weiss, 4ᶜ) to the effect that
the sacrifices of the proselytes were accepted whereas those of
Jewish apostates (משומדים) were rejected.[7]* Accordingly, the
missing ending probably read: וכן אתה מוצא שהגרים מביאין קרבנות
אבל לא ה מ ש ו מ ד י ם, מנין, ממה שקרינו בענין, אדם כי יקריב מכם וגו'.
Herewith there is the required return to the beginning of S,
thereby completing the first portion of the Y sermon.

In accordance with our procedure of investigation, there is
to be sought in the H a starting-point for the above Y question
and answer concerning ברכת המינים.[8] Now this benediction
commenced in its Palestinian version as follows: למשומדים אל
תהי תקוה (JQR, X, 657, cp. also HUCA, II, 296, 306), and these
apostates figure also in the conclusion of the homily (as pointed

---

[7] אדם, לרבות את הגרים; מכם, להוציא את המשומדים. Cp. the conclusion there:
ו ע כ ש י ו.*[3] הא אל תאמר אלא מה ישראל מקבלי ברית, אף הגרים מקבלי ברית, יצאו
המשומדים שאינן מקבלי ברית שהרי הפרו ברית, וכן הוא אומר זבח רשעים תועבה Buber,
TB, §3, note 21, rightly drew attention to this Sifra passage without, however, realizing the force of the contrast. The same applies to GS, l. c. See
further next note.

[8] Buber, l. c., writes: והרבה יגעתי לכוון טעם שאלה זו בהלכה לכאן כי אינו ענין
כלל עם הכתוב הזה (היינו וי' א', א'–ב'), אולם יגעתי ומצאתי תאמין, כי מצאתי בספרא ריש
ויקרא על הכתוב אדם כי יקריב מכם אדם, לרבות את הגרים, ואין ספק שגם בתנחומא היה
כתוב הדרש הזה, ועל זה הביא השאלה בהלכה זו בעבור הסיום שמדבר בענין גרים But
this accounts only for the conclusion of the Y homily as pointed out above
in the text, in order to encompass the return to the commencement of S.
However, for the beginning dealing with ברכת המינים an allusion has to be
found in the H to our S, as demonstrated throughout this work.

out before). Thus a H containing the verb שמד would have offered the Y preacher a clue for his initial theme.[28] The H listed above (p. 23) hardly fits the case in point, unless we assume that Mic. 6.13 read: וגם אני החליתי הכותך השמם על חטאותיך. The fact that H is mainly denunciatory and other considerations, that will become apparent subsequently, tend to the conclusion that the Midrashic homilies were based upon another H, viz. Is. 48.12: שמע אלי יעקב וישראל מקראי,[9]* tallying again by means of קרא with Lev. R. 1.1.[38] This H probably extended to v. 20 (עבדו יעקב)+49.7: (אמרו גאל ה' גאל כה אמר ה' גאל), (אני אני דברתי אף קראתיו :48.15 .ישראל וגו') Is., thus 10 verses. would afford a still further contact with the initial v. of S: ויקרא אל משה וידבר ה' אליו; it is indeed applied to Moses in Lev. (infra, p. 7). And altogether this lection contains indeed heartening consolation and encouragement of Israel, such as was the usual trend of the TC Haftarot. In this H we read: לוא הקשבת למצותי ויהי כנהר שלומך ... לא יכרת ולא ישמד שמו מלפני (48.18–19). On the other hand the wicked are excluded from the gift of peace (48.22: אין שלום אמר ה' לרשעים. This in skipped part of H). Hence the starting-point of the question and answer concerning the twelfth benediction of the Amidah which continues a denunciation of those who *broke God's commandments* such as the משומדים and other heretics; their speedy end was besought therein as against the promised perpetuation of the offspring of those who 'hearkened to the commandments' (Is. 48.19).[10]

Thus the first portion of Y sermon has been accounted for. It is difficult to find the direct continuation in TB and T. The point of proselytes is not raised again there (as to LR c. 1.2,

---

[9] The Genizah fragment, mentioned above (*l. c.*, vol. I, p. 426),[4]* indeed lists to Sidra ויקרא this verse next to Is. 43.22: ולא אתי קראת יעקב; the latter evidently being the commencement of the Babylonian AC H whereas the former of TC.

[10] It should also be added that this benediction also included a reference to the hated Roman government whose speedy uprooting was ardently wished for (ומלכות זדון מהרה תעקר בימינו). For this, too, an allusion was found in our H where the redemption from Babylon was promised (Is. 48.20); as is well known, the latter became in Talmudic times a synonym for Rome.

see further on).[4s] However, the remaining items, emphasizing
the high privilege of Moses in being summoned by God (Lev. 1.1),
tally with the above suggested H from Is. 48.12 ff. Thus the
Pet. on Prov. 29.23: גאות אדם תשפילנו ושפל רוח יתמך כבוד (TB,
§4, T, §3) corresponds to ואכבד בעיני ה' (Is. 49.5, this in skipped
part)[5s] whereas the one on Ps. 89.20: אז דברת בחזון לחסידיך
ותאמר שויתי עזר על גבור הרימותי בחור מעם (TB §5, T, §3,
end) has several points of contact with H (Is. 48.15: אני אני
דברתי, 48.16: ועתה ה' אלהים שלחני ורוחו which is tantamount
to God speaking in vision to the pious ones, and 49.7: קדוש
ישראל ויבחרך).[6s] The next item (TB, §6, T, §4) alludes to God's
love for Israel (בשביל אהבתן של ישראל) which is reflected in 48.14:
ה' אהבו. It further refers to Moses, leading down to the *perora-*
tion: א"ל הקב"ה: בעו"הז עשיתיך ראש (בת"ה נוסף: על כל ישראל), לעוה"ב,
כשיבואו הצדיקים ליטול, אתה בראש כולן, שנ' ויתא ראשי עם צדקת ה'
(דברים ל"ג, כ"א) עשה ומשפטיו עם ישראל. By means of 'righteousness' and 'judgment' this concluding v. links up with H (Is.
48.18, 49.4).[7s] — As to TB, §§1–2, T, §1, which contain the
same homilies as LR, c.1.1 and 1.5–6 (though with variations),
see further on. TB, §7, T, §5, being outside the sermon to our
S, need not be discussed. Likewise no further comment is
required on the conglomerate and late passage which originally
formed the only section to פ' ויקרא in the first two editions of T
and now given as §8 under the heading: כבר היה לעולמים.[11*]

2. *Other Homilies.* In LR, c.1, there are five Petiḥtot to the
S, all of which seem to tally with the above H. Thus the first
one is on Ps. 103.20: ברכו ה' מלאכיו גבורי כח עושי דברו לשמוע
בקול דברו, corresponding to דברתי in Is. 48.14–15 and to
the 'hearing' of God's words mentioned several times (48.12, 14,
16; 49.1).[8s] As to the employment of the same Pet. to S 96b,
see infra (p. 131). The second one introduces Hos. 14.8: ישובו
יושבי בצלו וגו', which links up with בצל ידו החביאני (Is. 49.2).[9s]
This item deals with proselytes, as was the case with the initial
portion of the Y sermon (above p. 23), and perhaps formed also
a part of the latter. However, the version in LR is apparently
truncated since there is no return at the end to the S so as to

---

[11] Cp. Buber, TB, §1, note 1, and מבוא, pp. 171–72.

indicate its relevance here.[11a] For the same Pet. to S 104[c] in
NR, c. 8.1, see infra (p. 219). The third Pet. (c. 1.4) from Ps.
89.20 has been mentioned before (above p. 27). There follows
the fourth one[12*] from Prov. 25.7: 'כי טוב א מ ר לך עלה הנה וגו,
which v. is reflected intrinsically by Is. 49.3, 5–7, containing in
addition the verb אמר.[10s] Finally there is the fifth Pet. by R.
Tanḥuma (b. Abba), which is developed by means of Prov.
20.15: יש זהב ורב פנינים וכלי יקר שפתי דעת; 'lips of knowledge'
correspond in essence to וישם פי כחרב חדה (Is. 49.2), thus a mouth
that speaks effectively owing to the knowledge in the utterances.[11s]

The remainder of LR, c.1, requires no further analysis, except
to draw attention to R. Abin's application of Is. 48.15 (a verse
of our H, see above, p. 26) specifically to Moses (§9[cw]).[13*] Finally
there is the *peroration* (§14, end): לפי שבעוה"ז שכינה נגלית על
היחידים, אבל לע"ל (בכ"י בריט' מוז': לעולם הבא מה כתיב) ונגלה כבוד
ד ב ר ' פ י ה' ה' וראו כל בשר יחדיו כ י פ י ה ' ד ב ר (Is. 40.5), tallying with
אני אני דברתי of our H (Is. 48.15).[12s] The final portion of LR,
c. 1 (viz. §15), is a later addendum and emanates from SER;[14*]
it is indeed missing in MSS. Vat. and Brit. Mus. (cp. above,
vol. I, p. 19).

LR, c. 2, is to Lev. 1.2: ד ב ר אל בני ישראל, and hence the
Pet. v. from Jer. 31.19: הבן יקיר לי אפרים אם ילד שעשועים כי מידי
ד ב ר י בו וגו' which is commented upon elaborately (thus §1 on
יקיר, §2 on לי, etc.). By the same tally Jer. 31.19 is to be connected with the above H from Is. 48.12 ff., viz. with אני אני
ד ב ר ת י (48.15).[13s] Indeed the whole trend of the Aggadot has

---

[11a] The passage תני ר ש ב" י למה נקרא שמו לבנון, שמלבין עונותיהם של
ישראל ...כצמר יהיו, indicates that it emanates from Sifre (Deut. §§6 and 28)
which has been attributed to this Tanna! In MS. Brit. Mus. of LR 1.2 תני
רשב"י is omitted, and likewise in NR, c. 8.1. In the latter place what is given
in LR as R. Tabyomi's view is attributed to R. Simon b. Yoḥai (and also
in Cant. R., c. 7.4, where the former is supposed to be the author of the above
statement, found anonymously in Sifre, *l. c.*, cp. also Yoma 39b where the
author is R. Isaac b. Tablai.[5*] See further infra, p. 218, note 256.

[12] The printed texts read: רבי יהושע דסיכנין בשם ר' לוי פ ת ר קרא, but MS.
Brit. Mus. reads פ ת ח קריה (hence קריה should be deleted).[6*]

[13] §9, end: ברם הכא אמר ר' אבין אמר הקב"ה אני הוא הקורא ואני המדבר, שנ' אני
אני דברתי אף קראתיו הביאותיו והצליח דרכו.[7*]

[14] Cp. ed. Friedm., p. 33, note 17.[8*]

been inspired by our H in glorification of Israel and a v. within
its compass is cited expressly.[15]* The chapter is incomplete
at the end (§7); the remainder (§§8–12) is again an addendum
from SER (*l. c.*, pp. 34–36) and is missing in the above-mentioned
manuscripts.

The section to our S in JTS MS. (§4) (infra, H. pt., p. ז)
contains Petiḥtot on Ps. 103.20 and on Prov. 29.23, as to which
see above (pp. 27–28). There is also the same peroration as in
TB, §6, T, §4. Further a new Pet. is cited on Is. 44.26: מקים
דבר עבדו ועצת מלאכיו ישלים, but the homily itself is missing owing
to curtailment. The Pet. v. would tally by means of עבדו with
Is. 49.5–7 containing the same noun.[14s] — Finally there is in
MHG (III, p. 2) the Pet. on Prov. 27.18: נוצר תאנה יאכל פריה
ושומר אדוניו י כ ב ד   which tallies with Is. 49.5: ואכבד בעיני ה'
(cp. above, p. 27).[15s]

Thus all the homilies analyzed here are to be connected with
the H from Is. 48.12 ff. The other H from Mic. 6.9 ff. (above,
p. 23) is accordingly late. Indeed it is one of denunciation and
not of consolation of Israel. Why the former was substituted
by the latter, cannot as yet be ascertained.[16]*

Seder 74a (1a)

The next regular Seder began at Lev. 4.1–2 (infra, sub
No. 75). However, from LR, c. 3, it appears that in Amoraic
times there was inserted a new S at Lev. 2.1: ונפש כי תקריב קרבן
מנחה לה' וגו'. Hence we read the formula (LR, c. 3.4): נפש כי
תקריב קרבן, מה כתיב למעלה מן העני0, והסיר את מראתה בנוצתה indicating

---

[15] LR, c. 2.5, end: כך א'ל הקב'ה למשה כל מה שאתה יכול לשבח את ישראל שבח,
לנדלן [נדל], לפארן פאר, למה, שאני עתיד להתפאר בהם, שנ' ויאמר לי עבדי אתה ישראל
אשר בך אתפאר (יש' מ'ט, ג').*

[16] However, it should not be overlooked that the Pet. on Ps. 103.20:
לשמוע ב ק ו ל דברו (above, p. 27) would also tally with H from Mic. 6.9:
ק ו ל ה' לעיר יקרא and altogether the Aggadah on God's voice (TB, §1, T, §1),
which is more fully developed in Sifra (Wayyikra, c. 2, ed. Weiss, 3d–4a)
seems to have had its inspiration from this verse. Hence this H may really
have been the original one. Owing to its being denunciatory in character
another H was chosen in Amoraic times, but prevailed even later on.[10]*

that Lev. 1.16 was outside the present S.[17]* Now the latter involves the difficulty that it renders the previous S (No. 74) to consist of only 17 verses, 4 short of the required minimum of 21. Recourse would then have to be taken to repeating the last verses so as to apportion 3 verses to each of the 7 persons called upon to recite from the scroll (cp. above, Vol. I, p. 8). Probably on account of this difficulty a variant custom developed in certain localities to commence the new S at Lev. 2.10: והנותרת מן המנחה וגו', in order that the previous one should fulfill the above requirement (viz. Lev. 1.1–2.9; 26 verses). This assumption will explain the interesting statement in LR, c. 3.6 (cp. Esther R., c. 3.6): ר' חנינא בר' אבא (באסתר ר': בריה דר' אחא, וכצ"ל) אזל לחד אתר אשכח הדין פסוקא ראש סדרא (שם: ראש הסדר): והנותרת מן המנחה לאהרן ולבניו, מה פתח עלה, ממתים ידך ה'... והניחו יתרם לעולליהם, והנותרת מן המנחה לאהרן ולבניו. Evidently in the locality, which R. Ḥan. b. Aḥa (a Pal. Amora of the 4th century) visited, the new S began at Lev. 2.10 differently from his own custom.[16s] Yet this Rabbi was able to evolve a ready Pet. to suit the situation. We have thus to assume that since Lev. 1 deals with עולה and c. 2 with מנחה, hence in some localities in Pal. the previous S was concluded at 1.17 (אשה ריח ניחוח לה'), with 2.1 forming the opening v. of a new S, in accordance with the division of the subject matter, although c. 1 comprised only 17 verses. On the other hand, in different localities the difficulty was solved by extending S 74 to Lev. 2.9 (also concluding with אשה ריח ניחוח לה') and commencing the next S (No. 74a) with v. 10.[18]*

Now, in accordance with our procedure of investigation, the respective Prophetic Lections to such variant Sedarim (Lev. 2.1

[17] Cp. also LR, c. 1.7: ד"א ויקרא אל משה, מה כתיב למעלה מהענין פרשת (צ"ל: בפרשת)*[11] משכן, כאשר צוה ה' את משה. Here the reference to Exod. 40 (viz. vv. 19, 21, etc.) which formed a part of the previous S (No. 73, above, vol. I, 549 ff.) and hence was outside the present one (No. 74).

[18] To assume that in the above item, Lev. 2.3 was meant (beginning too with והנותרת מן המנחה וגו'), and accordingly the previous S concluded at 2.2 (where again אשה ריח נחוח לה' occurs), would not help matters since there would still be lacking 2 verses (Lev. 1.1–17+2.1–2 — 19 verses). Cp. also פי' מהרז"ו where too Lev. 2.10 has been suggested for another reason. Theodor (MGWJ, Vol. 35, p. 309) strangely confuses this variant S with the one at 2.1.[12]*

or 2.10) have to be ascertained in order to account for the homilies in LR, c. 3. To the S at 2.1 one may suggest a H from Mal. 1.11: ומנחה טהורה וגו׳ . . . כי ממזרח שמש ועד מבואו thus tallying with the initial v. of S: ונפש כי תקריב קרבן מנחה לה׳. This H probably extended to 2.7 (11 verses).[19] Indeed Mal. 2.5–7 are expressly commented upon in LR, c. 3.6.[20*] The Pet. of R. Isaac on Koh. 4.6: טוב מלא כף נ ח ת (LR., c. 3.1) is homiletically connected on the one hand with מנחה in Lev. 2.1 (cp. the conclusion: ד"א טוב מ ל א כ ף נחת זה קומץ מ נ ח ת נדבה של עני ו כ ו׳),[17s] but on the other hand with the H v. (Mal. 2.5): ומפני שמי נחת הוא. The next Pet. (§2) is on Ps. 22.24–25: י ר א י ה ׳ הללוהו . . . . כי לא בזה ולא שקץ ענות עני וגו׳. The tally with H is by means of ו י י ד ר א נ י ואתנם לו מורא (Mal. 2.5). And altogether the explanation of ירא י ה׳ as referring to gentiles, who are either 'God fearing' (ירא י שמים, the so-called 'sebomenoi' or 'metuentes') or became full proselytes (גרי צדק),[18s] has been inspired by the initial v. of H (Mal. 1.11) alluding to the high reverence of God's name among the nations. LR, c. 3.3 comments on Is. 56.7 dealing with the repentance from sin which is reflected in the H v. (Mal. 2.6): ורבים השיב מעון. Then follow items (§§4–5) on Lev. 1.16–17 by means of the well-known formula of: מה כתיב למעלה מן העניין (cp. above, p. 29). In §6 Lev. 2.2 is explained and subsequently 2.3: והנותרת מן המנחה לאהרן ולבניו weaving in expressly Mal. 2.5–7 the final verses of the suggested H (cp. the conclusion: מה כתיב בו ב ס ו ף כי שפתי כהן וגו׳, this being the last v. of H[19s]). In connection with Lev. 2.3 there is cited the story of R. Ḥan. b. Aḥa and his Pet. on the S that began with והנותרת מן המנחה. However, this S really started with the identical v. 10, and not 3 (as pointed out above, note 18). LR, c. 3.7, is a later addendum from SER (ed. Fried., 37–38) and is indeed missing in MSS Vat. and Brit. Mus. (cp. also above, p. 28, with regard to LR, cps. 1 and 2).[20s]

What H was there to the S that commenced with והנותרת מן המנחה? One could argue that the same H from Mal. 1.11 ff.

---

[19] The same H is listed to S. 67 (above, vol. I, p. 507).

[20] אהרן זכה לבנים בין כשרים בין פסולים וכו׳. This is no longer a part of the Pet. of R. Ḥan. b. Aḥa (cp. the parallel in Esther R.), but is a continuation of the previous section in LR (see further on).[13*]

would have suited here too owing to the same tally מנחה as in
the case of the S at Lev. 2.1 (above p. 29). However, the Pet.
of R. Ḥan. b. Aḥa from Ps. 17.14: ממתים ידך ה' מ מ ת י ם מחלד
חלקם בחיים וגו' would afford no tally with this H²¹⁸ — an essential
requirement that necessitates the assumption of another H
having served for this exceptional S. I suggest Is. 4:3: והיה
הנשאר בציון והנותר בירושלם וגו', tallying with והנותרת in Lev. 2.10;
such H probably extended from Is. 4.3–5.4+16 (10 verses).²⁰ᵃ
Now in the initial v. we read: כל הכתוב לחיים בירושלם, hence the
Pet. from Ps. 17.14 containing the phrase: חלקם בחיים. No more
homilies have been preserved on this very rare S. More current
in Amoraic times was the S that began with Lev. 2.1 But this
too was later on omitted, and the next regular S (No. 75)
commenced at Lev. 4.1.

Seder 75 (2)

וידבר ה' . . . דבר אל בני ישראל לאמר נפש כי תחטא בשגגה מכל מצות ה'
אשר לא תעשינה וגו', Lev. 4.1–2.

Haftarah: הן כל הנפשות לי הנה כנפש האב וכנפש הבן לי הנה הנפש החטאת
היא תמות, Ezekiel 18.4–17 (14 verses, so B 42). No doubt there
was skipping, viz. 18.4–9 (where there begins a new Seder in
this prophetic book)+14–17 (10 verses); the tendency was to
omit the passage referring to the death of the sinner (verses
10–13) and rather to continue with such that described the doer
of good who would live (note the concluding phrase חיה יחיה
in v. 9 and v. 17). C 34 has 18.4–12, with the end missing
owing to a lacuna. C 35 lists (according to Abrahams' description) 18.4–13+16–17 (12 verses), but this fragment needs re-
examination. The same applies to CL, defective at the beginning, which is supposed to continue up to 18.10 (hence verses
4–10)+32 (thus 8 verses). However, the conclusion at v. 32
seems to be appropriate since the homilies discussed forthwith,
refer to the whole chapter, although a great deal of it was not
recited as H; as noticed frequently before, the Aggadists would
employ for their homiletic purpose also the portion skipped.

---

²⁰ᵃ About the same H to S 91, see infra, p. 97.

Hence it may be assumed that H extended from 18.4 to 13+32 (11 verses).[228]

Yannai in his Ḳerobah also seems to indicate Ezek. 18.4 as the initial v. of H to our S (see ed. Zulay, p. 123).

The connection between the former and the latter lies in the tally of a sinning soul. This afforded the opportunity for reciting in the synagogue the important doctrine of Ezekiel emphasizing individual responsibility. A portion of Ezekiel, c. 18, was recited too in connection with Seder 61 (as shown above, vol. I, pp. 475-79).[238]

STRUCTURE OF HOMILIES

1. *Y Sermon*. TB, Wayyikra, §8, T, §6:

וידבר ה' אל משה לאמר, נפש כי תחטא וגו'. ילמדנו רבינו: מהו שיכנס אדם
להר הבית במקלו ובאפונדתו, כך שנו רבותינו: לא יכנס אדם להר הבית
במקלו ובאפונדתו ובאבק שברגליו, שלא ינהג בו קלות ראש אפילו בחרבנו וכו'.[21]

The starting-point is to be found in the H v. (Ezekiel 18.6): אל ה ה ר י ם לא אכל, hence the suggestion for the Y question and answer concerning one's conduct when entering the Temple mount (הר ה ב י ת). The latter is to be held in reverence, even after the destruction of the Temple, by analogy to the Sabbath whose sanctity is perpetual. The homilist proceeds to introduce a verse from the Hagiographa (Koh. 3.16): מקום המשפט שם הרשע which is Aggadically first applied to the ruined Temple and subsequently to the soul that sins, though aware of the right (משפט). The end of the homily is curtailed, and there is missing the usual formula: מנין, ממה שקרינו בענין, נפש כי תחטא.[22] Now Koh. 3.16 tallies by means of 'justice' and its opposite 'wickedness' with the H where these topics are illustrated by the respective deeds of a righteous father and a wicked son, and vice versa (משפט recurs several times, Ezek. 18.5, etc., and

---

[21] Cp. M. Ber. 9.5 (see MY in §7, p. 60), and the variants in Tos. 7.19, Babli 62b, bottom, and Yer. IX, 14c, top. About the same Y topic to S see infra, p. 34.[14*]

[22] TB, §§8-9, should form a unit (as in T, §6, beginning), comprising the first part of the Y sermon.

corresponding to רשע cp. 18.20: ורשעת הרשע). The homily also weaves in the point concerning the soul being deposited in God's hand, citing Job 12.6: אשר בידו נפש כל חי. This thought has been suggested by the initial v. of H (18.4): הן כל הנפשות לי הנה! Thus there is clear evidence of the close relationship of this Y item with the H to our S.[23]

Further homilies concerning the sinning soul we have first in TB §10 (T, §6, middle), introducing Prov. 19.2: גם בלא דעת נפש לא טוב ואץ ברגלים חוטא, which tallies by the italicized words with both Lev. 4.2 and Ezek. 18.4. Then in TB, §11 (T, §6), Koh. 3.16, which was commented upon already in the first portion of the Y sermon, is again dealt with. Here the second half of the verse ומקום הצדק שמה הרשע is explained, viz. the soul originating from where neither sin nor guilt exists becomes addicted to sin.[24] For the tally of משפט and צדק with H cp. Ezek. 18.5: ועשה משפט וצדקה (see also v. 19). In this portion the initial v. of H is cited expressly (cp. T לפיכך פנה לגוף ונתן לנפש אפופסין. שנ' הנפש החוטאת היא תמות). The conclusion of the section (TB, §12, T, §6, end) treats of the future judgment of the sinning soul, leading down to the following *peroration*: אמר הקב"ה: בעוה"ז, על ידי שיצה"ר שולט בהם (צ"ל: בכם, כמו בת"ה),

---

[23] Owing to the total unawareness of the role of H in determining the trend of the homilies, our Y item is readily transferred in GS, I, 473, No. 56, to Lev. 5.1 (S 76), where *the H is quite different* (infra, p. 36) and thus offers no contact whatever. See also above, vol. i, p. 146, note 155.

[24] Cp. T, where the text is, on the whole, better than in TB: אמר הכתוב מקום המשפט שמה הרשע ומקום הצדק שמה הרשע, הנפש שניתנה מן הצדק, במקום (צ"ל: ממקום, כמו בת"ב) שאין שם לא עון ולא חטא, היא חוטאת להקב"ה. Similar to the item in TB, §11, T, §6, is the passage emanating from the section to our S in Midr. Yel. (as cited in 'Arukh s. v. פנן 2, ed. Kohut VI, 293): בי למדנו בסוף ויקרא: נפש כי תחטא (היינו וי' ד', ב', ולא ה', בא כמו שמציין קאהוט בטעות), לפולח ופנן שהכעיסו את המלך וכו' עד הפולח הזה יודע נימוסי והכעיס אותי לכן הרגתיו, אבל הפנן הדיוט הוא ואינו יודע נימוסי. לכן פניתי (=פיניתי). In v. דפקופלן (Kohut, III, 102, bottom) the sentence הפולח הזה וכו' is quoted as follows: בי למדנו בסוף ויקרא הפולח הזה יודע נימוסי ודיסקפלינא שלי. The fact that this Y section is indicated as being at *the end of* ויקרא פ' would tend to show that in Midr. Yel. (at least in the copy which R. Nathan b. Yeḥiel of Rome used) there was no section to the next S (No. 76) which in reality should have had the above designation (see infra, p. 37). Cp. further note 26. (For the expression פינה את, to free, see also infra, note 127.)

הייתם חוטאים, אבל לעוה"ב אני עוקרו מכם, שנ' [ונתתי לכם ל ב חד ש
ו ר ו ח ח ד ש ה אתן בקרבכם] והסירותי את לב האבן מבשרכם וכו'.‏²⁴⁸
This final v. cited here (Ezek. 36.26) is clearly reflected by Ezek.
18.31: ‏ועשו לכם לב חדש ורוח חדשה.‏²⁵

A further portion of the Y sermon to our S, missing in TB
and T, is found in YSH (קונדריס אחרון Jellinek, BHM, VI, p. 84,
No. 38).²⁶ The first item here emphasizes the need of repentance
for the sinner — a theme that is the *leitmotif* of our H which
concludes (18.32) with the summons: והשיבו וחיו! The second
item there comments on the reason why in Lev. 4.2 the singular
is used (נפש) and not the plural (נפשות).²⁷ This whole idea has
been suggested by the initial v. of H (18.4): הן כל הנפשות לי הנה!
(See also further on.)

2. *Other Homilies.* LR, c. 4, contains much of the same
Aggadic material, though in a variant manner. Thus in §1 there
is the Pet. on Koh. 3.16 and in §3 on Prov. 19.2. But in §2
there is a new Pet. on Koh. 6.7 where the word הנפש affords a
tally with both Lev. 4.2 and Ezek. 18.4. In §6 there is introduced Jer. 50.17: שה פזורה ישראל in order to develop the Aggadah
as to why in Lev. 4.2 the singular is used for soul and not the
plural. The verbal tally is in the name 'Israel' as compared to
בני ישראל in Lev. 4.1 and בני ישראל in Ezek. 18.6, etc., but the

---

²⁵ In Midr. Agg. (II, p. 9) there is a further addendum: ולא עוד אלא שאני
נותן ביניכם שלום, שנ' וכל בניך למודי ה' ורב שלום בניך (יש' נ"ד, י"ג).‏ In citing this
final v. which foretells the ideal state of affairs when *all* children will conduct themselves properly as being "taught of the Lord," there is a subtle
homiletic contrast to the topic of our H which deals with the sad case of a
wicked son of a righteous father (Ezek. 18.10 ff.).¹⁵*

²⁶ This passage has the heading: ונפש כי תחטא and accordingly Jellinek
gives the reference Lev. 5.1, with which v. there commences the next S (No.
76, infra, p. 36). However, the intrinsic analysis shows that the whole piece
belongs to our S, hence the heading should read: נפש כי תחטא (Lev. 4.2).
Indeed the homily there on Koh. 9.10 is also found, though in a variant
form, to our present S in MHG, III, p. 61. The assignment of this Y passage
to its proper place would further be in accord with the observation gained
from 'Arukh (above, note 24) that Midr. Yel. had really no section to
S 76.¹⁶*

²⁷ ד"א למה אינו אומר נפשות כי יחטאו," שכל ישראל נקראו נפש אחת וכו'.‏ The same
topic is also dealt with in LR, c. 4.6, though in a different form.¹⁷*

whole Aggadic point has been suggested by the initial v. of H
(18.4), as pointed out above.

LR, c. 5, is to Lev. 4.3 and seems to be of a secondary character not pertaining to the actual sermon to our S. There is a
long homily on Job 34.29 (§1–3) with the final point applicable
here to the effect that, unlike a human ruler, God makes no
distinction between a group and an individual; hence both the
anointed priest and the whole congregation of Israel offered some
sin offering (cp. Lev. 4.3 and 4.13–14). The Pet. v. itself (Job
34.29) has no bearing on the above H.[25s] The same applies to
the rest of LR, c. 5, a part of which was also incorporated in the
section in Midr. Yel. to our Seder.[27a]

SEDER 76 (3)

ונפש כי תחטא ושמעה קול א ל ה והוא עד או ראה או ידע אם לוא יגיד
ונשא עונו, Lev. 5.1.

Ḥafṭarah: ויאמר אלי זאת ה א ל ה היוצאת על פני כל הארץ כי כל
Zechariah 5.3–6.14, הגונב מזה כמוה נקה, וכל הנשבע מזה כמוה נקה
(23 verses, so B 42). No doubt there was skipping, viz. 5.3–11 +
6.14 (10 verses); at the last verse there begins a new S in Minor
Prophets. C 35 lists 5.3–11 + 6.11–12 (11 verses). CL, according
to Abrahams, gives 5.3–8 + 6.15 (7 verses). C 14 also begins
with 5.3, but the end is defective. Yannai's Ḳerobah to our S
(ed. Zulay, 124–26) is lacking the part indicating the initial v.
of H.

Between S and H there is only the linguistic tally of אלה,
but the point of swearing falsely (Zech. 5.4) has an intrinsic
connection with Lev. 5.4.

STRUCTURE OF HOMILIES

No Y theme has been preserved. Indeed from the indications
in Arukh (see above, note 24, and cp. note 26) it would seem

[27a] See 'Arukh, s. v. גל, 7 (Kohut, III, 279): ובי ל מ ד נ ו, ובויק'ר אם הכהן
המשיח, פרשת ומי ירשיע (פ'ה, ה'), מה לך פה ומי לך פה, גלוייא בר גליי וכו'. The reading
בבית הכנסת (as in 'Arukh), and not בבית הקברות (as in printed texts of LR),
is also found in MSS. Vat. and Brit. Mus. of LR.[18*]

that Midr. Yel. (at least the copy which R. Nathan b. Yeḥiel
of Rome had before him) contained no section to the present S,
and accordingly S 75 comprised Lev. 4–5, with the next one
commencing at 6.1 (No. 76a, infra, p. 38–42). Otherwise the
items in the section to our S in TB Wayyikra, §§13–18, T, 7,
reflect the above H. Thus the Pet. from Koh. 5.1: אל תבהל
על פיך...כי האלהים בשמים ואתה על הארץ tallies with the
H v.: בין הארץ ובין השמים (Zech. 5.9).²⁶ˢ Likewise the
next Pet. from Prov. 29.24: חולק עם גנב שונא נפשו אלה ישמע
ולא יניד (TB, §14, T, §7) supplies the connection with H: ובאה
אל בית הגנב (Zech. 5.4), in addition to אלה common to both S
and H.²⁷ˢ The point of swearing falsely (weaving in Jer. 7.9:
השבע לשקר and Mal. 3.15: ובנשבעים לשקר, TB, §§15, end, 16 and 17,
beginning, T, §7) has a direct contact with Zech. 5.4: ואל בית
הנשבע בשמי לשקר. There is no proper *peroration* at the conclusion
of the section (end of TB, §18, T, §7).

LR, c. 6, begins with a Pet. on Prov. 24.28–9: אל תהי עד
חנם ברעך והפתית בשפתיך אל תאמר כאשר עשה לי וגו'. The connection
with the intial v. of S is clear, viz. by means of עד,²⁸ˢ but with the
H there is only the weak linguistic link of אמר (viz. here אל תאמר
as compared to ויאמר אלי in Zech. 5.4, cp. further v. 5 and following). There follows (§2) the Pet. on Prov. 29.24 as to which
see above. In §3 Zech. 5 is expressly woven in.²⁸ The remainder
of LR, c. 6, is disjointed, and there has been tacked on at the end
a peroration²⁹ that seems to emanate from the conclusion of the
sermon to S 54 (see above vol. I, p. 416).²⁹ˢ A more suitable
ending than in either the versions of Tanḥuma or in LR seems
to be found in JTS MS. (infra, H. pt., p. יט) emphasizing the
importance of Truth and concluding with the designation of
God as Truth (והקב"ה אמת, שנ' ויי' אלהים אמת הוא אלהים חיים ומלך
עולם). This final v. cited (Jer. 10.10) would be in contrast to the
H v. which denounces him who falsely takes an oath in God's
name (Zech. 5.4: הנשבע בשמי לשקר) — the very Deity whose
characteristic is Truth.

²⁸ אל תהי שבועת שוא קלה בעיניך, שהרי זכריה חמי ליה, ואשא עיני ואראה וכו'. The
H. v. (Zech. 5.4) is mentioned at the end.¹⁹*
²⁹ Viz. the passage beginning with ר' אבא בר כהנא אמר חשך ואפלה וכו', as
compared to the one in PRK, 68a, PR, 90 a-b.²⁰*

Seder 76a (3a)

וידבר ה' אל משה לאמר, צו את אהרן ואת בניו לאמר זאת תורת העולה היא
העולה על מוקדה על המזבח וגו', Lev. 6.1–2.

The regular S commenced at Lev. 6.12 (No. 77, infra, p. 42),
and hence there could be none here since such a S would comprise only 11 verses (Lev. 6.1–11). However, the Midrashim
point to the latter S. Also the fact that the Babylonian AC has
its Sidra at 6.1–2 (פ' צו) indicates that originally there began
here a Torah lection also according to TC (see above vol. I,
pp. 8–9). There is thus apparent another case of shifting of the
Sedarim which probably was the consequence of the difference
in the previous Sidra (above, p. 36), viz. that the custom to
insert a new S at Lev. 5.1 (no. 76) resulted in extending it to
6.11, with the next one (no. 77) commencing at 6.12–13, whereas
the usage to combine Lev. 4–5 as one S (no. 75) had as its sequel
the commencement of the next S at 6.1–2 (no. 76a). In this
manner there was preserved a certain symmetry in the respective
lengths of the Torah readings. It may be further surmised that
the objection was raised to conclude a S with a word connoting
'guilt' (לאשמה בה, 5.26); by shifting the final v. of the lection to
6.11 which ends with יקדש, a more propitious finale was attained.
Anyhow, the arrangement to have S 76 followed by 77 prevailed,
as is evident from the Genizah lists and Yannai's Ḳerobah
(infra, p. 42). On the other hand S 76a seems to have been more
current in Amoraic times than 77 (which excluded each other),
since the former is represented more in the Midrashim than the
latter (see infra, p. 39). (Concerning the influence of the present
shifting of Sedarim on the subsequent ones, nos. 77a and 78, see
infra, pp. 42–46.) According to the Babylonian ritual, the
Prophetic lection for פ' צו began with Jer. 7.21: כה אמר ה' צבאות
אלהי ישראל עולותיכם ספו על זבחיכם וגו', thus tallying with
זאת תורת העולה (Lev. 6.2). One could assume that in Pal. too the
H for S 76a was similar, viz. 7.21–28+9.22 (also beginning with
כה אמר ה') and 23 (10 verses; at 23 there starts a new Seder in
Jeremiah). However, this H is essentially one of denunciation
and does not accord with the usual characteristics of a TC reading
from the Prophets in offering consolation of Israel (נחמת ישראל).

Furthermore the Midrashic homilies, to be analyzed forthwith, do not correspond to the above H from Jer. I therefore posit as such for our S Mic. 6.6: במה אקדם ה' אכף לאלהי מרום האקדמנו בעולות בעגלים בני שנה, affording the same tally of Olah.[30s] It probably comprised 6.6–8 + 7.14–20 (10 verses). The tendency was to omit the part foretelling punishment (פורענות), such as Mic. 6.9 ff., and complete the reading with cheerful and encouraging verses (cp. above, p. 23, concerning the H to S 74 from Mic. 6.9 ff., which in reality was not accepted in Amoraic times, see infra, p. 41 ff.).[31s] With the final v. of H (Mic. 7.20) there begins a new Seder in Minor Prophets.

Structure of Homilies

1. No Y topic has been preserved in the Tanḥumas. That Midr. Yel. contained a section to the present S, is evident from the passage cited in YSH (קונדריס אחרון BHM, V, p. 85, No. 39), which emphasizes the importance of a burnt-offering, as being one of voluntary character, unlike the sacrifices for sin or guilt (חטאת ואשם) which were for atonement.[29a] Another morsel is given in Arukh, s. v. צר 3 (Kohut, VII, 43).[29b] The latter is of special interest because it reveals that the redactor of T, Ṣaw, §§13–14 (containing much extraneous material), utilized the Y section under discussion.[29c] In view of this latter fact and

[29a] זאת תורת העולה היא העולה (היינו: על מוקדה על המזבח כל הלילה וגו'), שלא תזח מן המזבח, מפני שהיא חביבה מכל הקרבנות, לה"ד (= למה הדבר דומה) למלך שהיתה לו שמחה, והיו אריסין (צ"ל: אריסיו) ובני ביתו ואוהביו מביאין לו דורונות... כך אם חטא אדם מביא קרבן חטאת, ואם אשם מביא קרבן אשם, אבל העולה נדבה היא, לפיכך חביבה היא לפני.

[29b] בריש צו בילמדנו: וכשנגלה הקב"ה ליחזקאל ואמר לו: הגד לבית ישראל את הבית (יח' מ"ג, י', ולפנינו במקרא: את בית), אמר לו: רבש"ע, וכי עכשיו בונין אותו שאמרת וישמרו את (צ"ל: את כל צורתו ואת) כל חקותיו ועשו אותם (שם, י"א), אמר לו עכשיו יהיו קורין בצורת הבית, ואני מעלה עליהן כאילו בבנינו הן עסוקין, וכן בסדר קרבנות.

[29c] Cp. §14, towards beginning: וכן אמר שמואל בר אבא אמר הקב"ה לישראל: אעפ"י שבית המקדש עתיד ליחרב והקרבנות בטלין, לא תשכחו עצמכם לסדר הקרבנות... ואם רצונך לידע, בא וראה כשהקב"ה מראה ליחזקאל את צורת הבית, מה הוא אומר, הגד את בית ישראל... אני מעלה עליהם כאילו הן עוסקין בבנין הבית. In LR, c. 7.3, end, the topic is only briefly mentioned: שמואל אמר ... כאילו אתם בוני אותו, and there can be no doubt that in T the Y passage is quoted, however touched up it may be.[21*] In T, §13, another Y item is cited, viz. ארבעה הם חיים, וקראם הכתוב מתים, ואלו הן: האביון, והמצורע, והעור, ומי

also of the above item concerning Olah not being offered up for an actual transgression, it is reasonable to assume that in T §13, end, there has been preserved the missing Y topic of question and answer to our S (ד"א זאת תורת העולה, כך שנו רבותינו היתה עולה, (כולה קדושה שלא היתה באה על עונות . . . אלא על ההרהור הלב היא באה, וכו'. Of course in T, in its present form, the original Y language is much worn off by the redactor. Above (vol. I, 113–115 to S 12) the similar Y topic concerning a burnt-offering was discussed (ילמדנו: העולה על מה היתה באה, וכו'). Here, too, it probably began in the same manner, but in the reply emphasis was laid upon the fact that this sacrifice was not for an overt act of transgression but only for mental doubting, thus: ילמדנו רבינו: העולה על מה היתה באה, כך שנו רבותינו: לעולם אין העולה באה אלא על ההרהור הלב. Thereupon this latter theme was developed similar to LR, c. 7.3.[29d] The starting point would be the word *Olah* occurring both in S and H.

שאין לו בנים: המצורע מנין, שנאמר בשנת מות המלך עוזיהו (יש' ו', א'), ולמה כנהו הכתוב מת, אלא שנצטרע והיה נחשב כמת, וכן אתה מוצא במרים, שנ' אל נא תהי כמת (במ' י"ד, י"ב), הוי המצורע נחשב כמת; ומי שאין לו בנים מנין, מרחל, שאמרה ליעקב הבה לי בנים ואם אין מתה אנכי (בר' ל', א'); ומנין העור שחשוב כמת, שנ' במחשכים הושיבני כמתי עולם (איכה ג', ו'); ומנין האביון, שנ' כי מתו כל האנשים המבקשים את נפשך (שמ' ד', י"ט). The point about Uzziah is cited from *Yel.* in YSH to Is. 6 (§404): בשנת מות המלך, וכי מת היה. אלא שנצטרע, ומצורע חשוב כמת, שנ' אל נא תהי כמת. About the whole item see GR, c. 71.6 and parallels (ed. Theod. — Alb., 829–30). As reconstructed above, the Y item read originally; only a late redactor of T, §13, inserted the following extraneous matter: a) between אלא שנצטרע and והיה נחשב כמת a whole passage (from אף הצרעת זרחה במצחו to שנ' בשנת מות המלך עזיהו) emanating from Rashi to Is. 6.1–4 (as rightly pointed out by Reifmann, *Bet Talmud*, II, 184, No. 24); b) between הוי המצורע נחשב כמת and וכן אתה מוצא במרים a long passage in comment on Num. 12 which again is mostly based on Rashi, *a. l.*, (as pointed out already by the author of אות אמת).

[29d] See T, §13, where the passage should read: העולה היתה כולה קדושה, מפני שלא היתה באה על עונות, [חטאת היתה באה על החטאים], אשם היתה באה על הגזילות, אבל העולה היתה באה לא על חטאת (צ"ל: חטא), ולא על גזל, אלא על ההרהור הלב היא באה. Cp., TB, Ṣaw, §9, T, §7: והחטאת היתה באה על השגגה, and T, Teṣṣawweh, §15: החטאת היתה באה על החטא וכו' (see further, above, vol. I, H, pt., p. 257). In the former Tanh. item preference over all other sacrifices is given to Todah, and in the latter item incense (קטורת) is singled out. But here the importance of 'Olah is enhanced over that of either the sacrifice for sin or guilt because the former was only for mental doubting and not for an actual breach of the Law. For the same enhancement of 'Olah see the Y passage cited before (note 29a).

2. The sections in TB, Ṣaw, §§1–4, T, §§1–2, are now to be
analyzed. First there is the Pet. on Ps. 89.7: כי מי בשחק יערוך
לה' ידמה לה' בבני אלים which v., with its emphasis on God's
uniqueness in the skies, corresponds to the initial v. of H (Mic.
6.6) containing the phrase לאלהי מרום.[328] In this homily v. 7
(וכתיב הירצה ה' באלפי אילים) is woven in expressly. In TB, §2
(T, §1) Is. 61.8 is commented upon; the point of God loving
justice (אוהב משפט) links up with Mic. 6.8 wherein one of God's
demands on man is to do justice (עשות משפט) — a sort of *imitatio
dei*.[338] The further point of God hating robbery (שונא גזל בעולה),
which is the main shift of the homily warning man not to obtain
such illicit gain and then employ some of it for sacrifices, is also
reflected in our H where deceit, cheating and violence are strongly
denounced (Mic. 6.10 ff., this in skipped part which, however,
was utilized by the Aggadist). The ingenious comment on
היא העולה על מוקדה, to the effect that "he who exalts himself
will ultimately disappear by fire" (TB, §3, T, §2), has been suggested by the H. v. (6.8) which demands of man "to walk humbly
with thy God!"[348] This theme of arrogance resulting in destruction is extensively developed leading down to the *peroration*
that Israel, because of its humility (שעשו עצמם נבזים ושפלים)
will endure after the disappearance of Esau (TB, §4, end, T,
§2, end): כיון שעשו מסתלק מן העולם, הקב״ה וישראל משתיירין, שנ' אחת
היא יונתי תמתי, ואומר ה' ב ד ד ינחנו ואין עמו אל נכר. The last v. cited
(Deut. 32.12) corresponds to the H. v. (Mic. 7.14): רעה עמך
בשבט צאן נחלתך שכני ל ב ד ד וגו'. Thus the suggested H is well
woven into these homilies.

The same applies to LR, c. 7. First there is the Pet. from
Prov. 10.12: שנאה תעורר מדנים ועל כל פשעים תכסה אהבה which tallies
with ועובר על פשע in H (Mic. 7.18). There follow (§2) the comments on Ps. 51.18–21. By means of עולה (v. 21) there is the
verbal tally with both S and H; there is further the intrinsic
connection of Ps. 51.18 with Mic. 7.18–19.[358] In §6 the above
Aggadah is given concerning arrogance (שכל המתגאה אינו נידון
אלא באש). The *peroration* is curtailed at the end and there is
missing the addendum: כיון שעשו וכו' (as in TB and T) which
establishes the connection with H (as pointed out above). —
In JTS MS (infra, H. pt., p. כב) there is a further Pet. from

Hos. 6.6: כי חס ד חפצתי ולא זבח ודעת אלהים מעולות which tallies by means of חסד with Mic. 6.6 ואהבת חסד, in addition to the mentioning of Olah common to both S and H.[36s]

SEDER 77 (4)

וידבר ה' אל משה לאמר, זה קרבן אהרן ובניו אשר יקריבו לה' ביום המשח אתו עשירית האפה סלת מ נ ח ה תמיד וגו', Lev. 6.12–13.

Haftarah: וערבה לה' מ נ ח ת יהודה וירושלם כימי עולם וכשנים קדמניות, Mal. 3.4–12 (9 verses, 20 B 42 which breaks off with this item, see above, vol. I, p. 574). C15, beginning missing, ends with 3.10 (hence only 7 verses), but the conclusion at v. 12 is to be preferred (see infra, p. 43). C 14 also begins with 3.4, the end is missing. Yannai in his Ḳerobah too indicates this initial verse (see ed. Zulay, p. 128). About the same H to S 124 see infra, p. inc.

Only the word מנחה connects S with H.[37s]

STRUCTURE OF HOMILIES

No section is preserved in TB or T to our S, evidently because of the S at Lev. 6.1–2 (No. 76a) which made impossible an S here (above, pp. 38–42). We may also assume that in Midr. Yel., which contained a sermon to S 76a (above, pp. 39–40), the present S was not represented and hence the same situation obtained in TB and T. However, LR includes sections to both these Sedarim which excluded each other (thus c. 7 to No. 76a and c. 8 to No. 77). This fact tends to show that both Sedarim were current in Pal. in Amoraic times, of course in different localities, with the former one apparently having wider acceptance. But ultimately the latter prevailed, as is evident from the Genizah lists and from Yannai's Ḳerobah, due perhaps to the reason suggested above (p. 38).[30]

---

[30] About similar cases see above, vol. I, p. 52, and several times subsequently.

In LR, c. 8, there is the first Pet. on Ps. 75.8: כי אלהים שופט
זה ישפיל וזה ירים which has a verbal tally with H v. (Mal. 3.5):
וקרבתי אליכם למשפט.[38s] The next Pet. from Jud. 14.14:
ואמר להם מהאכל יצא מאכל וגו', also has a point of contact with
וגערתי לכם באוכל (Mal. 3.11).[39s] This shows that the conclusion
of H at 3.12 is to be preferred to the variant at 3.10 (above, p. 42)
since v. 11 is still regarded here as being a part of the Prophetic
lection. Finally, in the conclusion (§4, end), there is cited Mal.
1.11 which v. by means of ומנחה טהורה is connected with both S
and H containing the same tally.[40s] — In JTS MS. (infra, H.
pt., p. כה) the section to our S begins with a Pet. from Prov.
13.22: טוב ינחיל בני בנים וצפון לצדיק חיל חוטא.[41s] There is no direct
contact in this v. with H, except that the designation 'sinner'
(חוטא) can indeed be applied to each of the persons denounced
in the H v. (Mal. 3.5). But perhaps this whole item really belongs
to S 78 where it is more appropriate (see infra, p. 46). No further
homilies to the present S are available.

SEDER 77a (4a)

וזאת תורת זבח השלמים אשר יקריב לה', אם על תודה יקריבנו וגו'
Lev. 7.11–12.

This S, which is evident from the Midrashic sections (TB,
Ṣaw, §§5–10, T, §§3–7, LR, c. 9, and JTS Ms.), is the result of
the previous variant S (No. 76a). Thus those who read on the
previous Sabbath Lev. 6.1–2 ff., and hence could not have their
next S at 6.12–13 (above, p. 38), would have their lection on the
following Sabbath at 7.11–12. But those who adopted the
previous S to commence at 6.12–13 (No. 77) had their next S
at 8.1–2 (No. 78). Thus there was established a certain symmetry
in the respective lengths of the Sedarim. Moreover, there is
evident a certain harmonization of the sequence of the subject
matter involved; a S that began by זאת תורת העולה (Lev. 6.2,
No. 76a) was followed by one headed וזאת תורת זבח השלמים (Lev.
7.11, No. 77a), whereas the regular S (No. 77), that commenced
with the topic of the sacrifice of Aaron and his sons on the day
of their initiation, was properly succeeded by the next regular

S (No. 78) that described in detail that very ceremony. This will account properly for the shifting of the Sedarim in the present instance.

Haftarah. This has to be ascertained from the homilies to be discussed forthwith. On the basis of the latter, I posit as such Hos. 14.3: קחו עמכם דברים ושובו אל ה' אמרו אליו כל תשא עון וקח טוב ונשלמה פרים שפתינו, tallying by means of the verb שלם with שלמים in the initial v. of S. Such a H probably extended from 14.3 to 10+Joel 4.16–17 (10 verses).[31]

STRUCTURE OF HOMILIES

No Y topic has been preserved. In TB, §5, T, §3, there is given the Pet. from Prov. 3.17: דרכיה דרכי נעם וכל נתיבותיה שלום which tallies on the one hand with H referring to God's ways as being straight (Hos. 14.10: כי ישרים דרכי ה') similar to pleasant ways (דרכי נועם), and on the other hand שלום is connected with שלמים of S. The homily is curtailed at the end and there is no comment on Lev. 7.11 with which the item commences. Probably there was an additional remark that therefore these sacrifices are called שלמים because they 'establish peace between Israel and their Father in heaven' (cp. TB, §10, beginning, T §7, middle). The next Pet. (TB, §5, T, §4) is on Ps. 85.9: אשמעה מה ידבר האל ה' כי ידבר שלום אל עמו ואל חסידיו ואל ישובו לכסלה which in addition to the mentioning of *Shalom* tallies with Hos. 14.3 by way of contrast: there we have ואל ישובו לכסלה whereas here Israel is urged to return to God (ושבו אל ה'). There is moreover a linguistic tally of עמו as compared to מחסה לעמו וה' in the penultimate v. of H after the skipping (Joel 4.16). In TB, §9, T, §7, there is woven in Ps. 50.23: זובח תודה יכבדנני ושם דרך אראנו בישע אלהים which affords a point of contact on the one hand by means of זובח תודה with Lev. 7.12 (אם על תודה יקריבנו והקריב על זבח התודה), and on the other hand by means of ושם ד ר ך viz. 'he sets his way aright,' with Hos. 14.10: כי ישרים דרכי ה'. Also

---

[31] The same H, except for the concluding verses, has been suggested to S 66, but there the tally is different and also the corresponding homilies (Vol. I, 503–506).

'God's salvation' (אלהים י ש ע) is in contrast to אשׁור לא
יו שׁיענו in Hos. 14.4. The conclusion of the section dwells
on the importance of peace of which the sacrifices of שׁלמים were
a symbol (TB, §10, T, §7 end). The peroration deals with the
future restoration of the Diasporas to Jerusalem in peace. The
last verses cited (viz. Ps. 122.6 and Is. 66.12) mention Jerusalem
(in Is. 66.12: הנני נוטה אליה refers to v. 10: שׂמחו את ירושׁלים) and
thus supply a connection with the last verses of H (Joel 4.16–17)
containing the same word.

In LR, c. 9, there is first the Pet. on Ps. 50.23 as to which
v. see above.[42s] In §5 another one follows on Prov. 14.9: אוילים
יליץ אשׁם ובין ישׁרים רצון, in which v. the two contrasted groups
(אוילים and ישׁרים) correspond to those mentioned in Hos. 14.10
(צדיקים and פושׁעים), in addition to the linguistic tally of ישׁר
occurring in both places.[43s] Lastly in the *peroration* (§9, end)
the final verses cited are Is. 66.12(as to which see above) and
Is. 52.7;[44s] the latter v. tallies by its conclusion: אומר לציון
מלך אלהיך with the last v. of H (Joel 4.17): וידעתם כי אני ה' אלהיכם
שׁוכן בציון הר קדשׁי.

This peroration, which is a variant of the one in TB and
in T, has a still further modification in JTS Ms. (infra, H.
pt., p. כט): ואף לעתיד לבוא,[32] שׁיחזיר שׁדי שׁכינתו לירושׁלם ויחזיר כל
הגליות לתוכה, בתחלה בשׁלום הוא מבשׁרן, שׁנ' הנה על ההרים רגלי מבשׂר
משׁמיע שׁלום (נחום ב', א'),[33] וממלא ירושׁלם שׁלום, שׁנ' כה אמר י"י הנני נוטה
אליה כנהר שׁלום וכנחל שׁוטף וגו' (ישׁעיה ס"ו, י"ב). ומברך את עמו בשׁלום
שׁנ' יי" עוז לעמו יתן י"י יברך את עמו בשׁלום (תהלים כ"ט י"א).
This last v. (Ps. 29.11) cited here again tallies with the penultimate v. of H (Joel 4.16): וה' מחסה לעמו ומעוז לבני
ישׂראל.

Finally attention should be drawn to the Genizah fragment
(infra, H. pt., pp. כח–כט), comprising the end of a Midrashic section
to the present S and the beginning of one to the next S (No. 78).
This fragment forms a part of a new version of a Midrash to the
Pent. another portion of which to S 1 and 2 was published above

---

[32] This is to be preferred to the reading עוה'ב in the Tanhumas and
in LR.

[33] The similar v. Is. 52.7 is to be preferred, as in LR, because it contains
the name Zion.[22*]

(vol. I, H. pt., pp. 35–39). Here we have a homily on Ps.
116.17–19 ('לך אזבח זבח תודה וגו) tallying with Lev. 7.12: זבח
התודה). There is woven in the case of Jonah, citing 2.10: אשר
נדרי לה' אשלמה‌[45s] which v. is similar to Ps. 116.18: אשלמה‌נדרתי
both have a point of contact with the initial v. of H (Hos. 14.3):
וכל מי שהוא נודר :The *peroration*[33a] reads as follows. ונשלמה פרים שפתנו
ומשלם נדרו בעולם הזה, זוכה לשלם את נדרו לעתיד (היינו: לבוא) בירושלים
שנ' נדרי לה' אשלם נגדה נא וגו', בחצרות בית י"י בתוככי ירושלם וגו' (תהלים
קט"ז, י"ח–י"ט). Here again by means of Jerusalem there is a tally
with the last verses of H (above, p. 45). Thus the above suggested H clearly formed the background for the homilies to the
present S. (About the same peroration in LR, c. 37, end, to
S 100, see infra, p. 152.)

SEDER 78 (5)

וידבר ה' אל משה לאמר, קח את אהרן ואת בניו אתו ואת הבגדים ואת שמן
המשחה וגו', Lev. 8.1–2.

Haftarah: ובחר אתו מכל שבטי ישראל לי לכהן לעלות על מזבחי להקטיר
קטרת לשאת אפוד לפני וגו', I Samuel 2.28. CL has 2.28–31, skipping
to 3.5 and then to 3.20 (hence in all 6 verses). There is evident
the tendency to omit the denunciatory verses as much as possible, thus 2.32–4 and 36 (cp. also infra, p. 50). However, the
whole remainder of c. 2, viz. 28–36,+3.20 comprises 10 verses,
as was the usual practice, and hence the regular H to our S
should be reconstrued. This is borne out by C 15 which gives
2.28–33; no doubt the end is missing owing to a lacuna, although
not indicated by Abrahams, since it is inconceivable for a H to
end with such a terrible sentence of punishment (פורענות):
וכל מרבית ביתך ימותו אנשים. Hence the full H in this fragment was,
as suggested above, 2.28–36+3.20; with the last v. (3.20) there
begins a new Seder in this Prophetic book.

    Linguistically there is no tally between H and S unless we
take the particle את common to both, but intrinsically the Ephod
(לשאת אפוד לפני) was one of the garments put on Aaron at his

[33a] About the same peroration in LR, c. 37, end, to S 100, see infra,
p. 152.

initiation (See Lev. 8.7), hence there is a connection with the
commencement of the S (ואת הבגדים, 8.2).[46s]

STRUCTURE OF HOMILIES

No Y question and answer have been preserved. Yet in
YSH (קונדריס אחרון, Jellinek, BHM, VI, p. 85, No. 40) a passage
from Midr. Yel. to our S is cited which weaves in explicitly a
verse from the above H (1 S 2.30).[34] Another Y item is cited
in Jacob Sikilli's *Yalkut Talmud Torah* to Leviticus (see *REJ*,
XIII, p. 231, No. VI).

The sections to the present S in TB and T clearly presuppose
the above H. Thus the Pet. from Ps. 65.5: אשרי ת ב ח ר
ותקרב ישכון חצריך וגו', (TB, §11, T, §8) tallies with ובחור אותו in
the initial v. of H; it is indeed cited there expressly (מנין שבחרו
ובחור אותו 'שנ); the text here should be compared to the one in
NR, c. 3.2 (infra, p. 193).[47s] The next Pet. (TB, §12, 1, §9) on
Prov. 3.35: כ ב ו ד חכמים ינחלו וכסילים מרים ק ל ו ן clearly
reflects the H. v. (1 S. 2.30): כי מכבדי א כ ב ד ובזי יקלו.
The further homily (TB, §13, T, §10) introduces Prov. 20.7:
מ ת ה ל ך בתומו צדיק אשרי בניו אחריו corresponds to the same v.:
אמור אמרתי ביתך ובית אביך י ת ה ל כ ו לפני עד עולם which, however,
was not to be realized in the case of Eli and his sons owing to
the latters' misconduct; indeed, they are mentioned expressly
within the homily (ואף עלי היה צדיק ולא היו בניו כמוהו).[48s] The
conclusion of the section (TB, §16, T, §12), developing the theme
of God's walking in the future together with the righteous
(הקב"ה אומר להם: אני ואתם נ ה ל ך ב ע ו ל ם שנ' ו ה ת ה ל כ ת י
בתוככם), again reflects homiletically the above v.: י ת ה ל כ ו

---

[34] קח את הבגדים (צ"ל: קח [את אהרן ואת בניו ו[את הבגדים), שהן כבודו של אדם. בן
סירא אומר הדרים [הדר אלהים] בני אדם והבגדים מכבדין האדם. מעשה בחסיד אחד כשהיה
עולה מן השוק היה נוטל בנדיו ומקפלן, אמרו לו: כמה תלמידים יש לך ועבדים ובני בית
לקפלם, אמר להם: הבגדים מכבדים אותי בשוק, אף אני מכבד אותם בבית, כי מכבדי אכבד
(ש"א ב', ל'). About the above quotation from Ben Sira see *JQR*, III, p. 695,
No. 19 — The indication מדרש ילמדנו in YSH, Lev. §513, for the passage
commencing: א"ר סימון כשם שהקרבנות מכפרין כך הבגדים מכפרין וכו', is evidently
a scribal error since the whole item is found in LR, c. 10.6 (from ואת פר
החטאת in YSH, cp. LR, c. 10.9). See also infra, note 70b.[23*]

לפני עד עולם, and the same applies to the last v. cited there
לפיכך ישראל עתידים לומר (כמו בת"ה) כי זה אלהים (Ps. 48.15):
אלהינו עולם ועד הוא ינהגנו על-מות (cp. also infra, note
35).[49a]

As regards LR, c. 10, there is first the Pet. on Ps. 45.8:
אהבת צדק ותשנא רשע על כן משחך אלהים אלהיך וגו' (§§1–3). This v.
has been used frequently for the purpose of commencing there-
with a homily to a given Seder (thus to Nos. 10, 12, and 15b,
see above, Vol. I, pp. 152–3, and cp. there H. pt., p. 59, note 50).
Here the v. is applied among others to Aaron (§3) whose anointment (initiation) is described in our S (cp. Lev. 8.12).[50a] The
verbal connection with both S and H is to be found in משחך
as compared to שמן המשחה in Lev. 8.2 and משיחי in 1 S.
2.35 The next Pet. (§4) introduces Prov. 24.11: הצל לקוחים
למות ומטים להרג אם תחשוך and applies it to Aaron's four sons
two of whom perished whereas the other two were saved (מתו
שנים ונשארו שנים, cp. further §5, end). The whole point of the
death of Nadab and Abihu, which event is recorded in the *next S*
(cp. Lev. 10.1 ff.), is brought in here by reason of the H which
foretells the simultaneous death of Eli's two sons (1 S.2.34:
ביום אחד ימותו שניהם).[51a] Finally there is the *conclusion* (§9, end)
dealing with the spaciousness of the future Jerusalem.[35] The
last verses cited are Is. 54.2–3 wherein the sentence וזרעך
נוים יירש connects by way of contrast with the H v. (1 S. 2.31):
זַרְעֲךָ (taken as: וגדעתי את זרעך ואת זרע בית אביך מהיות זקן בביתך
ואת זֶרַע, as indeed in LXX). In JTS Ms. (infra, H. pt., p. לא)
this peroration is couched differently: אף לעתיד לבוא כך הוא עתיד
לעשות לציון, שכל אכלוסי ישראל מתכנסין לתוכה והן אומרין: צר לי המקום
נשה לי ואשבה (ישעיה מ"ט, כ'), ומה הוא [עושה], מרחיב את ירושלם, כמה
שנ' הרחיבי מקום אהלך (שם, נ"ד, ב'), וכשם שהלבֿיש את ישראל בגדים
יפים לשעבר, שנ' ואלבישך רקמה (יחזקאל ט"ז, י') וכל העניׄין הזה. ונטלו
מהן, שנ' ויתנצלו בני ישראל (שמות ל"ג ו'), עתיד הקב"ה להחזיר את הבגדים,
שנ' כי הלבישני בגדי ישע מעיל צדקה וגו' (ישעיה ס"א, י'). Then there is a

---

[35] אף לעתיד לבוא כן, שנ' בעת ההוא יקראו לירושלם כסא ה' ונקוו אליה כל הגוים וכו'.
In the Tanḥumas the enlargement of Jerusalem is also woven in (וכן אתה
מוצא לעוה"ב שהקב"ה מרחיב את ירושלם וכו'), but there is added another conclusion
about God's presence amidst the righteous (as to which see above, p. 47.)

return to the topic of Aaron's beauteous sacerdotal garments
mentioned at the beginning of S (ואת הבגדים Lev. 8.2) one of
which was the Ephod alluded to in the initial v. of H (see above,
p. 46). The point of garments enhancing man's dignity is also
discussed in the Y item cited above (note 34). — In conclusion
reference should be made to the Pet. from Prov. 13.22 (cited
above, p. 43), which deals among others with Aaron's merit to
hand down the priesthood to his progeny. It fits in here well,
and the v. cited (טוב ינחיל בני בנים) is reflected by the H (1 S.
2.30 ff.); only in the case of Eli an exception was to take place,
owing to the evil doings of his sons.

Seder 79 (6)

ויהי ביום השמיני קרא משה לאהרן ולבניו ולזקני ישראל, Lev. 9.1.

This Seder is missing in the usual Masoretic lists.[36] However, the Genizah lists of TC Haftarot (to be cited forthwith)
have a S here, which fact is also borne out by the commencement
of a new Sidra (פ' שמיני) at the same v. in the Babyl. AC (cp.
above, vol. I, pp. 8–9). Moreover, the Byzantine ritual had to
the latter Sidra Ezek. 43.27 ff. as a H, which practice has also
been adopted by the local Karaites (and subsequently by those
of Turkey and the Crimea). Now the same H was read in
Palestine in connection with the present Torah lection. It is
obvious that when the Byz. Jews changed from TC to AC they
retained, in accordance with the general procedure, the H of
the former to our Seder[37] This is further evidence for its cur-
rency, and the reason for its omission in the Masoretic lists is
not clear.[52s] It would be of interest to know whether Yannai
had a Ḳerobah to Lev. 9.1; unfortunately there is a lacuna here
in the fragments of his Maḥzor (see ed. Zulay, p. 129).

---

[36] Thus in *Adat Deborim*, fol. 27a; Meiri, *Kiryat Sepher*, II, 64b; and
Yemenite מחברת התינאן (in אבן ספיר, II, 230).
[37] See above, vol. I, p. 91. For a full substantiation of this development
cp. infra, vol. III.

Hafṭarah: ויכלו את הימים והיה ב י ו ם ה ש מ י נ י והלאה יעשו הכהנים
Ezekiel ,על המזבח את עולותיכם ואת שלמיכם ורציתי אתכם נאום אדני אלהים
43.27. CL has 43.27–44.5, skipping to 44.30 (7 verses). C 23
concludes, according to Abrahams, at 44.6. But this is hardly
likely since such an ending as רב לכם מכל תועבותיכם בית ישראל
is highly denunciatory, whereas the general practice was to
finish with a v. of consolation and encouragement of Israel. No
doubt there is a lacuna in this fragment which needs re-
examination. However, the H, as listed in CL, is rather short.
The skipping after 44.5 was obviously meant to omit the denunciatory verses (thus v. 6: ואמרת אל מרי אל בית ישראל, etc., cp. also
above, p. 46). Now it is more logical to assume that after the
skipped portion there were added 44.28–30 (and not merely v. 30),
thus completing the usual number of 10 verses for a Prophetic
lection of TC. With the initial v. of H (43.27) there begins a
new Seder in Ezekiel.[38] (See also infra, pp. 52–53)

H tallies with S, in addition to the italicized words, by means
of 'your burnt-offerings and peace-offerings' (Ezek. 43.27) parallel to Lev. 9.3–4 where the congregation of Israel is enjoined to
bring such sacrifices on the 8th day. In the H (44.4) is further
mentioned that the "glory of God filled the Temple" (והנה
מלא כבוד ה' את בית ה') similar to the statement in Lev. 9.24:
וירא כבוד ה' אל כל העם (cp. also 9.4). And altogether the ceremony
of the ordinances of the altar, as depicted in Ezek. 43.18 ff. of
which v. 27 is the conclusion, is essentially a replica of the ceremonies set forth in Lev. 8–9 during which the altar was sanctified
(see Lev. 8.11 ff., and cp. Exod. 40.10 ff.).[538]

STRUCTURE OF HOMILIES

No Y theme with question and answer has been preserved.
That there was a section to our S in Midr. Yel. is evident from
the citation in Arukh, s. v. קופלא רגיא (Kohut, VII, 165): בילמדנו

---

[38] Some codices transfer this S to 44.4 (see Ginzberg, Introd., p. 51), but
the former indication seems to be more correct since at 43.27 there begins a
H (see above vol. I, p. 10–11).

ב ר א ש   ויהי ביום השמיני, אינו עשוי לקופלא רגיא³⁹ הזו, הוי לא איש דברים
אנכי (שמות ד', י'). This passage evidently belongs to the homily
dealing with Moses' refusal to accept God's mission of which a
version is found in the section to our S in TB Shemini, §5, T,
§3 (cp. also LR, c. 11.6, end).

The first Pet. in the Tanḥuma (TB, §§1–2, T, §1) is on
Koh. 8.5: שומר מצוה לא ידע רע וגו'. By means of the procedure
מה כתיב למעלה מן העינין (although not cited here explicitly) there
is introduced in this homily the penultimate v. of the previous
S (Lev. 8.35): ופתח אהל מועד תשבו יומם ולילה שבעת ימים ושמרתם
את משמרת ה' ולא תמותו.⁵⁴ˢ Aggadically these seven days are
taken as days of mourning which symbolized God's regret for
the world before consummating the Flood.⁴⁰ They were also a
prognostication of Aaron's sorrow when on the 8th day Nadab
and Abihu died; on that occasion he and his remaining two sons
were not allowed to mourn (Lev. 10.1 ff., cp. v. 7 as compared
to Lev. 8.35). The whole drift of this homily is reflected linguistically by Ezek. 44.15: אשר שמרו את משמרת קדשי (see also
v. 8 ff., all this in the skipped part of H which, however, the
homilist would utilize for his purpose), and intrinsically by
44.25–26 where there is mentioned the waiting period of seven
days for a priest after the death of his nearest relatives among
whom there is also listed a son (ולבן).

The next Pet. (TB, §3, T, §2) on Ps. 75.5 affords no connection with our H.⁵⁵ˢ The whole item seems to me to have been
transferred from the sermon on Lev. 16 (אחרי מות) as to which
see infra (p. 88). However, the Pet. (TB, §4, T, §3) on Ps.
92.13–14: צדיק כתמר יפרח וגו', שתולים בבית ה' וגו' offers a good tally
with the same phrase בית ה' in Ezek. 44.4–5. Finally the peroration
(TB, §6, T, §4, end and §10) deals with the atonement of sins
which in the future is to be graciously granted even without
sacrifices: א"ל הקב"ה: בעוה"ז נתכפר להם ע"י קרבנות, ולעו"ה אני מוחל
(צ"ל: מוחה, כמו בת"ה) עונותיהם שלא בקרבן, שנ' אנכי אנכי הוא מוחה

---

³⁹ Brüll, *Jahrbücher*, VIII, 71, top, suggests the reading: קופאלוגיא, vain
talk. Cp. also Krauss, *Lehnwörter*, II, 517.

⁴⁰ אמר להם משה: שמרו אבילות ימים שבעה... שכך שימר הקב"ה ז' ימי אבילות עד
שלא הביא את המבול וכו'. Cp. Yer. M. K., III (82c), where this Agg. is cited
in the name of R. Zeira, and see also above, vol. I, II. pt., p. 285, No. 34.

פשעיך למעני וחטאתיך לא אזכור. Sin offerings are mentioned in the penultimate v. of H (44.29: החטאת והאשם), and as against the condemnation of bearing one's iniquity (cp. ונשאו עונם and מכשול עון in 44.10 and 12) if not atoned, there is cited the cheering promise (Is. 43.25) of blotting out transgression and sin.[56s]

The section in LR (c. 11) is very loosely constructed. The only Pet. that fits in with H is the one from Prov. 9.1 ff. (§§1–4): חכמות בנתה ביתה וגו', which is applied, in the homily of R. Abba b. Kahana (§4)[41] to the 'Tent of Meeting' (אהל מועד), thus parallel to בית ה' in the H (see above).[57s] The next item (§5) on Ps. 18.26–27, is apparently outside the sermon delivered on the Sabbath when our S and H were read; the verses cited offer no point of contact with the latter.[58s] — In Midr. Agg. (II, 20) and also in JTS Ms. (infra, H. pt., p. לב) there is a further Pet. on Koh. 11.2: תן חלק לשבעה וגם לשמונה וגו' which tallies by means of the numeral 8 with the initial verses of both S and H.

SEDER 80 (7)

וידבר ה' אל אהרן לאמר, יין ושכר אל תשת אתה ובניך אתך בבאכם אל אהל מועד וגו', Lev. 10.8–9.

Haftarah: ויין לא ישתו כל כהן בבואם אל החצר הפנימית Ezekiel 44.21–28 (8 verses), so C 23, but CL has 44.21 27, skipping to 46.3 (again 8 verses). Now either version is lacking the usual number of 10 verses. In the former instance it is strange that the H did not include at least 44.29: המנחה והחטאת והאשם המה יאכלום in view of Lev. 10.12 ff., forming a part of our S (see infra, p. 53). I thus suggest that this H really comprised 44.21–29, skipping to 45.15 (thus 10 verses). This final v. contains again the word מנחה (cp. also לכפר עליהם here and in Lev. 10.17), and it further forms the commencement of a new Seder in Ezekiel. The reason for the skipping is to be sought in the fact that the H

---

[41] In §1: ר ב אהבה בר כהנא פתח חכמות בנתה ביתה וכו' should read ר ב י רבי אבא בר כהנא פתר, thus referring to his homily in §4: א ב א בר כהנא פתח קריא באוהל מועד וכו'. In MSS. Vat. and Brit. Mus. the ch. in LR begins merely with the citation of Prov. 9.1, followed by: ר' ירמיה בר' אלעזר פתר קרייה בבריתו של עולם וכו'.[24*]

to the previous S concluded with Ezek. 44.30 (above p. 50),
hence in order to avoid confusion the ending of the H to the
present S was extended to 45.15. As regards the second version,
again we have to rectify its extent, viz. that after the skipping
there were added 46.1–3 (and not merely 46.3). The tendency
was to find in the added final verse or verses some connection
with the previous portion of H. Now here, with 44.21 referring
to החצר הפנימית, and likewise 44.27 after which v. the skipping
began, the conclusion of H started at 46.1 wherein we read
שער החצר הפנימית. Accordingly, the Prophetic lection really
comprised 44.21–27 + 46.1–3 (again 10 verses).

The initial v. of H tallies with that of S both linguistically
and intrinsically. We further read in H: ואת עמי יורו בין קודש
לחול ובין טמא לטהור יודיעם (44.23), parallel to Lev. 10.10–11:
ולהבדיל בין הקדש ובין החל ובין הטמא ובין הטהור ולהורת את בני ישראל וגו'.
The Torah lection also recounts how Aaron and his sons were
ordered by Moses to consume the meat-offering (Lev. 20.12 ff.)
and how the latter was aroused on learning that the goat of
sin-offering had been burnt instead of being eaten (10.16 ff.).
Likewise in H (Ezek. 44.29, see above, p. 52) these sacrifices
are designated for consumption by the priests: המנחה והחטאת
והאשם המה יאכלום. Thus the choice of this Prophetic lection, to
accompany the recital of the above Torah portion is eminently
appropriate.

STRUCTURE OF HOMILIES

Y Sermon. No introductory topic with question and answer
has been preserved in either Tanḥuma. That there was a section
to our S in Midr. Yel., is evident from the citation in Arukh,
s. v. כס 4 (Kohut, IV, 267), בילמדנו ויהי ביום השמיני,
כי יתן בכוס עינו (משלי כ"ג, ל"א), בכיס כתיב, אתה נותן עיניך, והחנוני נותן
עינו בכיס שלך. Though the indication is not exact the present S
is no doubt meant by reason of the parallel item in TB, Shemini,
§7, T, §5: בכיס כתיב, השכור נותן עינו בכוס וכו'. Furthermore, an
Oxford MS. (see Neub., REJ, XIII, 233 ff.) cites in connection
with פ' ויהי ביום השמיני the following passage: (*ibid.*, p. 238, No. 26)
כתוב בספר ילמדנו תניא אסור לאדם שיורה הוראה בפני רבו עד שיהיה

רחוק ממנו י"ב מיל, כנגד מחנה ישראל, הה"ד ויחנו על הירדן מבית
הישימון עד אבל השטים בערבות מואב. Now this passage is found
in TB, Aḥare Mot, §6, T, §6, and the author of the above
MS may have meant by his citation this very item. However,
essentially it pertains well here as the Y Halakhic topic
in view of the Tannaitic Aggadah that Nadab and Abihu
died because they dared decide a law (שהורו הלכה) in
the presence of their teacher Moses[42] and considering that
the H contains the sentence ואת עמי יורו וגו' parallel to
Lev. 10.11 ולהורות את בני ישראל (see above p. 53). Therefore one
may safely suggest that the Y sermon to our S began in some
such manner: ילמדנו רבינו: תלמיד (או: אדם מישראל) מהו שיורה הלכה
בפני רבו, כך שנו רבותינו: אסור לתלמיד (או: לאדם מישראל) להורות הלכה
בפני רבו עד שירחק ממנו י"ב מיל, כנגד מחנה ישראל וכו'. About this Bar.
see TB, Aḥare Mot, §6, and the parallels cited there note 85; it is
mentioned in some sources in the name of R. Eliezer b. Hyrcanus
who is also the author of the above Agg. concerning Nadab and
Abihu. Thus, after the Bar. stating the general rule, there was
added as an example the specific case of Aaron's sons who acted
contrary to this law and hence suffered their penalty. Subsequently there was added the other Aggadic reason for their
death as being due to their entering the Tabernacle while in a
state of drunkenness.[43] The conclusion of the first portion of the
Y sermon probably was similar to that of LR, c. 12.1, end:
כך ותצא אש מלפני ה', ותאכל אותם וימותו לפני ה', ואין אנו יודעים מפני
מה מתו, אלא ממה שמצוה את אהרן ואמר לו יין ושכר אל תשת (היינו: ולא
תמותו) אנו יודעין מתוך כך שלא מתו אלא מפני היין, לכך חבבו הכתוב
לאהרן וייחד אליו הדבור בפני עצמו שנ' יין ושכר אל תשת. Only in Midr.
Yel. the final sentence no doubt reads: לכך ... עצמו [מנין, ממה
שקרינו בענין, וידבר ה' אל אהרן לאמר] יין ושכר אל תשת וגו'.

[42] See Sifra, Shemini, ed. Weiss, 45c: רבי אליעזר אומר לא נתחייבו אלא על
שהורו הלכה בפני משה, וכל המורה הלכה בפני רבו חייב מיתה. (Cp. further TB, Aḥare
Mot, §6, and the parallels cited there, note 85).

[43] See the Baraita cited in LR, c. 12.1, in the name of R. Simon b. Yoḥai:
דתני רבי שמעון לא מתו בניו של אהרן אלא על שנכנסו שתויי יין (לאהל מועד); in §5, end,
the author is supposed to be R. Ishmael. See further TB, Aḥare Mot, §7,
and parallels cited there.[25*]

The section in TB Shemini, §§7–9 = T, §5, deals entirely
with the evil effect of inebriety. There are woven in Prov.
23.29 ff. where the word 'wine' (יין) occurs (vv. 30–31), thus
tallying with S and H. The same applies to the introduction of
Is. 5.11 and Prov. 23.20.[44] Finally there is the *peroration* (T,
§5, end, TB, §9, end): אמר להם הקב"ה לישראל :בעוה"ז היין סימן קללה
לעולם, אבל לעוה"ב אני עושה אותו עסיס, שנ' והיה ביום ההוא יטפו ההרים
עסיס... ומעין יצא מ ב י ת ה' והשקה את נחל השטים (יואל, ד', י"ח).
By mentioning the Temple this final v. cited has a point of
contact with the H v. (Ezekiel 44.27): וביום באו אל הקודש.[45] [59s]

LR, c. 12, again treats of the evil effect of wine. There is first
the Pet. on Prov. 23.31 ff.: אל תרא י י ן כי יתאדם וכו' yielding
forthwith the tally with S and H. The next Pet., by R. Isaac,
is on Jer. 15.16: נמצאו דבריך ואוכלם ויהי דברך לי לששון ולשמחת לבבי
כי נקרא שמך עלי ה' אלהי צבאות. While the main point of the homily
is that Aaron was singled out to receive alone God's command
without the intermediacy of Moses (Lev. 10.8),[46] there is also a
verbal connection with H by means of אכל (here ואוכלם and there:
המה יאכלום, Ezek. 44.29).[60s] The following item (§3) on Ps. 19.9:
פקודי ה' ישרים מ ש מ ח י ל ב וגו' does not seem to form a separate
Pet., but is rather a subsidiary Aggadah to the previous one on
Jer. 15.16 where we read: ויהי דברך לי לששון ו ל ש מ ח ת ל ב ב י,
hence the point of Aaron's rejoicing on receiving God's order,
after his sorrow on the death of his children.[47] And yet essentially
there is a point of contact between Ps. 19.9, referring to God's
precepts and commandments, with H where the teaching of
these is declared to be the duty of the priests (Ezek. 44.23–24).
Hence the above homily may be taken also as a separate Petiḥta.
This appears to be the case from JTS Ms. (infra, H. Pt., p. לה)
and further from MHG (III, p. 198). From §4 and following

---

[44] ישעיה אמר הוי משכימי בבקר וכו', שלמה אמר אל תהי בסובאי יין וכו' The latter
v. is cited in Midr. Agg., II, 24, as a regular Pet.: ד"א יין ושכר אל תשת, זה
שאמר הכתוב אל תהי בסובאי יין וכו'.

[45] About the same peroration to S 8, where the connection is different,
see above, vol. I, pp. 88–89.

[46] ומנין שקיבל שכר על שתיקתו, שזכה ונתיחד אליו הדיבור, שנ' וידבר ה' אל אהרן.

[47] ד"א פקודי ה' ישרים משמחי לב, זה אהרן, שהיה לבו עצוב עליו בשביל בניו שמתו,
כיון שנתיחד עליו הדיבור שמח, ומנין, שנ' וידבר ה' אל אהרן.

there is a return in LR to the theme of wine leading down to the *peroration* (§5, end) which is the same as in TB and T (above, p. 55).[48]

Seder 81 (8)

וידבר ה' . . . דברו אל בני ישראל זאת ה ח י ה אשר תאכלו מכל הבהמה אשר על הארץ, Lev. 11.1–2.

A S here involves the difficulty of rendering the previous one (No. 80) to consist of 13 verses only (Lev. 10.8–20). We have thus to assume that Nos. 80 and 81 were *different Sedarim to the same Sabbath*, viz. that in some localities in Palestine the Torah lection commenced at Lev. 10.8, and of course concluded at 11.47, whereas in other communities the custom was to extend the previous S (No. 79) to 10.20 (and not to 10.7), with the reading on the following Sabbath starting at 11.1. The present case will thus be a replica of the situation obtained with regard to Sedarim 6 and 7 (see above, vol. I, pp. 76–77). The reason for the variance in practice here may be surmised in the following manner. The conclusion of S 79 at 10.7 was intended as a sort of symmetrical parallel to the ending of the previous S (No. 78), as a comparison of Lev. 10.7 with 8.35–36 clearly reveals. However, such an arrangement really interrupts the context since 10.8 ff. certainly forms a unit with the preceding incident described in 10.1 ff. Moreover it was probably regarded as inauspicious to terminate a S with a v. containing a reference to death (פן תמותו), unlike the ending in 8.35 where it is stated negatively: (ולא תמותו). Hence a different arrangement was adopted by some, viz. to extend S 79 to 10.20, thus concluding the pertinent Biblical section and attaining at the same time a favorable ending (וייטב בעיניו), and consequently beginning the next S at 11.1. The Midrashim included sermons to both variant Sedarim for the same Sabbath, as we have noticed several times before (cp., e. g., vol. I, p. 52). (About the effect of the present

---

[48] Only the wording is a little different: אמר הקב"ה: לפי שבעוה"ז היין ת ק ל ה לעולם, לעתיד לבוא אני עושהו שמחה, הה"ד והיה ביום ההוא יטפו ההרים עסיס [וגו']. The expression תקלה is better than סימן קללה. Cp. also TB, Noaḥ, §21, end: עשוי לתקלה.[26*]

difference of Sedarim on the subsequent commencements of the
Torah portions, viz. S 82 and S 82a, see infra, pp. 61, 64.)

Haftarah: אין די עולה ו ח י ת ו אין די בער ולבנון, Isaiah 40.16. Thus
begins CL, end of col. 2, which is torn. Probably H extended to
v. 26 (11 verses), or it may be that verses 19–20 were skipped,
as merely describing the manner of manufacturing idols, and
accordingly H comprised 40.16–18+21–26+31 (10 verses; for a
similar arrangement of H to S 47 see above, vol. I, p. 365).

The H tallies with S merely by the word חיה. The Midrashic
sections presuppose another lection.

STRUCTURE OF HOMILIES

Y Sermon. The commencement of the Y sermon to the
present S is preserved in T, Shemini, §7, though in a very curtailed manner. Altogether this paragraph is corrupt in style,
and there have been amalgamated two Petiḥtot that should
follow the Y topic as separate items. (cp. also infra, p. 55). Of
the latter there is given the following: וידבר ה' . . . זאת החיה
אשר תאכלו, ילמדנו רבינו: כמה בהמות טהורות יש בעולם. כך שנו רבותינו:
עשר בהמות (צריך להוסיף) טהורות) הן: איל וצבי ויחמור, אקו ודישון
ותאו וזמר, ושור, שה כשבים ושה עזים (השוה דברים י"ד, ד'–ה'), יותר
מאלה אין בעולם.[49] אמר הקב"ה לישראל: הזהרו עצמכם שלא לשקץ את
עצמכם בבהמה טמאה ובשרץ טמא.

[49] This is evidently a Baraita, although not mentioned elsewhere. As to
its substance, cp. Sifra, Shemini, c. 2 (ed. Weiss, 48a, top): זאת החיה אשר
תאכלו מכל בהמה, משמע מוציא מיד משמע, מכלל שנא' כירק עשב נתתי לכם את כל (בר'
ט', ג', והסרה התחלת הפסוק: כל רמש אשר הוא חי לכם יהיה לאכלה), יכול הכל היה בכלל
היתר, ת"ל זאת הבהמה אשר תאכלו שור שה כשבים ושה עזים איל וצבי ויחמור אקו ודישון
ותאו וזמר. Hence only these ten kinds, enumerated in Deut. 14.4–5 are permitted. Cp. further R. Isaac's statement (Ḥull. 80a): עשר בהמות מנה הכתוב
ותו לא. In GS, I, 473–4 (No. 5), all this has been overlooked, and reference
is made instead to PRK, c. 6 (ed. Buber 57a) where the point involved is
quite different; viz. that out of the ten species only three are domesticated
(ox, sheep, and goat) and hence they alone have been designated as sacrifices because of God's consideration for Israel (א"ר יודן ב"ר סימון, אמר הקב"ה
לישראל: בני, עשר בהמות מסרתי לך, ג' ברשותך וכו'). To use this passage as evidence for the Y topic, as is done in GS, is indeed unwarranted. See further
notes 52–55. (Cp. also infra, p. 59.)

Now the above H does not contain the word בהמה at all to account for the topic chosen here.⁶¹⁸ This consideration, as well as others that will become evident in the course of the analysis pursued here, point to a different H, viz. כרע בל קורס נבו היו עצביהם לחיה ולבהמה וגו' tallying with Lev. 11.2 where both 'beast' and 'cattle' are mentioned. Such a H probably extended from v. 1 to 5+8–13 (11 verses; 6–7 were skipped as merely describing the manufacture of idols). The mention of בהמה in the initial v. of H, just as in S, served as the starting-point for the question concerning the number of clean (i. e., permitted) animals. It should be borne in mind that several of the enumerated ten kinds were classed as beasts (חיה) and not as cattle (בהמה),⁵⁰ which the homilist regarded as reflected in the juxtaposition of both in Is. 46.1 (לחיה ולבהמה).

After citing the above Hal., there is an abrupt turn: אמר הקב״ה ... ובשרץ טמא, which seems to constitute already the conclusion of the item with its usual return to the commencement of S, viz.: אמר הקב״ה ... טמא [מנין, ממה שקרינו בענין, זאת החיה אשר תאכלו מכל הבהמה וגו']. The phrase 'be careful not to make yourselves detestable' alludes to Lev. 11.43 (אל תשקצו את נפשתיכם), thus indicating the scope of the Torah lection which comprised the whole chap. 11, with the next S starting at 12.1 (infra, No. 82). There is thus missing the link which traced the transition from Hal. to Aggadah with the latter leading down to the above finale — a feature we notice regularly in these Y topics that have been preserved in full.

The next item in T, §7, beginning with כך אמר דוד האל תמים דרכו אמרת ה' צרופה, (תהלים י"ח, ל"א) בשביל לצרוף בריותיו וכו' should be regarded as a separate Pet., as evident from LR, c. 13.3: ד"א וזאת הבהמה, הדא הוא דכתיב כל אמרת ה' צרופה וכו' (here Prov. 30.5 is cited which is practically similar to Ps. 18.31).⁵¹ The verbal tally with H lies in the word צרופה as applied to God's word, in contrast to the human צורף employed for making an

---

⁵⁰ See Sifra, l. c., §8: זאת החיה אשר תאכלו מכל הבהמה אשר על הארץ, מלמד שהבהמה בכלל חיה, מנין שאף היה בכלל בהמה, ת"ל זאת הבהמה אשר תאכלו שור שה ... וגו. Cp. also ibid., 4c, §6, and Ḥull. 71a, top.

⁵¹ See also TB, §12, end, and Buber's note 81.²⁷*

idolatrous deity (Is. 46.6).[62s] Here the well-known Aggadah is introduced to the effect that the commandments were ordained for the purpose of testing (לצרוף) by them God's creatures. E. g., the ritual made of slaughtering (שחיטה) was intended only for this test, because really it is immaterial to God whether the animal is killed at the throat or at the neck.[52] In the hereafter, when the righteous will partake of the mythical Behemoth and Leviathan, Sheḥitah will no longer be obligatory.[53]

In the first two editions there followed a passage, beginning with: 'משל למה הדבר דומה, לרופא שעלה לבקר שני חולים וכו and concluding with: כך אמר הקב"ה אוה"ע שהן מוקצים ואין להם חלק לעוה"ב,

[52] The style is corrupt: (כך אמר דוד . . . לצרוף בריותיו, א מ ר ל ו ר' (כך בדפוס ראשון, קושטא 1522, בדפוס שני, ויניציאה 1545: אמר לו רבי) מה איכפת להקב"ה שיאכלו ישראל בלא שחיטה, שיהא ישראל נוחר ואוכל ושוחט מן הצואר ומן הירך. A comparison with the version of this Aggadah in GR, c. 44.1 (ed. Theod.-Alb., 424–5): ר ב אמר לא ניתנו המצות אלא לצרוף את הבריות, וכי מה איכפת לו להקב"ה מי ששוחט מן הצואר ומי ששוחט מן ה ע ו ר ף, readily suggests the correction here: In GS, .[28]*אמר ר' (=רב:) ו כ י מה איכפת . . . ושוחט מן הצואר ומן (—או מן) העורף l. c., the whole point has not been realized, and the corruption רבי מה איכפת להקב"ה is taken as an argument for the lateness of the Y item.

[53] The conclusion should read: מכאן שחיטה (כן בדפוס א) [אינה] אלא בשביל לבדוק ולצרוף את ישראל. As regards the interesting point concerning the abolition of Sheḥitah in the hereafter cp. the parallel passage in LR, c. 13.3: כיצד הם נשחטים, בהמות נותץ ללויתן בקרניו וקורעו, ולויתן נותץ לבהמות בסנפיריו ונוחרו, ו ח כ מ י ם אומרים זו שחיטה כשרה היא, ולא כך תנינן . . . חונקין, א"ר אבין (צ"ל: אבא) בר כהנא תורה ח ד ש ה (צריך למחוק) מאתי תצא (יש' נ"א, ו'), חדוש תורה מאתי תצא. Now for חכמים the correct reading (as given in YSH to Sam., 161, towards end) is: ו ה צ ד י ק י ם אומרים, viz. the righteous for whose entertainment the Behemoth and Leviathan are to be served as dainty courses of the banquet, ask in astonishment: Is this (to wit, the described manner in which these two gigantic creatures are doing each other away) the proper Sheḥitah? Answer (according to R. Abba b. Kahana): God says 'a different Torah will come forth from Me'. This right interpretation has already been given by R. David Lurya (חדושי הרד"ל, note 4).[29]* However, strangely enough in GR, l. c., the reading וחכמים אומרים is retained and the statement is taken in an affirmative manner, as if their view is different from that of R. Abba b. Kahana! Hence we have the following amazing criticism of the corresponding item in T, §7:ו ק ל ח נ ש שם נסמן ובנ ,'נ ,'ג י"ר וי"ר עיין ובהמות לויתן למלחמת שנוגע ובמה ונחלקו בדבר יחיד הוא כן והאומר תצא, חדשה תורה לבוא לעתיד אם היא יחיד של זו דעת בתנחומא שלפנינו המאוחר להדרשן אבל רבים, עליו הלכה פסוקה שאין לזמוגם בה. The italics are mine, and further comment is needless.

שנ' ואלה לחרפות לדראון עולם (דניאל, י"ב, ב'), יאכלו מה שירצו, ואתם
שחיים כולכם לעוה"ב תנו דעתכם מאי זו חיה תאכלו, שנ' דבר אל בני ישראל
זאת החיה. Subsequently there is found there the Pet. on Ps. 40.9
(now T, §8). This passage has been omitted since ed. Mantua,
because it really formed the end of the Pet. on Hab. 3.6: עמד
וימודד ארץ וגו' (T, §6, TB, §10). Thus we see again how T, §7,
has been curtailed and even mutilated, (see above, p. 33).[54]

To proceed now with the further analyses of T and TB.
There is a Y item which has been correlated with the suggested
H from Is. 46.1 ff., and likewise the Pet. from Ps. 18.31. A
second Pet. is from Hab. 3.6 where the sentence ע ו ל ם הליכות
זכרו ראשונות מ ע ו ל ם   כי אנכי אל וגו' corresponds to the H v.: לו
(Is. 46.8).[63a] In this Aggadah ויתר גוים is homiletically explained
by R. Tanḥum b. Ḥanilai to refer to the gentiles who were not
obliged to observe the dietary laws (התיר להם את האסורים וכו').
This is illustrated by the above story of a physician attending
two patients and issuing different orders as to their respective
diets.

A third Pet. (only in T, §8) is from Ps. 40.9: ל ע ש ו ת
ר צ ו נ ך אלהי ח פ צ ת י ותורתך בתוך מעי which tallies with H v.:
א ע ש ה אומר עצתי תקום וכל ח פ צ י (46.10).[64a] This item is
defective at the end, and also seems to have been subject to
later insertions.[55] Further there is a comment on Job 14.4:
מ י יתן טהור מטמא לא אחד (TB, §13, T, §8). The 'one' in this v.
is explained to refer to the One God (יחידו של עולם), thus reflecting
the emphasis in H (46.9) on the same fact (כי אנכי אל ואין עוד

---

[54] Hab. 3.6 suddenly is cited in the first two editions before the item:
היו"ד במילה שלא יחטא ג' דברים נתקשו למשה וכו' (T, §8, cp. TB, §11). Thus after יחטא
אדם וכו' we read ג' דברים וכו'. עמד וימודד ארץ. (since ed. Mantua this v. has
been omitted). In reality this v. belongs before the above passage משל למה
הדבר דומה וכו' of which the beginning is missing in these editions.

[55] Thus the original Pet. no doubt read: זש"ה לעשות רצונך אלהי חפצתי
ותורתך בתוך מעי, אשריכם ישראל שבכל אבר ואבר שבכם נתן מצוה, בראש לא תקיפו פאת
ראשכם וכו'. And later on there was inserted after מצוה the sentence: שרמ"ח
איברים באדם, ולכך אנו אומרים בכל יום בא"י אמ"ה אשר יצר את האדם... רמ"ח הוי כמניין
איברים שבאדם. Further the passage ועוד שחתם שמו שהוא שדי וכו' is probably a
later addition (see also T, Tazria, §5, and cp. TB, ibid., §7, note 34). This
addendum is incomplete towards the end: היו"ד במילה שלא יחטא אדם וכו', and
there is missing the indication of the real conclusion of the above Petiḥta.

אלהים ואפס כמוני).[65s] Finally there is the *peroration* (TB, §14, end;
T, §8, end, according to the first two editions, see Buber's note
95) citing as a final v. Is. 66.17: אוכלי בשר החזיר והשקץ והעכבר
י ח ד י ו יסופו נאום ה' which tallies with the initial v. of H (46.2):
קרסו כרעו י ח ד י ו וגו'.[66s]

In LR, c. 13, there is first introduced a Pet. from Prov. 15.32:
אוזן ש ו מ ע ת תוכחת חיים וגו' which affords a point of contact
with Is. 46.3: ש מ ע ו אלי בית יעקב.[67s] The next Pet. is on Hab.
3.6 as to which see above. This is followed by another one from
Prov. 30.6, so similar to Ps. 18.31 (above, p. 58). The section in
LR concludes with a cheering allusion to the downfall of hated
Edom (Rome), citing the last v. of Ob.: ועלו מ ו ש י ע י ם בהר
צ י ו ן לשפוט את הר עשו והיתה לה' המלוכה, which tallies very well
with the final sentence of H (Is. 46.13): ונתתי ב צ י ו ן ת ש ו ע ה
לישראל תפארתי.[68s]

The above analysis of the structure of the Midrashic sections
to our S *fully establishes*[69s] the validity of the suggested H from
Is. 46.1 ff. (above, p. 58). The other one from Is. 40.16 (p. 57)
is therefore to be regarded as a later substitution for reasons
that cannot as yet be ascertained. The fact that the Y topic
(T, §7) correlates with the earlier H is evidence for its compara-
tive antiquity, although its present form is curtailed. (See also
above, note 49).

SEDER 82 (9)

וידבר ה' אל משה לאמר, דבר אל בני ישראל לאמר אשה כי תזריע ו י ל ד ה
ז כ ר וגו', Lev. 12.1–2.

Haftarah: כי י ל ד י ו ל ד לנו ב ן נתן לנו וגו', Isaiah 9.5 (so CL,
col. 3, but its extent has not been indicated by Abrahams).
It may have comprised 9.5–13 (ending with יום אחד)+10.17
(having the same conclusion), thus 10 verses. However,
probably the final v. was 10.20, offering a more pregnant happy
ending. And altogether, because Is. 9.7 ff. consists chiefly of
denunciation, it may be surmised that the Prophetic lection
started merely at verses 5–6 and then skipped to 11.1 (where
there begins a new Seder in Is.), with the conclusion being at
v. 9 (hence 11 verses). Yannai's Ḳerobah to the present S is

defective at the beginning (see ed. Zulay, p. 129), but the
Ḳerobah of Simon Hakkohen b. Megas indicates Is. 9.5 as the
initial v. of H (Zulay's list); very likely the former composition
too, had the same reading.

The tally between the latter and the Torah portion consists
of the italicized words.

STRUCTURE OF HOMILIES

No Y question and answer have been preserved. That Midr.
Yel. contained a section to our S, is evident from the passage
cited in YSH (קונדריס אחרון=Jellinek, BHM, VI, 85, No. 42),
which introduces a Pet. from Job 14.1: אדם י ל ו ד א ש ה
וגו' a v. that has an obvious point of contact with the initial
verses of both S and H. The items in the Tanḥumas also can
be correlated with the latter as regards their linguistic tallies.
Thus in TB Tazria, §1, T, §1, there is a Pet. from Job 29.2–4
where the words קדם and ראשי offer parallels to Is. 9.11 (מקדם)
and 13 (ראש). The next homily is on Ps. 139.5: אחור וקדם צרתני
corresponding to Is. 9.11: מ א ח ו ר ופלשתים מ ק ד ם ארם. There
follows the item (TB, §3, T, §2) on 1 S. 2.2: אין קדוש כה' וגו'
affording an allusion to the final v. of H (either 10.17 or 10.20)
where God is designated the Holy One of Israel; and even if H
really consisted of Is. 9.5–6+11.1–9, the skipped part would be
used by the Aggadists for their homiletic purposes, as we have
noticed already frequently. In TB, §4, T, §3, there is woven in
Job 36.3: אשא דעי למרחוק ולפועלי אתן צ ד ק (cp. LR, c. 14.2,
where there begins a Pet. with this v.) which supplies a point of
contact with ובצדקה in Is. 9.6. The *peroration* seems to be contained in TB, §7, T, §5 (beginning), referring to the expenses a
Jewish father would incur at the ceremony of circumcision of his
son (cp. T, Teṣawweh, §1, and above, vol. I, p. 496). Because
of the joy evinced by the Jews in the fulfillment of the commandments, they were promised by God additional joy in the future:
אמר הקב"ה אתם משמחין את המצות (בת"ה: אתם משמרים את המצות ותשמחו
בהן)[70s] אף אני אוסיף לכם שמחה, שנ' ויספו ענוים בה' שמחה ואביוני אדם
בקדוש ישראל יגילו. The final v. cited (Is. 29.19) would thus
tally by the italicized designation of God with either Is. 10.17

or 12.20 (as above).[71s] Moreover, if H extended to Is. 11.1–9, there would be an additional correlation with דלים and עני ארץ in v. 4. The subsequent story of the argument of Tineius Rufus, the Roman governor of Palestine, with R. Akiba concerning circumcision (TB, §7, T, §5, end) thus belongs before the above *peroration* with which the section concludes.[56] In this story there is introduced the idea of the commandments having been ordained for the purpose of testing by them Israel's obedience, weaving in Ps. 18.31: אמרת ה' צרופה מגן הוא לכל החוסים בו (see above, p. 58). This v. too would be homiletically reflected by Is. 10.20: ונשען על קדוש ישראל באמת.

In LR, c. 14, the first Pet. is on Ps. 139.5 and the second one on Job 36.2, as to which see above. There follows the homily (§3) on Job 10.12: חיים וחסד ע ש י ת ע מ ד י ופקודתך שמרה רוחי, which may have a verbal tally with H v. (Is. 9.6): קנאת ה' צבאות ת ע ש ה זאת,[72s] Then comes the comment (§4) on Job 38.8–11: ויסך בדלתים ים בגיחו מרחם יצא וגו'; here the phrase בגאון גליך (v. 11) would have some contact with Is. 9.8: בגאוה ובגודל לבב. The next item (§5) on Ps. 51.7: הן בעון חוללתי ובחטא יחמתני אמי would also have some correlation with H, inasmuch as sin and transgression are implied in Is. 9.16: כי כולו חנף ומרע וגו' (cp. also v. 17: רשעה). The Pet. on Ps. 139.3 (§6) does not offer any connection.[73s] Perhaps it is really a part of the one on v. 5 (§1); note in both the Aggadic remarks of R. Yoḥahan and R. Simon b. Laḳish. The last Pet. (§7) is on Koh. 11.2: תן חלק לשבעה וגם לשמונה כי לא תדע מה יהיה רע על הארץ. This v. is homiletically applied in Koh. R., *a. l.*, to numerous instances among which also the one stated here is mentioned, viz. the number 7 being a symbol for the seven days of impurity of a menstruous woman and the number 8 corresponding to the day of circumcision of a newly born boy.[57] Now in this manner the first half of Koh. 11.2

---

[56] This conclusion is in connection with the comments on Lev. 12.3. The item on 12.6 (TB, §6, T, §4) is exegetical and seems to be outside the sermon. — The passage in T, §5, from חביבה המילה to חלל בריתו, is an insertion in late prints (see Buber's note 34 in TB, §7).

[57] Cp. MHG, III, p. 254, where the whole item is given (as in Koh. R.), concluding with: אמר הקב"ה: אם שמרה שבעת ימי הנדה כדאי א ם (צ'ל: א נ י נותן)

is connected with the beginning of our S[74a] (Lev. 12.2–3), whereas the second half (רעה על הארץ) would be reflected by Is. 9.18: בעברת ה' צבאות נעתם ארץ. Finally there is the *peroration* (§9, end): לפי שבעוה"ז אשה יולדת בצער, לעתיד לבוא מה כתיב, בטרם תחיל י ל ד ה בטרם יבוא חבל לה והמליטה ז כ ר, the final v. cited (Is. 66.7) offering a ready tally with the commencements of both S and H.

In considering the trend of the above homilies, we notice how the H supplied merely linguistic correspondence with the verses chosen for the Petiḥtot, due to the nature of the former which did not offer intrinsic material for the substance of the Aggadot dealing mainly with the topic of the wonderful process of birth. All the more one has to appreciate the ingenuity of the homilists who were able to discover in such an H suggestions for the choice of Pet. verses with which to develop their themes in order ultimately to connect them with the commencement of the Seder.[58] [75a]

Seder 82a (9a)

וידבר ה' . . . אדם כי יהיה בעור בשרו שאת או ספחת או בהרת והיה בעור בשרו לנגע צרעת, Lev. 13.1–2.

This S is evident from the respective sections in TB, Tazria, §§8–16, T, §§6–11, and LR, c. 15. But it renders impossible the previous S at 12.1 (No. 82) since the latter would thus comprise 8 verses only. Again we have an instance of shifting of the Sedarim, viz. *for the same Sabbath*. In certain localities in Palestine the custom was to commence the Torah lection at 12.1 (and consequently the previous S, No. 81, terminated at 11.47) whereas in other places S 81 was extended to 12.8 with the result that the new S (our No. 82a) began at 13.1. The former custom prevailed; also תזריע פ' in the Babylonian AC coincided

לך בן זכר ואת מולו לח' ימים, מנלן, ממה שקרינו בענין, אשה כי תזריע וילדה זכר (וצריך להוסיף: וטמאה ש ב ע ת י מ י ם כימי נדת דוחה תטמא) ו ב י ו ם ה ש מ י נ י ימול.

[58] Note the recurring formula at the end of the items: ביותר אם היה זכר שנ' (או: הה"ד, או: הוי) אשה כי תזריע וילדה זכר (LR, c. 14.3–6, TB, §1).[30*]

with that S.[59] The Midrashim included sermons to both Sedarim although the latter excluded each other, as has been noticed several times before (cp. above, pp. 42, 56).

It is difficult to account for the present difference in custom. We can only surmise that it was the result of the previous difference as to Sedarim 80 and 81 which also excluded each other (above, p. 56). Thus those who read on the previous Sabbath Lev. 10.8 ff. (No. 80) continued on the following Sabbath with 12.1 ff. (No. 82), whereas those who a week before started their Torah portion at 11.1 ff. (No. 81) would resume it a week afterwards at 13.1 ff. (No. 82a). In this manner there was preserved a certain symmetry as regards the respective lengths of the lections. Moreover, there was established also a certain parallelism in the commencements of the Sedarim involved, viz. S 80 has a heading mentioning God's command to Aaron *alone* (10.8), and correspondingly, the following S (No. 82) has the same feature applying to Moses *alone*, (12.1), whereas according to the other arrangement S 81 begins with God's instruction extended to *both* Moses and Aaron (11.1) and the same is the case with the subsequent 82a (13.1)! About the effect of the present pair of Sedarim (Nos. 82 and 82a) on the next ones (Nos. 83 and 84, which also excluded each other) see infra, p. 68.

Haftarah: On the basis of the homilies to be discussed forthwith, it seems to me that the H began with Is. 5.7: . . . . כי כרם ה' צבאות ויקו למשפט והנה ח מ ש פ לצדקה והנה צעקה, tallying by the italicized word with ספחת in Lev. 13.2.[60] The reading probably extended to 5.16 (10 verses).

---

[59] Similar instances we have had with regard to Nos. 4a and 5 (above, vol. I, p. 51–2), Nos. 10 and 10a (ibid., p. 102), Nos. 15 and 15a, (p. 142), Nos. 19b and 20 (p. 183), Nos. 23 and 23a (p. 205), Nos. 27 and 27a (pp. 229, 233 and 235–6), Nos. 42a and 43 (p. 340–41), Nos. 55a and 56 (p. 424), Nos. 62 and 62a (p. 487–8), Nos. 65 and 65a (p. 501), Nos. 67 and 67a (p. 508), and Nos. 70 and 70a (p. 533–34). Cp. also infra p. 68.[31*]

[60] Cp. Rashi to Is. 5.7: ד"א לשון נגע, and Kimḥi: נגע כמו ספחת פי' נגע, והיה משפח.

STRUCTURE OF HOMILIES

No Y topic has been preserved. That Midr. Yel. comprised also a section to this S is evident from the Pet. (cited in YSH to Job, §916, as from Y) on Job 28.25: לעשות לרוח משקל ומים תכן במדה.[61] The linguistic contact with H would be in the measures mentioned in Is. 5.10 (בת and איפה). In TB, §8, T, §6, there is introduced Job 38.25: מי פלג לשטף תעלה ודרך לחזיז קולות. Some kind of connection with H can be established by means of קולות as compared to צעקה in Is. 5.7 (crying produces a loud sound just as the thunder does on a still larger scale). There are also woven in Job 34.11: כי פעל אדם ישלם לו (reflecting Is. 5.12: כי אלהים שופט) and Ps. 75.8: (ואת פעל ה' לא יביטו) זה ישפיל וזה ירים (reflecting Is. 5.15–16.). The homily links up with the commencement of S in a similar manner as LR, c. 15.2, does in connection with the comments on Job 28.25.[62] The next Pet. (TB, §9 and §§11–13, T, §§7 and 9, cp. also above, vol. I, H, pt., pp. 276–7, Nos. 14–16) is on Ps. 5.5: כי לא אל חפץ רשע אתה לא יגורך רע. This v. is in accord with the initial v. of

---

[61] לעשות לרוח משקל ומים תכן במדה, כמה דאת אמר (אולי צ"ל: דאתאמר) מי מדד בשעלו מים (יש' מ', י"ב). ד"א לעשות לרוח משקל, כל נביא ונביא נותן בו רוה"ק כל אחד [ואחד] לפי כחו; ומים תכן במדה, שכל אדם נוטל תורה במדה, שאין מים אלא דברי תורה, שנ' הוי כל צמא לכו למים (שם, נ"ה, א'). ד"א לעשות לרוח משקל, יש אדם שדעתו ארוכה, ויש אדם שדעתו קצרה, ויש אדם שדעתו בינונית, והקב"ה משקל בדעתו וברוחו, אם נתן בו [כדי] צרכו הרי דעתו יפה, ואם יותר הרי הוא גס (היינו: דעתו גסה עליו) ואם פחות הרי דעתו קצרה; ומים תכן במדה, הגבל הזה שהוא גובל לבנין הטיט יפה (היינו שמעבד אותו היטב במים) היא טובה. אם פחת מים היא יבשה (הסרה כאן האפשרות השלישית שנתן בו מים יותר מדאי), כך האדם, אם נוהג בו כדי צרכו (היינו שבנופו נמצא מים באוחה מדה כמו הדם, השוה וי"ר, פט"ו, ב') הוא שוה לבריות, ואם פחות הוא יבש, ואם הוא יותר מצרכו הרי הוא לוקה בשחין, שנ' [שנ' אדם כי יהיה בעור בשרו]. The parallel homily in LR, c. 15.a (cited in YSH there immediately afterwards, cp. also to Tazria, §554, beginning) is couched differently. Also the conclusion here is unlike that in TB, §8, end, T, §6, end, which is in connection with Job 38.25 (see next note). About the further use of Job 28.25 as a Pet. to S 38a see above, vol. I, p. 318–19.

[62] The conclusion should read as follows: ד"א מי פלג לשטף תעלה, כשהקב"ה ברא את האדם בחכמה (יותר נכון: במדה*[32]) ברא אותו, כיצד אם בורא אותו חציו דם וחציו מים נעשה אדם שלם, אם בורא אותו רובו מים ומיעוטו דם נעשה אסטנים, אם בורא אותו רובו דם ומיעוטו מים נעשה מצורע [שנ' אדם כי יהיה בעור בשרו וגו']. See also, Midr. Agg., II, p. 33.[33*]

H (Is. 5.7), wherein the prophet disappointingly complains that
God hoped for 'righteousness (לצדקה, the opposite of רשע, רשעה)
and behold there is outcry (צעקה)' due to wrongdoing; the same
Pet. v. corresponds also to the final H v. (5.16) declaring that
God is 'sanctified by rightousness.' There follows (TB, §10,
T, §8) the item on Hab. 1.7: ו ש א ת ו משפטו ממנו הוא ונורא איום
יצא contacting with S by means of שאת (Lev. 13.2) and with H
by means of משפט (Is. 5.16). Finally there is the *peroration*
foretelling the future purification, sanctification and redemption
of Israel (TB, §16, and T, §11, end): מ ק ד ש אני ישראל אבל
גאולי ה', ש הקוד עם להם ויקראו שנ' מביניכם וגואלן ומטהרן אותם
וכן אמר שלמה כולך יפה רעיתי ומום א י ן ב ך. The penultimate v.
cited (Is. 6.2–12) links up with Is. 5.16 referring to the Holy
God (ש ה ק ד ו האל). The last one (Cant. 4.7), symbolizing Israel
(according to the Rabbinic view) as having no blemish, is by
contrast to the initial v. of H (Is. 5.7) wherein an ugly scab
משפח=מספחת, see note 60) in the body of Israel is figuratively
mentioned.

In LR, c. 15, there are given first Aggadot introduced by
Job 28.25 and 38.25 respectively, as to which verses see above.
In §4 Prov. 19.29: נכונו ללצים שפטים[63] is commented upon tallying
with משפט in Is. 5.16. Lastly there is the *peroration* (§9, end):
אני מטהר הקב"ה: אמר לעוה"ב אבל הנגעים, את רואה הכהן שבעוה"ז לפי
אתכם, הה"ד וזרקתי עליכם מים טהורים וטהרתם[64]. With this final v.
cited (Ezek. 36.25) there have to be included the following
verses (26–28) completing the picture of the future bliss as a
result of God's purification of Israel. Now in v. 27 we read:
ו מ ש פ ט י תשמרו ועשיתם, thus forming a homiletic parallel to the
last v. of H. (Is. 5:16): ב מ ש פ ט ויגבה ה' צבאות. Thus the suggested
H from Is. 5.7 ff. accounts for all the homilies to the present S
and is thereby *well substantiated.*[76s]

---

[63] About the homily in this v. in NR, c. 13.4, see infra, p. inc.

[64] This peroration is inserted in a different version into TB, §12, end,
T, §9, middle: לעתיד אבל מלאך, ע"י אלא עצמו ע"י הרעה את לעשות הקב"ה רצה ולא
לבוא הוא עושה הטובה ע"י עצמו, שנ' וזרקתי עליכם מים טהורים וגו'[34*].

Seder 83 (10)

Lev. 13.18. ,ובשר כי יהיה בו בעורו שחין ונרפא

Haftarah: בעון בצעו קצפתי ו א כ ה ו הסתר ואקצוף וילך שובב בדרך, לבו
Isaiah 57.17–18 ,דרכיו ראיתי וארפא הו ואנחהו ואשלם נחומים לו ולאבליו
(so CL, col. 3, where the S is listed only by its heading [ו]בשר (and
of the H only the above 2 verses are given, the rest being torn).
Probably the latter comprised Is. 57.17–19, skipping to 58.8–14
(10 verses); at the last v. there began in some Bible codices a new
Seder in this Prophetic book (see Ginsburg, *Introd.*, p. 46). The
tendency was to omit the denunciatory portion (57.20 ff.) so as
to have an entire lection of 'Consolation of Israel.'

The connection of H with S would be in the word ואכהו
which included also an affliction of a boil (cp. מכת שחין among
the ten plagues of Egypt), as well as in וארפאהו corresponding
to ונרפא. About the same H to S 85 see infra, p. 70.

A S here would only be possible if the previous one commenced at Lev. 12.1 (No. 82), and not at 13.1 (No. 82a), since
in the latter case there would merely be 17 verses from 13.1 to
13.17. And then the next S starts at 13.29 (infra, No. 84),
11 verses removed from 13.18 (No. 83). Hence Nos. 83 and 84
excluded each other. It is evident that we have here a difference
of custom as to the beginnings of the Sedarim which was the
result of the difference in the previous Sidra, viz. as regards
Nos. 82 and 82a (above, pp. 61–64); thus those who on the previous Sabbath had as their Torah lection 12.1 ff. continued on
the following Sabbath with 13.18 ff., whereas those who adopted
the other arrangement for the previous portion, viz. 13.1 ff.,
would have their next one at 13.29 ff. In this manner there was
maintained a certain symmetry in the respective lengths of the
Sedarim. The final fixation of the latter was to eliminate both
Nos. 82a and 83, and accordingly the Torah lection comprising
the Babyl. Sidra תזריע consisted of only two TC Sedarim, Nos.
82 and 84 (Thus Adat Deborim, fol. 27h, Meiri's קרית ספר, II,
65b, and the Yemen מחברת התיגאן in אבן ספיר II, 230). Likewise
with regard to Yannai's compositions there are preserved Ķerobot
only to S 82 and 84 (ed. Zulay, *l. c.*, pp. 129–33, and 133–36).
See further infra, p. 70.

No Midrashic sections are given to our present S (No. 83) either in LR or the Tanḥumas. However, in Arukh, s. v. ביאה בילמדנו . . . ובאשה כי תזריע: או ב ש ר, (Kohut, II, 45) we read: אמר הקב"ה לירמיה: ראה מה עשו לי בני, הביאו לי מצורע וסומא לתוך ביתי, צווח אני ביאה עליהם. Now the above indication is Lev. 13.24, but probably read ו ב ש ר (13.18), hence we have a morsel of the section in Midr. Yel. to our S. Also MS JTS seems to contain homilies pertaining to here (see infra, p. מב).

SEDER 84 (11)

ואיש או אשה כי יהיה בו נגע ב ר א ש או בזק ן, Lev. 13.29.

Haftarah: ביום ההוא י ג ל ח אדני בתער השכירה בעברי נהר במלך אשור את ה ר א ש ושער הרגלים וגם את ה ז ק ן תספה, Isaiah 7.20 (so C 14, end missing). Probably H extended to 8.3, skipping to a 10th v. of 'happy ending,' viz. either to 8.13 (where some codices begin a new Seder in Is. instead of at 6.3, see Ginsburg, *Introd.*, p. 46) or more likely to 9.6: למרבה המשרה ולשלום אין קץ וגו' (There a new Seder is generally accepted).

The linguistic connection of H with S is obvious from the italicized words. Moreover, the process of treatment of a plague on the head or on the beard (Lev. 13.29 ff.) involved *shaving* the hair around the infected place (v. 33: והתגלח ואת הנתק לא יגלח וגו').

Again no section is to be found either in LR or in the Tanḥumas. Only in JTS Ms. (infra, H. pt., p. מו) there would seem to be given a Pet. introducing Koh. 2.23: כי כל ימיו מכאובים וכעס ענינו וגו'. There would be some tally in ימיו as compared to ביום ההוא in Is. 7.20. However, the section there is in disorder and the context is more applicable to S 83 (see the notes, *a. l.*). Whether the morsel, cited in Arukh, s. v. דנסטס (Kohut, III, 97): בילמדנו ב ס ו ף אשה כי תזריע, לאחר שהיה חייב לדנסטס, emanates from the section in Midr. Yel. to our present S (No. 84), is difficult to ascertain since this Midr. had a section to No. 83 (above, p. 68), with the latter S excluding the former one (above, p. 68).

It is strange that LR and both Tanḥumas should have ig-nored both Nos. 83 and 84. One could surmise that there was

a custom to have only one long TC S, consisting either of Lev.
12–13 or of c. 13 (thus Nos. 82 and 82a). On the other hand
another usage was to have the section split up into 2 parts, viz.
either the pair comprising Sedarim 82 and 83 or the other one,
Nos. 82a and 84, with the final fixation being Nos. 82 and 84
(above, p. 68). This division of the previous long S which
increases the number of Sedarim, would perhaps have to do with
the requirement of a sum total of 154 items for a cycle covering
the same number of weeks during three years. The matter is
problematic and will be discussed further on in this work in
connection with the parallel lists of TC Sedarim.

Seder 85 (12)

וידבר ה'... זאת תהיה תורת המצורע ביום טהרתו... וראה הכהן והנה
נ ר פ א נגע הצרעת מן הצרוע, Lev. 14.1–3.

Haftarah: There is a gap in the Genizah lists of TC Haftarot
available to me. However, the Prophetic lection can be ascertained from Yannai's Ḳerobah to our S (ed. Zulay, p. 138,
ll. 36–38) where Is. 57.17–18 are given followed by Jer. 30.17.
Now the latter v. is not meant there as the commencement of
the H, but as a subsidiary Scriptural text conveying the same
thought as that expressed in the cited verses from Is. (thus
ואכהו... דרכיו וממכתך אר פ א ך in Jer. as compared to
ראיתי וארפאהו in Is.).[65] Accordingly the H to the present S
commenced: בעון בצעי קצפתי ואכהו הסתר ואקצף וילך שובב בדרך
לבו, דרכיו ראיתי ו אר פ א ה ו ואנחהו ואשלם נחמים לו ולאבליו tallying
verbally with והנה[77s] נ ר פ א in Lev. 14.3. The extent of the
Prophetic lection probably was as above (p. 68), viz. 57.17–19,
skipping to 58.8–14 (10 verses). Now it would indeed be strange
for those who had commenced the previous S at Lev. 13.18
(No. 83) and consequently had Is. 57.17 ff. as their H, to have

[65] For similar instances in Yannai's Ḳerobot see *l. c.*, p. 25, ll. 34–35
(to S 12, above, vol. I, p. 112–113), p. 42, ll. 30–31 (to S 30, ibid., p. 255),
p. 64, ll. 34–35 (to S 41, ibid., p. 328), p. 90, ll. 30–32 (to S 54, ibid., p. 411),
p. 96, ll. 27–28 (to S 55 ibid., Vol. I, p. 423), and p. 104, ll. 17–19 (to S 60,
ibid., p. 469). See further, infra, pp. 76, 79–80.[35*]

repeated in connection with the following Torah portion (No. 85;
as shown above, p. 68, Nos. 83 and 84 excluded each other) the
same accompanying reading from the Prophets.[78s] However,
as will be shown forthwith, the Tanḥuma sections as well as the
Y topic presuppose here *another H.* On the other hand, according
to the custom followed by Yannai there was no new S at Lev.
13.18 but at 13.29 (No. 84, see above, p. 69), and therefore the
H from Is. 57.17 ff. to the present S (No. 85) would offer no
difficulty.[79s]

STRUCTURE OF HOMILIES

1. *Y Sermon.* TB, Meṣora, §1, T, §1: זאת תהיה תורת המצורע,
ילמדנו רבינו: כמה בני אדם אין להם חלק לעולם הבא, כך שנו רבותינו: אלו
שאין להם חלק לעוה"ב [66] שלשה מלכים וארבעה הדיוטות אין להם חלק
לעוה"ב [67] ג' מלכים: ירבעם אחאב ומנשה... וד' הדיוטות: בלעם, ודואג,
ואחיתופל, וגחזי (מ' סנהדרין, י', ב') וכו'. As regards the three kings,
who forfeited the hereafter, there is inserted the interesting
legendary episode as to how the authors of the Mishnah
(חכמי המשנה) had endeavored to include also Solomon but were
prevented by heavenly disapproval.[68] However, the main drift
of the homily is concerning the 'four commoners'; they were
thrust into Gehinnom because of the utterance of their mouth
(אתה מוצא שהללו מפני דבור פיהם נדחפו לגיהנם). After substantiating
Aggadically this statement with regard to each of the four persons
enumerated, the Y homilist concludes his item by citing R.

---

[66] From אלו is redundant here; it belongs to M. Sanh. 10.1 wherefrom
emanates the Y topic to S 49 (above, vol. I, p. 380–1). See next note.

[67] So in TB, in accordance with the wording of M. Sanh. 10.2. In T
the sentence אין להן חלק לעולם הבא is missing because of the previous insertion
of אלו שאין וכו' (see note 66), but in reality the latter is superfluous here. The
different opinion, to the effect that the text in TB is confused (cp. GS, I,
474, No. 58), is incorrect.[36*]

[68] א'ר יהודה בר שלום בקשו חכמי המשנה לשנות ארבעה מלכים ולמנות שלמה עמהם,
אלא שיצתה בת קול ואמרה: אל תגעו במשיחי (תה' ק'ה, ט'ו), ואעפי"כ חזרו יום אחד ובקשו
(כמו בת'ה) לשנות, באת אש מן השמים וליחכה בספסליהם וחזרה (היינו: ב'ק) ואמרה:
המעמך ישלמנה כי מאסת בי אתה תבחר ולא אני ומה ידעת דבר (איוב ל'ד, ל'ד) וכו'. For
the parallels see Buber's note 2. The historical tradition underlying this
Agg. cannot be discussed here. Cp. Aptowitzer, *Parteipolitik d. Hasmonäer-
zeit*, p. 25–6, whose theories have to be accepted with caution.

Pedat's dictum that the punishment for slander is leprosy, as
evidenced from the Scriptural word המצורע (Lev. 14.2) which
by means of the hermeneutic formula of אל תקרי can be read
המוציא [שם] רע. Herewith there is a return to the beginning of
S thereby completing the first portion of the Y sermon.[69]

Now this Y topic has no starting-point at all in the above H
from Is. 57.17 ff., and another one has to be ascertained in
accordance with our procedure of investigation. In turning to
the Byzantine ritual, which was also adopted by the Karaites
of Turkey and the Crimea, we find listed as H 2 Kings, ch. 7,
the same as in the Babylonian rite and its derivative to Sidra
מצורע. As the former ritual retained the Pal. Hafṭarot of TC
in a modified form even after the adoption of AC for the Torah
lections (see above, vol. I, p. 91), one may safely assume that
to our S there was also prevalent in the Holy Land another H
(in addition to the one cited by Yannai), viz. beginning with
2 K. 7.3: וארבעה אנשים היו מצור עים פתח השער וגו' which tallies
linguistically with our S: זאת תהיה תורת המצור ע וגו' (Lev.
14.2).[80s] Such a lection probably extended to v. 11 (ויגידו בית
וה מל ך מדבר אל גחזי נער איש האלהים לאמר)+8.4 (ה מל ך פנימה
ספרה נא לי את כל הגדולות אשר עשה אלישע) and 5, hence 11 verses.
This story concerning the *four* lepers suggested the above Y
topic which enumerates the *four* commoners excluded from a
share in the future world! One of the latter was Geḥazi, mentioned explicitly in H (8.4). Moreover, according to an Aggadic
view the four lepers were Geḥazi and his three sons.[70]

In addition to the above first portion of the Y sermon,
there is the passage in allegorization of the ritual of purification
of the leper after his recovery from his affliction, cited by YSH
(קונדריס אהרון, BHM, VI, 86, No. 45)[70a], which allegorization is

[69] As in T: מניין, ממה שקראו (יותר נכון) בעניין, זאת תהיה תורת המצורע, אל
(שקראו) תקרי המצורע אלא המוציא ש"ר. In TB the characteristic Y phrase שקרינו
בעניין has been attenuated into שכתיב בעניין.

[70] Cp. Tanḥ. 107b: וארבעה אנשים היו מצורעים פתח השער, א"ר יוחנן נחזי וג' בניו.
[70a] ולקח למטהר צפרים (וי' י"ד, ד'), כשם שהוציא דברים של רוח מתוך
פיו כך מכפר עליו בצפרים שהן טסין על פני רוח, שהן (צ"ל: ושהן) מודיעות לשמים דברים
(היינו: של רוח), שנ' כי עוף השמים יוליך את הקול (קה' י', ב'); ועץ אר ז, למה,
שנמשלה תורה לעץ, שנ' עץ חיים היא (מש' ג', י"ח), וכן מרפא לשון עץ חיים (שם, ט"ו, ד'):

different from the parallel one mentioned in TB, Meṣora, §8,
T, §3. The *birds* flying along the wind symbolize the 'windy
words' (slander) which the erewhile leper had uttered; they
also are supposed to carry these words to heaven (citing Koh.
10.20).[70b] The *cedar wood* is used because the Torah is compared
to a tree of life and likewise a 'soothing tongue' (here מרפא לשון,
Prov. 15.4, is homiletically taken as the healing of the affliction
due to the evil tongue, viz. leprosy being the result of slander
according to אל תקרי המצורע אלא המוציא שם רע).[70c] The *scarlet
thread* symbolizes the retraction of the slander (שׁ שׁ ינה דבריו,
a homiletic play upon שני י תולעת), thereby meriting atonement
because of Jacob to whom the word תולעת is also applied in Is.
41.14.[70d] Finally the *hyssop* as a means of purging is in accordance with Ps. 51.9. — A further Y morsel is cited in Arukh
(s. v. מטרפלין, Kohut, V, 125): ובי ל מ ד נו זאת תהיה: הפסולת
של א"י טובה ממטרופולין של מצרים. However, it is doubtful whether
it really pertains to the present S and not rather to the next
one (No. 86, infra, pp. 76–79 ff.) which commences with a reference to "the land of Canaan" (Lev. 14.34).

2. The sections in the Tanḥumas also presuppose the above
suggested H from 2 K. 7.3 ff. In TB, §§2–3, T, §1, these are
given comments on Koh. 5.5 which v. offers a point of contact
by means of קולך with וקול אדם (2 K. 7.10).[81s] There are also

---

ושני ת ו ל ע ת, למה, בשביל ששינה דבריו וחזר בו, מתכפר בשני תולעת, בזכות יעקב,
אל תיראי תולעת יעקב (יש' מ"א, י"ד); וא ז ו ב, למה, על שם תחטאני באזוב ואטהר (תה'
נ"א, ט').

[70b] In TB this v. is cited in connection with שהן מוליכות קולן similar to
LR, c. 16.7: א"ר יהודה בר סימון אילין צפריא קולנין, אמר הקב"ה וכו'. In YSH to
Koh., *a. l.*, another version of Tanḥ. is given: ד"א קולם של מדברי לשון הרע,
לפיכך קולם של בעלי כנפים מכפר על אותו הקול (cp. further 'Arakhin 16b, top);
in YSH to Meṣora, §559, this passage from אמר רבי יהודה is listed as from
מדרש ילמדנו but this indication is no doubt a scribal error.[37*]

[70c] Cp. also 'Arakhin 15b: א"ר חמא ברבי חנינא מה תקנתו של מספר לשון הרע,
אם ת"ח הוא יעסוק בתורה, שנ' מרפא לשון עץ חיים, ואין לשון אלא לה"ר, שנ' חץ שחוט לשונם,
ואין עץ אלא תורה, שנ' עץ חיים היא למחזיקים בה.

[70d] A different Agg. from some unknown source is given in MHG, III,
p. 333: זה שאומר לו (כנראה הכהן למצורע): מה שני תולעת הזה תחילתו לבן ונשתנה ע"י
האור ונעשה שני תולעת, אף אתה שהגבהת עצמך תחלה ונעשית נס רוח, עכשיו חזור בך והשפל
את דעתך, כדי שיקוים עליך אם יהיו חטאיכם כשנים כשלג ילבינו (יש' א', י"ח).

woven in Mal. 3.16: אז נדברו יראי ה' איש אל רעהו
(as compared to 2 K. 7.3: ויאמרו איש אל רעהו)[82s] and
Ps. 139.2: אתה ידעת שבתי וקומי וגו' (as compared to 2 K.
7.3–5: מה אנחנו יושבים . . . ויקומו)[83s] But the main Pet. from the
Hagiogr. in illustration of the theme concerning the evil effect
of slander is the homily (TB, §§4–5, T, §2) on Prov. 18.21:
מות וחיים ביד לשון which v. links up with 2 K. 7.4: אם יחיֵנו נחיה
ואם ימיתֻנו ומתנו.[84s] Finally there is the *peroration* (TB, §9, missing
in T): א"ל הקב"ה בעוה"ז מפני העונות הייתם מתיסרין, ומטהרין וחוזרין
ומתיסרין, לעתיד לבא אני הוא שמטהר אתכם מלמעלן, שנ' וזרקתי עליכם
מים טהורים וטהרתם מכל טומאותיכם ומכל גלוליכם אטהר אתכם (יחזקאל
ל"ו, כ"ה). Here the homilist had also in mind the subsequent
verses in Ezekiel depicting the bliss in consequence of Israel's
purification, one feature of which being the disappearance of
famine (v. 29: ולא אתן עליכם רעב) in contrast to the story of the
terrible famine in Samaria as told in the above Prophetic lection
(cp. also 2 K. 8.1: כי קרא ה' לרעב).[85s]

3. *Other Homilies.* In LR, c. 16, the first Pet. is on Prov.
6.16–20 which does not provide a ready tally with the H, unless
we reflect that one of the seven sins abhorred by God is 'a heart
that deviseth wicked thoughts' (Prov. 6.18) such as was imputed
to the Arameans in their strategy to lure the Israelites to come
out from fortified Samaria (2 K. 7.12). However, the word און
in the former v. has a linguistic parallel in 2 K 7.9 (ומצאנו עוון).[86s]
The next Pet. introduces Ps. 34.13–15 where the phrase החפץ
חיים links up with אם יחיֵנו נחיה in 2 K. 7.4.[87s] In this homily there
is cited the famous story concerning the peddler selling the elixir
of life, which story is now found in a more original form in a
Genizah fragment of a new version of Midrash Tehillim.[71] There
follows in LR, c. 16.3, the comment on Job 20.6–7 which by means
of רואיו יאמרו איו correlates with והנה אין שם איש in 2 K. 7.5.[88s]
The next Pet. (§4) on Ps. 50.16: ולרשע אמר אלהים מה לך לספר
חוקי וגו' would tally with the last verses of H (2 K. 8.4–5) record-
ing how Geḥazi, upon the request of the King, recounted the

---

[71] Published by Mann, *HUCA*, XIV, 327.

great deeds of Elisha (...נא לי　ספרה ... והמלך מדבר אל גחזי
ויהי הוא מספר למלך וגו').[89s] Indeed this point is expressly
mentioned within this Midrashic item.[72] The following Pet. (§5)
is on Koh. 5.5, as to which see above (p. 73).

Thus LR again presupposes the other H. The different
prophetic lection from Is. 57.17 ff., listed by Yannai (above,
p. 70), must therefore be regarded as a later substitution.[90s]
It may be due to the Aggadic interpretation of these very
verses (57.17–19), as given in LR, c. 16, end, which applied them
to a leper.[73] Once this latter H was chosen, several of the above
Petiḥtot could be correlated with it by means of the flexible
method of tallying.[74] Also in JTS Ms. (infra, H. pt., p. מח)
there is a new Pet. on Job 34.10–11 which by means of
דרכיו וכאורח איש ימציאנו rather links up with Is. 57.18:
ראיתי וארפאהו.

---

[72] ... א"ר לוי מצינו בתורה בנביאים ובכתובים שאין הקב"ה חפץ בקילוסו של אדם רשע
מן הנביאים, ויהי מספר למלך את אשר החיה את המת... בכתובים מנין, שנ' ולרשע
אמר אלהים מה לך לספר חוקי.

[73] ואומר: לא על חנם הכיתי אותו, אלא בעון בצעו קצפתי [ואכהו]... דרכיו ראיתי
וארפאהו ואנחהו ואשלם נחומים לו ולאבליו, אלו איברין המתאבלים עליו... [בורא ניב
שפתים שלום שלום לרחוק ולקרוב], לרחוק, ר' הונא ור' יודן בשם ר' אחא זה מצורע שהיה
לגרמיה.[38*]רחוק ונתקרב, אמר ה' ורפאתיו, ואסיניה ליה לגרמיה.

[74] Thus the item on Koh. 5.5 (above, p. 73) where the same tally of
קולך would also apply to Is. 58.1 (cp. further קול ך למה יקצוף אלהים על
in the Pet. v. and קצפתי in initial v. of H). Likewise the Pet.
on Prov. 18.21, and altogether the emphasis on the beneficial or baneful
effect of the 'tongue' (speech) would be reflected by Is. 57.19: בורא ניב
שפתים. In the same manner some of the homilies in LR could be correlated
with this H; thus the one on Prov. 6.16–20 (above, p. 74) where one of the
misdeeds abhorred by God, viz. ומשלח מדנים בין אחים would correspond to
the denunciation in Is. 58.4: הן לריב ומצה תצומו, the one on Ps. 34.13–15
would have a point of contact with קרבת אלהים יחפצון (Is. 58.2) by means
of והחפץ חיים; and finally the homily on Ps. 50.16: ולרשע אמר אלהים
וגו' would be parallel to Is. 57.22: אין שלום אמר ה' לרשעים. It should
also be added that in MHG, III, 316 ff., there is given a new Pet. on Prov.
29.23: נאות אדם תשפילנו, ושפל רוח יתמוך כבוד which v., after being applied
to several instances, is employed in connection with the ceremony of purification of a leper who has been cured (p. 320, 1.19 ff.): ד"א נאות אדם תשפילנו,
זה מצורע שטהרתו בארז ובאזוב וכו'. Now by means of כבוד there would be a tally
with Is. 58.8: כבוד ה' יאספך.

Seder 86 (13)

וידבר ה' . . . כי תבאו אל ארץ כנען אשר אני נותן לכם לאחוזה ונתתי נגע
צרעת ב ב י ת א ר ץ אחוזתכם, Lev. 14.33–34.

Haftarah: הוי מגיעי ב י ת ב ב י ת שדה שדה בשדה יקריבו עד אפס מקום
והושבתם לבדכם בקרב ה א ר ץ, Isaiah 5.8. The initial v. is found in
Yannai's Ḳerobah to this S (ed. Zulay, p. 144, C. 33), and the
conclusion is given in C 22, viz. 5.10–16 (beginning missing).
Thus the lection comprised 5.8–16 (9 verses). Probably there
was also skipping to 6.3, thus linking up והאל הקדוש נקדש בצדקה
with קדוש קדוש קדוש ה' צבאות, and at the same time completing,
the usual number of 10 verses (cp. also infra, p. 79); with 6.3
there also commences a new Seder in Isaiah.

H tallies with S by means of the italicized words. Moreover, in the threatened punishment for expropriating other
people's property, to the effect that "many houses shall be
desolate, large and good ones without inhabitant" (Is. 5.9),
there was found a parallel to the baneful results of a plague of
leprosy appearing in a house (as described in our S); the occu-
pants had first to vacate the dwelling and ultimately the latter
had to be destroyed in case the plague resisted.

Structure of Homilies

1. *Y Sermon*. TB, Meṣora, §10, T, §4: כי תבאו אל ארץ כנען
וגו' ונתתי נגע צרעת בבית ארץ אחוזתכם,[75] ילמדנו רבינו: על כמה דברים
[ה]נגעים באים על האדם (כ"ה לנכון בת"ה, ובת"ב הנוסח קטוע: על כמה
דברים הצרעת באה). כך שנו רבותינו:[76] על אחד עשר דברים הנגעים באים

---

[75] Since ed. Mantua, T has the wrong heading: זאת תהיה תורת המצורע
(cp. Buber's note 42 to TB, §10).

[76] This phrase indicates that it is a Tannaitic Bar., although in NR,
c. 7.5, it is cited in the name of R. Judah b. Sholom (cp. also GS, I, 474,
No. 59);[39*] in 'Arakhin 16a, where 7 items are enumerated, the author is
R. Jonathan. Also in the Genizah fragm. of a new version of Midr. Ps. it is
introduced by תנו רבנן.

על האדם (בת״ב חסרות ב׳ מלות אלה), על עבודה זרה... ו ע ל ה נ כ נ ס
ב ת ח ו ם ש א י נ ו ש ל ו 77 וכו׳.

The starting point of the Y topic is clear. Since in the initial
v. of H there is the denunciation of those "that join house to
house, that lay field to field," viz. encroaching unlawfully upon
the property of others, hence the choice of the Y topic which
enumerates the causes of the plagues descending upon man
among which there is mentioned the sin of "entering (wrong-
fully) into the boundary that does not belong to one" (ועל
הנכנס בתחום שאינו שלו)!77 After citing evidence in substantiation
of each item,78 the homilist concludes with drawing a contrast
between the punishment meted out respectively to the gentiles
and to Israel; the latter are punished at first in their houses as a
warning, and only subsequently in their bodies.79 Herewith
there is a return to the beginning of S, thereby completing the
first portion of the Y sermon.

In TB, §11 (missing in T), there follow comments on Ps.

---

77 So also in NR, *l. c.*, but in the above fragm. and also in LR, c. 17.3,
the reading is: ועל הגוזל את שאינו שלו. Whereas the offense amounts to the
same, yet the former phraseology is more pregnant with reference to the H v.:
הוי מגיעי בית בבית שדה בשדה יקריבו.

78 The item of הנכנס בתחום שאינו שלו is illustrated here and in NR, by the
instance of King 'Uzziah who dared to assume also the office of priest (מן
עוזיהו שנכנס בתחום הכהונה), see 2 Chr. 26.16 ff.; in LR and in the above Genizah
fragment the case of 'Uzziah is connected with the sin of arrogance, נסות
הרוח, see *HUCA, l. c.*, 328, note 177).40* As a further comment on the leprosy
of this Judean king there is the Yel. passage (cited in YSH, קונדריס אהרון,
Jellinek, BHM, VI, 86, No. 43) which attributes this disease to his love of
earthly goods but not of the Torah: ג׳ לקו בצרעת, קין ואיוב ועוזיהו, על שהיו
אוהבין את הנכסים ולא תורה וכו׳. Cp. further T, Bereshit § beginning, and Noaḥ,
§13, and see above, vol. I, H. pt., p. 279, Nos. 18–19, and p. 288–9, no. 45.40a*

79 א״ל הקב״ה לישראל: ראו מה ביניכם לאומות העולם, כשהן חוטאין בגופן אני נוגע
תחלה ואח״כ בבתיהם, שנ׳ וינגע ה׳ את פרעה נגעים גדולים, ואח״כ (כמו בת״ה) את ביתו, אבל
אם אתם חוטאים בבתיכם אני נוגע (בת״ה: מלקה) תחילה, מנין, ממה שקראו (ויותר נכון: ממה
שקרינו) בענין, כי תבאו... ונתתי נגע צרעת בבית ארץ אחזתכם. The first part of this
Aggadah is in contradiction to the one concerning the plagues of Egypt
(see PRK, 66c and cp. LR, c. 17.4: וכן במצרים, בתחלה נגעה מדת הדין בממונם
ואח״כ ויך כל בכור... in illustration of R. Levi's general dictum that "the
Lord of Mercy does not strike forthwith at souls" (lives, ibid., 65b: אין בעל
הרחמים נוגע בנפשות תחלה וכו׳).

73.1–7 (cp. also LR, c. 17.1, where only verses 1–5 are dealt with). Whereas the connection with S is to be found in v. 5: ועם אדם לא יגעו (as compared to ונתתי נגע צרעת, see מהרז"ן 'פי, *a. l.*)[91s] the correlation with H is to be sought in v. 6: לכן ענקתמו גאוה (cp. also vv. 8–9 which probably the homilist also had in mind) as against which it is foretold in Is. 5.15 that "man will be bowed down and brought low and the eyes of the lofty (גבוהים) will be humbled."[92s] In TB, §12, T, §4, the section concludes with a homily on Prov. 19.29: 'נכונו ללצים ש פ ט י ם וגו which reflects the H v. (Is. 5.16): ויגבה ה' צבאות ב מ ש פ ט. Also within the item there is inserted Is. 26.9: כי כאשר מ ש פ ט י ך לארץ צדק למדו יושבי תבל (missing in TB, see Buber's note 61). This whole Aggadah concludes again in T (but not in TB) with the characteristic formula: 'מנין, ממה שקראו בענין, ונתתי נגע צרעת וגו although the previous Y topic had it already. It would thus seem as if the former emanates from a source other than Midr. Yel. No *peroration* has been preserved in either Tanḥuma.

2. *Other Homilies.* In LR, c. 17, we have first the Agg. of Ps. 73.1 ff., as to which see above. The next Pet. is on Job 20.28: 'יגל יבול ב י ת ו וגו, affording a tally by means of 'house' with the same word in both S and H (above, p. 76). In §3 there is found the enumeration of the causes of plagues, which item formed the above Y topic (p. 77). In this respect we have here a parallel to the procedure noticeable in certain parts of ER, to include within the section to a given Seder the theme which formed the initial portion of a Y sermon (see above, vol. I, pp. 372, 389, notes 419, 408, 429, and 547, and cp. *ibid.*, H. pt., p. 92). The last item of LR (§7) presents a symbolical interpretation of Lev. 14.33 ff. as referring to the desecration by idolatry of the first Temple and its resultant destruction. The 'happy ending' seems to form a sort of a curtailed *peroration*: יכול לעולם, ת"ל ילקחו אבנים אחרות, שנ' לכן כה אמר ה' אלהים הנני יסד בציון וגו'. If we add to this final v. cited (Is. 28.16) the beginning of the next v.: ושמתי מ ש פ ט לקו ו צ ד ק ה למשקלת, we obtain a fine point of contact with H (Is. 5.16): ויגבה ה' צבאות במשפט והאל הקדוש נקדש בצדקה.[93s] For another possible *peroration* see infra, H. pt., p. נא.

Finally it should be pointed out that in MHG (III, 344, ll. 5 ff.) there is apparently given a new Pet. to our S by R. Samuel (b. Naḥman) on Prov. 5.22: א"ר שמואל מאי דכתיב עוונותיו ילכדנו את הרשע ובחבלי חטאתו יתמך, רשע זה בעל לשון הרע, הקב"ה לוכדו ביסורין, שמא ירגיש ויחזור בתשובה וגו'. If we bear in mind that there was skipping in H from Is. 5.16 to 6.3 (as suggested above, p. 76), then the homilist had in mind Is. 5.18: הוי מושכי העון ב ח ב ל י השוא וכעבות העגלה חטאה as offering a fine parallel to the v. shown as a Petiḥta.

SEDER 87 (14)

וידבר ה ' . . . דברו אל בני ישראל ואמרתם אליהם איש איש כי יהיה זב מבשרו זובו טמא ה ו א, Lev. 15.1–2.

Haftarah: לכו ונשובה אל ה ' כי ה ו א טרף וירפאנו יך ויחבשנו, Hosea 6.1. C 22, as listed by Abrahams, gives verses 1–9, but it is hardly likely for a H to conclude with such a v. of denunciation. No doubt the fragment is defective at the end. Very likely the lection terminated with v. 11 (בשובי שבות עמי), hence 11 verses. Yannai in his Ḳerobah to this S also indicates Hos. 6.1 as the initial v. of H (ed. Zulay, p. 150, l. 34; the other v. following there, viz. Jer. 17.14, is only of a subsidiary character, cp. above, p. 70).

There is only a weak linguistic connection between the above cited verses of S and H by means of the italicized words. However, the sentence נטמא ישראל in Hos. 6.10 affords a tally with טמא הוא in Lev. 15.2.

STRUCTURE OF HOMILIES

None is preserved in either Tanḥ. version, probably because the present S was not accepted, with the result that the previous S (No. 86) was extended to 15.18 and the next one commenced at 15.19 (No. 88, see infra, p. 80). However, LR, c. 18, has a section to S 87. First there are given comments on Koh. 12.1–7; by means of ושבו העבים אחר הגשם (v. 2) there is the required point of contact with the H v. (Hos. 6.3): ויבוא כגשם לנו.[948] Also the phraseology at the end of the item: ואם לאו הריני ט ו ר פ ה[95ᵃ]

לפניך alludes to Hos. 6.1: כי הוא ט ר ף. The next Pet. (§2) is on
Hab. 1.7: איום ונורא הוא ממנו מ ש פ ט ו ושאתו י צ א which tallies
with Hos. 6.5: ו מ ש פ ט י ך אור י צ א.⁹⁶ˢ Also the following item
(§3) introduces Is. 17.11, which by means of וכאב אנוש links up
with Hos. 6.1: כי הוא י ך (cp. further the word בבקר in the
former v. with כ ש ח ר and נכון מוצאו and והסדכם כענן ב ק ר in Hos.
6.3–4). At the conclusion of the ch. we have a sort of 'happy
ending': בשר ודם מכה באיזמל ומרפא ברטייה, אבל הקב״ה במה שהוא
מכה הוא מרפא, שנ' כי אעלה ארוכה לך ו מ מ כ ו ת י ך. This final v.
cited (Jer. 30.17) affords a ready parallel to the initial v. of H
(Hos. 6.1): כ י ה ו א ט ר ף ו י ר פ א נ ו י ך ו י ח ב ש נ ו.

In JTS Ms. (infra, H. pt., p. נא) there seems to be a new
Pet. on Ps. 38.4: אין מתום בבשרי מפני זעמך אין שלום בעצמי מפני חטאתי
which links up, on the one hand, by means of חטאתי with פועלי
א ו ן in H (Hos. 6.8).⁹⁷ˢ

SEDER 88 (15)

ואשה כי יזוב זוב ד מ ה ימים רבים בלא עת נדתה . . . טמאה היא, Lev.
15.25.

Haftarah. There is a gap in the Genizah lists available to me.
However, the initial v. is indicated by Yannai in his Ḳerobah
(ed. Zulay, p. 156, l. 31), viz. Ezek. 16.9: וארחצך במים ואשטף
ד מ י ך מעליך ואסוכך בשמן, tallying by means of דם with the
commencement of S. The next v. cited there, viz. Is. 4.4, is
only of a subsidiary character (cp. above, p. 79). The Prophetic
lection probably comprised Ezek. 16.9–14 (concluding with
62, — (כי כה אמר אדני אלהים beginning with) 59 +(נאום אדני אלהים,
hence 10 verses. The tendency was to omit the denunciatory
portion as much as possible.

Finally attention should be drawn to the rather unusual
abundance of Sedarim in the section comprising Sidra Meṣora
of AC, viz. 3 lections (Nos. 85–87) plus the beginning of a fourth
one (No. 88). The latter makes impossible a new S at Lev. 16.1,
where in AC Sidra אחרי מות commenced, since from 15.25 to 33
there are only 9 verses; indeed the next regular S is listed at 17.1
(infra, No. 89). It appears to me that in olden times Sedarim 87

and 88 excluded each other, viz. on the *same Sabbath* in some
Pal. localities the custom was to read Lev. 15.1–33, with the
next S starting at 16.1 (אחרי מות infra, No. 88a), whereas in
other localities the fourth lection began at 15.25 (and of course
the previous S, No. 86, was extended to 15.24) with the result
that on the following Sabbath the new S commenced at 17.1
(No. 89). That Nos. 87 and 88 excluded each other, seems also
to be evident from the fact that the Tanḥ. versions have no
section to the former but only to the latter (above, p. 79).
The reason for this variance in custom seems to have been the
objection of some to have a S at Lev. 16.1 which was also the
reading for the Day of Atonement (infra, p. 88). Hence the
fixation of the S at 15.25 (No. 88) which made impossible S 88a
above, p. 80). For a similar case see above, vol. I, p. 455,
with regard to Nos. 58a and 59. Altogether we notice the tendency, according to some mode of arrangement of TC, to diverge
from the point where the Sidras of AC began (see above, note 59);
for a fuller discussion of this phase of the problem see the summary (infra, p. 85). However, in the final fixation of TC Nos.
87 and 88 were arranged to be read in succession, as evident
from the Geniz. lists, and from Yannai's Ḳerobot (above, pp. 79
and 80).[80] This procedure may have been in consequence of the
Agg. in LR. c. 19.3 (see infra, note 94).

STRUCTURE OF HOMILIES

1. *Y Sermon.* T, Mezora, §5, TB, §13: ואשה כי יזוב זוב דמה
ימים רבים, ילמדנו רבינו: מהו שתישן נדה בבגדיה[81] עם בעלה במטה אחת,
ואף בעלה בבגדיו זה לצד אחד וזו לצד אחד. כך שנו רבותינו: אסור לשכב

[80] Yet there is still a possibility that there too these Sedarim were meant
as variant ones for the same Sabbath. Cp. above, vol. I, pp. 76–77, with
regard to Nos. 6 and 7, and p. 315, with regard to Nos. 38 and 38a. Cp.
further infra, p. 94.

[81] In TB the reading is: מהו לנדה שתישן עם בעלה הוא בבגדו והיא בבגדה ...
זה לצד אחד וכו', but the plural בבגדיה is more in accordance with the phrase
in H and also with the Bar. (see above in text). The phraseology in TB is
already influenced by that of Babli (Sabb. 13a): איבעיא להו מהו שתישן עם בעלה
היא בבגדה והוא בבגדו (there also במטה אחת is missing and likewise in TB).[41*]

אפי' זה בבגדיו וזו בבגדיה,[82] שאין נותנין פרצה לפני הכשר, ביותר[83] לפני
הגנב, שמשלו חכמים את הדבר כאש בנעורת, ואומר ואל אשה בנדת טומאה
לא תקרב [לגלות ערותה][84] וכו'. In essence the Hal. cited here emanates from an old Bar. which reads as follows. הרי הוא אומר
ואל אשה בנדת טומאתה לא תקרב, יכול יחבקנה[85] וינשקנה וידבר עמה דברים
בטלים, ת"ל לא תקרב; יכול תישן עמו בבגדיה על המטה,
ת"ל לא תקרב; יכול תרחץ פניה ותכחול את עיניה,[86] ת"ל והדוה בנדתה וכו'.
The antiquity of this passage is evident from the last item concerning the 'make up' of the menstruous woman which represents
the strict view of the 'early scholars' (זקנים הראשונים) and which
R. Akiba later on modified in order that the woman should
retain her attraction in the eyes of her husband.[87] Accordingly
the Y homilist here has not made use of Babli (Sabb. 13a), as
is assumed by Buber (note 69) and by Ginzberg[88] (G S, I, 474,

[82] From אפילו to בבגדיה is missing in TB, but cp. YSH, Meṣora, §567
(Buber).

[83] See above, vol. I, H. pt., p. 80, l. 20; better וביותר; in TB: וכל שכן
(cp. also TB, Wayyishlaḥ, §12, note 55).

[84] Thus Lev. 18.19 is interpreted as prohibiting propinquity lest it lead
to intercourse.

[85] ARN, c. 2 (ed. Schechter, p. 8), cp. also NR, c. 10.8, and SER, ed.
Friedm., p. 76.

[86] In NR there is added: ויטול ממנה הכוס.

[87] Sabb. 64b: כדתניא והדוה בנדתה, זקנים הראשונים אמרו ש ל א תכחול ולא
תפקוס ולא תתקשט בבגדי צבעונין, עד שבא ר' עקיבא ולימד: א"כ, אתה מגנה על בעלה ונמצא
בעלה מגרשה וכו'. This Bar. emanates from Sifra, Meṣora, end (ed. Weiss,
79c, top).[42*]

[88] Ginzberg is inclined to designate the author of the Y topic as "a late
homilist who made use of Babli and Tanḥuma" (ונראה שדרשה זו היא לדרשן
מאוחר שהשתמש בבבלי ובתנחומא), but he entirely overlooked the above Bar. where
the inference is from Lev. 18.19, which v. is also cited here, whereas in Sabb.
13a the inference is from Ezek. 18.6: אל ההרים לא אכל וכו' which is not mentioned here at all, revealing that our Y homilist had not in mind this latter
passage.[43*] — Ginzberg's further assertion that the phrase שמשלו חכמים את
הדבר כאש בנעורת here emanates from Sanh. 37a is (certainly) not cogent,
since the metaphor (cp. Is. 1.31) was well-known in Palestine; in Sanh. *the
Min, who used it* (אפשר אש בנעורת ואינה מהבהבת), *argued with R. Abbahu of
Caesarea* (according to the reading cited in ס"ד, a. l., p. 79, note 4, end). Even
if we retain the version of R. Kahana, this disputation happened no doubt
when the latter lived in Palestine as a result of his flight from Babylon (see
B. K., 117a and cp. my remarks in הצופה לחכמת ישראל X, 203). Hence Resh

No. 60), however the copyists here and there may have touched
up the style (cp. above, note 81, with regard to TB).

The starting point for the above Y item is to be found in
Ezek. 16.16: ותקחי מבגדיך.[938] This is the portion skipped in H
which, however, the Aggadist utilized, describing the alluring
locale of the stripped harlot. (Cp. also v. 39: והפשיטו אותך בגדיך).
Hence the theme here in contrast concerning the sleeping of a
Niddah when fully covered up in her garments on the same bed
with her husband. The latter case is prohibited for fear that
it may lead to intercourse. The Aggadah is truncated towards
the end, and there is not evident the usual return to the beginning of the S by means of the formula: ממה שקרינו בענין. מנין?.

The remainder of the sections in TB and T is also defective,
and there is missing a Pet. that usually follows the first piece
of the Y sermon. On the other hand in TB, §17, T, §9, there
has been inserted another Y topic which is based on a different
H to our S. It should read: ואשה כי יזוב זוב דמה וגו'. [ילמדנו רבינו]
על כמה עבירות נשים מתות בשעת לידתן]. כך שנו רבותינו: על ג' עבירות
נשים מתות בשעת לידתן, על שאינן זהירות בנדה ובחלה ובהדלקת הנר[89]
(מ' שבת ב', ו'). [ו]למה בשעת לידתן, שאין השטן מקטרג אלא בשעת הסכנה.[90]
ושלשתן מן התורה...זו הדלקת הנר בשבת,[91] ולמה נמסרו לאשה, אמר
הקב"ה...נדה, אמר הקב"ה: היא שפכה דמו של אדם (בת"ב נוסף: הראשון),
והיא מתחייבת שתשפך דמה, שנ' שופך דם האדם באדם דמו ישפך (בר' ט', ו'),

---

Lakish and Zeira commented on this argument with inferences from other
verses. Ginzberg could have cited a better example for his argument from
Soṭah 48a, bottom, where R. Joseph of Pumbedita uses the phrase כאש
בנעורת, but again the deduction would hardly be justified that it was not
current in Palestine where our Y homilist lived.[44*]

[89] From על שאינן is missing in TB. As regards this topic here cp. also the
passage cited by Neubauer from MS. Oxford (REJ, XIV, p. 93, top): ואשה
כי תזוב זוב דמה, כתוב בספר ילמדנו: כך שנו רבותינו וכו'. Also Yannai in his Ḳerobah
to our S (ed. Zulay, p. 156, l. 34 ff.) introduces this theme: אומנם על ג' עברות
הנשים עוברות ומיתות עוברות (צ"ל: מעוברות), על חלת קודש, ועל נר שבת קודש, ועל נידת
עונש, כי לא שמרה בקודש וכו'.[45*]

[90] This reason is found in Yer. Sabb. II (5b, top): ומן דמר יולדות, מיכן
שאין השטן מקטרג אלא בשעת סכנה.

[91] From ושלשתן is a later insertion directed against the Karaites. Still a
larger passage in T, Noaḥ, §1, TB, §1, and cp. especially above, vol. I, p.
62, note 45. Indeed it is missing in REJ, l. c.

תשמור נדתה שתכפר לה על הדם ששפכה, הוי ואשה כי יזוב זוב דמה וגו'.
Here is the return to the beginning of the S but instead of the
usual formula: מנין? ממה שקרינו בענין ואשה, there is given the
modification הוי וכו', just as the beginning ילמדנו רבינו וכו' is
missing, due to the fact that another Y topic is heading the
sections to our S in both Tanḥumas. (Above, p. 83).

Now the same Y theme concerning the causes of the death
of a woman while giving birth to a child we have had above to
S 5 (vol. I, 61 ff.), where the main stress was laid on the point
of kindling the Sabbath lights (הדלקת הנר) in accordance with
the underlying H to that Torah lection. However, here the Agg.
properly concludes with the point of observing the laws of
menstruation in order to link up with the initial v. of the present
S (Lev. 15.25) where these laws are referred to (כימי נדתה תהיה
טמאה היא). If I am not mistaken, it is rather to link up with
ומולדותיך ... :4 .v also .cp ,(16.20 .Ez) ילדתי. דם ששפכה=זוב דמיה
ביום הולדת.

The underlying H here was not the one listed by Yannai,
viz. Ezek. 16.9 ff. (above, p. 80), since it does not mention at
all the word Niddah.[99s] Moreover, this Prophetic lection already
served as the starting-point for another Y topic (above, p. 83).
The pertinent different H was Ezek. 36.16–17: ויהי דבר ה' אלי
לאמר, בן אדם בית ישראל ישבים על אדמתם ויטמאו אותה בדרכם
ובעלילותם כטמאת הנדה היתה דרכם לפני tallying so well with
the initial v. of S (Lev. 15.25): ואשה...זוב טומאתה כימי
נדתה תהיה טמאה היא. The reading extended to v. 25 (11
verses) with which there begins a new Seder in Ezekiel. Thus
the item of Niddah in the Y theme corresponds to both S and
H. Furthermore the Aggadic point of the blood of menstruation
being in lieu of the blood of Adam that has been shed as a result
of Eve's action (viz. his condemnation to die and not live forever, היא שפכה דמו של אדם הראשון) is homiletically reflected
in the H v. (Ezek. 36.18): ואשפוך חמתי עליהם על הדם אשר
שפכו על הארץ.

The above suggested different H is indeed indicated in TB,
§17, T, §9, but in a curtailed manner because of the elimination
of the Y feature from the above passage concerning the causes
of demise at childbirth. After the sentence הוי ואשה כי יזוב זוב

דמה, with which in reality the new Y theme concluded, there has been tacked on: לפיכך הקב"ה מדמה טומאת ישראל לטומאת הנדה שנטמאה ונטהרת (וצריך להוסיף: שנ' כטומאת הנדה היתה דרכם לפני), כך עתיד הקב"ה לטהר את ישראל, שנ' וזרקתי עליכם מים טהורים וטהרתם. Here are given both *the beginning and the end* of our H. That the above insertion is essential is evident from the immediate sequence (TB, §18, T, §9, end): ד"א כטומאת הנדה היתה דרכם לפני which v. (Ezek. 36.17) has not yet been mentioned at all in our printed texts![100a] This v. thus became in the Tanḥumas a sort of a Pet. in connection with the previous portion of the section to our S based on the other H from Ezek. 16.9 ff. By means of the flexible procedure of tallying the phrase היתה דרכם לפני would supply a connecting link with Ezek. 16.61: וזכרתי את דרכיך (cp. also in skipped part וגם אני הא דרך ך בראש, v. 43, and see v. 47).[101a] Finally, there is the *peroration*: אמר הקב"ה לישראל: בעוה"ז הייתן מטהרין וחוזרין ומטמאין, אבל לע"ל אני מטהר אתכם שלא תטמאו עולמית, שנ' וזרקתי עליכם מים טהורים וטהרתם מכל טומאותיכם ומכל גלוליכם אטהר אתכם. The last v. cited (Ezek. 36.25) is really the final one of the other H, but by considering that the Aggadist had in mind the several verses of glorious promise following this v., as is only natural to assume, (cp. also above, p. 80), then in the sentence והייתם לי לעם ואנכי אהיה לכם לאלהים (v. 28) there is a point of contact with the concluding v of the above H (Ezek. 16.62): והקימותי אני את בריתי אתך וידעת כי אני ה'.

The structure of the sections in TB and T thus laid bare is again instructive for the process of redaction that becomes manifest. There existed two different Hafṭarot to our S, viz. Ezek. 16.9 ff. and 36.16 ff., and accordingly two separate Y sermons were based on the former respectively. When for some reason or other the H from 16.9 ff. prevailed and the other was eliminated, portions of the second sermon were amalgamated by the redactors of the current version of Tanḥ. with the sermon based on the prevailing H. Significantly, Yannai in his Ḳerobah (cp. note 89) seems already to have used this amalgamated form.[102a] The existence of two different Prophetic lections will also become clear from the consideration of the further Midrashic material to which we proceed forthwith.

2. *Other Homilies.* In LR, c. 19, there is first given the Pet. (§§1–3) on Cant. 5.11: ראשו כתם פז which tallies with the H v. (Ezekiel 16.12): ועטרת תפארת בראשך such a beauteous crown consisting of course of fine gold (cp. also v. 13: ותעדי זהב וכסף).[1038] The Pet. v. is applied homiletically to various instances the final one of which, viz. by R. Sam. b. Isaac (§3, end), pertains to our S here. This Agg. reflects the criticism levelled by ordinary congregants of the Synagogue services against the recital in public of such topics as contained in Lev., chs. 12–15.[92] One should bear in mind that as against the practice of AC, according to which Sidras תזריע and מצורע would be covered in ordinary years on one Sabbath and in leap years on two, the smaller weekly sections of TC resulted in these apparently unseemly subjects occupying the attention of the worshippers during 6 or 7 weeks in succession (Sedarim 82–88)! Hence the need for the Aggadist to emphasize the importance of these readings as being a part of God's Torah.[93] The next Pet. in LR, c. 19.4, is from Koh. 10.18: בעצלתים ימך המקרה ובשפלות ידים ידלוף הבית. Here there is only a linguistic tally with the H v. (Ezek. 16.11): על ידיך.[1048] The homily (§5) on 2 Chr. 15.3: וימים רבים וגו' although introduced by זה"ש, is not to be regarded as a Pet. since there is no correlation with H but rather only as another instance containing the same phrase "many days" as in the initial v. of S (ימים רבים, Lev. 15.25), this phrase being explained as denoting "days of pain" (ימים של צער).

---

[92] ר' שמואל בר יצחק פתר קרא בפרשיותיה של תורה, אעפ"י שנראות כאילו הן כעורות ושחורות לאומרן ברבים, כגון הלכות זיבה ונגעים נדה ויולדת, אמר הקב"ה: הרי הן עריבות עלי, שנ' וערבה לה' מנחת יהודה וירושלם וגו', תדע לך שהוא כן, שהרי פרשת זב וזבה לא נאמרו כאחת, אלא זו בפני עצמה וזו בפני עצמה, איש איש כי יהיה זב מבשרו, ואשה כי יזוב זוב דמה וגו'.[46*] It seems as if this Agg., referring to Lev. 15.1 ff. and 15.25 ff. as separate sections (פרשיות) was the cause for starting at these points respectively separate Sedarim, viz. Nos. 87 and 88 (see above, p. 79). However, cp. the expression שתי פרשיות with regard to Lev. 17.3 and 17.13 (infra, H. pt., p. נב) where certainly no separate Sedarim could at all be indicated (see note 2, p. נג,).

[93] In this homily the sentence ושחורות כעורב is explained that though these lections are "black" (unseemly, כעורות), yet they are pleasant in the sight of God (a play upon the word עורב as if being ערב, pleasant); for this meaning of ערב there is cited Mal. 3.4: וערבה (so rightly פי' מהרז"ו). (Marg. *a. l.*)

Other such instances are enumerated in T, §6 (cp. ER, c. 1.,
and Esther R., c. 2). Thus the section in LR seems to reflect the
H from Ezek. 16.9 ff. on which are based essentially also the
Tanḥ. portions discussed before. Yannai, whose Ḳerobah supplied this very H (above, p. 80), lists too Koh. 10.18, 2 Chron.
15.3 and Cant. 5.11 (ed. Zulay, p. 155, ll. 9–11), obviously
alluding thereby to the homilies on these verses as found in
LR.[105s]

On the other hand the suggested different H from Ezek.
36.16 ff., which was the occasion for the Y topic concerning
death at childbirth (a topic that has been curtailed in TB and
T), is apparently underlying the section to our S found in the
Genizah fragment (infra, H. pt., pp. נג–נד).[94] [106s] The emphasis
there at the beginning (recto, 1.13 ff.) is on God's anger at the
evildoers, who are destroyed from the land, whereas He turns
favorably to the righteous to restore them to their country.
This is reflected in the H speaking of His wrath at Israel for its
misdeeds and the resultant dispersion among the nations (Ezek.
36.18–19); however Israel's ultimate restoration to its land is
foretold (v. 24). Israel is warned in one text to keep pure, as
otherwise defilement of Palestine will result in the people being
ousted from there, parallel to what we read in H (vv. 17 ff.)
that "the house of Israel, while residing in their land, defiled
it . . . and I scattered them among the nations," etc. The new
Midrashic section also deals with the duty of the scholars to
instruct (verso, 1.4 ff.) the people in the law so that the latter
perish not, citing Ezek. 3.17: בן אדם צופה נתתיך לבית ישראל וגו'.
The *peroration* (verso, l. 27 ff.), too, fully presupposes the above
Prophetic lection. The future purification of Israel from sin is
promised, (citing Jer. 33.8: וטהרתם מכל עונם וגו' as compared to
Ezek. 36.25), whereupon God's greatness will be revealed to all
the nations (citing Ezek. 38.23 as compared to H v., 36.23),
when Israel will be restored to its land and the wrongs it underwent will be avenged. The final v. cited (Deut. 32.43) tallies
by means of וכפר אדמתו עמו with Ezek. 36.24: והבאתי אתכם אל
אדמתכם.[107s]

[94] Cp. the notes, *a. l.*, for the elucidation of several points not touched
upon here.[47*]

Seder 88a (15a)

,וידבר ה' אל משה אחרי מות שני בני אהרן בקרבתם לפני ה' וימתו
Lev. 16.1.

The existence of an old Seder here has been discussed above
(p. 51). It was ultimately discarded, evidently because the same
Torah reading was of yore designated for the Day of Atonement
(M. Meg. 3.5, Yoma 7.1) and hence the reading for the Sabbath
within TC was shifted to commence at another point (viz. at
Lev. 15.25). Now for the former occasion the H began at Is.
57.15 (Meg. 31a). Should we assume the same with regard to
our present S? This seems to me hardly likely. Rather another
H was used, viz. Is. 6.1: בשנת מות המלך עוזיהו וגו', tallying with
אחרי מות שני בני אהרן. This will be substantiated as a result of
a close examination of the extensive Midrashic material to Lev.
16, including that edited from manuscripts further on in the
Hebrew section, some of which is to be correlated with the former
H and some with the latter. In order to avoid repetition, the
discussion of the whole problem is reserved for the subdivision
ealing with the readings on Yom Kippur (infra, pp. inc.).

Seder 89 (16)

וידבר ה' . . . דבר אל אהרן . . . זה הדבר אשר צוה ה' לאמר איש
איש מבית ישראל אשר ישחט שור וגו', Lev. 17.1–3.

Haftarah: כה אמר ה' השמים כסאי . . . וחרד על דברי שוחט
השור מכה איש וגו', Isaiah 66.1–3. This lection is indicated in Bodl.
2610[7c], beginning missing, which ends at 66.11 That the H to our
S is meant there is evident from the next item (ibid., 7[d]) which
gives the H to the next S (No. 90, infra, p. 94). The intrinsic
connection between S and H, in addition to the italicized linguistic tallies, lies also in the fact that in the Torah portion the
injunction is made to do all the slaughtering of the animals at
"the door of the tent of meeting" as offerings to God "before the
Tabernacle" (לפני משכן ה') and in the initial v. of H the Temple

is referred to (אֵיזֶה בֵּית אֲשֶׁר תִּבְנוּ לִי). Moreover, the killing of an animal away from the locale of the Tabernacle was deemed as if blood had been shed (Lev. 17.4: דָּם יֵחָשֵׁב לָאִישׁ הַהוּא דָּם שָׁפַךְ), thus affording an association of ideas with the prophetic condemnation (Is. 66.3) that "he that killeth an ox is as if he slew a man" (שׁוֹחֵט הַשּׁוֹר מַכֵּה אִישׁ)! This association of ideas is expressly set forth in an Aggadah (infra, p. 92).

As to the extent of H (Is. 66.1–11), the same is also given to S 63 (above, vol. I, 489). However, from the Y item (to be discussed forthwith) as well as from the Pet. cited infra, (p. 90) it would appear that v. 12 too was included which final v. indeed would, by the sentence כִּי כֹה אָמַר ה', correspond to the commencement of H (66.1): כֹּה אָמַר ה'. One may thus surmise that verses 3–4, being of denunciatory character, were omitted (see infra, p. 91), thus reducing the Prophetic reading to the usual number of ten verses, viz. 66.1–2 (וְחָרֵד עַל דְּבָרִי) 5+ (שִׁמְעוּ דְבַר ה') 12. — (הַחֲרֵדִים עַל דְּבָרוֹ)[95] However, the skipped verses were implied by the homilists, as we have noticed frequently, and hence v. 3 (שׁוֹחֵט הַשּׁוֹר) afforded the starting point for the Y topic as also indeed this very v. supplied a tally with S: אֲשֶׁר יִשְׁחַט הַשּׁוֹר (Lev. 17.3).

The portion of Yannai's Ḳerobah to our S (ed. Zulay, pp. 158–159) is lacking the part indicating the initial v. of H, but no doubt the latter was identical with the one ascertained from the above Genizah fragment.

STRUCTURE OF HOMILIES

1. *Y Sermon.* From the citation in Arukh, s. v. בבואה (Kohut II, p. 6a, top), as found in יִלְמְדֵנוּ בְּאַחֲרֵי מוּת אֲשֶׁר יִשְׁחַט שׁוֹר, it appears that the Y topic to our S is to be reconstructed[96] as follows: אִישׁ אִישׁ מִבֵּית יִשְׂרָאֵל אֲשֶׁר יִשְׁחַט שׁוֹר וְגוּ', [יִלְמְדֵנוּ רַבֵּינוּ: מַהוּ לְאָדָם מִיִּשְׂרָאֵל שֶׁיִּשְׁחוֹט לְתוֹךְ הַיַּמִּים אוֹ לְתוֹךְ הַנְּהָרוֹת. כָּךְ שָׁנוּ רַבּוֹתֵינוּ:]

---

[95] Cp. also above, vol. I, p. 430, to S 56.

[96] See also GS, I, 493, No. 2, where, however, the Halakhic theme is only lightly touched upon.

אין שוחטין לתוך המים (צ"ל: הימים)[97] ולא לתוך הנהרות (מ' חולין ב, ט)
למה', שהוא עובד בבואה.[98] אתה מוצא בימי גדעון שהיה (צ"ל: שהיו) עובדין
את הבבואה שבאותן המים; שאותם שכרעו על ברכיהם היו עובדין לבבואה.[99]

The starting point is clear; since in Is. 66.3 the verb שחט is
mentioned and further on in v. 12 we read הנני נוטה אליה כ נ ה ר

[97] The reading הימים in M. is well authenticated (see ד"ס Ḥullin, p. 80,
note 5), and is also borne out by the continuation: אבל שוחט הוא לתוך עוגע
של מים (נ"א: עונן, אוגן). In Tos. Ḥull. 2.19 (ed. Zuckerm., p. 503) the text is
corrupt: אין שוחטין לא לתוך ימים, ולא לתוך נהרות, ולא לתוך מים עכורין, אבל שוחט
אבל שוחט לתוך מים עכורין (היינו אפילו לתוך :probably read; או לתוך אגן של מים
(אפי' צלולים). See ימים ולתוך נהרות אם המים שבהם הם עכורים) או לתוך אגן של מים
also Sifre, Deut., §71 (ed. Finkelstein, p. 136), and next note.

[98] Viz. that he is sacrificing to the reflection visible in the water (evidently involving the notion of a spirit residing therein. About the prohibition of worshipping the reflection see Mekh., Baḥodesh c. 6 (ed. Horov. —
Rabin, p. 225): (נ"א: הבבואה), להביא את הבוביא, דברי ר"ע), אשר בשמים מתחת לארץ.
Cp. further Sifre, Deut. §320: אבל הם עובדים לבבואה, and Mekh. of R. Sim.
b. Yoḥai (ed. Hoffman, p. 105, top): כשהוא אומר כל תמונה, לא בדמותן ולא בדמות
בבואה שלהן. Here the reason is different from the one given in Babli Ḥull.
41b, top: מאי שנא לתוך ימים דלא, דאמרי לשרא דימא קא שחיט לתוך עונה של מים נמי
שנו בעכורים. אמרי לבבואה קא שחיט, אמר רבא Here Rabba clearly meant that
muddy water in a basin was permissible (Finkelstein's remark to the contrary, l. c., note to l. 7, on the basis of the above corrupt passage in Tos.,
is impossible as Rabba's answer would make no sense here at all). In reality,
according to the statement in Tos., as emended, when the water is muddy
slaughtering of the animal is permitted even into sea or river, since no reflection (בבואה) is visible, whereas in the case of water in a basin, even a
clear one, it is permitted because there can be no suspicion of worshipping
a resident spirit at all in view of the fact that the basin serves only as a temporary container soon to be emptied of its water that produces the reflection.
Thus the Tos., as interpreted here, corresponds to the reason given in our
Y passage: למה, שהוא עובד בבואה, but in Babli the point involved has become
confused.

[99] A further morsel of this Y item is also cited in 'Arukh, s. v. לק 2
בילמדנו בריש אחרי מות: אמר הקב"ה לגדעון בשלש מאות :(Kohut, V, 56)
המלקקים בידם אושיע אתכם (השוה שו' ז', ו'–ז'), שאותם שכרעו על ברכיהם היו
עובדים לבבואה. The indication 'the beginning of אחרי מות' is somewhat in-
exact, since our section is to Lev. c. 17, and not to c. 16. However, the
former c. constituted the *first Seder* within Sidra אחרי מות because S 88a was
eliminated, with the result that c. 16 was a part of the lection that commenced at the end of מצורע (Lev. 15.25, above, No. 88). Yet in 'Arukh, s. v.
ספקל (Kohut, VI, 109) and s. v. תה (VIII, 205), the same indication obviously
refers to the section on Lev. 16.

שלום, hence the Hal. concerning 'slaughtering into seas and *rivers*' (viz. allowing the blood to be emptied from the animal into these places). This is prohibited because there is a suspicion that such an action involved worshipping the reflection visible from the water, evidently this being connected with a spirit supposedly making his habitat there (cp. note 98). Proceding from this Hal. the homilist mentions the Agg. that the reason Gideon was instructed to eliminate from his troop those who had knelt while drinking water from a brook (Jud. 7.4 ff.), was because by the act of kneeling they worshipped the image that was reflected in the water.[108s] Unfortunately no more has been preserved in the Arukh or elsewhere and there is missing the passage indicating the usual return to the beginning of S by means of the formula, מנין, ממה שקרינו בענין.

Whether the parallel section in TB, §§14–18, T, §§9–12, was part of the Y sermon cannot be ascertained at present. Anyhow, it comprises homilies which presuppose the above H. Thus, there are at first comments on Mal. 1.11: כי ממזרח שמש ועד מבואו ג ד ו ל ש מ י בגוים ובכל מקום מוקטר מוגש ל ש מ י ו מ נ ח ה טהורה כי גדול שמי בגוים אמר ה' צבאות affording several points of contact with H: כה א מ ר ה ' . . . מעלה מ נ ח ה . . . ל מ ע ן ש מ י . . . י כ ב ד ה ' (Is. 66.1, 3, 5).[109s] There follows a Pet. on Ps. 51.20–21: היטיבה ברצונך את ציון תבנה חומות י ר ו ש ל י ם או תחפוץ זבחי צ ד ק וגו'; the rebuilding of the wall of Jer. corresponds to the H v. (66.10): שמחו את י ר ו ש ל י ם וגו', whereas the promise of God's desire for 'sacrifices of righteous men' is in contrast to denunciation in H (66.3) of those who bring offerings in iniquity ((שוחט השור . . . שוחט השה וגו'.[110s] In TB, §16 = T, 10, end, the thought is developed, in connection with Lev. 17.2: זה הדבר, that after the cessation of sacrifices, as a result of the destruction of the Temple, the study of 'the *words* of the Torah' has become a substitute for sacrifice as a factor of atonement.[100] This emphasis on 'the *words* of the Torah' (דברי תורה) is reflected

---

[100] זה הדבר, צפה הקב'ה שביהמ'ק עתיד ליחרב, ואמר הקב'ה (היינו: לישראל, כמו בת'ה) . . . אין ביהמ'ק קיים במה מתכפר עליכם, התעסקו בדברי תורה, שהן משולין כקרבנות, והן מכפרין עליכם, שנ' זה ה ד ב ר, וכן הנביא אומר (הושע י'ד, ג') קחו עמכם ד ב ר י ם ושובו אל ה' (היינו: ונשלמה פרים שפתינו).

by the H v. (66.5); (שמעו ד ב ר ה ' החרדים אל ד ב ר ו) (cp. 66.3).
Concerning another item also dealing with the words of the
Torah, but in a different trend, see infra, p. 93. In TB, §18 = T,
§12, a verse from our H is cited expressly (ישעיה אמר שוחט השור
מכה אשי) and is used for an association of ideas with the prohibition
of slaughtering an animal outside the Tent of Meeting, (see
above, p. 89). In contrast to this, the fulfillment of this law
will be rewarded by the beholding of God's salvation.[101] The
v. cited as inference: זו ב ח תודה יכבדנני ושם ד ר ך אראנו בישע
אלהים is in contrast to Is. 66.3: ... השה זו ב ח ... שוחט השור
בחרו בדרכיהם; even the point of honoring God (יכבדנני)
links up with Is. 66.5: '(למען שמי יכבד ה. Proceeding from ישע
אלהים the theme of Israel's redemption is developed concluding
with the following *peroration*: אמר הקב"ה: בעוה"ז הייתם נושעים
ע"י בשר ודם (בת"ה: בני אדם)... (וע"י שהיו בשר ודם הייתם חוזרין
ומשתעבדין, אבל לע"ל אני בעצמי גואל אתכם ושוב אין אתם משתעבדין, שנ'
ישראל נושע בה' תשועת עולמים ל א ת ב ו ש ו ולא תכלמו עד עולמי עד.
This final v. cited (Is. 45.17) tallies by contrast with the H v.
(Is. 66.5): ונראה בשמחתכם והם י ב ו ש ו.

The Genizah fragment (infra, H. pt., p. unv.) offers quite new
homilies to our S. It seems to contain a version of Midr. Tanḥ.
quite different from TB and T. Where the text commences
there is found a homily on God's care for the poor. The Pet. v.
is missing, but it seems to me that such a one was Ps. 22.25:
כי לא בזה ולא שקץ ענות ע נ י ו ל א ה ס ת י ר פ נ י ו ממנו corresponding to the H v. (Is. 66.2): ו א ל ז ה א ב י ט א ל ע נ י וחרד על
דברי. There follows another Pet. on Prov. 25.2: כ ב ו ד א ל ה י ם
החרדים אל which links up with the H v. (Is. 66.5): הסתר ד ב ר
ד ב ר ו ... י כ ב ד ה'.[112a] The next homily is on Prov. 14.7;
by assuming that the next v. was also included, there would be
a point of contact in גם המה בחרו חכמת ערום הבין ד ר כ ו with
ב ד ר כ י ה ם, albeit by way of contrast.[112s] For further details
concerning this fragment, see the notes, *a. l.*[112as]

---

[101] אמר הקב"ה: מי שהוא מקריב שור חוץ מאהל מועד כמכה איש, כאילו נפש הוא שוחט,
שנ' דם יחשב לאיש ההוא דם שפך, וכל מי שהוא שוחט במשכן מכבדני, שנ' זובח תודה יכבדני,
ומה שכר אני פורע לו, כשאביא ישועה לישראל הוא זוכה לראות בה, שנ' ושם דרך א ר א נ ו
בישע אלהים. The last point is further reflected by Is. 66.5 ונראה בשמחתכם.

2. *Other Homilies.* LR, c. 22.1–5 (= Koh. R., c. 5, verses
8–9) is of a composite character. There are introduced Koh.
5.8–9 as a Pet.: ויתרון ארץ בכל הוא מלך לשדה נעבד, אוהב כסף לא
ישבע כסף ומי אוהב בהמון לא תבואה גם זה הבל, affording no tally
whatsoever with the above H from Is. 66.1 ff.[113s] Indeed §§1–2
are really the Pet. to the S beginning at Deut. 4.41: או יבדיל
משה (see Deut. R., c. 2.26, TB, ואתחנן, Addendum, and the
discussion, infra, p. inc.). The real part pertaining to our S,
viz. §5 concerning the prohibition of offering up sacrifices on
high places (איסור במה) has no connection whatever with the
preceding items, and one is at a loss to ascertain why it should
have been connected at all with the former.[114s] Rather §5 is to
be understood in conjunction with §6 where the H v. (Is. 66.3)
is cited; with this latter v. is combined the Agg. concerning the
high places in TB, §18, T, §12, mentioned above (p. 91). The
Pet. in §10 on Ps. 146.7: עושה משפט לעשוקים, נותן לחם לרעבים ה'
מתיר אסורים, again has no point of contact with our H, and indeed
the whole item has no proper bearing on our Seder.[115s] This
homily has to do with the similar S at Deut. 12.20 (see DR,
c. 4.9) as to which see infra (p. inc.). It was brought in here
because among the enumerated prohibited items, the counterpart of which are permitted,[102] there is mentioned the consumption of animal blood interdicted in our Torah lection
(Lev. 17.10 ff.) corresponding to the same prohibition in Deut.
12.23! Thus the whole section in LR seems to be in much disorder.[116s]

In JTS. Ms. (infra, H. pt., p. נו) there is given a new Pet.
from Prov. 3.1–2: בני תורתי אל תשכח ... כי אורך ימים ושנות חיים
ושלום יוסיפו לך affording a tally with the final v. of H (Is.
66.12): הנני נוטה אליה כנהר שלום. The emphasis of this homily
is on 'the words of the Torah' (דברי תורה), but the trend is different from that of the same topic as dealt with in TB, §16, T, §10
(above, p. 91).

[102] ה' מתיר אסורים, מה שאסרתי לך התרתי לך ... [אסרתי לך] את הדם, התרתי לך
טחול.

Seder 90 (17)

וידבר ה'. . .דבר אל בני ישראל. . .כמעשה ארץ מצרים אשר ישבתם
בה לא תעשו וכמעשה ארץ כנען אשר אני מביא אתכם שמה לא תעשו
ובחוקתיהם לא תלכו, Lev. 18.1–3.

Haftarah: כה אמר ה' אל דרך הגוים אל תלמדו ומאותות השמים אל
תחתו. . .כי חוקות העמים הבל הוא וגו', Jeremiah 10.2–10 (9 verses,
so Bodl. 2610ᵈ). C 45 also begins with 10.2, but its extent is
not indicated by Abrahams. From the homilies, to be discussed
further on, it appears that the H actually began with v. 1:
שמעו את הדבר אשר דבר ה' עליכם בית ישראל,[178] thereby
completing the usual number of ten verses and offering at the
same time further linguistic tallies with Lev. 18.1–2, as italicized.
The Prophetic warning 'not to learn the way of the nations'
was also taken as a parallel to the injunction in our S not to
imitate the deeds of Egypt and Canaan. Otherwise the latter
essentially deals with the topic of sexual immorality (Lev.
18.6 ff.) whereas the H is chiefly directed against idolatry.

    A new Seder here involves a difficulty in that it renders the
previous S (no. 89) to consist of 16 verses, 5 short of the required minimum, in addition to its inauspicious conclusion with
ונשא עונו (Lev. 17.16)! This would tend to show that S 89 really
ought to comprise Lev. 17 and 18, and hence the latter ch.
should not form a new S. Indeed there are no sections to the
latter in TB or T, indicating that it had no general acceptance.
Also in Midr. Agg. (II, 43–44) the comments on Lev. 18 are
incorporated within the section to c. 17 (S 89), with the *peroration* discussed above (p. 92) being placed there subsequently
(ibid., p. 92, top). Yet there is evidence that there existed a
Y sermon to our present S (No. 90), in addition to the respective
section in LR, c. 23.

    It seems that originally Sedarim 89–90 constituted *variable
lections on the same Sabbath*, as the result of the difference as to
the respective readings on the previous Sabbath, viz. Nos. 88
and 88a. Accordingly S 88, comprising Lev. 15.25–16.34, was
followed by S 89 which combined chs. 17–18 of Leviticus. On
the other hand, the different previous S at Lev. 16.1 (No. 88a)
really extended to 17.16, with the next one commencing at 18.1

(No. 90). In this manner there was preserved a certain symmetry
in the respective lengths of the Sedarim. There is further the
consideration whether No. 90 was not rejected as a S because
it coincided with the Torah lection at Minḥah of Yom Kippur,[103]
just as was the case with No. 88a in view of the same reading at
Shaḥarit of the same day (above, p. 88). However, there is
doubt whether in the former occasion the reading actually began
in Palestine at Lev. 18.1 and not at 18.6 (see infra, p. inc.).
Anyhow, in the final fixation of TC, Nos. 89 and 90 became
successive Sedarim, notwithstanding the shortness of the former
(16 verses) and its inauspicious ending (ונשא עונו). The reasons
for this procedure are still inexplicable.

STRUCTURE OF HOMILIES

No Y topic has been preserved. Yet the existence of a section to our S in Midr. Yel. is evident from the citation in Arukh
s. v. זמין (Kohut, III, 296): ובילמדנו בסוף אחרי מות אלו אומרין
תנו זימין, ואלו אומרין תנו פסין, ואלו מבקשין ארנונות ואלו מבקשין גולגליות.
Now the full passage is found in YSH to Cant., c. 2, §985, end
(without indication of source, as rightly pointed out by Kohut);
as part of a Pet. on Cant. 2.2: [104] כשושנה בין החוחים כן רעיתי בין הבנות

---

[103] Meg. 31a: ובמנחה קורין בעריות ומפטירין ביונה. As regards this H from
Jonah see infra, p. inc.[48*]

[104] כשושנה בין החוחים, מדבר בישראל בשעה שהיו במצרים, ומה השושנה הזו בין החוחים
קשה היא ללקטה מתוכן, כך היו ישראל קשים להגאל ממצרים, שנ' או הנסה אלהים לבוא לקחת לו
גוי מקרב גוי (דב' ד', ל"ד). ד"א מה השושנה הזו נכרת בין החוחים, כך היו ישראל ניכרים בין
המצריים, שלא שינו את שמם, ולא שינו מעשיהם, ולא היו שטופים בזימה ולא שינו את לשונם, ולא
היה בהם לשון הרע. ד"א מדבר במתן תורה, שהחזיר הקב"ה התורה על כל האומות ולא קבלוה,
וקבלוה ישראל. ד"א כשושנה בין החוחים, מה השושנה הזו שבין החוחים רוח דרומית באה והיא
לוקה בקוץ, רוח צפונית באה והקוץ מכה אותה, וכן מארבע רוחותיה, כך היו ישראל ויעש
להם בתים (שמ' א', כ"א; כאן ישנו איזה נוסח קטוע), ומשועבדים בין האומות, אלו אומרים
להם: תנו פיסים, ואלו אומרים להם: תנו לנו זימין, ואלו מבקשים מהם ארנוניות, ואלו מבקשים
להם החוחים בין כשושנה הוה ,(מילמדנו בערוך שמובא כמו) גולגוליות. Subsequently there is
given in YSH the parallel passage from LR, c. 23.1–7 (,החוחים בין כשושנה ד"א
ר' יצחק פתר קרא ברבקה וכו'). The first item in the above Y passage corresponds
to R. Eliezer's homily in LR, §2. However, in the latter Israel is represented
as having been outwardly indistinguishable from the Egyptians (ואלו אלו
ערלים, אלו מגדלי בלורית ואלו מגדלי בלורית, אלו לובשי כלאים ואלו לובשי כלאים, א"כ
לא היתה מדת הדין נותנת לישראל שיגאלו וכו' Cp. PRK, פ' החודש 52a, and PR, 76a)

just as there is a set of beautiful Aggadot on this v. in LR,
c. 23.1–7 (= Cant. R., c. 2). In order to obtain the requisite
connection with H, also the following v. (Cant. 2.3) is to be
included: כתפוח בעצי היער כן דודי בין הבנים which indeed completes
the comparison applied respectively to Israel and God, according
to the Rabbinic conception of the Song of Songs.[105] Now the
latter v., as allegorically taken to refer to God, affords a subtle
homiletic contrast to the H v. (Jer. 10.3) depicting *the fashioning
of an idol out of a tree from the wood* (כי עץ מיער כרתו וגו')![118s]

In LR c. 23, Cant. 2.2 is also applied by several Aggadists
to the various topics, the last of which, viz. that of R. Berakhyah,
pertains to the present S.[106] There follows in §7 another Pet.
by R. Isaac on Ezek. 23.2;[107] here again the previous v. ויהי דבר
ה' אלי לאמר is to be included in order to link up linguistically
with Lev. 18.1 and with Jer. 10.1.[119s] The next item (§8) is a

whereas in the former this point is omitted and, on the contrary, in the second
item Israel is depicted as *conspicuous* among the Egyptians by reason of
proper names, deeds, avoidance of unchastity, language and lack of slander
(cp. above, vol. I, H. pt., p. 211, note 570). The third item concerning the
giving of the Torah, which was offered to all the nations but which only
Israel accepted (cp. TB, §3, and the parallels indicated there in note 2a),
is quite different from R. Judah b. Simon's homily in LR, §3. Finally as
regards the fourth item here, cp. LR, §5.[49*]

[105] That Cant. 2.3 is also to be included seems to be implied in R. Abin's
statement (LR, §6) referring to 'the shade of Esau', which is detrimental to
Israel and will disappear in the hereafter (כך כל זמן שצלו של עשיו קיים, כביכול
ישראל נראין כאלו הם כמושים בעוה"ז, אבל לע"ל יעבור צלו של עשו וישראל מרטיבים
והולכים. Accordingly, Israel will henceforth enjoy 'the shade' (protection) of
God, thus alluding to Cant. 2.3: בצלו חמדתי וישבתי. However, it is ques-
tionable whether צל in the above passage is not a corruption for טל, as the
context would seem to require.[50*]

[106] אמר הקב"ה למשה: לך אמור לישראל, בני (כמו בשהש"ר ובי"ל"ש), כשהייתם במצרים
הייתם דומין לשושנה בין החוחים, עכשיו שאתם נכנסין לארץ כנען היו דומין לשושנה בין
החוחים, תנו דעתכם שלא תעשו לא כמעשה אלו ולא כמעשה אלו, הה"ד כמעשה ארץ מצרים
וגו'.[51*]

[107] In the printed texts: ר' יצחק פתר קריא בבן אדם שיש לו שתי
בנות מאם אחת וכו', as if continuing the comments on Cant. 2.2. However, the same Aggadist has already offered his explanation in §1 (ר' יצחק
פתר קריא ברבקה וכו'). The correct text is given in MSS. Vat. and Brit. Mus.:
ר' יצחק פתח בן אדם שתים נשים בנות אם אחת היו (יח' כ"ג, ב') שתיהן מאם אחת, שתיהן
משפיר אחת וכו' (viz. Egypt and Canaan originated from the same stock and
accordingly were immoral alike). Thus a new Pet. is meant here.[52*]

combination of Yer. passages based on the interpretation of
Job 37.21: ועתה לא ראו אור בהיר הוא בשחקים ורוח עברה ותטהרם viz.
Yer. Ber. IX (13d) and Sukkah IV (54c, top). Here would be a
linguistic connection between שחקים and השמים in the H (Jer.
10.2); also these passages deal with phenomena visible in the
skies, thus reflecting this very latter v.: ומאותות השמים אל תחתו.
However, it is very doubtful whether here really a Pet. to our
S is meant since there is no logical correlation with the latter[120s]
(the attempt in פי' מהרז"ו to establish such a connection does
credit to the ingenuity of the author, but essentially is hardly
acceptable). LR, c. 23.9–11, comprises further several Aggadot
concerning sexual immorality which is the main topic of our
Seder. There follows (§12) a homily introducing Job 24.15:
ועין נואף שמרה נשף לאמר לא תשורני עין וגו', as if it were a Pet. to our
S. However, there is no point of contact with H, and this Pet.
really pertains to the S dealing with a Soṭah (Num. 5.11 ff., see
TB, Naso, §6, T, §4, and NR, c. 9.1, and cp. infra, p. 227). It
was inserted here because of the previous items (§§9–11) dealing
with the same theme.[108] Finally there is given the Agg. (§13)
to the effect that refraining from deriving pleasure at the sight
of obscenity merits the beholding of the Shekhinah.[108a] This
item may have served here as the *peroration* of the section to
our S. The final v. cited (Is. 33.17): מלך ביפיו תחזינה עיניך וגו'
would be in fine homiletic contrast to the H v. (Jer. 10.4) depicting the process of beautification of the idol by means of a
layer of silver or gold (בכסף ובזהב ייפהו).

Seder 91 (18)

וידבר ה' ... דבר אל כל עדת בני ישראל ואמרת אליהם ק ד ו ש י ם
תהיו כי ק ד ו ש אני ה' אלהיכם, Lev. 19.1–2.

Hafṭarah: והיה הנשאר בציון והנותר בירושלים ק ד ו ש יאמר לו כל
הכתוב לחיים בירושלים, Isaiah 4.3 Bodl. 2610[7e] has 4.3–5 where

---

[108] This whole passage of LR (§§11–12) is also found in PR, c. 24 (124b–
125a) to לא תנאף[53*].

[108a] מצינו שכל מי שרואה דבר ערוה ואינו זן עיניו ממנו, זוכה להקביל פני השכינה, מאי
טעמא, ועוצם עיניו מראות ברע, מה כתיב בתריה, מלך ביפיו תחזינה עיניך
מרחקים[53a*].

the fragment breaks off. With 4.3 there begins a new Seder in
this Prophetic book. Probably the H extended to 5.5, skipping
to v. 16: ויגבה ה' צבאות במשפט והאל הקדוש נקדש בצדקה (thus
10 verses). C 13 and 14 also list 4.3 as the initial v. of H, but
their extent is not indicated by Abrahams (in his notebook the
statement that in C 13 this v. formed the *end* of H is no doubt
a scribal error for *beginning*). Yannai's Ḳerobah to our S (ed.
Zulay, pp. 159–161) is lacking the part wherein the H is cited.

The connection of H with S is by means of the italicized
words.

STRUCTURE OF HOMILIES

1. No Y topic has been preserved. Of course there was a
section to our S in Midr. Yel., as evident from the citations in
Arukh, s. v. אסרט (Kohut, I, 203) and קנת (VII, 141).[109] The
homilies in TB, Kedoshim, §§1–6 and 9 (which is misplaced) =
T, §§1–6 and 9, all presuppose the above H. In a rather unusual manner, there is first introduced the final v. of H (Is.
5.16) as a *Petiḥta* (TB, §1, T, §1, cp. also LR, c. 24.1), and in
what appears as a *peroration* (TB, §5, T, §5, end) the final v.
cited is the initial v. of H (Is. 4.3)![110] However, it is doubtful
whether the latter item is really the *peroration*[110a] since such may
be found in TB, §6, T, §6, which begins with comments on
Ezek. 3.12: ואשמע אחרי קול רעש גדול ברוך כבוד ה' [ותשאני רוח]
ממקומו affording a linguistic tally with the H: ברוח משפט
וברוח בער (Is. 4.4).[121s] There is also woven in Ps. 17.4: שמרני

<hr/>

[109] The citation, s. v. קפנדר (VII, 166): קדושים תהיו: ואם פירשת ממנו
לקפונדר, תהא יודע שאני מניחך, hardly corresponds to TB, Ḳedoshin, §8, T, §8:
וקרב לפני המלך בקפנדר (as Kohut suggests), since the latter belongs to the
next S (No. 92), unless we assume that in 'Arukh the reference was really
to קדושים פרשת which became corrupted into קדושים בריש. There is
another citation s. v. רא 2 (VIII, 233, top), which may belong to our S since
it refers to the topic of dualism (שני אלהות) also dealt with in TB, §4, T, §4.

[110] Cp. above, vol. I, p. 73, to S 6, where a homily on the initial v. of
the respective H follows directly on the Y topic. See further ibid., p. 112,
note 108, 166–7, and 360.

[110a] Theodor (*MGWJ*, XXXIV, 427, and XXXV, 410, No. 15) is ready
to assume it on the basis of one MS. that omits §6 (see also infra, note 120).

וסוכה תהיה 4.6: ‎.Is reflecting כאישון בת עין בצל כנפיך ת ס ת י ר נ י
ולמסתור ‎.... לצל יומם. The parable concerning a Galilean
having a *vineyard* in Judea and vice versa a Judean having such
in Galilee is appropriate here because of 'the song of my beloved
touching his *vineyard*' (Is. 5.1 ff.) forming a part of our Prophetic
lection. In the finale of the item God's protection of Israel is
assured by citing Ps. 121.7: ‎ה' ישמרך מכל רע ישמר את נפשך. There
the previous verses are also to be included (121.3–6) as well as
the last v. (8), all of which gloriously depict this theme of Divine
protection. Accordingly, verses such as 5–6: ‎ה' שומרך ה' צלך
על יד ימינך יומם השמש לא יככה homiletically link up with Is. 4.6
cited before.[110a] For quite a different *peroration* see infra, p. 100).
The Pet. in TB, §9, T, §9, (misplaced as part of the section of
the next Seder), is on Ps. 20.3: ‎ישלח עזרך מקודש ומציון
יסעדך and tallies with the initial v. of H ... ‎והיה הנשאר בציון
‎ק ד ו ש יאמר לו ... (see farther on to LR).

2. In LR, c. 24, there is first given the Pet. on Is. 5.16 as in
the Tanḥumas but in a different form. There follows another
one on Ps. 92.9: ‎ואתה מרום לעולם ה' reflecting this very final
v. of H (Is. 5.16) ‎ויגבה ה ' צבאות וגו'.[122s] In §§3–4, Ps. 20.3
is commented upon; here the text is fuller than in the Tanḥumas
where §4 has been entirely omitted, this very item emphasizing
the point that "all good things, blessings or consolations (of
Israel), which God is destined to give to Israel, would come from
Zion" ‎(כל טובות וברכות ונחמות, שהקב"ה עתיד ליתן לישראל, אינן אלא
‎מציון וכו'). One such aspect of *consolation* (of Israel) represents
the initial v. of H, which gave the inspiration for this homily,
viz.: ‎והיה הנשאר ב צ י ו ן והנותר בירושלים קדוש יאמר לו.

In MHG (III, 469) there seems to be found a new Pet. to
our S, viz. introducing 1 S 2.2: ‎אין ק ד ו ש כ ה ' כי אין בלתך
which links up readily with Lev. 19.2 and Is. 5.16. After enum-
erating the various appellations of ‎קדוש, as applied to several
beings and objects,[111] the homily concludes with the statement:

---

[111] ‎לפי שמצינו דברים הרבה שנקראו קדושים, המלאכים נקראו קדושים ... השמים
‎נקראו קדושים ... הנביאים ... נקראו קדושים ... והצדיקים נקראו קדושים, שנ' והיה
‎הנשאר בציון והנותר בירושלם קדוש יאמר לו ... ישראל נקראו
‎משנת Cp. also קדושים ... השבתות נקראו קדושים ... הקרבנות נקראו קדושים ... וכו'

ולפיכך הוא אומר למשה: אני קדוש ומחנותי קדושים, קדש את ישראל ואמור
להם שיהיו קדושים, כדי שאשרה את שכינתי ביניהם, מנין ממה שקרינו בענין,
קדושים תהיו כי קדוש אני וגו'.¹¹²

3. Finally attention is drawn to the conclusion of the section
to our S in the Genizah fragment (infra, H. pt., p. unv.). In the
lacuna evidently the proximity of Lev. 18, dealing with sexual
immorality, to 19, dealing with holiness was discussed, similar
to the Agg. of R. Judah b. Pazzi in LR, c. 24.6 (בן יהודה א"ר
פזי מפני מה נסמכה פרשת עריות לפרשת קדושים וכו'). Hence where the
leaf commences Lev. 18.3 is cited, this being at the commencement of the previous S (No. 90, above p. 94). Thereupon
follows the *peroration* of the section to the present S: להן אמר
הא': בניי, אם מבקשין אתם לירש את הארץ הזאת, שמרו עצמכם מן העריות
ומכל דבר של קלקלה, והיו טהורין ו ק ד ו ש י ם, ואתם יושבים לבטח שנ'
ונטעתים על אדמתם (עמוס ט', ט"ו). This final v. in its completeness is
in contrast to Is. 5.8–9, (being the skipped part of H, yet utilized
by the homilists) where the devastation of the land is prophesied
because of wrongdoing. This *peroration* is quite different from
either of the two in the Tanḥumas discussed above (p. 99).¹²³ˢ

אליעזר 'ר, ed. Enelow, which in reality is construed on Prov. 30.1–3. Hence
on ד ב ר י (30.1) we have the Bar. of R. Eliezer b. R. Yose Ha-Gelili introduced by the statement 'כל מקום שאתה מוצא ד ב ר י ו של רבי אליעזר וכו (p. 9,
cp. p. 57: אף כאן אתה אומר ד ב ר י אגור בן יקה); on אגור we have ch. 4 אגור זה
שלמה (p. 65), etc. Now in connection with ודעת ק ד ו ש י ם אדע several chapters are given beginning with these appellations of קדוש (pp. 243, 263, 279,
299, 341, 363). See also Enelow's note to p. 225, to l. 1. About the structure
of this Midr., cp. also Liebermann, גנזי קדם, V, 186 ff., who could not yet
account for the placing on R. Eliezer's Bar. in front, as pointed out above.
Accordingly the designation מדרש אגור by R. Menaḥem di Lonsano is not
exact, and should be מדרש ד ב ר י א ג ו ר.

¹¹² The subsequent passage in MHG: ומפני מה הוא מזכיר בישראל ב' קדושות,
ב ת ח ל ת ה פ ר ש ה (היינו: וי' י"ט, ב') ובסופה (היינו: כ', כ'ו), משל למה"ד, לאחד שהיה
לו מרתף של יין וכו', is already modified by the redactor of MHG to suit *his*
arrangement according to AC; in LR, c. 24.8, wherefrom the parable emanates,
the introductory question מפני . . . ובסופה is missing, and the inference for
'two sanctifications' (שתי קדושות) is not from 19.2 and 20.26 but from 20.7:
והתקדשתם והייתם קדושים (cp. חידושי רש"ש, note 8).⁵⁴* Cp. also the Genizah fragment of a *Midr. according to AC* (infra, H. pt., p. רט, 11.25 ff.), where the
same observation is made concerning 19.2 and 20.26 in connection with
quite a different homily.

Seder 92 (19)

וכי תבאו אל הארץ ונטעתם כל עץ מאכל וערלתם ערלתו את
ערלו לא יאכל, Lev. 19.23. פריו שלש שנים יהיה לכם ערלים לא יאכל

Haftarah: לא יבנו ואחר ישב לא יטעו ואחר יאכל כי כימי העץ
ימי עמי ומעשה ידיהם יבלו בחירי, Isaiah 65.22. C. 13 gives 65.22,
with the end missing. C. 21 (beginning missing) gives 65.23–
66.2, skipping to verses 5–7 and then to 10–11 (hence 11 verses).
The skipping of verses 3–4 is due to the tendency of omitting
denunciatory verses (see above, p. 89). Moreover, v. 2 (וחרד)
(שמעו דבר ה' החרדים על דברו) links up well with v. 5 (על דברי).
In order to obtain a finale of glorious consolation of Israel, viz.
verses 10–11, verses 8–9 were skipped; perhaps also v. 7 was
omitted, hence 65.22–66.2+4–5+10–11 (10 verses).

The italicized words form the tallies between S and H.

Structure of Homilies

1. No Y topic has been preserved. A morsel of the section in
Midr. Yel. to our S is found in YSH (קונדריס אחרון BHM, VI,
p. 87, No. 47) wherein Lev. 19.23–24 is allegorized as referring
to the subjection of Israel by 'four kingdoms,' with the redemption to take place during the dominion of the last one, (viz.
Edom, Rome): שלש שנים יהיו לכם ערלים, א"ל הב"ה: אם שעבדו בכם
שלש מלכיות לא תצפו לגאולה, לא יאכל, אין לכם גאולה אלא בשנה
הרביעית, תאכלו את פריו,[113] שבמלכות הרביעית ישם לכם גאולה. א"ר ינאי
הוא שכתיב תחת שלש רגזה ארץ וגו' לא יוכל שאת (משלי ל', כ"א), כביכול
אין הקב"ה יכול להטה (צ"ל: להניח) את ישראל, אלא מיד הוא גואלם ונוטעם
באַרצם, שנ' ונטעתים על אדמתם.[114] Am. 9.15 is also woven into the
different Agg. in TB, §11, T, §11 (see further on). Further in the

[113] Actually, Lev. 19.24 reads: ובשנה החמישית תאכלו את פריו, hence we
read here: *[55]אלא ובשנה הרביעית יהיה כל פריו קודש הלולים לה'.

[114] R. Yannai's statement is curtailed here, but is more fully given in
YSH to Prov., a. l. (§963, from Yel.): תחת שלש רגזה ארץ, אלו ג' מלכיות
שמשעבדות לישראל, ותחת ארבע לא יוכל שאת, זו אומה רביעית, כביכול אין הקב"ה יכול
להניח את ישראל, אלא מיד הוא גואלם, וכן הוא אומר שלש שנים יהיו לכם ערלים, אלו ג'
מלכיות שלא תצפו לגאולתכם, אין לכם [גאולה] אלא בשנה הרביעית תאכלו את פריו,
שבמלכות רביעית יהיה לכם גאולה. About a similar allegorization of the law of
Shemita, see infra, p. 104.

latter Midrashim (§14) the allegorization of Lev. 19.23–25 is different from that of the above Y passage (see further on).

2. The first Pet. in TB and T (Kedoshim, §7) is on Zech. 8.11–12, containing by means of כימים ... העם ... יבולה linguistic tallies with the initial v. of H: ... כי כימי העץ ימי עמי יבלו בחירי, in addition to the intrinsic affinity of the verses in question.[124s] In §8 there is developed the theme of sustained attention to plantations; even if a person is not likely to enjoy them in his lifetime, he should prepare them for his progeny. All this is well reflected in the H v. (Is. 65.23): 'They will not labor in vain nor bring forth in terror, for they are the seed blessed by God and their offspring with them.' (cp. the sentence: ולמה אני לא יגעו לריק וגו' יגע בשביל אחרים in the homily as compared to in the above v.). In §10 the Pet. is from Koh. 2.5: עשיתי לי גנות ופרדסים ונטעתי בהם עץ, affording a ready point of contact with both Lev. 19.23 and Is. 65.22. In §11 the comments are on Ps. 105.44–45 which link up by means of ארצות גוים with הארץ in Lev. 19.23 and ארץ in Is. 66.8 (this in skipped part). In the conclusion the initial v. of H is woven in expressly וכשעושים תשובה לא יבנו ואחר ישב לא יטעו ואחר יאכל, למה שהן נוטעין ואינן נותשין, שנ' ולא ינתשו עוד מעל אדמתם אשר נתתי להם אמר ה' אלהיך. With this final v. (Am. 9.15) also the previous one there (v. 14) is to be combined, viz. ובנו ערים נשמות וישבו ונטעו כרמים ושתו את יינם ועשו גנות ואכלו את פריהם, thus supplementing so well Is. 65.22. Am. 9.15 was also cited in the Y passage (above, p. 101).[115] The next Pet. (§12) is from Jer. 3.19: ואנכי אמרתי איך אשיתך בבנים ואתן לך ארץ חמדה, correlating with S and H by means of ארץ (as above) and further by means of 'children' with Is. 65.23.[125s] Further §13 introducing Prov. 31.16 מפרי כפיה נטעה כרם, affords a verbal tally with S and H by reason of the verb נטע common to all three. Finally in §14, Lev. 19.23–25 are allegorized (in a different manner from the Y passage above, p. 101) as referring to a child which in the

---

[115] In JTS. MS. p. 28 (infra, H. pt., p. 92) the section to our S concludes with this Agg., in a variant form, as the *peroration*: בעוה"ז היו ישראל נוטעין ואומות העולם אוכלין, אבל לע"ל מה שהן נוטעין זוכין לאכול אותו, שנ' לא יבנו ואחר ישב וגו', והקב"ה נוטען על אדמתן נטיעת עולמים, שנ' ונטעתים על אדמתם [56*].

fourth year of its life is dedicated to the Torah and in the fifth
year it actually begins to study the Bible.[116] This leads down to
the *peroration* which uses Is. 66.23 expressly as its final verse:
אמר להן הקב"ה: בעוה"ז, ע"י שיצר הרע מצוי בכם, אתם חוטאים ובניכם
מתים, אבל לעתיד לבוא אני מסיר יצה"ר מכם ומבניכם (אולם בת"ב רק:
מביניכם) ואתם מולידים ושמחים (צריך להוסיף: "בהם" כמו במדרש אגדה),
שנ' לא יגעו לריק ולא ילדו לבהלה וגו'. However, in YSH to Lev.
(§615) the *peroration* is different, referring not to the death of
children but rather to their forgetfulness of the Torah which
they had been taught — this forgetfulness to disappear in the
hereafter: בעוה"ז אדם מלמד בנו תורה ומשכחה, אבל לע"ל הקב"ה מלמדה,
שנ' וכל בניך למודי ה' ורב שלום בניך (יש' נ"ד, י"ג). This final v. would
link up well with Is. 65.23 also dealing with children (cp. further
the parallel of למודי ה' and ברוכי ה'). This version is an improve-
ment upon the one in the Tanḥumas, since it involves more
skillful homiletic technique to cite a v. from elsewhere and
connect it with II rather than quote a v. from the latter itself.
Perhaps this version in YSH really emanates from Midr. Yel.,

---

[116] מדבר בתינוק, ש ל ש ש נ י ם י ה י ה ל כ ם ע ר ל י ם, שאינו יכול לא להשיח ולא
לדבר; ו ב ש נ ה ה ר ב י ע י ת י ה י ה כ ל פ ר י ו ק ד ש, שאביו מקדישו לתורה;
ה ל ו ל י ם ל ה', מהו הלולים, משעה שמהלל להקב"ה (כן בת"ב, ובב' דפוסים הראשונים
של ח"ה רק: מהלל להקב"ה, ובדפוס מנטובה: שמשעה שהוא מהלל להקב"ה, ובעל עץ יוסף
מנסח: שבשעה ההוא מהולל להקב"ה); ו ב ש נ ה ה ח מ י ש י ת ת א כ ל ו א ת פ ר י ו,
משעה שהוא מתחיל לקרות בתורה, מכאן ואילך ל ה ו ס י ף ל כ ם ת ב ו א ת ו, מכאן שנו
רבותינו בן חמש למקרא בן עשר למשנה (אבות פ"ה, כ"א). The point of dedication of
the child to the Torah in the fourth year is rather vague; there is also no
indication how the child praises God (as is the correct reading in TB, cp.
the subsequent משעה שהוא מתחיל וכו' also referring to the same). Buber offers
no comment. It seems that the Aggadist had in mind here the Bar. (Tos.
Hag. 1.2, cp. Babli Sukkah 42a: קטן... יודע לדבר (היינו: בשנה הרביעית), אביו
מלמדו שמע ותורה ולה"ק. In Babli 'Shema' is explained as meaning Deut. 6.4,
and 'Torah' as referring to Deut. 33.4, viz. the father teaching his child to
recite these verses. Although this interpretation of the Bar. is by the Babyl.
Amora R. Hamnuna, the tradition behind it is Palestinian, thus R. Yehuda
Hannassi's reading of the Shema consisted only of Deut. 6.4 (Ber. 13b)
whereas Deut. 33.4 was taught the little children in school (evidently the
beginners, cp. the story of R. Yannai in LR, c. 9.3: חד זמן הוה עבר קמי בית
ספרא ושמעית קלהן דמיניקא אמרין תורה צוה לנו משה מורשה קהלת יעקב), and by the
child's recital of Deut. 7.1 declaring God's unity, the latter is praised. The
child was also taught to recite the blessings over food, etc., involving further
praise of God.

viz. at first Lev. 19.23–24 were allegorized as referring to the subjugation of Israel by the 'four kingdoms' (above, p. 101) and then (as a דבר אחר) the allegorization concerning the early education of a Jewish child was added (as also given in the Tanḥumas) leading down to the *peroration* as found in YSH.

3. In LR, c. 25, the first Pet. is on Prov. 3.18: עץ חיים היא למחזיקים בה ותומכיה מאושר, affording a tally by means of עץ with Lev. 19.23 and Is. 65.22. R. Judah b. Simon (§3) applies Deut. 13.5 as a Pet. to our S, viz. one of the instances of *imitatio Dei* being that just as God attended to the planting of a garden in Eden soon after the creation, so the Jews were enjoined to start planting trees soon after their arrival in Canaan (about this Aggadic parallelism cp. also TB. Now this v. by the sentence ובקולו תשמעו is homiletically reflected in the H v.: והרד על דברי (Is. 66.2, cp. also v. 5).[126s] The next Pet., by R. Levi (§4) introduces Koh. 2.4–5 which verses offer ready tallies with both S and H. The following item (§5) begins with Job 38.36[127s] which is hardly meant as a Pet., but rather is cited in connection with another remark of R. Levi in order to apply the parable of the hen and her chicks to the case of Israel before and after the possession of Canaan. Likewise Cant. 5.15, introducing the Agg. in §8, is not meant as a Pet., but is introduced in connection with Bar Kappara's comment comparing the sections of the Torah to a pillar having a chapter above and a basis below (cp. also Cant. R., *a. l.*, and NR, c. 10.1, as to which see infra, p. 135. See further infra, p. 234). Finally there is the *peroration* which weaves in expressly the initial verses of H (the citation here is according to the version in Cant. R., c. 5, end, which is more correct than in LR, c. 25, end): ר' שמעון בר' יוסי בר לקוניא (ובכת"י וטיקן וברימיש מוזיאום לויק"ר: בן יוסי בן לקוניה) לפי שבעוה"ז אדם בונה בנין ואחר מכלה אותו, אדם נוטע נטיעה ואחר יאכל (צ"ל: אוכל) אותה, אבל לע"ל מה כתיב, לא יבנו ואחר ישב לא יטעו ואחר יאכל וגו' לא יגעו לריק ולא ילדו לבהלה כי זרע ברוכי ה' המה [וכתיב] ונודע בגוים זרעם וצאצאיהם בתוך העמים כל ראיהם יכירום כי הם זרע ברך ה'. The last v. (Is. 61.9) has been added because of its tally with Is. 65.23, as italicized.

4. Finally the novel section in the Genizah fragment (infra,

H. pt., p. unv.) is to be discussed. It begins with the Pet. on
Prov. 3.18, but in quite a different manner from the one in LR,
c. 25.1–2. A new allegorization of Lev. 19.23–25 is given, viz.
the three years, during which the fruit of a newly planted tree
is forbidden for consumption, correspond to the three Patriarchs; the fourth year, during which the fruit is 'holy' as praise
to God (הלולים לה'), corresponds to Judah, Jacob's fourth son,
whose name means 'thanking God'; the fifth year, when the
unrestricted eating is allowed, symbolizes Israel consumed by
the nations. Another parallelism is developed concerning the
Pal. trees; the number 3 reminds of the Torah given in the
3rd month (Sivan), with the recipients being the *fourth* generation (cp. Gen. 15.16) corresponding to the *fourth* year (Lev.
19.24), and because the Pent. consists of *five* books, the fruit
of the tree is unrestrictedly permissible in the fifth year (Lev.
19.25) to symbolize the enjoyment of the fruit of the Torah.
Thereupon follows a new Pet. on Ps. 94.20–21 which by means
of כסא (היחברך כסא) has a linguistic tally with H v. (Is. 6.1):
השמים כסאי.[128s] Our fragment breaks off after the development of
the comments on this Pet., and the conclusion of the section is
missing. (For further details see the footnotes, *a. l.*).

SEDER 92a (19a)

וידבר ה' . . . ואל בני ישראל תאמר איש איש מבני ישראל ומן הגר הגר בישראל
אשר יתן מזרעו למלך מות יומת עם הארץ ירגמהו באבן, Lev. 20.1–2.

From the Y items, to be discussed forthwith, it appears that
a new S began here, and accordingly there could not have been
such at 19.23 (above, No. 92) since the latter would thus have
contained fifteen verses only (19.23–37). We have here another
case of shifting of Sedarim. One custom was to have S 91 comprise Lev. 19.1–22, with the next one (No. 92) beginning at
19.23 and extending to 20.27. But another usage was to prolong
S 91 to the end of Lev. 19 and start the rendering of the next
Sabbath at 20.1 (No. 92a). The conclusion of S 91 with Lev.
19.37 is certainly better than with 19.22. Yet the former custom
prevailed, and the existence of the latter (of very limited vogue)

is discernible only from the few following Midrashic data. About the influence of the present shifting of the Sedarim on the next one, viz. Nos. 93 and 93a see infra, pp. 108, 112).

Arukh, s. v. חך 4 (Kohut, III, 380, bottom), cites: ‏ב י ל מ ד נ ו‏ פ ' ק ד ו ש י ם ת ה י ו, חכו ממתקים (שה"ש ה', ט"ז), אין חיך מתוק משל הקב"ה, שהוא מצוה את ישראל להנאתן ולטובתן ונותן להן שכר עליהן, כיצד, מזהיר לישראל שלא יאכלו שקצים ורמשים, וכן הדם שהוא מאכל לכלבים, קונדריס) וכן נבלות וטרפות. Now the whole item is given in YSH (אחרון, BHM, VI, 87, No. 48) as a Pet. to Lev. 20.2: ‏איש אשר‏ יתן מזרעו למולך זש"ה חכו ממתקים, הב"ה מצוה את ישראל להנאתן ולטובתן לעשות מצוה ונותן להם שכר, כיצד, מזהיר שלא יאכלו שקצים ורמשים, שנ' אל תשקצו [את] נפשותיכם (וי' י"א, מ"א) ונותן להם שכר, יש חיך מתוק מזה: וכן הדם אינו אלא מאכל לכלב, ואומר וכל דם לא תאכלו (שם ג', י"ז, וז', כ"ו); ‏[וכן]‏ הרחיקם מן הגבלות וטרפות; וכן ושרט לנפש לא תתנו וגו' וכתובת קעקע לא תתנו בכם אני ה' (שם, י"ט, כ"ח),117 ליתן לכם שכר, יש חיך מתוק מזה;117 וכן אומות העולם מעבירין את בניהם באש, וכתיב לא ימצא בך מעביר בניו (צ"ל: בנו) ובתו באש (דב' י"ח, י'). The above citation in Arukh does not indicate where exactly in קדושים פ ' the Yel. passage belongs, but this is evident from YSH. However, Arukh itself, s. v. גיא בן הנם (Kohut, II, 274), produces another passage from the section to the present S dealing with Moloch worship: בילמדנו בס' (= בסוף) פרשת קדושים, ובמגלת איכה טומאתה בשוליה (צ"ל: בשוליה, איכה א', ט'), אמרו רבותינו אעפ"י שהיו כל בתי ע"ז בירושלם, המולך חוץ לירושלים היה, והיה עשוי צלם, והיו לו ז' קנקלים, והוא לפנים ממנו (הוצ' רצא: מהן) וכו' (for the same item cp. also YSH, Jerem, §277, from Yel., and Arukh, s. v. קנקל II, (Kohut, VII, 139), where again the reference is בילמדנו קדושים תהיו without further specification).[118]

A ready H for such a S, the beginning of which contains the prohibition of the worship of Moloch, would be Jer. 32.35: ‏ויבנו את במות הבעל אשר בגיא בן הנם ל ה ע ב י ר א ת ב נ י ה ם ו א ת‏ ‏ב נ ו ת י ה ם ל מ ו ל ך וגו'‏, tallying with Lev. 20.2. This H extended to v. 44 (10 verses). It thus comprised predominantly words of

---

[117] Read [נאמן] ליתן וכו'. Cp. TB, ויצא §22: נאמן לפרוע לכם שכר, למה אני ה'. and Cant. R., to 5.16 (§4): אני ה' נאמן לשלם לכם שכר טוב לעולם הבא.

[118] See further the similar passage in TB, ואתחנן Addendum (p. 17), כיצד, היה המולך בגיא בן הנם וכו'.57*

'consolation of Israel' (viz. 35–44), except the initial v. of denunciation. Now in v. 36 there is a reference to 'Jerusalem' (העיר
הזאת cp. also v. 44: ובסביבי ירושלים), there the Pet. v. from 5.16:
חכו ממתקים וכולו מחמדים, זה דודי וזה רעי בנות ירושלים could be tallied
with H by means of the same locality.[129s] Furthermore, since
v. 35 contains the indication of the locale of Moloch worship
at גיא בן הנם, hence the above Y item depicting graphically this
worship and giving an Agg. interpretation of the name הנם.[119]

A portion of a Midrashic section to our S is also preserved
in TB, §15, T, §15, beginning with comments to Lev. 20.9 It
can hardly be assumed that there was once a S there since its
commencement would be very abrupt, viz. כי איש איש אשר יקלל
אביו ואמו וגו'. Rather we have here the latter part of the section
that commenced with comments to Lev. 20.2 ff. In connection
with Lev. 20.9 there is cited the similar v. from Prov. 20.20:
מקלל אביו ואמו (but not as a Pet., cp. the introduction אמר שלמה
מקלל וכו' and not the usual זש"ה וכו'). The present item leads
down to the *peroration*: (ובת"ב: בשביל) אמר הקב"ה: בעוה"ז על ידי
יצה"ר בני אדם לוקין, אבל לעתיד [לבוא] אני עוקרו מכם (ובת"ב: אבל
לעוה"ב אני מסיר יצה"ר מכם); שנ' והסירותי את לב האבן מבשרכם ונתתי
לכם לב בשר, ואת רוחי אתן בקרבכם ועשיתי את אשר בחוקי תלכו ומשפטי
תשמרו ועשיתם (Ezek. 36.26–27).[130s] To these two verses the following one (28) should be added as the culmination of the new
order: וישבתם בארץ אשר נתתי לאבותיכם והייתם לי לעם ואנכי אהיה לכם
לאלהים. This whole passage of Ezek. corresponds so well to that
of our H (Jer. 32.37 ff.): והשיבותים אל המקום הזה והושבתים לבטח,
והיו לי לעם ואני אהיה להם לאלהים, ונתתי להם לב אחד ודרך אחד ליראה
אותי כל הימים . . . ונטעתים בארץ הזאת וגו'. Again the procedure of
investigation pursued here makes it possible to establish the
proper whereabouts of a Midrashic item that otherwise seems
out of place.[120]

---

[119] 'Arukh, *l. c.*: ולמה נקרא שמו תפת והנם, שהיו מתופפים ומנהמים בתופים שלא
ישמע אביו קול הנער וירחם עליו, ד"א הנם, שהיה תינוק מנהם וקול נהמותיו עולות. ד"א (הנם)
שהיו הכומרים אומרים: י ה נ ה לך, י ע ר ב לך, יתבסם לך.

[120] Cp. Theodor, *MGWJ*, XXXIV, 427, and XXXV, 410, No. 16, whose
remarks are now untenable (see also above, note 110a).

Seder 93 (20)

ויאמר ה' אל משה אמר אל הכהנים בני אהרן ואמרת אליהם ל נ פ ש ל א
י ט מ א בעמיו כ י א ם לשארו הקרב אליו ל א מ ו ו ל א ב י ו ולבנו
ולבתו ולאחיו, ולאחתו הבתולה הקרובה אליו אשר לא היתה לאיש לה יטמא,
Lev. 21.1–3.

Haftarah: ואל מת אדם לא יבוא לטמאה כי אם לאב ולאם ולבן ולבת לאח
ולאחות אשר לא היתה לאיש יטמאו, Ezekiel 44.25 (so C 21, but its
extent is not indicated by Abrahams); probably the lection
extended to 45.2 skipping to v. 15 wherewith there begins a new
Seder in Ezek. (hence 10 verses). Yannai's Ḳerobah (ed. Zulay,
pp. 161–64) is lacking the part which lists the initial v. of H.

The linguistic and intrinsic connection between the commencements of S and H is obvious.

Structure of Homilies

1. *Y Sermon*. The Halakhic topic, although not included in
the Tanḥ. sections, can be ascertained from the citation in
Arukh, s. v. חמש (Kohut, III, 439): ב י ל מ ד נ ו ב ר י ש א מ ו ר
א ל הכהנים: ה' דברים חייבים בחלה מן המקרא, וכבר פירש בערך חט.
In the latter place (s. v. חט Kohut, III, 369) the passage from
Yer. Ḥallah (c. 1, 57b) is given, viz. R. Samuel b. Naḥman's
statement inferring from Is. 28.25 the five species from which
Ḥallah is given (M. Ḥallah 1.1). From these indications it
appears that the Y question and answer began as follows:
ילמדנו רבינו: כמה דברים חייבים בחלה: החטין והשעורין והכוסמין, ושבולת
שועל ושיפון (מס' חלה א', א'). הרי זה מן המשנה, מן המקרא מניין.[121] שנ'
ושם חטה שורה ושעורה נסמן וכוסמת גבולתו (יש' כ"ח, כ"ה), ושם חטה, אלה
החטים (בערוך: כמשמעה); שורה, זו שבולת שועל, ולמה נקרא שמה שורה,
שהיא עשויה כשורה; שעורה, אלו השעורים (בערוך: כמשמעה); נסמן, זה
השיפון, וכוסמת, זה הכוסמין; גבולתו (בירוש' נוסף: לחם, אבל חסר לנכון
בערוך), עד כאן גבולו של לחם.

The starting point of the above topic concerning Ḥallah is
clearly to be found in the H v. (Ezek. 44.30) which contains the
injunction to give to the priests *the first of your dough* (ראשית
עריסתיכם, cp. Num. 15.20).[131s] Wheat and barley, forming two
of the five species from which this priestly perquisite was due,
are also mentioned in the part skipped in the H (Ezek. 45.13)
which, however, the homilist utilized for his purpose. The
further development of this item, viz. the transition from Hal.
to Agg. leading down to the beginning of the S by means of the
formula: ממה שקרינו בעניין מניין has not been preserved.

Another morsel from the section in Midr. Yel. to our S is to
be found in Arukh, s. v. למד (Kohut, V, 42, bottom): ב י ל מ ד נ ו
בריש אמור אל הכהנים, ולמדנה בנותיכם נהי (ירמיה ט', י"ט),
מה ראו הקינים והנהיות להנתן לנשים, בשביל שהביאו מות לעולם. Death
is the topic of the beginnings of both S and H setting forth the
regulations for a priest when confronted with a case of demise.
Perhaps the above morsel was towards the end of the Y sermon
leading down to a *peroration* that contained the cheerful assurance
that in the future death would disappear altogether. A passage
such as found in M. Moed Ḳaṭan, end, *which also weaves in the
above v. from Jer.* 9.19, would fit in well here: איזהו עינוי, שכולן
עונות כאחת, קינה שאחת מדברת וכולן עונות אחריה, שנאמר ולמדנה
בנותיכם נהי, ואשה רעותה קינה, אבל לעתיד לבוא הוא אומר בלע ה מ ו ת
לנצח ומחה ה' אלהים דמעה מעל כל פנים וגו'. The final v. cited (Is.
25.8) would tally by means of 'Death' with the initial v. of H:
ואל מ ת א ד ם לא יבוא.[132s] The same final v. is also given in the
similar *peroration* in T, Emor, §3, end, as to which see infra
(p. 110).

2. In the sections in the Tanḥumas (TB, Emor, §§1–6, T,
§§1–4) the first Pet. is from Ps. 12.7: אמרות ה' אמרות ט ה ו ר ו ת
וגו' affording a linguistic point of contact with the H v. (Ezek.
44.26): אחרי ט ה ר ת ו.[133s] The general remark is added that "all,
that God warns Israel about, is for their sanctification and purification" (בשביל קדושתן וטהרתן). These two qualifications are
reflected in Ezek. 44.26–27 (ט ה ר ת ו ... לשרת בקודש) in addition to the respective v. of our S (Lev. 21.6). Another Pet.
(TB, §2, missing in T, cp. LR, c. 26.4–5) is on Ps. 19.3: י ו ם

ליום יביע אומר וגו' which can be correlated with the latter H
v., viz. וביום בואו.[134s] By means of the formula of מה כתיב
למעלה מן הענין (TB, §3, T, §2) there is introduced (Lev. 20.27):
ואיש או אשה כי יהיה בהם אוב או ידעוני and in connection with the
latter v. we have comments on Is. 8.19–20: וכי יאמרו אליכם
דרשו אל האובות ואל הידעונים... בעד החיים אל ה מ ת י ם וגו'. By
means of המתים there is a tally with the initial v. of our H:
ואל מ ת אדם לא יבוא וגו'.[135s] Because of the topic of divination by
a ghost or familiar spirit there is the long Agg. on Saul and the
witch of En-Dor (TB, §4, T, §2). Finally there is the comment
(TB, §5, T, §3) on the repetition of אמר in the initial v. of S
(אמור אל הכהנים... ואמרת אליהם). This leads down already to the
peroration (T, §3, end): ואף כאן אמור אל הכהנים בני אהרן ואמרת,
אמירה ראשונה למת מצוה יטמא, והשנייה לאחרים לא יטמא, לפיכך אמור
ואמרת,[122] לפי שבעוה"ז כהן מטמא למת מצוה, אבל לעתיד [לבוא] אין אתם
מטמאין כל עיקר, למה, שאין מיתה לעתיד, הה"ד בלע המות לנצח (יש',
כ"ה, ח'). The passage from לפי onwards has been added in T,
ed. Mantua; it is also missing in TB and in LR, c. 26.8.[136s]
However, the addendum is from a genuine source and forms the
proper conclusion of the section of our S and H that began with
regulations concerning the conduct of priests when confronted
with a dead person (cp. also above, p. 109, with regard to the Y
item). This *peroration* neatly terminates LR, c. 26, according
to the correct MSS.[123] Hence the parallel passages in Lam. R.

---

[122] About the different reading in Lam. R. and in Midr. Sam. see Buber's
note 48 to TB, §5. This different reading is also found in the MSS. of LR
to be cited in the next note.

[123] A Genizah fragment (T.-S Box C1, No. 19, one vellum leaf) contains
the end of ch. 26 of LR and the beginning of ch. 27. The former concludes
thus: והדין ויאמר ה' אל משה אמר אל הכהנים, למה אמר ואמרת, אלא באמירה ראשונה
אמר להם לנפש לא יטמא, ובאמירה שניה אמר לו: אם בא מת מצוה על ידך הטפל בו, לפי
שבעוה"ז כהנים מיטמאים למת מצוה, אבל לעתיד לבוא, מה כתיב, בלע המות לנצח. The
same ending of ch. 26 is found in MS. Vienna of LR (the only variant being:
אם בא מת מצוה לידך הזקק לו, לפי שבעוה"ז כהן מטמא למת מצוה). In MSS. Vat. and
Brit. Mus. the whole passage in LR, from §7 is curtailed, thus: מה כתיב
למעלה מן הענין... זו בעלת אוב כל עינ(י)נא דשמואל עד ובלע המות לנצח. The copyist
evidently referred to the parallel item in Midr. Samuel and hence omitted
it here. Subsequently there begins in both MSS. ch. 27 without the passage
מה כתיב אחר הענין, LR, c. 26.9.

and in Midr. Samuel have the same conclusion. The omission of the *peroration* is due to the fact that there had been added later on a passage concerning the High Priest (מה כתיב אחר העניין והכהן הגדול מאחיו, LR, c. 26.9, TB, §6, T, §4) with a sort of conclusion of its own (אמר דוד ... אף בשרי ישכון לבטח). Hence the real *peroration* has been left out. However, this passage is really a part of the *section to an 'irregular' Seder, which commenced with Lev. 21.10* and which excluded the regular S at 21.1, as will be shown infra, sub No. 93a (p. 112).

3. LR, c. 26, needs only a brief discussion. It begins with the Pet. of R. Tanḥum b. Ḥanilai on Ps. 12.7; as to the correlation with H see above (p. 109). The whole portion till §2, end, is a replica of what is found in PRK to פ' פרה (30a–33a, cp. also NR, c. 19.2). Indeed in MSS. Vatican and Brit. Mus. of LR we have the following interesting rubric: ר' תנחום בר חניליי פתח אמרות יי' אמרות טהורות וגו' ... מלך בשר ודם נכנס למדינה כל פיתחה (בכ"י בריט. מוז.: פתיחא) דהפסיקתא[124] עד שאתה מגיע על ידי שהיה סיפק בידו למחות בשאול על נוב עיר הכהנים ולא מיחה (היינו: סוף סי' ב').[137ᵃ] א"ר תנחום בר חנילי שתי פרשיות וכו' (היינו: סי' ג'). The pertinence of this Pet. in connection with the Torah reading on Sabbath Parah (viz. Num. 19) will be discussed infra (p. inc.). There follows in LR (§§4–5) the Pet. on Ps. 19.3 as in TB, §2

[124] The same designation of Pesiḳta is also found in both MSS. to LR, c. 28: מה יתרון לאדם וגו', א"ר בנימן בר לוי בקשו לגנוז ספר קהלת שמצאו בו דברים שהן מטין לצד מינות כוליה פרשתא דהפסקתא עד .א"ר פנחס ובקרית שמע היה עוסק ולא הפסיק, למען יזמרך כבוד ולא ידום", thus referring to Pisḳa העומר (PRK, 68b–72b, PR, 90b–93b); further to c. 29: דברך נצב בשמים, תני בשם לעולם יי' ר' אליעזר בכ"ה באלול נברא העולם כל פיתחה דההפסקתא עד כשאתה מגיע, ועשיתם אשה, מקום שהקרבנות קרבין", א"ר תחליפא קיסרייא ... והארץ החדשה referring to Pisḳa השביעי בחדש (PRK, 147b–155b); finally to c. 30: ר' אבא בר כהנא פתח קחו מוסרי ואל כסף ... למה תשקלו כסף בלא לחם וגו' כל פיתחה דההפסקתא עד שאתה מגיע ארחץ בנקיון כפי, במקח ולא בגזל, דתנינן תמן לולב הגזול (היינו: סי' ה' בויק"ר, פ"ל) ... ואם היה גזול צווח לפני הקב"ה כל פיתחא דההפסקתא עד שאתה מגיע, וערבי נחל, אלו ישראל, מה ערבה זו אין בה לא ולקחתם טעם ולא ריח" וכו' (היינו באמצע סי' י"ב בויק"ר שם) לכם (PRK, 178a–181b and 182b–185a).

The above form הפסקתא viz. that *the so-called Pesiḳta contained sections on the readings that interrupted the regular Sedarim,* is apparently the original designation of this Midrashic work (for fuller discussion see infra, vol. III).

(above, p. 109). In §6 there is the Pet. on Ps. 19.10: 'יראת ה
טהורה וגו' which again tallies with H v. (Ezek. 44.26): ואחרי
טהרתו just as in the case of the Pet. on Ps. 12.7 (above, p. 109).
The homilies, in connection with Lev. 20.27 by means of מה
כתיב למעלה מן העניין (7), are the same as in the Tanḥumas, and
likewise §8 containing also the *peroration* which has been omitted
in the printed text. Finally there is a §9 which is part of the
section to S 93a (infra, p. 112).

In MHG (III, 519–20) the Pet. on Ps. 19.10 (cp. LR, c.
26.6) is extensively developed leading down to the same comment as that of R. Levi in LR, though in a variant form, to the
effect that Aaron, because he feared God, merited to receive the
command to keep himself and his offspring free from the so-called
levitical impurity.[125] The sentence עומדת לעד in Ps. 19.10 is
further commented upon to emphasize the validity of this law
of priestly purity even after the destruction of the Temple.[126]
The whole passage in MHG seems to emanate from some
Midrash unavailable to us now. The further passage in MHG
(520–22), introducing the Pet. from Koh. 8.1, does not belong
to our S here, but has been taken over from the Pesikta on
פ' פרה.

Seder 93a (20a)

והכהן הגדול מאחיו אשר יוצק על ראשו שמן המשחה ומלא את ידו ללבוש
את הבגדים וגו', Lev. 21.10.

In Arukh there are three citations from the section in Midr.
Yel. beginning with the above verse, viz. 1) s. v. אסטרטיני

[125] ד"א יראת ה' טהורה, יראה מביאה לידי טהרה, וכן אתה מוצא באהרן שהיתה בו יראת
שמים, שנ' ואתנם לו מורא וייראני, לפיכך ניתנה לו פרשה שאינה זזה ממנו ומבניו לעולם, זו
טהרת המת, שאין אחד מהן מיטמא במת, ממה שקרינו בענין, ויאמר ה' אל משה אמר אל
הכהנים.

[126] א"ל הקב"ה: אעפ"י שעתיד ביהמ"ק ליחרב, והקרבנות בטילים, וכהונה גדולה נפסקת,
הטהרה אינה בטילה לעולם, לכך נאמר יראת ה' טהורה עומדת לעד, א"ר שמואל טהרה
כתיב, לפיכך הקב"ה אומר למשה: אמור לאהרן ולבניו שלא יהא (צ"ל: יהו) סבורין שמא ע"י
הקרבן הזהרתי אתכם, אלא אעפ"י שבטלו הקרבנות יטהרו (צ"ל: יזהרו) עצמן מלא
(צ"ל: שלא) יטמאו למתים, מנין, ממה שקרינו בענין, ויאמר ה' אל משה אמור
אל הכהנים.

בילמדנו והכהן הגדול מאחיו, לאיסטרטינוס :(Kohut, I, 175)
(Kohut, V, 145): דריה .s. v (2 ;גבור שבקשו למנות על אסטרטיא
ובילמדנו והכהן הגדול מאחיו, מוחל לעונות ישראל
ונוטל דוריה שלימה, הוי לפי שהוא מוציא דוריה לעולם יקרא (צ"ל: נקרא)
בילמדנו והכהן הגדול :(Kohut, V, 176) מנייק .s. v (3 ;גדול
מאחיו, היה הכרוז לפניו והמונייק בידו, א"ל אילו זכית, היה המונייק
הזה שלך. With the second quotation, dealing with the designation
of גדול for the chief priest, there is to be connected the Y passage
from the same section in YSH (קונדרים אחרון, BHM, VI, p. 87,
No. 49), wherein the role of the High Priest, in bringing about
the atonement of Israel in consequence of his entrance into the
Holy of Holies on Yom Kippur, is depicted as greater than that
of the angel Michael or of Moses.[127]

From the above items it would appear that at Lev. 21.10
there was in olden times a new Seder which of course excluded
the one at 21.1 (above, No. 93). This difference in custom was
apparently the result of the previous one with regard to Nos. 92
and 92a (above pp. 101, 105). Accordingly, the 'regular' S at
Lev. 19.23 (No. 92), had as its next S Lev. 21.10. The irregular S
at Lev. 20.12 listed here as No. 92a, had as its next S Lev. 21.10
(No. 93a) which excluded No. 93. In this manner there was
preserved a certain symmetry in the respective length of the
Torah lection. Furthermore, there is noticeable with regard to
No. 93a, which excluded No. 93, a tendency to have the reading
at a point different from where the Babylonian section of AC
commenced (viz. אמור 'פ). This tendency has been noticed
several times before (see above, note 59). It may have been the
earlier custom, whereas the later one was to reconcile TC with

[127] והכהן הגדול מאחיו, זה גדול ממיכאל השר הגדול, שנ' ובעת ההוא יעמוד מיכאל השר
(צריך להוסיף: הגדול העומד על בני עמך, דניאל י"ב, א'), שמיכאל סניגור בדברים, וכהן
גדול עושה מעשים, שהוא נכנס בבית קה"ק ואינו זז עד שאני מוחל עונות ישראל, ד"א והכהן
הגדול, שגדול ממשה רבינו, לשני סניגורין, אחד מהן עומד [בפני] הדיין מ' יום ומבקש על אוהבו,
ולא פנה (—פינה) אותו עד שהכניס עמו עוד ג' סניגורין, והשני נכנס שעה אחת לפני הדיין
ופינה את אוהבו, הוי אומר השני גדול מן הראשון, כך משה, ואתנפל לפני ה' [את] ארבעים
יום (דב' ט', כ"ה), ולא אמר (היינו: ה') סלחתי (השוה במ' י"ד, כ') עד שהכניס (היינו: משה)
עמו ג' סניגורין שנ' זכור [לעבדיך] לאברהם וגו' (דב', שם, כ"ז), וכה"ג נכנס שעה אחת, וכתיב
(וי' ט"ז, י"ז) וכפר בעדו ובעד ביתו וגו'. (About the expression פינה את, to acquit,
cp. also the Y passage cited above, note 24).

AC at least where there was a new Sidra according to the latter. A fuller discussion is reserved for vol. III of this work. (inc.)

A ready H for such a S beginning with והכהן הגדול would be Zech. 3.1: ויראני את יהושע הכהן הגדול עומד לפני מלאך ה' וגו' extending to v. 10 (hence the normal number of verses). In this Prophetic passage is described how Yehoshua was ordered to remove his dirty garments, as a symbol of forgiveness of his sins (v. 4), and to don the beautiful garments of his high office (v. 5 וילבישוהו בגדים) parallel to Lev. 21.10 ומלא את ידו ללבוש את הבגדים. I surmise that the above Agg. about the great role of the High Priest in bringing about on Yom Kippur speedy atonement was homiletically derived from the H v. (Zech. 3.9): 'For behold the *stone* which I have placed before Yehoshua ... and I will remove the sin of the land *in one day.*' The stone (האבן) was taken as referring to אבן שתיה in the Holy of Holies, whereon in the period of the Second Temple the High Priest would place the censer of incense (M. Yoma 5.2), and the 'one day' (ביום אחד), on which the removal of our sin would take place, was taken to mean that unique day in the Jewish calendar, viz. the Day of Atonement.[128] Also the point of the role of Michael, as pleader (סניגור) for Israel, mentioned in the above homily has been suggested by our H, where Yehoshua is depicted as standing before God's angel, as long as he was in dirty garments (viz. as long as the sins were not atoned for, Zech. 3.1 and 3), but after putting on the beauteous garments of his dignity he evidently was sitting with the angel *standing before him.* (v. 5: ומלאך ה' עומד וילבישוהו בגדים). This suggested the Aggadic idea of the rule of the High Priest being more important than that of Michael (notice this very verse as compared to Dan. 12.1: ובעת ההיא יעמוד מיכאל השר הגדול העומד על בני עמך). Altogether the notion of a defender (סניגור) in this homily — presupposing an *accuser* whose charges

---

[128] Cp. the similar Agg. on Ps. 139.16: ימים יוצרו ולו אחד בהם to the effect that the *one* day belonging to God is Yom Ḳippur (according to R. Levi in PR, c. 23, 115a); cp. further SER, c. 1, pp. 4–5: ד"א ימים יוצרו ולו אח, זה יוהכ"פ לישראל שנתנו הקב"ה באהבה רבה ובשמחה, ולא זו בלבד אלא בשעה שהוא מוחל לעונותיהן של ישראל וכו'.

necessitate the pleading of the former — has been suggested by
Zech. 3.1–2: 'והשטן עומד על ימינו לשטנו וגו. Thus the
surmised H would well account for the theme of the portion of
the Y sermon discussed here.

Finally attention should be drawn to the item in TB, §6,
T, §4, and LR, c. 26.9, beginning with the unusual formula:
מה כתיב אחר העניין הזה, והכהן הגדול מאחיו,[129] and also dealing
with the reason why this priest is called הגדול. This homily has
really no connection with the previous sections in the Tanḥumas
and LR, especially after the *peroration* found in T, §3, end, and
in LR §8, end (above, p. 114). Moreover, the very formula:
אחרי הענין הזה shows that Lev. 21.10 was regarded as outside the
Torah readings which included Lev. 21.1 ff. The whole passage
actually is a portion of a Midrashic section to our present S
(No. 93a) and was later on attached to the one to S 93 which of
course included also Lev. 21.10 ff. (covering indeed Lev. 21.1 to
22.16). However, S 93a at 21.10 meant that the previous S
(No. 92a) extended to 21.9, with the result that 21.10 actually
was outside the lection dealt with in S 93. And this fact was still
further indicated here by מה כתיב אחרי הענין הזה notwithstanding
the amalgamation of the item pertaining to S 93a with the
previous section pertaining to S 93.

[According to some codices the next 'regular' S was at Lev.
22.1–2 and not at 22.17 (infra, No. 94); cp. Ginzberg, *Introd.*,
p. 37, and his edition of Massor. Bible to 22.1 (בס"א יש כאן סדר
ולא בפסוק י"ז). However, there is no other evidence for the existence
of such a S, and there seems to have taken place a confusion of
Lev. 22.18 beginning with דבר אל אהרן ואל בניו with 22.2 commencing in *the same manner*. Consider such a rubricum as in Meiri's
קרית ספר II, 69b, top: יש בה (היינו בפ' אמור) ג' סדרים וחצי, א' מהתחלת
הסדר עד וידבר דדבר אל אהרן, ב' משם עד וידבר דכי תבאו וכו' which
easily lends itself to such a misunderstanding.]

---

[129] About the formula[59]* מה כתיב למטה מן הענין in TB, Shelaḥ, Addendum,
§17, see infra, p. 134, to S.

Seder 94 (21)

וידבר ה'... דבר אל אהרן... איש איש מבית י ש ר א ל ומן הגר בישראל
אשר יקריב קרבנו לכל נדריהם ולכל נדבותם אשר יקריבו לה' ל ע ו ל ה,
ל ר צ נ כ ם תמים זכר... כי לא ל ר צ ו ן יהיה לכם, Lev. 22.17–20.

Haftarah: והביאותים אל הר קדשי ושמחתים בבית תפילתי ע ו ל ו ת י ה ם
וזבחיהם ל ר צ ו ן על מזבחי... נאם אדני אלהים מקבץ נדחי
י ש ר א ל ונו', Isaiah 56.7–8. The commencement is indicated in
Yannai's Ḳerobah (ed. Zulay, 165, l. 29). C 20, defective at
beginning, ends with 56.12–57.4+19 (11 verses).

The H tallies with S by means of the italicized words. Moreover, the v. preceding the initial one of H deals with strangers
who 'attached themselves to the Lord to serve Him and to live
in the name of the Lord,' (56.6), thus becoming proselytes;
they will be rewarded by *their* sacrifices being accepted 'favorably
upon my altar' (v. 7). Therein there is a further parallel to
Lev. 22.18 referring to 'the stranger who is in Israel' (הגר בישראל)
with regard to sacrifices.[138s]

STRUCTURE OF HOMILIES

None are to be found in either Tanḥuma or in LR, probably
because of the Seder at Lev. 22.26–27 (שור או כשב, infra No. 94a)
which excluded one here at vv. 17 18, only nine verses previously.
However, Yannai's composition to the present S presupposes
the existence of a corresponding Midrashic section the items of
which contained Petiḥtot from various parts of Scripture. These
Pet. verses Yannai inserted at the conclusion of each of the first
three portions of his composition.[139s] Thus Ps. 51.21 is cited
(ibid., p. 164, l. 8): ונ' אז תחפוץ ז ב ח י צדק ע ו ל ה וכליל אז יעלו
על מ ז ב ח ך פרים, tallying with the initial v of H (Is. 56.7);[140s]
further Ps. 22.31 (l. 9): ונ' ז ר ע יעבדנו יסופר ליי' לדור, which is
in contrast to the evil offspring denounced in Isaiah 57.3–4;[141s]
then Ps. 76.12 (l. 10): ונ' נדרו ושלמו ליי' אלהיכם כל סביביו יובילו שי
למורא, which v. by means of נדרו links up with נדריהם in Lev.
22.18,[142s] and by the sentence 'let all those round about Him
(viz. all nations) bring presents to [Him Who is the object of]
awe' reflects Is. 56.7 wherein God's house is declared to be 'a

house of prayer for all peoples.' In connection with Ps. 76.12, which admonishes to fulfill one's vows, there probably was given the Aggadah found in JTS. Ms., p. 30 (infra, p. ‫סא‬), the only Midrashic morsel to our S which has been preserved. At the end of the second part of his Ḳerobah (p. 165, lines 20–22) Yannai cites Ps. 66.15: ‫עולות מחים וגו'‬ tallying with both Lev. 22.18 and Is. 56.7, and Ps. 145.19 as well as Ps. 19.15 (wherein the word ‫רצון‬ affords the connection with the same word in S and H). Finally in the third part (ibid., ll. 29–30) Ps. 100.4 is cited (‫ב ו א ו שעריו בתודה וגו'‬) next to the indication of the initial v. of H (‫והביאותים אל הר קדשי וגו'‬). Thus all these citations correlate with both S and H, and must emanate from a Midrashic section to the present S which Yannai utilized. Such a section seems also to have been the source for the further passage there (p. 165, ll. 32 ff.) drawing a parallel between the regulation governing the sacrifices and the status of those who bring or offer up the latter.[130] The same applies to the remainder of the Ḳerobah, as far as preserved.

SEDER 94a (21a)

‫ וידבר ה' . . . שור או כשב או עז כי יולד והיה שבעת ימים תחת אמו ומיום‬
‫ השמיני והלאה ירצה לקרבן אשה לה'‬, Lev. 22.26–27.

The question of a Seder here is complicated by the fact that at the same point there also commenced the lections on the first days of Passover and of Tabernacles respectively (cp. above, vol. I, p. 412, with regard to the former). A careful analysis of the Midrashic sections, in accordance with our procedure of investigation, is the prerequisite of any possible classification of the whole matter. This analysis will be offered infra (pp. inc.) in connection with the discussion of the reading and the homilies pertaining to the above Festivals.[143s] It should only be added here that S 94a precludes S 94 which began at Lev. 22.17, nine verses previously (above, p. 116). This difference of custom

---

[130] ‫מאום היפה אשר אין בה מום, חפצתה קרבן אשר אין בו מום, קרבנות תמימים וכהנים‬
‫תמימים וכו'.‬

is apparently the result of the previous one with regard to Nos. 93 and 93a (above, p. 113). Thus the 'regular' S at Lev. 21.1 (No. 93) was followed by the one at 22.17 (No. 94), whereas the 'irregular' S at 21.10 (No. 93a) was followed by a similar one at 22.26 (No. 94a). In this manner there was maintained a symmetry in the corresponding lengths of the Torah lections.

SEDER 95 (22)

וידבר ה'... דבר אל בני ישראל ואמרת אליהם כי תבאו אל הארץ אשר אני נתן לכם וקצרתם את ק צ י ר ה והבאתם את עומר ראשית ק צ י ר כ ם אל הכהן, Lev. 23.9–10.

This S is possible only as a sequence of the previous one at 22.17 (above, No. 94), but not of the different one at 22.26 (No. 94a) 16 verses previously. Indeed some codices indicate a new S at 23.15 instead of at 9–10,[131] this variant evidently being due to the previous variant; thus those who read on the Sabbath before Lev. 22.17 ff. would continue on the following one with 23.9 ff., whereas those who followed the different custom of S 94a, viz. 22.26 ff., necessarily had to extend their lection to 23.14 (22 verses) and accordingly would commence on the next Sabbath with 23.15 ff. (infra, No. 95a). As to the influence of the present pair of mutually exclusive Sedarim on the next pair, Nos. 96 and 96a, see infra (p. 120).

Haftarah: שלחו מגל כי בשל ק צ י ר באו רדו וגו', Joel 4.13–21 (9 verses, so C 20). The present H is also referred to in the Genizah fragment to be discussed infra (p. סב).

The word 'harvest' (קציר) supplies the connecting link between S (Lev. 23.10) and H. Otherwise the latter is a characteristic TC Prophetic lection of 'consolation of Israel.'

---

[131] See Masoretic Bible, ed. Ginzberg, note to v. 9: בספרים אחרים הסדר בפסוק ט"ו. See also his *Introduction*, p. 37.

STRUCTURE OF HOMILIES

No sections are preserved in either Tanḥuma. However, in Midr. Agg. (II, 60) there is a passage (misplaced there, see Buber's note 4) which begins with א"ר תנחומא בוא וראה טובתיו של הקב"ה וגו', and clearly emanates from a Tanḥ. version that contained homilies to the present S (see also infra, H. pt., p. unv.). There is further the section in LR, c. 28 (=PRK, c. 8, 67b–72b; PR, c. 18, 90b–93b). The first Pet. from Koh. 1.3: מה יתרון לאדם בכל עמלו שיעמול תחת ה ש מ ש וגו' tallies by means of the word 'sun' with H v.: ש מ ש וירח קדרו וגו' (Joel 4.15).[144s] There is further introduced Jer. 5.24 (LR, §3) which by means of ק צ י ר correlates with both S and H. The same applies to the Pet. from Job 5.5: אשר ק צ י ר ו רעב יאכל (ibid. §4). The remainder of the Midrashic comments deal with the importance of the commandment of Omer. There is no proper *peroration*, indicating that the section has been curtailed towards the end.

Finally it should be remarked that Lev. 23.9 ff. was also the Torah reading in Palestine on Nisan 16th, forming there the first day of Ḥol-Hamoed of Passover (above, vol. I, p. 419). However, since no H was recited on that day, probably also no sermon was delivered on that occasion.[132] Hence the section in LR really pertains to the TC Seder and from there it was transferred to the Pesiktas,[145s] probably because the Piska on שור או כשב (PKR, c. 9, 73a ff.) is also found in LR, c. 27, preceding there immediately the section in our S in c. 28.

SEDER 95a (22a)

וספרתם לכם ממחרת השבת מיום הביאכם את עומר התנופה שבע שבתות תמימת תהיינה, Lev. 23.15.

The point of view of a S here instead of one at 23.9–10 (No. 95) has been mentioned above (p. 118). However, there is

---

[132] Buber's remark to the contrary (PRK, 68b, note 1), notwithstanding (he was altogether unaware of the problem of TC and its connection with the Midrashim).[60*]

no further evidence for its existence testifying to the very limited vogue of such a S. The interpretation of the first two verses of the latter (23.15–16) of course formed a subject of dispute between the Pharisees and the Sadducees (Boethusians) with regard to the date of Pentecost, which, according to the latter, should always fall on a Sunday. (Meg. Taanit, c. 1, cp. Men. 65a). Should we say that, in view of this issue involved, the H for the present S was Josh. 5.11: ויאכלו מעבור הארץ מ מ ח ר ת הפסח מצות וקלי בעצם היום הזה. This v. was explained by some to mean the 16th of Nisan, thus corresponding to the Pharisaic interpretation of ממחרת השבת as denoting the same day.[133] Such a H probably comprised Josh. 5.11–6.4+v. 27 (10 verses; with the concluding v. there commences a new S in this Prophetic book). However, all this must remain problematic because of the lack of Midrashic data concerning the whole present TC S at Lev. 23.15.

SEDER 96 (23)

וידבר ה' . . . צו את בני ישראל ויקחו אליך שמן זית זך כתית למאור להעלות נר תמיד, Lev. 24.1–2.

The only Genizah list of TC Haftarot available viz. C 20, contains no H to this S, indicating apparently the non-recognition of the latter. However, such a Torah lection is listed in Yemen. מחברת התיגאן (*Eben Sappir*, II, 231), in Meiri's *Ḳiryat Sepher* (II, 69b) and in *Adat Deborim* (fol. 27a). In view of the fact that in C 20 the next S is listed at Lev. 25.14 (infra, no. 97), thus rendering the previous S there (viz. No. 95 at 23.9) to be of unusual length (Lev. 23.9–25.13, 72 verses), the omission of the present S (No. 96) may be regarded as a scribal *lapsus*

---

[133] See Yer. Ḥallah, III (58b): התיב ר' בון בר כהנא והכתיב ויאכלו מעבור הארץ ממחרת הפסח, לא בששה עשר. However, R. Elazar b. Yose argues that in Josh., the 15th of Nisan is meant. Cp. further Babli, R. H. 13a: ממחרת הפסח אכול מעיקרא לא אכול, דאקריבו עומר והדר אכלי, and see Tosafot, ibid., s. v. דאקריבו עומר. The variant interpretation of Josh. 5.11–12 was used extensively in the literary feuds between Rabbanites and Karaites concerning the dates of swinging the Omer and the resultant date of Pentecost.[61*]

calami. Yet in some Biblical codices too Lev. 24.1 is omitted as a S.[134] This omission is due to the different S at 24.10 which precludes one at v. 1 (see infra, sub No. 96a).

Haftarah: To the parallel S beginning with Ex. 27.20 (No. 65, above, Vol. I, pp. 495 ff.) two Prophetic lections were listed, viz. one comprising Hos. 14.7–Joel 1.5+14 (or + 2.14) and another from Jer. 11.16–12.2 skipping to 15.15–16. With either of these readings the respective Midrashic homilies there have been correlated. The available Aggadot here seem to presuppose the same underlying variant Haftarot.

STRUCTURE OF HOMILIES

No section has been preserved in either Tanḥuma version, unlike the case with S 65 (T, Teṣawweh, §§1–8, TB, §§1–6). There is only to be considered LR, c. 31. The first Pet. introduces Ps. 71.19 וצדקתך אלהים עד מרום אשר עשית גדולות אלהים מי כמוך. The same v. was employed in the homily to S 65 (above, vol. I, H. pt., p. 255), and the correlation with either of the above Haftarot, especially with the second one, was pointed out there in the body of the work[146s] (p. 498). The trend of the Agg. both there and here is that God, notwithstanding His being the Fountain of Light, so-to-say yearns for the light kindled in the menorah of the Tabernacle.[135] Here the reason for this yearning is not indicated, but in the above mentioned Agg. to S 65 the commandment is motivated as being an act of Ṣedaka on the part of God to Israel in order that the light atone for their soul which is compared to a light.[136] The second Pet. by R. Isaac (LR, c. 31.2) is on Ps. 119.140: צרופה אמרתך מאד ועבדך אהבה. In content this v. links up with the final one of the H from Jer.,

---

[134] See Maso. Bible, ed. Ginzberg, note to v. 1: בס״א אין כאן סדר.

[135] Cp. the conclusion of the item here in LR, c. 31.1: אתה מאיר לעליונים ולתחתונים, אתה מאיר לכל באי עולם, ואתה מתאווה לאורן של ישראל, הה״ד צו את בני ישראל [וגו׳].

[136] Above vol. I, (H. pt., p. 255): ועם כל האור הזה הוא מצוה את ישראל שיקחו שמן זית זך להדליק לפניו, כמה שנ׳ ואתה תצוה וגו׳, למה בשביל לזכות את ישראל ולכפר על נשמתן, שהיא משולה בנר, שנ׳ נר ה׳ נשמת אדם וגו׳.

viz. 15.16, wherein the Prophet describes how satisfactory God's
words were to him (נמצאו דברך ואכלם ויהי דברך לי לששון ולשמחת
לבבי). The homilist comments here on the repetition of the same
command concerning the light of the Menorah in three different
parts of the Torah (Ex. 27.20, Lev. 24.1–4, and Num. 8.1 ff.)
in order to emphasize the importance of God's behest. There
follows in LR (§3) the Pet. on Job 14.15: תקרא ואנכי אענך למעשה
ידיך תכסוף. For similar items, cp. ER, c. 34.4, and T, Teṣawweh,
§2. The tally with H is found in אענך as compared to אני ע נ י ת י
ואשורנו in the H from Hos. (viz. 14.9 see above, vol. I, p. 497).[147s]
Bar Kappara's Pet. (LR, c. 31.4) introduces Ps. 18.29: כי אתה
תאיר נרי ה' אלהי יגיה חשכי. While by means of נרי there is a ready
connection with S: להעלות נר תמיד (Lev. 24.2), such one is not
apparent with regard to either H.[148s] One could find some correlation by way of contrast with Joel 2.4: יום חשך ואפלה וגו' (this
in the skipped part of H from Hos. 14.7 provided it concluded at
Joel 2.4 instead of at 1.14, above, p. 121). By the same procedure
the skipped part of Jer. H could be utilized viz. in contrast to
the gloom and darkness foretold in Jer. 13.16: תנו לה' אלהיכם כבוד
בטרם יחשיך . . . וקויתם לאור ושמה לצלמות וגו'. However, it is doubtful
whether the Pet. on Ps. 18.29 really does not belong to the S
at Num. 8.1 ff. (בהעלותך, infra, p. inc.) where the same verse is
also employed for a different Agg (cp. TB, Behaaloteka, §5, T,
§4, NR, c. 15.5); the correlation there is due to a different H
(ibid., p. inc.). Moreover, the gist of the homily here that God
says to man: 'I have your light and you have mine,' etc.,[137] is
given in the name of the same Aggadist in a different matter in
DR, c. 4.4.[138] There Prov. 6.23 is woven in: כי נר מצוה ותורה אור
ודרך חיים תוכחת מוסר, which v. indeed links up well with H from
Hos. (see above, vol. I, p. 498). Accordingly, it could be argued

---

[137] אמר הקב׳ה לאדם [הזה, כן נוסף בכ״י רומי ובריט׳ מוז׳]: נרך בידי ונרי בידך, נרך
בידי, שנ׳ נר ה׳ נשמת אדם, ונרי בידך, להעלות נר תמיד, אלא אמר הקב׳ה: אם הארת נרי,
הריני מאיר נרך.

[138] ד׳א כי אם שמור תשמרון, אמר בר קפרא הנפש והתורה נמשלו בנר, הנפש דכתיב נר ה׳
נשמת אדם, והתורה, דכתיב כי נר מצוה ותורה אור, אמר הקב׳ה לאדם הזה: נרי בידך ונרך
בידי, נרי בידך, זו התורה, ונרך בידי, זו הנפש, אם שמרת את נרי, אני משמר את נרך, ואם כבית
את נרי, אני מכבה את נרך וכו'. See further Midr. Ps., c. 17 (ed. Buber, p. 131):
אמר אלעזר הקפר וכו', and anonymously ER, c. 36.3.

that the Pet. of Bar Kappara really was on Prov. 6.23 instead
of on Ps. 18.29. And yet since the latter v. somehow or other
could by the flexible means of tallying be connected with either
of the Haftarot to our present S, such a chance would not be
justified. The next Pet. in LR (§4) is on Cant. 7.6 as to which
see above (ibid. pp. 499–500). In §5 Prov. 21.22 is introduced
as a Pet.:[139] עיר גבורים עלה חכם ויורד עוז מבטחה which seems to
tally with the H v. (Hos. 14.10): מי חכם ויבן אלה וגו'.[148s] In §6[140]
the comments are on Job 25.3: היש מספר לגדודיו ועל מי לא
יקום אורהו, which v. corresponds to Joel 1.6: כי גוי עלה על ארצי
ואין מספר (this in the skipped part of H).[149s] The remainder
of LR is not susceptible to further analysis in accordance with
our procedure. There is no proper *peroration* in §11, unless we
take as such R. Hanin's statement: בזכות להעלות נר תמיד אתם
זוכים להקביל (פני, חסר בכ"י וטיקן ובריט' מח') נרו של מלך המשיח,
מ"ט שם אצמיח קרן לדוד וגו',[150s] (תה' קל"ב, י"ג), ואומר שמחתי באומרים
לי בית ה' נלך. The last v. cited (Ps. 122.1) would tally by means of
נלך with Hos. 14.10: ילכו בם or by means of: שמחתי
ויהי דברך לי לשון with the final v. of the Jer. H: וצדיקים ילכו בם באומרים לי
ולשמחת לבבי (15.16). Finally it should be added that the
homily in TB, Teṣaweh, §1, T, §5, to S 65, is also given in
MHG, III, 594–5 to the present S. The correlation of the Pet.
v. from Cant. 1.15 with the initial v. of the Jer. H (11.16) has
been pointed out above (vol. I, p. 499).

SEDER 96a (23a)

ויצא בן אשה ישראלית והוא בן איש מצרי בתוך בני ישראל וינצו
במחנה בן הישראלית ואיש הישראלי, Lev. 24.10.

This S, the existence of which is apparent from the Midrashic
homilies to be discussed forthwith, renders impossible a S at

---

[139] Instead of אמר אחא ר' יהושע דסכנין בשם ר' in the printed text, MSS.
Vat. and Brit. Mus. read: פ ת ח; cp. also YSHM to Prov. (ed. Grünhut, 23a).

[140] Instead of the reading in printed text, which erroneously conveys the
impression that Rabbi and Rabbanan commented on Lev. 24.2: את צו ד"א
בני ישראל, רבי ורבנן וכו', MSS. Vat. and Brit. Mus. correctly read: צו את בני
ישראל, היש מספר לגדודיו, רבי ורבנן, thus their remarks pertain to the first half
of the Job verse, whereas the subsequent homiletic interpretation of the
second half (ועל מי לא יקום אורהו) really links up with Lev. 24.2.[62*]

24.1 (above, No. 96) only 9 verses previously. It is clear that
Nos. 96 and 96a excluded each other, or in other words they
represented different commencements of the Torah lections for
the same Sabbath. This difference of custom is the result of the
previous one with regard to Nos. 95 and 95a (above, p. 118);
thus those who read on the previous Sabbath Lev. 23.9 ff.
(No. 95) would begin their lection on the next one at 24.1 (No.
96), whereas those who a week before did so at 23.15 (No. 95a)
would on the following week have their S at 24.10 (No. 96a).
In this manner there was preserved a certain symmetry in the
respective lengths of the Sedarim, as has been noticed several
times before.

Haftarah. From the analysis of the available Aggadot it appears that such commenced at 1 Sam. 17.4: ויצא איש
הבינים ממחנות פלשתים גלית שמו וגו'; it probably extended to
v. 12: ויאמר דוד ודוד בן איש אפרתי וגו', skipping to v. 45
(אל הפלשתי וגו') — 47 (11 verses). In addition to the italicized
words which form the tallies with the initial v. of S there is the
parallel of blasphemy common to 'the son of the Egyptian' of
the S and Goliath of the H (cp. v. 45 where the Prophetic lection
resumed). Their lot was the same, as both were killed by
stoning (cp. Lev. 24.23 and 1 S. 17.49). This last point seems
to be indicated in R. Levi's comment (infra, p. 127).

STRUCTURE OF HOMILIES

No Y topic with question and answer has been preserved.
However, from citations in Arukh (and in YSH) the existence of
a section to the present S in Midr. Yel. is established. Thus
there has been preserved a Pet. introducing Jer. 9.24–25: הנה
ימים באים נאם ה' ופקדתי על כל מול בערלה על מצרים ועל יהודה ועל
אדום ועל בני עמון ועל מואב ועל כל קצוצי פאה היושבים במדבר כי כל
הגוים ערלים וכל בית ישראל ערלי לב.[141] The whole point of

---

[141] 'Arukh, s. v. מל, 6 (Kohut, V, 142): בילמדנו ויצא בן אשה:
ופקדתי על כל מול בערלה, מה מול בערלה, שהיו מולין ומשכו להן ערלה. וחמשה היו: על
מצרים שהיו מהולין בימי יוסף, וכשמת יוסף משכו להן ערלה; ועל יהודה, זו יהויקים מלך
יהודה; ועל אדום, זה עשו; ועל בני עמון, [צריך להוסיף: ועל מואב], אלו שילדו בנות לוט:

non-circumcision dealt with in this Agg. is due to the fact that
in the H Goliath is referred to as 'the uncircumcised Philistine'
(הפלשתי הערל), 1 S. 17.26, 36; this in the skipped part, which,
however, the homilist would utilize for his purpose).[1518] Another
Pet., preserved in YSH (Prov. §961), is from Prov. 25.8–10:
אל תצא לריב מהר וגו' where the verb יצא affords the link with the
initial verses of S and H.[141a] [152s]

In the Tanḥ. versions our S is hardly represented. What is
given in T, Emor, §§23–24, TB, §§31–32 is really a part of the
larger section in LR, c. 32 (viz. §§3–4 as to which see further on);
indeed MS. Rome of Tanḥ. omits the whole passage (see TB,
§31, note 217). Towards the end of these items there is added
abruptly a *peroration* which is also to be found at the end of LR,
c. 33, to S 97 (see infra, p. 136). The proper conclusion of the

The ועל על (צ'ל: כל) קצוצי פיאה, זה חירם מלך צור, ויש אומרים אלו הישמעאלים
continuation is found s. v. קטידיקי (Kohut, VII, 78): בן ויצא בילמדנו
אשה הישראלית, ובאל תצר את מואב (דב' ב', ט', עי' להלן צד 127): ה' שמשכו
להן ערלה, כמפורש בערך מל (ו'); ולכולם נתחי קטידיקי; על מצרים נתחי קטדיקי, ויקם
מלך חדש (שמ' א', ח'), שחידש עליהם שיעבוד; וליהויקים נתחי קטדיקי, והגליתי אותו לבבל;
ועל אדום נתחי קטדיקי, כי אני חשפתו את עשו (יר' מ"ט, י'); ולבני עמון (וצ'ל: ומואב] נתחי
קטדיקי, לא יבא עמוני [ומואבי] (דב' כ"ג, ד')
given in YSH, Jer, §285, from ילמדנו (viz. from the section to our S): זש"ה
ופקדתי על כל מול בערלה, מהו מול [בערלה], שהיו מולים ומשכו להם ערלה, וכולהו בענין
אחד, שנ' על מצרים ועל יהודה ועל אדום ועל בני עמון ועל מואב ועל כל קצוצי פאה: על
מצרים, שהיו מולין בימי יוסף, וכשמת יוסף משכו להן ערלה, שנ' כי בנים זרים ילדו (הוש'
ג', ז', השווה שמ"ר פ"א, ז', ות"ה שמות ה', ות"ב ז'); ועל יהודה, זה יהויקים מלך יהודה; ועל
אדום, זה עשו; ועל בני עמון וגו', אלו שילדו בנות לוט; ועל כל קצוצי פאה, אלו הישמעאלים.
אמר הקב"ה: מצרים, מה עשיתי להם, ונער פרעה וחילו (תה' קל"ה, ט"ו); יהויקים, הגליתי
אותו (היינו לבבל); עשו, נבעו מצפוניו (עובדיה, פס' ו'); עמון ומואב, לא יבא עמוני ומואבי;
(וחסר הפרט על אודות העונש על כל קצוצי פאה); לכלם נתחי קרטקי (צ'ל: קטדיקי),
שמשכו להם ערלה, אתם לא תעשו מעשיהם, אלא המולו, והסירו ערלת לבבכם וערלת בשרכם,
ומה שכר אני נותן לכם, ונתתי לכם לב בשר ואת רוחי אתן בקרבכם וגו' (יח' ל"ו, כ"ו–כ"ז).
For a further morsel from the Y section to our S see 'Arukh דבר, 6 (Kohut,
III, 13): בילמדנו שלמית בת דברי, שהיתה דברנית, מתוך הדבור עינה אותה, מכאן שהשיחה
רעה לאשה.
[141a] אל תצא לריב מהר, מדבר בבן הישראלית, דכתיב ויצא בן אשה ישראלית, התחיל
מחרף ומגדף, אמר שלמה אל תצא לריב מהר, למה שסוף שבטו של דן להכלים אותך,
בהכלים אותך רעך; היה לך ריב ביני ובין רעך, למה היית מחרף, ריבך ריב את רעך וסוד
אחר אל תגל. מה היית מזכיר בסוד אחרונו של עולם, שנאמר ואת אחרונים אני הוא (יש' מ"א, ד')
אני ראשון ואני אחרון (שם, מ"ד, ו'); פן יחסדך שומע, וסמכו כל השומעים את ידיהם על ראשו
(וי' כ"ד, י"ד). ודבתך לא תשוב, ורגמו אותו כל העדה (שם). Subsequently in YSH are
given comments from PR, ed. Friedmann, p. 111a.

Aggadic portion to the present S seems to be in LR, c. 32.8, end, as to which anon. However, if we assume that the *perora-tion* in Tanḥ. is pertinent here — with the preliminary passage having been curtailed —, then some connection with our H could be ascertained. Thus: אמר הקב״ה בעולם הזה בעונות אתם נמסרים ביד אומות העולם, אבל לעתיד לבוא (בת״ב: לעולם הבא) והיו מלכים אומניך ושרותיהם מניקותיך אפים ארץ ישתחוו לך ועפר רגליך ילחכו ו י ד ע ת כ י א נ י ה ' אשר לא יבושו קוי; the last v. cited (Is. 49.23) would link up by means of the italicized sentence with the final verses of H: ו י ד ע ו כ ל ה א ר ץ כ י י ש א ל ה י ם ל י ש ר א ל, ו י ד ע ו כ ל ה ק ה ל ה ז ה ו ג ו ' (1 S. 17.46–47).

And now for the analysis of LR, c. 32. The first two Petiḥtot (§§1–2) are really in connection with Lev. 24.14 (הוצא את המקלל) and not with the initial v. of S (v. 10: ויצא בן אשה). We have therefore to assume that underlying these items was the homiletic tally of the same verb employed in both these verses (הוצא and ויצא). The first Pet. introduces Ps. 12.9: סביב רשעים י ת ה ל כ ו ן ונושא כרום זלות לבני אדם, correlating verbally with the H v.: הצנה ה ו ל ך לפניו (1 S. 17.7);[153s] here is a subtle Aggadic allusion to 'the wicked strutting about' just as Goliath and his armor-bearer did. The Pet. v. is developed in the item (as in Midr. Ps. *a. l.*) leading down to the pertinent conclusion that connects it with the case of the blasphemer, the offspring of an illegitimate marriage.[142] The second Pet. is on Koh. 10.20: גם במדעך מלך אל תקלל... כי ע ו ף ה ש מ י ם יוליך את הקול affording a link with the H. v. (1 S. 17.46): ל ע ו ף ה ש מ י ם.[154s]

In LR, §§3–4 there are given the items which were taken over in the Tanḥ. versions (above, p. 125). In the printed text of LR (§3) there is inserted after נאכל לי״א the rubric: כדאיתא בתנחומא, which should by no means be taken to mean that the redactor of LR used Tanḥ., since this is only a scribal indication that there has been omitted here the remainder of the passage (till נאכלות לשלשה), the whole in reality emanating from M. Men. 11.9.[155s] Moreover, in MSS. Vat. and Brit. Mus. of LR

---

[142] LR, c. 32.1, end: ד׳א איתמי כרום זלות, לכשיפרסם הקב״ה כרמן (בכ״י וטיקן ובריט׳ מוז׳: כרומן) של ממזרים, וכבר פרסמן ע״י משה, שנ׳ הוצא את המקלל אל מחוץ למחנה (היינו שממזר אסור לבוא בקהל ה' [דב׳ כ״ג, נ׳]).

there is merely the statement: אמר: דרכו של מלך להיות אוכל פת
חמה או שמא צוננת, כההיא דתנינן לחם הפנים אינו נאכל לא פחות מט' ולא
יתר על י"א. This seems indeed to be the correct text since, for the
Aggadic point involved here, there is only needed this brief
quotation from M. Men. to the effect that the showbread was
eaten at the earliest nine days after baking, hence when already
cold. There is certainly nothing gained in citing the remainder
of the M. (till יום הצום) and *subsequently* even the regulations
concerning the 'two loaves' (שתי הלחם) on Pentecost, which
regulations are found in the M. *prior* to those concerning the
showbread! LR, §4, is fuller than the corresponding item in
Tanḥ., the latter clearly being a modification of the former.[143]

Interesting is R. Levi's comment (LR, §3) wherein 1 Sam.
17.4 is cited, this v. forming in our opinion the commencement
of the H to the present S: ויצא בן אשה ישראלית, מהיכן יצא, יצא
מעולמו כמד"א ויצא איש הבינים. The meaning is that in each case
the person involved forfeited his world (i. e., his life) as a result
of his action — a parallel that constituted one of the reasons for
the choice of this H (above, p. 124).[156s] At the beginning of LR,
§4, the view of the Rabbanan reads correctly in MS. Vat.:
אעפ"י שלא היו ממזרין באותה שעה, הוא היה כ מ מ ז ר. Thus, corresponding to the anonymous statement in Sifra, Emor, *a. l.* (ed. Weiss,
104c). But R. Levi differs by declaring the son of the Egyptian
as entirely illegitimate. <cf. Luria's note 15, *a. l.*>

In LR, §5, the item introducing Cant. 4.12–13 seems to have
been transferred from the section on ויהי בשלח (see PRK, 83a–b,
and parallels, and cp. above, vol. I, 428, top). The verses cited
offer no tally with H here, and the whole homily is given here
because of its allusions to Shelomit bat Dibri of our S (Lev.
24.11).[157s] The last Pet. (LR, §8) is from Koh. 4.1: ו ש ב ת י אני
ואראה which affords a point of contact with 1 S. 17.15: ודוד
הולך ו ש ב (this in the skipped part of H). The former v. is
commented upon in various ways in Midr. Koh., *a. l.*, but here
only the last instance is given, viz. as applied to Mamzerim such
as 'the son of the Egyptian' of our S was taken to have been.

---

[143] In T there even remained untranslated into Hebrew the Aramaic
sentence: הוה מחי ליה כל יומא, ואמר ליה, ליענות טבאות, ליענות טבאות.

This Agg. leads down already to the *peroration*[144] to the effect that in this world Israel reveals in its body base matter (such as illegitimate offspring), but in the future it will be pure gold, citing Zech. 4.2: 'והנה מנורת זהב כלה וגלה על ראשה וגו which tallies with the H v. (1 S. 17.5):וכובע נחשת על ראשו.[158a] The above analysis of the Midrashic homilies thus tends to the conclusion of the existence of a TC S at Lev. 24.10 with its accompanying H from 1 S. 17.4–12+45–47.

Seder 96b (23b)

וידבר ה' אל משה בהר סיני לאמר, דבר אל בני ישראל ואמרת
אליהם כי תבאו אל הארץ אשר אני נותן לכם ושבתה
הארץ שבת לה', Lev. 25.1–2.

The fact that in the Babylonian AC there begins here a new Sidra indicates that at some time there was here also a new TC Seder (cp. above, vol. I, pp. 8–9). There is the evidence for the latter in the Midrashic data to be discussed forthwith. Now, such a S is only possible as the sequence of S 96 at Lev. 24.1 but not of S 96a at 24.10, 11 verses before. According to the latter custom the Torah lection on the following Sabbath commenced at 25.14 (infra, sub No. 97). We thus notice again how the previous different pair of Sedarim (viz. Nos. 96 and 96a) caused the next such pair (viz. Nos. 96b and 97a). Further on the resultant subsequent variance in custom (viz. Nos. 97a and 98) will be pointed out (infra, p. 136).

לפי שבעוה"ז יש בהן פסולת, אבל לע"ל אמר זכריה: אנא חמיתיה אלו כורסוון (צ"ל: [144]
אולוכרוסון — ὀλόχρευσον), כולו דהב נקי (זהו תרגום של המלה היונית הנ"ל), הה"ד
ראיתי והנה מנורת זהב כלה וגלה. Subsequently the second half of the v. is commented upon: (צ"ל: שנלו) תרין אמוראין: ח"א גולה וח"א גואלה; מאן דאמר גולה, שגולה (צ"ל: שנלו)
לבבל ונלתה שכינה עמהן כדאמר למענכם שלחתי בבלה (יש' מ"ג, י"ד; פה שלחתי נדרש כמו
שולחתי), ומ"ד גואלה, פרוקא, שנ' גואלנו ה' צבאות שמו קדוש ישראל (שם, מ"ז, ד'), וכתיב
עלה הפורץ לפניהם, פרצו ויעברו שער ויצאו בו ויעבור מלכם לפניהם וה' בראשם
(מי' ב', י"ג). All these verses can be correlated with H. Thus Is. 43.14 where God is called the Holy One of Israel (קדוש ישראל) as compared to 1 S. 17.45: אלהי מערכות ישראל. Is. 47.4 yields a still better tally by reason of בשם ה' צבאות, corresponding to ה', צבאות שמו קדוש ישראל אלהי מערכות ישראל in H (ibid.); and finally Mic. 2.13 by reason of the verb יצא (ויצאו בו) which formed the connecting link between S and H (above, p. 126).[63*]

Haftarah. From the Aggadot to be analyzed it appears to me
that such began at Ezekiel 37.21: ודבר אליהם כה אמר
ה' אלהים, הנה אני לקח את בני ישראל מבין הגוים אשר הלכו שם
וקבצתי אותם מסביב והבאתי אותם אל אדמתם, tallying with
Lev. 25.2 as italicized, and also intrinsically in that just as in
the past God brought Israel to the promised land so will He do
in the future. This H extended to Ezek. 37.28 (8 verses; with the
last one there commences a new Seder there). In the portion
comprising our S the fulfilment of God's statutes and ordinances
is declared as being rewarded by dwelling securely on the land
(Lev. 25.18: ועשיתם את חקתי ואת משפטי תשמרו ועשיתם אתם וישבתם
על הארץ לבטח) and the same is foretold in the Prophetic lection
(Ezek. 37.24–25): ובמשפטי ילכו וחקותי ישמרו ועשו אותם וישבו על
הארץ אשר נתתי לעבדי ליעקב וגו'. This establishes a still further
contact between S and H. Moreover, the emphasis on God
being Israel's divinity occurs in both (Lev. 25.17: כי אני ה'
אלהיכם and Ezek. 37.23: ואני אהיה להם לאלהים, cp. also vv. 27–28).

STRUCTURE OF HOMILIES

There is no section at all in LR or in TB and T. However,
there is one in Midr. Agg. (II, 58–60), beginning with an item,
attributed to *R. Tanḥuma*, which seems to emanate from a
novel version of the Midr. bearing the name of this famous
Aggadist. The same section is also partially preserved in JTS
Ms. (infra, H. pt., pp. סו–סג). Further Midrashic data bearing on
our S are to be found in MHG (III, 609–11).

To begin with the above homily, there is introduced a Pet.
v. from Joel 2.21: אל תיראי אדמה גילי ושמחי כי הגדיל ה' לעשות
which tallies by means of אדמה with the initial v. of H (אדמתם
in Ezek. 37.21),[1598] and by means of the sentence that 'God has
done greatly' (כי הגדיל ה' לעשות) corresponds to the great act
foretold of restoring Israel as one nation on its land (Ezek. 37.22:
ועשיתי אותם לגוי אחד בארץ וגו'). In connection with this Pet. v.
there is cited R. Tanḥuma's Aggadah concerning the earth's
fear at the giving of the Torah lest Israel's neglect of the latter
would result in the former's punishment (weaving in Ps. 76.9:
משמים השמעת דין ארץ יראה ושקטה thus linking up with אל

(תיראי אדמה).[145] The homily is curtailed at the end and there
is no return to the Pet. v. and through it to the S (Lev. 25.1).[146]
However, it is clear that the introduction here of the topic of
the giving of the Law is due, on the one hand, to the mention of
'Mount Sinai' at the commencement of S (וידבר ה' אל משה בהר
סיני),[147] and, on the other hand, to the assurance in H of the
observance of God's statutes and ordinances (Ezek. 37.24, cp.
above, p. 130). The allegory concerning the anxious role of the
earth, as affected by obedience to the commandments on the
part of the creatures or vice versa, is further graphically depicted
in the available section.[148] Another Pet. (l. c., pp. 58–59) introduces Koh. 9.18: טובה חכמה מכלי קרב וחוטא אחד יאבד טובה
הרבה which tallies with H v. (Ezek. 37.23) referring to the
previous sins of Israel (אשר חטאו בהם). The homily, too, leads
down to the transgression in not keeping the Sabbatical and the
Jubilee years, which sin resulted in the land lying waste in consequence of the exile of the population.[149] The whole item is
also found in LT (a. l.), with the author, R. Tobias b. Eliezer,
using the Pet. v. (Koh. 9.18) as the heading of his section on
Sidra Behar because of its commencement with the word טובה
in accordance with his scheme to use an introductory v. having
an allusion to his own name טוביה. It may be argued that this
item is an original composition of the author of LT and that
from the latter it was taken over in Midr. Agg. (about several
such borrowings see Buber's Introd. to Midr. Agg., XVI–XXII),
in view also of the fact that it is missing in the parallel passage

---

[145] וידבר ה' אל משה בהר סיני לאמר, זש"ה אל תיראי אדמה . . . כי הגדיל ה' לעשות,
א"ר תנחומא בשעה שבא הקב"ה ליתן תורה לישראל ולהשמיע את הדינין לישראל, אותה
שעה נתייראה הארץ, שנ' משמים השמעת דין ארץ יראה ושקטה, אם יראה למה שקטה, וכו'.
Cp. PR, c. 21 (ed. Friedm. 99b–100a), and notes there.

[146] Also in JTS MS., which is unfortunately defective here, the conclusion is lacking (but see infra, H. pt., p. דּר, note 1).

[147] Concerning this point, see ibid., note 1, (סג).[64*]

[148] Midr. Agg., II, 59: וכיון . . . ונם הארץ מתפללת לפניו יותר מכל הנבראים
שהבריות עושין רצונו של מקום היא מזמרת בכנפיה, שנ' מכנף הארץ זמירות שמענו, וכשהם
חוטאים היא לוקה למענם וכו'. Cp. the parallel in JTS MS.

[149] ד"א בהר סיני, זש"ה טובה חכמה מכלי קרב וחוטא אחד יאבד טובה הרבה . . . והם
לא עשו כן, אלא חטאו ולא שבתו שמיטות ויובלות, וגרמו להם גלות וכו'.

in JTS Ms. However, the above tallying of the Pet. v. with the
TC H militates against such an assumption, and rather tends to
the conclusion that both used a common source, viz. a Midr.
version which contained a section to the present S.

This section has only partially been used in Midr. Agg.[150]
No *peroration* has been preserved. But such seems to be found
in JTS Ms. (infra, H. pt., p. סב) to the effect that because the
Sabbatical year had not been observed, the land has been for-
saken and the Temple destroyed; however, the assurance is
given that in the future God will restore Israel to the country
and will plant them thereon eternally. The last v. cited is
Am. 9.15: ונטעתים על א ד מ ת ם ולא ינתשו עוד מעל אדמתם א ש ר
נ ת ת י ל ה ם אמר ה' אלהיך tallying both with Ezek. 37.21 and 25
and further with Lev. 25.2.

In MHG (III, 609) there is a Pet. on Ps. 103.20: ברכו ה'
מלאכיו גבורי כח עושי דברו לשמוע בקול דברו. Now the same item,
with variants, is found in LR, c. 1.1 and TB Wayyikra, §1, T,
§1, to S 74 (above, p. 27). However, the above v. also links
up by means of ע ו ש י ד ב ר ו with the H v. here (Ezek. 37.24):
ובמשפטי ילכו וחקותי ישמרו ו ע ש ו אותם.[160a] Hence this Pet. is
legitimate here too, especially R. Isaac's application of the Pet.
v. to those "who observe the Sabbatical year," despite the
constant monetary loss involved.[151] This may have also been
the case with R. Aḥa's homily referring to the event of the
giving of the Law on Mount Sinai (see above, p. 130).[152] In

---

[150] The passage on p. 60: כי תבאו ... זש"ה מה יתרון לאדם ... א"ר תנחומא וכו':
does not belong here, but to the section on S 95 (above, p. 118).

[151] LR. c. 1.1: גבורי כח עושי דברו, במה הכתוב מדבר, א"ר יוחנן בשומרי שביעית
הכתוב מדבר. בנוהג שבעולם אדם עושה מצוה ליום אחד, לשבת אחת, לחודש אחד, שמא
לשאר ימות השנה וכו'.[65*] In TB and T, *l. c.*, R. Isaac's statement is couched
somewhat differently. Here in MHG (*l. c.*, 11.5–9) the item is given anonymously and also in a variant form, probably emanating from a Midrashic
section to our S (perhaps from Midr. Yel., see anon.).

[152] LR, *l. c.*: ר' הונא בשם ר' אחא אמר בישראל שעמדו לפני הר סיני הכתוב מדבר,
שהקדימו עשייה לשמיעה וכו' (see TB and T). Here again in MHG (11.3–4) anonymously. The point of Israel's acceptance of God's word even prior to hearing
is also woven into R. Tanḥuma's homily in Midr. Agg. (II, 58) concerning
the earth's reassurance after its disquiet at Sinai (above, p. 129): מיד שקטה
הארץ.[66*] ... ושמעה שישראל אמרו נעשה נעשה ונשמע וכו'.

MHG there is given subsequently a characteristic passage (*l. c.*, l. 10 ff.: 'מעשה באדם אחד וכו) allegorizing the seven years ending with the Sabbatical one as corresponding to the seven nations that subjected Israel; with the passing of the seventh oppressor, viz. *Edom*, Israel will be recompensed abundantly, just as the soil is profusely productive in the eighth year after its having been left uncultivated during the seventh.[153] The whole item seems to me to emanate from Midr. Yel. wherein also the law of Orlah was symbolized as referring to Israel's subjection and ultimate restoration (see above, p. 131).[161s] There follows in MHG (p. 610, l. 1 ff.) a statement by R. *Yose* comparing the Sabbatical year to the Sabbath and elaborating upon the beneficial or the injurious result of observing or disobeying respectively the former law. The lower part of this item is similar to R. *Yose* b. Ḥanina's dictum in Tos. Arakhin 5.9 (and parallels),[154] but here seems to be given a larger version of this Aggadah emanating from a Midrashic section.

Finally in MHG (p. 610, l. 15 ff.) there is the statement that Israel's exile was due to non-observance of the commandment of Shebiit. This is substantiated by citing a Baraita concerning the three things given to Israel on condition, viz.: the kingdom of the house of David, the Temple and Palestine, and subsequently there is the return to the initial verses of S by means of the formula ממה שקרינו בענין. Here in my opinion, there has been woven in the first portion of the Yel. sermon to our S,

---

[153] In MHG the text has been subjected to change: אעפ"י שנשתעבדו ששה שעבודין: מצרים, ואדום (צ"ל: ואשור), ובבל ומדי, ויון, ופרס (צ"ל: ופרס ויון), ובא השביעי ואיבד כל מלכיות שלפניו, והשבית מישראל ששה דברים: שכינה, ואורים ותומים, וקרבנות, ומלכות, ונבואה, ואיזה הוא שביעי, זה י ש מ ע א ל, ומנין שנמשלה מלכותו בשביעית... אמר הקב"ה יעבור השביעי הזה, ואני אשפיע לכם טובות יתירין מן הראשונים וכו'. The reading 'Ishmael' is clearly a scribal change for 'Edom',[67*] the next oppressor in order after Yavan, the sixth of the list. A different Agg. in Mekh. of R. Sim. b. Yoḥai (ed. Hoffm., p. 118) enumerates 6 kingdoms: בבל ומדי ופרס ויון ואשור ורומי (this in the name of דורשי רשומות), but cp. the parallel item in Midr. Agg., I, 155, where seven are mentioned: גלות מצרים, גלות סנחריב (אשור—), וגלות ארבע מלכיות, הרי שש, ובשביעית יצא, זה מלכות גוג ומגוג (cp. further ibid., p. סו).

[154] א"ר יוסי בר חנינא בא וראה כמה קשה אבקה של שביעית וכו' which cp. to MHG (l. 7 ff.): וכל מי שאינו משמר שביעית כראוי, סוף שהוא מוכר נכסיו וכו' (cp. infra, p. 134, to S. 97).

which originally read as follows: 'וידבר ה' אל משה... שבת לה'. ילמדנו רבינו: כמה דברים ניתנו לישראל על תנאי. כך שנו רבותינו: שלשה דברים ניתנו לישראל על תנאי, ואלו הן: מלכות בית דוד, ובית המקדש, וארץ ישראל[155] וכו'. Now the starting points for these three items are all to be found in H; thus for the royal house of David see Ezek. 37.24: ועבדי דוד מלך עליהם (cp. also v. 22), for the Temple see v. 26: ונתתי את מקדשי בתוכם לעולם (cp. also v. 28), and for the land see vv. 21–22 and 25. The respective verses cited in the homily in substantiation of each item easily can be correlated with our H (viz. Ps. 132.11–12; I K. 6.11–13; and Ps. 105.44–45). One may thus safely assume that the whole section in MHG (609–11, top) has been taken over from Midr. Yel. to our S, however the sequence of the homilies may have been changed and their style touched up by the redactor of this work which in reality is a Yemenite Yalkuṭ to the Pent. on a large dimension.

SEDER 97 (24)

וכי תמכרו ממכר לעמיתך או קנה מיד עמיתך אל תונו איש את אחיו, Lev. 25.14.

About this S, which is the direct sequence of the one at 24.10 (No. 96a), see above (p. 124).

Hafṭarah: והיה כעם ככהן כעבד כאדוניו כשפחה כגבירתה כקונה כמוכר כמלוה כלוה כנושה כאשר נושה בו, Isaiah 24.2. C 20 has 24.2–11, with the end missing; probably there was added v. 15 in order to conlude the Prophetic lection with a 'happy ending' (hence 11 verses). A better arrangement would have been 24.2–8, adding the three last verses of consolation and encouragement (13–15), in all 10 verses. Also Yannai in his Ḳerobah to the present S indicates Is. 24.2 as the initial v. of H (ed. Zulay, p. 168, l. 32).

---

[155] This is a Bar. emanating from Mekh., Yitro (ed. Horov.-Rabin, p. 201), cp. Midr. Tannaim, ed. Hoffm., p. 39. There the v. cited in substantiation of the item concerning the land of Israel in Deut. 11.16–17, but here Ps. 105.44–45 is cited, and likewise in the Genizah fragment edited in GS, I, 152: שלשה דברים ניתנו על תנאי, אלו הן: ארץ ישראל, ומלכות בית דוד, ובית המקדש, [68]*ארץ ישראל, שנאמר בעבור ישמרו חקיו ותורתיו ינצרו הללויה וכו'

S and H tally verbally by means of the italicized words. Moreover, in contrast to the assurance in the former, that "the observance of God's statutes and ordinances results in prosperity, plenty, and security" (Lev. 25.18–19), there is in the latter the prophetic lament over transgression of the Laws, violation of the statute and breaking of the covenant, with the sequence that 'a curse consumed the land' and the inhabitants waste away (Is. 24.5–6).

The Midrashic homilies to be discussed do not tally at all with the above H. From the emphasis on not wronging one's fellow-men in LR, c. 33, in connection with the injunction in the initial v. of S (אל תונו איש את אחיו), it would appear that the Prophetic lection underlying these Aggadot also contained the same topic.[162s] I therefore suggest as such Ezekiel 18.7: ואיש לא יונה הבולתו חוב ישיב גזלה לא יגזול וגו', extending to v. 14 and skipping to 31–32 (10 verses). There is a further contact in v. 9: בחקותי יהלך ומשפטי שמר לעשות אמת as compared to ועשיתם את חוקותי ואת משפטי תשמרו in S (Lev. 25.18).

STRUCTURE OF HOMILIES

1. No Y topic has been preserved. In TB, Behar, §1, T, §1, there is a Pet. from Prov. 28.22: נבהל להון איש רע עין ולא ידע כי חסר יבואנו[156] which tallies by means of איש with the same word in both S and H.[163s] The v. is homiletically applied to several instances, the last of which pertaining to our Torah lection, viz. those dealing illicitly with produce of the Sabbatical year (אלו סוחרי שביעית) who, because of their greed, are ultimately punished with loss of their wealth being even forced to sell their belongings. Here there is applied the well-known formula of מה כתיב למעלה מן העניין, thus linking up a v. of the previous S with the initial one of the present S (viz. Lev. 25.2 with 25.14). The next item (TB, §2, T, §1) introduces Bar Kappara's comment on Cant. 5.15: שוקיו עמודי שש מיוסדים על אדני פז which is not meant as a Pet. (since this v. has no connection with H), but

---

[156] About the same Pet. to S 61 (which, too, had a similar H from Ezek. 18), see above, vol. I, 477, and concerning the Pet. in connection with עשר תעשר (Deut. 14.22) see infra, p. inc..

rather as an illustration of the comparison of the sequence of
the chapters of the Torah to a pillar adorned by a chapter above
and a basis below (the same case we had above, p. 104, in
connection with S 92).¹⁵⁷ The remainder of the section in TB
and T requires no further analysis for our purpose here, except
the conclusion (TB, §4, T, §1, end) which would seem to contain
the *peroration*: 'שנ, כשתקרב שנת הגאולה אני גואל אתכם :אמר הקב"ה
כי יום נקם בלבי ושנת גאולי באה.¹⁵⁸ There is no clear correlation in this
last v. cited (Is. 63.4) with H, unless we find it in בלבי as compared to H v. (Ezek. 18.31): ועשו לכם לב חדש.¹⁶⁴ˢ However, it is
doubtful whether the above is really meant as a *peroration*
since quite another one is found in LR, c. 33, end (see anon);
here it may be merely a comment in connection with Lev. 25.24:
גאולה תתנו לארץ. At any rate, herewith concludes in the Tanḥumas the section to S 97, the next one (TB, §§5–9, T, §§2–4)
being to S 97a (infra, p. 136).

2. In LR (c. 33.1) there is first the Pet. on Prov. 18.21:
מות וחיים ביד לשון ואהביה יאכל פריה which, on the one hand, tallies
with S (Lev. 25.19: ונתנה הארץ פריה ואכלתם לשובע) and, on
the other, with H where living and dying as a result of good and
evil conduct respectively are mentioned several times (cp. Ezek.
18.9: במות המת... ;חיה יחיה, v. 13: מות יומת and v. 32: והשיבו וחיו;
see further the skipped part, vv. 15–30).¹⁶⁵ˢ In §§2–3 there are
comments on Amos 7.7–8 (כה הראני והנה אדני נצב... מה אתה) and 9.1
(ראיתי את אדני נצב וגו') and 9.1 (ראיה וגו'). The point of contact
with H seems to be in the designation of God as אדני (see Ezek.
18.9: נאום אדני אלהים, cp. vv. 23, 25, 29, 30, and 32); but perhaps
also the use of ראה affords further correlation with Ezek. 18.14:

¹⁵⁷ In LR, c. 25.8 (cp. Cant. R. to 5.15 and NR, c. 101), this comparison
is entirely by Bar Kappara: ולמה הן דומות (היינו לעמוד), רב הונא בשם בר קפרא
אמר כעמוד הזה שיש לו בסיס מלמטן וקיפלוס (קיפלים, κεφαλίς) מלמעלה, כך הן
פרשיותיה של תורה, נדרשות לפניהם ונדרשות לאחריהם. However, here in TB and T
the text is different: א"ר אלעזר הקפר כתיב שוקיו עמודי שש מיוסדים על אדני פז וגו',
העמוד הזה אם אין לו כותרת מלמעלה ובסיס מלמטה אינו נראה נאה, א"ר שמואל בן גדליה
⁶⁹*(בת"ה: גוריא) אין לך פרשה בתורה שאין לה כותרת מלמעלה ובסיס מלמטה וכו'
¹⁵⁸ In Midr. Agg., (II, 63) the reading is: (צ"ל) אמר הקב"ה לישראל: כך אם (צ"ל:
אני) אוציא אתכם ואת ארצכם מעבדות לחירות משתקרב (צ"ל: לכשתקרב) הגאולה, שנ' יום
⁷⁰*נקם בלבי וגו'.

ו.[166a] וירא ... את כל ... וירא וגו' In §4 there is a curtailed homily in connection with Num. 2.34: ויעשו בני ישראל ככל אשר צוה ה' וגו' which v. fits in with H only in a general way, viz. insofar as the righteous person depicted in the latter is conducting himself in accordance with God's behest (the verb עשה is used there several times).[167a] The next item (§5) introduces 2 Chr. 13.17–20: ויכו בהם אביה ... ויגפהו ה' וימות, the last word of which links up with H where dying is frequently mentioned (see above).[168a]

Finally we come to the *peroration* (§6, end) which in the printed texts is in double form: לפי שבעוה"ז ישראל משועבדין לאו"ה, ול"ל (ולעתיד לבוא) מה כתיב, והיו מלכים אומניך ושרותיהם מניקותיך וגו' (יש' מ"ט, כ"ג) לפי שבעוה"ז או"ה מונין לישראל, אבל לע"ל אמר הקב"ה עתיד אני להאכילם מבשרם ולהשכירם מדמם, הה"ד והאכלתי את מוניך את בשרם וגו' (שם, כ"ו). The first form is missing in MS. Brit. Mus. and also in a Genizah fragment (T.-S. Box C 2, No. 135) containing parts of LR, c. 33–34. It is the same conclusion as found in TB and T to S 96a (above, p. 125). The v. cited (Is. 49.23) does not tally with the H here,[169a] and hence the whole item is out of place. The proper *peroration* is the second form referring to the oppression of the Jews by the gentiles and concluding with the assurance that the oppressors will be punished in the future. By the word מוניך in the cited v. (Is. 49.26) there is the ready link with אל תונו in S and לא יונה in H (above, p. 134). The suggested H from Ezek. 18.7 ff. accounts thus for all the available Midrashic data whereas the other one from Is. 24.2 ff. (above, p. 133) is not represented at all.[170a] The latter must therefore be regarded as of late origin, but the reason for its supplanting the former cannot as yet be ascertained.

SEDER 97a (24a)

כי ימוך אחיך ומכר מאחזתו ובא גאלו הקרב אליו וגאל את ממכר אחיו,[159] Lev. 25.25.

This S is apparent from the parallel section in TB, Behar, §§5–9, T, §§2–4. Now, a S here is only possible in case the

---

[159] Several codices read וכי (as in v. 39), and likewise in the Tanḥumas (cp. Masor. Bible by Ginzberg).

previous one was at Lev. 25.1 (No. 96b, above, p. 128), but
not if at 25.14 (No. 97), merely 11 verses before. The next
'regular' S (infra, sub No. 98) at 25.35 in its turn, is permissible only as the direct sequence of S 97, but not of 97a which
began 10 verses previously. Thus we notice again the cause of
this shifting of the respective commencements of the above
Torah readings. Those whose lection on the previous Sabbath
started at 25.1 would on the following one continue with 25.25,
whereas those who adopted the practice of beginning at 25.14
on the Sabbath before (above, p. 133) necessarily had on the
subsequent one to shift their S from 25.25 to 25.35, in order to
obtain the required minimum of 21 verses for the reading of the
week before (viz. No. 97, comprising Lev. 25.14–34). At any
rate, whether the present S commenced at 25.25 (No. 97a) or
at 25.35 (No. 98), the still further S was at 26.3 (אם בחקותי) to
be discussed further on (sub. No. 99).

Haftarah: The Prophetic portion evidently commenced with a
reference to God as the redeemer (גואל) of Israel, in order to
tally thereby with גואלו in Lev. 25.25 and furthermore to accord
with the characteristics of the TC Haftarot in offering consolation
and solace to a people burdened heavily with the sorrows of
subjection. Now, several such references to God can be found
especially in Isaiah (from c. 40 and subsequently). However in
view of the Midrashic data to be considered forthwith — the
only criteria available with regard to the present S — , it seems
to me that the H began at Is. 49.7: כה אמר ה' ג ו א ל ישראל
קדושו, probably extending to v. 13+24–26 (10 verses); the last
v. again concludes with: כי אני ה' מושיעך ו ג ו א ל ך אביר יעקב,
and furthermore forms the commencement of a new Seder in
this Prophetic book. One could also suggest as H Is. 41.14
(10 22+27 - (אל תיראי תולעת יעקב . . . ו ג ו א ל ך קדוש ישראל)
verses); with the last v. a new Seder is again indicated in the
Masoretic codices. Yet the former surmise is to be preferred.

STRUCTURE OF HOMILIES

No Y topic has been preserved. The citation in Arukh, s. v.
חסד (Kohut, III, 452), from י ל מ ד נ ו פ' כ י י מ ו ך really

belongs to S 98 (see infra, p. 139), and hence for כי the reading
should be וכי (Lev. 25.35). In TB, §5, T, §2, there is the Pet.
from Prov. 22.22–23: אל תגזל דל כי דל הוא ואל תדכא עני בשער
כי ה' יריב ריבם וקבע את קובעיהם נפש. By means of the
italicized words there is a tally with H, to wit with Is. 49.13
(וענין) and 25 (ואת יריבך אנכי אריב).[172s] A similar tally, though
somewhat less cogently, could be established with the other
suggested H, viz. with Is. 41.17 (העניים) and 21 (קרבו ריבכם).
There is also woven in (TB, §6, T, §3) Jer. 50.33–34, where the
sentence: גאלם חזק ... ריב יריב את ריבם affords correlation with H.[173s] There follows (TB, §§7–8, T, §3) the Pet.
on Ps. 106.43; the same item is partially found, too, in LR,
c. 34.6, to S 98 (see infra, p. 142). It is apparent that in addition
to v. 43, the following ones (44–47) are to be included since they
elaborate the statement in the former in accordance also with
the trend of the homily to the effect that God vouchsafes help
to Israel whenever they repent and beseech divine succor.[160]
Accordingly by means of וימוכו (Ps. 106.43) there is on the one
hand the verbal parallel to כי ימוך of S (Lev. 25.25) and by
means of וינחם ברוב חסדיו ויתן אותם לרחמים (Ps. 106.45–46)
there is on the other hand a tally with H (Is. 49.13): 'כי נחם ה
עמו ועניו ירחם.[174s] Likewise the plea 'Help us, O Lord our
God' (הושיענו ה' אלהינו וגו', Ps. 106.47) would correspond to
Is. 49.25–26: מושיעך ה' אני כי ... אושיע ואת בניך אנכי. As
regards the other suggested H, one could find some connection
in בקדוש ישראל תתהלל (Is. 41.16) as compared to Ps.
106.47: להודות לשם קדשך להשתבח בתהלתך. The Midrashic
section concludes (TB, §9, T, §4) with an allegorical interpretation of the initial v. of S as referring to Israel and God. The
former were brought low on account of their sins (again weaving
in Ps. 106.43: וימוכו בעונם corresponding to כי ימוך) and were put
under subjection, but their Redeemer will surely come; here
Jer. 50.34: גואלם חזק ה' is cited, thus establishing a link with
גואלו in S and especially with H where God is designated as such
(above, p. 137). He is further alluded to in our homily as Israel's
relative (הקרוב אליו), and in substantiation there is cited as a

---

[160] אתה מוצא בימי שפוט השופטים שהיו ישראל עובדים ע"ז, והיו משועבדים בידי אומות
העולם. . . ומה עשו, ויזעקו בני ישראל אל ה' . . . מיד עשו תשובה ונגאלו וכו'.

final v. Ps. 148.14: עם ישראל לבני חסידיו לכל תהלה לעמו קרן וירם
קרובו הלויה linking up with the reference to Israel as God's
people in H (Is. 49.13): עמו ה' נחם כי.[175a] As for the other H,
there would be a rather weak tally in תתהלל ישראל בקדוש
(Is. 41.16) as compared to חסידיו לכל תהלה here.

The above analysis of the accessible Midrashic data thus tends
to justify the conclusion that the Prophetic lection was Is.
49.7–13+24–26.

SEDER 98 (25)

עמך וחי ותושב גר בו החזקת והה עמך ידו ומטה אחיך ימוך וכי,
Lev. 25.35.

Haftarah: אמצו כושלות וברכים רפות ידים חזקו, Isaiah, 35.3.
The beginning is found in Yannai's Ḳerobah to our S (ed. Zulay,
p. 172, l. 33) and the conclusion in C 12 listing 35.9–10, hence
8 verses; with v. 10 there commences a new Seder in this Prophetic book.

In addition to the italicized verbal tally of H with S, there
is the further parallel that just as in the latter there is a reference
to the Exodus from Egypt as the forerunner of the acquisition
of the land of Canaan (Lev. 25.38), so in the former there is the
assurance of the deliverance of Israel from Exile and the joyful
return to Zion (Is. 35.10). Corresponding to the redemption
(גאולה) of the needy Jew, who had to sell himself into servitude
(cp. Lev. 25.51–52), the Prophetic lection gloriously depicts the
triumphant journey of God's redeemed (Is. 35.9: גאולים והלכו).
The former's return to his patrimony (ישוב אבותיו אחוזת ואל,
Lev. 25.41) links up so well with the promised restoration of
Israel to Zion (Is. 35.10: וגו' ברנה ציון ובאו ישובון ה' ופדויי).

STRUCTURE OF HOMILIES

In considering these one cannot escape the impression that
they presuppse another H, although some of them are capable
of correlation with the lection from Is. 35.3 ff. by means of the
flexible method of tallying. The commencement of the S deals
with the economic support of a needy brother, who is in straitened
circumstances, and the same is the trend of the Aggadot in LR,

c. 34, whereas this whole theme is missing in the latter H which
is a typical one of 'consolation of Israel.' One has to look for
a Prophetic portion that concretely emphasizes the same topic
as that of S.[176s] I suggest that the H, underlying the Midrashic
homilies, began with Ezek. 18.17: מעני השיב י ד ו נשך ותרבית
לא לקח משפטי עשה בחקותי הלך הוא לא ימות בעון אביו חיה יחיה.
In addition to the italicized words by which there is a linguistic
tallying with Lev. 25.35 (ומטה ידו ... וחי עמך) we have a
parallel to the prohibition in the S of taking usury from an
impoverished Jew (Lev. 25.36–37). This H probably extended
to 18.23+30–32 (10 verses), just as in the case of S 61 (above,
vol. I, pp. 475–6). In comparing these two instances, (viz. S 61
and our present one), we notice alike how the earlier H was later
on substituted by lections of purely consolatory character, viz.
there Is. 48.10 ff. and here Is. 35.3 ff. As regards the respective
Aggadot, there is much that is common to both, viz. the general
topic of kindness to the needy, but there particular emphasis is
put on the sin of usury (in accordance with the initial v. of S 61,
Ex. 22.24) whereas here the aspect of charity to the poor is
predominant (again corresponding to the initial v. of the present
S, Lev. 25.35).[177s]

And now for the analysis of the homilies. In the Tanḥumas
the present S is not represented at all, evidently because of
S 97a at Lev. 25.25 which excluded one here, only 9 verses
subsequently (above, pp. 136–137). However, Midr. Yel. contained a section to the Torah lection, here, as evident from two
citations in Arukh, viz. one s. v. טמיון (Kohut, IV, 42) and another s. v. חסד (Kohut, III, 452). The former is a morsel of a Pet.
from Prov. 29.7: יודע צדיק דין דלים רשע לא יבין דעת, which tallies
with H from Ezek. not only on account of צדיק and רשע mentioned in the latter several times, but also by means of דלים
as compared to מעני in 18.17.[177s] [161] The full Pet. is given in

---

[161] Cp. the eight synonyms for 'poor' in the Hebrew language as pointed
out in LR, c. 34.8: שמונה שמות נקראו לעני: עני, אביון, מסכן, רש, דל, דך, מך, הלך וכו'.
In MS. Vat. the reading is: שבעה שמות with הלך not listed, thus corresponding
to the number in T, §3, TB, §6 (cp. Buber's note 18). The same reading
in LR is also cited in 'Arukh, s. v. אביון (Kohut, I, 10–11). See further the
Genizah fragment (infra, H. pt., p. סו).[71*]

YSH, to Prov., §961.[162] The second citation in Arukh[163] is the
same Aggadah about kindness as found in LR, c. 34.8, as to
which anon.

In LR, c. 34.1, there is the Pet. on Ps. 41.1–3 where the
word דל (אשרי משכיל אל דל) links up with עני in H. The same
applies to the next Pet. (§2) on Prov. 19.17: ד ל מלוה ה' חונן.
וגמולו ישלם לו. By the flexible method of tallying, the word
וגמולו would furnish a connection with the other H from Is.,
viz. 35.4: גמול אלהים. However, there 'requital' means retribution whereas here in Prov. it denotes reward, in addition to the
fact that in the latter H the poor are not mentioned at all.
Hence the correlation with the suggested lection from Ezek.
is to be preferred. In §3 there is introduced Prov. 11.17:
גומל נפשו איש חסד ועוכר שארו אכזרי which reflects the dictum in
H that the sinful soul dies whereas he that repents preserves his
soul (Ezek. 18.20: החוטאת היא תמות ה נ פ ש as against v. 27:
הוא את נ פ ש ו יחיה). Here again the word גומל would link up
with גמול אלהים (Is. 35.4),[178s] but the same objection as above
can be put forward here. In §4 the comments are on Prov. 29.13:
עשיר ור ש and on 22.2: ר ש ואיש תככים נפגשו מאיר עיני שניהם ה'
נפגשו עושה כולם ה' where רש tallies with עני in Ezek. 18.17 by
reason of their being synonyms (see above, note 161).[179s] The
former v. could somehow be connected by means of מאיר ע י נ י,
שניהם with Is. 35.5: אז תפקחנה ע י נ י עורים, but not at all the

<hr/>

[162] In 'Arukh (s. v. טמיון) the text is somewhat corrupted: וביל מדנו
וכי י מו ך אחיך: ורשע לא יבין ד ר כ ו (במקרא שלפנינו: רשע לא יבין ד ע ת; אולם
השווה מש' י"ד, ח': חכמת אדם הבין דרכו, וב', כ"ד: ואדם מה יבין דרכו), זה עשו הרשע,
(ד"א) יודע .שהיה (צ"ל: שהוא) מכניס ממונו של אדם לטמיון והורגו In YSH we read:
צדיק דין דלים, א"ר ברכיה בא וראה היאך הפרשיות הללו כתובים, מה כתיב למעלה, ושבחה
הארץ (וי' כ"ה, ב'), אמר הקב"ה: אם שמרת את השביעית, וצויתי את ברכתי לכם (שם, כ"א),
ואם לאו, אתה מוכר את נכסיך (היינו: שם, כ"ה), ואף אתה סופף מוכר את עצמך*[72] (היינו:
שם, ל"ט ומ"ז), למה, בשביל שלא השמיט שנה אחת, הוי יודע צדיק דין דלים (היינו באופן
אנדתי: י ו ד ע — כמו מודיע — צ ד י ק — היינו: ה', צדיקו של עולם — ד י ן — משפט —
ד ל י ם: הודיע ה' בתורתו מפני מה אדם מישראל נעשה דל), רשע לא יבין ד ע ת,*[73] זה
עשו הרשע, שהוא מכניס ממונו של אדם לטמיון והורגו, והוא סבור שכל מה שהוא מבזבז הוא
שלו, ואינו יודע שהן מושלשין אצלו, שנ' והיה סחרה ואתננה קדש לה' וגו' (יש' כ"ג, י"ח).
וביל מדנו פ' כי (צ"ל: וכי) י מו ך: ואתה עשית חסד עם כל בני[163]
ישראל (ש"א ט"ו, ו'), וכי עם כל בני ישראל עשה והלה (צ"ל: ו ה ל א) לא עשה חסד אלא
עם משה לבד, שנ' קראן לו ויאכל לחם (שמ' ב', ו') אלא כל העושה עם אחד מגדולי ישראל
חסד כאילו עושה עם כל ישראל (cp. infra, note 165).

latter. In this homily there is woven Koh. 5.12–13 (see also §7)
which v. pertains to the H from Ezek., as pointed out above
(vol. I, p. 476).[180s] In §5 R. Tanḥum b. Ḥiyya employs as a Pet.
Koh. 7.14: 'ביום טובה היה בטוב וגו which is in contrast to Ezek.
18.18: 'ואשר לא ט ו ב עשה וגו. There follows (§6) the comment on
Ps. 106.43 where וימוכו בעונם supplies on the one hand a link with
ימוך in S and on the other hand with בעוני in H (Ezek. 18.18),[181s]
as for the same Aggadah in a more elaborate version, see above,
p. 138. In §8 R. Simon reports in the name of R. Elazar (b.
Pedat) four homilies concerning doing kindness to the needy.
There is no clear indication as to the actual connection of these
items with our S.[164] It seems as if his comments were on Prov.
11.17: גומל נפשו איש חסד, which v. served above as a Pet., hence
the theme concerning him who does kindness (מי שעושה חסד).
Indeed this is apparent from the presentation in MHG (III,
635) which may emanate from Midr. Yel.[165] In §9 there is
woven in Ps. 109.31: כי יעמוד לימין א ב י ו ן להושיע משופטי נפשו
which v. by means of אביון supplies a ready synonym with עני
of H[182s] and in §11 a v. from the latter is expressly cited (הנפש
החוטאת וגו', Ezek. 18.20).

It seems that Ps. 109 served as the *Mizmor* for our S since
it denounces him 'who has not remembered to do kindness and
pursued a poor and needy person' (v. 16) and, on the other hand,

---

[164] It merely states: אומר בה ד' שיטין.

[165] In LR, c. 34.3 after the story concerning Hillel, the further application of Prov. 11.17 is curtailed: ד"א גומל נפשו איש חסד ועוכר שארו אכזרי, א"ר
אלכסנדרי זה שמגעת לו שמחה ואינו מדביק את קרוביו עמו משום עניות וכו', with no comment whatever on the first part of the cited verse. In YSH, *a. l.*, §947, this
omission is partially rectified: ד"א גומל נפשו איש חסד, דמפלג מצוון, ועוכר שארו
אכזרי, זה מי שהגיעה לו שמחה וכו'. However, in the version given in MHG the
contrast in the two halves of the verse, as exemplified by one's attitude
toward needy relatives, is fully brought out: ד"א גומל נפשו, זה המקרב קרוביו
ועושה חסד עם קרוביו, כאילו הוא עושה עם עצמו, שקרוביו של אדם כנפשו; ועכר שארו אכזרי,
זה שאינו מידבק בקרוביו, מכאן אמרו לעולם יתעסק אדם בגמ"ח עם כל אדם, וכ"ש בקרוביו,
ואפי' עם מי שאינו צריך, שכן מצינו מי שעשה חסד עם מי שאינן צריכין ופרע לו הקב"ה, ואיזה
זה, זה אברהם אבינו וכו'. Herewith are given the examples of Abraham and
Jethro which are also mentioned in R. Elazar b. Pedat's homilies. As the
example of Jethro is cited in 'Arukh from Midr. Yel. (above, note 163), the
above version in MHG probably emanates therefrom. Also the remainder
of the passage in MHG (till p. 636, l. 11) is different from LR.

it concludes with the assurance that God 'will stand at the
right hand of the needy' (v. 31). Therefore we have an extensive
passage in LR, c. 34.11–16, which resembles the chapters headed
Ketubim in AB (as analyzed seriatim above in vol. I). In the
name of R. Joshua b. Levi there is introduced the Aggadah concerning the importance of 'the commandment about (the treatment of) the poor'; the neglect of this law is punished by 24
curses whereas its reward are 24 blessings.[166] The curses are
enumerated in Ps. 109.6 ff., with the reason for them stated in
v. 16 ('וגו ואביון עני איש וירדוף חסד עשות זכר לא אשר יען)
whereas as a result of furnishing aid to the hungry and needy
(as stated in Is. 58.7: מרודים ועניים לחמך לרעב פרוס הלא
וכו' בית תביא) 24 blessings are promised, 14 of which being listed
in Is. 58.8–14 and the remainder in Gen. 27.28–29. The contrasting here of Is. 58.7 with Ps. 109.16 in LR, c. 34.12, is the
occasion for an extensive Aggadic interpretation of Is. 58.7–14
taken up in LR.

Finally attention should be drawn to JTS Ms. (infra, H.
pt., p. סו) where the section to our S is introduced by a Pet.
from 1 S. 2.7: 'וגו ומעשיר מוריש יי'; here the next v. is to be included: 'וגו אביון מאשפות ירים דל מעפר מקים thus established
a tally with עני in H (Ezek. 18.17).[183s] Indeed 1 S. 2.7–8 are
cited by Yannai in his Ḳerobah (ed. Zulay p. 170, ll. 8–9).

SEDER 99 (26)

אם בחקתי תלכו ואת מצותי תשמרו ועשיתם אתם ונתתי גשמיכם בעתם ונתנה
הארץ יבולה וגו', Lev. 26.3–4.

Hafṭarah: תאכלו הארץ טוב ושמעתם תאבו אם, Isaiah 1.19;
c. 8 and 12 have this beginning, but in both the end is missing.
However, c. 7, whose commencement is defective, ends with
1.31–2.1+5. Yet this would render the lection to consist of
15 verses, unusually long for a TC H. One may safely assume
that there was skipping; probably the very denunciatory verses
21–23 were omitted, and likewise vv. 29–30, thereby restoring
the reading to the usual number of 10 verses.

[166] LR, c. 34.12: בשם (סימון בר' יהודה ר' :229 צד לישעיה, (בילה"מ סימון רבי
'וכו ברכות כ"ד שכרה ומתן קללות, כ"ד שהפסדה בעיניך, קלה עני מצות תהי אל לעולם ריב"ל.

Yannai in his Ḳerobah to the present S also lists Is. 1.19 as the initial v. of H (Ed. Zulay, p. 173, l. 10). The same is the case in the Ḳerobah according to AC (published by Zulay, *Zur Liturgie d. Babyl. Juden*, p. 74, top) as to which see infra, H. pt., p. unv. S and H tally by means of the italicized words, in addition to the intrinsic parallel of obedience to God's will being rewarded whereas disobedience results in dire punishment. Just as in the initial v. of H it is stated that the latter is to be effected by the sword (חרב תאוכלו), so in the course of the Torah lection 'the avenging sword' (חרב נוקמת) is listed among the means of retribution (Lev. 26.25). Furthermore, there is the promise in the S of God having His residence amidst Israel (v. 11: ונתתי משכני בתוככם, cp. infra, p. 146), and the Lord's house (i. e., Temple) as the attraction for all the nations in order to obtain there instruction of His Torah (Is. 2.2 ff.). Again, in the former, there is the assurance of peace established in the land, with the sword never to pass through it (Lev. 26.6), and in the latter there is the expression of the sublime ideas of mankind to 'beat their swords into ploughshares and their spears into pruning hooks; nation shall not lift up sword against nation, neither shall they learn warfare any more ' (Is. 2.4)! This will account for the choice of the above Prophetic reading.

STRUCTURE OF HOMILIES

No Y topic with question and answer has been preserved. Citation from the Y section to the present S are to be found in Arukh. Thus s. v. מגרס (Kohut, V, 78): בי למדנו בראש בחקות י: תרי (צ"ל: הרי) המגרוסין עד שלא יבשלו בחצי היום הן מבשלין של ערב, והשיג לכם דיש את בציר (ויקרא כ"ו, ה') and s. v. קתר (Kohut, VII, 229): בי למדנו: והרי הארץ מתקנת לכם קתרין,[167] ונתנה הארץ יבולה (ויקרא, כ"ו, ד'); ואין הארץ מתקנת לכם קתרין, ואת ארצכם כנחושה (שם, י"ט). From the same section no doubt emanates the citation ובי למדנו באם בחקות י א"ר s. v. אם 2 (Kohut, I, 110):

---

[167] See Jastrow, *Dictionary*, קתר, who emends the text to read: ונתנה הארץ יבולה, ואין הארץ מתקנת לכם קתרין ואת ארצכם כנחושה, והרי הארץ מתקנת לכם קתרין. See further, Löw, *Zeitschr. f. Assyr.*, XXII, 84, No. 3.

אחא רביעה אחת יורדת מיד האמאות עולות .Perhaps also the one, s. v.
סדר 1 (erroneously omitted in ed. Kohut, VI, 26, and not rectified in Krauss, תוספת הערוך השלם, p. 290[148s]): ב י ל מ ד נ ו ב פ ר ש ת
א ם ב ח ק ו ת י: כיון שיעלו הסידורין ויעטפו אותן הן נעשין שוין, הן נדין,
ואומר (צ״ל: ואומרין) לו שירה יתרועעו אף ישירו (תה׳, ס״ה, י״ד).

In the Tanḥumas the H is reflected throughout. The first
Pet. (TB, Beḥukkotai, §1, T, §1) is from Job 14.15: א ם חרוצים
י מ י ו ומספר חדשיו אתך ח ק י ו עשית ולא יעבור tallying on the one
hand with והיה באחרית הימים in H (Is. 2.2, this in skipped part).[185s]
The point of keeping the Torah and the commandments (אדם
הראשון אילו שמר את התורה ואת המצות) links up again with Lev. 26.3
(ואת מצותי תשמרו) as well as with Is. 2.3 (כי מציון תצא תורה). The
second Pet. (TB, §2, T, §2) introduces Hos. 9.17: ימאסם אלהי
כי לא ש מ ע ו לו ויהיו נודדים ב ג ו י ם; which is in contrast to what
is stated in H: אם תאבו ו ש מ ע ת ם וגו׳ (Is. 1.19) and ונהרו אליו
כל ה ג ו י ם (2.2), thus all the nations streaming towards God's
house in the land of Israel instead of the latter being wanderers
among the former.[186s]   In TB, §3, T, §2, there is woven in
על כן עליכם כלאו שמים מטל ו ה א ר ץ כלאה י ב ו ל ה :Haggai 1.10
being the opposite of the promise foretold in S (ונתנה ה א ר ץ
י ב ו ל ה Lev. 26.4) and in the initial v. of H (טוב ה א ר ץ תאכלו).
The interesting Agg. in this connection, in the name of R.
Joshua b. Levi, that the gentiles ought to take measures that
the Jews kept their law, instead of preventing them from doing
so,[168] is reflected by the promise in H that the 'many peoples will
come and say: Let us go up to the Lord's mountain, to the house
of the God of Jacob, in order that He may teach us of His ways
and that we may walk in His paths.' (Is. 2.3). There follows in
TB, §4, T, §3, the item on Prov. 1.20–21: חכמות בחוץ תרונה
ברחובות תתן קולה, ב ר א ש הומיות ת ק ר א בפתחי שערים ב ע י ר
אמריה ת א מ ר, affording by means of the italicized words a connection with H, viz. י ק ר א לך ע י ר הצדק (Is. 1.26) and בראש
ההרים . . . ו א מ ר ו (2.2–3).[187s] In this homily the role of the Torah
is dealt with, due to Is. 2.3: כי מציון תצא ת ו ר ה וגו׳. Interesting

[168] אמר ריב״ל אילו היו האומות יודעין כשיחטאו ישראל אף הן לוקין, היו מעמידין שני
איסטרטיוטין כדי שיהיו משמרין כל אחד ואחד מישראל שלא יחטאו, ולא דיין שאין האומות
משמרין את ישראל, אלא עוד מבטלין אותן מן המצות.

is the mention here of the custom of having the synagogue building occupy the highest spot in the city,[169] thus corresponding to what is promised in H that 'in the end of days the mountain of the house of God will be established on top of the mountains and exalted above the hills.' (Is. 2.2). In TB, §5, T, §3, the topic is concerning God's Shekhinah, which abideth within Israel (in commenting upon Lev. 26.11: ונתתי משכני בתוככם, cp. above, p. 144) and which withdrew in consequence of Israel's sins resulting in the destruction of the Temple. The Shekhinah will return after Israel's repentance when God will return to his former locale, viz. the sanctuary at Jerusalem.[170] All this is reflected by the glorious vision in Is. 2.1–5. And at the conclusion of the section here the *peroration* cites as a final v. Is. 59.20: ובא לציון גואל ולשבי פשע ביעקב נאם ה' which corresponds to the v. in H: ציון[188s] במשפט תפדה ושביה בצדקה (Is. 1.27). Thus the above analysis reveals how the H has entered the web and woof of the Aggadot to the present Seder.

The same is the case with regard to LR, c. 35. In §1 there is a Pet. from Ps. 119.59: חשבתי דרכי ואשיבה רגלי אל עדתיך where there is a tally with ויורנו מדרכיו in Is. 2.3.[189s] The same applies to the next Pet. (§2) from Prov. 8.32: ועתה בנים שמעו לי ואשרי דרכי ישמרו, in addition to the verb שמעו as compared to ושמעתם in Is. 1.19.[190s] In §6 the latter v. is cited expressly together with the following one. The topic of occupying one's self with the Torah recurs several times in the Aggadot of LR, c. 35, due to Is. 2.3: כי מציון תצא תורה וגו'. Finally there is the *peroration* (§12, end) concerning rain (in connection with Lev. 26.4): לפי שבעוה"ז נשמים טורדים לעולם, יוצאי דרכים מצירין בהם, מפרשי ימים מצירין בהם דורכי גתות וטחי גגות (צריך להוסיף: מצירין בהם), אבל

---

[169] בראשונה היו עושין בתי כנסיות בגבהה של עיר, לקיים מה שנאמר בפתחי שערים בעיר אמריה תאמר. Here the beginning of the v. should be added, viz. ברא ש הומית תקרא (parallel to ההרים ברא ש in Is. 2.2). Indeed in Tos. Meg. 4 (3).23, wherefrom this passage emanates, we read: אין פותחין (בנ"א לנכון: בונין) אותה אלא בגובה של עיר, שנ' בראש הומית בפתחי שערים בעיר. The phrase בראשונה here reflects already the time (during the Byzantine period) when the Jews in Palestine were not allowed to build their synagogues in such a conspicuous manner.

[170] אלא אמר הקב"ה: אעפ"י שאני הולך, יעשה תשובה ואני חוזר... מתוך צרה שהיא בא[ה] עליהם, הן עושין תשובה, ואני מחזיר שכינתי וכו'.

לעתיד לבוא הקב"ה עושה אותן ברכה, מה טעמא, ונתתי אותם וסביבות גבעתי
ברכה והורדתי הגשם בעתו גשמי ברכה יהיו.[171] This final v. (Ezek. 34.26)
links up by means of גבעתי with מגבעות in Is. 2.2[191s] And according
to the variant (see note 171), which has instead Joel 4.18, there
is a tally in מבית ה' with הר בית ה' in Is. 2.2

In Midr. Agg. (II, 65) there is found an additional Pet. from
Prov. 3.11–12 where the sentence כי את אשר יאהב ה' יוכיח
tallies with והוכיח לעמים רבים in Is. 2.4, but the style of this
homily stamps it to be of rather late origin.[192s] [172] Subsequently
there is inserted the comment on Lev. 26.3 in Sifra (ed. Weiss,
110c)[173] which again reflects our H; God desires that Israel labor
in the Torah (an allusion to Is. 2.3: כי מציון תצא תורה) and in
substantiation Ps. 81.14–15 and Is. 48.18–19 are cited, which
verses again have point of contact with the above lection. The
latter fact is evidence for the prevalence of our H to the present S
already in Tannaitic times.[193s]

SEDER 99a (26a)

וזכרתי את בריתי יעקוב ואף את בריתי יצחק ואף את בריתי אברהם אזכר
והארץ אזכר, Lev. 26.42.

[171] In MS. Vat. the reading is: דורכי . . . לפי שבעוה"ז נשמין סימן טרחות לעולם
נרנות מצרין בהן, טחי גנות מצרין בהן, אבל לע"ל א"ר שמען בן חלפתא לע"ל הקב"ה עושה
אותן ברנה, ונתתי אותם וסביבות גבעתי וגו' But in MS. Brit. Mus. the final v. given
is: והיה ביום ההוא יטפו ההרים עסיס וגו' (יואל ה', י"ח).

[172] אם בחקותי תלכו, זש"ה מוסר ה' בני אל תמאס וגו', כי הקב"ה עושה טובה עם מי
שאוהבו ומייסרו בזה העולם, כדי שילך נקי לעוה"ב, כי לא יתכן האדם להיות נקי מן העוונות
ובעבור זה מביא עליו הייסורין כדי לצרפו, כמו הכסף המזוקק שבעתים.

[173] אם בחקותי תלכו, מלמד שהמקום מתאוה שיהו ישראל עמלים בתורה, וכן הוא אומר
לו עמי ש ו מ ע ל י ישראל ב ד ר כ י יהלכו כמעט א ו י ב י ה ם אכניע ועל צ ר י ה ם
א ש י ב י ד י (תה' פ"א, י"ד–ט"ו) לו ה ק ש ב ת למצותי ויהי כנהר שלומך וגו' (יש'
מ"ח, י"ח–י"ט); וכן הוא אומר מי יתן והיה לבבם זה להם ליראה אותי ולשמור את כל מצותי
כל הימים למען י י ט ב להם ולבניהם לעולם (דב' ה', כ"ו), מלמד שהמקום מתאוה שיהיו
עמלים בתורה.[174*] In addition to their connection with Lev. 26.3, these cited
verses, as italicized, link up as well with H; thus Ps. 81.14–15 with ו ש מ ע ת ם
. . . הוי אנחם מ צ ר י ואנקמה מ א ו י ב י ו א ש י ב ה י ד י עליך. . . ויורנו מ ד ר כ י ו
(Is. 1.19, 25–26 and 2.3); Is. 48.18–19 (to which should be added v. 17:
ו ש מ ע ת ם . . . ושביה ב צ ד ק ה . . . ו נ ה ר ו אליו with: (מדריכך ב ד ר ך ת ל ך
ויורנו מ ד ר כ י ו ו נ ל כ ה בארחותיו . . . (Is. 1.19, 27 and 2.2–3); and Deut.
5.26 with ט ו ב הארץ תאכלו (Is. 1.19).

A S here is rather strange as it involves an inauspicious conclusion of the previous one (No. 99), viz. at Lev. 26.41. Yet
LR, c. 36, presupposes such a Torah reading since there is a
whole section of Aggadot in v. 42 together with a *peroration*
Of course such a S would render impossible the next 'regular'
S at Lev. 27.1–2 (infra, No. 100), only a few verses subsequently.
We would thus have another variant in custom with regard to
the respective commencement of the lection following directly
the one recited on the Sabbath before (viz. Lev. 26.3 ff.), with
some starting at 26.42 ff. while others did so at 27.1 ff. The
latter practice prevailed. As to the question of reading ברכות
וקללות on fast-days (M. Meg. 3.6) and the possibility of LR,
c. 36, consisting of homilies delivered on such occasions, see infra,
p. inc.[194s]

Haftarah. On the basis of the homilies to be analyzed forthwith — the only criteria available —, it appears that the Prophetic portion commenced at Jer. 31.30: הנה ימים באים נאום ה'
וכרתי את בית ישראל ואת בית יהודה ברית חדשה, thus tallying with
the same word 'covenant' in Lev. 26.42. The H probably continued to v. 36, skipping to 33.25–26 which verses continue the
point of the reassurance that God will never reject Israel; in the
last v. the Patriarchs are mentioned (זרע אברהם יצחק ישראל),
just as they are in the initial v. of S. At 33.26 there also begins
a new S in Jer., according to some codices instead of at 33.15
(see Ginzberg, *Introd.*, p. 49). Our H thus comprised 9 verses
(31.30–36 — 33.25–26). For a similar H to S 70 see above,
vol. I, p. 530.

There are several other points of contact between the present
reading from Torah and Prophets. As against the expiation of
Israel's sin for not keeping God's laws (Lev. 26.43), there is the
promise of His Torah being inscribed upon the people's heart,
with all their transgressions pardoned (Jer. 31.32–33). The
Exodus from Egypt and the acceptance of the Lord as Israel's
Divinity is reiterated both in Lev. 26.45 and in Jer. 31.31–32.
The comforting assurance that, even while in exile in the hand of
their enemies, the people will not be rejected by their God (Lev.
26.44: לא מאסתים ולא געלתים לכלותם וגו') is still more strongly

reaffirmed in Jer. 31.35–36: ... נם זרע ישראל ישבתו מהיות גוי לפני
גם אני א מ א ס בכל זרע ישראל (cp. further 33.26).

STRUCTURE OF HOMILIES

In LR, c. 36.1, there is the Pet. from Ps. 102.26: לפנים
הארץ יסדת ומעשה ידך השמים which links up with the H v.:
אם ימדו שמים מלמעלה ויחקרו מוסדי ארץ למטה (Jer. 31.36,
cp. also 33.25).[195s] The next Pet. (§2) introduces Ps. 80.9–11:
נפן ממצרים תסיע וגו' corresponding to the event of the Exodus
from Egypt mentioned in S and H (Lev. 26.45 and Jer. 31.31).[196s]
This homily contains a series of beautiful parallels between the
vine and Israel.[174] In §3 the comment is on Prov. 11.21: יד ליד
לא ינקה רע וזרע צדיקים נמלט corresponding to Jer. 33.26:
זרע יעקב ודוד עבדי ... זרע אברהם ישחק ויעקב (cp. זרע ישראל
in 31.35–36).[197s] Ps. 80.9–11 and Prov. 11.21 were also employed
in the section to S 68 d, (above, vol. I, p. 520) which Torah
lection, too, began with a reference to the Patriarchs (Ex. 32.13)
as here in Lev. 26.42, thus giving rise to the introduction of the
same Aggadic theme of the efficacy of 'the merits of the Fathers'
(זכות אבות). However, there the H was different and the respective correlation of the Pet. verses not as pregnant as here, especially with regard to Ps. 80.9–11 (see above, l. c). Indeed the
latter homily seems to have been transferred from here (LR,
c. 36.2) to there (viz. ER, c. 44.1).[175] Also the item on Prov.

---

[174] About the same Pet. to S 103, see infra, p. 189.

[175] In the latter place we read: ד'א גפן ממצרים, אתה מפרנס כל אותן הדעות
האמורות בו, והנה גפן לפני (בר' מ', ט'), גפן ממצרים תסיע ובסוף אתה
מפרנס: מה הגפן היא חיה ונשענת על עצים מתים, כך ישראל הם חיים וקיימים ונשענין
על המתים, אלו האבות. The citation of Gen. 40.9 in juxtaposition to Ps. 80.9
would seem to refer to the Aggadah in GR, c. 88.5 (ed. Theod. — Alb., p.
108): (cp. פ"ש מהרז"ו to ER, c. 44.1). והנה גפן לפני, אלו ישראל, גפן ממצרים תסיע וגו'
However, this seems to me to be an unwarranted scribal insertion. What was
really meant by the sentence 'you furnish all the views expressed concerning
it' (viz. Ps. 80.9) was *a reference to all the Aggadic applications of this v. as
found here in LR, c.* 36.2.[75*] This is clear from the continuation 'and at the
end you supply (the item that) just as the vine is living and is supported
by dead pieces of wood', etc., thus clearly alluding to the conclusion of the
homily here in LR: מה גפן זה נשענת ע"ג עצים יבשים והיא לחה, כך ישראל נשענין בזכות
אבותם, אעפ"י שהן ישנין, הה"ד וזכרתי את בריתי יעקב וגו' (cp. the reading in Midr.
Sam, c. 16, ed. Buber, p. 94, which is similar to that in ER).

11.21 in ER, c. 44.3, is curtailed as compared to the one here in LR, c. 36.3. Next comes in our section (§4) the Agg. on Is. 43.1: ועתה כה אמר ה' בוראך יעקב ויוצרך ישראל which v., in addition to the mentioning of Jacob and Israel common to our H (Jer. 31.30, 32, 35–36 and 33.26), also tallies with the latter by means of the phrase כה אמר ה' employed three times therein (31.34, 36, and 33.25).[198s] The whole point of the world having been created by the merit of Jacob seems to have been suggested by the juxta-position in the H of the continued existence of the laws of nature and of 'the seed of Jacob and Israel' (33.25–26, cp. 31.34–35 and 36). The *peroration* seems to be contained in the statement in the name of R. Berakhyah (§6), to the effect that if the merits of the Patriarchs and the Matriarchs were of no avail, acts of kindness should be accomplished instead so as to merit God's benevolence.[176] There is woven in Is. 54.10: כי ההרים ימושו והגבעות תמוטינה וחסדי מאתך לא ימוש וברית שלומי לא תמוט אמר מרחמ ך ה' linking up with ברית in both S and H as well as with אם ימושו in Jer. 31.35 and ורחמתים in 33.26. But R. Aḥa differs and main-tains that *Zekhut Abot* is to endure forever,[177] citing Deut. 4.31: כי אל רחום ה ' אלהיך לא ירפך ולא ישחיתך ולא ישכח את ברית אבותיך אשר נשבע להם. In addition to רחום as compared to ורחמתים in H, there is in this v. the reference to 'the covenant of thy fathers' as in *both S and H*. From the parallel passage in Yer. (Sanh., c. 10, 27d) it appears that R. Aḥa's statement should really be placed before R. Berakhya's, thereby concluding

---

[176] אם ראית זכות אבות שמטה (צ"ל: שמש ה, כמו שהוא בכי"י וטיקן) וזכות אמהות שנתמוטט ה, לך והטפל בחסדים (ובכ"י וטיקן: בגמילות חסדים, ויל"ש ליש' נ"ד, סוף סי' תע"ז: לך הדבק בג"ח), הה"ד כי ההרים ימושו והגבעות תמוטינה וכו'. But from the parallel passage in Yer. Sanh., c. 10 (27d): לכו והדבקו בחסד, it would seem that the meaning of חסד is God's kindness (viz. to rely on it), thus correspond-ing to וחסדי מאתך לא תמוש in the cited verse.[76*] However, the sense seems to be as stated above in the text, viz. that acts of kindness performed by the Jews will result in God's benevolence towards them, or, in other words, their own good deeds will constitute 'the merit' formerly furnished by the Fathers.[77*]

[177] לעולם זכות אבות קימת, לעולם מזכירין ואומרין כי אל רחום ה' אלהיך וגו'. This reading would indicate as if R. Aḥa referred to some liturgical custom of reciting Deut. 4.31. However, a better reading is found in Tosafot (Sabb. 55a): ולעולם אנו מזכירים אותם (היינו: האבות), וכן הוא אומר כי אל רחום וכו' (ושמואל אמר ולעולם מזכירין (צריך להוסיף: אותם), וכה"א כי אל וגו'. See also YSH, *l. c.*;

the enumeration of the various opinions as to how long 'the merit of the Fathers' is to be efficacious.[178] Thereupon R. Berakhyah commented that even if the latter failed, there is recourse to deeds of kindness in order to obtain Divine favor, citing Is. 54.10 which links up well with H. Thus we obtain the proper *peroration* of the section to the present Torah lection.

Seder 100 (27)

וידבר ה'. . . דבר אל בני ישראל ואמרת אליהם איש כי יפלא נדר בערכך נפשות ל ה', Lev. 27.1–2.

Haftarah: וידר יפתח נדר לה' ויאמר אם נתון תתן את בני עמון בידי, Judges 11.30. This beginning is found in C 7, but the end is missing (also C 8 has a fragment of Jud. 11). Probably H extended to v. 40 (thus 11 verses), but perhaps vv. 33–34 were omitted (hence 9 verses). There is a portion of Yannai's Kerobah to the present (cd. Zulay, pp. 175–6), but the part indicating the initial v. of H is missing.

In addition to the verbal tally of 'vow' in S and H, there is an intrinsic parallel though of a contrasting character, inasmuch as in the former are given the rules concerning vows of 'souls to God,' which involved only the payment of their monetary value (Lev. 27.2–8), whereas in the latter there is the sad story of Jephthah's rash vow to offer to God as a burnt offering 'whatsoever comes forth of the doors of my house to meet me' (Jud. 11.31), a vow that resulted in the death of his daughter.[199a]

Structure of Homilies

No Y question and answer have been preserved. Citations from the Yel. section to the present S are found in Arukh (s. v. טרש 3, Kohut, IV, 98, and s. v. אפרכוס, I, 240).[179] The first one

---

[178] עד היכן היתה זכות אבות קיימת; in Yer: עד מתי זכות אבות קיימת.

[179] This latter citation reads: ובילמדנו בסוף אם בחקותי: מלך ששלח אפרכוס שלו מי מספיק לאפרכוס צרכי (צ"ל: צרכיו),*[78] בני מדינה, אמר הקב"ה: אפרכין שלחתי (היינו: משה ואהרן ומרים), והן מספיקין להן. (היינו: האפרכין של העם להפך ועני, באר, מן: מספיקין לבני ישראל את צרכיהם). Cp. the Y passage in YSH, Micah, §554, end, and TB, Bammidbar, §2 T, §2.

reads:[180] בי למדנו בסוף אם בחקתי, ובפרשה וישב ממנו שבי

אמר ר' לוי מהולתך טרשא אקיש עלה, א"ל הקב"ה ליעקב: יעקב שכחת נדרך.

Concerning this statement see GR, c. 81.2 (ed. Theod. — Alb., p. 972), and T, Wayyishlaḥ, §8, to S 32b (above, Vol. I, 280–81). Also to our S there is in LR, c. 37.1, a reference to the cause of Jacob's delay in fulfilling his vow. One may therefore venture to suggest that the same Y topic as in the case of S 32b served here, too, because of the item of הנודר ואינו משלם. From the instance of Jacob there was a transition to the present S, with the emphasis on being careful to carry out one's vow, similar to the Y passage in YSH, Num., §784, as applied to S (infra, p. inc.).

The continuation would be the Pet. from Koh. 5.1: טוב אשר לא תדור משתדור ולא תשלם dealing with vowing as in S and H. This Pet. is found here in LR, c. 37.1, and indeed also in T, *l. c.*, to S 32b, following immediately the Y topic mentioned before (cp. also infra, p. 153). To continue with the section in LR, there is another Pet. (§2) from Job 34.11: כי פועל אדם ישלם לו וכאורח איש ימציאנו, thus linking up with איש in Lev. 27.2 and in H (Jud. 11.39: איש לא ידעה).[200s] In §4 the story of Jephthah and his vow is introduced, leading down to the *peroration* which terminates with Ps. 116.18: נדרי לה' אשלם וגו',[181] again linking up by means of 'vow' with both S and H.

When we turn to the section in TB, Beḥuḳḳotai, §§6–8, T, §§4–6, we are confronted with homilies that presuppose another H, although the story of Jephthah and his daughter is brought in (TB, §7, T, §5). Neither the two Petiḥtot nor the *peroration* offer points of contact with the Prophetic lection from Jud. 11.30 ff. It seems that there was raised objection by some to

---

[180] Num. 21.1; there, too, vowing is mentioned (v. 2: וידר ישראל נדר לה'). About this S see infra, p. inc.

[181] The following sentence: ואומר הודו לה' כי טוב כי לעולם חסדו is a later scribal addition thanking God for His kindness on the completion of the copy. Indeed in MS. Vat. Ps. 118.1 is cited (without ואומר) on a separate line (in the middle) followed by another such line with the rubric: חסלת אגדתא דויקרא רבה. Accordingly, from הודו וכו' is the colophon of the scribe. Cp. further the same peroration to 77a (above, p. 46) where, too, Ps. 118.1 is omitted.

read in the Synagogue the bitter story which was an abhorrent
reminder of the practice of human sacrifices, so much denounced
in the Bible (cp. the opposition to the Molokh service). Thus a
different H was selected, viz. 2 Kings 12.5: כל כסף הקדשים אשר
יובא בית ה' כסף עובר איש כסף נפשות ערכו כל כסף אשר יעלה
על לב איש להביא בית ה', thus tallying with בערכך נפשות
in Lev. 27.2 (also כסף is mentioned several times subsequently).
The lection probably comprised verses 5–13+17 (10 verses).
Hence we have in TB, §6, T, §4, the Pet. from Ps. 89.7: כי מי
בשחק יערוך לה' ידמה לה' בבני אלים, linking up with בערכך in
S and ערכו in H.[201S] The next Pet. (TB, §7, T, 5) introduces
Prov. 11.30: פרי צדיק עץ חיים ולוקח נפשות חכם, affording the
contact with both, S and H, by means of נפשות.[202S] In this latter
homily there is developed the theme of Jephthah's vow, and
towards the end there is woven in Jer. 19.5: אשר לא צויתי
ולא דברתי ולא עלתה על לבי which is in contrast to אשר
יעלה על לב איש in the initial v. of H. Finally there is the
peroration (TB, §8, end, T, §6, end) which introduces verses
containing the verb ערך[182] thereby tallying with S and H (as in
the case of the above initial Pet. from Ps. 89.7).[203S] Thus the
analysis of the Midrashic data to our S reveals the existence of
two Prophetic readings, with the first one (Jud. 11.30 ff.) represented in LR and probably also in Midr. Yel. (above, p. 152),
and the second one (2 K. 12.5 ff.) in the Tanḥ. section.[204S] The
former one prevailed, as is evident from the Genizah lists cited
before.

Herewith concludes the examination of the Sedarim, Hafṭarot and corresponding sermons to Leviticus. We proceed
forthwith to the discussion of the next part of the Pentateuch.

---

[182] אמר הקב"ה: בזכות ה ע ר כ י ם אני מציל אתכם מ ע ר י כ ת נהינם, שכתב (צ"ל:
שכתוב) בה כי ע ר ו ך מאתמול תפתה (יש' ל', ל"נ), ו א ע ר ו ך לפניכם שלחן, כמו שאמר
דוד ת ע ר ו ך לפני שלחן נגד צוררי דשנת בשמן ראשי כוסי רויה (תה' כ"נ, ה').

NOTES BY SONNE ON LEVITICUS

[1] This, in my opinion, is a case in point exemplifying the "magnetic field" suggestion which would allow us the search for the main link beyond the limits of the H proper. In fact, we need to extend our exploration to a couple of verses before the beginning of the Hafṭarah, namely to Mic. 6.6–7, and we hit the very topic of our S: במה אקדם ה'...האקדמנו בעולות... באלפי אילים הירצה ה'. Here we have the center of attraction through which the whole area is linked up with our S, yes, with the whole book of Leviticus. This becomes transparent in the last Tanḥuma homily on Leviticus. There the cited Micah passage serves as a means of connecting the beginning of Leviticus with the end: האומות אומרים במה אקדם...א"ל הקב"ה... לבני נתתי פרשת ערכין ופרשת קרבנות...תדע לך שתחילתו של ספר...אדם כי יקריב מכם...ולא מן האומות. It appears clearly that in the mind of the homilist this passage of Micah puts its stamp on the whole book of Leviticus. No wonder that whoever was looking for a prophetic reading based on a verbal link with ויקרא, could not fail to be attracted by the Micah verse 6.9: קול ה' לעיר יקרא.

[2] The twelfth benediction may begin with למשומדים in the earliest fragments available, yet in the Tannaitic and earlier Talmudic sources it is, to my knowledge, never referred to as ברכת המשומדים, but often either ברכת המינים (as in our Y passage) or, less frequently, ברכת מכניע זדים (cp. Yer. *l. c.*) because of the conclusion: שובר אויבים ומכניע זדים (רשעים). One might be tempted to suggest a link between ברכת המינים and our S based merely on assonance: מן הבהמה מן הבקר ומן הצאן (Lev. 1.2). If we insist on a link with H, I would consider a term such as אויב or רשע a more suitable link than the verb שמד. The Micah H, indeed, can be linked up with the *Minim*-benediction by means of רשע (three times in vv. 10–11) as well as by means of אויבתי (Mic. 7.8: last verse of H).

There may also be a subtle reflection of our Y topic — that of proselytes being more acceptable than Jewish heretics — in the first v. of the H. The second clause of the v.: ותושיה יראה שמך is interpreted by the Karaite Yaphet b. Ali (cp. Ezra *a. l.*) as יראי שמך "those who fear Thy name." So does Pseudo-Jonathan: דחלין לשמא'. Now according to certain teachers יראי השם are identical with גרי הצדק — "proselytes of righteousness" (cp. LR. 3.2). Of interest to our Y. passage is Tosefta Ber. III.25: כולל של מינים בשל פרושין (generally corrected: בשל פושעין, cp. Lieberman, *Tosefta Ki-pshuṭah*, I, 53–54) ושל גרים בשל זקנים. We have here the same juxtaposition of "heretics-proselytes" as in our Y homily.

154

[3] The proposed H contains really no reference to sacrifices, nor could we find any reference to this topic in the whole chapter 48 of Isaiah.

[4] Here again, as above note 1, the exploration of the area of the Y Halakhah reveals a close connection between the following items and the first portion of the Y homily. The Y topic, as stressed above, is clearly related to M. Ber. V. 3, dealing with a reader who erred in the recital of the *Amidah*. There the statement of the Mishnah that such a reader should be replaced by another one is followed by the exhortation: "And in such a moment (occasion) he, the other reader, should not refuse the honor" (ולא יהא ס ר ב ן באותה שעה), the implication being that under normal circumstances one should first refuse honors. This is indeed expressly stated in a Baraita (Ber. 34a): העובר לפני התבה צריך לס ר ב. Now the topic which follows immediately the first Y portion is that of Moses having been rewarded for his refusal to accept high offices. In other words Moses is styled as a סרבן, one who refuses honors and runs away from leadership בורח מן השררה. There could hardly be a better continuation of the first portion of the Y topic if we only bear in mind its close association with the warning ולא יהא ס ר ב ן באותה שעה.

I would suggest the tally with the Micah H by means of הגיד לך א ד ם (Mic. 6.8) in the proximity of the H. Through the same term אדם the Pet. is linked up with S: אדם כי יקריב.

[6] One could find a verbal link in the Micah H: אבד חס יד (7.2). If we further apply the magnetic field pattern to the Pet. vv., and consequently admit links with the area of the cited Pet., it should not be difficult to perceive a resonance of the Micah H area: במה אקדם ה'...כי אם עשות משפט (Mic. 6.6–8) in the area of the Pet.: צדק ומשפט מכון כסאך ואהבת חסד (Ps. 89.15). חסד יקדמו פניך

[7] By the same means of "righteousness" and "justice," the peroration tallies also with Micah H through v. 7.9: ועשה משפטי אראה בצדקתו. A still closer link can be found in the H area, i. e., Mic. 6.4–5: ואשלח לפניך מ ש ה...למען דעת צדקות ה'.

[8] There is of course a much better link with the first v. of the Micah H by means of 'ה and קול (cp. author's note 16). The periphery of the Micah H (6.1): ק ו ל ך ...אמר ותשמענה ' ה אשר...שמעו offers a still closer tally with Ps. 103.20.

[9] The end of the Hos. v.: יחיו דגן זכרו כ י י ן לבנון forms a contrast to Mic. 6.15: תזרע ולא תקצור...ולא תשתה י י ן.

[10] Assuming that Prov. 25.7 forms a new Pet., the immediate area of the Micah H (6.6): הגיד לך א ד ם מ ה ט ו ב would provide a perfect tally with כי טוב אמר לך. But I doubt whether it really was meant as a separate Pet., and not rather as a supporting piece to the Pet. from Prov. 29.23 discussed before. The latter, as seen above, has as its main topic Moses' refusal to assume leadership. The same idea is implied in the midrashic nterpretation of Prov. 25.7 (cp. TB. W.§2).

[11] This seems forced. I would rather suggest a graphical and phonetical

link with S as well as with Micah H by means of ויקרא and יקרא respectively. We should bear in mind that in the Palestinian idiom the *Aleph* was often dropped so that ויקר(א) and יקר(א) (H) could well tally with וכלי יקר. This is especially true with regard to S, since the Masora remarks that the *Aleph* of Wayyiḳra is a small one (א' זעירא) and could therefore be disregarded.

[12] The *peroration* seems rather to be linked up, intrinsically as well as verbally, with our S. in contrast to "this world" where the Lord spoke to *Moses solely* (ויקרא אל משה וידבר ה' אליו), "in the future" *every flesh* shall see that the mouth of the *Lord has spoken* (וראה כל בשר כי פי ה' דבר). As to the lack of a link with H, we may take into consideration the following: Admitting the pattern of the homilist to connect the S. with the Pet. through the intermediary of the Hafṭarah, it [is] reasonable to assume that such pattern was followed only when the Pet. v., or the *peroration v.*, was taken, as usually, from the Hagiographa. The preachers might have felt some hesitation to ascend from the lowest level, that of the Hagiographa, directly to the highest elevation, the Torah, leaving out the middle link the Prophets, in the hierarchal order. But when the Pet. v. or the peroration verse was taken from the Prophets, as in our case, there seems to be no reason why it should not be connected directly with the Seder.

[13] Here again, since the link with S is manifest and the Pet. v. is taken from Jer. there seems to be no reason why we should search for a link with H. But even if we insist on such a link, one might suggest Mic. 7.6: בן מנבל אב tallying by contrast with הבן יקיר לי.

[14] If Is. 44.26 is to be treated as a separate Pet., one could surmise a tally with Micah H by means of כי נפלתי קמתי, (7.8). A still more suitable link could be established with the area of the Micah H (6.5): זכר נא מה יעץ בלק ומה ענה אותו בלעם which tallies with Is. 44.26 by means of ועצת מלאכיו ישלים. Moreover, Mic. 6.5 tallies intrinsically with Is. 44.25 — immediately preceding our Pet. v.: מפר אתות בדים וקוסמים יהולל, Balaam being the prototype of a קוסם.

But since the Pet. v. seems to have no connection with what follows immediately, it is possible that the v. is here out of place, and originally served as supporting v. to Pet. LR. 1.1 (— JTS, §1) where מלאכיו is explained as meaning Moses.

The passage of the JTS will be discussed in our note *a. l.*

[15] It also tallies with the Micah H by means of: תאכל ולא תשבע ... תזרע ולא תקצור. Besides the common verb אכל the whole forms a contrast to נוצר תאנה יאכל פריה.

[16] Concerning the text of the Midrashic passage under consideration, cp. LR ed. Marg., p. 69, *v. 1.* and notes to 11.4–5.

Though generally referred to as evidence of different Sedarim in various localities, I doubt whether the story really speaks of a local Seder in its strict sense, namely as beginning of the Torah reading. We should bear in mind that very often the second verse of the S, not the first, was taken as point of departure by the homilist. In such case the second verse would be considered, for homiletical purposes, the "heading of the S" (ראש סדר). This is manifest in Yannai's compositions where the second verse forms a counterpart to the first in the structure of the Ḳerobah. In certain cases the "heading of the Seder," for homiletical purposes, extended also to the third verse of the Seder. And this seems to me is meant here by ראש סדר. V. 2.3 was designated as point of departure for the sermon, though the S proper started 2.1. R. H. b. Aḥa was therefore asked to find a Pet. which would be linked up with the third verse of the S, which he did.

On the other hand there is one conclusion to be derived from this story overlooked by most scholars, viz. that the Pet. verse was supposed to tally verbally with "the heading of the Seder." Indeed R. H. b. Aḥa's improvised Pet. contains the word יתרם which tallies with והנותרת.

[17] A better tally with S is: מלא כף (H)+קמצו מלא (S).

[18] Cp. LR, ed. Margulies, p. 60 editor's note to line 2.

[19] It should be noted that the word בסוף is missing in some MSS (cp. ed. Margulies, v. 1. a. 1.).

[20] Cp. LR, ed. Margulies, p. 72, editor's note to line 4.

[21] The A seems to have overlooked Mal. 2.5: ברית היתה אתי החיים (H, according to the A, extends to 2.7) which affords a tally with חלקם בחיים.

[22] According to our point of view the use of v. 32 as linkage does not necessarily imply its inclusion into the H; the entire area of the H may be used for this purpose.

[23] This H is not recorded in any list known to us; it is only a plausible suggestion made by the A based on the premise that a link with H is indispensable for a Pet. no matter how close its connection with S.

[24] We should include also Ezek. 36.27: ועשיתי את אשר בחקי תלכו ומשפטי תשמרו ועשיתם, and we will obtain a fitting link, by way of contrast, with S: נפש כי תחטא מכל מצות ה' אשר לא תעשנה ועשה אחת מהנה.

[25] A survey of the area may help us to find some link between Pet. and H. Indeed, Job 34.29 והוא ישקט ומי ירשיע forms the conclusion of the main theme of the entire chapter which is best formulated in vv. 11–12: כי פעל אדם ישלם לו...אף אמנם אל לא ירשיע, namely that of just retribution for man's deeds, and this is also the leading idea of H, Ezek. 18.

[26] There is also a close relation between Koh. 5.1 and S. Indeed, אל תבהל על פיך may well refer to Lev. 5.4: או נפש כי תשבע לבטא בשפתים להרע.

[27] It should be stressed that the main connection of this Pet. with S is not the common term אלה alone, but rather the whole phrase שונא נפש ונפש...ושמעה אלה ישמע ולא יגיד which echoes beginning of S: קול אלה...אם לא יגיד. Accordingly the link with S should be regarded as the main one, and the H tally as subsidiary.

[28] Here again the Pet. tallies with S not only by means of עד, but also through והפיתות בשפתיך which resounds לבטא בשפתים.

[29] The middle of the peroration reads: אבל ישראל שקיימו את התורה...היך. מה דאת אמר והיה כשמעכם את הקול which seems rather to reflect ושמעה קול אלה in S.

[30] In substance Jer. 7.21–28, 9.22–23 evolve almost the identical theme as Mic. 6.6 ff., and there seems to be no compelling reason to substitute the latter for the former, the less so since Micah was used in S 74.

[31] See our remarks *a. 1.*

[32] The main connection here is of course with S: העולה עליה וערך (Lev. 6.5). The Midrashic paraphrase of the Pet.: היית לא קרבן מבקש היית אילו אומר למיכאל שיקריב לי? seems rather to echo Jer. 7.22: לא כי דברתי ... על דברי עולה ... (*I spoke not ... concerning sacrifices*). There might even be some token link with the area of H(J) by means of השמים למלכת (Jer. 7.18, only 3 vv. remote from the beginning of H).

[33] By the same token Is. 61.8: משפט אוהב ' ה אני כי is connected H(J), viz. Jer. 9.23: משפט חסד עושה ' ה אני כי.

[34] The theme of humility is also inherent in the H(J), viz. Jer. 9.22: יתהלל אל חכם יתהלל אל ... הגבור יתהלל ואל ... עשיר יתהלל אל.

[35] The same holds good for Jer. 7.22, 9.22–23. Moreover, there is also a verbal tally by means of the verb חפץ (ח ם פ — ת י פ צ ח).

[36] A still closer relation is manifest between Hos. 6.6 (ח ס ד ח פ צ ת י) and Jer. 9.23 (עושה חסד... באלה חפצתי).

[37] If we take into consideration also v. 11, immediately preceding beginning of S, we obtain another link by means of עולם (עולם חק—עולם כימי).

[38] Judging from the entire homily, one gets the impression that its structure is based on the contrast of זה — וזה (בלשון זה הושפל ובלשון זה הוגבה). The main link is therefore זה at the beginning of S. The homiletical function of the word זה is also manifest in Yannai's composition (PY, p. 126, bottom): טינפו בשמצת עגל זה // יה בכך הורית לכי זה / כי אם נתרחקו בזה / לקורבם בו ב ל ש ו ן ה ז.

[39] It seems to me that the main tally is י א כ ל נ ה בבני אהרן כל זכר (Lev. 6.11), preceding immediately beginning of S. Indeed, the conclusion of the homily reads: כ ל הקרבנות כ ך אהרן ובניו אוכלין which clearly refers to Lev. 6.11.

[40] Cp. LR, ed. Margulies, p. 172, editor's note 8.

[41] Here again the main tally, in my opinion, is with S, viz. by means of אהרן ובניו. Similarly Yannai (PY, p. 127) cites Is. 38.19 (... יודיע לבנים אב) as a supporting verse to beginning of S. (זה קרבן אהרן ובניו).

[42] Cp. LR, ed. Margulies, p. 173, editor's notes.

[43] The derivation of the H from the Midrashic material is ingenious and convincing. In view of the fact that most Petiḥtot are linked up with H by means of the term שלום which is also common to S, we may consider most of the Petiḥtot dependent mainly on S, and secondarily on H. The only Petiḥta primarily dependent on H is that of Prov. 14.19. However, even here S is not entirely out of the picture. We should bear in mind that our S, dealing with peace-thanksgiving offering (*Shelamim-Todah*), is preceded by the section which deals with guilt offering (*Asham*). Now in the mind of the homilist the juxtaposition of Asham-Shelamim in S is reflected *Asham-Rezono* (אולים יליץ אשם ובין ישרים ר צ ו נ ו) in the Pet.

[44] Both vv. contain the term שלום common to S and H.

[45] We should of course include the first half of the verse: ואני בקול ת ו ד ה א ז ב ח ה which links it up with זבח תודה in S.

[46] The whole ceremony of the initiation of Aaron and his sons as described in our S is alluded to in the first verse of H. There is also a linguistic tally between H (ובחור אותו...לי ל כ ה ן) and Lev. 7.35 (ביום...זאת משחת אהרן הקריב אותם ל כ ה ן ל י) which remains in the area of our S.

[47] There is also a secondary tally with S by means of the verb קרב (Lev. 8.6: ויקרב משה את אהרן, and ת ק ר ב in H).

[48] The main link, as rightly pointed out by A is H, but there is also some connection with S by means of בניו which appears repeatedly in our S.

[49] Ps. 48.15 may tally with S by means of the word עולם which occurs in Lev. 7.36 (...חקת עולם). This v. refers to the ceremony described in our S, and might have been considered by the homilist as part of the S. Cp. above our note 46.

[50] Cp. LR, ed. Margulies, p. 195 f., editor's notes and references.

[51] It should not be overlooked that the Pet. tallies verbally with the beginning as well as with the end of S: ל ק ו ח י ם — ק ח את אהרן ואת בניו; ל מ ו ת — ושמרתם את משמרתי ולא ת מ ו ת ו.

[52] I surmise that the reason of its removal from "head of Seder" (ריש סידרא) was the fact that Lev. 9.2 (קח לך עגל) became closely associated with the "making of the (Golden) Calf." Already in the Tannaitic period (Sifra) it was commented: "Let the calf atone for the making of the Calf" (יבוא עגל ויכפר על מעשה עגל). Now, there is a ruling that the second part of the story of the Golden Calf (Ex. 32.21 ff.) where Aaron is the target of reproach, should be only read in the synagogue, but not interpreted, or preached on (cp. Tosefta Megillah, 4, §36): מעשה עגל השיני נקרא ולא מתרגם, ואלו הן...ויאמר משה אל אהרן...כי הבאת עליו חטאה גדולה...כי פרעה אהרן...את העגל אשר עשה אהרן). As long as the connection between Lev. 9.1 f. and "the making of the Calf" by Aaron remained within a restricted circle of scholars no objection was raised against our S. As soon, however, as such association penetrated into the popular circle of interpreters (cp. Pseudo Jonathan a. l.), it was thought that the rule of the second part of the story of the Golden Calf (מעשה עגל השני) should be applied also to Lev. 9.2, viz. not to preach upon it. Consequently, the passage was considered unfit to be "head of Seder" (ריש סידרא).

[53] Here we have a typical example of the *magnetic field* pattern. The entire chapter echoes our S, but the last v. is taken as point of departure because of its linguistic tally.

[54] I doubt whether this Midrash falls under the category of מה כתיב למעלה מן הענין. The formula is generally used when the topic of the new S seems entirely disconnected from that of the preceding S, and poses the question: What has the one topic to do with the other (וכי מה ענין זה לזה)? In our case no such problem exists. The present S continues to evolve the topic of the preceding S, viz. the description of initiation ceremonies of Aaron and his sons.

What we really have here is nothing but the usual pattern of linkage with the *area* of the S. Koh. 8.5 (שומר מצוה) tallies with Lev. 8.35 (ושמרתם

(את משמרת ה'). The latter gravitates towards our S, and is considered as a part of it.

55 The last v. of S (Lev. 9.24: וירא כל העם וירנו) may afford some link with (לחוללים —) אמרתי להוללים, since חוללים corresponds to וירנו.

56 The *peroration* seems to refer mainly to S. Indeed, Lev. 9.7 affords not only a verbal link with the *peroration* by means of חטאת, but also an intrinsic one. As a matter of fact, בעוה"ז נתכפר להם על ידי קרבנות in the *peroration* is but a paraphrase of ועשה את קרבן העם וכפר בעדם, and forms a contrast to it. 43.25: אנכי אנכי הוא מחה פשעיך. In comparison with such close connection the H link appears rather weak, and should therefore be considered as a subsidiary one.

57 We should of course supplement the second half of Prov. 9.1 (הצבה עמודיה שבעה) which tallies with Lev. 8.35 (ופתח אהל מועד תשבו שבעת ימים), considered as part of our S (cp. our note 54).

58 There is a point of contact with S by means of *Tamim* (עם גבר תמים . . .) which echoes *Temimim* (Lev. 9.2). The area of H (Ezek. 43.22–25 — only two vv. removed from H) affords the same tally by means of תמים or תמימים.

59 There is no need for such forced tally. The point of contact with S as well as with H is obviously עסיס, synonym of יין. This identification of עסיס is given in Joel 1.5: והילילו כל שתי יין על עסיס which v. forms a contrast to Joel 4.18 cited in the *peroration*.

60 Like in all other Petiḥtot to the present S, here too the link is formed by means of יין or its synonyms. On the basis of Ps. 104.15: ויין ישמח לבב אנוש, שמחת לבב became a synonym of יין, and afforded a link with S and H. Jer. 15.16 is then interpreted homiletically that the word of God was the substitute wine (שמחת לבב) which was prohibited to Aaron and his sons. This holds good also for the following Pet. from Ps. 19.9 where משמחי לב is linked up with יין.

61 In view of the fact that the Y topic is so directly and intrinsically related to S, a verbal link with H can be dispensed with. If nonetheless we insist on some token connection with H, I venture to suggest that the homilist might have taken the word בער in Is. 40.16 in the sense of בעיר, the Aramaic equivalent of בהמה. The term בעיר for cattle seems to have appealed to the Palestinian preachers (cp. PRK, ed. Buber, p. 58a: אית בעיר אכיל בעיר). The first v. of H: וחית בער די אין would afford a link with "cattle and beast."

62 The same tally, by means of צורף, exists of course also in the corresponding passage of Is. 40.18: וצרף בזהב . . . כסף צורף which is but a variation of Is. 46.6.

63 The link by means of עולם is unlikely. The Hab. Pet. starting עמד וימדד ארץ ראה ויתר גוים is best linked up with Is. 40. In the first place, by means of גוים (Is. 40.17: כל הגוים כאין נגדו). The term ארץ affords another link with H (Is. 40.22–24) as well as with S (הבהמה אשר על הארץ). The most striking tally, however, one finds outside the H proper, but within its area, i. e. Is. 40.12: מי מדד בשעלו מים וכל בשליש עפר הארץ which reechoes in Hab. 3.6: עמד וימדד ארץ.

[64] There is also a link with S (Lev. 11.46–47: ...זאת תורת הבהמה... החיה הנאכלת ...בין להבדיל— last two vv. of S) which is reflected in the second half of Ps. 40.9 (ותורתך בתוך מעי— Thy *law* concerning the food in my stomach).

[65] There seems to be a better connection with Is. 40 by means of the particle מי, expressing a rhetorical question. As matter of fact מי is a favored figure of speech in Is. 40 (cp. vv. 12, 14: מי מדד; מי תכן in the area, and 26: מי ברא אלה in H proper).

[66] Is. 66.17: אוכלי בשר החזיר is so intimately related to our S that a tally with H can be dispensed with. If one still insists on such a link, we may refer to Is. 41.1: יחדו למשפט נקרבה.

[67] By the same token it is also linked up with Is. 40.21: הלא תשמעו, or with Is. 40.28: אם לא שמעת.

[68] The theme of the future kingdom of God resounds in the entire chapter of Is. 40, and no specific verbal link is needed.

[69] There is no denying that to a certain extent Is. 46.1 ff. would afford smoother links with the various Petiḥtot than does Is. 40.16 ff. But this is hardly sufficient ground to introduce a new H, not otherwise recorded. Is. 40.16 ff. accounts, as we have seen, for most of the Petiḥtot; others are so closely related to the Seder that the preacher might have felt free to dispense with H link.

Moreover, we should bear in mind that Is. 40 and 46 evolve partially a common theme, consisting in the attack against the worship of idols. It is thus well possible that in the mind of the homilist the two chapters became welded together. In this way, though the H was taken from Is. 40, the preacher might have used as linkage some vv. from Is. 46. We are far from having established the validity of the suggested H from Is. 46.1 ff.

[70] Cp. Buber, note 33.

[71] The *peroration* verse: ...ויספו בה' שמחה (Is. 29.19) seems rather to echo Is. 9.2: הרבית הגוי הגדלת השמחה which is outside the H proper, but remains within its area.

[72] This faint tally could hardly have been the source of inspiration for the homilist. In all probability the center of attraction was vv. 8–11 (ידיך ...ועצמות ונידים תשככני) which speak clearly of the formation of the embryo, and are thus intrinsically connected with our S speaking of the birth of a child. There is also a linkage between the last v. of Job 10 (צלמות ולא סדרים) and the first v. of Is. 9 (ישבי בארץ צלמות) within the area of H.

[73] This Pet., like the preceding from Job 10.12, contains a clear reference to the formation of the embryo, and is consequently directly and intimately linked up with our S, so that a link with H may not be compelling. One may be satisfied with the assonance of תזריע — זרית.

[74] We may add that the numbers *seven* and *eight* form only a subsidiary link between Koh. 11.2 ff. and S. The real point of contact consists, in all probability, in the term זרע which occurs in 11.4, 6. בטן המלאה in v. 5.

[75] We have tried to show that the linguistic links with H were not neces-

sarily the main instruments which effected the connection of the Petiḥtot with S; in most instances they seem to have been of secondary order.

[76] The suggested H from Is. 5.7 is at best a plausible and workable conjecture, and I would hesitate to call it an established fact. There are, in all probability, other prophetic passages which would also account for all the homilies to S, supposing that such links are indispensable. Let us take, for example, Hab. 1.7: יצא ו ש א ת ו משפטו ממנו ונורא איום which tallies with S by means of שאת, or Hab. 2.15: חמתך ...מ ס פ ח הוי which could also be linked up with S through ספחת. In either case we could consider the entire book of Habakkuk as the area of H, and it would be easy to account for all the homilies, their Petiḥtot and perorations.

Let us take the first suggestion, Hab. 1.7.

1) Pet. from Job 28.25: ב מ ד ה לעשות לרוח משקל ומים תכן במדה is reflected in Hab. 3.6: ארץ ע מ ד וימדד.

2) Job 38.25: ק ל ו ת ודרך לחזיז tallies with Hab. 3.10: נתן ההום ק ו ל ו.

3) Job 34.11: לו ישלם אדם פעל כי tallies by means of פעל with Hab. 1.5 (בימיכם פ ע ל פ ע ל) and 3.2: (שנים בקרב פ ע ל ו). Moreover, the theme of retribution in kind is often implied in Hab. (cp. 2.8: ...ת ש ל ו ת אתה כי י ש ל ו ך; cp. also 2.12, 16, 17).

4) Ps. 75.8: וכו' שפט אלהים כי is linked up with Hab. 1.7 by means of מ ש פ ט ו.

5) Ps. 5.5 רע ינרך לא אתה רשע חפץ אל לא כי is linguistically and intrinsically linked with Hab. 1.13: ע ר ש ר כבלע תביט למה רע מראות עינים טהור.

6) *Peroration*: (י"ב 'ס"ב ,'יש) הקדש עם להם וקראו ... אותם מקדש אני is reflected in Hab. 1.12: ק ד ש י א ל ה י 'ה מקדם אתה הלא.

7) Prov. 19.29: שפטים ללצים נכונים tallies by means of שפט with Hab. 1.7, 12.

Thus the Hab. suggestion would also do justice to all homilies, though, it must be admitted, in a less satisfactory way than does the H suggested by the A. We should bear in mind that many of the known Hafṭarot do not present the best possible choice from our point of view.

[77] It should be noted that the real tally consists in the combination of [H]). ו א ר פ א ה ו ר א י ת י ד ר כ י ו—[S] נ ר פ א ו ה נ ה ה כ ה ן ה ר א ה ו and רפה (ראה).

[78] I wonder whether the two Sedarim were not originally established as alternates for the same Sabbath. The choice might have been left to each congregation, or perhaps to the individual reader. As a matter of fact, the halakhic Midrash (Sifra) unites both Sedarim under the heading of "Section of Plagues" (דנגעים מכילתא). Such division is also reflected in the redaction of the Mishnah which contains a "Tractate of Plagues" (נגעים מסכת). It is therefore possible that the H was meant for the section of *Negaim* no matter which of the two Sedarim was read. Indeed, in the Agadic field the topic of *Negaim* was that of *suffering* (ייסורין), its origin and meaning, and Is.

57.17: "For the iniquity of his covetousness was I wroth and smote him" seems a most fitting motto for this subject.

[79] The same holds good for the Tanḥumas and LR; neither of them has any homily on S 83, and probably had no S at Lev. 13.18. We should therefore hesitate to assume a new H for these collections.

[80] This is one of the most persuasive suggestions made by the A. aiming at introducing a non-recorded new Hafṭarah. We, nonetheless, shall see that it remains a most plausible conjecture, but is far from being an established fact.

As to the Y topic, we may be able to find some connection also with H from Is. 57.7. Indeed, we need only extend our search for contacts to the immediate area, the verse preceding the beginning of H, viz. Is. 57.6: לא כי לעולם אריב ולא לנצח אקצף to establish a connection with the Y topic by means of the underscored terms (ל ע ו ל ם ה ב א). True the tally suggested by A. is much more transparent, but that is not enough to make it an established fact.

[81] As realized later by the A. (note 74) Is. 57.17 (בעון בצעו ק צ פ ת י), and we may add also Is. 57.16 (כי לא ל ע ו ל ם א ק צ ף) afford a perfect link with the second half of Koh. 5.5: למה יקצף האלהים.

[82] The second half of Mal. 3.16 (ו י ש מ ע) is reflected in Is. (ו י ק ש ב ה') 58.9 (או תקרא וה' יענה).

[83] Is. 58.3: ולא תדע עינו נפשנו affords a clear contrast to Ps. 139.2, besides a verbal tally.

[84] We should include the second half of Prov. 18.21 (והאכלתיך נחלת יעקב) which tallies with Is. 58.14 (ואהביה יאכל פריה). This verse may still be included in the H; if not, it surely belongs to its area.

[85] Intrinsically the peroration tallies better with Is. 57.17–18. Indeed מתיסרין ומיטהרין is but a paraphrase of דרכיו ראיתי וארפהו, קצפתי ואכהו. There may also be some linguistic tally with cited v. by means of Is. 58.11 (וכמוצא מים).

[86] As realized later by the A. (his note 74) Prov. 6.19 (משלח מדנים) is reflected in Is. 58.4: לריב ומצה תצומו.

[87] Ps. 34.13 ff. tallies better with Is. 58.2 by means of (ודעת דרכי ו י ח פ צ ו ן) — so A. in note 74. If we include also v. 15 (בקש ש ל ו ם ורדפהו), we have a ready tally with Is. 57.18 (ש ל ו ם ש ל ו ם לרחוק ולקרוב).

[88] We should include the first half of Job 20.7: כגללו לנצח י א ב ד, and we obtain a perfect contrast to Is. 57.16: ולא ל נ צ ח א ק צ ף. This v., as noted above, was regarded as an integral part of the following v., the beginning of the H.

[89] As realized later by the A. (note 74) there could hardly be a better counterpart to Ps. 50.16 than Is. 57.21: אין שלום אמר אלהי לרשעים.

[90] I readily admit that in this case the "presupposed other H" seems to rest on solid ground, especially the Y topic and the H to our Parasha in AC. On the other hand, however, the absorption by Yannai, who lists Is. 57.17 as H, of much of the Midrashic material, must caution us against overcon-

fidence in "new Haftarot" derived from the homilies. The A.'s explanation of the phenomenon is ingenious and plausible, but cannot be considered as conclusive.

[91] Cp. LR, ed. Margulies, p. 368, editor's introductory remark to 17.1.

[92] There is also a linguistic tally between Ps. 73.1 (אך טוב לישראל) and Is. 5.20 (הוי האומרים לרע טוב).

[93] Needless to say, the main connection of Is. 28.16 is with S by means of אבן — אבנים. The last clause of the Is. verse (המאמין לא יחוש) forms a striking contrast to Is. 5.19 (ימהר יחושה).

[94] I would suggest the tally of ימי הרעה (Koh. 12.1) with יחיינו מימים ביום השלישי (Hos. 6.2).

[95] All known MSS have the reading: שורפה (cp. LR, ed. Margulies, p. 400, v. l.

[96] Here the main link seems to be with S: ואיש כי תצא ממנו which resounds in ממנו משפטו ושאתו יצא.

[97] Here again the main connection is to be looked for in S, viz. זב מבשרו, corresponding to אין מתום בבשרי.

[98] The Y topic was obviously suggested by S with which it is linked up not only intrinsically, but also by linguistic tallies (Lev. 15.33: והדוה בנדתה...ולאיש אשר ישכב).

[99] If I am not mistaken, the main link of this Y topic is also S. The center of attraction here is not טומאת נידה, as in previous Y, but rather דם נידה and שפיכת דם which is clearly reflected in Lev. 15.23: ואשה...זוב (ש פ ך—). דמה...בלא עת נדתה. There may be some link with the Y H by means of דמיך (Ezek. 16.9) or דם ושפכת דם (Ezek. 16.38). משפטי נאפת

[100] The formula דבר אחר seems rather to indicate that the v. under consideration already was used as Pet. before, and that there is a lacuna before לפיכך. Since it is unusual, to say the least, for the homilist to utilize the first verse of the H as Pet., the appearance of Ezek. 36.16 as Pet. can hardly lend assistance to the new H suggested by the A.

[101] The main tally, as pointed out by the A. above, is with S by means of כימי נדתה...טמאה (Lev. 15.25); a token link with H is satisfactory.

[102] In fact, section IV of his Ḳerobah (PY, p. 156, ll. 34 ff.), which follows immediately the citation of Ezek. 16.9 as H verse, is but a versification of the second Y topic (אמנם על שלש עבירות הנשים עוברות ומתות). Interesting Yannai's version of the last part: ונידה כי טימאה טהרת אדם / אשר הוא היה דם העולם.

[103] It is more likely that the term *Ketem* which is often used in connection with *Niddah* (cp. M. Niddah 6.13: הרואה כתם & *passim*) suggested this Pet. This seems to be borne out in Yannai's Ḳerobah mentioned above. In section I, line 2 (PY, 54) we read: נילית סוד לחכמי מראות / דמים וכתמים ליראות, and in the corresponding line in section II we have: סודרים כראוי בלא כזבים / עיטרתם לך בכתמי זהבים (—כתם פז).

[104] Here again the main link seems to be with S, viz. by means of ידלף considered as synonym of יזוב (cp. Targum Jonathan on Koh. a. l.). This too

seems to be indicated by Yannai, *l. c.* section I, 1. 6: / כי בשפלות דמיה מרובים
לעת הזוב . . .

[105] But Yannai also inserted into his Ḳerobah the second Y topic which, according to the A., is based on H from Ezek. 36.16 ff. (see above our note 99).

[106] Unfortunately none of the A.'s notes on this fragment could be found. In our own notes we mostly pointed out the connections with S (Lev. 15.25, 31).

[107] Deut. 32.43: הרנינו גוים עמו כי דם עבדיו יקום tallies by means of דם with S as well as with H from Ezek. 16.9. Also by means of וכפר אדמתו there would be a link with S (Lev. 15.30: וכפר הכהן), and also with Ezek. 16.62 (בכפרי לך) which may be included in the first H, and surely is in its area.

[108] Exploring the area of the Gideon Story, one discovers a link H by means of חרד. In Jud. 7.3 (one v. remote from the beginning of H) those who had knelt while drinking water are styled "fearful and trembling" (מי ירא וחרד). They form a contrast to those who are "trembling at His word" (החרדים אל דברו: Is. 66.5).

[109] Intrinsically Mal. 1.11 stating that "in every place offerings *are presented to My name*" (בכל מקום מוקטר מוגש לשמי) forms a contrast to S prescribing "to *present an offering to the Lord*" (Lev. 17.4: להקריב קרבן לה') only within the "tent of meeting." On the other hand, Mal. is in accordance with H. Being so intimately linked up with S and H, the verbal tallies are of little weight.

It may be noted that our Midrash seems to belong to the group of Midrashim aiming at reconciling Biblical verses which appear to be contradictory to one another (מדרש שני כתובים המכחישים זה את זה).

[110] Ps. 51.20 forms a parallel to S, insofar as acceptance of sacrifices is restricted to Jerusalem, and by the same token is in contrast with H. Apart from this, there is a linguistic tally with S (by means of זבחי שלמים — Lev. 17.5, and זבחי צדק — Ps. 51.21).

[111] By the same token, viz. by means of דבר, it tallies also with S (זה הדבר).

[112] Prov. 14.7 proper: לך מנגד לאיש כסיל affords a linguistic tally with S by means of איש (איש איש . . . דם יחשב לאיש).

[112a] As indicated above in our note 106, none of the notes to the Genizah fragments could be found.

[113] There is a linguistic tally by means of ארץ (Is. 66.1, 8).

[114] Cp. LR, ed. Margulies, p. 494, editor's introductory remarks to section 22.

[115] If we take into consideration also the preceding v. of Ps. 146.6 (עושה שמים וארץ), we obtain the required link with H (השמים כסאי והארץ). There is also a tally with Ps. 146.7 by means of עושה (עשתה . . . ואת— ידי עשתה עושה) Is. 66.1).

[116] Cp. LR, ed. Margulies, p. 521, editor's remarks to 22.10.

[117] According to our suggestion, v. 1 being within the area of the H, was

sufficient to be utilized by the homilist as point of departure for his homily. There is no compelling reason to include the v. into the H proper.

[118] Intrinsically the relation of Cant. 2.2 to S is quite obvious. Israel stands above other peoples "as a lily among thorns," and consequently "the children of Israel shall not walk in the statutes" of the gentiles.

[119] The main link is obviously with S, viz. through Ezek. 23.3 where the theme of "fornication" (ותזננה) is introduced which runs through the whole chapter. In fact ותזננה במצרים besides the linguistic tally with S contains almost an allusion to it (כמעשה ארץ מצרים).

[120] Cp. LR, ed. Margulies, p. 536, editor's remark at the beginning of LR 23.8.

[121] Both Tanḥumas have מהו דכתיב ואשמע אחרי וכו', and it appears strange that they should have omitted the beginning of the verse which forms the point of contact. I therefore suggest that it tallies by means of ברוך כבוד ה' with Is. 4.5 (על כל כבוד חפה).

[122] Cp. LR, ed. Margulies, p. 549, editor's remark on LR 24.1. According to Marg. Pet. 1 is dependent on Pet. 2. It seems that מרום was considered synonym of קדוש (in Is. 37.23b מרום forms a parallel to קדוש ישראל). Hence the tally with our S.

[123] This peroration seems rather to allude to the following S beginning: וכי תבאו אל הארץ ונטעתם (Lev. 19.23). The homilist endeavors to connect Lev. 19.23 with the two preceding Sedarim dealing with "purity" (טהרה) and holiness" (קדושה). The observance of the precepts contained in these two Sedarim is a prerequisite of taking the land in possession.

[124] Zech. 8.11–12 tallies mainly with S by means of פרי (Lev. 19.23, 24, 25: את פריו, and Zech. 8.12: הגפן תתן פריה).

[125] The link with H is more likely to be by means of נחלת צבי צבאות גוים, re-echoing Is. 66.12: וכנחל שוטף כבוד גוים. The center of attraction, however, seems to me to lie in Jer. 3.18 (the verse preceding the Pet.): בימים ההמה ילכו...ויבאו יחדו...על הארץ אשר הנחלתי את אבותיכם which corresponds to S: כי תבאו אל הארץ.

[126] Deut. 13.5: אחרי ה' אלהיכם תלכו is obviously linked up primarily with S where אני ה' אלהיכם is used repeatedly as a refrain (Lev. 19.25, 27, 34). As a matter of fact, a Pet. taken from Pent. we should expect to be directly connected with S, and not through the intermediary of the H.

[127] Here again the exploration of the area is the key to the real link. Indeed, the entire chapter of Job 38 abounds in rhetorical questions: "Who did that" (cp. vv. 5, 25, 36, 41), to which Is. 66.2: "For all these things hath My hand made" (ואת כל אלה ידי עשתה) sounds a fitting response.

[128] Ps. 94.20: ק חק עלי is linked up by contrast with S (Lev. 19.37: ושמרתם את כל חקתי).

[129] There may be a token tally with S by means of דוד, viz. Lev. 20.20: ערות דודו גלה.

[130] Ezek. 36.27 quoted in the *peroration* is primarily connected with S by means of the refrain ושמרתם את חקתי (Lev. 19.37; 20.8, 22). Moreover Lev.

ושמרתם את כל חקתי ואת כל משפטי ועשיתם אותם ולא תקיא :20.22
אתכם הארץ אשר אני...לשבת בה tallies intrinsically as well as linguistically with Ezek. 36.27–28: ועשיתי את אשר בחקי תלכו ומשפטי
תשמרו ועשיתם, וישבתם בארץ אשר נתתי...

[131] It should not be overlooked that לחם אלהים occurs five times in our S
(Lev. 21.6, 8, 19, 21–22) which might have contributed to the introduction
of our Y topic (Ḥallah). It is, in all probability through the term לחם that
Is. 28.25–28 became associated with the Ḥallah topic. This would explain
the above mentioned Yerushalmi reading: גבולתו לחם, to indicate the beginning of v. 28 as the point of departure.

[132] By the same token it also tallies with the corresponding v. in S: ועל כל
נפשות מת לא יבא (Lev. 21.11).

[133] The main connection of Ps. 12.7 is obviously with S by means of
אמרות corresponding to אמור...ואמרת.

[134] Here again the main point of contact is with S by means of אמר.

[135] By the same token it is also linked up with the corresponding v. in
S: על כל נפשות מת לא יבא (Lev. 21.11). But the real connection seems to
be by means of וכי יאמרו in contrast אמור...ואמרת in S.

[136] Cp. Buber's note 48 a. l.

[137] Cp. LR, ed. Margulies, p. 587, editor's introductory remark to sect. 26.

[138] Here the A. inadvertently comes very close to the principle of the
"magnetic field," in so far as a phrase outside the H proper is being utilized
as link because of its proximity to the H. We must, however, admit that
in the present case the "strangers" (בני נכר) of the previous verse are actually
referred to in the suffix of והביאו תים.

We may also add that the real point of contact between Is. 56.6 and
our S is not so much the beginning (Lev. 22.18: הגר), but rather 22.25 stating
that offerings "from the hand of foreigners shall not be accepted (ומיד ב
נכר...לא ירצו לכם). Is. 56.6 seems to refer to this rule saying that it
does not apply to those foreigners "that join themselves to the Lord," their
offering will be accepted.

[139] Here for the first time the A. rightly recognized that the verses which
follow each of the first three sections of Yannai's Ḳerobot contain besides
S(1), S(2), H(1) also Petiḥtot, point of departure for various homilies. The
Midrashic material indicated by these citations is often evolved, sometimes
only alluded to, in the paitanic compositions which precede such verses and
follow them.

[140] By the same token it tallies also with S by means of עולה.

[141] & [142] Ps. 22.31 as well as Ps. 76.12 tally primarily with S by means
of 'לה common to all three ('יסופר לה ;'ושלמו לה, corresponding to 'יקריבו לה).

[143] This seems to imply that the A. shares the generally accepted opinion
that the midrashic material to this S originated in the Pesiḳta, and from
there transferred to LR. This opinion has been recently challenged by Prof.
Albeck (cp. Louis Ginzberg Jubilee Volume [Hebrew sect.], 1946, pp. 36 ff.).

[144] The main point of contact here seems to be the term לדרתיכם which

occurs several times in our S (Lev. 23.14, 21, 31, 41, 43), and which is re-echoed in Koh. 1.4: דור הולך ודור בא. By the same token the Pet. is also connected with the H: (ב', ד' יואל) דור ודור לדור וירושלם. As a rule we should always prefer a common link with S and H.

145 In this particular case the A. agrees with Albeck that LR was the source for the Pesiḳta, and not vice versa (see above our note 143).

146 Here we have, in my opinion an instructive example of the working of the "magnetic field" principle in the selection of a Pet. v. One of the conspicuous terms of our S. is that of *Tamid*; it appears three consecutive times in the first three vv. (Lev. 24.2, 3, 4). *Ner Tamid* must have had a special appeal to the preacher and the audience. Now if we explore Ps. 71, we find that like our S this Ps. too contains the term *Tamid* three times (vv. 3, 6, 14). Moreover the first time (v. 3), *Tamid* is accompanied by the verb *tzaw* (צוית תמיד) which connects it still closer with our S (צ... להעלות נר תמיד). It is reasonable to assume that the center of attraction linking up Ps. 71 with our S was the term *Tamid*; the choice of the particular verse within the "magnetic field," might have been determined by a certain token link with H.

147 In a case like this where the connection with S is so manifest, we could, in my opinion, dispense with a H-link. The attempt to remove the Pet. from here because no reasonable tally with H could be established, seems to me unwarranted. I may add that some kind of link between כי אתה נרי תאיר and the H from Hos. 14.7: ויהי כזית הודו could be established if we take into consideration the rendering of the Hos. v. by Pseudo Jonathan (ויהי כזיו מנרת קודשא זיוהון).

148 By means of עלה Prov. 21.22 tallies also with S echoing להעלות. Moreover, the term חכם in the Pet. v. could have been associated, or confused, by the homilist with the same term in Prov. 21.20, only two vv. removed from our Pet., where it is connected with שמן (חכם בנות ושמן), the main topic of S.

149 Job 25.3 tallies with S by means of אורהו, corresponding to למאור. It is interesting to note that in the small chapter of Job 25, consisting of six verses, there occurs twice the term זך (vv. 4, 5) which echoes שמן זית זך in our S.

150 Considering the two verses cited in the *peroration*, we find the first, Ps. 132.17 ([ערכתי נר למשיחי]) שם אצמיח קרן לדוד) clearly linked up with S (Lev. 24.4: יערך את הנרות); the second, Ps. 122.1, related to the H, as pointed out by the A. Is this a mere accident?

151 It should be noted that Jer. 9.24 tallies also with S by means of מצרים echoing מצרי in Lev. 24.10.

152 However, the point of contact seems to be S with which the Pet. v. tallies not only by means of יצא, but also through לריב, equivalent of וינצו.

153 In Ps. 12.9: "The wicked walk around," the homilist might have sensed an allusion to our S, Lev. 24.14: "Bring forth him that has cursed without the camp," i. e., to "walk around" the camp.

[154] Here obviously the main tally is with S, viz. by means of תקלל, the very topic of our S (cp. Lev. 24.11, 14, 15).

[155] Cp. Ch. Albeck, Midrash Wayyikra Rabbah, Louis Ginzberg Jubilee Volume (Hebrew section), 1946, p. 36, note 67.

[156] Similarly the commentators (cp. מתנות כהונה and רד"ל a.l.). But they fail to explain how this meaning can be derived from the Goliath passage. I would suggest that "he went out from his world" means "from his own environment, his own camp." The curser being a son of an Egyptian, was supposed to live in an Egyptian camp among Egyptians, and not to mingle with Israelites in the camp of Israel. This meaning we can well derive from the Goliath passage which reads: "And there went out . . . from the camp of the Philistines" (ויצא איש הבינים ממחנות הפלשתים).

[157] There might be some phonetic linkage between Cant. 4.11 (וריח שלמתיך) and S (Lev. 25.11: שלמית ושם אמו). In fact the homily concludes with the explanation of the דברי בת שלמית.

[158] By the same token it tallies also with S (Lev. 24.14: וסמכו כל השומעים את ידיהם על ראשו).

[159] By the same token it also tallies with S where הארץ (ושקטה—ושבתה) is synonym of האדמה. This is made clear in the course of the homily where אל תיראי אדמה is contrasted with ארץ יראה. Ps. 76.9 (ארץ יראה ושקטה) woven into the homily affords a perfect parallel to ושבתה הארץ.

[160] By the same token it also tallies with S (Lev. 25.18: ועשיתם את חקתי ואת משפטי תשמרו ועשיתם אותם).

[161] Cp. MHG, Lev., p. 610, editor's note 5.

[162] The rejection of the given H on the ground that there is no intrinsic, topical connection with S and homilies, seems somewhat strange, since on other occasions the A. seems to imply that we should be satisfied with linguistic tallies.

[163] We may perhaps take into consideration some kind of phonetical link with S by means of להון. In the Palestinian dialect the He was usually dropped, so that להון might have had some resonance of לא חונו.

[164] But שנת גאלי is a most fitting link for our S. As a matter of fact, "years" (שנים) and "redemption" (גאל, גאלה) are special features of our S. We may also add that בשנת היובל (Lev. 25.13, immediate area of S) affords a perfect parallel to שנת גאלי.

[165] The real link with S as well as with H from Is. 24 is given expressly by the homilist himself. He quotes Akila's rendering of עקילס תרגום which reads: מיצטרא מכירין. Akila employs here the Greek word *maxaira* (swords, knives) which re-echoes מכר in S and H.

It may be noted that the play on the Hebrew root מכר as identical with the Greek *maxaira* seems to have been a favored one with certain exegetical circles in Palestine. Various Midrashic sources interpret מכרתיהם in Gen. 49.5 "swords," as if it were the Greek *maxaira* (cp. Midrash Aggada, ed Buber, 1894, I, 109a, note 12).

[166] Here again the homilist provided us with the key to the tally with S

by quoting this time the Aramaic rendering of חומת אנך which reads: שורא
דאוניתא, related to אונאה cheating, fraud, and, of course, intimately connected
with אל תונו.

[167] By the same token Num. 2.34 tallies also with S (Lev. 25.18: ועשיתם
את חקתי...ועשיתם אותם). However, it seems to me that we have here
again a more artificial tally. We should include in the Num. v. also the
clause כן חנו לדגליהם. In the Palestinian dialect *Heth* and *He* are interchange-
able, and it sounds as if it were written: כן הונו לדגליהם, linking it up with
אל תונו in our S.

[168] By means of מכה רבה there is a linguistic link with S and H from
Is. 24 (cp. Lev. 25.16: ...לפי רב; Is. 24.22: ומרב ימים).

[169] The peroration v. from Is. 49.26 tallies with the H from Is. by means
of אמונת אמן in Is. 25.1. This v. may be included in the H, and in all events
remains within its area.

[170] In our notes we have tried to show that the H from Is. 24 is not entirely void of links with the Midrashic material, and that the S accounts
for almost all the material. The need for a new Ezek. Hafṭarah remains
therefore problematic, the more so since no reasonable explanation is given
for the dropping of the "old H."

[171] With regard to the H to this S, we should bear in mind that this S
is but an alternate to the previous one, starting 25.14, and that the topic
remains the same. It therefore would seem logical that we should try to
ascertain whether the same H, viz. Is. 24.2: כקונה כמוכר...והיה כעם ככהן
could not have been used also by those who started the S Lev. 25.25. There
is the same tally, as in the previous S, by means of כמוכר, re-echoing כי ימוך
אחיך ומכר in the new S.

As to the arrangement of the H, I would suggest Is. 24.2–3 (כי ה')
דבר), 25.1–8, concluding with a similar phrase (כי ה' דבר את הדבר הזה.
In this way H would include Is. 25.4: כי היית מעוז לדל מעוז לאביון בצר לו, a most
fitting motto for both Sedarim, and which might have been the magnetic
center, the determining factor in the choice of the H in this area.

As to the כי motif, this is well furnished by our S.

In the sequel we shall investigate whether the suggested H from Is. 24.2
would account for the Midrashic data.

[172] Concerning Prov. 22.22 f., there is in the first place the obvious tally
with S by means of דל, עני synonym of כי ימוך. Still more striking is the tally
with Is. 25.4: מחסה לאביון מעוז לדל כי היית מעוז which constitutes a perfect
counterpart to אל תגזל דל כי ה' יריב ריבם.

[173] Jer. 50.34 f. tallies in the first place with S, where the term גאל occurs
several times, by means of גואלם. Moreover, the clause למען הרגיע את
הארץ in the Pet. v. affords a striking contrast to Is. 24.18–20: וירעשו
מוסדי ארץ; רעה התרועעה ארץ; נוע תנוע ארץ... within the
suggested H.

[174] The link with Ps. 106.44 is provided by the clause: וירא בצר להם
בצר לו...כי היית מעוז לדל which reflects Is. 24.14: בשמעו את רנתם, and
Is. 25.4: המה ישאו קולם ירננו.

[175] Ps. 148.14: וירם קרן לעמו tallies perfectly with the last v. of the
suggested H (Is. 25.8): וחרפת עמו יסיר which in negative terms expresses
the same thing that Ps. 148.14 does in positive terms.

Thus all the Midrashic material could be accounted for by S and the H
from Is. 24.2, 25.8, and there seems to be no compelling reason for any non-
recorded H.

We readily admit that the H proposed by the A. affords easier connections with the Petiḥtot and with the substance of the homily, but this
is not sufficient ground to consider the introduction of a non-recorded H as
an established fact.

[176] We have here a reversal, to a certain extent, in the A.'s approach to
the problem of the relationship between S and H. Thus far the A. seems to
have shared Büchler's opinion, viz. that the Hafṭarot to TC, their main
purpose being consolation, were not always selected on the basis of intrinsic
affinity with the corresponding S, but often by mere linguistic tally. It
seems therefore strange to see the A. stating that "we must look for a prophetic portion that emphasizes the same topic."

This shift of emphasis seems to have been the result of overemphasizing
the weight of the H in the formation of the homilies. In order to carry such
weight the H must absorb the substance of S. But if we consider S as essential a factor in the structure of the homily as H, so that linkage with S may
sometimes dispense with a H tally, we should have no difficulty in assuming
that occasionally mere linguistic tally was decisive in the selection of a prophetic portion as H.

[177] In the preceding S beginning with כי ימוך we found several Petiḥtot
containing the term דל or some synonym of it which served as direct link
with S. In these cases we thought that any "flexible" link with H would
suffice, and that we might even dispense with a H tally altogether. The
same holds good here with regard to the two Petiḥtot, i. e., from Ps. 41.1
and from Prov. 19.17; both are linked up directly with S by means of דל.

[178] While the first half of Prov. 11.17 גמל נפשו איש חסד affords a tally with
the Is. H, as pointed out by the A., the second half: ועכר שארו אכזרי
tallies with S (Lev. 26.49: יגאלנו...בשרו מששאר או).

[179] The latter is obviously a supporting v. connected with the former by
means of verbal and intrinsic links.

[180] Not necessarily. We should bear in mind that the last clause of Koh.
5.13 reads: ואין בידו מאומה which is but a circumlocution for דל and its
synonyms. Accordingly, it is linked up directly with S (cp. our note 139).
There is also a token tally with H Is. by means of ידים (רפות ידים חזקו).

[181] As for Ps. 106.43, we should include also v. 44: וירא בצר להם בשמעו
את רנתם, and we obtain also a link with H Is. by means of רנה (Is. 35.10:
ובאו ציון ברנה).

[182] By the same token it also tallies with S because of כי ימוך which is
equivalent to אביון; the second half of the v.: נפשי משפטי מששיע להושיע reflects H: גמול...יבא וישיעכם (Is. 35.4).

[183] As in most of the other Pet., 1 Sam. 2.7 is primarily connected with S by means of מוריש, synonym of כי ימוך. Moreover, the second half of the v.: וכסא כבוד ינחילם reflects Is. 35.2: (כבוד ה') (המה יראו כבוד ה') which precedes transmitted H.

[184] The A. has overlooked that, in accordance with all MSS and earlier editions, this item is placed before סדום (Kohut, VI, p. 23).

[185] It seems that something has been omitted here. I suggest to add: "on the other hand with אם בחקתי in S."

[186] Here the principal association is with S. Indeed, Hos. 9.17 is but a variation of Lev. 26.14, 33. ·

[187] Though the verbal tallies with H are manifest, they are only secondary ones; the real link is with S, and has to be looked for in the area of the Pet. v. Indeed, it is the term תוכחה which occurs twice in the area (Prov. 1.23: תשובו לתוכחתי; 1.25: ותוכחתי לא אביתם) which constitutes the center of attraction for our S that is known by the name of תוכחה or תוכחות.

[188] We readily admit that technically the structure of this homily seems to be dependent on H. But it should not be ignored that the theme is indicated in our S (Lev. 26.44), and more articulated in the corresponding תוכחה S in Deut. 30.1–10 which passage was, in all probability, in the mind of the homilist.

[189] The main intrinsic connection of this v. is with S, since ואשיבה (אם בחקתי, ואלכה בחקתיך is but a variation of רגלי אל עדותיך תלכו).

[190] The main association is obviously with S, viz. paralleling ואת מצותי תשמרו (Lev. 26.3), and contrasting ואם לא תשמעו לי ולא תעשו את כל המצות (Lev. 26.33).

[191] As to the peroration, it should be added that we find it in LR joined to a comment on Mal. 3.10: והריקתי לכם ברכה עד בלי די. This v. is, in all probability, linked up with S because it forms a contrast to והריקתי אחריכם חרב (Lev. 26.33). Moreover, there seems to be a hint to the S as a whole in the word ברכה, our S being known under the name of ברכות וקללות.

There is no need to stress that the *peroration* v. from Ezek. is primarily connected with S, since והורדתי הגשם בעתו is almost a citation of ונתתי גשמיכם בעתם (Lev. 26.4).

[192] The choice of this Pet. v. containing the verb זבה, may be due to the name תוכחה attached to our S (cp. above our note 184).

[193] Both supporting vv., Ps. 81.14 (לו עמי שומע לי ישראל בדרכי) & Is. 48.18 (לו הקשבת למצותי וכו') (יהלכו כמעט איביהם אכניע) mentioned by the A. as well as Deut. 5.26 (מי יתן והיה לבבם זה...ולשמור את כל מצותי) are so intimately related to our S (Lev. 26.3: ואת מצותי...אם בחקתי תלכו; 26.14: וכו'; 26.8: ונפלו איביכם לפניכם (ואם לא תשמעו לי וכו'; תשמרו) that there seems to be no need for any intermediary link of the H.

[194] It is to be greatly regretted that no traces of the discussion referred to here could be found in the A.'s notes. The suggestion seems to me rather well taken. We should bear in mind that, according to a Baraita (Meg. 31b),

such reading on fast-days started at Lev. 26.13 and concluded at 26.42 (תנא
כשהוא מתחיל מתחיל בפסוק שלפניהן וכשהוא מסיים מסיים בפסוק שלאחריהן). Instead of
the beginning of a new S, we would have here the conclusion of a Torah
portion serving as point of departure for a homily. The Midrashic material,
as we shall see, is well linked up with this Torah portion.

The existence of a new S here and its H derived from LR, c. 36, should
be considered as a plausible suggestion, but not as an established fact.

[195] It should be added that by means of הארץ the Pet. v. tallies directly
with S (והארץ אזכר).

[196] Assuming that we have here a homily for S(f), comprising Lev.
26.12–42, our Pet. v. would be linked up with the beginning and conclusion
of this Torah portion; both contain the mention of the Exodus from Egypt
((מצרים).

[197] Intrinsically Prov. 11.21 is closely related to S. Indeed, the promise
in Lev. 27.42 that Israel will be saved for the sake of its ancestors is but a
particular case of the general maxim in Prov. 11.9: זרע צדיקים נמלט.

[198] Is. 41.1 is also linked to S, or S(f), by means of the name "Jacob."
We should, in all probability, include also the last clause of the Is. v.: קראתי
בשמך לי אתה which corresponds to Lev. 26.12: ואתם תהיו לי לעם.
This v. is closely related to the following v., the beginning of S(f).

[199] It should be added that if we take into consideration the verse וכל
חרם אשר יחרם מן האדם מות יומת (Lev. 27.29), we obtain a perfect parallelism
with the Jephthah topic (cp. Naḥmanides' commentary on Pentateuch, a. l.).

[200] An additional tally with S can be obtained by means of אדם (Lev.
27.29: האדם מן חרם וכל= אדם פעל). There might also be a more subtle
connection through the similarity of פ(ע)ל and יפל(א). We should keep in
mind that in the Palestinian idiom אלף and עין are often dropped. As to the
intrinsic link, see מהרז"ו a. l.

[201] The correspondence of the Pet. v. (יערך לה') to S (בערכך לה') being
obvious, the homilist might have thought that he could dispense with a substantial H link. He contented himself with a "slim" tally, consisting of the
word יערך לה' to Pet., S and transmitted H (Jud. 11.30, 31: נדר לה', והיה לה').

[202] As pointed out by the A., the Pet. v. is linked up with S. by means of
נפשות. There was no need to allude to the transmitted H by any artificial
device, since the homilist introduced the Jephthah topic expressly into his
homily and dwelled on it at some length.

[203] An exploration of the area of the first v. in the peroration, viz. Is.
30.33, reveals a surprising tally with the transmitted H. In fact, the preceding v., Is. 30.32, reads: והיה כל מעבר... אשר יניח ה' עליו בתפים ובכנרות
ויעבר יפתח... , ובמלחמות..., re-echoing Jud. 11.32, 34: נלחם בה בה
להלחם בם... והנה בתו יצאת לקראתו בתפים ובמחלות.

It should be added that the Tanḥuma section which contains the
peroration introduces Mic. 6.6–7. Through במה אקדם לה' can be linked up
with S (בערכך לה') as well as with the transmitted H (נדר לה').
Moreover, the homilist seems to have intentionally directed our attention to

the passage containing the phrase האתן פרי בטני חטאת נפשי because of its allusion to the Jephthah story, the transmitted H.

[204] In view of our last few remarks, it would appear that the second
Hafṭarah should not yet be admitted to the realm of "necessary" existence,
but should, for the time being, be confined to the region of probabilities.

NUMBERS

Seder 101 (1)[183]

'וידבר ה' אל משה במדבר סיני באהל מועד וגו, Num. 1.1.

Haftarah: לכן הנה אנכי מפתיה והולכתיה המדבר ודברתי על
לבה, Hosea 2.16 (so C 8, but the extent is not indicated by
Abrahams). Probably it comprised 2.16 to 25 (10 verses). For
the same Prophetic lection to S 48a see above vol. I, pp. 374 ff.
Concerning the possibility of a different H to the present S
which commenced at Hos. 2.1, see infra, p. 183.

H links up with S by reason of the italicized expressions.
Moreover, in the former there is an allusion to the exodus from
Egypt (Hos. 2.17: וכיום עלותה מארץ מצרים) just as in the latter,
(Num. 1.1: לצאתם מארץ מצרים).

Structure of Homilies

No Y topic with question and answer has been preserved.
The citations in Arukh from the Y section to our S[184] correspond
partially to what is found in TB (and parallels), viz. the quotation s. v. אפופסין (cp. TB, Bammidbar, §7, end) and the one
s. v. אפרכיא (cp. TB, §5, beginning).[185]

---

[183] The figure in parenthesis indicates the respective number of the S in
Numbers proper. See above, note 1, with regard to Leviticus, and cp. vol.
I, p. 358, note 380, with regard to Exodus.

[184] S. v. סנמוס, 2 מסא, איפרכיא, אפופסין.

[185] The latter passage (ed. Kohut, I, 240) needs rectification: ובילמדנו בריש
וידבר ה' אל משה במדבר סיני: כתוב לך (צ"ל: לה, וכן לפי נ"א: כתוב ל ך כתובה, צ"ל:
כתוב ל ה כתובה) באי זה כתובה, באי זו שנה, באיזה חודש, בכמה בחודש,
אמר (צ"ל: שבוע) באי זה שבועה. This corresponds to TB, §5, beginning (see NR, c. 1.5) איפרכיא
לשושבינו: אל תנהוג בה כבראשונות . . . כתוב לה כתובה באיזה שבוע, באיזו שנה, וכו'.

175

There is a parallel section in TB, §§1–8, T, §§1–8, and NR, c. 1.1–9, which presupposes the above H from Hos. 2.16–25. The first Pet. introduces Ps. 36.7: צדקתך כהררי אל משפטיך ואָרשׂתיך לי בצדק ובמשפט :H which v. tallies with תהום רבה (Hos. 2.21).[18] The second Pet. is from Jer. 2.31: הדור אתם ראו דבר ה' המדבר הייתי לישראל אם ארץ מאפליה מדוע אמרו עמי רדנו וגו'. In addition to the word 'wilderness' common to both S and H, this Pet. v. contains also a reference to Israel as God's people (עמי), corresponding to the final v. of the Prophetic lection (Hos. 2.25): ואמרתי ללא עמי עמי אתה. The whole Agg. depicting Israel's refusal to rejoin God, because of His departure from their midst, and the latter's nostalgia so-to-say for the scenes of the wilderness[186] is reflected by the initial v. of H which describes so tenderly God's reconciliation with Israel while alluring it to follow Him into the wilderness in order to speak there upon its heart (Hos. 2.16). There is a further Pet. on Cant. 7.3 wherein the mentioning of 'wheat' (ערמת חטים) links up with the more comprehensive noun of 'grain' (דגן) in the H v. (Hos. 2.24).[28] There follow comments on Ps. 147.20 and 148.14 wherein there is the tally of משפטים (in the former v.) with ובמשפט in Hos. 2.21 and of עמו . . . עם קרובו (in the latter v.) with עמי אתה in 2.25. Ps. 148.14 is also mentioned at the end of the Midrashic section under discussion (TB, §8, T, §8, NR, c. 1.9).[38] This conclusion offers no proper *peroration*, with the usual allusion to the happy state of affairs in the future. Such seems rather to be found where §3 terminates: או"ה רואים לישראל (ולעתיד) בת"ה: ולעוה"ב היאך הקב"ה עמהם, והם באים להתדבק בהם שנ' בימים ההמה אשר יחזיקו עשרה אנשים מכל לשונות הגוים והחזיקו בכנף איש יהודי לאמר נלכה עמכם כי שמענו אלהים עמכם. This final v. cited (Zech. 8.23), with its promise of the universal recognition of God's presence among Israel, reflects well the final v. of H which foretells the mutual acknowledgment of each other as to the special relationship of Deity and people: ואמרתי ללא עמי עמי אתה והוא יאמר אלהי. Moreover, there is a tally in בימים ההמה with והיה ביום ההוא in H (Hos. 2.18 and 23).

---

[186] אמרו לו: נתת לנו ביהמ"ק, וסילקת שכינתך ממנו, ומה אתה מבקש ממנו עוד, לא נבוא עוד אליך (יר' ב', ל"א). אמר להם: ומי יתן לי והייתי כמדבר עכשיו, היכן שעשיתי לכם כל אותן הנסים . . . היכן שהייתי מתקלס. See also infra, p. 177.

The remainder of NR, c. 1, viz. §§10–12 (missing in the Tanḥumas), contains comments on the last verses of the S (to wit Num. 1.46 ff.) which are of an Aggadic-exegetical nature and require no analysis for our purpose. About similar comments in NR, cps. 2–3, see infra, pp. 184 and 194.

In MHG, IV (ed. Fisch, Manchester 1940, pp. 146–8), the section to the present S begins with a Pet, from Hos. 2.25: זש"ה וזרעתיה לי בארץ . . . והוא יאמר אלהי, נאמר הפסוק הזה כנגד ישראל, שהן עושין רצונו של מקום ולפיכך יש להן זריעה. . . ויש להן שורש . . . ויש להן נטיעה וכו'. Such a Pet. is rather strange since the v. forms the final one of H; the sermonic technique consisted rather of using an extraneous v. (mostly from the Hagiogr.) and linking it up with S and H (yet see above, vol. I, pp. 73, 166, and 360; cp. further above, p. 103). There follows in MHG a comment which is really based on Cant. 7.3, without, however, citing this v. as a Pet. as in Tanḥ. and in NR (ibid., p. 147, top: וכן את מוצא שנמשלו ישראל בחטים ואוה"ע נמשלו בקש וכו'). Subsequently (pp. 150–53) Cant. 7.3 is used as such but in this item the main point is not in connection with ערמת חטים but with סוגה בשושנים (see further on). Lastly there is given the same Agg. as in TB, §5, T, §5, NR, c. 1.5, without prefacing the Pet. verses from Ps. 147.20 and 148.4 (pp. 147–8: מלה"ד למלך שנשא אשה ולא היתה הגונה וכו'). This last item is also couched differently and concludes: אבל ישראל כשעמדו לפני הר סיני וקבלו את התורה, אמר הקב"ה למשה איני נוהג בהם כראשונים, הואיל וקבלו את תורתי הריני מקרבם לתחת כנפי שכינתי, פקוד אותם והודע באיזה מקום, באיזה חנייה, באיזה חדש, בכמה בחדש, באיזו שנה, באיזה פרק נכנסו תחת כנפי השכינה, מניין ממה שקרינו בענין, וידבר ה' וכו'. The whole homily seems to emanate from a new version of a Midr. to Num. which the author of MHG had before him.[48] We have further there (l. c., pp. 149–50) the Pet. from Jer. 2.31, headed by ר' יהודה פתח and concluded by the formula: מנין, ממה שקרינו בענין, which again reveals a different presentation of the homily (see above, note 186, as compared to here, p. 176: ולמה אתם אומרים לא נבוא עוד אליך, הלא המדבר מעיד בכם, שבו עשה לכם הקב"ה כמה נסים, ובו ייחס אתכם ע"י משה, מנין, ממה שקרינו בענין וידבר ה' אל משה וגו'). Finally there is given (pp. 150–53) the Pet. from Cant. 7.3 which too is differently treated. Whereas in Tanḥ. and NR the main point is the preciousness of Israel which is being counted as wheat is (commenting on ערמת חטים), in MHG the homily is continued also with regard to סוגה בשושנים (incorporating much of the material also found in Cant. R., *a. l.*), and *in connection with the latter* there is the return to the beginning of S: הא לפי שהיו גדורין מן העריות זכו להתיחס למשפחתם לבית אבותם, שהן שקולין כאבותיהם: אברהם, יצחק ויעקב, ולפיכך נמנו בכניסתן למצרים וביציאתן ממצרים, כשבאו להכנס תחת כנפי השכינה, מנין, ממה שקרינו בענין וידבר ה' אל משה...שאו את ראש כל עדת בני ישראל למשפחותם לבית אבותם. Anew we gather the impression that in MHG a new version of a Midr. to Numbers is offered (cp. also infra, p. 189).[5s] About a further new version see infra, H. pt., p. סח.

SEDER 102 (2)

וידבר ה' אל משה ואל אהרן לאמר איש על דגלו באותות לבית אבותם יחנו בני ישראל מנגד סביב לאהל מועד יחנו, Num. 2.1–2.

Ḥafṭarah: None is available from the Genizah lists at our disposal. Also Yannai's Ḳerobah (ed. Zulay, pp. 177–78) is defective, with the part indicating the initial v. of H missing. However, the Midrashic data, to be analyzed forthwith, presuppose a Prophetic lection, that commenced with Is. 55.13: תחת הנעצוץ יעלה ברוש ותחת הסרפד יעלה הדס והיה לה' לשם לאות עולם לא יכרת tallying with S by means of the noun 'sign' (אות). This reading extended to 56.8 (hence 9 verses). With 56.9 there begins a new Seder in Isaiah, testifying to the fact that a H started here.[6s]

This lection is essentially of a consolatory character, with the linguistic connection with S consisting merely of a common noun. However, there is intrinsically a fine correlation of the two, inasmuch as Num. c. 2 depicts the encamping of all the tribes of Israel around the Tabernacle, and correspondingly there is the promise in H that God's Temple will be a universal house of prayer (Is. 56.7) and the scattered ones of Israel will be gathered (v. 8) — thus resulting in Palestine becoming again the home of the whole Jewish people with the Temple of Jerusalem being the national center, as was the case with the Tabernacle in the wilderness. This will account for the choice of the above H here.[78]

STRUCTURE OF HOMILIES

1. *Y Sermon.* TB, Bammidbar, §9, T, §9[187] . . . 'וידבר ה
איש על דגלו באותות לבית אבותם וגו', ילמדנו רבינו: בתוך כמה אמות מותר
לאדם (היינו: מישראל) להלך בשבת (ובת"ה: בתוך כמה אמות אדם יכול
להלוך בשבת), כך שנו רבותינו השובת בדרך עושה לו עגולות עד ארבע
אמות, דברי ר' חנניא בן אנטיגנוס וכו'.[188]

The starting point is to be found in H where the observance of the Sabbath and the refraining from desecrating it are commanded (Is. 56.2, 4, and 6). Hence the question and answer concerning one's conduct when compelled to spend the Sabbath on the road outside an inhabited locality. As an example for the limit of 2,000 cubits in each direction there is cited the injunction of Joshua to the people to keep the same distance away from the Ark (Josh. 3.4). This is explained here as contemplated for the stay in front of Jericho so that on Sabbath the people should be able to approach the Ark in order to pray in front of it.[189] The allusion to praying on Sabbath is due to H where, in conjunction with the observance of this day of rest (Is. 56.6), there is the promise of being brought to 'My Holy Mountain' and made happy 'in My House of *Prayer*' (v. 7). Likewise the encampment of the tribes under their banners around the Tabernacle was at a distance of 2,000 cubits. Here-

---

[187] In NR, c. 2.9, the Y topic is placed within the section (see infra, p. 181) with the question omitted and the answer introduced by: תמן תנינן השובת בדרך וכו'. Cp. also infra, notes 217, 224, 269. The present Y item is also reproduced in YSH, Num, §684, and partially is cited in 'Arukh עבר 5 (Kohut, V, 162): בילמדנו בריש וי ד ב ר: השובת במדינה וכו' (the indication 'at the beginning of וידבר' is not exact since the passage belongs already to the section for the second Seder of Numbers).[79*]

[188] Concerning the sources of this Hal. see Buber's notes, *a. l.*, and GS, I, 475, No. 61.

[189] אמר להם יהושע: עתידים אתם לעשות שם את השבת, אל תרחקו מן הארון יותר מן אלפים אמה לכל רוח, למה, שתהיו רשאין לבוא להתפלל לפני הארון בשבת.

with there is a return to the beginning of the S,[190] thereby completing the first portion of the Y sermon.

Here follows in TB, §10, T, §10 (as the parallel section in NR, c. 2, see further on), a Pet. from Ps. 20.6: נרננה בישועתך ובשם אלהינו נדגול וכו', which v. tallies, on the one hand, with S by means of נדגול (as compared to איש על דגלו) and, on the other hand, with H by means of בישועתך (as compared to Is. 56.1: כי קרובה ישועתי לבוא). The sentence 'and in the name of our God we shall set up standards' is homiletically interpreted to mean that He 'inserted His name into ours (viz., El forming the end of Israel) and grouped us into banners'.[191] This comment is reflected by the initial v. of H (Is. 55.13): והיה לה' לשם לאות עולם לא יכרת. There is also woven into this item Cant. 2.4 הביאני אל בית היין ודגלו עלי אהבה supplying again a link with S (by means of ודגלו) and with H (by means of הביאני as compared to Is. 56.7: והביאותים אל הר קדשי). This v. is also used as a Pet. in TB, §15, T, §14=NR, c. 2.3 (end).[8s] A further Pet. (TB, §11, T, §11) introduces Cant. 6.10: מי זאת הנשקפה כמו שחר יפה כלבנה ברה כחמה איומה כנדגלות the point of connection with H being זאת as compared to Is. 56.2: אשרי אנוש יעשה זאת (in addition to the con-

---

[190] The conclusion in TB and T is defective: כן אתה מוצא כשאמר האלהים למשה שישרה את ישראל דגלים (וכן בבמ"ר, וביל"ש ובת"ה: שיעשה לו דגלים), א'ל: השרה (וכן בבמ"ר וביל"ש, ובת"ה: השוה) אותם לדגליהם לכל רוח (וצריך להוסיף כמו ביל"ש: מנין אלפים אמה, או כמו בבמ"ר: רחוק אלפים אמה). מנין? ממה שקראו בענין, איש על דגלו יחנו באותות לבית אבותם. Now there is no explanation of how Num. 2.2 indicates the distance of 2,000 cubits. However, this is found in NR: א'ל: השרה אותם לכל רוח רהוק אלפים אמה, שנ' מנגד סביב לאהל מועד יחנו, מה מנגד, אמר ר' יצחק מרחוק מיל, שהם אלפים אמה. This passage evidently was also inserted in the original Y item prior to the concluding formula: מנין? ממה וכו'. In the present version of Tanḥ. R. Isaac's inference is found farther on (TB, 3.16, beginning, T, §14, middle): מהו מנגד, א'ר יצחק מרחוק מיל, אמר הקב"ה: יהיו ישראל רחוקים מן הארון אלפים אמה, שנ' אך רחוק יהיה ביניכם וביניו כאלפים אמה וגו' (יה' ג', ד').

[191] ובשם אלהינו נדגול, שקבע הקב"ה שמו בשמותינו ועשה אותנו דגלים, שנ' איש על דגלו באותות, so in TB and in NR, c. 2.2. In T (in the early editions): ושהקב"ה שהקב"ה שם שמו בשמותינו, but in YSH, Num. §684: שמו כשמותינו ועשה עמנו דגלים ועשה אותנו דגלים. See also the reading in YHM, to Ps. 20 (ed., Buber, I, 142): שהקב"ה הבב את ישראל, שם שמו בשמותינו ועשה אותנו דגלים דגלים.

tact with S by means of כנדגלות).⁹⁸ ¹⁹¹ᵃ The next item (TB, §12,
T, §12) employs Job 36.3: אשא דעי למרחוק ולפועלי אתן צדק
tallying with H v. (Is. 56.1): וצדקתי להגלות. Thereupon
(TB, §14, T, §13) Deut. 32.10 is dealt with Aggadically; here
the verb נצר (יצרנהו) is a synonym of שמר in H (Is. 56.1 ff.).¹⁰⁸
Finally there is the *peroration* (TB, §16, end, T, §14, end):
א"ל הקב"ה: בעוה"ז עשיתי אתכם דגלים, שנ' איש על דגלו (ובת"ה: בעוה"ז
נתאויתם לדגלים ומצאתי משאלותיכם),¹⁹², ולעוה"ב אני מדלג וגואל אתכם
(ובת"ה: ולע"ל בזכות הדגלים אני גואל אתכם ומדלג על הקץ בזכות אבות
שנקראו הרים), שנ' קול דודי הנה זה בא מדלג על ההרים מקפץ על הגבעות.
In this final v. cited (Cant. 2.8) מדלג is evidently taken homiletically as akin to מדגל so as to link up with דגלו in S, but the
connection with H would be in ההרים as compared to ה ר קדשי
in Is. 56.7 (cp. also בא here and והביאותים there).¹¹⁸

2. As regards NR, c. 2, the first part is essentially the same
as the section in the Tanḥumas. The initial Y topic (above,
p. 179) is placed within this part (§9) and is introduced by
תמן תנינן, with the formula ילמדנו רבינו וכו' being omitted. This
procedure is noticeable several times in NR, up to C 14 inclusive,
and resembles the one in ER.¹⁹³ The first item (§1) concerning
God's order being directed simultaneously to Moses and Aaron
(as in Num. 2.1) eighteen times in the Pentateuch, corresponding
to the same number of benedictions in the Amidah, is late (as
is apparent from the style) and does not belong to the section
under discussion. There follow the Petiḥtot (§§2–4) on Ps. 20.6,
Cant. 2.4 and 6.10 respectively. From §5 it would seem as if

---

¹⁹¹ᵃ Here again MHG, IV, p. 161–2, offers a different version of this
Pet. resembling more Cant. R., *a. l.* It begins: זש"ה מי זאת הנשקפה כמו שחר
יפה כלבנה ברה כחמה מדבר בכנסת ישראל, ולמה נמשלה כנסת ישראל בלבנה, ללמדך כשם
שהלבנה היא שולטת ביום ובלי לה וכו'.

¹⁹² The reference here is to the Agg. at the beginning of the item (TB,
§15, T, §14) that at Sinai the hosts of angels appeared grouped under banners, and that Israel, on beholding them, desired the same arrangement
which request was granted unto them (כיון שראו אותם ישראל שהם עשוים דגלים
דגלים היו מתאוים לדגלים...א"ל הקב"ה: נתאויתם לדגלים, חייכם שאני עושה שאלתכם
וכו').

¹⁹³ See above, vol. I, pp. 372; 389, note 419, 408, 429 and 547, and cp.
ibid., II. pt., p. 92.

there was another Pet. from Cant. 6.4. However, this item is
really an adjunct to §4 (on Cant. 6.10) because both verses conclude with איומה כנדגלות. In TB, §13, end, T, §12, end, the former
is given in a different connection (ורוה"ק אומרת ע"י שלמה יפה את
רעיתי כתרצה וגו') without being intended as a separate Petiḥtah.
In NR (§8) we have further the homily on Job 36.3. The long
piece concerning the order of the banners (§10) is extraneous to
the sermon discussed here, but herein is found a passage (from
חגי יהודה חגיך to את מוצא בכל מקום) which pertains to the end of our
section (see TB, §16, T, §14) preceding directly the *peroration*
(above, p. 181). The latter itself is missing altogether in NR
(about the further analysis of NR, c. 2, 19 ff., see infra, p. 185).

3. In connection with Num. 2.32: אלה פקודי בני ישראל וגו'
there is given in NR a Midrashic section (c. 2.11–18) which
would seem as if meant for a separate Seder. There is even
listed the initial v. of a H (Hos. 2.1) upon which several Aggadot
are being developed (thus §12: אלה פקודי בני ישראל וגו', הה"ד
והיה מספר בני ישראל וגו'. והיה מספר בני ישראל, הה"ד לעולם ה' דברך
נצב בשמים וכו'). We have thus a replica of the chapter headed
Nebiim in AB which is also traceable elsewhere.[194] Yet it is
very difficult to assume that Num. 2.32 formed the commencement of a new Torah lection for which there is no other evidence
whatever. It would indeed be a peculiar procedure, since verses
32–34 naturally conclude the topic of c. 2; cp. the parallel in
c. 2 v. 34: ויעשו בני ישראל ככל אשר צוה ה' את משה to 1.54, which
latter v. constituted the ending of the previous S (No. 101) just
as 2.34 should be the same of the present S. Indeed the next
regular S is at 3.1 (No. 103, infra, p. 185). It is true that with
regard to the latter there was a shifting either to 3.5–6 (No. 103a,
infra, p. 190), or to 3.14–15 (No. 103b, infra, p. 195), but neither
instance involves the breaking up of c. 2 as would be the case
of an assumed S at 2.32.

It therefore appears that the Midrashic section under discussion has been originally intended for the beginning of the

---

[194] Above, vol. I, p. 57, and frequently in connection with the analysis
of AB to each S in Genesis; and with regard to ER, pp. 421, 474, 500–1,
505–6.

fourth book of Moses, viz. to S 101. It has been inserted here
in NR because of the tendency of this Midrash (viz. till c. 14
inclusive) to incorporate extensively the available Aggadic material wherever there was room for it (see infra, p. 194). In
other words, these homilies are based on a different H to this S,
to wit Hos. 2.1 ff. instead of Hos. 2.16 ff. (above, p. 175).[128]
With Hos. 2.1 there started the Prophetic lection not only
according to the Babylonian AC ritual, but also according to
the Byzantine Rabbanite custom, later on adopted by the
Karaites of Byzantium, Turkey and the Crimea. The latter
usage was to retain for each Sidra one of the several previous
Haftarot of TC to the Sedarim comprised within the compass
of that Sidra (see above, vol. I, p. 91). There is thus evidence
in the present case for the conclusion that according to TC there
were two different lections to S 101, viz. one being Hos. 2.16 ff.
and another Hos. 2.1 ff. To the latter pertains NR, c. 2.11–18,
whereas NR, c. 1.1–9 was based on the previous H (above, p. 176),
corresponding to the structure of AB where occasionally the
chapter headed Torah presupposed one Prophetic lection to the
respective S while the chapter headed Nebiim had another one
as its basis (above, vol. I, p. 57).

Now, Hos. 2.1: והיה מספר בני ישראל וגו' would tally
verbally with Num. 1.2: ... שאו את ראש כל עדת בני ישראל
במספר שמות וגו'. Furthermore, there is the intrinsic contrast
that whereas in the S there is recorded the sum total of the
census of the Israelites in the wilderness, in the H we read the
Prophetic promise of Israel's multitude becoming as numerous
'as the sand of the sea that cannot be measured nor counted.'
As regards the extent of this TC H, it certainly did not comprise
22 verses (viz. till וארשתיך לי באמונה וגו') as according to the
AC ritual followed by that of Byzantium. We have rather to
assume that in Palestine the lection comprised Hos. 2.1–9,
skipping to v. 25 in order to conclude with a verse of consolation (נחמת ישראל). Moreover, the end of v. 25: ואמרתי ללא עמי
עמי אתה והוא יאמר אלהי would link up with that of the initial v.
of H (2.1: והיה במקום אשר יאמר להם לא עמי אתם יאמר להם בני אל חי).
Thus the H contained 10 verses, as was the usual procedure.

To continue with the analysis of the respective homilies in

NR, c. 2. In connection with Hos. 2.1 there is (§12) the Pet.
from Ps. 119.89: לעולם ה' דברך נצב ב ש מ י ם which tallies with
Hos. 2.23: אענה את ה ש מ י ם (this in the skipped part). The
beginning of the item is curtailed and has to be reconstructed by
means of the partially parallel passage in ER, c. 38.6.[195] There
follow Aggadic comments on Hos. 2.1 proper (§§13–15 and 18),
but in §16 there is given a further Pet. from Cant. 8.7–8 where
the expressions אהבה and אחות afford links with אחותיכם and
מאהבי in Hos. 2.3 and 7. Another Pet. (§17) is from Ezra 8.34:
ב מ ס פ ר במשקל לכל וגו'. Finally §11 should be added which may
have formed the conclusion of this section, except that it is
curtailed towards the end with the *peroration* missing. There
we have the Agg. concerning the census of Israel taking place
ten times, the last one being in the hereafter (citing Jer. 33.13).[196]
Now the last item would contradict the promise in Hos. 2.1 of
Israel being uncountable. However, from the *peroration* in TB,
Ki Tissa, §8 (and parallels listed there),[197] it is evident that all
these censuses are meant as human ones, with the last one done
by orders of the Messiah.[198] But the final one in the still more
distant future will be done by God Himself as a result of which
Israel's numbers will be limitless; here Hos. 2.1 is cited explicitly
as proof of the case in point.

4. The remainder of NR, c. 2, needs only brief remarks, as it
is of an Aggadic-exegetical nature and does not pertain to the
sermons discussed here (cp. also above, p. 177, and infra, p. 194).
In §10 there is a running comment on Num. 2.3–31, allegorizing

---

[195] Here there is the abrupt statement: הה"ד לעולם ה' דברך נצב בשמים, מפני
הה"ד לעולם ה' דברך נצב בשמים, but in ER we read: שהבטיח הקב"ה את אברהם וכו'
וכי אין דברו של הקב"ה נצב בארץ אלא בשמים, (א'ר חזקיה בר חייא) מפני שהבטיח הקב"ה
דבר בשמים וכו'.[80]*

[196] בעשרה מקומות נמנו ישראל... ואחד לעתיד לבוא, עוד תעבורנה הצאן על ידי
מונה (יר' ל"נ, י"ג).

[197] אתה מוצא י' פעמים נמנו ישראל... ואחת לע"ל, שנ' עוד תעבורנה הצאן על ידי
מונה, אמר הקב"ה: בעוה"ז היו בני אדם סופרים (בפסדר"כ: מונין) אתכם, אבל לעולם הבא
אני אספור אתכם (ובפסדר"כ: אבל לע"ל אני מברך אתכם), ואין מי יספור אתכם, והיה מספר
בני ישראל כחול הים אשר לא ימד ולא יספר.

[198] Cp. the Genizah text (above, vol. I, H. pt., p. 130): י' פעמים נמנו ישראל
ט' לשעבר, ועשירי לעתיד לבוא שימנו על ידי משיח... לעתיד, עוד תעבורנה הצאן על ידי
מונה.

the arrangement of the four banners with the respective tribes
gathered around them as corresponding to the four sides of the
universe and to the four angels surrounding God's throne. This
item is introduced by the citation of Prov. 3.20 which however,
should not be taken as a Pet. proper; it was the tendency of this
extensive Midr. to expatiate on its detailed exegesis (see especially, infra, p. 196). Therein has been incorporated a passage
which belongs to the end of the sermonic section to S 102 (above,
p. 178). Following the unit comprising §§11–18, discussed above,
we have in §19 and till the end of the chapter Aggadot on Num.
2.32–34 and 3.1–4. The S, which began at 3.1 (infra No. 103),
is not represented at all in NR nor in the Tanḥumas. In these
Midrashim there are instead sections to different commencements
of the S in lieu of No. 103, as will be pointed out in due course
(infra, p. 190).

SEDER 103 (3)

Num. 3.1, ואלה ת ו ל ד ו ת אהרן ומשה ביום ד ב ר ה' את משה בהר סיני

About the choice of this S and the objections raised against
it, see infra, pp. 186, 190.

Haftarah: לא בסתר ד ב ר ת י במקום ארץ חשך לא אמרתי ל ז ר ע
Is. 45.19 (so C 12, יעקב תהו בקשוני אני ה' ד ב ר צדק מגיד מישרים
with the end missing). Also Yannai in his Ḳerobah to the
present S lists this initial v. of H (ed. Zulay, p. 180, top). The
lection probably extended to 46.2, skipping to v. 13 which
concludes in a 'happy' manner that 'I will place salvation in
Zion, to Israel, My glory' (hence 10 verses).

The connection with S is by means of the italicized words.
The choice of this H may also be due to the homiletic explanation of Is. 45.19 as referring to the giving of the Torah openly
on a mountain in the wilderness of Sinai,[199] thus corresponding
to Num. 3.1 which mentions 'the day when God addressed Moses

---

[199] See Mekh., Yitro, Baḥodesh, c. 1 (ed. Horov-Rabin, p. 205–6):
ויבואו מדבר סיני ויחנו במדבר, נתנה תורה דימוס פרהסיא במקום הפקר... ר' יוסי אומר
הרי הוא אומר לא בסתר דברתי במקום ארץ חושך, כשנתתיה אני בתחלה לא נתתיה בסתר,
וכי' (cp. further, c. 5, p. 220).

on Mount Sinai.' Otherwise H is a typical one of consolation of Israel.[138]

STRUCTURE OF HOMILIES

1. Whereas in the Tanḥumas and in NR the present S is not represented,[200] owing to its having been shifted to 3.5–6 or 3.14–15 (infra, p. 190), there has been preserved a Midrashic section in a Genizah fragment (edited infra, H. pt., pp. unv.). The introductory Y topic is as follows: [ילמדנו רבנו האחים השותפין שהשביחו הנכסים מהו, כך] שנו רבותינו: האחים השותפין שהשביחו הנכסים אפילו לא הניח להם אביהן אלא מטה או קרדום חולקין בשוה, למה ששניהם אחים.[201] From this Hal. concerning brothers, who were partners as heirs of their father's estate, the homilist turns to the spiritual 'partnership' of the two brothers Moses and Aaron who, unlike so many other brothers at feud, cherished each other and rejoiced in each other's attainment of leadership. Herewith there is a return to the initial v. of S (Num. 3.1) which mentions Aaron even before Moses to indicate their equality.

This topic has no connection whatever with the above H from Is. 45.19 ff., and therefore presupposes another Prophetic lection which would also account for the other Aggadic items contained in this fragment.[148] I suggest Mic. 6.4: כי העלתיך מארץ מצרים ומבית עבדים פדיתיך ואשלח לפניך את מ ש ה א ה ר ן ומרים thus tallying with Num. 3.1 by means of Moses and Aaron. The H probably comprised verses 4 to 11, skipping to 7.14–15 in order to lead down to a 'happy ending.' Moreover, the final verse (7.15), with its promise that 'as in the days of your going out from Egypt I will show him wonders' (כימי צאתך מארץ מצרים אראנו נפלאות) would link up with the initial v. of H (6.4) referring to this historic event. The latter was brought about by the last of the plagues, the death of the firstborn (cp. Ex. 11.1 ff., 12.29 ff.), and this decisive plague is alluded to in the present S

---

[200] See infra, p. 188, concerning a Genizah version of NR which contained a section to the present S.[81*]

[201] A Baraita in this form is unknown from elsewhere. Cp. M. B. B. 9.3: הניח בנים גדולים וקטנים, השביחו הגדולים את הנכסים, השביחו לאמצע, and the comment in Yer., a. l. (16d bottom): רב אמר אפילו סל, אפילו ק ר ד ו ם. The expression האחים השותפין occurs in M. B. B. 9.4.

(Num. 3.13). Thereby is established also an intrinsic connection between the lection from Torah and from Prophets.

As demonstrated so abundantly in the course of our study, the skipped part of H was throughout utilized for sermonic purposes. Now in Mic. 7.2 there is denounced the faithlessness of one towards another, with even 'a person hunting his brother with a net' (איש את אחיהו יצודו חרם). This afforded the homilist his starting-point of the Halakhic theme concerning the appreciation in value of the property belonging to brothers as partners in an inheritance; this appreciation is to be divided equally between these brothers, hence one is not to have advantage over the other, a crime denunciated in the Prophetic verse concerning a person dealing treacherously with his brother. From this point the preacher proceeded to depict the ideal spiritual partnership of the two brothers, Moses and Aaron, which was so precious in the sight of God.

The latter theme is further developed in the main Pet. from Ps. 133.1: הנה מה ט ו ב ומה נעים שבת אחים גם יחד (infra, H. pt., p. unv.), which v. tallies verbally with מה טוב in Mic. 6.8.[158] The former v. is applied to Moses and Aaron as against the several cases enumerated in the Bible of feuds among brothers, such as Cain and Abel, Ishmael and Isaac, Esau and Jacob, and so on. This item also concludes in our text with the characteristic formula ממה שקרינו בענין, just as the initial Y passage. This repetition reflects the combination of two types of sermonic compositions with the one introducing at the head a Y topic whereas the other only using a Pet. verse, mostly taken from the Hagiographa, to be developed homiletically so as to evolve the main sermonic lesson. The latter procedure is older, and the former was an innovation, though already in Amoraic times, to achieve the same purpose by means of a theme (mostly of an Halakhic nature) introduced by the formula of ילמדנו רבנו . . . כך שנו רבותינו.[202]

To proceed with the analysis of our Genizah text, there is another Pet. from Prov. 17.6: עטרת זקנים בני בנים ותפארת בנים

---

[202] Cp. vol. I, H. pt., p. 92, and infra vol. III, where the subject will be fully treated, inc.

אבותם which again is in contrast to Mic. 7.6: כי בן מנבל אב.[16s]
A further Pet. is from Cant. 4.5 supplying by means of ה ר ו ע י ם
בשושנים the virtual link with H v.: רעה עמך וגו' (Mic. 7.14).[17s]
The homily concerning the successive stages of God's discourses
with Moses, first at the burning bush, then in Midian and in
Egypt, followed by the scenes at Sinai and lastly by addressing
him in the Tabernacle, is expressly based on Mic. 6.8: והצנע
לכת עם אלהיך. Thus because humility towards God is proper,
therefore He finally addressed Moses out of the privacy of the
Tent of Meeting. There follows a passage dealing with the three
good leaders of Israel, Moses, Aaron and Miriam, wherein the
initial v. of H (Mic. 6.4) is mentioned explicitly.[18s]

Thus the suggested underlying Prophetic lection is manifest
from the section preserved in the Genizah and its substitution
by another one from Is. 45.19 ff. (above, p. 186) must be regarded
as late, viz. in the Byzantine period when Christianity was the
state religion. A verse like Is. 45.20: הנושאים את עץ פסלם ומתפללים
אל אל לא יושיע could easily have been turned as an allusion
directed against the Christian worship of the Cross (a piece of
wood) and of Jesus (ישוע) as the saviour (σωτήρ), ironically
styled here as 'a god who does does not save.' And in the same
strain there is in the H the further emphasis on there being no
Saviour but the Jewish God (Is. 45.21: ומושיע אין זולתי) and that
'only I am God and none else' (v. 22: כי אני אל ואין עוד). This
substitution of the H thus reveals an interesting point of the
self defense of the synagogue against the claims and assumptions
of the church in using the Jewish Bible for its own christological
purposes.[19s]

It is interesting to note that Yannai in his Ḳerobah though
already listing the later H from Is. 45.19 ff., cites several verses
from the Hagiogr. found in the Genizah text (thus Ps. 133.1 and
Cant. 4.5, ed. Zulay, p. 178, bottom; Ps. 122.8 and Prov. 17.6,
ibid., p. 179). These verses, as well as the others cited by him,[203]

---

[203] Thus Koh. 4.9: טובים השנים מן האחד אשר יש להם שכר טוב בעמלם
(p. 179, top) tallies by means of שנים with both S and H wherein these two
famous brothers are mentioned. However, Is. 2.3 (p. 180, top), cited immediately after Is. 45.19 (the initial v. of the other H), is mentioned because
the preceding v. was explained as referring to the giving of the Torah openly

all are to be correlated with the H from Mic. 6.4 ff. This shows
on the one hand that Yannai was familiar with the Midrashic
section analyzed here, and on the other hand that the latter
was retained in his time for sermonic purposes, although the
underlying H was different from the one adopted later on for the
synagogue service.[204]

2. Another Genizah fragment (GS, I, 91–95) seems to be
from a version of NR which contained a section to our S,[205]
unlike the current printed version of this Midrash (above, p. 178).
In this text figures the Pet. from Ps. 80.9: גפן ממצרים תסיע
תגרש גוים ותטעה containing a series of beautiful parallels drawn
between the vine and Israel. The same Agg. is found in LR,
c. 36.2, to S 99a, as to which see above (p. 149). This Pet. v.
poetically describes Israel's exodus from Egypt as a vine removed from that country and planted elsewhere (viz. in Palestine), and thus readily tallies here with the initial v. of H alluding
to the same event (Mic. 6.4, cp. also the final v., 7.15).[208] Since
in Num. 3.1 there is a reference to "the day when God spoke to
Moses on Mount Sinai," hence the Pet. v. is first applied to the
scene at this mount when Israel readily declared to act according
to God's word.[206] The reason for the assumption that this Geniz.

and publicly (above, p. 185) and accordingly in the future the nations will
flock to Zion to obtain there the teachings of the Torah (כי מציון תצא תורה).[82*]

[204] The same procedure can be observed several times in the Ḳerobot of
this Paitan (cp. the summary in vol. III). Inc.

[205] The editor was unaware of S 103, and thus after hesitating between
assigning the text either to S 101 or 102, decided in favor of the latter because
one of the parallels between the vine and Israel mentioned the grouping of
the latter under banners (ibid., p. 91). However, this item occurs also in
the parallel text in LR, c. 36.2, to S 99a. We find it strange to have an Agg.,
supposedly to Num. 2.2, followed forthwith by comments on Num. 3.1–2
(ibid., p. 94, l. 12 ff.) and prefer to assign the whole to Num. 3.1, the initial
v. of our S.

[206] GS, I, 91–92: ותתלשת [רע]*[83] גפן ממצרים תסיע, מה הגפן הזאת נעקרת ממקום
(צ"ל: ונשתלת) במקום טוב, כך ישראל כל זמן שהיו במצרים לא עשו פירות, כיון שנסעו
ממצרים ובאו להר סיני, התחילו ועושין פירות ואומרין כל אשר דבר יוי נעשה ונשמע
(here 'דבר ה again tallies with 'דבר ה ביום in Num. 3.1). Prior to this passage
there probably was in the text the comment concerning Aaron being mentioned here before Moses as against the usual procedure vice versa (cp. the
text in H. pt., p. unv.: ד"א ואלה תולדות אהרן ומשה, בכל מקום הוא מקדים משה לאהרן

text emanates from a version of NR is on account of C. 3 of our
printed edition (to S 103a which was in lieu of the present S,
infra, p. 192) which contains a Pet. from Ps. 92.13–14, with a
similar series of beautiful parallels between the date palm and
Israel (infra, p. 192). It thus stands to reason that the above
Pet. concerning the vine constructed in the same manner was in
the section that preceded the one in c. 3 of NR, viz. to the
present S at Num. 3.1. Thus the Genizah finds have supplied
two Midrashic texts to the latter Torah lection which hitherto
was lacking entirely in Sermonic productions following in its
train.

Seder 103a (3a)

וידבר ה' . . . הקרב את מטה לוי והעמדת אותו לפני אהרן הכהן ושרתו אותו,
Num. 3.5–6.

This S, which is evident from the homilies in NR, c. 3.1–3,
was in lieu of the one at 3.1 (No. 103), only 4 verses previously,
that is not represented at all in NR and in the Tanḥumas (above,
p. 185). But the same Aggadot, though in a curtailed form, are
found in TB, §17, T, §15, to Num. 3.14–15 where apparently
another commencement of the S is indicated. To the latter there
is in the Tanḥumas a whole Midrashic section concluding with
a *peroration* (end of TB, §20, T, §17). Now this lection would
again exclude the one at 3.1 (only 13 verses before) as well as the
alternative at 3.5 (only 9 verses previously). We notice thus
another instance of the variance of custom as regards the beginning of the S on the same Sabbath, with three resulting usages:
1) Num. 3.1 (No. 103), 2) 3.5–6 (No. 103a), and 3) 3.14–15
(listed here sub No. 103b).[218]

In the absence of concrete data in explanation of these differences, we can only advance the following surmises. The adoption
of S 103 was probably motivated by the fact that its initial v.
(Num. 3.1) afforded linguistic parallels to the two previous
Sedarim; thus by means of ביום דבר ה' את משה בהר סיני to Num. 1.1:

וכו'). In LR, c. 36.1, too, this topic (among the other instances of this kind)
precedes the Pet. homily on Ps. 80.9 (ibid. §2).

וידבר ה' אל משה במדבר סיני באהל מועד וגו' (No. 101),[207] and by reason
of mentioning together Aaron and Moses (אלה תולדות אהרן ומשה)
to Num. 2.1: וידבר ה' אל משה ואל אהרן (No. 102). However,
objection was raised against this arrangement inasmuch as Num.
3.1–4 contains an isolated brief account of Aaron's progeny, two
of whom died prematurely. The main topic of the lection pertains to the assignment of the tribe of Levi to the service of the
sanctuary under the supervision of the priesthood (from 3.5 ff.).
Hence another custom developed to conclude S 102 at 3.4 and
begin the reading on the following Sabbath with 3.5–6 ff. S 103a,
with its injunction at the head concerning the Levites: ה ק ר ב
את מטה לוי וגו', would thus constitute a parallel to S 65a containing a similar order concerning the selection of Aaron and
his sons for the priesthood: ואתה ה ק ר ב אליך את אהרן וגו' (Exod.
28.1, see above, vol. I, pp. 501–2). Indeed the same H is to be
presupposed in both instances, as will be shown forthwith. But
S 103a involved the difficulty of terminating the previous one
(No. 102) with an inauspicious v. recounting the death of Nadab
and Abihu (3.4). Hence, a different solution was offered, viz.
to start the Torah section at 3.14–15 containing the command to
hold the census of the sons of Levi (פקוד את בני לוי לבית אבותם
וגו'). Thereby a certain intrinsic symmetry in the sequence of
the first three Sedarim in Numbers was established. On the first
Sabbath there was read the portion concerning the census of
Israel (No. 101: Num., c. 1; cp. the specific exclusion there of
the tribe of Levi, v. 48 ff.). On the next Sabbath there was
recited the passage dealing with the grouping under their respective banners of those who had been included in the census (No.
102: Num., c. 2). And now on the third Sabbath the lection
commenced with the order to count and group the Levites (No.
103b: Num. 3.14 ff.; cp. v. 23 as regards the encampment of
the sons of Gershon, etc.). A further reason for the choice of
No. 103b instead of 103a was the fact that 3.14 reads: וידבר ה'
אל משה במדבר סיני (similar to Num. 1.1) whereas in 3.5 the mention
of the locality is omitted. The former S seems to be a later

---

[207] This parallel is indeed commented upon in the Genizah text to S 103
(infra, H. pt., p. unv.).

innovation, as evident from the fact that the homilies to the latter S were subsequently transferred to the former and adapted to its H (see infra, p. 195). But neither lection prevailed, and S 103 was still in vogue in the time of Yannai and subsequently.

We discuss here first the alternative S 103a, and subsequently No. 103b.

Haftarah: Just as in the case of S 65a mentioned before, so with regard to the present S the Prophetic lection began with Jer. 30.21: ‏;והיה אדירו ממנו ומושלו מקרבו יצא והקרבתיו ונגש אלי וגו'‏ tallying with Num. 3.6: ‏הקרב את מטה לוי‏; it probably extended to 31.4 skipping to v. 13 (10 verses).[208] This H is a typical one of consolation of Israel. Yet in 31.5 the sentence 'arise and let us go up to Zion, to the Lord our God' evidently means to the Temple, the house of God (cp. Is. 2.3). Thus there is a parallel to the Tabernacle where the Levites were to do service (Num. 3.7–8). Moreover in the final v. (31.13) there is a reference to the priests under whom the former were to serve (see Num. 3.9).

STRUCTURE OF HOMILIES

In NR, c. 3.1, there is given the Pet. from Ps. 92.13–14: ‏צדיק כתמר יפרח כארז בלבנון ישגה שתולים בבית ה' בחצרות אלהינו‏ ‏יפריחו‏, where v. 14 tallies with Jer. 31.5: ‏קומו ונעלה ציון אל ה'‏ ‏אלהינו‏ in the meaning of ‏אל [בית] ה' אלהינו‏, as has just been pointed out. This Agg. contains at first a series of beautiful parallels drawn between Israel and the righteous on the one hand and the date palm on the other, and thus resembles the similar Agg. to S 103 with regard to the vine, as found now in the Genizah text discussed above (p. 189). This application of the Pet. verses to Israel is due to the fact that the latter forms the main topic of H (see Jer. 30.25 ff.); further the distinction of the righteous is in contrast to the denunciation of the wicked in Jer 30.23–4.[228] The homily then proceeds to apply Ps. 92.13–14 to the tribe of Levi with whom the S deals.[209] This whole item

---

[208] To S 65a the H comprised Jer. 30.21–31.4+19.

[209] ‏ד"א צדיק כתמר וגו', מדבר בשבטו של לוי... שלא בחר בכל השבטים לעמוד‏ ‏בשימושו אלא בני לוי בלבד... שתולים בבית ה', שלא היו זזים מביה"מ לעולם, בחצרות‏ ‏אלהינו יפריחו, אלו השירות, תדע לך שהוא כן שנ' (היינו: ממה שקרינו בענין) הקרב את מטה‏ ‏לוי וגו' ושמרו את משמרתו וגו'.‏

thus originally belongs to the present Torah lection and was
later inserted into Midr. Ps., c. 92 (ed. Buber, pp. 409–11).[210]
There follows (NR, c. 3.2) a Midrash on Ps. 65.5: אשרי תבחר
ותקרב ישכון חצריך נשבעה בטוב ביתך קדוש היכלך, affording
a link with both S and H by means of the verb קרב and further
with the final v. of the latter (Jer. 31.13): ועמי את טובי ישבעו.
That the Temple was meant in 31.5 has been stated before.[238]
This Pet. has been employed to several Sedarim (thus to S 68a
in ER, c. 37.3, above, vol. I, p. 502; to S 78 in TB, Ṣaw, §11,
T, §8, above, p. 47).[211] The remainder of NR, c. 3, is loosely
constructed, with running comments on Num. 3.6–39 (§§3–13),
some of which are parallel to the items in the Tanḥumas comprised within the section to S 103b. Thus to Num. 3.14–15
there is in NR, c. 36, the Pet. from Ps. 68.7 as in TB, §18, T,
§16, (as to which cp. infra, p. 196). Likewise §§7–9 of NR contain the same material although in a more extended form, as
found in TB, §§19–20, T, §§16–17. One notices how in the
Tanḥumas the Aggadic items have been compressed so as to
form a more compact sermonic unit.[212] Only the *peroration* (end
of TB, §20, T, §17) is omitted in NR, and yet essentially it
pertains better to the present S, as its analysis farther on (p. 197)
will show. Thus the whole section was originally intended for
No. 103a (as in NR). But after the commencement of the Torah
lection had been shifted to 3.14–15 (No. 103b, which took the
place of No. 103a), the same Aggadot were applied to the new S
and were adjusted to suit in turn its H which was different from
the one to S 103a. This adjustment we notice in the Tanḥ.
section to S 103b to be discussed soon.

To conclude the remarks on the remainder of NR, c. 3, there
is noticeable again the detailed Aggadic exegesis of the verses, in
addition to those items incorporated into the sermon to the S,

[210] About the same Pet. but in a curtailed form, to S 10a see above, vol.
I, p. 103. As to its version in TB, §17, T, §15, to S 103b see infra, note 212.

[211] See further above, vol. I, pp. 100 and 539–40.

[212] This process of compressing the homilies in TB to S 1 as compared
to the larger version of Midr. Tanḥ. has been pointed out above, vol. I, p.
34–35. See also ibid., H. pt., p. 8–9.

a procedure that obtains also in the first two chapters of this Midrash (see above, pp. 177 and 184). The passage here (§12) about the respective positions of the divisions of the tribe of Levi around the Tabernacle, in their relationship to the grouping of the other tribes under their banners, presupposes the allegorization of the latter arrangement as found in NR, c. 2.10 (above, p. 182).

Here a general statement should be made on the first part of NR (viz. till c. 14 inclusive). In its present form it shows evidence of several extraneous insertions (cp. Epstein, מקדמוניות היהודים, 70 ff.). That it contains material that is also found in Midr. Yel. has been noticed so far in our investigation, and the same will be the case in the subsequent analysis (Epstein, too, observed this, though in an incomplete manner). Moreover, in its extensive coverage of the Aggadic material, it resembles the larger version of Midr. Tanḥ., parts of which (to Gen.-Exod.) were dealt with in vol. I (pp. 29 ff., 514; H. pt., 1, pp. 7 ff., 69 ff., 122 ff.). The parallel homilies in TB and T on the one side and in NR on the other can be traced all along, as has been done here so far and as will be continued afterwards. R. Tanḥuma b. Abba is also cited several times in NR, c. 3 (thus twice in §1, and see the story of his discussion with R. Huna Hakkohen b. Abin in §7); in c. 7.1 there seems to be given his Pet. to a S (see infra, p. 214). Because of the manner of the larger version of Midr. Tanḥ. to comment fully on each verse of a given Bible section, there was also placed at the head of each item an extraneous verse which need not be taken as a real Petiḥta to be correlated with the H; such is only the case when the respective homily pertains to the beginning of the S and not when it is a part of running comments on the subsequent verses. One has only to examine the text edited above (vol. I, H. pt., pp. 112 ff.) to realize this point, and the same applies to the early part of GR for example (above, vol. I, p. 35). Accordingly, here too in NR, c. 2.10 and 12, we observe a similar procedure (see above, pp. 181, 182, and infra, p. 196). Now the part of NR under discussion contains a good deal of extraneous matter. Also in style it was subject to much change. However, it is clear that there has been incorporated a considerable portion of the larger

version of Midr. Tanḥ. which is older than the versions that
assumed their form in TB and T (for a fuller discussion of this
topic see infra, vol. III, inc.).[248]

Finally, attention should be drawn to MHG, IV (ed. Fisch,
pp. 178–9), wherein there is given a Pet. from Prov. 22.22:
וידבר . . . הקרב את מטה לוי, זש"ה אל תגזול דל כי דל הוא, זה שבטו של לוי,
מפני שהן דלין, מפני שהן רואין את השכינה ונושאין את הארון, וכן עזרא אומר
ואבינה בעם ובכהנים ומבני לוי לא מצאתי, שהן מעטין. ועוד נקראו דלין,
שהן דלים מן המתנות. This whole item is out of place here, and really
belongs to S 104, as evident from TB, §27, T, §23, NR, c. 5.2
(see infra, p. 203). It has no connection whatever with what
follows in MHG: ר' יהודה אומר וכו', this latter being a comment on
Ps. 103.3–6 (see Midr., Ps., a. l.); because in v. 6 we read הוא
י שׁ ר ת נ י, there is a tally with Num. 3.6: הקרב את מטה לוי . . . ,
ו שׁ ר ת ו אותו (see also infra, note 213).

<h2 style="text-align:center">SEDER 103b (3b)</h2>

וידבר ה' . . . פ ק ו ד את בני לוי לבית אבותם למשפחותם כל זכר מבן
חדש ומעלה ת פ ק ד ם, Num. 3.14–15.

About the shifting of the commencement of the S to here,
see above, p. 182.

Hafṭarah. By reason of the Aggadot to be analyzed forthwith,
the Prophetic lection seems to have begun with Zech. 10.3:
על הרועים חרה אפי ועל העתודים אפקוד כי פ ק ד ה' צבאות את עדרו
וגו'. It extended to v. 12 (10 verses). The tally with S is only
by means of the verb פקד. Otherwise the H is of a purely consolatory character.[258]

<h2 style="text-align:center">STRUCTURE OF HOMILIES</h2>

In TB, §17, T, §15, there is the Pet. from Ps. 92.13: צדיק
כתמר יפרח כארז ב ל ב נ ו ן ישגה, which affords the link with the
H v. (Zech. 10.10): ואל ארץ גלעד ו ל ב נ ו ן אביאם.[268] This Pet.
was originally constructed to S 103a, as evident from NR,
c. 3.1 (above, p. 192), and was transferred to the present S in a
curtailed form. This curtailment is evident from the conclusion of the item here bringing in points that were legitimate

there including the Pet. from Ps. 65.5 (above, p. 193) which would offer no tally with the present H and hence was changed in such a manner as to remove this difficulty![213] The next Pet. (TB, §18, T, §16) introduced Ps. 68.7: אלהים מושיב יחידים ביתה מוציא אסירים בכושרות אך סוררים שכנו צחיחה which offers by means of מושיב a point of contrast with the H v.: והושבתים כי רחמתים וגו' (Zech. 10.6).[27s] In NR, c. 3.6, the Agg. on this v. is extensive and is really connected with Num. 3.14.[214] It was not meant there as a real Pet., but was in accordance with the manner of this Midrash to comment in a running homiletic exegesis on the numerous verses comprising the Torah lection (see above, p. 193).[28s] However, in the Tanḥumas the Agg. has been curtailed and so shaped as to fit Num. 3.15 (and not 3.14)![215]

[213] ד"א צדיק כתמר יפרח, מדבר בשבטו של לוי, שהפרישן (צ"ל: שהפריחן) הקב"ה במעשיהם הטובים, מה כתיב אחריו שתולים בבית ה' בחצרות אלהינו יפריחו, ללמדך שלא היו זזים מביה"מ, שנ' עיני בנאמני ארץ לשבת עמדי הולך בדרך תמים הוא ישרתני (תה' ק"א, ו'), לכך נאמר שתולים בבית ה', שלא היתה עזרה חסרה מהם, שנ' בחצרות אלהינו יפריחו, מה ו בחצרות, זש"ה אשרי תבחר ותקרב ישכון חצריך וגו'. Here Ps. 65.5 is cited indeed by the introductory formula זהו שאמר הכתוב, but in a subsidiary connection with Ps. 92.14! But the legitimacy of the Pet. from Ps. 65.5 in NR, c. 3.2, to S 103a has been made manifest above (p. 193). Here, too, Ps. 101.6 is woven in artificially, but in NR, c. 3.3, we logically read the comment on Num. 3.6: והעמדת אותו לפני אהרן הכהן ושרתו אותו, ויטנה מהם גזברין ואמרכלין ושרתו אותו, עליהם הכתוב אומר עיני בנאמני ארץ... הוא ישרתני. Buber, in his notes to TB, §17, constantly belittles the value of the text in NR claiming insertions from Midr. Ps. by some copyist. While the current printed text was no doubt "touched up" here and there, the originality of its homilies (to S 103a) under discussion is clear. Buber, on the one hand, was unjustifiably prone to regard his version of Tanḥ. (TB) as the most ancient and original and, on the other hand, was unaware of the problem involved here as to the respective Aggadot to Nos. 103a and 103b.

[214] ד"א... במדבר סיני לאמר, הה"ד מושיב יחידים ביתה... מוציא אסירים בכושרות בכושרות, בזכות מה יצאו ישראל ממצרים, אריב"ל מפני שצפה הקב"ה... ושבטו של לוי בזכות מה יצאו... לפיכך כיון שהוא בא למנות את ישראל בראש הספר הוא מזכיר אהל מועד ויציאת מצרים, שנ' וידבר ה' אל משה במדבר סיני באהל מועד, מזכיר מיד. לצאתם מארץ מצרים', להודיעך שלא יצאו ישראל ממצרים אלא בזכות אהל מועד, אבל בני לוי שיצאו בזכות עצמן, כיון שהוא בא למנותן אינו מזכיר בפרשתן לאהל מועד ולא יציאת מצרים, הה"ד וידבר ה' אל משה במדבר סיני לאמר (במ' ג', י"ד).

[215] פקוד את בני לוי (במ' ג', ט"ו), זש"ה אלהים מושיב יחידים ביתה, שאלה מטרונא גואלנא אחת... אמר הקב"ה: האיל והשבט הזה למוד הוא להיות מעמידים (צ"ל: מעמיד) גואלים, לך וספור אותם, פקוד את בני לוי.

Finally there is the *peroration* (end of TB, §20, T, §17): אמר
הקב״ה: בעוה״ז היו מתכלין על שהיו רואין את כבודי שנ' כי לא יראני אדם
וחי (שם' ל"ג, כ'), אבל לעוה"ב (ובת"ה: לע"ל) כשאחזיר שכינתי לציון, אני
נגלה בכבודי על כל ישראל ורואים אותי וחיים לעולם, שנ' כי עין בעין יראו
בשוב ה' ציון (יש' נ"ב, ח'), ולא עוד אלא מראים (צ"ל: שמראים) את כבודי
זה לזה באצבע (ובת"ה: שמראין אותו [צ"ל: אותי] באצבע), ואומרים כי זה
אלהים אלהינו עולם ועד הוא ינהגנו על מות (תה', מ"ח, ט"ו), ואומר ביום
ההוא הנה אלהינו זה קוינו לו ויושיענו זה ה' קוינו לו נגילה ונשמחה בישועתו
(יש' כ"ה, ט). Now the whole point of the danger of perishing in
this world on account of beholding the Deity is abruptly introduced here. There would be a slight connection with the present
S by reason of the injunction towards its end, (Num. 3.38):
והזר הקרב יומת, or by reason of 4.15: ולא יגעו אל הקודש ומתו if this
Torah lection extended to 4.16 (see infra, p. 200). However,
there is no real intrinsic contact with H, and only the very last
v. cited in the *peroration* (viz. Is. 25.9) would somehow linguistically link up with H: ו ג ב ר ת י את בית יהודה ואת בית יוסף א ו ש י ע
כ י א נ י ה ' א ל ה י כ ם. But if the *peroration* is applied to S 103a,
there is a natural suggestion for the topic of this *peroration* since
on the one hand, quite at the beginning of this S there is the
warning: והזר הקרב יומת (Num. 3.10), and, on the other hand, in
the corresponding H (Jer. 30.21 ff.) the appearance of God is
mentioned (31.2: נ ר א ה ה' ל י מרחוק ה') together with the promise
of flocking to 'Zion, to the Lord, our God' (31.5: קומו ונעלה
ציון אל ה' אלהינו). Hence the assurance in the *peroration* that
'in the hereafter I shall restore My Shekhinah to Zion, I shall
be revealed in My glory to all Israel who will behold Me and
yet live forever' citing Is. 52.8: כי עין בעין י ר א ו בשוב ה' צ י ו ן
further Ps. 48.15 (where כי זה אלהים א ל ה י נ ו corresponds to
Jer. 31.5 referring to visiting God at Zion), and finally Is. 25.9
which v., in addition to its phrases הנה א ל ה י נ ו זה ... זה ה ה '
speaks of God's saving and the resultant joy of His people
(ו י ו ש י ע נ ו ... נגילה ו נ ש מ ח ה ב י ש ו ע ת ו) and thus links up
with the final v. of H (Jer. 31.6): רנו ליעקב ש מ ח ה ו צ ה ל ו
ה ו ש ע ה' את עמך ....[298] There is thus ample evidence for the
assumption that the above *peroration* originally pertained to
S 103a, just as the other homilies analyzed before, and was later
on transferred to S 103b. The above discussion of these two

Sedarim and their respective homilies is very instructive for the understanding of the changes the Midrashic material underwent in connection with its employment for the sermons delivered during the service of the synagogue.

SEDER 103c (3c)

ויאמר ה' אל משה פקוד כל בכור זכר לבני ישראל מבן חדש ומעלה ושא
את מספר שמותם, Num. 3.40.

The 'regular' S following directly the one at 3.1 (No. 103), commenced at 4.17 (infra, sub No. 104). But from the Midrashim a Torah lection here (at 3.40) is apparent, and the same applies to Midr. Yel. as cited in Arukh (בילמדנו פקוד כל בכור זכר).[216] Now such a S could be a direct sequel of either No. 103, 103a or 103b since in each case there would be the required minimum of 21 verses prior to 3.40.

Haftarah. By reason of the Midrashic material to be analyzed forthwith the following Prophetic lection is to be presupposed, viz. Is. 66.7: בטרם תחיל ילדה בטרם יבוא חבל לה והמליטה ז כ ר tal- lying by means of זכר with the initial v. of S (פקוד כל בכור ז כ ר). The extent of H probably was 66.7–12+20–23 (10 verses). The promise in v. 21: וגם מהם א ק ח לכהנים ל ל ו י ם אמר ה' would link up with Num. 3.41, where the selection of the Levites for God's service is mentioned (ולקחת את הלוים לי אני ' ה), while the final v. (66.23) would offer by means of חודש another point of contact with Num. 3.40 (מבן חודש). Further- more, the phrase אמר ה' recurring several times (66.12, 21 and 22, cp. also אמר ה' in v. 9), corresponds to ויאמר ה' with which the S commenced. Otherwise the Prophetic rendering is one of 'consolation of Israel,' so typical of the Haftarot of TC.

[216] S. v. איקונין (Kohut, I, 257), ארנון (I, 294) and סנודיא (in Kohut, VI, 84, erroneously סנוריא).

Structure of Homilies

1. *Y Sermon*. TB, Bammidbar, §21, T, §18:[217] ויאמר ה' אל
משה פקוד כל בכור זכר וגו', ילמדנו רבינו: תינוק שנולד לשמונה חדשים[218]
מחללין עליו (בת"ה: מהו לחלל עליו) את השבת, כך שנו רבותינו:[219]
תינוק שנולד לח' חדשים אין מחללין עליו את השבת וכו'. The whole item
has been skillfully developed on the background of the H wherein
the sudden restoration of Israel is compared figuratively to the
birth of a baby (Is. 66.7 ff.). Mother Zion is depicted as bringing
forth her children in a surprisingly rapid manner (v. 8), with the
latter 'sucking' and being satisfied from 'the breast' of her
consolations (v. 11: למען תינקו ושבעתם משד תנחומיה). In a subtle
homiletic contrast, the Hal. is cited here concerning a *premature
human birth* which sometimes is fatal (as in the case of a birth
at eight months); this law also contains a detail about giving
to suck (אבל אמו גוחה עליו ומניקתו). Unlike such a birth, the
rebirth of Israel is to last as long as the new heaven and earth
(v. 22). The juxtaposition of this promise (כן יעמוד
זרעכם ושמכם) and the following one (v. 23) concerning worshipping God in the sanctuary every month and every Sabbath
(והיה מדי חודש בחדשו) suggested the conclusion of the Y item
here to the effect that a babe ceases to be of premature birth[220]
after having lived a month. Hence the counting of the first
born males was to be 'from a month old and upwards' (מבן
חודש ומעלה).[221] [308] Herewith there is a return to the initial v. of
S, thereby completing the first portion of the Y sermon.

There follows (TB, §22, T, §19) a Pet. from Is. 43.4: מאשר
יקרת בעיני נכבדת ואני אהבתיך, which links up by means of

---

[217] In NR, c. 4.3, this item is placed within the section and is introduced
merely by תנין תמן (cp. above, p. 181). See also infra, note 224.

[218] In T erroneously לששה (see Buber's note 168).

[219] About the Hal. cited here see Tos. Sabb. 15 (16).5 and 7, and Babli
135a. The variants need not be discussed. It should only be added that,
in connection with the statement of R. Simon b. Gamliel (at the end of the
item), for ובמה סמכה דעתו וכו' in TB (in T: וכמה) read (as in NR):
ולמה? סמכה דעתו של רשב"ג לדבר תורה, לפי שאין הבכורות נפדין אלא לאחר ל' יום וכו'.
[220] נ פ ל, the opposite of which being styled בן קיימא.

[221] TB, §21, end (omitted in T, §18, end): לפיכך אמר הקב"ה למשה שלא יהו
הבכורות נפקדים אלא מבן חודש. מנין? ממה שקראו (ויותר נכון: שקרינו) בענין, פקוד כל
בכור זכר בבני ישראל. מבן חודש ומעלה וגו'.

נכבדת with the H v. (66.10): ה ו ד ב כ מזיו והתענגתם.[318] Moreover,
God's love of Israel (ואני אהבתיך) is so tenderly depicted in 66.13:
'As a person whom his mother comforts, so will I comfort you.'
This latter v. also supplies the tally (אמו) for the next Pet.
(TB, §23, T, §20) from Cant. 6.8–9: אחת . . . מלכות המה ששים
וגו׳ ה מ א ל היא.[328] There is no proper *peroration* preserved. The
item (TB, §26, T, §21, end) concerning the several kinds of
'visitation' (פקידה) does indeed conclude with a reference to the
peace (יש פקידה לשלום שנ׳ ושמתי פקודתך שלום) and thereby seems to
allude to the promise in H (Is. 66.12) that 'I will extend to her
peace like a river.' However, this should hardly be taken as the
real termination of the sermon, since such usually contained a
contrast between the present state of affairs and the ideal one in
the hereafter (לעוה"ז . . . אבל לעתיד לבוא לעוה"ב). Thus the section
in the Tanḥumas is defective.

2. In NR, c. 4, there are first given the above 2 Petiḥtot
followed by the Y Halakhic topic placed here within the section
(§3, cp. above, note 217), and subsequently by the above Agg.
concerning the kinds of 'visitation' (§4). The remaining two
items of the section to our S in the Tanḥumas (TB, §§24–25,
T, §20, end, and §21) have their parallel in NR, §§5 and 10.
But the latter Midr. contains an extensively running exegesis of
Num. 3.40 to 4.16 where the Torah lection ended. While there
are several extraneous insertions, a good part of c. 4 seems to
emanate from a larger version of Midr. Tanḥ., as pointed out
before (pp. 194, 195).[222]

[Arukh, s. v. סמרטין (Kohut, VI, 78) cites a passage from Yel.
to קח את הלוים,[223] which Buber (TB, מבוא, p. 200) took to refer to
במדבר (viz. Num. 3.45, yet on p. צ"ט he stated: או במדבר
בהעלותך, 8.6), followed by Kohut (SHL, IV, 7a, No. 18). This
would presuppose a Seder at Num. 3.44–45 for which there is
no other evidence whatever. There can be no doubt that the

---

[222] In §20 (to Num. 4.16) there is a passage introduced by Prov. 25.6
(הה"ד אל תתהדר לפני מלך וגו׳) which certainly cannot be taken as a Pet. in the
proper sense since no Y commenced at Num. 4.16. In this item there is an
insertion from SER (c. [13] 14, ed. Friedm., 65–66): כל :ר מ ו א אליהו
המרבה כבוד שמים וכו׳. See also infra, p. 204.

[223] בילמדנו בקח את הלוים: ואפילו סמריטין, ואפי׳ ברברײם.

above citation refers to Num. 8.6, since a new S actually began there according to a variant custom (see infra, p. inc., sub No. inc.). The latter is specifically mentioned in Arukh, s. v. ארגליא (I, 271: בילמדנו בהעלותך את הנרות בפסוק קח את הלוים) where the respective Halakhic topic from Y is quoted (see infra, l. c.).]

SEDER 104 (4)

Num. וידבר ה', אל ת כ ר י ת ו את שבט משפחות הקהתי מתוך הלוים
4.17–18.

Haftarah. None is preserved in the available Genizah lists. From the Midrashic data, however, it is clearly evident that the Prophetic lection started with Zeph. 3.7: אמרתי אך תיראי אותי תקחי מוסר ולא י כ ר ת מעונה וגו' tallying with S by means of the italicized sentence. It extended to v. 15, skipping to v. 20 with which there commences a new S in the Minor Prophets. Hence H consisted of 10 verses.

Besides the above tally, there is an intrinsic connection between S and H, inasmuch as the former deals with the details of the specific labor (עבודה) assigned to the three clans of the Levites (cp. 4.19: איש איש על עבודתו וגו', 23, etc.), of whom the clan of Ḳehat (mentioned at the beginning of the Torah lection) had to carry their loads on the *shoulder* without the assistance of carts (see Num. 7.9). In contrast to this state of affairs, limiting the physical service of God to one tribe, there is the glorious promise in H (Zeph. 3.9) to the effect that in the future all the nations will 'call upon the name of the Lord, to serve Him with one consent' (literally: with one *shoulder,* ל ע ב ד ו ש כ ם אחד) — this service of course being meant as spiritual.[338]

STRUCTURE OF HOMILIES

1. *Y Sermon.* TB, Bammidbar, §28, T, §23:[224] אל תכריתו וגו', ילמדנו רבנו: העובר על כריתות שבתורה במה הם מתכפרים (בת"ה בטעות: מתרפאין — Buber n. 205) ויוצאין מידי כריתותן, כך שנו רבותינו: כל חייבי כריתות שלקו נפטרו מידי כריתתן, שנאמר והפילו השופט

---

[224] In NR, c. 5.4, this topic is placed within the section: וזו ששנינו כל חייבי כריתות וכו' (see above, notes 187 and 217).

וגו', ארבעים יכנו לא יוסיף וגו', ונקלה אחיך (דברים כ"ה, ב—ג), כיון שלקה
הרי הוא אחיך (מס' מכות ג', ט"ו),‎225 ולמה ארבעים, אלא האדם הזה וכו'.
The verb כרת, by which H tallies with S, suggested the topic
concerning the transgressor of a law punished by כרת.‎348 Moreover, the point of such a culprit obtaining atonement after being
flogged has been ingeniously inspired by the initial v. of H:
תקחי מוסר ולא יכרת מעונה. Chastisement (מוסר) was
taken as referring to flogging, and מעונה was homiletically taken
to read מִעֲוֹנָה hence: 'you will take chastisement, so that he will
not be cut off on account of her sin,' or in the words of the
Mishnaic law: 'all guilty of כרת, who have been flogged, are
freed from their impending punishment' (כל חייבי כריתות שלקו
נפטרו מידי כריתתן)! From the Hal. the homilist turns to explain
symbolically the reason for the number of the stripes (40 in all)
constituting the punishment of flogging. Man, whose formation
in the womb after the conception lasted 40 days and who trans-
gressed the Torah that Moses received during 40 days on Mount
Sinai, shall atone for his sin by 40 stripes. Adam's offense
which was to be punished by death (Gen. 2.17), was expiated by
40 kinds of afflictions imposed on the world, viz. ten on him,
ten on his wife, ten on the serpent and ten on the earth — these
symbolizing the similar number of the stripes.‎226 After the event
in the wilderness of the gathering of wood on the Sabbath
(see Num. 15.32–36), whose penalty was death, Moses pleaded
with God to absolve from כרת anybody who underwent flogging.
Likewise after the untimely death of two of Aaron's sons the
clan of Ḳehat was afraid of the same dire result because of their
approaching the Deity too closely in consequence of their particular labor. Accordingly God directed Moses to order this clan
not to approach the Holy of Holies but to wait for Aaron and
his sons. Thus a remedy was contrived to save the former from

---

225 In TB only ונקלה אחיך is cited, but this is evidently due to shortening
by the copyists. In T the concluding sentence: כיון שלקה הרי הוא אחיך is enlarged so as to explain it: כיון שלקה, חסה התורה עליו ואמרה ונקלה אחיך לעיניך,
הרי הוא אחיך. In NR, c. 5.4, a further section of the M. is continued (ומה העובר
עבירה וכו') which is really not needed here.

226 About this allegory, see above, vol. I, H. pt., p. 277–78.

threatening כרת (אל תכריתו).²²⁷ Herewith there is a return to the
beginning of the S, thereby completing the first portion of the
Y sermon.

In the continuation there is the Pet. (TB, §29, T, §24) from
Ps. 33.18–19: הנה עין ה' אל י ר א י ו linking up with the initial v.
of H: אמרתי אך ת י ר א י אותי וגו'.³⁵⁸ This Pet. has been applied
to several other cases, but here it is limited to the instance of
the tribe of Levi with whom the S deals.²²⁸ The Agg. is curtailed in
the Tanḥumas, and there is no connection evident between the
commencement of the S with its particular reference to the clan
of Ḳehat. This connection becomes apparent from the further
version in NR, c. 5.1, where we have the comment of R. Elazar
b. Pedat that the sentence 'and to save their soul from death'
(Ps. 33.19) is to be applied especially to the Ḳehatites because
they had to carry the Ark which task involved mortal danger.
Hence special regulations had to be given so as to avoid destroy-
ing this group from among the Levites (Num. 4.17 ff.).²²⁹

The next Pet. (TB, §27, *T*, §23, misplaced before the Y topic)
is from Prov. 22.22: אל תגזל ד ל כי דל הוא ואל תדכא ע נ י בשער

---

²²⁷ There is woven in a comment on the expression וזאת in Num. 4.19:
א'ל הקב"ה למשה: כשם שעשיתי תקנה לאהרן, שנ' ב ז א ת יבא אהרן וגו' (וי' ט"ז, ג'), ואף
למשפחות הקהתי כך אני עושה תקנה שלא ימותו בבואם אל קדש הקדשים (מן בבואם חסר
בת"ה ובמ"ה), שנ' וזאת עשו להם וחיו ולא ימותו, מנין, ממה שקראו (ויותר נכון: שקרינו) בענין,
אל תכריתו את שבט משפחות הקהתי. This comment on וזאת is further found separately in NR, c. 5.7, to Num. 4.19, in accordance with the procedure of this
Midrash to comment in detail on the verses of the S.

²²⁸ זש"ה הנה עין ה' אל יראיו וגו', להציל ממות נפשם [וגו'], מדבר הכתוב בשיטין הרבה,
אלא למה שאנו צריכין (היינו שאנו מציעין כאן רק מה שנצרך לעניננו: מדבר בשבטו של לוי.
The allusion here is to such a passage as found in TB, Toledot, §5, where
these verses are applied to Abraham, Isaac, Jacob and the tribe of Levi
(Buber has failed to point this out).

²²⁹ א'ר אלעזר בן פדת, מאיזו מיתה היו נצולים, אם ממיתה של עולם, הרי אין בריה שאין
מתה, מהו להציל ממות נפשם, אלא ממיתת הארון וכו'. א'ל הקב"ה למשה ולאהרן: עשו להם
לפי שמנינם :Cp. further NR, c. 6.8. תקנה לבני קהת כדי שלא יכרתו מן העולם וכו'
היה לשם טעינת הארון, צירף הקב"ה שמו עמהם כדי שלא יכלו, ה"א בראשו ויו"ד בסופו (היינו:
הקהתי), הרי י"ה, לומר י"ה יצילם ממיתה [משונה, כמו בילח"מ לתהלים ל"ג, י"ט], לקיים מה
שנ' להציל ממות נפשם. Buber has not realized at all the lacuna in TB and T.
About the addition of ה"א and יו"ד see also TB, §30, end, and T, §24, end,
NR, c. 5.6, end.

tallying with the H v. (Zeph. 3.12): עני עם בקרבך והשארתי
ודל ל ונו'.[368] The former v. is applied here to several cases, only
the item in the Tanḥumas is curtailed, and has to be supplemented by NR, c. 5.2, with the latter in turn also deficient in
our printed texts (as is evident from the complete version in
YHM, Prov., ed. Grünhut, 32a–33a). Combining all these data,
we find Prov. 22.22 at first interpreted as referring to the per-
quisites due to the poor, such as gleanings, forgotten sheaves of
grain, corner-ears and poor-tithe.[230] Subsequently the Pet. v.
is applied to other items leading down to the tribe of Levi.[231]
The latter are called 'needy' because they obtained no portion
of Palestine and also because their service in the sanctuary,
fraught with danger, diminished their numbers. As the text is
in the Tanḥumas, there is no special application to the clan of
Ḳehat with whom the S deals as its commencement; only *the latter*
handled the Ark, which harmed those who were disrespectful
towards it, and not the whole tribe of Levi, as it appears from
the Tanḥumas.[232] But in NR we have the logical development
of the Agg., viz. first treating of the tribe of Levi as a whole and
then turning specifically at the end to the Ḳehatites.[233] Only

---

[230] NR, c. 5.2: הה"ד אל תגזול דל כי דל ונו', אמרו רבותינו במה הכתוב מדבר, אם
הוא דל מהו גזל לו, אלא לא דיבר אלא במתנות עניים, שהוא חייב ליתן להם מן התורה: לקט,
שכחה, ופאה, ומעשר שני וכו'. Different is the Agg. on this same v. in TB, Behar,
§5, T, §2 (cp. above, p. 41).

[231] TB, §27, T, §22, fuller in the version of NR given in YHM (32b):
א"ר תנחומא (in the Tanḥumas: ד"א אל תגזול דל כי דל. א"ר לוי זה התורמוס ונו'
בר אבא א"ר לוי וכו', but in YSH, Num. §695, only R. Levi as in YHM).
Interesting is the citation (in the version in YHM) of a passage from SER:
אליהו אומר כל מי שאינו אומר דבר וכו' (as above in NR, c. 14.16, note 222,
and in c. 5.9, end, see infra, note 237). About this particular item in YHM,
see the rather profuse remarks of Friedmann, SER, מבוא, pp. 143–144.

[232] ד"א אל תגזול דל, הוא מדבר ב ש ב ט ו ש ל ל ו י, והוא קורא לשבטו של לוי דל,
וכי דלים היו, ר"י בר סימון ורבותינו, אחד מהם אמר: למה נקראו דלים, לפי שהיו דלים
מנחלה ... ואחד אומר: שהיו דלים מן המנין, למה, שהיה ה א ר ו ן מ כ ל ה ב ה ן, לפיכך
הקב"ה מצוה את משה ואומר: אל תכריתו את שבט משפחות ה ק ה ת י.

[233] NR, c. 5.2: ד"א אל תגזול דל, מדבר בשבטו של לוי, למה קורא אותן דלים, שהיו
דלים במנין מכל השבטים ... למה שהיו ס מ ו כ י ם ל ק ו ד ש ... ועוד שהם דלים
מנחלה ... [ד"א] אל תגזול דל, מדבר ב ב נ י ק ה ת, למה קורא אותן דל, שהיו משבט
לוי שלא נטלו חלק בארץ (כאן הוא סוף הסימן בבמ"ר שלפנינו).

this end is again truncated in the printed texts, with the proper conclusion found in YHM.[234]

The next Pet. (TB, §30, T, §24, end) introduces Is. 48.9: למען שמי אאריך אפי ותהלתי אחטם לך לבלתי הכריתך. Whereas by לבלתי הכריתך there is an obvious tally with the initial verses of both S and H, there is a further connection with the latter by means of the contrast in God being long-suffering towards Israel as against the pouring out of His wrath on the nations. (Zeph. 3.9: לשפוך עליהם זעמי כל חרון אפי.) In the final v. of H (3.20) Israel is promised to have name and renown among the nations (לשם ולתהלה).[378] The Agg. is again truncated in the Tanḥumas, and the whole application of the Pet. v. to Israel, as conditioned by the H, is missing. Again NR, c. 5.6, rightly supplies the lacuna, and its conclusion that, in order to glorify His name through Israel, God will restore Israel to its land, has been inspired by the last v. of H (3.20).[235] Subsequently the Pet. v. if applied to the Ḳehatites whom God decided to spare, in spite of Ḳoraḥ and his group belonging to them; hence at the beginning of the present S there is the form הקהתי (Num. 4.18), thus adding to the name ה and יוד=יה half of the full Tetragrammaton (cp. also above, note 229). Another Pet. is from 2 K. 14.27: ולא דבר ה' למחות את שם ישראל מתחת השמים וגו' linking up with Zeph. 3.13 which mentions 'the remnant of Israel' (שארית ישראל) and with v. 20 where Israel is assured to have a 'name' (fame) among the nations. In TB, §31, T, §25, the introductory formula is: הרי יפה אמר הכתוב ולא דבר וגו', but in NR, c. 5.3, the usual phrase הה"ד is used.[38s] The next item

---

[234] YHM, l. c., 33: שהיו דל, ולמה קורא אותם דל, שהיו ק ה ת, אל תגזול דל מדבר ב ב נ י. משבטו של לוי שלא נטלו חלק בארץ. ד"א שהיה משאם בכתף ולא בעגלות כשאר אחיהם (עיין במ' ז', ט'). כי דל הוא, ולא עוד אלא שהיו מתדלדלים מכל משפחות הלוים, שהיה הארון מכלה בהם. אמר הקב"ה למשה ולאהרן: הזהרו בהן בבני קהת, אל תגזלו חייהם מהם, עשו להם תקנה שיחיו, הה"ד אל תכריתו את שבט משפחות הקהתי מתוך הלוים, וזאת עשו להם ויחיו ולא ימותו.

[235] הה"ד למען שמי אאריך אפי ותהלתי אחטם לך לבלתי אכריתך, מדבר בישראל . . . ותהלתי אחטם לך, כדי שלא יתהלל שמו של הקב"ה בהם (ויותר נכון הנוסח בילה"מ לישעיה, צד 166: כדי שיתהלל שמו של הקב"ה בהם) יביא להם קץ הגאולה החתום, שנ' וקדשתי את שמי הגדול המחולל בגוים וגו', ולקחתי אתכם מן הגוים וקבצתי אתכם מכל הארצות והבאתי אתכם אל אדמתכם (יח' ל"ו, כ"ג, כ"ד), thus reflecting Zeph. 3.20: בעת ההיא אביא אתכם ובעת קבצי אתכם כי אתן אתכם לשם ולתהלה וגו'.

(TB, §32, T, §25, NR, c. 5.3, end) is based on Nah. 1.7: 'טוב ה
למעוז ביום צרה ויודע חוסי בו which tallies with the H v.
(Zeph. 3.12): 'וחסו בשם ה.[398] Finally there is the *peroration*
(end of TB, §33, T, §26, and NR, c. 5.9) to the effect that the
fear of God and the doing of His will result in honor and in
everlasting preservation.[236] This theme, as applied to Israel,
clearly reflects our H, viz. Zeph. 3.7 as regards revering God
(אך תיראי אותי), 3.13 as regards refraining from doing evil (שארית
ישראל לא יעשו עולה), and 3.20 as regards fame and honor (כי אתן
אתכם לשם ולתהלה).[408]

2. NR, c. 5, requires little further analysis, since it contains
the whole sermon discussed above. It should only be pointed
out how the component parts of TB, §28, T, §23, forming the
first portion of the Y sermon (above, p. 201), are differently
arranged in NR, in accordance with its procedure of commenting
extensively on the verses of the S. In §4 there is a discussion as
to why with regard to the clan of Ḳehat the Divine injunction is
directed to both Moses and Aaron (Num. 4.17) whereas concerning the other clans only Moses was addressed (vv. 21–22
about the sons of Gershon, cp. v. 29 about the sons of Merari).
This is obviously the purport of the statement here: ד"א אל
תכריתו וגו', מה כתוב למעלה (היינו במ' ד', י"ז), וידבר ה' אל משה ואל
אהרן, א"ר לוי מה עסקו של אהרן נזכר כאן וכו'. Of course the same
question applies also to Num. 4.1 wherewith the Biblical portion
concerning the sons of Ḳehat began (v. 2: 'נשא את ראש בני קהת וגו).

---

[236] As to the version in TB and T see the reading in YHM to Is. 48.19
(ed. Spira, p. 170) which resembles more closely that of NR and which we
cite here: אמר הקב"ה: ומה בני קהת בשביל שהיו יראים אותי כבדתים, וחלקתי להם
ולבניהם כבוד (בבמ'ר: כשם שעשיתי לבני קהת, על שהיו יר א י ם אותי, כבדתים וחלקתי
להם כבוד והזהרתי עליהם להציל ממות נפשם, כך כל מי שהוא מ ת י ר א ממני אני מכבדו
ואיני מ כ ר י ת ש מ ו מן העולם. ממי אתה למד, מבני יונדב בן רכב, על ידי שעשו רצוני,
מה כתיב בהם, לא י כ ר ת א י ש ליונדב בן רכב לפני כל הימים (יר' ל"ה, י"ט). ומה
אם אותם שהם גרים, ע"י שעשו רצוני כך עשיתי להם לישראל, שהם בני אהובי, בני ידידי,
עאכ"ו כשהן עושין רצוני, שהם עומדים לפני כל הימים, שנ' לוא הקשבת למצותי וגו' ויהי כחול
זרעך וצאצאי מעיך במעותיו ל א י כ ר ת ולא ישמד שמו לפני (יש' מ"ח, י"ח–י"ט), ואו'
ואתם הדבקים בה' אלהיכם חיים כלכם היום (דב' ד', ד'). The last v. (Deut. 4.4) is
cited only as an addendum, the real finale is meant to be Is. 48.19 containing the expression לא יכרת as in S and H; the latter (Zeph. 3.7) also mentions
the point of fearing God (אמרתי אך תיראו אותי).[84*]

Since, however, no S commenced at the latter place but only at
4.17–18 (No. 104), the above comment in NR is in its proper
place.[237]　Now R. Levi and the Rabbis explain the mentioning
of Aaron here in addition to Moses, in different ways, and the
opinion of the latter is woven into the above Y item anonymously
and also without indication of the proper connection with Num.
4.17.[238]　In illustration of that opinion of the Rabbis, to the effect
that God ordered a remedy for the Ḳehatites in order to prevent
their premature death, there is cited in NR the instance of even
an evildoer being given a chance of reprieve such as the case of
one guilty of כרת expiating his punishment by means of flogging
(quoting also M. Makkot 3.15).[239]　This has been shaped into a

[237] The commentators (see חדושי הרד"ל and פי' מהרז"ו) have difficulty with
R. Levi's question as to why Aaron is mentioned here, inasmuch as to Num.
4.1 there is found in NR, c. 4.12, a statement that explains this very point:
לפי שכל מעשה הפרשה באהרן, הביא את אהרן לכלל דיבור וכו' (and the same difficulty
would apply to the same question of the Rabbis further on: ורבותינו אמרו
למה כתיב כאן אהרן). However, this whole item in c. 4.12 emanates from Sifre
in connection with quite a different situation, viz. where Scripture reads:
וידבר ה' אל משה לאמר, דבר אל אהרן ואל בניו לאמר (see §39 to Num. 6.22–23, ed.
Horov., p. 42; §59 to Num. 8.1, ibid., p. 57). R. Levi and the Rabbis are
certainly not responsible for the above insertion in c. 4.12 which is out of
place, since in Num. 4.1 (and 4.17) Aaron is addressed directly in conjunction
with Moses, and not through the intermediacy of Moses, as in 6.22–23 etc.
Cp. further NR, c. 6.5: לפי שאהרן ממועט הוא וכו' which also is subject to
criticism.

[238] NR: ורבותינו אמרו למה כתיב כאן אהרן, לפי שבשעה שנצטוו בני קהת על משא
הארון נתייראו, התחילו צווחין על משה ואומרים הרי אנו מתים כשם שמתו בני אהרן, אמר
כך כשמתו בני אהרן. This became in TB and T: הקב"ה למשה... וזאת עשו להם וגו'
ראו אותן שבטו של קהת, התחילו צווחין על משה. The version in NR is obviously
more logical and original.

[239] NR: ואל תתמה על זו שעשה לחם חקב"ח תקנה שלא ימותו, [ש][בשעה שפירש הקב"ה
למשה ל"ו כריתות שבתורה (השוה מ' כריתות א', א'), אמר משה לפני הקב"ה: רבון העולמים,
אם יחטא אדם בהם, כך הוא נטרד (היינו: מן העולם), א"ל הקב"ה: ילקו ארבעים ויצאו ידי
כריתתן, וזו ששנינו (מס' מכות ג', ט"ו), כל חייבי כריתות שלקו נפטרו מידי כריתתן וכו'. In
the Tanḥumas, Moses' plea is stated to have been made in consequence of
the condemnation of the stoning of the gatherer of wood on the Sabbath:
באו למדבר ומצאו מקושש... רגום אותו באבנים, מיד עמד משה בתפלה, ואמר רבש"ע: אם
יחטא אדם מישראל כך הוא נ ס ק ל, הרי הם מתכלים, עשה להם תקנה, א"ל: ילקו ארבעים
ויצאו ידי כריתתן. This is not a logical development, since the remedy does
not apply at all to a transgression involving stoning. One could argue that,
since desecration of the Sabbath, as it occurred in the above case, was one

Y topic by placing the Mishnaic passage at the head and proceeding from it to develop the Aggadic theme. One can but obtain the distinct impression that the item in NR presents an earlier stage of the Aggadic construction and was reshaped subsequently by the Y homilist.[41s]

There are further comments in NR (§§7–9) on Num. 4.18–19, not included in the Tanḥumas. There must have been more running exegesis on v. 21 ff., as indeed found in NR, c. 6. This would be in accordance with the procedure noticed before with regard to the previous chapters of this Midr. (above, pp. 183, 193, 194, and 196). Only there has been inserted in c. 5, end, the *peroration* discussed above (p. 206)[240] because at Num. 4.21–22 there began a new S, according to a variant custom, in lieu of No. 104 (see infra, sub 104a), and hence by means of the *peroration* there was indicated that in c. 6.1–2 were contained homilies to the new Torah lection (for further analysis of c. 6, see further on).

SEDER 104a (4a)

וידבר ה' אל משה לאמר נשא את ראש בני גרשון גם הם לבית אבותם למשפחותם, Num. 4.21–22.

The fact that according to AC a new Sidra commenced here, also tends to show that at some time there began here a new S according to TC. Of course the latter would exclude No. 104 at Num. 4.17, only four verses previously. The reason for the substitution of No. 104 for 104a may have been the inauspicious ending of 4.20 (ומתו) which was the concluding v. of the previous S. Hence the latter was terminated at 4.16, with the new Torah

---

of the 36 types of כרת (see M. Kerit. 1.1: והמחלל את השבת, there would be established a sort of connection with the plea of Moses. However, כרת applies to a sin committed without warning (התראה) whereas the gatherer of wood received warning (according to the Rabbinic interpretation, see Sifre, Num., §113). The version in NR seems to be more original.[85*]

[240] In TB, §33, T, §26, the peroration is the result of a logical homiletic development whereas in NR, c. 5, end, it is tacked on abruptly after a previous passage with which it has no connection at all, testifying that it has been inserted here as an afterthought. It is curious that the whole homily in TB and T preceding the peroration is found in NR, c. 1.12, to Num. 1.49.[86*]

lection starting at 4.17 instead of at 4.21. Here we have another case of shifting of the Sedarim, involving especially a divergence between AC and TC (see above, p. 65, note 59, and pp. 49–50, 80–81).

Haftarah. There are only scanty Midrashic data to enable the ascertaining of the underlying Prophetic lection. I hesitatingly suggest Mal. 2.3 where the sentence: אֹתָם אֵלָיו נ ש א ו would link up with נשא in S. Of course, there is the difficulty of the former v. being entirely derogatory. However, who knows whether the above sentence, which is very difficult in the present context, really should not form the commencement of the next v., viz. 'And He (God) raised you up to Him, and know ye that I sent to you his commandment, that My covenant be with Levi, saith the Lord of Hosts.' In this manner the 'raising' meant honor and prestige just as the metaphor נשוא את ראש (literally 'to count') was Aggadically interpreted as bestowal of dignity.[241] Be this as it may, this H probably comprised Mal. 2.3–10, skipping to 3.3–4 which verses furnished the 'happy ending' (thus 10 verses). Although essentially there is depicted in this lection the ideal of the priesthood (cp. 2.6–7), yet there is employed the general term of God's 'covenant with Levi' (2.4: ברית הלוי 2.8: ;ברית את בני לוי 3.3: וטהר את בני לוי) and thereby there is an intrinsic connection with S which describes in detail the functions of the Levites under the supervision of 'Aaron and his sons' (cp. Num. 4.27–28, 33).

STRUCTURE OF HOMILIES

In NR, c. 6.1, there is a Pet. from Prov. 3.15: יקרה היא מפנינים וכל חפציך לא ישוו בה. While the linguistic tally would be in חפציך as compared to חפצים in Mal. 3.1 (this in the skipped

---

[241] Cp. the comment on Num. 1.2: שאו את ראש וגו' in TB, Bamidbar, §8, T, §8, NR, c. 1.9: אמר הקב"ה לישראל: לא חבבתי לבריה יותר מכם, לכך נתתי לכם .תלוי ראש ודמיתי אתכם לי, שכשם שיש לי תלוי ראש על כל באי העולם וכו' Cp. further, NR, c. 4.12 (to Num. 4.2): נשוא את ראש, וגו', אינו אומר פקוד, אלא נשוא את ראש, ומנין אתה למד שנגרשון לא אבד גדולתו, לפי שהיה and see c. 6.2, end: לשון נשיאות וכו', בכור, שכן את מוצא כשם שאמר בקהת נשוא את ראש בני קהת", כך אמר בגרשון נשוא את ראש בני גרשון. See further, infra, note 247.

part), the main point of the Agg. as to the superior importance
of the Torah has been inspired by the H (Mal. 2.6–7: תורת
אמת היתה בפיהו . . . ותורה יבקשו מפיהו). There is a subtle homiletic
turn in the particular point concerning a scholar, though of
illegitimate birth, having precedence over a High Priest who is
an ignoramus,[242] inasmuch as the Priest according to the Prophetic ideal, should have been the one from whose mouth the
Torah was being sought (ותורה יבקשו מפיהו)! Now this item in
NR, after citing the Pet. v., introduces a Tannaitic passage by
the formula תנינן תמן,[243] and one would be tempted to assume that
there has been inserted the topic which formed in Midr. Yel.
the initial one of the sermon to the present S, in view of the
previous similar examples in this Midrash (above, notes 187, 217,
224).[244] But in the latter cases the particular Y topic is not connected at all with a Pet. v. and there is no reason for a new
procedure here. Moreover, there would have to be a starting-
point in H for the Y question upon which there follows the
answer introduced by כך שנו רבותינו.[245] As the Tannaitic statement deals with the respective precedence of the various per-
sonages when in need of sustenance (see note 243), the Y question
would thus have to be couched in some such form as follows:
ילמדנו רבנו: מי קודם למי להחיות ולהשיב אבידה, לכסות ולפדות, כך
שנו רבותינו: חכם קודם וכו'. While the conclusion of the topic, with

---

[242] אבל אם היה ממזר ת"ח קודם לכה"ג ע"ה, שנ' יקרה היא מפנינים . . . אפי' מזה שהוא
נכנס לפני ולפנים (here there is a play upon the Ketib מפניים).

[243] נשא את ראש בני גרשון וגו', הה"ד יקרה היא מפנינים וכל חפציך לא ישוו בה, תנינן
תמן: חכם קודם למלך, מת חכם אין לנו כיוצא בו, מלך שמת כל ישראל ראוין למלכות וכו'
(in ed. Romm, Wilna, ישראל after מלך is an insertion due to the censor). About
this Bar. see Tos. Horayot 2.8–11, Yer. III, 9 (48b) and Babli 13a. The
point of the respective precedence is with regard to support, restoration of
lost articles, etc. (להחיות ולהשיב אבידה וכו' cp. M. Hor., 3.7 and Tos. 2.5). The
text here resembles that of Yer.; thus the insertion here: ר' הונא בשם ר' חנינא
אמר נביא כופף ידיו ורגליו וכו' is to be compared to that in Yer. (l. c., l. 57,ff.):
ר' יונה בשם ר' חמא בר' חנינה נביא מכפת (וצ"ל: מכפף) ידיו ורגליו, and the passage
here: סברין מימר לפדות וכו' as to which see there (48c, bottom).

[244] See also Epstein, מקדמוניות היהודים, p. 72, who could not account for
a S here.

[245] Epstein, who was entirely unaware of the dependence of the Y on TC H,
writes facilely: (אף שאינו סדר בשום מקום) נראה שבילמדנו היתה דרשה גם על ראש נשא
עם שאלה יל"ר מי קודם למי, והשיב חכם קודם וכו' מירושלמי או תוספתא הוריות סוף פ"ג.

its climax that an illegitimate scholar has precedence over an
ignorant High Priest, would link up with H (as pointed out
before), the commencement would lack such a link unless we
reason that the H. v.: ה ח י י ם והשלום (Mal. 2.5) inspired the
question which contained a reference to sustenance (להחיות).
But it is still difficult to explain why M. Horayot 3.8 was not
cited, but instead the longer statement from Tos. or Yer. The
latter fact rather seems to indicate that the main purpose was
to make use of the Pet. v. from Prov. 3.15 (see note 242), which
v. is subsequently applied to the case of the sons of Gershon
with whom the S deals.[246] It thus seems to be unjustified to
detect a hidden Y topic in this passage in NR (as Epstein does;
his further examples will also be shown further on to be unwarranted, see infra, pp. 229–230, note 269, 296, inc.).[42s]

There follows in NR, c. 2, another Pet. from Job 36.7–8:
לא יגרע מצדיק עיניו וגו', affording a point of contact with
בצדקה in Mal. 3.3[43s] The remainder of the chapter is of an
Aggadic exegetical nature giving comments on Num. 4.23–49
that do not require further analysis for our purpose. Finally
the passage in MHG (IV, ed. Fisch, pp. 215–17) is to be discussed. It offers a novel Pet. to the present S which seems to
emanate from a version of a new Midr. to Num. (as has also been
noticed with regard to previous items in MHG, above, pp.
177–8, 195). Ps. 132.16: וכהניה אלביש ישע וחסידיה רנן ירננו, is applied
to the tribe of Levi which was designated for God's service
because of humility and piety and because of devotion to the
study of the Torah. Therefore God concluded with the tribe a
covenant that 'the words of the Torah will never cease from their
mouth'. Now, in addition to the verbal tally of וכהניה with כהן
in Mal. 2.7, the points of the covenant with Levi and the study
of the Torah clearly reflect the sentiments expressed in our H
(2.4–7). A v. from the latter, viz. 3.3, is expressly woven into this
item.[247] In MHG (pp. 226–7) there seems to have been also pre-

---

[246] ד"א יקרה היא מפנינים, מדבר בקהת וגרשון, אעפ"י שגרשון בכור וכו'.

[247] זש"ה וכהניה אלביש ישע וחסידיה רנן ירננו, הכ' מדבר בשבטו של לוי שהובדלו לעבודת
המקדש ונתקדשו יותר מכל ישראל, לפי שהיו ענוים וחסידים ועמדים בברית אבות ... לפי
שהן הוגין בתורה ומפלפלין בטומאה וטהרה ובסדרי קרבנות. ולפיכך כרת להם הקב"ה ברית
שלא יפסקו ד"ת מפיהם לעולם, וכה"א ולכהנים הלוים לא יכרת איש מלפני מעלה עולה ומקטיר

served from this Midr. a *peroration* of the section to the present S. In connection with the comment on the sentence לעבוד עבודת עבודה towards the end of the S (Num. 4.47), as denoting the task of singing by the Levites (p. 201, cp. NR, c. 6.10, end), there is given (pp. 209–11) the well-known list of the daily Psalms recited by them in the Temple (cp. M. Tamid 7.4 and the Bar. in R. H. 31a). Thereupon is added a passage that in consequence of the destruction of the Temple the Holy Spirit ceased from Israel and the melody of song (טעם השיר; cp. the expression טעמים for the signs of cantillation) disappeared. A novel Agg. on Ps. 137.3–4 is cited to the effect that, when asked to sing by their Babylonian captors, the Jews could only produce words of lament. But Jerusalem will be ultimately restored to its pristine glory and then a new song will be heard there (concluding with the quotation of Is. 65.19 and 12.6).[248] Now the reference to

מנחה ועושה זבח כל הימים (יר' ל״ג, י״ח), והלא כבר חרב המקדש ופסקו קרבנות, אלא שלא יפסקו מהן ת״ח מורין הורייה והוגין בסדרי קרבנות, ומעלה עליהם הכתוב כאלו מזבח בנוי והן מקריבין עליו כל הקרבנות . . . ולפיכך הן עתידין להתיחס תחלה לימות המשיח, שנ' וישב מצרף ומטהר כסף וטהר את בני לוי וגו' (מל' ג', ג'), מהו בצדקה, בשכר שציּדקו את ישראל בעוה״ז, שהיו מורין להם הלכה, וזכו להיות משמשין בצדקה לפני הקב״ה לעתיד לבוא . . . הא לפי שיש בהן כל המדות המשובחות הללו זכו להתיחס וניתנה להם נשיאות ראש. מנין, ממה שקרינו בענין, נשא את ראש בני גרשן. Now, this final formula occurs in MHG frequently (thus 3 times to the beginning of Num., above, p. 177) and is not by itself evidence for the assumption of the editor that this whole item emanates from Yel. (*l. c.*, p. 217, note c, and pp. 66–7). More important is the insertion here of the comment on Jer. 33.18, which is similar in substance to the item from Yel. in YSH, Jer. §321. However, in form the latter is different (ולכהנים הלוים לא יכרת איש מלפני וגו', א״ר לוליינא שאל קריטיס אחד את ר' יוסי וכו', cp. GS, I, 220, ll. 34.6, where Hadrian is supposed to have the same question of R. Josh. b. Ḥan.), and it is difficult to ascertain whether it was the Y section to the present S. By means of לא יכרת this v. would tally with S 104 and its corresponding H, *which S indeed took the place of No. 104a and to which we have an established Y section* (above, p. 201 ff.). Accordingly the above passage cited in YSH may be a portion of the latter section.

וכשחרב ביהמ״ק בעוונותינו, פסקה רוה״ק וניטל טעם השיר, שכן את מוצא כשהגלו [248] כשדים את ישראל, אמרו להם: נגנו לנו בשיר שלכם, שנאמר כי שם שאלונו שובינו דברי שיר, אמרו להם: אין אנו יכולין לשיר בארץ טמאה, ולא עוד אלא שכבר שכחנו השיר ונהפך שירנו לקינה, אמרו להם: אף על פי כן אין אנו מניחין אתכם, מתוך הדוחק פתחו פיהם לומר שירה, ולא בא על פיהם אלא איכה ישבה בדד . . . בכה תבכה בלילה, אמרו להם: אין זה טעם שיר, אמרו: איך נשיר את שיר ה' על אדמת נכר. ועתיד הקב״ה להחזיר את ירושלים לקדמותה, ומשמיע בה שיר חדש, שנאמר ולתי בירושלים . . . ואומר צהלי ורוני יושבת ציון כי גדול בקרבך קדוש ישראל (כן יאמר רחום, this is addition of copyist).

Jerusalem is due to the final v. of H (Mal. 3.4) where there is mentioned מנחת יהודה וירושלים. The point of the new song at the time of the Messianic restoration is also mentioned in the above Pet. item introducing Ps. 132.16 (p. 217: וחסידיה, אלו הלוים ...). רנן ירננו, שהן עתידין לומר שירה חדשה). Thus there is good reason for the assumption that the author of MHG had before him a Midr. which contained a full section to a S that began with Num. 4.21, from which he excerpted the initial Pet. as well as the conclusion, whereas in NR (being of different construction) we have two Petiḥtot for the commencement of S, but no further parts of the sermon.

SEDER 104b (4b)

The regular Sedarim were No. 104, comprising Num. 4.17–5.10, followed by No. 105. As to the length of the latter, viz. whether it consisted only of the passage concerning the ordeal of a woman suspected of adultery (סוטה 'פ, Num. 5.11–31, just the minimum of 21 verses) or combined also the section dealing with the laws of the Nazirite (נזיר 'פ, Num. 6.1–21, again the bare minimum), see infra sub No. 105a (p. 232). Now as to S 104 we have noticed the alternative S 104a that began with Num. 4.21 (instead of 4.17). And with regard to the commencement of the next Torah lection the considerable sections in NR, cps. 7 and 8, suggest variants in customs, viz. that instead of the S starting at Num. 5.11 (No. 105) one usage was to do so at 5.1 while another was to begin reading at 5.5

For the former practice there is the evidence of NR, c. 7, to be analyzed forthwith. There is a further consideration inasmuch as Sifre to Num., as well as Sifre Zutta, commenced at Num. 5.1, which must have formed at some time a new S (and not the end of S 104 or 104a), and hence afforded an appropriate starting point for this Tannaitic Midrash in addition to the fact that there was the first Halakhic topic in the fourth book of Moses. This commencement would thus resemble that of Mekh. of R. Ishmael at Exodus, c. 12, where there was, if not a Seder, a distinct special lection for the so-called Sabbath החודש (see above, vol. I, p. 406, and especially, infra, p. inc.). And

Mekh. of R. Simon b. Yoḥai began with Ex., c. 3, which formed
a S (above, vol. I, p. 365). Of course, Sifra to Lev. and Sifre to
Deut. both started at the very beginning of these parts of the
Pentateuch respectively where Sedarim were naturally in general
acceptance (above, p. 23, and infra, p. inc.). The validity of an
alternative S at Num. 5.5 will become evident from the analysis
of NR, c. 8 (infra, p. 218). We thus have three different commencements of the same S which we list here under Nos. 104b
(Num. 5.1), 104c (Num. 5.5) and 105 (Num. 5.11) respectively.
The reasons for these various differences are entirely obscure.[44s]

וידבר ה' . . . צו את בני ישראל וישלחו מן המחנה כל צרוע וכל זב וכל ט מ א
לנפש, Num. 5.1–2.

Haftarah. On the basis of the Midrashic data it appears to me
that the Prophetic lection began with Is. 52.1: עורי עורי לבשי
עוזך ציון לבשי בגדי תפארתך ירושלים עיר הקדש כי לא יוסיף יבא בך עוד
ערל ו ט מ א; it probably extended to v. 10, in making up the
usual length of a TC H. In addition to the tally of טמא, there is
the intrinsic parallel that just as in S the Levitically impure was
to be sent out from the camp in order not to defile it (Num.
5.2–3), so also in H it is promised that Jerusalem the holy city,
will no longer be frequented by 'the uncircumcised and the
impure.' The camp of the wilderness was the locale of the
Divine residence (Num. 5.3: אשר אני שוכן בתוכם), and correspondingly Zion — Jerusalem was again to become the place where
God ruled (Is. 52.7: אומר לציון מלך אלהיך, cp. v. 8: בשוב ה' ציון).
Otherwise the H is a typical one of 'consolation of Israel.'

STRUCTURE OF HOMILIES

NR, c. 7, evidently incorporated a good deal from the larger
version of the Midr. Tanḥ. (as noticed before with regard to the
portions of the former, see above, p. 194). Thus section 1 here
commences with a Pet. of R. Tanḥ. b. Abba. Furthermore,
there is here the characteristic use of אלהים (אמר אלהים) which is
also common to Yel, and kindred compositions (more about this
point infra, vol. III).[45s] The above Pet. (§1) introduces Prov.
25.4: הגו סיגים מכסף which tallies linguistically with the H v.:

ולא ב כ ס ף תגאלו (Is. 52.3). The former v. is applied to Israel on
leaving Egypt; among them were many invalids from the
effects of the hard labor there, but prior to the giving of the
Torah at Sinai they were healed.[249] Yet the blemishes returned
upon the worship of the 'Golden Calf.' Thus there were in the
wilderness persons afflicted with gonorrhea and leprosy that had
to be sent out from the camp (thereby linking up with S, Num.
5.2–3). The introduction here of the point of the Exodus from
Egypt has been inspired by the H v. (Is. 52.4): מצרים ירד עמי
בראשונה וגו'.[46s] In §2 the placing of the commencements of the S
(Num. 5.1–4) next to the section concerning the Levites is
discussed (למה נסמכה פרשת מצורעים לפרשת הלוים). Here again the
sin of the 'calf' is woven in. It was committed by a part of
Israel, but not by the Levites; therefore the latter were honored
by being chosen to God's service, whereas the former were
smitten by leprosy and were put to shame by being sent out
from the camp. The Agg. here is developed on 1 S. 2.30: כי
מכבדי אכבד ובוזי יקלו,[250] which v. in its second half has an affinity
to the H v. (Is. 52.5): ותמיד כל היום שמי מנואץ. Whereas the above

---

[249] The printed text of NR, c. 7.1, is defective, and has to be rectified
by the citation in YHM to Prov., a. l. (ed. Grünhut, 53b–54a). Thus after
א'ר יהודה בר הריני משהא במתן תורה there has been left out in the printed NR:
סימון משל למלך שהיה לו בן והיה מבקש להשיאו...ואם נמתין לבניהם, הריני משהא
במתן תורה. See PRK, 12 (ed. Buber 106b). Grünhut's remark (l. c.,
note 7) that the redactor of NR took this passage from PRK (ואין ספק שהמסדר
הבמ'ר לקח זה מפסיקתא) is incorrect. Rather R. Tanḥ. b. Abba wove into his
Pet. here the Agg. of R. Judah b. Simon concerning the healing of the afflicted Jews prior to the giving of the Torah which Agg. belonged originally to
S 50a (see above, vol. I, p. 456–7).

[250] NR, c. 7.2: אמר הקב"ה: כי מכבדי אכבד ובוזי יקלו, בני לוי שכבדוני, שלא כפרו
בי, להם אני מכבד, אבל ישראל שביזוני, שאני העליתי אותם ממצרים, והם אמרו לעגל שהוא
העלם (השוה שמ' ל"ב, ד'), בדין הוא שיקלו. מה כבוד כיבד הקב"ה את הלוים, שלקחם
להלקו...אמר הקב"ה: הלוים שכבדוני יהיו אצלי. From here the printed text is
truncated, and should be rectified by the citation of NR, in YHM to Ps.
101 (ed. Buber, II, 124, No. 12): יהיו אצלי, כמד"א עיני בנאמני ארץ לשבת עמדי
וגו' (תה' ק"א, ו'), אבל אותן שטעו בעגל יתרחקו מעלי. הם (צ"ל: ומי הם) שטעו בעגל, אלו
שלקו בצרעת, שנאמר וירא משה את העם כי פרוע הוא (שמ' ל"ב, כ"ה), וצריך להוסיף כאן
כמו בבמ'ר, כ"ז, א': [ואין פרוע אלא לשון צרוע, כמא דתימא והצרוע אשר בו הנגע וגו' וראשו
יהיה פרוע וגו' (וי' י"ג, מ"ה)]. הוי ובוזי יקלו, מה קלון היה להם, וישלחו מן
המחנה כל צרוע וגו' (במ' ה', ב'), וכן הוא אומר עשה שטים שנאתי (תה' ק"א, ג').

homilies take it for granted that the lepers to be excluded from
the camp were the devotees of the Calf, in §4 there is given a
difference of opinion between R. Judah b. Simon and the Rabbis
as to the cause of this affliction, with the former ascribing it to
this deed and the latter to the grumbling about the Manna
(Num., c. 11). Long Aggadot are developed in support of each
theory.[251] While these do not lend themselves to detailed analysis
for our purpose here, it should only be pointed out that the one
Agg. concerning the grumblers weaves in the feature of 'spurning'
God (thus Num. 14.11 is cited, although this v. really pertains to
the evil report of the spies); it concludes with the statement
that anyone who contemns God becomes leprous and thus is
excluded from the community.[252] This feature seems to have
been suggested by our H containing the statement: ותמיד כל
היום שמי מנואץ (Is. 52.5). In §5 there is given, in the name of
R. Judah Hallevi b. Shalom, a list of the causes of leprosy.
This item is really a Tannaitic statement, and has been used as
a Y topic to S 86 (see above, p. 76, and cp. there note 76).
But here it is cited in order to conclude with one of the enum-

---

[251] וישלחו מן המחנה וגו', מהיכן באת עליהם הצרעת? ר' יהודה בר סימון :NR, c. 7.4
אמר מן מעשה העגל, ורבותינו אומרים מן המתאוננים. לדעת רבותינו (צריך להוסיף: שהן
אומרין, כמו בילה"מ ליש' י"ז, י"א, הוצ' שפירא, צד 103) מן המתאוננים באת עליהם הצרעת,
כיצד? בשעה שהוריד להם אלהים את המן וכו', ועל דעתיה דר"י בר סימון דאמר מן מעשה
העגל באת עליהם הצרעת מפיק ליה מהאי קרא וכו' .In LR, c. 18.4, the authors of
these opinions are reversed (see חדושי הרש"ש here, note 2). According to the
version in NR, c. 13.8, already R. Sim. b. Yoḥai ascribes the existence in
the camp of זבים ומצורעים to the sin of the Golden Calf, but according to the
version in LR, l. c. (cp. also Cant. R. 4.7) this Tanna only uses the general
term of sinning (וכיון שחטאו לא עברו ימים קלים עד שנמצאו בהם זבים ומצורעים).
Thereupon follows a discussion as to the kind of sin that caused these afflictions, with three reasons being advanced: 1) slander, 2) the sin of the Calf,
and 3) the grumblers: מהיכן נתחייבו ישראל בזיבות וצרעת? ר' הונא בשם ר' הושעיא
ע"י שהיו מליזין את גדוליהן ... ללמדך שאין הנגעים באים אלא על לה"ר, ר' תנחומא אמר
ע"י שהיו מליזין אחרי הארון ... ואין נגעים באים אלא על לה"ר, ורבנן אמרי מן העגל ...
ר"י ב"ר סימון אמר ממתאוננים.

[252] באותה שעה אמר אלהים למשה: איני יכול לסבול ולכבוש, עד אנה ינאצוני
וגו' ... כך כל מי שניאץ לאלהים נעשה זר, והיאך נעשה זר, אלא שבאת עליהם (צ"ל:
עליו) הצרעת. א"ל (היינו: למשה) האלהים, למה הם נאצו אותי, הרי הם זרים מן הקהל,
וישלחו מן המחנה כל צרוע וגו'.

erated causes that pertains to our S, viz. that leprosy is caused by idolatry.[253]

In NR (§§6–9) we have insertions from Sifre and Sifre Zutta to Num. 5.1–4 that require no further comment here. But interesting is §10 wherein this whole Biblical passage is interpreted in an allegorical manner as applying to the exile and the subjection by the 'four dominions' and the leading down to the ultimate salvation of Israel.

While such allegorizations are frequent in the Midrashic literature, (cp. also infra, p. 223, concerning the same procedure with regard to the portion about a Soṭah, Num. 5.11 ff.), the specific inspiration for this theme here is to be sought in the H referring to Israel having been sold into captivity and to its subsequent redemption (Is. 52.3, about which v. see further on, note 255). The exile has been caused by three sins: idolatry, sexual immorality and bloodshed.[254] Israel's subjection to Babylon was succeeded by that to Media (and Persia), Greece and Rome. The redemption will be the result of repentance (weaving in Is. 30.15: בשובה ונחת תושעון which v. is reflected by the theme of 'salvation' in our H, Is. 52.7 and 10).[255] On that

---

[253] NR, c. 7.5, end: ועל ע״ז, אלו ישראל, כשעשו אותו מעשה (היינו: העגל) נעשו מצורעים... לפיכך אמר אלהים למשה: הפרש המצורעים שביניכם ממחנה ישראל, שהם עשו אותו המעשה, וישלחו מן המחנה כל צרוע.

[254] NR, c. 7.10: ד״א צו את בני ישראל, רבנן פתרין קרייה בגלות. צו את בני ישראל, על שעברו ישראל על המצות נתחייבו שילוח, זה גלות, הה״ד וישלחו מן המחנה, אין וישלחו אלא גלות... מן המחנה, זו ארץ ישראל, ששם השכינה שורה. כל צרוע וכל זב וכל טמא לנפש, רמז להם שאם יעברו ישראל על ג' עבירות הללו: עבודה זרה, גלוי עריות, ושפיכות דמים, יתחייבו גלות... ותנינן כן גלות באה לעולם... ומסתלקת השכינה (השוה אבות ה', ט', ל״ח נתן פרק ל״ח). In the continuation there has been inserted between: ושילוח הזה אמור בגלות בבל and ודברים הללו היו במקדש ראשון a passage that emanates from Yoma 9a and Sabb. 139a.

[255] כאשר דבר ה' אל משה (במ' ה', ד'), מה דבר הקב״ה למשה, שאם יעשו תשובה במלכיות שיהיו שם, הקב״ה מקבצם... כן עשו בני ישראל (שם), שעתידין ישראל שיעשו תשובה באחרית הימים והם נגאלים, שנאמר בשובה ונחת תושעון. This v. (Is. 30.15) is one among others cited by R. Eli‘ezer b. Hyrcanos in his argument that repentance was the indispensable prerequisite of redemption, whereas his colleague, R. Josh. b. Ḥan., quoted among others Is. 52.3 to the effect that the latter would be consummated even without the former (see Yer. Taan. I, 63d, bottom: ר' אליעזר אומר: אם אין ישראל עושין תשובה אין נגאלים לעולם, שנ' בשובה (היינו כמו בתשובה) ונחת תושעון. א״ל ר' יהושע: וכי אם יעמדו ישראל ולא יעשו

happy occasion Israel will be purified by God from all un-
cleanness and imperfection. As a final v. Ezek. 34.25 is cited
with which some of the subsequent ones are to be included (as
noticed several times before, cp. above, pp. 200, 206).

Thus the assurance of Israel's restoration to its patrimony,
with the re-establishment of the former relationship between
God and His people (Ezek. 36.28: והייתם לי ל ע ם ואנכי אהיה
לכם לאלהים), links up with the announcement of the har-
binger of good tidings to Zion that 'thy God ruleth' (Is. 52.7:
מלך אלהיך, cp. v. 5: כי לוקח ע מ י). The conclusion of the section in NR, c. 7, is thus in the form of a *peroration*, affording further evidence for the validity of our assumption that Num. 5.1
formed the commencement of an alternative S, with a H of its
own, and accordingly in NR there has been preserved a regular
Midrashic portion comprising a Pet. as well as a proper termination, in addition to the other Aggadic material, on the construction of which the influence of the Prophetic lection could be
definitely traced.

Seder 104c (4c)

וידבר ה'. . . א י ש או אשה כי יעשו מכל ח ט א ת האדם למעול מעל
בה', ואשמה הנפש ההוא, והתודו את חטאתם אשר עשו וגו', Num. 5.5–7.

About the commencement of the S here, instead of at 5.1 or
5.11, see above (p. 214).[256]

(in Babli, תשובה, אין נגאלין לעולם? . . . א"ל ר"י: והא כתיב חנם נמכרתם ולא בכסף תגאלו
Sanh. 97b, bottom the reading is: חנם נמכרתם, בע"א, ולא בכסף תגאלו, לא בתשובה
ומע"ט).

[256] איש או אשה כי יעשו מכל חטאת וגו'. ר' אבהו אומר ישובו יושבי בצלו, אלו הגרים
שהם באים וחסים בצילו של הקב"ה; יחיו דגן, בתלמוד; יפרחו כנפן, באגדה; זכרו כיין לבנון,
אמר הקב"ה חביב עלי שמותן של גרים כיין שהוא מתנסך על גבי המזבח . . . דבר אחר יחיו
דגן, יעשו עיקר (הם) כישראל . . . וכן את מוצא כשם שכתובה פרשה בתורה בין ישראל לחבירו
. . . כך הקב"ה כתב פרשה בתורה בין ישראל לגרים, שאם גוזל אדם מישראל לגר דינו כגוזל
מישראל . . . הא למדנו שהגרים עיקר הם כישראל, הוי יחיו דגן ויפרחו כנפן. It should be
pointed out that in YHM to Is. 56.6 (ed. Spira, p. 214) there is rightly missing
the passage: רשב"י אומר שכל הלבבות שמחים בו . . . והיו עיני ולבי שם כל הימים which
is unnecessary here (see also, above, note 11a).

Haftarah. The extensive section in NR (c. 8) deals with proselytes to Judaism concerning whom some beautiful Aggadot are given. This topic here is in accordance with the Tannaitic interpretation of Num. 5.5 ff. as applying to the restitution made by an Israelite who robbed a stranger (cp. Sifre, Num. §2: למה נאמרה פרשה זו ... בא הכתוב ולמד על גוזל הגר וכו'). This suggests a Prophetic lection wherein the non-Jew was mentioned and which thus suggested the whole topic of proselytes.[478] Bearing in mind other data, to become evident from our discussion here, the following H. is proposed: את אשר יחטא איש לרעהו ונשא בו אלה להאלתו ובא אלה לפני מזבחך בבית הזה (1 Kings 8.31), extending to v. 39 (concluding with כי אתה ידעת לבדך את ל ב ב (להטות ל ב ב נ ו אליו) 58+(כל בני אדם), hence 10 verses (with v. 38 there begins a new Seder in this Biblical book). In addition to the linguistic tally in 1 K., 8.31 with Num. 5.6, as italicized, there is the further parallel of confessing one's sin in Num. 5.7 (והתודו את חטאתם) and in 1 K. 8.33, 35. Moreover, the point of a false oath implied in the initial v. of H, connects it with the guilt dealt with in the S, as the parallel law in Lev. 5.20 ff. shows (cp. v. 22 there: ונשבע על שקר). Now in the skipped part of the lection, which the homilists would utilize, there is a reference to the Gentile who, on hearing of God's fame, came to worship at the Temple (1 K. 8.42–3). This afforded the starting point for the theme concerning the proselytes (גרים) who accepted Judaism.

STRUCTURE OF HOMILIES

The first Pet. in NR. (c. 8.1) introduces Hosea 14.8: ישובו יושבי בצלו יחיו דגן ויפרחו כגפן זכרו כיין לבנון, which v. R. Abbahu applied to the proselytes 'who came and took protection in the shadow of the Holy One.' The verbal link with H. here would be in ישובו as compared to ושבו אליך in 1 K. 8.33. The same Pet. we have in LR, c. 1.2, to S 74 (above, p. 27), where, however, the item is truncated. Here this homily concerning the neophytes to Judaism who became as important in God's eye as native Jews, is further illustrated by the commencement of the S, the laws of which were explained as referring to robbery perpetrated by a Jew towards a Ger (above, p. 219). As pointed out there, the whole introduction to this topic has been inspired by the H where (in the skipped part) there is mentioned the non-Jew who came to pray in the Temple because of the reputation of God's name (1 K. 8.41–43), and such a sentence as contained in v. 43 concerning the former 'that he fear Thee as Thy people Israel' (ליראה אותך כעמך ישראל). On account of this close relationship between H. and Pet., it would seem that the latter was originally composed to the present S and not to S 74 where its relevance is not apparent; it is true that in LR the item begins with ר' אבהו פתח whereas here in NR with ר' אבהו אומר, but in YSH, Hos. §533, where the passage in LR is cited, the reading is: אמר ר' אבהו.[48s]

The next Pet. (NR, c. 8.2) is on Ps. 146.8–9: ה' פוקח עורים ...ה' אוהב צדיקים, ה' שומר את גרים ... ודרך רשעים יעות which verses afford several points of contact with H; thus with להרשיע רשע לתת דרכו בראשו ולהצדיק צדיק וגו' 1 K. 8.32: and with 8.41 where 'the stranger who is not of Thy people Israel,' is mentioned as having come to join the worship of God. The Latter's love of the righteous can be considered as a manifestation of the fact that the acquisition of the praiseworthy moral qualities is not dependent on lineage or class, but 'anybody who wants to become a righteous person, even a gentile, can do so.' Here there is woven in comment on Ps. 135.20: יראי ה' ברכו את ה' (a later special designation for non-Jews attached to Judaism, cp. *metuentes*), thus reflecting what is stated in 1 K. 8.43 concerning 'the peoples of the earth' ליראה אותך כעמך ישראל.[257] There follows in NR (§3) a homily on 1 S. 2.30: לכן נאום ה' אלהי ישראל אמור אמרתי ביתך ובית אביך יתהלכו לפני עד עולם ועתה נאום ה' חלילה לי כי מכבדי אכבד ובוזי יקלו. In addition to the linguistic connection with H by means of ובית אביך as compared to I K.

<hr>

[257] איש או אשה, הה"ד ה' אוהב צדיקים וגו' ... ולמה הקב"ה אוהב צדיקים, שאינם נחלה ואינם משפחה. את מוצא הכהנים בית אב הם, שנ' בית אהרן ברכו את ה' בית הלוי ברכו את ה', אם מבקש אדם להיות כהן, אינו יכול, להיות לוי, אינו יכול, למה, שלא היה אביו לא כהן ולא לוי, אבל אם מבקש אדם להיות צדיק, אפילו גוי, יכול הוא, שאינו בית אב, לכך הוא אומר יראי ה' ברכו את ה', בית יראי ה' לא נאמר, אלא יראי ה', אינו בית אב אלא מעצמם נתנדבו ואהבו להקב"ה, לפיכך הקב"ה אוהבם, לכך נאמר ה' אוהב צדיקים וגו', הרבה הקב"ה אוהב את הגרים וכו'.

8.38: אשר צוה את אבותינו, this item follows logically the preceding
one where emphasis was laid on good action and not on descent,
and here in the cited v. likewise Eli's sons, in spite of their
priestly lineage, are to be punished because of their deeds which
are tantamount to despising God; indeed 1 S. 2.30 is woven into
the previous homily (§3 beginning: כך אמר הקב"ה: אני אוהבי אהב
אכבד מכבדי כי וה"א ,(י"ז ,ח' משלי השוה)). Now this Pet. v. is first
applied to other instances (for the whole passage in §3 from
אומר יוסי ר' תני to ויך במחנה אשור וגו' see ARN, c. 27, ed.
Shechter, pp. 83–4) and then to the topic pertinent here, viz.
the proselytes. Because the latter honor God by 'forsaking their
evil deeds and coming to seek shelter under the wings of the
Shekhinah,' He in His turn honors them, whereas the wicked
He esteems lightly because of their departure from Him. This
item, too, reflects in its structure the underlying H to the
present S.²⁵⁸

In §4 there is a further Pet. from Ps. 138.4: כל ה' יודוך
מלכי ארץ כי שמעו אמרי פיך, affording a tally with את והודו
שמך in H (1 K. 8.33 and 35).⁴⁹ˢ Bearing in mind the plural
'words' R. Pinḥas developed an interesting Agg. concerning two
items in the Torah which especially had found approval by the
non-Jewish rulers, the one being the command in the Decalogue,
of honoring one's father and mother and the other being the
regulations concerning the restitution of monetary trespasses
committed respectively towards the sanctuary and towards an
individual; the latter case was regarded as more serious and
applied not only to a Jew but also to the proselyte (in accordance with the above-mentioned interpretation of the commencement of our S).²⁵⁹ The same Pet. is also to be found in PR

---

²⁵⁸ ד"א כי מכבדי אכבד וגו', מדבר בגרים, הם מכבדים להקב"ה, שמניחים מעשיהם
הרעים ובאים וחסים תחת כנפי השכינה, הקב"ה מכבדם, ללמדך שכל המיישר אורחותיו,
הוא מכבד להקב"ה שנ' זובח תודה יכבדנני [ושם דרך אראנו בישע אלהים] (תה' נ', כ"ג)
וכו' מקילם, הקב"ה המקום, מאחרי סרים שהרי הרשעים, אלה יקלו. ובוזי .... The allusion
to him "who sets his paths straight" reflects the final v. of H. (I K. 8.58):
ללכת בכל דרכיו, and the reference to the wicked links up with I K. 8.32:
להרשיע רשע לתת דרכו בראשו.
²⁵⁹ איש או אשה וגו', הה"ד יודוך ה' כל מלכי ארץ כי שמעו אמרי פיך, א"ר פנחס ב' דברים
שמעו או"ה מפי הקב"ה ועמדו מכסאותם והודו. As regards the first half of R. Pinḥas'

(ed. Friedm., p. 101a–b) in connection with the fourth commandment of the Decalogue, but there it is curtailed and the
point that links it up with our S is missing. In view of the
above tally of the Pet. v. with the H here, the whole item pertains well to the present Midrashic section and should not be
regarded as having been transferred from PR to NR (as Friedm.
assumes, *l. c.*, note 4). Following this Pet. there is given a long
discourse concerning the Gibeonites and their terrible demand of
vengeance on Saul's descendants (2 S. 21),[260] which to analyze
would be beyond our scope here. The same applies to §§5–8
which emanate from Sifre and Sifre Zutta. But interesting is
§9 which contains an Aggadic interpretation of Ps. 128 as
applied to proselytes. In NR the whole item is connected with
Num. 5.10, but in reality it formed a special section dealing with
the *Mizmor read on the Sabbath when our S was recited* — thus
corresponding to the chapter headed Ketubim in AB which ch.
was also traceable elsewhere (see above, vol. I, pp. 57, 94,
note 85, 220). Now the 'God-fearing' in Ps. 128.1 (אשרי כל ירא)
(ה' ההולך בדרכיו) was taken as referring to the neophyte to
Judaism, thus linking up with our H (1 K. 8.43, as above, p. 220
and 8.58: ללכת בכל דרכיו). This correlation was the
reason for the choice of this Ps. for the present Sabbath and
in the Aggadah this Mizmor was accordingly entirely interpreted to suit the righteous proselyte (גר צדק)[261] to whom also

statement, see the text in YHM, to Ps., *a. l.* (ed. Buber, II, p. 265, No. 4),
which corrects the printed one in NR (thus: איזה מלך רוצה שלא יהו מכבדין
איזה מלך רוצה שלא יהיו הבריות instead of the corrupted יום גנוסיא שלו, וכן הקב"ה
מכבדים את יום השביעי). It would be out of place to discuss this passage in
which there is an echo of the analysis and appreciation of the Decalogue
by the heathen. It should only be added that R. Pinḥas seems to have
modified and enlarged an earlier Agg. which Ullah once preached (Kidd. 31a:
דרש עולא רבה אפיתחא דבי נשיאה מאי דכתיב יודוך ה' כל מלכי ארץ כי שמעו אמרי פיך,
מאמר פיך לא נאמר אלא אמרי פיך, בשעה שאמר הקב"ה אנכי ולא יהיה לך, אמרו או"ה
לכבוד עצמו הוא דורש, כיון שאמר כבד את אביך ואת אמך, חזרו והודו למאמרות הראשונות).
ולא תאמר בגירי הצדק שנתניירו לש"ש קירב הקב"ה, אלא אפי' אותן שנתניירו שלא [260]
לש"ש מצינו שתבע הקב"ה עלבונם, הה"ד ויהי רעב בימי דוד וגו'. After this long insertion §4 of NR concludes: הא למדנו כמה קירב הקב"ה את הרחוקים, אפילו שנתניירו
שלא לשם שמים, ואצ"ל על גירי הצדק, הוי יודוך ה' כל מלכי ארץ וגו'.
ד"א ואיש את קדשיו לו יהיו, הה"ד אשרי כל ירא ה' ההולך בדרכיו, [261] NR, c. 8.9:

there was applied the law that formed the beginning of the S
under discussion. The above analysis of NR, c. 8, laying bare
its warp and web again justifies our assumption of a new Torah
lection here with its corresponding reading from the Prophets.[508]

Seder 105 (5)

וידבר ה' . . . דבר אל בני ישראל ואמרת אליהם איש איש כי תשטה אשתו
ומעלה בו מעל, Num. 5.11–12.

Haftarah: לא אפקוד על בנותיכם כי תזנינה ועל כלותיכם כי תנאפנה כי
הם עם הזונות יפרדו ועם הקדשות יזבחו ועם לא יבין ילבט, Hosea 4.14.
This initial v. is evident from Yannai's Ḳerobah to the present
S (see ed. Zulay, p. 181, top). Moreover, the Byzantine ritual,
which retained one of the Hafṭarot of the Sedarim of TC comprising within the section forming the Sidra of AC (see above,
vol. I, p. 91), has to פ' נשא a Prophetic lection consisting of
Hosea 4.14–6.2; the latter was also taken over by the Karaites
of Byzantium, Turkey and the Crimea (see infra, vol. III).
Now, while a TC H did not cover 23 verses, it may safely be
assumed that it extended from 4.14 to 5.2 (and in ושחטה ש ט י ם
there was a verbal tally with כי תשטה in Num. 5.12) and then
there was skipping in order to lead down to a 'happy ending';
thus there were added 6.1–2 to complete the usual number of 10
verses. With Hos. 6.2 there begins a new Seder in Minor Prophets, indicating that here was the termination of a H.

The initial v. of H links up with the beginning of the S intrinsically, only inasmuch as the adultery of one's daughter-in-law
is that of a married woman. The verbal tally is found only in
Hos. 5.2, as pointed out above. However, the coupling of
Hos. 4.14 with the ordeal of 'the bitter water' is already old.
When this ordeal was abolished by R. Yoḥanan b. Zakkai (not
long before the destruction of the Second Temple) because of
the increase of immorality among the men, this v. was evi-

אינו אומר: אשרי ישראל, אשרי כהנים, אשרי לוים, אלא אשרי כל ירא ה', אלו הגרים שהם
יראי ה' . . . ובאיזה גר אמור אשרי, בגר שהוא גר צדק . . . ש ה ו א י ר א מ ן ה ק ב ' ה
ו ה ו ל ך ב ד ר כ י ו ש ל ה ק ב ' ה ו כ ו '.

dently used by that eminent Pharisee in justification of his
step in abolishing a practice ordained in the Torah.²⁶² ⁵¹ˢ

Structure of Homilies

1. *Y Sermon.* TB, Naso, §1, T, §1: אִישׁ אִישׁ כִּי תִשְׂטֶה אִשְׁתּוֹ,
ילמדנו רבינו: מי שמקנא לאשתו (ובת"ב: מי שהיה מבקש לקנאות לאשתו) ...
כיצד היה מקנא לה, כך שנו רבותינו: המקנא לאשתו היה מוליכה לב"ד
הגדול שבירושלים, וכו'.²⁶³ In looking for a starting point in H for
this Halakhic item — a characteristic feature of Midr. Yel. by
now abundantly proven —, it seems to me that in addition to
the general case of adultery involved (in Hos. 4.3: ועל כלותיכם

²⁶² M. Soṭah 9.9: משרבו המנאפים פסקו המים המרים, ורי"ז הפסיקן, שנ' לא
אפקוד על בניכם כי תזנינה ועל כלותיכם כי תנאפנה כי הם וגו'. Cp. further the comment
on Num. 5.31 in Sifre, Num. §21, end (ed. Horov., p. 25): למה נאמר ונקה
האיש מעון, כשהאיש מנוקה מעון, האשה ההיא תשא את עונה, ולא [כשאין האיש מנוקה מעון,
כנוסח היל"ש, נשא סי' תש"י], כענין שנ' לא אפקוד על בניכם וכו'. See further the better
version of this Sifre passage in NR, c. 9.43, end. See also the Bar. in Babli
Soṭah 47b and Yer. I, c. 9 (24a).
²⁶³ The initial phrase המקנא לאשתו is taken from M. Soṭah 1.1 and the
continuation is from 1.3–4, etc. (for the sources see Buber's notes and GS,
I, 475, No. 64). Neither Buber nor Ginzberg have noticed that the statement here 'he (the husband) leads her to the High Court at Jerusalem' would
be in accordance with R. Judah's opinion in M. Soṭah 1.3: בעלה נאמן עליה
which, however, has not been accepted by the redactor of the M. since it
was a minority view. See the discussion between R. Judah and the majority
scholars in the Bar. cited (in the best version) in Yer. c. 1 (17d); in Tos.
1.2–3 (ed. Zuckerm., p. 293) and in Babli 7a the text is not preserved so
well. It seems that in the Y answer a passage has fallen out due to a scribal
skipping from one לב"ד to another לב"ד. Thus it should read: המקנא לאשתו
(מס' סוטה א', א'), היה מוליכה ל ב " ד [שבאותו מקום, ומוסרין לו ב' ת"ח שמא יבוא עליה
בדרך (שם, ג') והיו מעלין אותה ל ב " ד] הגדול שבירושלים (שם, ד') וכו'. That the
Tanḥ. text is defective is still more evident from the first two editions where
also the Y question is truncated: ילמדנו רבינו מי שמקנא אשתו היה מוליכה לב"ד
הגדול שבירושלים. Only since ed. Mantua has this question been properly inserted, but the answer has remained deficient requiring rectification as suggested above. The verb מעלין is essential here as affording the specific link
with H (as shown forthwith). The author of YSH (Naso, §904) had already
the deficient version. See also Wehizhir (ed. Freimann, II, p. 286–7):
והזהיר הקב"ה את ישראל שכל מי שמקנא אשתו היה מוליכה לב"ד הגדול שבירושלים, and
especially p. 293: והזהיר הקב"ה את ישראל שכל מי שמקנא לאשתו היה מביא אותה לב"ד
הגדול שבירושלים ומאימין עליה וכו'.⁸⁷*

כי תנאפנה and in the Hal. המקנא לאשתו, viz. the accusation by
the husband of such conduct on the part of his wife), the Y
homilist found a specific allusion in the Prophetic lection for
his theme which describes the ordeal of such a suspected
woman.[528] This ordeal began with her being brought to the
High Court at Jerusalem (והיו מעלין אותה לב"ד הגדול
שבירושלים וכו', see note 263) and subsequently to the eastern
gate of the Temple (ואח"כ מעלין אותה לשער המזרחי וכו', cp.
M. Soṭah 1.5). Now in H we read: ולא תעלו בית און, (Hos. 4.15),
with בין און being a derogatory nickname for Bethel (בית אל).
Hence the *Y preacher* ingeniously utilized this v. for his topic
which began with the statement that the Soṭah was brought
for her ordeal to Jerusalem and then to the genuine *Beth-El*,
the Temple![53s] He then proceeded to depict briefly the ordeal
by citing appropriate passages from M. Soṭah and elsewhere,[264]
leading down to a general statement that "God said to Moses:
Commit the section concerning a Soṭah to writing, so that she
may know which Divine Name the priest has to erase (viz.
from the scroll), and what kind of death will befall her, and how
she will become publicly known" (משה כתוב: אמר הקב"ה למשה
פ' סוטה, כדי שתהא יודעה איזה שם הכהן מוחה (עפ"י הפסוק בבמ' ה, כ"ג:
ומחה אל מי המרים, ובת"כ: מוחק, והיינו הך) בשבילה, ומהו מיתה (צ"ל:
מיתתה, ומאי בת"ה), והיאך היא מתפרסמת, מנין ממה שקראו בענין, איש
איש כי תשטה אשתו. Herewith there is a return to the beginning of
S, thereby completing the first portion of the Y sermon.

There follows (TB, §3, T, §1, end) a homily based on Prov.
6.16–19 which verses R. Yose the Galilean (but in YSH, Prov.,
§938, the author is R. Eliezer the son of R. Yose the Galil.)
applied to the case of a Soṭah. Now, it is difficult to find a

____

[264] What is given in TB, §2, and T, §1, as a separate item (with Buber
even inserting as a lacuna איש איש כי תשטה אשתו), really belongs after שלא
תטמא את העזרה (see M. Soṭah 3.4) as the continuation of the M. there: יש אם
לה זכות וכו'. [There follow the opinions of R. Simon and R. Meir taken from
M. Soṭah 3.5.] Subsequently we have (in TB, §1, T, §1) the citation from 5.1
(כשם שהמים . . . ונטמאה ונטמאה). Finally there is stated the contrast in case the
suspected woman underwent the ordeal while innocent: אבל אם שתת ונמצאה
טהורה, אם היתה עקרה נפקדת וכו' (see the Bar. in Yer. Soṭah, c. 3, 18d, bottom,
and cp. Sifre, Num., §19 ed. Horov., p. 23–24, where the parallels are cited).

linguistic tally between these verses and H, and it is altogether doubtful whether this Tanna originally commented on
the former in connection with the present S. Hence the item
should not be taken as a Pet. proper.[548] Buber inserted in front
of it the heading (איש איש כי תשטה אשתו) but at the conclusion
there is no return to this S v., as is usual with regular Petiḥtot.
In NR, c. 9.11, the Agg. is connected with Num. 5.14: ועבר
עליו רוח קנאה וגו', and hence at the conclusion (after הוי ומשלח
מדנים בין אחים) there is given a different finale so as to link it
up with the above verse.[265] In TB, §4, T, §2, there is given the
item setting forth how the adulterer and his paramour break
all the laws of the Decalogue. The very first point concerning
the denial of God (weaving in Jer. 5.9–12) would be reflected
by Hos. 5.7: בה' בגדו כי בנים זרים ילדו (this in the skipped part of
H). Thereupon is added the homily on Koh. 7.26 (ועליה אמר
שלמה ומוצא אני מר ממות את האשה וגו') the final sentence of which:
וחוטא ילכד בה would link up with Hos. 5.5: יכשלו בעונם. In NR,
c. 9.12, the former v. is even listed as a Pet. (however in connection with Num. 5.14: ועבר עליו רוח קנאה, הה"ד ומוצא אני מר
וגו').

The first real Pet. in the section to the present v. is in TB,
§6, T. §4, introducing Job 24.15: ועין נואף שמרה נשף לאמר
לא תשורני עין וסתר פנים ישים, which affords a ready tally by means
of the verb נאף with the initial v. of H: כי תזנה פנה (cp. also
פנים in the Pet. v. with בפניו וענה גאון ישראל in Hos. 5.5).[553]
The same Pet. in a different version, is also found in the Genizah
fragment of the Midr., each section of which began with the
formula: זו היא שנאמרה ברוח הקודש (infra, H. pt., p. חסר). There
is woven in Is. 29.15 where the self-assurance of the evildoers,
who say: "Who sees us and who knows about us (מי רואני ומי
יודעני)?", is in contrast to the declamation in Hos. 5.3:
אני ידעתי אפרים וישראל לא נכחד ממני. There follows (TB, §8,
T, §5) another Pet. from Jer. 23.24: אם יסתר איש במסתרים ואני
לא אראנו וגו', which v. again links up with Hos. 5.3 where it is

---

[265] Instead of the finale in TB and T: הרי ז' דברים קשים שהסוטה עושה
we read in NR: אף כאן הוא אומר ועבר עליו רוח קנאה, אין קנאה אלא לשון כעס וכו'.
However, see infra, p. 231, concerning the version in MHG.

emphatically stated that God is aware of Ephraim's whoredom and Israel's pollution. Towards the end of the homily
there are woven in Jer. 17.10 (where כפרי מעלליו offers a verbal
point of contact with מעלליהם in Hos. 5.4) and Mal. 3.5 (cp.
במנאפים there with תנאפנה in the initial v. of H.).[56s] The Pet.
from Jer. 23.24 was apparently in the section in Midr. Yel. to
our S, as evident from the citation in Arukh (see TB, §8, note
55). Finally we come to TB, §13, T, §7, which contains the
peroration. The first part (from אמרו רבותינו to והודה מלך הערביים
(לר' עקיבא וכו') is really an exegetic comment on Num. 5.20:
ואת כי שטית תחת אישך וכי נטמאת וכו', as is evident from NR, c. 9.34.
Similar such comments are interspersed in the Tanḥ. section
(thus to Num. 5.13 in TB, §§10–12, T, §§6–7, and to Num.
5.15 and 17 in TB, §5, T, §§3–4). All this belongs to the
exegetic part emanating from Sifre, etc., which hardly formed
an integral part of the sermon. In NR, c. 9, such comments are
given in abundance. We are here interested in the *peroration*
proper which is rather abruptly tagged onto the story concerning the king of the Arabs (i. e. Nabateans) and R. Akiba
(thus after והודה מלך הערביים לר' עקיבא we read: הוי כל אשה
שמתייחדת עם בעלה בקדושה וכו', which is not a logical sequence of
the preceding). This conclusion is to the effect that just as in
the past God chose Israel because of its being from the 'true
seed' (זרע אמת, weaving in Jer. 2.21), so in the future He will
select it for the same reason: שאתם, איני בוחר אלא בכם ואף לע״ל
זרע קודש (בת״ה: זרע קדושה, ברוכי ה'), שנ' לא יגעו לריק ולא ילד ו
לבהלה, כי זרע ברוכי ה'. This final v. cited (Is. 65.23) would be
in contrast to the denunciation of Israel in Hos. 5.7: בה' בגדו
כי בנים זרים ילד ו.[57s]

2. *The Homilies in NR, c. 9.* This extensive chapter requires
an analysis for our purpose only as far as the items pertaining
to the sermon on the present S are concerned. We notice therein
the tendency to give running comments on the whole Torah
lection (Num. 5.11–31), and this has been accomplished not
only once, but even twice; thus one set of such comments is
completed in §27 with the interpretation of 5.30–31, and another
such set is commenced in §28 (on 5.12) extending to §43 inclusive.

Material from Sifre, Sifre Zutta and other sources has been incorporated, which to examine in detail would be beyond our scope here. But to deal with the Petiḥtot and other kindred homilies, there is first (§1) the item placing at the head Deut. 32.18 (צור ילדך תשי ותשכח אל מחוללך) and Job 24.15. Only the latter v. figures in the parallel Pet. in the Tanḥumas (above, p. 226) whereas the former v. is woven into the Aggadah. Also the ending of the item in NR (from [לארכיטקטון [צ״ל: לארכיטקטי] משל לארכיקיטי) is really a part of the Pet. on Jer. 23.24 (above, p. 226) which is found, in a different version, also in NR, §9 (for the passage there מלה״ד, למי שנכנס לגנוב וכו' see TB, §9, T, §5, end, in connection with the comment on איש איש also found in NR, §2). There is thus disorder in the printed version of NR (cp. also §4 which is really a morsel of the item on Koh. 7.26 given in §12, see further on, p. 230). In §6 there is introduced a Pet. v. נואף אשה חסר לב וגו' (Prov. 6.32) and a subsidiary to it מעוות לא יוכל לתקון וחסרון לא יוכל להמנות (Koh. 1.15). The latter v. tallies with the former one by means of the verb חסר, but the main Agg. is developed on the basis of Prov. 6.32 in order to conclude with the statement that adultery is the result of insane passion. This verse links up by means of the verb נאף with the initial verse of H: כי תנאפנה; also חסר לב in the former would correspond to ועם לא יבין ילבט in the latter. There is also woven in Prov. 9.13 to prove the same state of mad passion with regard to the profligate female, and finally there is the comment on כי תשטה, which could also be read תשטה, in order to arrive at the same conclusion of madness (שטות) being involved in this case.[266] Here we have the larger homily which seems to be given, in a shortened form in TB, §7, T, §5, beginning.[267]

In NR (§7) we have further a long item headed by verses

---

[266] NR, c. 9.6, end: וכן הוא אומר נואף אשה חסר לב משחית נפשו הוא יעשנה, מהו חסר לב, מכאן שאין אדם הולך אצל אשת איש עד שיצא מדעתו, וכן הוא אומר מי פתי יסור הנה וחסר לב ולא ידע וגו' (מש' ט', ט"ז–י"ז) . . . וכשם שהוא נקרא פתי, כך הזונה נקראת פתיות, שאינה מזנה עד שתצא מדעתה, שכן כתיב אשת כסילות הומיה פתיות ובל ידעה מה וגו' (שם, י"נ–ט'ו).

[267] שנו רבותינו אין המנאפין מנאפין עד שתכנס בהן רוח שטות, שנאמר איש איש כי תשטה (היינו: תשטה). למדנו לאשה, לאיש מנין, שנ' נואף אשה חסר לב (cp. R. Simon Lakish's statement in Soṭah, 3a, top).

from three different places: Gen. 17.8, Deut. 23.15 and Prov.
5.7–10. The homily proceeds first with the Aggadic interpretation of the last mentioned verses, then with that of Deut.
23.15, and finally returns to the v. listed first.[268] Here we have
a concatenation of homilies on verses, all of which have points
of contact with H. Thus the emphasis on ולזרעך אחריך (Gen.
17.8) as legitimate progeny (זרע שיהיה מיוחס אחריך) would be in
contrast to כי בנים זרים ילדו in Hos. 5.7   The explanation of Deut.
23.15, with its injunction that 'thy camp be holy lest He behold
an unseemly thing in thee and turn away from thee,' as referring
in particular to sexual immorality[269] would be reflected by such
verses as Hos. 5.3–4 and 6 denouncing Ephraim's harlotry and
Israel's defilement; is a result of 'the spirit of whoredom that is
in their midst,' God 'has withdrawn Himself from them.' And
as regards Prov. 5.7–10, the words בנים (v. 7) and זרים (v. 10)
offer verbal tallies with Hos. 5.7.[58s] In §9 of NR, there is the
Pet. on Jer. 23.24, as to which see above. It should only be
remarked concerning the story of the two sisters (given at the
end of this item, cp. also TB, §10, T, §6) that in the citation of
Koh. 8.8: אין אדם שליט ברוח לכלוא את הרוח there is involved a point
of אל תקרי, viz. for רוח read ריח, scent, hence when the guilty
sister died from the scent of the 'bitter water,' which her innocent sister imbibed, there was fulfilled the above mentioned

---

[268] ד"א איש איש וגו', הה"ד ונתתי לך ולזרעך אחריך את ארץ מגוריך וגו'. ונתתי לך,
הה"ד כי ה' אלהיך מתהלך וגו', הה"ד ועתה בנים שמעו לי וגו' ... מהו ועתה בנים שמעו לי,
מדבר בעשרת השבטים ובשבט יהודה ובנימין ... וכן אמר להם משה לישראל: בשעה שאתם
יוצאים למלחמה הזהרו שלא יהיה בכם עון ניאוף ... לכך כתיב והיה מחנך קדוש וגו', שלא
יהיה ביניכם ממזרים ולא נולדים שלא בקדושה, לפי שאין הקב"ה מיחד שמו עליהם ואינו
מסייעם במלחמה, כן אמר הקב"ה לאברהם אבינו ונתת לך ולזרעך אחריך וכו'.

[269] In connection with this homily there is cited M. Kidd. 4.5 together
with the corresponding comment thereon in Yer. (66a): ד"א והיה מחנך קדוש,
תמן תנינן אין בודקין לא מן המזבח ... מה כתיב בתריה, כי תצא מחנה על אויביך וכו'.
Curiously enough, Epstein, מקדמוניות היהודים, p. 72, has taken this item to
emanate from the Yel. to the Seder that commenced with Deut. 23.10!
While it is true that in the first half of NR *the Y item to the S, with which
the particular chapter is connected* is sometimes introduced by תמן תנינן (see
above, notes 187, 217, 224) it would be very strange to do so with a theme
so far removed from the present S. Moreover, the connection of the topic
with a Pet. v. militates against such an assumption (as pointed out above,
p. 211). And as regards the S at Deut. 23.60, see infra, p. inc.

verse.[270] The latter in its turn, tallies by means of רוח with Hos.
5.4: כי רוח זנונים בקרבם.[598] As to Pet. (§11) from Prov. 6.16–19,
see above (p. 225). Finally there is in §12 the homily on Koh.
7.26 (cp. also §4, above, p. 228): ומוצא אני מר ממות וגו' wherein
the sentence וחוטא ילכד בה correlates with יכשלו בעונם in
Hos. 5.5.[608]

We have thus accounted for all the Petiḥtot in NR on the
basis of the underlying H to the present S. Omitting the further
running comments on the whole Torah lection (see above, p. 227)
the conclusion of the chapter in NR (§§44–49) remains to be
considered. Here the whole portion concerning a Soṭah is allegorically interpreted as referring to the worship of the Golden
Calf and its consequences (§4: רבנין פתרין קרייה במעשה העגל וכו');
for a similar procedure in NR, c. 7, to S 104b, see above, p. 215.
Now, the introduction of this theme, which involved treason
against God by substituting the recognition of an idol for
allegiance to Him, has been suggested by the whole tenor of H
(cp. especially Hos. 4.17: חבור עצבים אפרים and 5.7: בה'
בגדו). After the detailed application of Num. 5.12 ff. to this
allegorical topic, there is the explanation of the final v. of S
(Num. 5.31) in such a manner as to offer a sort of *peroration*
(§49, end). In the latter are woven in verses which reflect the
H[271] — a procedure common to similar 'happy' terminations of
the sermons to given Sedarim. Thus the promise of Israel's
purification from its defilement and of its obtaining a *new
spirit* (Ezek. 36.25–29) is in contrast to the denunciation contained in Hos. 5.3–4 (כי רוח זנונים בקרבם ... ישראל נטמא).[618]
There is further cited Ezek. 36.32 (בושו והכלמו מדרכיכם) to

[270] כיון שנשקו זו לזו, ה ר י ח ה במים המרים ומיד מתה לקיים מה שנ' אין אדם שליט
ב ר ו ח לכלוא את ה ר ו ח וגו' (היינו: קרי „בריח ... הריח").

[271] ונקה האיש מעון, זה הקב"ה שינקה את ישראל שלא יעשו (לו) עוד עון לפניו, שכך
אמר להם ע"י יחזקאל: וזרקתי עליכם מים טהורים וגו', ונתתי לכם לב חדש ורוח חדשה וגו',
ואת רוחי אתן בקרבכם וגו', והושעתי אתכם מכל טמאותיכם וגו' (יח' ל"ו, כ"ו-כ"ט). והאשה
ההיא תשא את עונה, כמה דתימא לא למענכם אני עושה ... בושו והכלמו מדרכיכם בית
ישראל (שם, ל"ב). וכשם שמחל להם הקב"ה בעגל ונתרצה להם ושכן בתוכם, והכניסם לארץ,
כך נבא יחזקאל שכך יעשה הקב"ה לבסוף, שנאמר דבר עליהם כה אמר ה' אלהים הנה אני
לוקח וגו', ולא יטמאו עוד בגלוליהם וגו', והיה משכני וגו', כי אני ה' מקדש את ישראל בהיות
משכני בתוכם לעולם (שם, ל"ו, כ"א-כ"ח).

which cp. Hos. 4.19 (ויבושו מזבחותם). And lastly there is the
promise of the reunion of the two houses of Israel (Ephraim and
Judah, both of whom figured in our H), their restoration to their
land and God's residence among them (Ezek. 37.21–28) — all
this being the opposite of what is depicted as punishment in the
present Prophetic lection.

3. *Other Homilies.* Above (p. 225), the Aggadic application
of Prov. 6.16–19 to the case of Soṭah has been discussed. Here
attention should be drawn to the version in MHG, IV, (ed.
Fisch, pp. 246–7), which seems to indicate that in the Midrash,
from which the item emanated, there was a proper Pet. from
the above verses.[272] In order to establish the necessary connection with H, we have to assume that in the sentence: לב
חורש מחשבות און (Prov. 6.18) which was homiletically taken as
referring to lascivious thoughts there was the link with כי רוח
זנונים בקרבם in Hos. 5.4. Subsequently there is found in MHG
a novel Agg. concerning the wording of the third commandment
of the Decalogue (לא תשא instead of לא תשבע) as alluding to a
feature of the ordeal of the Soṭah.[273] Whereas in other sources
there is depicted how both adulterer and adultress break every
law of the Decalogue (see TB, §4, T, §2, NR, c. 9.12), the emphasis here on the third one is due to the H v.: ואל תשבעו חי ה'
(Hos. 4.15), in addition to Num. 5.27 (cited in this item)
wherein a curse (=oath) is mentioned (והיתה האשה לאלה, cp. the
parallel v. 21 לאלה ולשבועה).
  In Soṭah 2a it is reported that R. Simon b. Lakish introduced his discussion of the subject of Soṭah with the remark:
No person is predestined to obtain a helpmate except in accord-

---

[272] זה ש'ה שש הנה שנא ה' ושבע תועבת נפשו, שש הנה שנא ה' מדות הללו מצויין בנואף
עם אשה... לב חורש מחשבות און, שהן מהרהרין בדבר עבירה תמיד, ואומרין באיזו שעה
נלך לנאוף... ומשלח מדנים בין אחים, שכל ישראל נקראים אחים, והנואף עם אשת חבירו
ושומע בו בעלה, הוא שונאו. לכך משה מזהיר את ישראל איש איש כי תשטה אשתו (This
ending is missing in the other sources, see above, note 265).

[273] ועליה הוא מזהיר בעשרת הדברות, לא תשא את שם ה' אלהיך לשוא, היה למקרא
לומר "לא תשבע" ומהו לא תשא, אמר לה הקב"ה: אל תגרמי לעצמך לטעון את השם, שאין
בך כח לטעינו, עד שלא נכנס לתוך מעיה היתה מתקלקלת, שנאמר וצבתה בטנה (ושם נאמר
ג'כ: והיתה האשה לאלה [—שבעוה] בקרב עמה). אמר הקב"ה למשה: הואיל והדבר בא
לידי כך, הזהיר (—הזהר) את ישראל על פרשת סוטה, שנאמר איש איש כי תשטה אשתן.

ance with his deeds (weaving in Ps. 125.3).[274] It is doubtful
whether there is meant here a synagogal sermon on the Sabbath
when our S was read; the v. cited offers no contact with H.
Rather the discussion in the house of study of the laws concerning
an unfaithful wife may have been the occasion for this scholar's
opening the debate with the above Aggadic remark.[628]

Seder 105a (5a)

וידבר ה' ... דבר אל בני ישראל ואמרת אליהם איש או אשה כי יפלא
לנדר נדר נזיר להזיר לה', Num. 6.1–2.

A new S here would render the previous one (No. 105) to
conclude in an inauspicious manner (והאשה ההיא תשא את עונה,
Num. 5.31). There is no section in either Tanḥuma version to
the portion concerning the Nazirite (Num. 6.1–21). This would
seem to indicate that S 105 really comprised Num. 5.11–6.21,
with the next 'regular' S commencing at 6.22 (infra sub No. 106).
Also Yannai seems to have composed Ḳerobot to Nos. 105 and
106, but not to the portion concerning the Nazirite (listed here
as No. 105a).[275] Furthermore, some Biblical codices have no
rubric of סדר at Num. 6.1 (see Ginzberg, *Massor. Bible, a. l.*).
However, the latter is listed in Meiri's *Kiryat Sepher* (II, 74b,
bottom), in the Yem. מחברת התיגאן (אבן ספיר, 11, 231) and in
Adat Deborim (fol. 27b); in the last two sources there is the same
erroneous omission of S 105, although the sum total cited there
requires its inclusion. There is further an extensive section in
NR, c. 10, which testifies to the existence of such a Seder. We
are thus confronted with another instance of the shifting of the

---

[274] כי הוה פתח ר"ל בסוטה כשהיה בא לדרוש בפרשת סוטה, אמר הכי: אין מזווגין לו
לאדם אשה אלא לפי מעשיו, שנ' כי לא ינוח שבט הרשע על גורל הצדיקים.

[275] What is printed in ed. Zulay (pp. 181, bottom, to 187) emanates from
one Genizah leaf (see his ידיעות המכון לחקר השירה העברית, מחקרי יני, II, p. 330,
No. 29, and cp. ibid., p. 298–9, Nos. 82–83). Now this leaf contains the end
of the Ḳerobah to Num. 5.11 ff. (S 105), *followed directly by that to Num. 6.22 ff.*
(S 106); the small lacuna between the two Ḳerobot in ed. Zulay, p. 184, is
due to the faintness of the writing. It is thus manifest that this MS. contained no Ḳerobah to Num. 6.1 ff. (S 105a).

Sedarim. Some terminated S 105 at Num. 5.31 and began a
new S at 6.1 (No. 105a), thus resulting in each of them consisting
alike of 21 verses (5.11–31 and 6.1–21). But others objected to
the inauspicious conclusion of 5.31 and combined both portions
as one Torah lection. The latter custom prevailed in the time of
Yannai.[63s] As to the difference concerning the commencement of
the next S, whether at 6.22 or at 7.1, see infra, p. inc.

Hafṭarah. The Babylonian Prophetic lection to פ' נשא was Judges
13.2–24 containing the story of the birth of Samson dedicated
as a Nazirite from his very birth (see v. 5). To our present TC S
the present lection would be very appropriate, too. Only such
a H would not comprise 23 verses, but the usual number of about
10. We may thus safely assume that it extended from v. 2 to
v. 10+v. 24; the latter formed a proper conclusion (ויגדל
הנער ויברכהו ה') and also was *the beginning of a new Seder in
Judges* — an indication that herewith terminated the lection,
as we have noticed so frequently before (see above, vol. I,
pp. 10–11). As regards the required linguistic tally between
S and H, such is to be found in ויהי איש אחד מצרעה ...
איש או אשה (Jud. 13.2) as compared to ואשתו עקרה וגו'
כי יפלא (Num. 6.2). There is a further intrinsic connection
inasmuch as both the wife of Mano‘ah and her husband were
to refrain from wine and strong drink and defilement during
the period of pregnancy of the former (see Jud. 13.3 and 14) —
thus both *man* and *woman* were in the status of a Nazirite until
the birth of their child who was to remain as such for the rest
of his life (נזיר עולם).[64s] And just as a Nazirite offered up
sacrifices in connection with his peculiar status (Num. 6.19 ff.),
so Manoah and his wife beheld their offering of food to the angel
being consumed by the flame as a sacrifice (Jud. 13.15–20).
This will amply account for the choice of this H as the com-
panion of the present S.

STRUCTURE OF HOMILIES

In NR, c. 10.1, there is a long Pet. on Cant. 5.15–16
wherein the expression מראה (מראהו בלבנון), denoting appearance,
would tally with ומראהו כמראה מלאך ה' in H (Jud. 13.6). There

is no need here to analyse the composite structure of this item
(cp. Cant. R., *a. l.*). Its pertinent part is the point concerning
the comparison of the Torah to pillars, just as the latter have a
a chapter above and a basis below, so the sections of the former
are to be combined with what precedes and follows, or, in other
words, each given section can have the preceding one as a sort
of chapter and the succeeding one as a sort of basis. This statement is illustrated among others by the case of the present S
concerning the Nazirite being placed between the lection concerning the Soṭah and the one containing the Priestly Blessing
(Num. 6.22 ff., infra, sub No. 106).[65s] [276] In §2 there follows a
long homily on Prov. 23.26–35 which verses are interpreted in a
twofold manner, first as applying to Israel and the nations and
subsequently to the more legitimate theme of sexual immorality
and of inebriety. The evil effect of wine is depicted as leading to
profligacy, leading down again to the reason as to why the section about the Nazirite follows that of Soṭah.[277] Since in the
Pet. verses 'wine' is mentioned (Prov. 23.29–30), there is a ready
tally with S (Num. 6.3) and H (Jud. 13.4). For the same reason
there is given in §3 the homily on Am. 6.1–7 because of v. 6
(השותים במזרקי יין), and in §4 the one on Prov. 31.1–9 because of
v. 4 (אל למלכים שתו יין). In §5 the story of the birth of Samson,
which formed the Prophetic lection in conjunction with the
present S, is commented upon in detail.[66s] In §8 another v. referring to wine and strong drink is introduced (Is. 5.22–23) for
homiletic interpretation. In this item there is woven in M.
Abot 1.1 סייג ועשו הרבה, תלמידים והעמידו בדין, מתונים הוו תנינן (תמן

---

[276] עמודי שש . . . ר' הונא בשם בר קפרא אמר מה העמודים הללו יש להם קופליות
מלמעלן ובסיסיות מלמטן, כך הן פרשיותיה של תורה, נדרשת (צ"ל: נדרשות) לפניהם
ולאחריהם . . . ודכוותה פרשת נזיר נדרשת לפניה ולאחריה. כיצד לאחריה, זאת תורת הנזיר
וגו', מה כתיב אחריו, כה תברכו את בני ישראל . . . כיצד נדרשת לפניה, איש או אשה כי
יפלא וגו' מה כתיב למעלה, זאת תורת הקנאות וגו'. About the similar Agg. see above,
pp. 232 and 233.
* [277] NR, c. 10.2, end: נזיר פ' בתורה הקב"ה כתב ולכך לזנות, גורם שהיין למדנו הא
אחר פ' סוטה, שלא יעשה אדם מעשה נואף ונואפת ששתו יין ונתקלקלו, אלא הירא מן החטא
למה נסמכה Cp. Soṭah 2a: יפלא כי אשה או איש נאמר לכך היין, מן עצמו את יזיר.
See .פרשת נזיר לפרשת סוטה, לומר לך שכל הרואה סוטה בקלקולה יזיר עצמו מן היין
further ER., c. 16.2.

לתורה) and the corresponding comment thereon in ARN, c. 2
(ed. Schechter, pp. 8–9). Therein Epstein (מקדמוניות היהודים,
p. 72) has discovered a Y topic to our S which the author of NR
excerpted from Midr. Yel. However, such a topic would require
a starting-point in the H — a point Epstein was entirely unaware of — and as none is to be found in the latter, the whole
suggestion is nothing but a figment (cp. also, above, p. 211).[67s]
The remainder of NR, containing running comments on the
whole Torah portion that emanate from Sifre, Sifre Zutta and
other sources, require no further analysis for our purpose.

SEDER 106 (6)

Num. 6.22–23.

Haftarah.

NOTES BY SONNE ON NUMBERS

¹ At first the Pet. from Ps. 36.7 appears void of any connection with S. On closer consideration, however, it becomes clear that Num. 1.1: וידבר ה' אל משה במדבר סיני...באחד לחדש בשנה השנית לצאתם ...ממצרים מארץ directed the homilist's attention to the parallel passage in Ex. 19.1 f.: באו...ממצרים מארץ ישראל בני לצאת השלישי בחדש מדבר סיני ויחנו במדבר...ויחן שם ישראל נגד ההר ומשה עלה מן ההר ה' אליו ויקרא האלהים אל. Here the association of מדבר סיני with האלהים הר or אל הררי is established. Hence the link between S (במדבר) and Ps. 36.7 (בהררי אל). The link with H, as pointed out by the A., is direct and conspicuous, but is only verbal; the link with S is indirect, but intrinsically much more significant. In fact, the sermonic conclusion of this Pet.: אבל כשהוא בא לגדל את בני ישראל הוא מפרסם באיזה יום באיזה מקום באיזה חדש וכו' is equally fitting for Ex. 19.1 ff. which passage must have been present in the mind of the homilist.

² There is no proper verbal link between S and Cant. 7.3, but neither is there a verbal link in the strict sense of the word between H and Cant. 7.3. We should perhaps take into consideration the rendering of שרך by ריש מתיבתא in the Targum. This would afford a tally with ראש את שאו in S (Num. 1.2).

³ Ps. 147.20 (תהלה לכל חסידיו) and 148.14 (לא עשה כן לכל גוי וכו') seem to me subsidiary vv. to Pet. 1 on Ps. 36.7. In this case what is needed is a link between Ps. 147.20 and Ps. 36.7; such link consists in the common term משפט (...משפטיך תהום — ומשפטים בל־ידעום). Ps. 148.14 in turn is linked up with 147.20 through the contrast of לכל גוי against לכל חסידיו. The whole homily forms a kind of chain reaction. That this Pet. is but a variation of Pet. 1 appears clearly in the conclusion (לפיכך כתוב להם באיזה חדש, בכמה בחדש ובאיזו שנה ובא) אפרכיא, באיזו מדינה רוממתי קרנם) which is almost identical with that of Pet. 1.

⁴ Here is a still clearer indication that this homily is but a variation of Pet. 1 which, as noted above (note 1) has as its background the scene of "matan Torah" described in Ex. 19.1 ff.

⁵ Here again in the italicized close we sense the presence of the *"matan Torah"* scene in the mind of the homilist.

⁶ Assuming, as does the A., that H tallied with S by means of אתות, I would suggest as beginning of H Is. 8.18: לאתות ה' לי נתן אשר והילדים אנכי הנה. ולמופתים בישראל מעם ה' צבאות השכן בהר ציון. We would of course have the verbal tallies of לאתות and ישראל. We should furthermore bear in mind that the term צבא (לצבאתם) runs all through our Seder. The H would consist of Is. 8.18–20 (skipping to the end of c. 8), 9.1–6 (together 9 verses). The finale would revert to the term צבאות (זאת תעשה צבאות ה' קנאת) which forms the keynote of our S. We shall see in the sequel whether such H could account for the Y topic as well as for the Petihtot, especially those without manifest connection with S.

[7] There is no denying that the tally is perfect which should surprise no one, since H was chosen by the A. to suit the Y. In view of the fact, however, that the connection of the Y with S is quite natural, the latter dealing with the location of the tribes in the encampment and the distance of each of them from the center, it seems that a token link with H would suffice. The suggested H from Is. 8.18 ff. affords a verbal link with Y by means of הלך (העם ההולכים, 19.1). Furthermore, the Halakhah referred to in the answer (כך שנו רבותינו) is the Mishnah 'Erubin IV.7–8 (so rightly indicated by Buber, note 72) which reads: מי שבא בדרך וחשכה לו...נמצא מהלך מ שחשך ה re-echoing Is. 9.1: העם ההולכים בחשך ארבעת אלפים אמה.

[8] Ps. 20.6 (ובשם ה' נדגול), as well as Cant. 2.4 (. . . ודגלו עלי) are so manifestly linked up with S (איש על דגלו) that no tally with H seems necessary.

[9] Cant. 6.10 seems equally to be mainly connected with S by means of דגל (כנדגלות), but tallies also with the suggested Is. H by means of שחר (כמו) in contrast to שחר אשר אין לו שחר in Is. 8.20.

[10] The tally of Job 36.3 (אשא דעי למרחוק ולפועלי אתן צדק) by means of צדק, holds good also for the suggested Is. H (9.6: במשפט ובצדקה).

As to Deut. 32.10, we should bear in mind that a Pet. v. from Pentateuch is in all probability connected with S rather than with H. In fact, through יסובבנהו it tallies with S (סביב לאהל יחנו). The real link with S, however, one finds in Deut. 32.8–9 immediately preceding the Pet. v.: יצב גבלות עמים למספר בני ישראל. Here we have a resonance of the main theme of S consisting in the assignment of the "boundaries" of the tribes in the encampment, the places they should occupy. In the immediate area of this center of attraction, the homilist found the Pet. with a verbal tally.

There seems to be some link with the suggested H from Is. by means of בתהו ויל(ה) which the Midrash seems to equate with (בתהו ויל(ה) (cp. Buber, note 128 where such reading is termed erroneous, but not necessarily, since it agrees with Targum Yerushalmi: . . . ובצודתא דליל). This would tally with Is. 8.22.

Finally, we may add that the whole trend of the sermon (תהו וליל ה היה העולם עד שלא קיבלו ישראל את התורה, כיון שיצאו ממצרים וקבלו את התורה האיר העולם) seems to reflect Is. 8.22–9, 2: ואל הארץ אביט והנה צרה . . . חשכה . . . העם ההולכים בחשך ראו אור גדול.

[11] Concerning the supposed peroration verse Cant. 2.8, the main link is with S by means of דגל (ודגלו עלי), as rightly pointed out by the A. A secondary, token link with the suggested Is. H may be seen in the particle הנה common to both Cant. 2.8 and H (הנה אנכי והילדים, ה נ ה ז ה ב א).

[12] The suggestion that Hos. 2.1 was originally the H of our S appears very plausible. The fact is that the way we perceive the process of linkage, Hos. 2.1 remains the main link behind the scenes also in the transmitted H of Hos. 2.16. There is reason to believe that in adopting a H for the first S of the fourth of the Pentateuch the name of the book played an important role, and was supposed to be reflected in the first verse of the H. As is well

known there are two names by which the book is referred to: a) Numbers (in the Septuagint and other translations, but also in earlier rabbinic writings — חומש הפקודים), indicating the main theme of the first sections of the book, the mustering of the Israelites; b) *Bamidbar*, after the first characteristic word of the book. There can be little doubt that Hos. 2.1 (והיה מספר בני ישראל) tallying with S by means of the term מספר is the most fitting H for the first S of a book called Numbers or its equivalent (חומש הפקודים). However, when the name במדבר supplanted that of Numbers, and a H tallying with S through מדבר was looked for, it was still in the area of Hos. 2 which was preferred. We may assume that Hos. 2.1 was never lost sight of by the homilists even after it has been discarded as H beginning. A similar process, according to our suggestion, took place in the H on the first S of the book of Leviticus. There too, the H fitting for the name "Leviticus," we assumed Mic. 6.6 (. . . במה אקדם ה' . . . האקדמנו בעולות), but when the name ויקרא prevailed, and a tally by means of קרא was looked for, they took the first ויקרא in this area, viz. Mic. 6.9: קול ה' לעיר יקרא. Cp. also above note 10.

Finally, it should be noted that this section of NR might have been taken from a Midrash based on the AC in which Hos. 2.1 was retained as the beginning of H.

[13] It is apparent that the mere linguistic link did not quite satisfy the A. I wonder whether we could not apply here too our device, i. e., to look for a more substantial contact at the background. Such contact could indeed be found at the beginning of chapter 45 of Is.: כה אמר ה' למשיחו . . . אשר החזקתי בימינו . . . הקורא בשמך which tallies verbally (אלה שמות בני אהרן), as well as intrinsically with S. In both reference is made to the act of consecration by anointment. This was the point of attraction for those who were looking for a H tallying with the first v. of S. They found such H in the area, namely Is. 45.19.

[14] The Y topic is quite fitting and natural for our S in which three pairs of brothers are mentioned, Moses and Aaron, Elazar and Ithamar, Nadab and Abihu, the last dying together. Moreover, the Mishnah referred to in the answer (כך שנו רבותינו) starts מי שמת (B. B. א.ט.מ.) which affords a linguistic tally with S: וימת נדב ואביהו.

It may be noted that the substitution מטה for סל in the original source (cp. Wertheimer, notes) could be due to the endeavor of the preacher to link up the topic with Num. 3.6: הקרב את מטה לוי.

[15] The main tally is, of course, with S by means of בני אהרן המשוחים, as compared with כשמן היורד על זקן אהרן. Should we insist on some verbal tally with H, the Is. H affords one by means of יחדו התנגשו and יועצו יחדו (Is. 45.20, 21) contrasting with שבת אחים גם יחד.

[16] Prov. 17.6 (. . . עטרת זקנים בני בנים ותפארת בנים) is also primarily linked up with S by means of בני אהרן . . . ובנים לא היו להם. Besides the verbal tally, there is also the indication of Aaron's lack of עטרת זקנים, since his sons died without children. It should be added that there is also a verbal link with the H from Is. in the very finale: לישראל תפארתו.

[17] The connection with S can be established through the Targum on the Cant. verse. There שני עפרים תאומי צביה is rendered תרין פריקין...דמיין ואההר ן למשה. Also Miriam is mentioned in the Targum. The homilist did not have to think of Micah.

[18] Direct reference to and commenting on H is rather unusual. Consequently, the explicit mentioning of Micah rather casts doubts on the suggestion of a Micah H.

[19] Ingenious and attractive as this explanation sounds, it is not quite convincing. If certain Jewish authorities wanted to use the Isaiah passage as an anti-Christian manifesto, they had better occasions to do so; there are many other Sedarim where the passage would fit much better as H. It certainly does not explain why those authorities would remove the Micah H which is so much better fitted for our S in order to insert this Isaiah passage here where it seems entirely out of place.

As indicated above, I am not convinced that there are reasons enough to assume the existence of a second Micah H not otherwise transmitted. But assuming the existence of such second H, I would consider it as the later one, and the Isaiah H as the earlier. It seems to me that as early as the first century the book of Isaiah, the prophet of consolation *par excellence*, was used as the main source for Haftarot, and all kinds of artificial tallies were admissible in order to obtain a H from this book. Only later when the use of the other prophetic books became more and more frequent, were some of the Isaiah Haftarot supplanted by Haftarot from other prophetic books with less artificial links. And this might have taken place in our S. Such changes, however, were not always universally accepted; more conservative groups would continue to retain the older Isaiah H. This is reflected in the fact that the Karaites, representing a conservative trend, still have more Isaiah Haftarot than the Rabbinists.

The fact that Yannai has the Isaiah H does by no means prove that this H is the later one. It simply means that Yannai represents a more conservative trend which did not accept the change. It is interesting to note that also in his Halakhic elements scholars, especially Lieberman, pointed out that Yannai often follows older traditions.

[20] There is no certainty that the Pet. from Ps. 80.9: נפן ממצרים ... really originated in our S. And even if so, the Is. H affords some verbal tally, as for instance פנו אלי (v. 22) as compared with פנית לפניה (Ps. 80.10).

[21] The existence of a S in Num. 3.5, not otherwise transmitted, seems to me doubtful. It is well known that the homilist usually took the first two verses of the S as point of departure for his sermon. This is manifest in Yannai's *Kerobot* where the first two verses follow the first two sections of the *Kerobah* respectively. But sometimes, when the first two verses did not touch the topic of the S, the homilist built his homily on the third verse of the S. Moreover, in certain *Kerobot* of Kalir the third verse is treated in the same way as the two first vv. of the S (Cp. Menaḥem Zulay, *Zur Liturgie der babylonischen Juden* — "Bonner orientalische Studien" — 1933, p. 12 ff.).

Now, if we read carefully Num. 3.3–4 we can not fail to realize that they are to a certain extent out of place here, and form a parenthetical insertion. For the story of Nadab and Abihu remains, as pointed out by the A., "an isolated brief account" entirely divorced from the main topic — the assignment of the tribe of Levi to the service of the sanctuary.

This being the case, it is quite possible that although the S started 3.1, the homilist felt justified to disregard the parenthetical vv. (3–4) and build his sermon on v. 5 f. Needless to say that in such case no other H besides that of Is. 45.19, transmitted in the list and by Yannai, would be required. In the sequel we shall see whether such assumption would account for the Midrashic material.

[22] It is by no means certain whether the Pet. from Ps. 92.13 (צדיק כתמר יפרח... שתולים בבית ה' בחצרות אלהינו יפריחו) actually originated here. But in case it did, we have to give priority to the intrinsic connection with S by means of "planted in *the house of the Lord, in the courts of our God* they shall blossom," which reflects the assignment of the Levites "to keep the charge of the congregation *before the tent of meeting* (— court of our God) and "to do the service of the tabernacle" (— the house of the Lord). There might also be a subtle, indirect linguistic connection by means of "blossom" (יפרח), alluding to Num. 17.23 which reads: "And behold the rod of Aaron for the house of Levi was blossoming" (והנה פרח מטה אהרן לבית לוי). The homilist associated מטה לוי with "blossom" (פרח) tallying with יפרח.

There is also a verbal link with H from Is. 45 by means of צדיק in Is. 45.21: אל צדיק ומושיע. The topic of the Agg. could have been suggested by Is. 45.25: בה' יצדקו ויתהללו כל זרע ישראל.

[23] Ps. 65.5 (אשרי תבחר ותקרב) tallies, as has been rightly noted by the A., mainly with S by means of הקרב. The finale of the Isaiah H affords also a tally (צדקתי לא תרחק, Is. 46.13). Alluding to Num. 17.20: והיה האיש אשר אבחר בו מטהו יפרח, the homilist might have associated מטה לוי with "being chosen" (אבחר), and subsequently linked up מטה לוי with אשרי תבחר. Both Petiḥtot, that from Ps. 92.13 and from 65.5 would then have a common source of inspiration, viz. the scene of the blossoming of the rod of Aaron in Num. 17.20 ff. It may be added that the two Pet. verses are linked together by means of ישכן חצריך נשבעה בטוב ביתך which is but a variation of שתולים בבית ה' בחצרות אלהינו...

[24] Unfortunately nothing of this larger discussion could be found in the A.'s manuscript. On the basis of the material thus far presented, the existence of an earlier, larger Tanḥuma version, though probable, is far from having been definitely established. Still less certain is the assumption that a great deal of it has been incorporated into NR. At present, all I would dare to affirm is that it seems to be a valuable working hypothesis.

[25] As H for S 103b (Num. 3.14 f.), I would suggest Is. 62.6: על חומתיך ירושלם הפקדתי שומרים. Besides the tally by means of the verb פקד, there is also an intrinsic connection with S, since it deals with the assignment of the Levites as custodians of the tent of meeting (ושמרו את משמרתו...).

לפני אהל מועד, Num. 3.7). The H would consist of Is. 62.6–63.1 (אני מדבר
(בצדקה רב להושיע), 7–8 (ויהי להם למושיע).

[26] The suggested H from Is. 62.6 affords a better tally through בחצרות
קדשי (Is. 62.9) as compared with בחצרות אלהינו.

[27] The suggested Isaiah H affords a tally with Ps. 65.5 by means of
בחצרות קדשי as compared with ישכן חצריך. It is, however, in all probability only subsidiary to the preceding Pet. Cp. above note 23.

[28] The Pet. from Ps. 68.7 (אלהים מושיב...מוציא אסירים) seems to me
to have originated in S 101 (Num. 1.1) where it was linked up with לצאתם
מארץ מצרים. It was probably due to a conflation of Num. 3.14 (אל 'וידבר ה
משה במדבר סיני) with Num. 1.1 which likewise starts with (וידבר ה' אל משה
במדבר סיני) that the Pet. found its way to our S.

[29] The suggested H from Is. 62.6 could well account for the peroration
vv. of Is. 52.8 (כי עין בעין יראו בשוב ה' ציון) and Is. 25.9 (...ואמר
(הנה אלהינו זה קוינו לו ויושיענו). Both tally with Is. 62.11: אמרו
לבת ציון הנה ישעך בא. Nonetheless, the A. is quite right in suggesting
that the whole sermon was originally conceived for Num. 3.5 (see infra).

[30] This derivation of the H from the Y through an ingenious penetration
into the subtle connections between H and Y is one of the most brilliant
and convincing combinations of the A. Nevertheless, we should not neglect
the link with S since R. Simon ben Gamaliel bases his opinion on our verse.

[31] Concerning the Pet. from Is. 43.4, the quotation should be extended
to the second part of the verse: ואתן אדם תחתיך ולאמים תחת נפשך
"And I will give men *instead* of thee and peoples instead of thy life," reflecting
Num. 3.41: "And thou shalt take the Levites for me . . . instead of all the
first born in Israel, etc." (ולקחת את הלוים לי אני ה' תחת תחת כל בכור...ואת
(בהמת הלוים תחת....

[32] Cant. 6.8 f. is primarily linked up with S by way of ושא את מספר שמותם,
as contrasting with ועלמות אין מספר. עלמות is taken by the homilist as abbreviation for אומות העולם, "the nations of the world" that have no "counting,"
i. e., are of no account.

[33] The proposed H, its subtle linkage with S, is undoubtedly suggestive,
yes captivating. But I still would hesitate to call it "clearly evident," because it does not preclude other possibilities. So, for instance, Is. 56.5 (ונתתי
להם בביתי ובחומתי יד ושם...שם עולם לא יכרת "And I will give unto them
in My house and within My walls a monument and a memorial . . . an everlasting name that *shall not be cut off*," seems to me a fitting H for our S. We
would have the same verbal tally by means of לא יכרת, its meaning in Is.
much more in conformity with that of S than is that of Zeph. 3.7. Also the
whole background, "in My house and within My walls," in Is. reflects our
S which deals with the service of the Ḳehatites around the tabernacle. We
shall see in the sequel whether this H can do justice to the Midrashic material.

[34] This of course holds good also for the suggested H from Is. 56.5.

[35] The Pet. from Ps. 33.18, 19, especially the second verse, (להציל
ממות נפשם ולחיותם) is in the first place connected with S, re-echoing

וזאת עשו להם וחיו ולא ימתו (Num. 4.19). It is interesting to note that the preceding Y section concludes with this very verse: 'וזאת עשו להם וחיו וכו. The concluding verse is at the same time the point of reference for the following Pet., a pattern of concatenation well known in Yannai's *Ḳerobot*.

We may add that there is also a token verbal tally with the suggested Is. H by means of ואותי לא תיראי, Is. 57.11.

[36] The contact of Prov. 22.22 (אל תדכא עני בשער) with (אל תגזול דל...וא ל) S seems to me to have been established through the common negative לא (א ל תגזול...וא ל תדכאו) instead of לא. (א ל תכריתו — א ל תגזול...וא ל תדכאו)

This would explain the fact that this Pet. was placed ahead of the Y topic, because the latter is connected with S by means of the word תכריתו, while our Pet. tallies with the preceding word לא.

The suggested Is. H affords also a verbal link in Is. 57.15: מרום וקדוש אשכן ואת דכא — ולהחיות לב נדכאים.

[37] The tally of the Pet. from Is. 48.9 by means of כרת holds of course good also for the suggested H from Is. 56.5. There moreover is also a linguistic tally by means of שם (ש ם עולם — ש מ י למען).

[38] The Pet. v. from 2 K. 14.27 (ולא דבר ה' למחות את שם ישראל מתחת השמים) tends rather to support the suggested Is. H. Indeed, "I will give them an everlasting name" (שם עולם אתן לו) in the initial v. of the Is. H is but the positive counterpart of, "And the Lord said not that He would blot out the name of Israel, etc." However, I doubt whether 2 K. 14.27 should be considered as a new, separate Pet. It seems rather only a subsidiary to the preceding homiletical explanation of Is. 48.9 (למען שמי...) with which it is connected by means of שם. Only so would the formula in T. הרי יפה אמר which is never used to introduce a new Pet., make sense. The insertion of the S v. at the beginning may be the work of a copyist who mistakingly took the v. for 2 K. 14.27 as a new Pet.

[39] A still better tally for Naḥ. 1.7 (טוב ה' וידע חוסי בו) is offered by the suggested Is. H (והחוסה בו ינחל ארץ, Is. 57.13).

[40] With regard to the peroration vv. we may note in the first place that Jer. 35.19 is linked up by means of לא יכרת with S as well as with H (whichever we may choose), and this threefold cord of לא יכרת accounts for the theme of "everlasting preservation," which is most explicitly expressed in the initial verse of the Is. H. The theme of reverence of God is also present in the suggested Is. H where Israel is reproached for the lack of fear of God (ואת מי דאגת ותיראי...ואותי לא תיראי, Is. 57.11).

[41] One might be inclined to argue that the fact that the anonymous opinion in Tanḥ. is attributed to the Rabbis (*rabotenu*) in NR is rather an indication of the latter being dependent on Tanḥuma. For it would seem that the name "Rabotenu" in NR is but a reference to כך שנו רבותינו in Tanḥuma.

I cannot share the impression that the version in NR presents an earlier stage than that of the Tanḥuma. The fact is that the transformation of a Y formula into a simple quotation (*taman taninan*) is also otherwise observed and generally recognized. But there is no other known instance to indicate the reverse process, viz. the reshaping of a simple quotation into a Y topic. Consequently, even if we were to accept the A.'s thesis that NR reproduces an earlier version of the Tanḥuma, we would still assume that already this older version had the Y formula, preserved in the later Tanḥuma, which NR transformed into a mere quotation.

[42] The objections raised against Epstein's suggestion that the idiom *taman taninan* may indicate a Y source do not justify the harsh qualification of "figment."

a) As far as the first objection is concerned, namely that there is no tally of the question with H, we should bear in mind that neither the H nor the question formula has been definitely established. Indeed, the proposed H from Mal. was "hesitatingly" suggested by the A., and at best can be considered as very plausible, yet does by no means preclude other possibilities. Nor is there any certainty about the question formula. It seems improper to speak of contact, or lack of it, between two unknown entities. But assuming the proposed H from Mal. and the question formula מי קודם למי proposed by Epstein, we find a verbal link in the very finale of H which reads וכשנים קדמוניות.

b) Still less compelling is the second objection, viz. why was the longer version of the Tosefta preferred over the shorter in the Mishnah. This is not unusual even in genuine and original Y homilies, and should be still less surprising in the version of NR which, as is generally known, tends to expand its sources. Besides, the question formula might have read: ילר׳, חכם מלך וכהן מי קודם, and since חכם proper does not figure in the Mishnah (there is only תלמיד חכם towards the end), the homilist rightly quotes the Tosephta which starts with חכם. For all these considerations it would seem that Epstein was in his right to *suspect* not to *affirm*, that the quotation (תמן תנינן) is a transformed Y topic.

We noted above that the proposed Mal. H does not preclude other suggestions. I would, for instance, suggest Is. 52.13: הנה ישכיל עבדי ירום ונשא וגבה מאד, tallying with S by means of ונשא. Such H would consist of Is. 52.13–53.3, 10–12 (together 9 vv.), terminating with נשא והוא חטא רבים ולפשעים יפגיע. There would be a tally with the Y question as formulated by us above by means of מלך (פיהם מלכים עליו יקפצו, Is. 52.15). This H would also tally with the Pet. from Prov. 3.15 (לא יקרה היא מפנינים וכל חפציך) by means of contrast to חפץ ה׳ (ישוו בה) (Is. 53.10).

[43] Job 36.7 (לא יגרע מצדיק עיניו ואת מלכים לכסא וינבהו) tallies with the suggested H from Is. 52.13 in many ways. First by means of (בדעתו יצדיק צדיק, Is. 53.11); secondly by way of מלכים (Is. 52.15 quoted above), and finally through גבה (cp. initial v. of H quoted above).

[44] If we consider carefully the position chapters five and six occupy in the fourth book, we may perhaps find the key to the dispelling of the obscurity. Indeed, it should not be difficult to realize that Num. 4.47 (end of chapter four) brings to a conclusion the first topic of the book, consisting

in the main of narrative-descriptive matters, such as the counting of the
children of Israel, the assignment of places and functions to the various
tribes within the encampment and the like. It is due mainly to this part
of the book that it obtained the name of Numbers (חומש הפקודים). Beginning
with chapter five the narrative is interrupted by certain legalistic matters.
It is here where the Halakhic *Midrash, Sifre,* starts. There are five topics in
the two following chapters (5–6): 1) lepers and those who are unclean should
be sent forth out of the camp (5.1–4); 2) how to redress certain acts of unfaithfulness against God (5.5–10); 3) laws concerning a woman suspected
of unfaithfulness against her husband (5.11–31); 4) laws concerning a
Nazirite (6.1–21); 5) priestly blessing (5.22–27). After these five topics of
Halakhic nature, the book resumes the narrative-descriptive form, describing
the consecration of the tabernacle. A glance at the five topics shows that
the first two are too small to constitute a S; so is the last one, the fifth.
Only three and four are large enough to form a Seder. The authorities plan-
ning the arrangement of the Sedarim for the TC had to face the problem
what to do with the two small topics separating the first narrative-descriptive
section of the book from the first larger Halakhic theme.

There were three alternatives: a) To treat the first two small topics as
appendices joined with the preceding Seder; b) to follow the arrangement
of the Halakhic Midrash, and put them at the beginning of the first S of
Halakhic character; c) finally, the third alternative is to consider the first
small topics as a bridge between the narrative and Halakhic section, and to
add the first (5.1–4) as appendix to the preceding Seder, while attaching the
second (5.5–10) as introduction to the following Seder. This indeed, appears
the most logical arrangement. For one cannot fail to realize that Num.
5.1–4 remains tied up with the previous section dealing with the organization
of the camp, the assignment of place and duties to the people within the
camp. The logical sequel is to deal with those who have no right to stay
in the camp, and this is precisely the theme of Num. 5.1–4. Seen from this
angle this topic actually remains within the narrative frame. On the other
hand the second small topic (5.5–10) dealing with acts of *unfaithfulness
against God* (למעל מעל בה') is clearly joined to the theme of unfaithfulness of a woman against her husband (ומעלה בו מעל) in the following
Seder.

The three different customs mentioned by the A. represent these three
alternatives. Those who started the S at 5.11 adopted the first alternative;
those who started the new S at 5.1 followed the second alternative, while
those who started at 5.5 preferred the third most logical alternative.

It is interesting to note that what prevailed was not the most logical
alternative, but the first one which followed a pattern in vogue. It should be
remarked that the redactors of the Mishnah often had to cope with the same
problem, how to dispose of small secondary items, and in most cases adopted
the first alternative, viz. to add them as appendices, to the preceding section

[45] This is explicitly stated by Epstein, מקדמוניות, p. 72, top: נשארו בו רשמים
של הילמדנו, נמצא מלת האלהים בהרבה מקומות.

[46] On the basis of this Pet. from Prov. 25.4, I would suggest as H Is.
52.11: סורו סורו צאו משם טמא אל תגעו צאו מתוכה הברו נשאי כלי ה'
which tallies perfectly, verbally and intrinsically, with our S. The H would
consist of Is. 52.11–53.1, 10–12 (together 9 vv.). The link with the Pet.
(הנו סינים ויצא לצורף כלי) would be by means of (הברו נשאי כלי ה') in the
initial v. of. H.

[47] It probably might be more correct to say that the topic of proselytes
was introduced by the Halakhic interpretation of v. 5.8, and it was the topic
that suggested the area of the H. The starting point was then determined
by the usual linguistic tally.

[48] The reasoning is hardly convincing. The fact is that the topic of
proselytes, here as well as in Lev. 1.2 was introduced by the Halakhic Midrash, here in Sifre, there in Sifra, and it is therefore justified there just as
here. Add to it the other fact that S 74 (Lev. 1.1) was universally accepted
while our S seems to have been of a limited, local use, and we will be rather
inclined to consider S 74 as the genuine place of the homily. Cp. LR., ed.
Margulies, 1.2, editor's note.

[49] It should be noted that by the same token the Pet. tallies also with S
(והה תודו את חטאתם, 5.7).

[50] While we can only admire this brilliant, painstaking analysis, we
hesitate to consider the conclusions as definite, incontestable. I doubt that
the Petiḥtot are genuine, belonging to this S, because their links with S are
extremely weak. It would seem to me possible to perceive the whole of NR 8
as a collection of Midrashim on the topic of proselytes, an Aggadic supplement to "Parashat Gerim" in the Halakhic Sifre. The compiler might have
gathered whatever Midrashic material on this topic was available to him.
A certain indication to this effect can be seen in the fact that when referring
to the text of our Seder, the compiler does not use the standard term עינן
לכך נאמר ואיש בפרשת גרים; ממה שקדרינו בעניין (למעלה מן העניין), but פרשה (גרים)
לאחר פרשת גזל הגר כתיב), a term which seems to refer to the topic
rather than to the S.

[51] The fact that this apparent old H shows no linguistic, but only intrinsic connection with S seems to corroborate Buchler's theory that the
pattern of linguistic tally represents a later stage of development. However,
the use of the Hos. v. by R. Yoḥanan ben Zakkai to justify the abolition of
the Soṭah ordeal does not prove that already at that time the Hos. v. was
the beginning of the H for this S. It is well possible that it was because R.
Yoḥanan ben Zakkai's use of the Hos. v. in connection with Soṭah that
this verse was later adopted as starting point for the H to our S.

[52] A Y topic like that of our S which is so intimately and manifestly
related to the substance of the S may not require any tally with H, as has
been rightly pointed out by Lieberman.

[53] The connection with H is quite ingenious, and if there were a need for
it, I would not hesitate to accept the suggestion. But I am not convinced
of the need of any link with H, I hesitate to ascribe that much of ingenuity
to the homilist.

[54] It seems to me that Buber was justified to consider the verse as a Pet. since it is introduced by the specific formula זה. שאמר הכתוב. True no linguistic tally with H is to be found, but there is a linguistic tally with S by means of עינים רמות (cf. Num. 5.13: ונעלם מעיני אישה). Even should we admit that at a certain period the pattern of linking the Pet. v. with H was generally accepted and followed, we still may doubt whether this was the case at such an early period as the middle of the first century (the time of R. Yose, the Galilean). As a matter of fact, contemplating all these formalistic word linkages one has the impression of being at the threshold of the Byzantine period.

[55] The Pet. from Job 24.15 (ועין נואף שמרה נשף לאמר לא תשורני עין) ונעלם מעיני אישה :was manifestly suggested by S (וסתר פנים ישים ונסתרה (5.13). This is also the case with Jer. 23.24 (אם יסתר איש במסתרים) and Is. 29.15 (הוי המעמיקים מה' לסתיר עצה). The tallies with H are secondary, token links.

[56] In Mal. too the main link is, in all probability, with S, namely by means of ובמנאפים, ועד אין בה, as against והייתי עד ממהר במכשפים in S (v. 5.13).

[57] The peroration verses of Is. 65.23 (זרע ברוכי ה') and Jer. 2.21 (זרע אמת) allude clearly to S, and precisely toward the end of it, v. 5.28: אם לא נטמאה האשה וטהורה היא ונקתה ונזרעה זרע. It is worthy of note that this verse is the last one of the S to be commented upon in Sifre, the Halakhic Midrash on Num.

[58] The quoting of several verses from different places after each of the first three parts of the composition is a familiar feature of Yannai's *Ḳerobot* as well as those of all the earlier *Paitanim*. They seem to be united by a great variety of linkages, and not exclusively through the H. In many cases the first verse is linked up with S, and the second verse tallies with the first; often the various verses are linked up with S, but through various words of the S verse, either starting with the end and ending up with beginning or vice versa. We are therefore hardly justified to reduce the complicated scheme of various combinations to one single method of linkage, viz. that by means of the H.

I am inclined to see here too a more complicated combination than the simple link of all three verses with H. There is in the first place the connection of the first quoted v. (Gen. 17.8: ולזרעך אחריך) with S by means of 5.28 (ונקתה ונזרעה זרע) which v., as we surmised, was also used as link in the peroration; the second verse quoted (Deut. 23.15: כי ה' אלהיך מתהלך בקרבך...ושב מאחריך) is linked up with Gen. 17.8 through the italicized words. Finally, Prov. 5.7 ff., speaking of a "strange woman," is intrinsically connected with S as well as with H, and verbally tallies with H.

[59] Koh. 8.8 (אין אדם שליט ברוח) tallies in the first place with S by means of ועבר עליו רוח קנאה (5.14).

[60] Needless to say that the main contact of Koh. 7.26 (ומוצא אני מר ממות את האשה) is with S where we find the suspect woman repeatedly referred to

as את האשה, and especially in connection with the bitter cursed waters (5.24: והשקה את האשה את מי המרים המאררים).

[61] The peroration vv. from Ezek. 36.25 ff.: וזרקתי עליכם מים טהורים ...ורוח חדשה אתן...) form also a contrast to the מי המרים המאררים destined for a woman "being defiled" (והיא נטמאה), and the "new spirit" in contrast to the "spirit of jealousy" (רוח קנאה).

[62] It is doubtful whether a verbal link with H was indispensable already at the time of Resh Lakish, first half of the third century (cf. above, notes 51 and 54). Intrinsically, R. Lakish's statement that one gets a wife he deserves is reflected in the first v. of H: "I will not punish your daughters, etc., when they commit adultery, for they themselves consort with lewd women," in other words they do not deserve better wives.

It should be noted that in a larger sense R. Lakish's saying is but a variation of the principle of "measure for measure" (מדה כנגד מדה). Now this principle was already in Tannaitic time developed and illustrated in connection with "Soṭah" (cf. Tosephta, Soṭah, c. 3).

[63] The question whether the Torah portion dealing with the laws of the Nazirite should form a separate Seder or not, entailed something more significant than the inauspicious ending of the previous S. It involved the attitude towards the Naziriteship, especially that of life long ascetic conduct (Nazir 'Olam). In the first two centuries C. E., when various heretic sects, Jewish and Christian, assumed an ascetic, Nazirite coloring, Jewish authorities endeavored to degrade Naziriteship as something desirable in itself. Only under certain circumstances, to combat one's excessive passion, was it considered advisable to subject oneself to a temporary Naziriteship (usually for 30 days). It was, in all probability, at that time that the Torah portion dealing with the laws of the Nazirite was dropped from the list of Sedarim, and placed as an appendix to the S dealing with the laws of Soṭah. However, even within authoritative Judaism there still were certain circles which assumed a positive attitude towards the Nazirite status. Among them the Torah portion concerning the Nazirite continued, in all probability, to form a separate S. The different views about the Nazirite status among the teachers of the second century is reflected in the controversy in the last Mishnah of tractate Nazir whether the prophet Samuel was a Nazirite or not. The first opinion is maintained by R. Nahorai, the second by R. Yose. This last Mishnah is, in all likelihood, a later addition, because the authoritative Mishnah code did not care to mention the opinion of a sectarian tinge, that of R. Nahorai.

[64] I was unable to find the source of the statement that not only his wife, but also Manoaḥ was in the status of a Nazirite until the birth of Samson. I suspect here a lapsus. As to Samson, it should be noted that in its technical-Halakhic sense, he was not a נזיר עולם; Mishnah Nazir 1.2 explicitly contradistinguishes נזיר שמשון from נזיר עולם.

[65] There might be here an allusion to the different customs with regard to our S, i. e., those who combined it with the previous one, and those who

started here a new S, terminating in the following topic, the priestly blessing.

[66] This is rather an exception; the general pattern being, as often pointed out by the A., to let the H work behind the scenes. One might therefore be tempted to suggest that we have here a relic of an earlier sermon which, according to Rapoport's suggestion, consisted in commenting the H proper. This earlier homily would reflect the older tradition concerning the Nazirite, i. e., before his status was challenged, at which time our Torah portion formed, of course, a Seder by itself. All this, however, is but mere guess.

[67] The A.'s objection does not carry enough weight to justify such harsh judgment. The fact remains that the suggested H, though plausible, is far from being definitely established. Nor do we know how the question could have been formulated. Under these uncertainties, a categoric assertion such as: "None is to be found in H," seems out of place.

ADDITIONAL NOTES BY SONNE ON
LEVITICUS AND NUMBERS

[1] This is also stated by Ginzberg, GS, *l. c.*: ומי שפירש שמחזירין בירושלמי הוא
מסלקין אינו אלא טועה. It should be noted that in the earlier Talmud editions
(Bomberg 1520 to Basel 1579), the passage in Babli reads: אין מחזירין
אותו מחזירין...אותו. Solomon Luria in his critical notes (חכמת שלמה)
corrects the text (צ"ל אין מעלין אותו...מעלין). In the later Talmud
edd. which made use of Luria's corrections מעלין...אותו...מעלין אין מעלין
was substituted for אין מחזירין אותו...מחזירין אותו.

[2] On the other hand the reason given by M. for the omission of the second
benediction in the Y is hardly tenable, since the Baraita quoted as basis of
our Y states expressly טעה בכל הברכות כולן אין מחזירין אותו, in contradiction to the opinion which makes a distinction between the first three
benedictions and the others.

It seems to me that essentially Ginzberg is right, namely that the omission was due to the lack of interest by the author of our Y. The reason for
this lack of interest in the second benediction is rather obvious, because it
was not actual any more. Indeed, the only sectarians who might have been
tempted to skip intentionally the second benediction, containing the belief
in resurrection, were the Sadducees, and they disappeared soon after the
destruction of the Temple. On the other hand, Judaeo-Christians, various
Gnostic sects as well as Samaritans who would contrive to skip the benediction containing a curse against sectarians (ברכת המינין) and the prayer for
the restoration of Jerusalem (בונה ירושלים) respectively, continued to linger
on and to trouble the Jewish communities in Palestine for many more
centuries.

[3] M. follows all commentators who consider ועכשיו as the beginning of a
new sentence, introducing the conclusion. However, a Genizah fragment
(VI, §16, note 7) seems to indicate, rightly in my opinion, that ועכשיו should
be connected with the preceding sentence. The whole passage would read:
אי מה ישראל בני מקבלי ברית אף המשומדים...יצאו הגרים שאינם בני מקבלי ברית,
ת"ל מכם—ועכשיו (כלו' אלה שהם עכשיו מקבלי ברית ולא די שאבותיהם היו
מקבלי ברית).

[4] The Genizah fragment referred to is said (vol. I, 426) to be "edited
and discussed infra vol. III." We regret to say that we were unable to find
it. Since I have not seen the fragment, it is of course impossible for me to
say anything positive about it. Yet it seems that it is not a list of Haftarot,
but a list of verses vaguely connected with the AC of Parshyyot or TC
Sedarim. I am inclined rather to consider both vv., one as H v. the other as
Pet. v. or as supporting v. in the same fashion as Yannai adds to the S vv.
and H v. some "supporting," or better "Pet. vv."

249

⁵ Concerning the text of R. Simon's saying, cp. LR, ed. Marg., p. 7, *v. l.* The references are given in the editor's notes.

⁶ Cp. LR, ed. Marg., p. 16, *v. l.* and notes.

⁷ It may be noted that Yannai (Zulay, PY, p. 121), though citing the Micah H, alludes to this saying of R. Abin: כי אתה הוא הקורא והמדבר (section I, line 6).

⁸ Cp. also LR, ed. Marg., p. 32, editor's note.

⁹ Cp. also LR, ed. Marg., p. 44, *v. l.* and notes.

¹⁰ One sees the uncertainty of M. in deciding the chronological relationship between the transmitted Micah H and the suggested new H from Isaiah. First, in the text, priority in time was given to the Is. H, whereas here the Mic. H is considered likely to be earlier. In our own notes we have endeavored to show that all midrashic data can be linked up with S and the Mic. H, so that there is no compelling reason to assume the Is. H. But admitting the existence of two Hafṭarot, they might have been used at the same time in different congregations, and not necessarily in subsequent periods.

¹¹ So Ms Brit. Mus. (cp. LR, ed. Marg., p. 19, line 7, *v. l.*).

¹² I assume that Theodor understood ראש סדר in the sense we suggested, viz. the third v. of the S used as heading for the sermon. Similarly Samuel Jafe Ashkenasi in his commentary: שהתחילו לישא וליתן בפסוק זה יפה האר.

¹³ Cp. LR, ed. Marg., p. 70, note 4. The suggestion to connect the phrase with עולליהם has been made also by מהרז'ו *a. l.*, but M. is quite right, there is no connection whatsoever.

¹⁴ Cp. now Tosefta, ed. Lieberman, vol. I, p. 38 f. and Lieberman's commentary, *Tosefta Ki-Fshutah*, p. 121.

¹⁵ The Is. v. may also be considered as connected with Ezek. 36.26 (והסירתי את לב הא ב ן) through the preceding v. (Is. 54.12): ושמתי כדכד שמשתיך ושעריך לא ב נ י אקדח וכל גבולך לא ב נ י חפץ, וכל בניך...

¹⁶ In fact the conclusion of the homily (p. 85) reads: כך נ פ ש כי תחטא.

¹⁷ Cp. LR, ed. Marg., p. 91. In his introductory note to 4.6, the editor also rightly remarks: ודרוש נפש כי תחטא, נפש לשון יחיד, but it has already been noted by Luria (רד'ל) *a. l.*: בא לדרוש מ'ש נפש לשון יחיד.

¹⁸ Cp. LR, ed. Marg., p. 116, line 1, *v. l.* and note.

¹⁹ Cp. LR, ed. Marg., p. 130, *v. l.*; see also p. 135–136, editor's note to 135, line 4.

²⁰ Variants and references are given in LR, ed. Marg., p. 146.

²¹ Cp. LR, ed. Marg., p. 156, editor's note to line 4.

²² This may indicate that the compilers of the later Midrashim to which JTS belongs, were not aware any more of the connection between peroration vv. and H. Thus they felt free to substitute Naḥum 2.1 for Is. 52.7.

²³ See ed. Marg., p. 210 (editor's note), 215.

²⁴ Concerning the text of this passage in LR, cp. ed. Marg., p. 219, *v. l.* and notes.

²⁵ Cp. commentary מהרז'ו *a. l.*; see also ed. Marg., p. 255, *v. l.* and notes.

²⁶ It also echoes והיו למ כ ש ו ל ע ו ן, rendered by Pseudo-Jonathan

לתקלת חובין, in Ezek. 44.12 which verse could be considered as being within the area of H (Ezek. 44.21).

[27] Cp. also LR, ed. Marg., p. 277, note 1.

[28] I would suggest that originally the text had: א"ל ל א"ר to be read אמר לוי אמר רבי (או: רב), meaning that Levi ben Sisi, disciple of Rabbi and colleague of Rab, transmitted the saying in the name of Rabbi (or Rab). But when the abbreviation א"ל was misread אמר לו the Aleph of א"ר had to be dropped, and we got the corrupted text: אמר לו ר'.

[29] To a certain extent, this interpretation has been suggested already by Samuel Yaphe, a sixteenth century commentator, in Yephe Toar a. l. Concerning the text, cp. now LR, ed. Marg., p. 277–278, v. l.

[30] The recurrence of this formula may perhaps be considered as indication that the homily was delivered on the occasion of the birth of a son, at the Sabbath preceding the circumcision, as suggested by us infra (see following note).

[31] Concerning the existence of a S at Lev. 13.1–2, cp. LR, ed. Marg., p. 318, introductory note to 15.1.

It should be noted that in most of the cases mentioned above, we observe that some of the main Midrash compilations, like TB, T, LR, have homilies on the one S, but none or only very few on the other. In our S, however, all three collections, TB, T, LR, have almost an equal number of homilies to each of the two Sedarim. It seems to indicate that both Sedarim were in use at the same time and within the same circle. I wonder whether the beginning at least of this S might not have constituted a special Torah reading for the occurrence of the birth of a son. Such Torah portion would be read by the father on the Sabbath preceding the circumcision. It is interesting to note that in the Sephardic communities the Ḥazan recites the verse of Is. 9.5, the beginning of the H to our S, Friday evening preceding a circumcision. We know of a special Torah section for a bridegroom (Gen. 24.1 ff.) on the Sabbath preceding the wedding, and it would appear logical to have also a special Torah section for the Sabbath preceding a circumcision. If our Torah portion was used for this purpose, viz. for one person alone, then 8 verses would be sufficient. It would also explain the fact that most of the homilies have circumcision as their main theme.

In this connection I venture to suggest that the two Hafṭarot to Gen. 24.1, as indicated by M. (vol. I, 184–186), should be as to two different occasions. The one transmitted in the H lists, Is. 51.2 ff., was used in the normal TC; the other, 1 K. 1.1 ff. is most appropriate for the reading of the bridegroom.

[32] במדה, so have MS Vat. and YSH, as quoted by Buber, TB, p. 35, note 81.

[33] Cp. also LR, ed. Marg., pp. 323–324, v. l. and notes.

[34] Almost the same peroration is to be found in TB Messora, §9, as rightly pointed out by Marg. in his LR, p. 339 end.

[35] It seems that M. has not yet had a clear idea of the function verses, besides those from S and H, which Yannai attached to the first three parts

of the *Ḳerobah*. Only later, as we shall see, did he become aware of the fact that for the most part these vv. represent *Petiḥtot* of homⁱlies that furnished Yannai the material for his compositions. As such they of course are linked up with S or H, or with both.

³⁶ The repetition of the phrase אין להם חלק לעולם הבא requires its removal from one place. But whether from the first place, as suggested by M. (preceding note), or from the second, as proposed by Ginzberg, cannot be ascertained.

³⁷ Cp. TB *a. l.*, editor's note 31; see also LR, ed. Marg., p. 361, where editor remarks: ציון בטעות ילמדנו.

³⁸ Concerning text and meaning, cp. LR, ed. Marg., pp. 365–67, *v. l.* and notes.

³⁹ Ginzberg (GS, *l. c.*) suggests that there might have been an old tradition, perhaps of Tannaitic origin, that leprosy is caused by eleven sins, but without any further specification. R. Judah *ben* Shalom expanded this tradition by specifying the eleven sins and deriving them from Scripture. This suggestion seems to me well taken.

⁴⁰ The difference is only in appearance; in reality however this version is but an expansion of the cause given here, namely Uzziah's usurpation of the rights of priesthood by offering incense. This was the immediate cause of his punishment. Yet the remote cause, which led the king to this usurpation, was his arrogance. This appears quite clearly in the version of T. Noaḥ, 13: בעוזיה כתיב כי אוהב אדמה היה (דהי״ב, כ״ו, י׳), שהיה מלך והפקיר עצמו לאדמה ולא נזקק לתורה. יום אחד נזקק לבית הועד, אמר להם במה אתם עוסקין, אמרו לו בהזר הקרב יומת (במד׳ א׳, נ״א), א״ל עוזיה הקב״ה מלך ואני מלך נאה למלך לשמש פני מלך ולהקטיר לפניו... ויאמרו לו, לא לך עוזיהו להקטיר לה׳ כי לכהנים בני אהרן...ובזה פו ע ם הכהנים והצרעת זרחה במצחו...

It is evident that the direct cause of king Uzziah's leprosy is here attributed to his quarrel with the priests. But at the same time it is also emphasized that the conflict with the king's arrogant behavior toward the members of the academy.

⁴⁰ᵃ Cp. also LR, ed. Marg., p. 374, editor's introductory remark to 17.3.

⁴¹ במטה אחת is not missing in TB, but it is shifted after הוא בבגדו והיא בבגדה.

⁴² The appearance of the strict view of the earlier teachers can hardly prove that we have here an old Baraita. It is well known that this strict Halakhah found entrance to quite later sources, as *Seder Elijah Rabba* and *Baraita d'Masekhet Niddah*. Saul Lieberman has shown that some "earlier Halakhot" found their way to Yannai's Ḳerobot (*Hazanut Yannai*, "Sinai").

⁴³ M. failed to take into consideration: a) The Baraita from ARN, c. 2 is not necessarily old. The B is found only in the A version, but is missing in B. According to Schechter (Introd. c. 5) passages which appear in A alone are for the most part later additions. b) As to the derivation of the Halakhah in Babli from Ezek. 18.6 which is not mentioned here, we should

bear in mind that what we derive from Ezek. is but the meaning of לא יקרב,
viz. that it includes also הוא בבנדיו והיא בבנדיה. Consequently לא תקרב in Lev.
18.19 also embraces הוא בבנדיו והיא בבנדיה. The homilist therefore, even if he
"made use of Babli," could have omitted the middle link, Ezek. 18.6, and
referred directly to Lev. 18.19.

⁴⁴ Ginzberg's argument is based on the phrase שמשלו חכמים ה ד ב ר, "our
sages have compared *this thing* . . ." which seems to indicate that the preacher
refers to a place in which this metaphor was applied to our topic, i. e., a
Niddah sleeping beside her husband in her garments. In Sanh. 37a the
metaphor is actually applied to quite a similar case, namely to a Niddah
being alone with the husband in a room. But in Soṭah 48a the metaphor
is used with reference to a woman's song. It is true that there is no proof
that Palestinian sources did not apply the metaphor also to the Niddah
topic, but thus far such Palestinian sources have not been discovered.

It should be noted that already N. Brull in his review of Buber's Tanḥuma
(*Jahrbücher*, VIII, 126) pointed out that our Y passage made use of Sanh.
37a, and that it therefore belongs to the later elements of the Midrash.

⁴⁵ In the same piece we find an allusion to Ezek. 16.9 and its supporting
v., Is. 4.4: עד תלבין אדמנו ותרחץ צואתנו.

⁴⁶ Concerning the text, cp. LR, ed. Marg., p. 424, *v. l.*

⁴⁷ We regret to have been unable to find the notes referred to here.

⁴⁸ Refers to the third vol., planned, but not executed.

⁴⁹ Concerning the relation of LR, c. 23 to other similar Midrashim, cp.
now LR, ed. Marg., pp. 526–535, editor's notes.

⁵⁰ Concerning the text, cp. LR, ed. Marg., p. 534, end, *v. l.* The most
likely correct text: עבר צילו של עשו . . . כל זמן שצילו של עשו קיים. Margulies'
reference to Giṭṭin 17a רחמנא או בטולך או בטולא דבר עשו is to the
point. Accordingly, the phrase should be understood as follows: "As long
as Israel is under the *protection* of Rome (Edom). . . . When Rome's pro-
tectorate is terminated (and replaced by the protection of God). . ." It is
probable that the homilist has interpreted Hos. 14.6: אהיה כ ט ל as אהיה כ צ ל.

⁵¹ Concerning the text, cp. ed. Marg., p. 535, *v. l.*

⁵² Cp. now ed. Marg., *l. c.* where the correct text is given; see also editor's
note to line 7. It should be noted that the correct sense has been rendered
already by the commentator.

⁵³ Cp. now ed. Marg., p. 545, introductory remark to 23.12.

⁵⁴ Cp. ed. Marg., p. 562 f., editor's note.

⁵⁵ The text seems to me correct; we should only set a dot (period) at
הרביעית. The following תאכלו את פריו is a new quotation which should not be
connected with the fourth year. This suggestion is corroborated by YSH to
Prov. §963 quoted in the following note.

⁵⁶ It is worthy of note that while the first v. is linked up with H, the
second v. points manifestly to S (ונטעתם).

⁵⁷ All the sources discussed by M ('Arukh, Yalḳuṭ, and Midrash Ekha)
are mentioned by Buber, note 4.

[58] About the term מקרא in the sense of Scripture except Torah (Prophets and Hagiographa), cp. W. Bacher, *Die exegetische Terminologie*, I, p. 119; cp. also I. Sonne, Book List, I, "Studies in Bibliography," I, p. 76, note 28.

[59] I was unable to locate the place referred to.

[60] About the relationship between LR and PRK, cp. Albeck, *Midrash Vayikra Rabba*, "Louis Ginzberg Jubilee Volume," (Hebrew section), p. 36 ff.

[61] References to Karaitic sources are given by Ginzberg, GS, II, 478, 493–94.

[62] Cp. commentator מהרז"ו *a. l.*

[63] It should be added that not only does the last v. (Mic. 2.3) tally with S, but also the two Is. vv. mentioned above. Is. 43.14 tallies with S by means of *Israel*; as to Is. 47.4, צבאות שמו ' ה echoes ' ה שם ונקב which constitutes the core of S.

[64] I was unable to find the notes referred to in these notes.

[65] Concerning the text and the references, cp. now LR, ed. Marg., pp. 4–5, *v. l.* and notes.

[66] This too is best conceived as contrast to Jer. 32.22: לא שמעו בקולך ... צויתה להם לעשות לא עשו in the inverted order.

[67] The change was, in all probability, introduced by a copyist living under Arab (Ismael) domination.

[68] It should be noted that all the references are also given by Ginzberg in his note 24.

[69] Concerning the text of this passage and the references, cp. now LR, ed. Marg., p. 584, *v. l.* and notes.

[70] The text is corrupt. We should take into consideration also the preceding sentence. I venture to suggest the following reading: לפיכך אם (לא נמצא לו גואל, יפה. ואם לאו, משלקחה עשה לפניו עד היובל ומוציאה ביובל ... אמר הקב"ה לישראל, כך אם [נמצא לך גואל, יפה. ואם לאו אני] אוציא וכו'. God is waiting for a redeemer (גואל) to redeem Israel before the jubilee year, the year of redemption, arrives. But when none presents himself, then He Himself at the appointed time, will be the גואל. This is derived from Is. 63.4, to which v. 5 should be added: ואביט ואין עוזר.

[71] I was unable to identify the fragment referred to.

[72] את עצמן is missing in the earlier edd. (Ven. 1566, Cracow 1595), and is, in all probabilty, a correction by some later corrector. But I surmise that originally it read: סופך נ מ כ ר.

[73] The earlier edd. mentioned above have דרכו as in 'Arukh.

[74] Cp. Buber's note 1 *a. l.* where references to Sifra and Lekaḥ-Ṭob are given.

[75] So already explained by Buber in his ed. of Midrash Samuel, c. 16, note 1: וכן כאן צ"ל מפרנס כל אותן הדעות האמורות בויקרא רבה [פ' ל"ו].

[76] So פי' מהרז"ו *a. l.*: צפה וקנה (ק': וקוה) לחסדי ה' (ק': וקוה).

[77] Both interpretations are said by Samuel Yaphe (יפה תואר) equally possible.

[78] 'Arukh ed. Pesaro 1517 has צרכו which would be as correct as צרכיו; ed. Ven. 1531 *corrected* צרכי (!), and all later edd. followed suit.

79 Cp. Epstein A., מקדמוניות, p. 72: ומובא בערוך ערך עבר ה' בשם הילמדנו.

80 It seems that only the name (א"ר חזקיה בר חייא) was omitted; as to the rest, we have here, in all probability, a typical homoioteleuto skipping by a copyist. The text read: לעולם ה' נצב ב ש מ י ם [וכי אין דברו של הקב"ה נצב בארץ אלא ב ש מ י ם [מפני ...

81 The Genizah fragment referred to here was published by Solomon Wertheimer, בתי מדרשות, III, Jerusalem 1895, pp. 15–19 (recently re-edited by his son, בתי מדרשות, I, Jerusalem 1950, pp. 215–218). There is a copy of this fragment which seems to have been made by the A. from the original. But I could find no other information about the use of the original.

82 As to Is. 2.3 (כי מציון תצא תורה) which follows H v. (Is. 45.19), it should be noted that besides the intrinsic connection rightly pointed out by the A., there are various verbal links, the most characteristic with the finale of H (ונתתי ב צ י ו ן תשועה, Is. 46.13).

83 Ginzberg notes that it could not be רע, because there is more space than needed for two letters, and proposes פחות. I would suggest גרוע.

84 Last v. of peroration (Deut. 4.4: ואתם הדבקים ... ח י י ם כלכם היום) is linked up with S by means of Num. 4.19: ו ח י ו ולא ימתו. It is worthy of note that the two vv. of the peroration are linked up with two subsequent vv. of S. Is. 48.18 f. tallies with Num. 4.18 by means of תכריתו; Deut. 4.4 tallies, as mentioned above, with Num. 4.19.

85 A smoother and more logical text is no criterion of being original. I am inclined to see in the version of NR a later attempt to remove the difficulty raised by the A. The reference to the case of the gatherer of wood is, in all probability, genuine, because, being illogical, no later copyist would have introduced it. The same remark holds good for the previous note.

86 The language of the peroration in NR (אמר הקב"ה כשם שעשיתי לבני קהת על שהיו יראים אותי כבדתים וחלקתי להם כבוד והזהרתי עליהם להציל ממות נפשם) reflects clearly Ps. 33.18–19 (הנה עין ה' אל יראיו להציל ממות נפשם), the first Pet. in NR c. 5.

87 The homilist, as rightly noted by Ginzberg, does not quote the Mishnah verbatim, and seems to be following closely the Sifre, where it is stated מן התורה האיש מביא את אשתו. Being mainly interested in the description of the Soṭah ordeal according to the Torah, the homilist skipped the passage in the Mishnah dealing with a later rabbinic enactment. The same seems to be the case with the author of והזהיר.

ימלל (שם, ק"ו, ב').   תנן סדר נחלות כיצד (מ' ב"ב, ח', ב').   יש נוחלים ומנחילים (שם, א').   בנות צלפחד נטלו שלשה חלקין בנחלה (שם, ג').

ראשי המטות.   יש בוטה כמדקרות חרב (מש' י"ב, י"ח).   אלהים בציון ולך (תה' ס"ה, ב').   השמים מספרים (שם, י"ט, ב').   נחית כצאן עמ' (שם, ע"ז, כ"א).   תנן כל כינוי נדרים (מ' נדרים א', א').   נערה המאורסה אביה (שם, י', א').   ארבעה נדרים התירו חכמים (שם, ג', א').

(דף ס"ז, ע"ב) ספר אלה הדברים.   ולמוכיחים ינעם (מש' כ"ד, כ"ה).   זכרתי לך חסד נעוריך (יר' ב', ב').   מי זאת עולה מן המדבר (שה"ש ג', ו'; ח', ב').   תנן חמשה דברים אירעו את אבותינו (מ' תענית ד', ו').   משכונים אב ממעטים בשמחה (שם, ז').   כל שאינן לא במקרא ולא במשנה (מ' קדושין א', י').

ואתחנן.   בהתעטף עלי (תה' קמ"ב, ד').   בקראי עניני (תה' ד', ב').   תחנונים ידבר (מש' י"ח, כ"ג).   למרבה המשרה (יש' ט', ו').   פנה אלי וחנני (תה' כ"ה, ט"ז; פ"ו, ט"ז; קי"ט, קל"ב).   תפילת השחר עד חצות (מ' ברכות ד', א').   אין עומדים להתפלל (שם, ה', א').   ר' אליעזר אומר העושה תפילתו קבע (שם, ד', ד').

והיה עקב.   טובה תוכחת מגולה (מש' כ"ז, ה').   אם לא תדעי לך היפה בנשים צאי לך (שה"ש א', ח').   עקב נוה (מש' כ"ב, ד').   יראת י"י תוסיף ימים (שם, י', כ"ז).   הקורא את שמע (מ' ברכות ב', ג').   כל העושה מצוה אחת (מ' קדושין א', י').

ראה.   מי חכם ויבין אלה (הו' י"ד, י').   ברוך הגבר (יר' י"ז, ז').   לי"י הארץ ומלואה (תה' כ"ד, א').   אשכילך ואורך (שם, ל"ב, ח').   אשרי נשוי פשע (שם, ל"ב, א').   ראה חיים עם אש' (קה' ט', ט').   י"י בעזך ישמח מלך (תה' כ"א, ב').   ברכות וקללות כיצד (סוטה ז', ה').   הכל שוחטין ובכל (מ' חולין א', ב'; כאן סוף הקטע).

ט"ו, א'). שימני כחותם (שה"ש ח', ו'). שאו מרום עיניכם (יש' מ', כ"ו). תנן עשרה
ייחוסין (מ' קדושין ד', א'). אמ' ר' עקיבא מנין לפולטת שכבת זרע (מ' שבת
ט', ג'). הכונס צאן לדיר בפניהם (מ' ב"ק ו', א').

נ ש ו א. אלהים י"י חילי (חב' ג', י"ט). נכון לבי אלהים (תה' ק"ח, ב').
מצרף לכסף וכור לזהב (מש' י"ז, ג'; כ"ז, כ"א). היחתה איש אש (שם, ו', כ"ז).
לא יבוזו לגנב (שם, ל'). כהניה ילבשו ישע (תה' קל"ב, ט"ז). ראשך עליך ככרמל
(שה"ש ז', ו'). תנן המקנא לאשתו (מ' סוטה א', א'). ברכת כהנים כיצד, שוטה
(היינו: מ' סוטה ז', ו'). ארבעה אבות נזיקים (מ' ב"ק א', א').

ב ה ע ל ו ת ך. נר י"י נשמת אדם (מש' כ', כ"ז). כי נר מצוה (שם, ו', כ"ג).
ויאמר והנה ראיתי מנורת (זכ' ד', ז'). נר לרגלי (תה' קי"ט, ק"ה). על כן באורים
(יש' כ"ד, ט'). והיה אור הלבנה (שם, ל', כ"ו). הנה מה טוב ומה נעים (תה'
קל"ג, א'). תנן שלשה זתים (מ' מנחות ח', ד'). סנהדרין גדולה (מ' סנהדרין א', ו').
שבעה קני מונרה מעכבין זה את זה (מ' מנחות ג', ז'). מי שהיה טמא או בדרך
רחוקה (מ' פסחים ט', א'). במה מדליקין ובמה אין מדליקין (מ' שבת ב', א).

(דף ס"ו, ע"ב). ש ל ח ל ך. שש הנה שנא י"י (מש' ו', ט"ז). שלחו כר ומשל
ארץ (יש' ט"ז, א'). כחומץ לשנים (מש' י', כ"ו). הושיעה י"י כי גמר חסיד (תה'
י"ב, ב'). השולח בים צירים (יש' י"ח, ב'). יבש חציר נבל ציץ (שם, מ', ח').
תנן סנהדרין גדולה היתה שלע' ואחד (מ' סנהדרין א', ו'). התכלת אינה מעכבת
את הלבן, מנחות (היינו: מ' מנחות ד', א'). אילו שאין להם חלק לעולם הבא
(מ' סנהדרין י', א').

ו י ק ח. אח נפשע מקרית עוז (מש' י"ח, י"ט). כי אני י"י השפלתי עץ גבוה
(יח' י"ז, כ"ד). חלק לכם עתה יאשמו (הו' י', ב'). לפני שבר גאון (מש' ט"ז, י"ח).
לפני שבר יגבה לב איש (שם, י"ח, י"ב). אך איש אל ירב (הו' ד', ד'). מי ימלל
גבו' (תה' ק"ו, ב'). כי באש י"י נשפט (יש' ס"ו, ט"ז). לדויד אודך בכל לבי (תה'
קל"ח, א'). תנן עדת קרח אינה עתידה לעלות (מ' סנהדרין י', י"ג). כל התדיר
מחבירו הוא קודם (מ' זבחים י', א'). זר ששימש (מ' סנהדרין ט', ו').

ז א ת ח ו ק ת. וישב מטהר ומצרף (מלא' ג', ג'). יען טיהרתיך (יח' כ"ד,
י"ג). חנינו אלהים כחסדך (תה' נ"א, ג'). וזרקתי עליכם (יח' ל"ו, כ"ה). מי יתן
טהור מטמא (אי' י"ד, ד'). אל אלהים י"י דיבר ויקרא (תה' נ', א'). י"י מלך
ירגזו עמים (שם, צ"ט, א'). שני שדיך (שה"ש ד', ה'). (דף ס"ז, ע"א) תנן עושין
כל צרכי המת (מ' שבת כ"ג, ה'). שבעת ימים קודם שריפת הפרה (מ' פרה ג', א').

ו י ר א ב ל ק. צפור שמים ודגי הים (תה' ח', ט'). רשע יראה וכעס (שם,
קי"ב, י'). עמי מה עשיתי בך (מי' ו', ג'). עמי זכר נא (שם, ה'). כי התרפים
דברו און (זכ' י', ב'). ונדע בגוים זרעם (יש' ס"א, ט'). כל העמים תקעו כף (תה'
מ', ב'). תנן הפוער עצמו לפעור (מ' סנהדרין ז', ו'). ואילו דברים שלגוים
אסורים (מ' ע"ז ב', ג'). הגונב את הקסוה והמקלל (מ' סנהדרין ט', ו').

פ י נ ח ס. פרי צדיק עץ חיים (מש' י"א, ל'). בריתי היתה איתו (מלא' ב', ה').
חמת מלך מלאכי מות (מש' ט"ז, י"ד). כי י"י אוהב משפט (תה' ל"ז, כ"ח). מי

אחרי מות. אל י"י בצרתה לי (תה' ק"כ, א'). אמרי האזינה י"י (שם,
ה', ב'). לדויד ברכי נפשי את י"י (שם, ק"ג, א'). מחיתי כעב פשעיך (יש'
מ"ד, כ"ב). יקר בעיני י"י המותה (תה' קט"ז, ט"ו). לשחוק אמרתי מהולל (קה'
ב', ב'). שבתי וראה (שם, ט', י"א). כי בראותו ילדיו (יש' כ"ט, כ"ג). אשרי
נשוי פשע (תה' ל"ב, א'). כהן גדול דן ודנין אותו (מ' סנהדרין ב', א'). כהן גדול
משמש בשמונה בגדים (מ' יומא ז', ה'). חמש עשרה נשים פוטרות צרותיהן (מ'
יבמות א', א'). אמ' להם הממונה צאו וראו, כפורים (היינו: מ' יומא ג', א').

קדושים. לקדושים אשר בארץ המה (תה' ט"ז, א'). אל נערץ בסוד
קדושים רבה (שם, פ"ט, ח'). את י"י צבא' (דף ס"ה, ע"א) אותו תקדישו (יש'
ח', י"ג). והיה הנשאר בציון (שם, ד', ג'). בשנת מות (שם, ו', א'). י"י מי יגור
באהליך (תה' ט"ו, א'). כל הפרשה כולה נאמרה בקדושה (עמוד ר"ט). תנן עשר
קדושות הן (מ' כלים א', ו'). כל מצות הבן על האב (מ' קדושין א', ז'). אין
מוכרין להם במחובר לקרקע, עב' זר' (היינו: מ' ע"ז, א', ח').

אמר. אימרות י"י אמרות טהורות (תה' י"ב, ז'). הושיעה י"י כי גמר חסיד
(שם, ב'). והכהנים הלויים מבני צדוק (יח' מ"ד, ט"ו). אלפצל והיה כעם ככהן
(יש' כ"ד, ב'). כי שפתי כהן ישמרו דעת (מלא' ב', ז'). כי כה אמר י"י שאל
נא את הכהנים תורה לאמר (חגי ב', י"א). תנן אף עלפי שאמרן בתולה גובה
מאתים (מ' כתובות ה', א'). כהן גדול ונזיר אין מטמין בקרוביהן (מ' נזיר
ז', א'). כהן גדול לא ישא את האלמנה (מ' יבמות ו', ד'). אי זהו משיח, המשוח
בשמן המשחה (מ' הוריות ג', ד'). תנן משמיתו נביאים הראשונים בטלו אורים
(מ' סוטה ט', י"ב).

בהר סיני. ואני אמרתי איך אשיתך בבנים (יר' ג', י"ט). לו עמי שומע
לי (תה' פ"א, י"ד). (דף ס"ה, ע"ב) רצית י"י ארצ[י]ך (תה' פ"ה, ב'). ועל הר
סיני ירדתה (נחמ' ט', י"ג). הרים רקדו (תה' קי"ד, ד'). כשושנה בין החוחים
(שה"ש ב', ב'). וזה לך האות אכול השנה ספיח (יש' ל"ז, ל'). תנן ארבעה ראשי
שנים הם (מ' ר"ה א', א'). אילו דברים שאין להם אונאה, בבא קמא (היינו: מ'
ב"מ ד', ט'). המלוה את חבירו על ידי משכואן, בגרא (היינו: מ' ב"מ ט', י"ג).
איזו הוא נשך ואיזהו מרבית, מצעא (היינו: מ' ב"מ ה', א').

אם בחקותי. חשבתי דרכי ואשיבה (תה' קי"ט, נ"ט). אשרי איש ירא את
י"י (שם, קי"ב, א'). אם תאבו ושמעתם (יש' א', י"ט). לו הקשבת למצותי (שם,
מ"ח, י"ח). שומר מצוה (קה' ח', ה'). כי איננו יודע (שם, ז'). נודע י"י משפט
עשה (תה' ט', י"ז). תנן אנטיגנס איש סוכו (מ' אבות א', ג'). מאמתי מזכירין
גבורות גשמים (מ' תענית א', א'). תנן חזקת בתים בורות ושיחים ומערות, ביתרא
(היינו: מ' ב"ב ג', א').

ספר וידבר י"י. שררך אגן הסהר (שה"ש ז', ג'). הביאני אל בית
היין (שם, ב', ד'). והיה מספר בני ישראל (הו' ב', א'). רועה ישראל האזינה
(תה' פ', ב'). ואנכי נטעתיך שורק (יר' ב', כ"א). (דף ס"ו, ע"א) לכן הנה אנכי
מפתיה (הו' ב', ט"ז). על משמרתי אעמודה (חב' ב', א'). מי יגור באהליך (תה'

ו י ק ה ל. מי כהחכם ומי יודע פשר (קה' ח', א'). אם תשיב משבת רגליך
(יש' נ"ח, י"ג). במקהילות ברכו אלהים (תה' ס"ח, כ"ז). ברב עם הדרת מלך
(מש' כ"ח, כ'). תנן כלל גדול אמרו בשבת (מ' שבת ז', א'). אבות מלאכות
ארבעים חסיר אחת (שם, ב').

א ל ה פ ק ו ד י. (דף ס"ג, ע"ב) זכור י"י לדויד את כל עונותו (תה' קל"ב,
א'). י"י בחכמה יסד ארץ (מש' ג', י"ט). בחכמה יבנה בית (שם, כ"ד, ג').
בידך אפקיד רוחי (תה' ל"א, ו'). איש אמונות רב ברכות (מש' כ"ח, כ'). אלו
הן הממונים שהיו במקדש (מ' שקלים ה', א'). ואלו נשבעין שלא בטענה (מ'
שבועות ז', ח'). עד שלא הוקם המשכן היו הבמות (מ' זבחים י"ד, ד'). באתי
לגני א' (שה"ש ה', א').

ו י ק ר א י"י. אל אלהים דיבר ויקרא ארץ (תה' נ', א'). ולא אותי קראת
יעקב (יש' מ"ג, כ"ב). שמע אלי יעקב וישראל מקוראי (שם, מ"ח, י"ב). קרא
אלי ואעניך (יר' ל"ג, ג'). אשרי תבחר ותקרב (תה' ס"ה, ה'). יענך י"י ביום צרה
(שם, כ', ב'). ויקרא וידבר הקדים קרויה לדיבור (ספרא, ויקרא, פ"א, א').
תנן עד שלא הוקם המשכן (מ' זבחים י"ד, ד'). שבעת ימים קודם ליום הכפורים
(מ' יומא א', א'). כלל גדול אמרו בשבת כל השכיח (מ' שבת ז', א'). השוחט
אחד בעוף (מ' חולין ב' א').

צ ו א ת. יענך י"י ביום (תה' כ', ב'). שנאה תעורר מדנים (מש' י', י"ב).
במה אקדם (מי' ו', ו'). פחדו בציון חטאים (יש' ל"ג, י"ד). מי זאת עולה מן
המדבר (שה"ש ג', ו'). תנן אור לארבעה עשר בודקין את החמץ (מ' פסחים
א', א'). תנן המזביח מקדש את הראוי לו (מ' זבחים ט', א').

(דף ס"ד, ע"א) ו י ה י ב י ו ם ה ש מ י נ י. הנה מה טוב ומה נעים (תה'
קל"ג, א'). חכמות בנתה ביתה (מש' ט', א'). ויכלו את הימים (יח' מ"ג, כ"ז).
י"י לא גבה לבי (תה' קל"א, א'). תן חלק לשבעה (קה' י"א, ב'). תנן אילו
טרפות בבהמה (מ' חולין ג', א').

א ש ה. זכור נא כי כחומר עשיתני (אי' י', ט'). י"י חקרתני ותידע (תה' קל"ט,
א'). רני עקרה לא ילדה (יש' נ"ד, א'). לא יגעו לריק (שם, ס"ה, כ"ג). הלא
כחלב תתיכני (אי' י', י'). דרכיו ראיתי וארפאיהו (יש' נ"ז, י"ח). הרעיפו שמים
ממעל (יש' מ"ה, ח'). תנן המפלת טמטום ואנדרוגינס (מ' נדה ג', ה'). שמאי
אומ' כל הנשים דיין שעתן (שם, א', א'). האשה שמיתו ילדיה בתוך מיעיה (מ'
חולין ד' ג').

ז א ת. לדויד בשנותו (תה' ל"ד, א'). כי כה אמר י"י רם ונשא (יש' נ"ז, ט"ו).
חנינו י"י כחסדיך (תה' נ"א, ג'). שש הנה שנא י"י (מש' ו', ט"ו). רעה עמך
(דף ס"ד, ע"ב) בשבטיך (מי' ז', י"ד). תשב באחיך תדבר (תה' נ', כ'). תנן כיצד מטהרין
את המצורע (מ' נגעים י"ד, א'). ובמוציא שם רע להקל ולהחמיר, בערכין (היינו:
מ' ערכין ג', ה'). מראות נגעים שנים שהן ארבעה (מ' נגעים א', א'). ארבעה
מחוסרי כפרה וכול' (מ' כריתות ב', א').

בעלה (מ' פסחים ח', א'). ותנן יש בכור לנחלה (מ' בכורות ח', א'). ותנן ארבע
פרשיות שלתפלין (מ' מנחות ג', ז'). ותנן המקבל שדה מחבירו ואכלה חגב (מ'
ב"מ ט', ו').

ו י ה י ב ש ל ח. אנכי העירותיהו בצדך (יש' מ"ה, י"ג). לאמר לאסורים
צאו (שם, מ"ט, ט'). שמח מצרים בצאתם (תה' ק"ה, ל"ח). אמרו לאלהים מה
נורא (שם, ס"ו, ג'). רועה ישראל האזינה (שם, פ', ב'). משכני אחריך נרוצה
(שה"ש א', ד'). ויוציא עמו בששון (תה' ק"ה, מ"ג). למכה מצרים בבכוריהם
(שם, קל"ו, י'). כי [כימי] צאתך (מי' ז', ט"ו). כי פדה י"י את (יר' ל"א,י'). הנותן
בים דרך (יש' מ"ג, ט"ז). תנן בו ביום דרש ר' עקיבא אז ישיר משה (מ' סוטה
ה', ד'). משה זכה בעצמות אביו (שם, א', ט'). שיירה שחנתה בבקעה (מ'
עירובין א', ח').

ו י ש מ ע י ת ר ו. שירו לי"י שיר חדש (תה' צ"ח, א'). שמעו רחוקים אשר
(יש' ל"ג, י"ג). לץ תכה ופתי יערים (מש' י"ט, כ"ה). י"י שמעתי (דף ס"ב, ע"ב)
שמעך יראתי (חב' ג', ב'). תפילה לחבקוק הנביא (שם, א'). י"י עוזי ומעוזי
(יר' ט"ז, י"ט). י"י מלך תגל הארץ (תה' צ"ז, א'). תנן גר שבא להתגייר (יבמות
מ"ז, ע"א–ע"ב). הרואה מקום שנעשו בו נסים לישראל (מ' ברכות ט', א').
שבועות שתים שהן ארבע (מ' שבועות א', א').

ו א ל ה ה מ ש פ ט י ם. אלהים נצב בעדת אל (תה' פ"ב, א'). ואשיבה
שופטיך (יש' א', כ"ו). ציון במשפט (שם, כ"ז). באורח צדקה (מש' ח', כ').
מלך במשפט (שם, כ"ט, ד'). כי טוב זמרה אלהינו (תה' קמ"ז, א'). לא עשה כן
לכל גוי (שם, כ'). אלהים שופט צדק (שם, ז', י"ב). תנן עבד עברי נקנה בכסף
ובשטר ובחזקה (מ' קדושין א', ב'). ארבעה אבות נזיקים (מ' ב"ק א', א'). דיני
ממונות בשלשה (מ' סנהדרין א', א').

ו י ק ח ו ל י. כל העמים תקעו כף (תה' מ"ז, ב'). מה ידידות משכנותיך (שם,
פ"ד, ב'). כי נער ישראל ואוהביהו (הו' י"א, א'). לי הכסף ולי הזהב (חגי ב',
ח'). כי לקח טוב נתתי (מש' ד', ב'). ונדיב נדיבות יעץ (יש' ל"ב, ח'). תנן
חמשה לא יתרומו (מ' תרומות א' א'). בשלשה פרקים תורמים את הלשכה (מ'
שקלים ג', י"א). הקורא את שמע ולא השמיע לאזנו (מ' ברכות ב', ג').

(דף ס"ג, ע"א) ו א ת ה ת צ ו ה. מזמור לדויד י"י רועי לא (תה' כ"ג, א').
דשנת בשמן ראשי (שם, ה'). ילכו יונקותיו (הו' י"ד, ז'). וצדקתך אלהים עד
מרום (תה' ע"א, י"ט). זית רענן (יר' י"א, ט"ז). נר לרגלי דבריך (תה' קי"ט, ק"ה).
רחש לבי דבר טוב (שם, מ"ח, ב'). תנן תקועא אלפא לשמן (מ' מנחות ח', ג').
שלשה זתים ובהם (שם, ד'). כלי הקודש שניקבו (מ' זבחים ט', ז').

כ י ת ש א. יסודתו בהררי קודש (תה' פ"ז, א'). רבים אומרים (שם, ג', ג').
כה אמר י"י שמרו משפט (יש' נ"ו, א'). ואתה י"י מגן בעדי (תה' ג', ד'). כופר
לצדיק (מש' כ"א, י"ח). י"י מה רבו צרי (תה' ג', ב'). י"י חקרתני ותדע (שם,
קל"ט, א'). תנן באחד באדר משמיעין על השקלים (מ' שקלים א', א'). תנן ראש
חדש אדר שחל להיות בשבת (מ' מגלה ג', ד'). כופין אותו לבנות (מ' ב"ב א', ה').

חכמת יראת י"י (שם, קי"א י'). כחלום מהקיץ י"י (שם, ע"ג, כ'). אל תבטחו
בנדיבים (שם, קמ"ו ג'). אודך י"י כי אנפת בי (יש' י"ב, א'). הלעולמים יונח י"י
(תה' ע"ז, ח'). למרבה המשרה (יש' ט"ו, ו'). תנן המוכר פירות לחבירו ולא
צימחו (מ' ב"ב ו', א'). ותנן אין גוזרין תענית על הצבור בתחילה (מ' תענית
ב', ט').

ו י ג ש. בני אם ערבת לריעיך (מש' ו', א'). ערב עבדך לטוב (תה' קי"ט,
קכ"ב). מענה רך ישיב חימה (מש' ט"ו, א'). אשרי נשוי פשע (תה' ל"ב, א').
נודע ביהודה אלהים (שם, ע"ו, ב'). כי יהודה גבר באחיו (דה"א ה', ב'). שמחה
לאיש במענה פיו (מש' ט"ו, כ"ג). תנן אומר לו בן ננס (דף ס"א, ע"א) אינו גובה
לא מנכסים (מ' ב"ב י', ח'). ותנן המלוה את חבירו על ידי ערב (שם, ז').

ו י ח י י ע ק ב. אברכה י"י בחיי (תה' קמ"ו ג'). תפלה למשה (שם, צ', א').
יקר בעיני י"י (שם, קט"ז, ט"ו). חי חי הוא יודיך (יש' ל"ט, י"ט). יחיו מתיך (שם,
כ"ו, י"ט). אליך י"י אקרא (תה' ל', ט'). טוב אחרית דבר (קה' ז', ח'). שבתי
וראה תחת (שם, ט', י"א). ביראת י"י מבטח עז (מש' י"ד, כ"ו). מכתב לחזקיהו
מלך יהודה (יש' ל"ח, ט'). תנן האומר איש פלוני בני בכור (מ' ב"ב ח', ה').
המחלק נכסיו על פיו (שם, ט, ז').

ו א ל ה ש מ ו ת. שיר השירים אש' עד שמן תורק (שה"ש א', א'–ג'). טוב
שם משמן טוב (קה' ז', א'). מצרים ירד עמי (יש' נ"ב, ד'). ואעבור עליך ואראך
(יח' ט"ז, ו'). והנה עתך (שם, ח'). ואת כל אלה ידי עשתה (יש' ס"ו, ב').
הנה מה טוב (תה' קל"ג, א'). דור הולך (קה' א', ד'). תנן עשר יוחסין עלו מבבל
(מ' קדושין ד', א'). הבאים ישרש יעקב (יש' כ"ז ו'). נבחר שם מעשר רב
(מש' כ"ב, א'). רחש לבי דבר טוב (תה' מ"ה, ב'). ותנן אין מילדין את (דף
ס"א, ע"ב) הבהמה ביום טוב (מ' שבת י"ח, ג'). ותנן שנים שהיו בעיר (מ' ב"ב
י', ז').

ו א ר א. תתן אמת ליעקב (מי' ז'). גדול י"י ומהולל מאד (תה' קמ"ה, ג').
אלהי תהילתי אל תחרש (שם, ק"ט, א'). אודה י"י בכל לבב (שם, קי"א, א').
אני י"י הוא שמי (יש' מ"ב, ח'). למנציח על הגתית מזמ' לדויד י"י אדונינו (תה'
ח', א'–ב'). שיר מזמ' לבני קרח גדול י"י ומהולל (שם, מ"ח, ב'). וירא בצר
להם (שם, ק"ו, מ"ד). תנן המגדף אינו חייב עד שיפרש את השם (מ' סנהדרין
ז', ה'). ותנן יש שימות שנחקים (שבועות ל"ה, ע"א, למטה). שבועות העידות
נוהגת באנשים ולא בנשים (מ' שבועות ד', א'). ותנן שבועת הבטוי נוהגת (שם,
ג', י').

ב א א ל פ ר ע ה. ברוך הגבר (יר' י"ז, ז'). אלהים באזנינו שמענו (תה'
מ"ד, ב'). ויקרא רעב (שם, ק"ה, ט"ז). י"י בקר תשמע קולי (תה' ה', ד').
למנצח על מות לבן מזמ' לד' אודה י"י בכל לבי (שם, ט', א'–ב'). ולמה תכבדו
את לבבכם (ש"א ו', ו'). בסעפים מחזיונות לילה (אי' ד', י"ג). עד אנה י"י תשכחני
נצח (תה' י"ג, ב'). (דף ס"ב, ע"א) עשרה נסים נעשו לאבותינו (מ' אבות ה', ד').
ותנן כל המצות הבן על האב (מ' קדושין א', ז'). ותנן האשה בזמן שהיא בבית

ו י ר א. קומי אורי (יש' ס', א'). וכת' אשרי איש ירא את י"י (תה' קי"ב, א').
אני י"י הוא שמי (יש' מ"ב, ח'). אתה הוא י"י לבדך (נחמ' ט', ו'). ברוך הגבר
(יר' י"ז, ז'). מלך ביפיו (יש' ל"ג, י"ז). תפילה למשה איש האלהים (תה' צ', א').
כי לא יעשה י"י אלהים דבר כי אם גלה סודו (עמ' ג', ז'). כל העמים תקעו כף
(תה' מ"ז, ב'). ותנן קטן נימול (מ' שבת י"ט, ה'). מפני אפילו ארבע וחמש
קפות (שם, י"ח, א').

ו י ה י ו ח י י ש ר ה. (דף נ"ט, ע"ב) שמעו זאת כל העמים (תה' מ"ט, ב').
שמח בחר בילדותיך (קה' י"א, ט'). כי החיים יודעים שימותו (שם, ט', ה').
יומם יצוה י"י חסדו (תה' מ"ב, ט'). וזרח השמש (קה' א', ה'). בן אדם הנני
לוקיח (יח' כ"ד, ט"ז). יודעי י"י ימי תמימים (תה' ל"ז, י"ח). תנן האיש מקדש
בו ובשלוחו (מ' קדושין ב', א'). ותנן מי שמיתו מוטל (מ' ברכות ג', א').

ו א ל ה ת ו ל ד ו ת י צ ח ק. י"י רועי לא אחסר (תה' כ"ג, א'). אהבתי
אתכם נאום י"י (מלא' א', ב'). בבטן עקב את אחיו (הו' י"ב, ד'). ואני אמרתי
גואלי חי (אי' י"ט, כ"ו). הלך ילך ובכה נושא משך הזרע (תה' קכ"ו, ו'). בבקר
זרע את זרעיך (קה' י"א, ו'). זרע יעבדנו (תה' כ"ב, ל"א). בן חכם ישמח אב
(מש' י', א'; ט"ו, כ'). שתה מים מבוריך (קה' י"א, ו'). תנן האב זוכה לבן בנואי
(מ' עדיות פ"ב, ט'). ותנן לא יבטל אדם מפריה (מ' יבמות ו', ו'). ותנן לפני
אידיהן שלונים (מ' ע"ז א', א').

ו י צ א. שיר למע' אשא עיני (תה' קכ"א, א'). וכת' אורח לצדיק משרים
(יש' כ"ו, ז'). וכת' הולך בתום (דף ס', ע"א). ילך בטח (מש' י', ט'). ויברח
יעקב שדה ארם (הו' י"ב, י"ג). ואור צדיקים כאור נוגה (מש' ד', י"ח). תנן תפילת
השחר (מ' ברכות ד', א'). הוצאיה ממסגר נפשי (תה' קמ"ב, ח'). ותנן בני העיר
שמכרו רחובה שלעיר (מ' מגלה ג', א').

ו י ש ל ח י ע ק ב. כי מלאכיו יצוה לך (תה' צ"א, י"א). בשלוח שאול
(שם, נ"ז, א'). ישלח ממרום יושיעני (שם, י"ח, י"ז). חזון עובדיה (עו' פס' א').
כאשר ינוס איש (עמ' ה', י"ט). שלח אורך (תה' מ"ג, ג'). ועלו מושיעים (עו'
פס' כ"א). ישלח עזרך מקדש (תה' כ', ג'). תנן השולח סבלואות לבית חמיו
(מ' ב"ב ט', ה'). ותנן השוליח את הבעירה (מ' ב"ק ו', ד'). ותנן גיד הנשה (מ'
חולין ז', א'). ותנן אילו דברים אמרו מפני דרכי שלום (מ' גטין ה', ח').

ו י ש ב. יושב בסתר עליון (תה' צ"א, א'). שיר למע' אשא עיני (תה'
קכ"א, א'). וענוים יירשו ארץ (שם, ל"ז, י"א). נודע ביהודה אלהים (שם, ע', ב').
חלצני י"י מאדם רע (שם, ק"מ, ב'). בטח בי"י ועשה טוב (שם, ל"ז, ג'). אל תרבו
תדברו גבוהה (ש"א ב', ג'). (דף ס', ע"ב) וישב עמי בנוה (יש' ל"ב, י"ח).
בזעקך יצילוך (שם, נ"ז, י"ג). ואתה אל תירא עבדי (יר' ל', י'). אחת שאלתי
(תה' כ"ז, ד'). י"י מי יגור באהליך (שם, ט"ו, א'). תנן הרואה מקום שנעשו (מ'
ברכות ט', א'). ותנן גץ היוצא מתחת הפטיש (מ' ב"ק ו', ו').

ו י ה י מ ק ץ. אמרתי אשמרה דרכי (תה' ל"ט, ב'). הודיעני י"י קצי (שם,
ה'). קץ שם לחושך (אי' כ"ח, ג'). לעולם י"י דברך נצב (תה' קי"ט, פ"ט). ראשית

ומה קטטה היתה שם, ישפוט י"י ביני וביניך וגו'. יצחק בירך ליעקב
ומכוין לעשו, שנ' הן גביר שמתיו לך וגו'. יעקב אב' בירכו המלאך
שנ' ויאמר [לא א]שלחך כי אם ברכתני, ומה קטטה היתה שם,
והוא צולע על יריכו, ואף יעקב בירך את בניו, ומה קטטה, שנ'
ארור אפם וגו'. וכן בלעם בירך לישראל, ומה קטטה הית' שם, שנ'
וע[ותה] הנני הולך וגו'. אבל הברכה שבירך משה לישר' לא היתה
[שם] קטטה אלא ברכה שלימה, שנ' **וזאת הברכה** וגו'. **ויאמר**
י"י מסיני

בא, בארבעה מקומות הופיע הקב"ה בשעה שנתן התורה ליש'
שנ' **הופיע מהר פראן**, השנייה, כשהוא פורע מן הרשעים, שנא'
אל נקמות י"י אל נקמות הופיע. השלישית, כשהוא נותן שכר
לצדיקים, שנ' רועה ישראל [הא]זינה נוהג כצ' [ויס]ף יו[ש]ב הכרובים
הופיעה. הרביעית, בעת שיבוא משיח ישראל, ויושיע הקב"ה
[עמו יש]ר', וישכלל היכלו, שנ' מציון מכלל יופי. **מימינו אש דת למו,**

(דף נ"ח, ע"ב) בשמ' רחמ'. **פהרסת פואסין והלכות על פרשיות
ה ת ו ר ה.**

בראשית. שמע אלי יעקב וישראל מקוראי (יש' מ"ח, י"ב). וכת' ברכי
נפשי את יו' וכל קרובי (תה' ק"ג, א'). וכת' י"י בחכמה יסד ארץ (מש' ג', י"ט).
בדבר י"י שמים נעשו (תה' ל"ג, ו'). תנן אין דורשין בעריות (מ' חגיגה ב', א').
אלה תולדות נח. י"י צדיק יבחן (תה' י"א, ה'). כי שמש ומגן י"י (שם,
פ"ד, י"ב). כי מי נח זאת לי (יש' נ"ד, ט'). יראה אל עבדיך פעליך (תה' צ',
ט"ז). מזמור לדויד הבו לי"י בני אלים (שם, כ"ט, א'). לכן אנשי לבב שמעו לי
(אי' ל"ד, י'). יומם יצוה י"י חסדו (תה' מ"ב, ט'). כל הנקרא בשמ' (יש' מ"ג, ז').
לך עמי בא בחדריך (שם, כ"ו, כ'). ותנן דור המדבר (מ' סנהדרין י', ג'). ותנן
הגוזל את חבירו שוה פרוטה (מ' ב"ק ט', ה').

(דף נ"ט, ע"א) לך לך. י"י מי יגור באהליך (תה' ט"ו, א'). מי העיר
ממזרח צדק (יש' מ"א, ב'). שמעו אלי יודעי צדק (יש' נ"א, א'). הביטו אל אברהם
אביכם (שם, ב'). תתן אמת ליעקב (מי' ז', כ'). הולך את חכמים (מש' י"ג, כ').
אמרי האזינה י"י (תה' ה', ב'). נתתה ליראיך נס להתנוסס (שם, ס', ו'). אשכילך
ואורך בדרך זו תלך (שם, ל"ב, ח'). ותנן הכל מעלין לארץ ישראל (מ' כתובות
י"ג, י"א). ותנן שמעון הפקולי הסדיר שמונה עשרה ברכות על הסדר (ברכות
כ"ח, ע"ב, למטה, מגלה י"ז, ע"ב).

(עמוד ב')

קרא ראשון, לוי שני, יש שלישי. ומפני מה כהן קרא ראשון,
שכן שנו חכ הכהנים משמרים מבפנים והלוים מבחוץ,
לפיכך קודם ללוי. ומפני (!) לוי קו יש, שהלוים נכנסין לבית המק
ויש אין להם רשות להכנס, לפיכך לויים קודמין ליש. והקֹבֹה
5 יעמיד כהנים על משמרתם ולוים על דוכנם וישראל על
מחלקותם, וכן יהי רצון. ויֹא יֹי אל משה הנך שוכב ג, אֹמ לו
הק למשה: הביא לי ה זוגות יֹי יֹי. אֹמ לפניו: אלף אחד, טית
תשעה, זו עשרה; בית שנים, חית שמנה, זו עשרה; גימל
שלשה, זין שבעה, הרֹי יֹי; דל ארבעה, וֹ ששה, הרֹי יֹי; הֹא
10 חמשה, לֹא מצא לה זוג. אֹ לו הֹק: הניחהו מצד. אֹ לו: הבא לי
ה זוגות מאה מאה. אֹ לפניו: יוד עשרה, צד תשעים, הרי
מאה; כף כפיפה עשרים, פֹא כפיפה שמונים, זה מאה;
למד שלשים, עֹאן עֹ, זו מאה; מים פתוחה ארבעים, סמך
ששים, זו מאה; נון כפופה אין לה זוג. אֹ לו הֹק הניחהו
15 בצדו. שלהֹי אֹ לו: הבא לי ה זוגות אלף אלף. אֹ לפניו: קוף

(סוף הקטע)

[דף אחד של נייר ב–1 T.-S. Box C, מס' 54]

[לסדר (הסר): דברים ל"ג, א'.]

(עמוד א')

. . . הוי וחרפה לא [נ]שא וגו'. יעקב אבינו בא ובירך את בניו, כיון
[שביר]כן חתם את ב[ור]כתן בזאת, שנ' וזאת אשר דבר להם וגו'
ובא משה וברכן פתח בזאת, שנ' וזאת הברכה. כך שנו רבו' ז"ל
העובר לפני התיבה ות[ו]עה, יעבור אחר תחתיו, מהי[כ]ן חוזר,
מתחיל מתחלת ברכה שטעה זה. כך יעקב אב' [בי]רך את
בניו בזאת. בא משה רבינו ע"ה וברכן בזאת ה[בר]כה, ועליהם נאמ'
מזקנים אתבונן. ד"א וזאת הברכה, אמ' רבו' ז"ל, למה וזאת, שכן
מצינו בכל הברכות כולן מתחלת ברייתו של עולם ועד ברכתו
שלמשה רבינו ע"ה בכולן כתוב[ה קטטה] מתחלה בירך הב"ה אדם
וחוה, שנ' ויברך אותם אלהים [וגו', ומה קטט]ה היתה שם, שנ' ולאדם
אמר כי שמעת. בירך [לנח ולבניו, שנ'] ויברך י"י את נח ואת בניו, ומה
קטטה היתה שם, שנ' וי[אמר ארור] כנען וגו'. בירך את אברהם, שנא'
ואעשך לגוי גדול וגו', וכן [בירך את] שרה אשתו, שנ' וברכתי אותה,

(דף ב', ע"ב)

כשאני מלקט עצים שורפים אתי, וכשהוא מלקט עצים
שרפין אתו. אמר לו: עד מתי דינכם? א' לי: רבי, כשבאתי
לכן הנחתי אשתי מעוברת, ועכשו איני יודע אם זכר ילדה
או נקבה, בבקשה ממך הוי זהיר בו כשיגדל לה שנים, את
5 מוליכו לבית הכנסת ומלמדו תפלה וקרית שמע, ומלמדו
ג פסוקים ויעלה ויקרא בספר תורה ויענו הקהל אחריו ברכו
ברוך יוי המבורך, ואני פטור מן הדין הזה. מיד ר' יוחנן
ועשה כך. לאחר כן יצא ר' יוחנן, מצא אתו האיש באתו
המקום שפגע בו. א' לו: תנוח נפשך כשם שהנחת אתי
10 ואת נפשי, נפטרתי מאתו הדין. מיד פתח ר' יוחנן וא' י'י
שמך לעולם ג'. ר' או על התורה, לאהבה את י'י אלה ג', שכל
מי שהוא בעל תורה ומשפיל עצמו בין הבריות, ויודע משא
ומתן בשוק, הוא מאהב שם שמים על הבריות. הא כיצד?
כשאדם קורא ושונה, ומכבד אביו ואמו, ומכבד את רבו ומי
15 שהוא גדול ממנו, ודבריו בנח[ת ע]ם הבריות, ויודע משא

(סוף הקטע)

[דף אחד של נייר ב־2 T.-S. Box C, מס' 22]

[לסדר (חסר): דברים כ"ט, ט'.]

(עמוד א')

מה החול כל הגדולים מגיעים בו ועוברים, ואינו זז ממקומו,
כך הן יש. בא סיסרא ונגע בהן והלך לו, וכן סנחריב, וכן פר'
ואחרים. מה החול הוא מקהה שני כל מי שהוא אוכל ממנו,
כך עתידין יש עתידין להקהות שני כל האומות במלך המשיח,
5 ש' לא יסור שבט מיהודה ג'. טעם אחר אתם נצבים, א' יהוש'
בן לוי למה ראשיכם קודם לזקניכם וקודם לשטריכם, מפני
שהראש קודם לזקן, ש' אתם נצבים ג', וכת' ויאסוף יהושע ג'.
מפני מה הקדים ראשים לזקנים ויהושע הקדים זקנים
לראשים, משה שהיו הכל תלמידיו הקדים ראשים לזקנים,
10 ויהושע על ידי שלא היו הכל תלמידיו הקדים זקנים לראשים;
משה על ידי שלא היה צריך להם בכבוש הארץ הקדים ראשים
לזקנים, ויהושע על ידי שהיה צריך לכבוש את הארץ הקדי'
זקנים לראשים; משה על ידי שלא נתנגע בתלמוד תור'
הקדים רא' לזק', ויהושע על ידי שנתנגע בת' תו' הק' זקנ' לרא'
15 תנו רב חכם קודם למלך, כך אמ' חכ' מפני דרכי שלום כהן

(דף א', ע"ב)

```
. . . . .      . . .      . . . . .      . . .      . . . . .
. . .      . . .      . . . . .      . . .      . . . . .
. . .            . . . .                  . . . .      . . . . .
```

[שלח] תש[לח] . . . .

5 [את האם] . . . .   אני נותן לך בנ[ים]
[. .] ואם שלחת את הא[ם]ם אני מטיב לך ואני מפרנסך שֹ
[למען ייטב לך ג, אמרֹ] הקֹ; אל תהי אכזרי, יהי רחמיך על הכל, שאם
אתה מרחם, הרח[מן] ירחם עליך, שֹ ונתן לך רחמים גֹ. וכֹת כרחם
[אב על בנים גֹ הטיל] הקֹ אימתו על יֹש כעבדים ורחמיו עליהן
10 [וכבנים . . . כעבדים²] שֹ כי יש לי בני יֹש גֹ, כבנים, שֹ כרחם אב על
[בנים גֹ . . . .] על הכל רחמיו שלהקֹ, שֹ טוב י"י לכל וגו'
[וכשם שהוֹ]א רחמן כך צוה ליֹש שיהיו רחמנין, דכֹ שלח תשלח גֹ
[וא]ם עשיתן כן, למען ייטב לך גֹ. אֹר ירמיה, בא וראה רחמיו
שלהקֹ על יֹש, שהוא מצוה אותם על התורה, שלא תתפוס
15 מדה אחת ממדה טובה, ומצוה על המצות כדי לרבות בהן

(דף ב', ע"א)

שכר ורחמים בכל דבר ובכל מלאכה, שהן עושין בשביל שהן
חביבין, ובחיבתן שליֹש רבה להן מצות כדי לצדקם, שֹ י"י חפץ
למען צדקו גֹ. אמֹ רבו על גֹ דברים העולם עומדֹ: על התורה,
ועל העבודה [ועל גמי]לות חסדים. על התורה, אֹר שמעון בן
5 לקיש כל המצער עצמו על דברי תורה ועוסק בה בלילה
מושכין עליו חוט של חסד ביום, שֹ יצוה יוי חסדו גֹ והתורה
מגינה על אדם כל אותן השנים שהוא מוטל בעפר, שֹנֹ
בהתהלכך תנחה אותך, וגֹ, בעולם הזה; בשכבך תשמר עליך
בשעת המיתה, והקיצות היא תשיחך, לעתיד לבֹ, שהיא מלמדת
10 עליה סנגוריה. אֹר יוחנן בן זכאי פעם אחת הייתי עובר
בדרך, פגעתי באדם אחד שהוא מלקט עצים, נתתי לו שלום
ולא החזיר לי שלום. אמֹ לו: מן החיים אתה. אמֹ: למן המתים
אתו האיש, אמֹ לו: אם מן המתים אתה, עצים שאתה מלקט
למה לך, אמר לי: האזין ממני דבר אחד, כשהייתי באתו העולם
15 אני וחברי בלטיר אחד [היינו] עוסקין, נגזרה עלינו שרפה
```

(סוף העמוד)
```

20 בן יעקב צריך אדם להחזיק [טובה] לה'[קב'ה] בזמן שהיסורים באין עליו,
למה, שהיס[ורים]

מרצים את האדם לה'[קב'ה] [ודוקא ביסורים שלא]הבה. אמ' ר' שמעון בן יוחי
אם מת לא[דם]

בן לא יהיה קורא תיגר, למה ש[הבן מרצה אותו ל]ה'[קב'ה], למה הדבר דומה,
למלך שכעס

על בן ביתו, בא אחד וריצה המ[לך לבן ביתו, אות]ו בן ביתו שלמלך צריך
להחזיק

טובה [לאות]ו שצוה(!) אותו המלך, כך [אם מת בן אדם] יחזיק טובה
לה'[קב'ה] שירצה הבן

25 [אל] אביו. בוא וראה שהוא כן, שנ' [כי את אשר יאהב] י'י יוכיח וכאב את
בן ירצה. לכך אמר

[דו]ד אשרי הגבר אשר תיסרנו יה. [כשבאים יס]ו[רים על אדם יעמוד
בהשכמה, שאין סוף לשכר

(סוף הקטע)

[שני דפים של נייר ב־2 T.-S. Box C, מס' 144]

[לסדר (חסר): דברים כ"ב, ו'.]

(דף א', ע"א)

. . . .
. .   . .
. . .   .
. . .   .
. . .   . . "
5 . . . . . . שאמר הק'

שבתי לירוש' ג'. (ס) כי יקרא צפור, זש"ה אורח חיים פן תפלס ג',
א' ר' אבא בר כהנא מהו שתהא יושב ומש[קל במצותיה של תורה]
לומר: זו איני עושה, שהיא גדולה וזו אי' עושה ש[היא קטנה]
את תועה, למה, נעו מעגלותיה לא תד[ע מתן שכר שיש]
10 עליהן, שיש מצוה שהיא גדולה ושכרה [קטנה, ויש מצוה שהיא]
קטנה ושכרה גדולה. מכבוד אב ואם, ו[מה שכרה, כבד את]
אביך ג'. ואין לך מצוה שהיא קטנה משלוח הקן, ומ[ה שכרה],
שלח תשלח את האם ג', השוה הק' שכר שתיהן כאחד, [למה],
שלא תעמד על דרכה של תורה, הוי אורח חיים פן תפלס. א' ר'
15 אחא לא לא פרש ה'ב' מתן שכרן שלמצות חוץ מכבוד אב ואם

20 ע מ ך רוח תזזית נכנסת בהן, והן מור[דין במלך המ]שיח, מיד הוא הורגם,
שנֹ והכה

ארץ בשבט פיו וברוח שפתיו ימ[ית רשע, ולא מש]תייר אלא הֹקֹבֹה ליֹש, שנֹ
יי בדד

ינחנו ואין עמו אל נכר.   [כי יקרא קן צ]פור לפניך
ב ד ר ך ב כ ל ע ו ץ א [ו ע ל ה א ו ר ץ]

זה הוא שאמ הכתוב אורח חיים פן [תפלס נעו מעג]לותיה לא תדע, אור [ח
חֹיֹים]פֹן]

תפלס. אמֹ רֹ אבא בר כהנא לא תהא יו[שב ומשקל] מצותיה שלתורה לומר
שֹאני [עושה].

                 (עמוד ב')

. . . .

. . . .

. . . . מיֹשׁ . . . .

ופריב(?) נוט . . . .

5 . . . . מי שזור [ע נוטל] שכר זריעה שק. . . . .

. . . יטול שכרו [ש]קיים לא תחרוש בשור וב[חמור] . . . .

ששחט . . . . ש[ו]קיים לא תאכלו כל נבלה . . . .

שכרו . . לא תלבש שעטנז, מי שומטית(?) . . . .

. . . . לפניך מצות קן צפור לפניך. לפיכך אמֹ כי יקרא קן צפ[ור].

10 . . . ביר' יש מצות שהן מצי[לות] את האדם מידי דברים רעי[ם]. . .

. . . . לילה מחץ יעוף יומם, מהוא מחץ יעוף יומים, יש מ[ז]ק. . . .

. . . . יתכפר על אותו המזק, מצות קן צפור, מיד נפל ומת, לפיכך אמֹ. . .

. . . . בא לתוך ידיך אל תדאה אתה בראש האילן ותעלה, שלח תשלח
את [האם . .

. . [אשרי] הגבר אשר תייסרנו יה ומתורתך תלמדנו, אמֹ רֹ יהושע בן לוי
אם באו [עליך יסורין]

15 [והוא] יכול ליגע בתורה יסורים שלאהבה הן, אבל אם לא היה יכול ליגע
בתורה [יסורים]

שלפורענות הן, לכך נאמֹ אשרי הגבר אשר תייסרנו יה ומתורתך תלמדנו.
ד"א אשרי [הגבר]

וג', אמֹ רֹ חגיי בן אלעזר אשריו אדם [ש]הי[סורים באין עליו ויש להם סוף
והֹקֹבֹה . .

. . . . לכ[ך] נאמֹ אשרי הגבר, למה, שהיסורים מרצים את האדם להֹקֹבֹה,
שנֹ וכאב א[ת בן]

ירצה, [ואי]ן ירצה אלא שהן חביבין בקורבנות, שנֹ ונרצה לו לכפר עליו.
אמֹ רֹ אלי[עזר]

[דף אחד של קלף, ב־1 C Box .S.-T, מס' 8. קרוע למאד מלמעלה]

[לסדר (חסר): דברים כ', י']

(עמוד א')

....

.אחשורש....................................

ואסתר ....

5 ....כה, ומנין ש[כתוב] קימו [ן קיבלו.....................

....................ג ומנין ש[הסכים ה]בה אחריהם

...............[אש]ר החלו לעשות   ב[ני] הגולה

.............מעשרות. וכיון שעלו מיד גזרו על עצמם להיות

מ[ביאים]

.................ואת ראשית עריסותינו ותרומותינו ופרי כל עץ

שנה ..

10 ...א ונתנו ונתנו וכתבו ספר ונתנו א.... ....לש[כת בית אלהינו.

ובכל זאת אנחנו כרתים אמנה וכותבים ועל החתום

שרינו לוינו כהנינו

חתום, ומנין, שכתוב ועל החתומים נחמיה התרשתא למעלה

הוא [אומר]

[ו]על החתום ש[ר]ינו לויינו כהנינו, הוי אומ שהסכים ה'בה אחריהם. אמ' ר' לוי

[שלשה דברים]

[עש]ה משה והסכים ה'בה אחריו, אילו הן: ה'בה כתב ואמר פוקד עון אבות

[על בנים]

ויאמר לו לך לשלום, הולך וחוזר, שנ ויאמר יתרו למשה לך לשלום, מדבר

[במלך]

ב   נמשלו מיד ערים

15 [המש]יח, שהוא פותח להם לשלום, שנ וד[בר ש]לום עם הגוים שנ' והיה

אם ש[לום תענך]

[ופת]חה לך ג', הם כופפים אצ עצמם, שנ וכתתו חרבותיהם לאיתים

וחנית[ותיהם]

[למ]מרות ולא ישאו גוי אל גוי חרב ולא ילמדו עוד מלחמה, וכת והיה

כל [העם ה]נמצא

[בה] יהיו לך למס ועבדוך, יהיו לך למס, שהם מביאים לו

דורון, שנ יאתיו חשמנים מיני

מצרים כוש תריץ ידיו לאלהים, שהן [באין מהרה] במתנותיהם. ואם לא

תשלים

עבודו ואת שם קדשי לא תחללו עוד, אמׄ לו הבׄה לדוד
בתחלה אתה אומׄ אחת שאלתי שבתי בבית יׄי, וחזרת
ואמרת לחזות בנועם יׄי ולבקר בהיכלׄ. אמׄ לפניו: רבונו
שׄע, לא יהא העבד שׄה לרבו, לכתחלה לא כך שאתה(!) די לי
20 באחת, שׄנׄ ועתה ישׄרׄ מה יׄי שואל מעמך כי אם
לׄ יׄראׄה את יׄי אלהׄיך, ואחר כך אמרת: ללכת בכל דרכיו
ולׄ אׄהׄבׄה אותו ולעבוד את יׄי אׄלׄהׄיׄך בׄכׄל לׄבׄבׄך
ובׄכׄל נׄפׄשׄך
לשמׄר את מצות יׄי ואת חוקותיו אשר אנכי מצוׄך
הׄיׄום

(עמוד ב׳)

[לטוב לך ...., א״ל(?) הב״הׄלׄטׄוׄבׄ ׄלׄך]
........ך הכל הוא לטוב לך, ליתן לך
שכר [בעולם] הבא ולשמרך בעולם הזה. ללכת בׄכׄל
דׄרׄכׄיׄו, אלו הם דרכי יׄ״י: רחום וחנון, מה הוא רחום אף
5 אתה תהא רחום, מה הוא חנון אף אתה תהא חנון, ועשה
מתנת חנם, וׄשׄ״י והיה כל אשר נקרא בשם יׄי ימלט,
וזהו ללכת בכל דרכיו. לׄאׄהׄבׄׄה אׄׄותׄׄו, שלא תאמר הריני למד
תורה בשביל שאהיה עשיר, או בשביל שאקרא רׄ, שאשב
בישיבה, או בשביל שאאריך ימים, או בשביל שאקבל שכר
10 לעולם הבא, ת״ל לאהבה, למוד מ״מ וסוף הכבוד לבא.
ולׄ ׄעׄבׄׄוׄד, זה תלמוד תורה, ולׄ ׄשׄׄמׄׄרׄׄׄה, אלו המצות. וכשם
שעבודת מזבח קרויה עבודה, כך עבודת תלמוד קרוׄי׳(?).
ד״א ולׄ ׄעׄבׄׄוׄד, זו תפלה, או אינו אלא עבודה, כשהוא אומר
בכל לבבך, בעבודה שבלב הכתוׄ׳ מדבר, הוי אומׄ זו תפלה.
15 אמׄ דוד: כל זה אמרת לנו, א׳׳כ דיו לעבד שיהיה כרבו. א״ל
הב״ה: לׄ ׄטׄׄוׄׄבׄ ׄלׄך, כדי לזכותך ולהביאך אל הארץ. ועל ידי
התורה והמצות האדם נשמר מן הנזקין. והב״ה הוא לׄיׄשׄׄרׄ
כמו האב המצוה את בנו: שמור נפשך מזה, עשה כן
והנצל, כן הב״ה צוה לנו לתת מזוזה לפתחינו, שלא יוכלו
20 המזיקין להזיק, ומלאך המשחית זז משם, והיינו מזוזה,
זז מות, שלא ניתן לו רשות לחבל, למה, ששכינה עומדת
על פתחו, והיינו מזוזה, שזזה מלמעלה למטה על יׄשׄׄרׄ(?).

(סוף הקטע)

נטל את הלוחות והשליכן מידיו ושברן. אמ' לו הק' את
שברת אותן, את עשה תחתיהן. מנין ממה שקראו

5   בעניִן: ב ע ת ה ה י א א מ' י"י א ל י פ ס ל ך ש נ י ל ו א ב.
זה שה': עת להשליך אבנים ועת כנוס אבנים
(קה' ג', ה'), עת שישליך משה את הלוחות וישברם, ועת כנוס
אבנים, עת היא שיעשה תחתיהן אחרים. מנין, ממה
שקראו בעניִן: כעת ההִ אמ' י"י אלי פסל לך שנ לוחֹ.

10   כתֹ' חמת מלך מלאכי מות ואיש חכם יכפֿ' (משלי, ט"ז, י"ד)
מהו כן? אלא חמ' שנתמלא הק' על יש' כשעשו יש' אותו
המעשה גרמו למשה שיזדוגו לו ה' מלאכי חבלה
ואילו הן [אף] וחמה וקצף ומשחית והשמד
וכיון שהזכיר שלשה אבות מיד] [נסתלקו] קצף ומשחית והשמד, נשתירו אף
וחמה

15   שנ' כי יגרתי מפני האף והחמה (דב' ט', י"ט), אף וחמה התחיל
משה מפיס שיגרעו (?) ממנו(?). אמ' משה עמוד את ואחיך(?)
ואני מבקש. אמ' הק' במה את מבקש שאעבור ...

דף אחד של נייר ב־2 C‏ T.-S. Box, מס' 143]

[לסדר (חסר): דברים י', י"ב]

(עמוד א')

‏.. ן כעניִן כהן לוי ישרֿ, ואף ....
[הנש]ַמֹה תהלל יֹה הלֲלויה בגֹמֹ מֹ ....
השם יֹתֹ שלשמו אנו מברכין קֹ ברכות, וכש[אין מברכ]ין
קֹ ברכות הם נידונין ביסורין, כמדֿא על מה תוכו, על מה,

5   דהיינו מאה, אי נמי עֿל קֹ בגֹמֹ. וכשמברכין אותם בכל
יום, הבֿה מברכן, דֿא ו ע ת ה י ש רֿ מ ה ו ג ו', זֿשה אחת שאלתי
מאת י"י אותה אבקש שבתי בבית י"י כל ימי חיי לחזות
בנועם י"י ולבקר בהיכלו. אמרֿ אבא בר כהנא מלכות שאל,
אתה מוצא דוד שאל שאל אחת, ושלמה שאל שתים, שֿנ אך

10   שתים שאלתי מאתך אל תמנע ממני שוא ודבר כזב הרחק
ממני רֹש ועושר אל תתן לי הטריפני לחם חוקי, פן אשבע
וכחשתי ואמרתי מי י"י פן איורש וגנבתי ותפשתי שם
אלהי. איזוהיֿא קשה, ראשונה או שניה, הוי אומר שניה, ולמה
שויתר הבֿה על עֿז וגלוי עריות ושפיכות דמים, ולא ויתר

15   על חילול השם, שנֿא כה אמר י"י צבאות איש גילוליו לכו

(עמוד ב')

מרובים רבים, אינן חשובין לפני כלום, לכך כ[י]

תאמר בלבבך רבים וג', לא תירא מהם, למה, כי י"י

אליך עמך, י"י אלהיכם בהיותכם עמו. ואומ' י"י לי לא

אירא, ומה יעשה אדם לי, המעלך מארץ מצרים,

5   למה הזכיר יצי[א]ת מצרים כאן, אלא אמ': כמה מכות

עשיתי במצרים ושקעתי אותם וראיתם פגרים

מתים על שפת הים, שנ' ונע[ר פר]עה וחילו וג'.

וכיון שראו אותן יש[ראל מתי]ם על שפת הים

הה' וירא ישראל את מצר', אמ' להם משה: לא אמרתי

10   לכם התיצבו וראו, י"י ילחם לכם וא' ת'. כיון שבאו

[ישראל] למדבר, אמרו ישראל: מצרים אומ' א[חת]

ו[הלקי]ת א[ותה][(?) כמה מכות וכמה אותות ומופתים,

עד שיצאו ישראל ממצרים, ואנו באים לאומות

הרבה ושל[ש]ים ואחד מלך, היאך אנו יכולין ל'

15   לע[ש]ות מלחמה עם האוכלסים הללו. אמר להם

הק': אל תתיראו מהם, אפילו כמה אוכלסים כאילו

עמהם אין יכולים לכם, למה, שאני עמכם. כשם

שעשיתי במצרים כך אני עושה עם האומות,

לכך כי תאמר וג', כי י"י אליך עמך וג', כן יעשה

20   י"י אליך לכל העמים, יש לי להביא עליהם, שנ' את

אמתי אשלח וג', ואם אין אמתי, אני משלח מלאך,

שנ' הנה אנכי שולח מלאך, ואם אין מלאך, צרעה,

שנ' וגם את הצרעה וג'. וכן עשה, התחיל במלחמה

תחלה, וכן אמ' למשה: ראה החלותי, שאסר לשרו

וה'

(סוף הקטע)

לדברים י', א'. (ס'. . . .)

[ב' דפים של נייר ב–T.-S. Box C 2 מס' 171. ד' א', ע"א וד' ב'
ע"ב מטושטשים לגמרי ואינם בקריאה. מד' א', ע"ב אפשר לקרוא
רק מלות בודדות. דף ב', ע"א לבד ניתן לקריאה, אם כי בקושי,
ואותו אנו מוסרים כאן. מתוכו ניכר שהדרשה היתה שונה מזו
שבדברים רבה, פרשה ג', י"ב וכו']

וית[ן אל] משה ככלותו (שמ' ל"א, י"ח). וכיון שקבל משה את הלוחות
ירד לתנם ליש'. כיון שהרגיש שעשו יש' את המעשה

20 שמוע תשמעו בקול יי' אליך, שמור ושמעת וגו', והיה
עקב תש ושמרתם ועשיתם וגו', יש שומר וא[ינו]
עושה, שא[ם] ושמרתם ועשיתם, א' להן: שמרו
עד שלא תבוא אל ידכם, כשתבוא עשו אותה

(כאן סוף הקטע)

[דף אחד של נייר ב־2 T.-S. Box C, מס' 24. מטושטש]

[לסדר (חסר): דברים ז' י"ז]

(עמוד א')

[א]ני מברך אות[ן], שנ' יי' יב[ר]ך את עמ[ו] בשלום.
[ר] אבא בר כהנא בש ר יוחנן והגוי[ם] חרוב יחרבו
מהו חרז, מחורב יחרבו, מחורב נטלו אפופוסים
שלהם, נפסלו ואין חשובים לפניו כלום, שנ כל הגוים
5 כאין. דא כל הגוי[ם] וג, מעשה בגוי אחד מחלק
צדקה, ובא לפני ר עקיב ואמ לו: אני גדול ממך ש'
שאני [מחבב א]ת הצדקה, והק מחבבני ומרוממני
דכתי צדקה תרומ[ם] גוי, אמ לו ר עקיב: זה כח לישראל
שעושים המצות, שנ בהם ומ[י]ן כעמך ישראל גוי אח וג,
10 אבל כל מצות שתעשו תקלה היא לכם, דכ[ת] וחסד
לאומים חטאת. פעם אחת יצאו האסטריטון ל[נצ]ק
בקינפון, והיה ר עקיב יושב ודורש, [והיה רואה]
אותם שווריון, וכל הקופץ יתר מ[חב] נוטל ארנונא
יתר מחבירו. אמ עקיב לאותו הגוי: מ[פ]ני מה עושין
15 כון? אמ לו: כל מי שיש בו כח יותר מחב[י ושו]ו[ר]
נוטל פרס יותר מחבירו הרבה. אמ לו ר עקיב[ה]:
אני שוור יותר מכולם, תן לי ארנונא. אמ לו אותו
הגוי: אתה גדולם שליהודים, שאין אתה יודע
שכל מי שאינו באוני שלמלך אינו נוטל ארנונה.
20 אמ לו ר עקיב: לא ישמעו אזניך מה שידבר
פיך, אף הק [ול]א כרת ברית מ[ני]לה אלא בישראל
שהיא חותמו שלהק, והוא זונין שלישראל, אבל
האומות אין זוני שלהק עליהם. לפיכך אינם
חשובים אצלו כלום, שנ כל הגוים. כך אמר
25 הקב[ה] לישראל: א[ע]פ שאתם רואים אותם שהם

[נל]ידע איזה לשון חביב לפני הקׄ להוכיח את ישראל,
[ש]אין לך בכל הלשונות שחביב כלשון עקב. למד מאברהם
אבינו שעשה רצונו של הקׄ בלבב שלם, ובקש הקׄ
להקים ליצחק שבועת אברהם לא שבחו הקׄ אלא
בלשון עקב, שנׄ והרבתי את זרעך וגו׳ ככוכבי השמים
וגו׳, וכתו אחריו עקב אשׄ שמע אברהם בקולי וגו׳, וכן
כלב כשפרש ממרגלים ונדבק [בש]כינתו של הקׄ,
[לא] שבחו אלא בלשון עקב, שנׄ ועבדי כלב עקב
[הי]תה וגו׳. לפיכך פתח משה בלשון עקב והוכיח
[את] ישׄ, שנׄ והיה עקב תשמעון. ומפני שהיה משה
[או]הב את ישׄ מסר נפשו עליהן כמה פעׄ, וכשהו
[נתו]נין בצער בעון שהיה גורם להם, היה מבקש
[עלי]הן רחמים, ומזכיר זכות אבות, ומזכיר חירוף
[אומו]ת העולם, שכך אׄ (?) זכור לעבדיך לאברהם,
זכר לאברהם ליצׄ וליש׳ עבדיך וגו׳ פן יאמרו
[הארץ] וגו׳, למה יאמרו מצרים וגו׳. ומאהבתו אותן גילה
[את ה]דבר, והוכיחם על כל מה שעשו, והודיעם

(עמׄ בׄ)

המצות ומתן שכרם בעולם הזה ושכר גדול לעולם
הבא, מה שאין לו שיעור; והודיען הפסד מצוה
מה גרם, לכך אׄ טובה תוכחת מגולה. אׄ להן
משה ליש׳: דעו שדור ראׄשׄון ראשון שיצאו
ממצרים הייתי סבור שנכנסין הן לארץ
ואני עמם, ומעון שבא לידם(?) תמו הם במדבר,
ואני נגרם לי בשבילן שלא אכנס לארץ, אבל
אתם אם תקבלו על נפשכם לשמור מצותיו שלהקׄ
מתנות רבות הוא נותן לכם, וממשלכם בכל
האומות. לכך פתח ואמר והיה עקב תׄשׄ וגו׳, היה ראוי
לומר והיה עקב תעשון, מה תלמ׳ לומר תשמעון,
אלא ללמדך שבשעה שקרבו ישׄ לקבל תורה סביבות
הר סיני קבלו עליהן שני דברים, שכך השיבו
ואמרו כל אשׄ דבר יׄי נעשׄ, הקדימו עשיה לש[מיעה],
לא עברו ימים מעוטים עד שביטלו את העשׄ[יה],
שנׄ עשו להם עגל וגו׳, נשתיר בידן זכות שמ[יעה].
לפיכך משה רבׄ בכל מקום ומקום שצוה את
ישׄ לא ציום אלא בלשון שמיעה, שנׄ שמע ישׄ יׄי
אלוהׄ, והיה אם שמוע תשמעו אל מצותי, והיה אם

היום בלילה ויש באומות, אתה יכול לחלק
על הכהנה, ואם ליו, אין אתה יכול, שכשם
שכת̇ באלו הבדיל כך כת̇ באהרן הבדלה

(דף ג', ע"ב)

לכך נא̇ בקר. זאת עשו, הרי לכם המחתה
שהיא חביבה לפני הקב̇ה מן הכל, שבה נשרפו
נדב ואביהוא. מה ראה לומר להן כן, מלמד
שהתרה בהן ואמ̇ להן היו יודעין שכשם
שחטאו נדד(!) ואביהו, והקריבו לפני הקב̇ה
שלא ברצון נשרפו, כך כל העושה במעשידן
הו נשרף, לכך נאמ̇ קחו לכם וג̇. ותנו בהן אש,
וכי אין אנו יודעים שמו(!) שיבחר בו המקום
הוא הקדוש, אלא אמר להם מש̇: היו יודעין
שאם יבחר אחד מכם יהא יוצא, וכולכם
אובדין. רב לכם בני לוי, כך אמ̇ להם
מש̇: אין מידותיהן שליש לפני הקב̇ה כמידת
אומות העולם, שמידת אומ̇ הע̇ כל מי
שהוא מבקש עושה לאלהו מזביח וכהן
שנ̇ כל הבא למ̇ ידו בפר וג̇, אבל יש אינן

(כאן סוף הקטע).

[דף אחד של נייר, ב־T.‑S. Box 2 סימן 77]

[לסדר דברים . . . .]

(עמ' א')

הצדיקים ה̇ק נותן שאילתכם, ואם נתאחרה בעולם הזה
נתן להן בעולם הבא, וכן הוא או̇ עיני י̇י אל צדיקים וגו'.

[סדר: דברים ז', י"ב]

והיה עקב, פ̇ר̇ש̇. כת̇ו טובה תוכחת
מגולה וגו', כשאמר שלמה את המקרא הזה לא אמרו
אלא כנגד אותה שעה שבקש משה להוכיח את ישראל,
[ש]בשעה שבקש להוכיחן חזר על כל לשונות

שהיה חוטא על אביו היה אוהבו שלמלך
מפיס עליו, חטא ראשונה שניה ושלישית
ופיס עליו, כיון שהגיע לרביעית, אמ׳ אוהבו
שלמלך בדעתו: כמה אטריח על המלך,
נקטה נפשו ממני, כך אמ׳ משה רבנו
חטאו יש במעשה העגל, בקשתי עליהן
שנ׳ ויחל משה וג׳, וינחם י״י, והיה העם כמתאוננים וגו׳

(דף ב׳, ע״ב)

עמד ובקש עליהם, שנ׳ ויצעק העם אל משה וגו׳.
במרגלים אמ׳ הקב״ה עד אנה ינאצוני וג׳ אכנו
בדבר וג׳, עמד ובקש על, ויחל מש׳, אמ׳ לפניו
רבונו שלעולם, מה תעשה לשבועת אבות, אמ׳ לו
הקב״ה אתה מבניהם, ואעשה אותך לגוי גדול וג׳,
נשא בדבר אחר, אמ׳ לפניו: רבונ שלע׳, עכשיו
המצרים אומ׳ במלך אחד היה לו כוח לעמוד
בשלשים ואחד מלך לא היה לו כוח לעמוד
שנ׳ ושמעו מצרים וג׳, שמעו עמים ירגזון וג׳
פן יאמרו הארץ וג׳, ונתרצה, ויאמר י״י סלחתי
כדבריך. וכשבאו לסירחון הזה אמ׳ משה:
איני מטריח על הקב״ה, לכך ויפול על פניו.
וידבר אל קרח, בקר, מה ראה לומר
בקר, שלא היה משה רבנו נכנס לפני הקב״ה
אחר אכילה ושתיה. ד״א ב ק ר, אמ׳ משה
בדעתו שמא מתוך מאכל ומשקה עשו

(דף ג׳, ע״א)

כך אלא ימתינו עד הבקר, שמא יפוג מהן
היין ויעשו תשובה, לכך אמ׳ ב ק ר.
דבא בק׳, אמ׳ משה לקרח כשברא הקב״ה
את עולמו הציב גבולות בעולם שנ׳ אתה
הצבת כל גבולות וג׳, הבדיל בין אור לחשך,
שנ׳ ויבדל אלהים, והבדיל בין המים העליונים
לתחתונים, שנ׳ ויבדל בין המים אשר מתחת,
והבדיל בין יש לאומות הע׳, ואבדיל אתכם
מן העמים וג׳, וכשם שהבדיל בן(!) אלו
כך הבדיל בין אהרן ליש׳, שנ׳ ויבדל אהרן להקדישו וג׳,
המתינו עד הבקר, אם אתה יכול לערב

(דף א', ע"א)

הא לפי שהיה ראובן שכן לקרח נשתתפו עמו
במחלוקת. ויקומו לפני משה, מה עשה להן
קרח, הלך וזבח זבחים הרבה, וזימן אותם לסעודה,
בנו(!) בניו שלאהרן מבקשין ל[ויקח חזה התנ]ופה
ושוק התרומה, עמד כנגדן ולא [רצה] ליתן
אותן. באו ואמרו למשה .... עכב
את ה[מת]נות שנתנו לנו [ועד עתה. הל]ך משה
לפיסו, מתוך כך עמו(!) לפני משה שנ' ויקומו
לפני משה. כל הסנהדריות שלשבטים
ושלנשיאים, אליצור בן שדיאור וחביריו
היו עם קרח במחלוקת, ואף על פי שלא
פרסם הכת' שמותן, כבר נתן כל הסימנין
שלהם. משל למה הדבר דומה, לבן

(דף א', ע"ב)

טובין שנמצא גונב כלום(!) מן המרחץ ולא היה
בעל הגניבה רוצה לפרסמו, לפי שהיה בן
טובין. ואף על פי שלא פרסמו בשם כבר נתן
כל הסימנין שלו: אותן(!) בעל הקומה, אותו בעל
שער [ושחור א]ו הלבן, ואף על פי שלא פרסמו
כבר נתן סימנין, כך אלו, אף על פי שלא פרסמן
.... [ונתן כל הסימנין שלהן: נשיאי
עדה קריא(י) מועד אנשי שם, אלו ראשי השבטים
שנ' אלו קרואי העידה וגו'. ויקהלו, הקהילו עליהם
כל העדה ואמרו להן, הרביתם עלינו יתר מדיי
כל העדה עמדו על הר סיני ושמעו אנכי
וענו שפה אחת נעשה ונשמע והישרה
שכינתו הקב"ה ביניהם, שנ' ועשו לא מקדש
ושכנתי וגו'. וישמע משה, מלמד שנזדעדע(!)

(דף ב', ע"א)

לאחור ונתרשלו ידיו בחטאו של קרח, לכך
ויפול על פניו. והלא הוא שעמד בששים
רבו ושברו וכתתו, ושבר את הלוחות, וכאן
לא היה יכול למחות, אלא מלמד שזה היה
סרחן רביעי שלהן. משל למה הדבר
דומה, למלך שהיה לו בן סרחן, וכל זמן

להתיחס עד כאן, אלא אמ הכת בסודם אל תבא וג
בקש יעקב רחמים עליו, שלא ישתתף עם שמעון
ולוי בקלקלה. בסודם אל ת, כשנגלה זמרי סוד
ישראל וחילל שם שמים לעיני אומות העולם
לא יהי מתיחס נשיא לשמעון בן יעקב אלא נשיא
בית אב לשמעוני. בקהלם אל ת, כשהקהיל קרח
את יש למחלקות לא יהי מתיחס בן לוי בן יעקב
אלא בן יצהר בן קהת בן לוי, וכשהיו בניו עומדין

(דף ו', ע"א)

על הדוכן יהיו מתיחסין עד אצלי, בן קהת בן לוי בן
ישראל. לפיכך לא ניתחס (!) קרח אלא עד לוי.
ו ד ת ן שעבר על הדת. ו א ב י ר ם, ועבירם, הנה רבים אלף
תחלף בעין. ו ד ת ן ו א ב י ר ם, מהו ודתן ואבירם,
הן הן מנעורתן ועד זקנותן, הן שברח מהן
משה, הן שא לו הקבה כי מיתו האנשים וגו',
לומר שירדו מנכסיהן, הן שפגעו במשה
ואהרן והטריחו עליהם בדברים, שנ ויפגעו וגו'
הן שהותירו את המן, שנ ולא שמעו אל משה וג,
הן שיצאו ביום השבת ללקוט, הן שהיו במחלקתו
של קרח. ר שמעון בן יוחי אומ' כל מה שאתה
יכול לתלות ברשע תלה. למה לקו שבט
ראובן עם קרח במחלוקת, שכך אמרו חכ

(דף ו', ע"ב)

אוי לרשע אוי לשכינו, אשרי צדיק אש שכינו,
לפי שהיו שבטו של ראובן שכנין לקרח, לפיכך
לקו עם קרח במחלקת. ומנין שהיו שכנים לקרח,
שנ משפחות בני קהת יחנו וג, וכת דגל מחנה
בני ראובן וג, אלו שרוין בתימן ואלו שרוין בתימן.
אשרי צדיק אש שכינו, שבט יהודה יששכר
וזבולון, שהיו שכנין למשה רבנו, נטלו כולם
ריח טוב מן התורה. ומנין שהיו שכנין למשה,
שנ והחנים לפני המשכן וגו', והחונים קדמה
מזרחה, אלו שרוין במזרח ואלו שרוין במזרח
לפיכך זכו לתלמוד תורה. יהודה כת בו
מחוקקי, יששכר כת בו יודעי בינה. זבולון
כת בו ומזבולון מושכים בשבט סופר.

(דף ד', ע"ב)

כיוצא בו את אומ שאל הקב'ה על הבל, אלו
הודה מיד, נתקבלה תשובתו, אלא אמ השומר וג'
אחי. וכשראה הקב'ה שהוא עומ ברשעו קללו
שנ ועתה ארור וג. כך שאל אלישע לגחזי מאין
גחזי, אילו עשה תשובה והודה מיד, נתקבלה ממנו
תשובתו, אלא ויאמר לא הלך וג, וכשראה שהוא
עומ ברשעו קיללו, שנ וצרעת נעמן וג'.
והכבוד הוציא את ירבעם מן העולם שא' בלבו
שנ ויאמר ירבעם בלבו וג, אמ אני עולה
לירושלים אהיה עומד ומלכי בית דויד
יושבין, שכך שנ חכ אין ישיבה בעזרה אלא
למלכי בית דויד בלבד, שנ ויבוא המלך דויד
וישב לפני י", ואומ כי שמה ישבו כסאות וג
ואם אני עומד ורחבעם יושב יהו אומרין

(דף ה', ע"א)

זה אדון וזה עבד ויהרגוני. וכן הו אומ
אם יעלה העם הזה וג ויועץ המ וג, מהו ויועץ
מלמ שמשך את יש בדברים: אתם יודעין
שאחיה השילוני משח אותי והוא צדיק
וחסיד וישר. אמ לו: הין. אמ להם: אין אתם יודעין
שנתנבא עלי' שהוא בונה לי בית המקדש,
שנ והייתי עמך ובניתי לך בית נאמן וג
מי שהיה בו חכמה היה אומ לו: אין הקב'ה
בוחר אלא במקום אחד ומזבח אחד,
והטפשין אומ: הין, לכך ויועץ, שבעצה
בא עליהן אבל הכהנים לא קבלו ממנו.
וכיצד נתיעץ עד שעשה
שני עגלים, אמ להן: הכרובים שעשה
משה הין עגלים, כת אחד אומ ודמות

(דף ה', ע"ב)

פניהם פני אדם וג ובת אומ וארבעה
פנים לאחד פני האחד פני הכרוב וג, במקום הוא
קורא שור, ובמקום הוא קורא כרוב, לכך ויועץ
המלך. מפני שבקש כבוד לעצמו אבד עצמו מן
העולם. וכן קרח, כלך נאמ ו י ק ח   ק ר ח וג. מה ראה

חרפה לגוים וקלסה לכל הארצ[ות, וכן]
הוא אומ׳ אוי לנפשם כי גמלו להם [רעה]
ולא אמ׳ קרבו ימיך אלא ותקרבי [ימיך],
ובאת עד שנותיך אין כת׳ אלא ותב[וא]
עד שנותיך. וקרח ועדתו הם הבי[או ועל]
נפשם ועל עצמן צרה, שחלקו על מ[שה]
ועל אהרן ונתגאו ובקשו גדולה ל[עצמן]
וכל המבקש גדולה לעצמו גדולה זו
בורחת ממנו. וכן אמ׳ הכת׳ פי יחזקאל
וידעו כל עצי השדה כי אני י״י השפלתי
עץ גבוה הגבהתי עץ שפל הובשתי
עץ לח והפרחתי עץ יבש אני י״י ד׳
דברתי ועשיתי. השפלתי עץ גבוה,
זה נמרוד שהיה גבור חיל והשפילו
הקב״ה, שיעץ עצה רעה ואמ׳ הבה
נבנה לנו עיר וראשו בשמים ו[גו׳]

(סוף הקטע)

[ששה דפים של נייר ב—, מס׳ 28]

[לסדר (חסר): במדבר ט״ז, א׳.]

(דף ד׳, ע״א)

ולמה לא קבל ממנו אלישע מנחתו, מפני חילול
השם, שלא יאמרו מפני חילול נביאי יש עושין כן
אלא בשכר, לכך ויאמ׳ אלישע חי י״י וגו׳. וכשראה
גחזי שלא קבל מנחתו ממנו נתאוה הו ורץ
אחריו, הה׳: וירדף גחזי וגו׳, וכשחזר עמד
לפני רבו. אמ׳ לו: מאין באתה גחזי, ולאין הלכת.
והלא כבר ידע אלישע לאיכן הלך, מה ראה
לשאל אותו. והלא לא למדו הנביאים דרך
הארץ אלא מן הקב״ה ששאל לאדם הראשון
כשחטא, לא אמר לו כבר חטאת, אלא שאלו
ואמ׳ לו איכה, והלא לית ידע אנה הוא,
אלא לימד הקב״ה דרך ארץ שיהא החוטא
נשאל על חטאו, אם הודה מיד, זו היא תחילת
תשובה, ואם לא, עד עכשו הוא עומד בחטאו.

הברכות רבות והקללות מעוטות, מנין שהוא כן, בוא
20   וראה מה שכ֗ת אם בחקתי תמאסו, עד געלה נפשם,
נמצאו מעוטות, למה, שהק֗ רוצה שלא יבאו ישראל
לידי קללה, ומנין שהוא כן, הן מאלף ועד מים; תח[ולה]
אלף, אם בחקתי תמאסו, ובסוף מ֗ם, געלה נפשם [לכך]
נאמר חשבתי דרכי וג֗ו'. ונתתי גשמיכם בע[תם]

(כאן סוף הקטע)

[דף אחד של נייר, קרוע בחציו העליון, ב־ T.-S. Box C 2, מס' 43. פסוקי
התנ״ך מנוקדים]

[לסדר (חסר): במדבר ט״ז, א'.]

(עמוד א')

[זה קרח שפשע בתורה], שנקראת עז,
[שנ֗] י֗י עז לעמו י[תן י]֗י יברך את עמו
[בשלום]. וכן הקהיל קהילות על משה
[ועל אה]רן, וגרם לעצמו שנשה בו מלאך
[המות] שנ֗ פי מגלה כאיל ישי מות
[עלימ]ו ירדו שאול חיים כי רעות במגורם
[בקר]בם. עבארה דלך: פלינסא אלמות
. . . ביעי ענהם בל ירדו אלי אלתרי. חיא
[לא]ן אלשר פ[ין] גוארהם ופי גופהם . . . . .
. . . . וירדו שאול חיים, הוא מה שא֗ם הכתוב
וירדו הם וכל אשר להם חיים שאולה.
כי רעות במגורם בקרבם, שטמנו עצות
רעות בלבבם, שהרבו מחלוקת בישראל.
ומדינים כבריח ארמון, שהעלתה הארץ
בריחיה בעדו. אמ֗ ר֗ יוחנן חלילה לפני
הק֗ב֗ה שמגלגל ומביא פורענות על
בני אדם, אלא הם מביאים על נפשם
שכן מצינו מיחזקאל שהוכיח את ישראל

(עמוד ב')

ואמ֗ בדמך אשר [שפכת אשמת ובגלוליך]
אשר עשית טמאת [ותקרבי ימיך]
ותבוא עד שׁנוֹתׁיך שנותיך על [כן נתתיך]

10 אחד או שנים. והלך רש אצל איש תככים, אמר לו: שנה לי

פ[רק א]חד או שנים, ושנה לו, מאיר עיני שניהם ייי, שניהם

[זכו] בחיי העולם הבא. עשיר ורש נפגשו, זה עשיר בתורה,

[ורש, זה שרש] בתו[רה, ו]הלך רש אצל עשיר ושנה לו פרק

אחד או שנים, אמ לו: מה אנא מתנינא לך, מ[ש]קין או

15 אנא מתנינא לך מאימתי קורין ותני עם מן דכותך.

עשה כלם ייי, מי שעשאו לזה חכם יכול לעשותו טיפש.

דא רש ואיש תככים, רש, זה שרש בנכסים, איש תככים,

זה שהוא פועל ואוכל מעמלו, הלך רש אצל [איש תככים],

אמ לו: תן לי פרוטה, ונתן לו, מאיר עיני שניהם ייי, שניה[ם],

20 קנו חיי העולם הבא. עשיר ורש נפגשו, הלך רש אצל

עשיר, אמ לו: תן לי פרוטה, אמ לו: חמי שקין, חמי כר [עין],

[חמי קפרין], לית את אזיל ולאי ופרניסי, אמ לו הק: [לא]

[דייך שלא] נתתה לו משלך מאומה, עד שאתה מכניס ע[ין]

[רעה במה] שנתתי לו, עשה כלם ייי, מי שעשאו לזה עני,

(דף ב', ע"ב)

ויכול לעשותו עשיר. ביום טובה היה בטוב וגו', ביום טו'

טובתו של חברך, היה בטוב, וביום רעתו ראה היאך

לפרנסו, כדי שתקבל שכר. גם את זה לעמת זה, אמ הק:

למה בראתי בעולמי עשירים ועניים, אילא כדי שיהו

5 זוכים אילו עם אילו. שבעה שמות יש לעני: עני,

כשמועו; אביון, שהוא תואב לכל; מסכן, שהוא בזוי

לפני כל; דל, שהוא מדלדל; דך, שהוא מדכדך; רש,

שהוא מתרושש; מך, שמך לפני כל, ועשוי כאסקופה

התחתונה. הרחמן יזכינו לבשורות הטובות, וחסדי

10 מאתך לא ימוש וברית שלומי לא תמוט אמר מרחמך.

אם בחקתי

[זה שהוא נא[מר]

חשבתי דרכי וגו', לא נאמר הפסוק אלא כנגד מצות [ומתן]

שכרן ועונשן, כך אמר דוד: חשבתי דרכי, [וחשבתי]

שכרן שלמצות והפסידן שלעבירות, ואשיבה

15 רגלי אל עדותיך; חשבתי מה שכח בתורה אם בחקתי

תלכו, מה כתוב, ונתתי שלום ושאר הברכות עד

קוממיות, מאלף ועד תיו, תחלה אם – אלף, וסוף קו'

קוממיות – תיו, מכן אמ הכח חשבתי דרכי, כלומר

זוכרו נפשו ולבו הם משתוקקים עליו, ש[נ] כזכר בניהם
מזבחותם וגו'. אמ' ר' יצחק כיון שהיה לאדם בן כבן שנים
20　[עשה לו] עבודה זרה כיוצא בו, שנ' ועתה יוסיפו לחטוא
(בדף הראשון חסרות ד' שורות למטה)

(דף א', ע"ב)

מהם וגו', אמר ישעיה לעתיד לבוא בא גרמני ומחזיק בידו שלכושי
[ובא] כושי ומחזיק בידו שלגרמני, ונשלח ידו שלזה על ידו שלזה
והולכים ומעידים ב
נסים ונפלאות שהק עושה לישר', שנ' והגידו את כבודי ב[גוים].
5　ולפי שאין אומ העו' יודעים שבחו וגדלתו שלהק עד [אותה]
שעה, לפיכך הם נטרדים לגיהנם מאלתר, שהק [אומ] להם
בשעת הדין: הביאו עבודה זרה שלכם, אם יש בה ממש תציל
אתכם מ[דינה] שלגהינם.　[והם מביאין] עבד' זר' שלהם, ומשליכים
אותה ואותן לגהינם, וגהינם נגעלת בפניהם, והם מ..
10　וחזר ואומר להן לישראל: עברו בתוך גהינם,
[מה ז]ה שלהם עברה תחלה והיא בסוף אתה עב[ור ל]פנינו
תחלה ואחר כך נעבור אחריך, שנ' כי כל העמים ילכו איש וגו'.
והק עובר לפניהם　תחלה, שאלמלא הדבר כתוב אי אי[פשר]
לאומרו, שנ' כי באש י"י נשפט וגו', כביכול הק עובר וישראל
15　[עוברים] אחריו, אבל רשיעי ישראל וצדיקי האומות משתיירים
בגהינם. והק עולה ויושב בגן עדן, וצדיקים יושבין לפניו,
ומעמיד תורגמן　　　　　　על ידו, שנ' בעת ההיא אקחך
זרובבל בן שא[לתי]אל וגו', וכיון שהוא פותח ואומר יהי
י"י הגדול מבורך, רשיעי ישראל עונים אמן מגהינם, והק
20　[ש]ומע ואומ': מיהן הללו שנשתיירו בגיהנם, אמ[רים לו]
(כאן חסרות ארבע שורות)

(דף ב', ע"א)

שומעין ועונין אמן, הק מעלה אותם מגהינם ואינן נדו
נדונין בה כל עיקר, שנ' כי תעבר במים אתך אני וגו', כת'
גומל נפשו איש וגו', אמרו עליו על הלל הזקן כשהיה הולך
מטייל(?) תלמידיו בכל יום אמרו לו: רבינו, לאיכן אתה הולך,
5　אמ' להם: למינמל חסד עם הדא אכסניא, פעם אחת אמ' לו: רב
רבינו, אית גבך אכסניא ולית את מהודע לן אמ' להון: הדא
נפשי לא אכסני היא; היום עמי ולמחר אינה עמי. ועוכר
שארו אכזרי, זה שאינו מדבק בקרובותיו.　רש ואיש
תככים וגו', זה שרש בתורה, איש תככים, זה ששונה פרק

ברית אבות זכור [ה להקב"ה] ומרחם עליהים ומושיעם

שנ' ויחן י"י אותם וגו' .... עתיד לרחם עליהם

20 ולהושיעם בזכות ב[רית] אבות, שנ' וזכרתי את בריתי

אברהם ואף את [בריתי] יצחק ואף את יעקב. א מ ו ר

א ל ה כ ה נ י ם, מה כתי' למעלה מן העניז, ואיש או אשה כי

יהיה בהם אוב וגו', ראה מיום שהז[היר הקדוש ב]ה על אוב

וידעוני לא מצאנו אדם ש[ב]יק[ש]ש[ם אלא ש]אול בלבד, שנ'

25 ויאמר שאול אל עבדיו בקשו לי וגו'. ובשע[ה] שמלך שאול ה'

הכרית אבות וידעונים מן הארץ. משל למה הדבר דומה,

שנכנס למדינה, ואמר כל המעינות שיש כן יסתמו.

אחר כך בקש המל' לרחוץ את רגליו, אמ' הביאו לי מים, אמ'

לו עבדיו: לא כך אמרת כל מעין שיש כן יסתם. כך שאול

30 בשעה שמלך כתי' בו ויסר שאול את אוב וידעוני מן הארץ,

כיון שהצר לו אמ' לעבדיו: בקשו [לי]

[אשת בע]ל [ת או]ב

(כאן סוף הקטע)

[ב' דפים של נייר, קרועים ומטושטשים, ב-T.-S. Box C 2, סימן 61; בדף א'

חסרות ד' שורות האחרונות]

(דף א', ע"א)

אך שקר נחלו אבותינו וגו'. מהוא אך שקר, אמרו לפניו כל

מעשין שעשו אבותינו אינם אילא הבל בעולם, ולא יגעו אילא(?) לריק

והבל, אילא שבע מצות צויתנו אמת הן מתחילה הן אמת,

ואנו עברנו עליהן, שנ' היעשה לו אדם אלהים וגו'. ר' יהודה

5 היה דורש כנגד ישר', ור' נחמיה היה דורשן כנגד אומות

העו', שמתחרטין על מה שעשו, אומרים: אי לנו, אדם בן

מאה שנה או בן חמשים שנה ילך וישתחוה לעבודה זרה

בת יומה, ואילו יש לה פה או עינים עדין לא היה לה

שנעבדה, אילא שפה להם ולא ידברו וגו', לפי כך והמה לא

10 אלים. הררי בשדה חיליך וגו', אמר ר' יצחק בר אחא אמ' להם

הק' לישראל: עבודה זרה שעבדתם על ההרים ועל הגבעות,

שנ' על ההרים יזבחו ועל הגבעות וגו', גרמתם לשני הרים

[גד]ולים, שמים שבראתי את עולמי שכינה שרויה עליהם,

ואילו הם: הר סיני והר המוריה, שסילקתי שכינתי מ[הם]

15 ועשיתים הפקר כשדה, לכך נאמר הררי בשדה. אמר ר'

אלעזר בן פדת בוא וראה כמה חיבתה שלעבד [ז]רה על

ישראל, כאדם שיש לו בן ו[ש]רוי במ[דינת] הים, וכשהוא

חלק הקב̇ה̇ כבוד לאב ואם שוה, שהקיש כבודם לכבודו,

מוראתם למוראתו, כדכת̇ כבד י̇י̇ מהוניך. אם תעשה כן
15

מה סכרך(!), למען יאריכון ימיך, במורת(!) הקב̇ה̇, את י̇י̇ אלהיך

תירא, מה שכרך, לעתיד לבא וזרחה לכם יראי שמי. במוראת

אב ואם כת̇ א י ש א מ ו ו א ב י ו ת י ר א ו, מה שכרך, וראו כל עמי הא̇.

ו א ת ש ב ת י ת ש מ ו ר ו, למה נסמכה מצות שבת לאב

ואם,]וא[מר הקב̇̇ה: מי שמכבד את אביו ואמו אני מענגו בכבוד שבת, ומי
20

שמקלל אביו ואמו

מיתתו בסקילה, שנ̇ מחלליה מות יומת, שכבוד אב ואם

שקול כשמירת שבת ולול̇(!) (וחלזול̇) אב ואם שקול כחלול שבת. לכך

נסמכה זו לזה. א נ י י̇ ̇י, משלם שכר לשומרי שבת ואני

משלם שכר ל]מ[כבדי־אב ואם. הדברות שנאמרו בסיני

חזר הקב̇ה̇ ושנם באוהל מועד, ואלו הן: בסיני כת̇ אנכי י̇י
25

אלהיך, באוהל מועד כת̇ אני י̇י̇ אלהיכם; בסיני כת̇ ל א י ה י ה ל ך

א ל ה י ם וגו̇, כאן כת̇ אל תפנו אל האלילים; בסיני כת̇ לא תשא,

כן כתי̇ ולא תשבעו בשמי לשקר; בסיני כתי̇ זכור את יום

השבת, כאן כת̇ ואת שבתותי תשמורו; בסיני כת̇ כבד

את אביך ואת אמך, כאן כת̇ א י ש א מ ו ו א ב י ו ת י ר א ו; בסיני]כת̇
30

(דף ב׳, ע״ב)

לא תרצח, כן כת̇ לא תעמוד על דם רעך; בסיני

לא תנאף, כן כת̇ א ל ת ח ל ל א ת ב ת ך; בסיני כת̇ לא תגנוב, כן

כת̇ לא תגנובו; בסיני כת̇ לא תענה ברעך, כן כת̇ לא תשקרו;

בס]יני כ[ת̇ לא תחמוד, כן כת̇ לא תעשוק את רעך וגו̇. בא וראה

שהגדיל הקב̇ה̇ את ישראל מכל האומות בכל מעשיהם: בזריעתן,
5

]בח[רישתן, בקצירתן, בעמרן, בדישתן. בזריעתן, כת̇ לא תזרע

כרמך, וכן הוא אומ]ר את ח[]ו[קותי תשמורו. בקצירתן נאמר

ולקט קצירך לא ת ל ק ט. בחרישתן כת̇ לא ת ח ר ו ש ב ש ו ר.

בדישתן, לא תח]סום שור[בדישו. בעמרן נא̇מ ושכחתה עומר

בשדה. לפיכך]הבדיל]ם הקב̇ה̇ בשלש קדושות, תחלה אמ̇
10

ק ד ו ש י ם ת ה י ו וגו̇, וכן]הוא[אומ̇ והתקדשתם והייתם קדו̇

וגו̇, ולבסוף אמ̇ והיתם]לי קדוש[ים. למה בשלש קדושות, כנגד

שלוש מונים שנשתלחו,]כהניא ו[]לויי[ה וישראל; וכנגדם נא̇מ

שלשה מאמרים: תורה,]נביאים ו[כתובים. וכנגדם נתחזקו

בשלוש בריתו]ת[, ברית א]ברהם[יצחק ויעקב, שנ̇ אשר
15

כרת את אברהם וש]בוע̇ ליצ̇ ויעמדיה[ליעקב. וברית והחסד לאוהביו

אלף דורות, שנ̇ שומר הברית והחסד וגו̇. ובכל דור ודור

10 וישלחו מן המחֿ כל צרוע וכל זב. אומות העולם מלכלכין
בעבודה זר, אבל ישראל נאמֿ להם: ושמרתם את משמרתי.
אם הקֿבֿה לישראל: דעו שהגוים שהייתם ביניהם מטמאין
בכל שקוצין ומלכלכין בכל העבודות, תועיבות שנעשו
לפניכם לא תתאוו להם, עבירות שנעשו לפניכם לא תטמאו
בהם אני יֿי אלהיכם, אני דין ליפרע ממי שעשה כן. אמר להם:
כשם שאני טהור כך תהיו טהורים, כשם שאני קדוש כך
תהיו קדושים. והכלילם בפסוק אחד, שֿנ דבר אל בני ישראֿל
כל עדת בני ישראל, ללמדך שהקֿדושה חלה על קטון וגדול
20 על נשים ואנשים. כשם שהאנשים חיבים לטהר מכל עבירות כך נשים חיבים
לטהר עצמן מכל טמאות ומכל עבירות, ושלא לעבוד עבודה
זרה, ולהבדל מזבים ומצורעים, ולכבוד אב ואם, ולקדש
השבת ולשמרה, ושאר עבירות וֿוֿ]ומצות הזכרות
בפרשה הזאת חיבין לשמרם. לכך התחיל ואמֿ דבר
אל כל עדת בני ישראל וגוֿ, שיהיו זריזים בקדושה ובנקיות,
25 שֿנ והזרתם את בני ישראל וגוֿ. קדושים תהיו, בא וראה
כשמתחיל הקֿבֿה בענין בלשון קדושה, ובסוֿף העניין חתם
בקדושה. התחיל בקדושה תחלה, אמֿ: קדושים תהיו; בסוֿף
אמֿא: והיתם לי קדושים וגוֿ, כשם שהבדלתי אתכם מעברות
אומות העולם, כך קדשו את עצמן והטהרו ועבדוני בקדושה.
30 כ י ק ד ו ש א נ י יֿ י א לֿ ה, שאם אתם עושים רצוני, אני משליט
אתכם על כל האומות, וכשם שאני עליון על כל, שֿנ כי יֿי עליון

(דף בֿ, עֿֿא)

עליון נורה(!) וגוֿ, כך אני משימכם עליון על כל העמים, שֿנ ונתנך
יֿי אלהיך עליון וגוֿ. בא וראה שלש פרשיות כתובות לנו יש
בכל אחת ואחת עֿ מצות, ואלו הן: פרשת פסחין, פרשת נזיקים,
פרשת קדושים, ושאר כל המצות בשאר פרשיות. פרשת
5 פסחים, מן ויאמר יֿי אל משה ואהרן זאת חוקת ועד והיה
לאות על ידך, עֿ מצֿו אזהרות יש בה. פרשת נזיקים, מן
ואלה המשפטים ועד הנה אנכי שולח מלאךֿ, עֿ מצות
יש בה. וכך פרשת קדושים, עֿ מצות קבועות בה. איש
א י מ ו ו א ב י ו ת י ר א ו, מפני מה בסיני הקדים אב לאם, ובאוהל
10 מועד הקדים אם לאב? בסיני בשביל ששמעו אומות העולם
את הדבור הקדים אב לאם, ובאוהל מועד שלא שמעו אלא
ישראל הקדים אם לאב. באוהל מעד שנשים מתפללות, כענין
שֿנ במראות הצובאות וגוֿ, הקדים מדת האם למדת האב.

והם בני חם, שנ' ו[בני] חם כוש ומצרים. ומאת עדת בני ישר',
מהכן, מתרומת הלשכה. ולקח את שני השעירים. היה כהן
גדול מביא שני שעירים וקושר אותם פתח הבית, וקושר
לשון של זהורית בראשן עד שלא יעלה לשם י"י אחד ולשלח
10 אחד, היה לשון זהורית שבראשן [מלבין]. כך היה המנהג
עד סוף בית האחרון. אר[ב]עים [שנה לפני] חרבן הבית לא היה
לשון זהורית מלבין (יומא, ל"ט, ע"ב). כשהיה [כהן גדול מעלה הגור]ל מביטים
שהו
אדום והיה נלבן והיו ידע[ין] שהקב"ה נ[תרצה ע]מהם. כיון שלא היה
נלבן היו יודעין הכהנים אותו לחיים מן
15 הבית, לפי(?) שבתחלה היו צ[די]קי[ם] כראוי, ובסוף
התחילו למרות עין, ועליהם נאמר וימרו וימרדו [בך]. וכך
בתנאין בא הקב"ה עם ישר', שנ' רחצו הזכו הסי[רו], למדו הטיב,
אמ' להם הקב"ה: אם אתם עושין כך, אם יהיו חט[אי]כם כשנים
כשלג ילבינו. אבל לעתיד לבא למעניהו [ע]ושה ומעביר עונותן
20 שלישראל, לא לצדקתן, שנ' אנכי [אנכי הוא] מוחה פשעך למעני
וחטאתיך לא אזכור. קדושים. כתוב כי יעקב
בחר לו י ה וגו'. עשה [הקב"ה טובה] עם [ישראל] מה שלא עשה עם כל
בריה ואומה ולשון, והנחילן חקיו ומשפטי ותורותיו
האצורים בבית גנזיו קודם יצירת עולם, והבדילם מן
25 אומות עולם, שהן נושאין אחד את אחותו ואחד את
אחות אמו ואחות אביו, וכל העריות מתרות להם.
אבל ישראל אמ' להם הקב"ה: ובחקותיהם לא תלאכו(!).
וכך הנחילם משפטים לא כמשפטי אומות העולם,
שאו[מו]ת העולם חורשים בשור ובחמור, לובשים
[שעטנ]ז, אבל ישראל לא תחרוש בשור ובחמור יחדיו,

(דף א', ע"ב)

לא תלבש שעטנז. וכך למדם תורותיו, אלו התורות של
בהימות חיות ועופות ושרצים, והיולדות, ונגעים וזבים
זבות, ומ ה (ונדה?), שלא נצטוו בהם אומות העולם, מלכלכין בבהימ'
וחיות, בין טמאים ובין טהורים, אינם אסורים כלום, אבל
5 ישראל נאמ' להם זה לכם הטמא וגו', זה טמא וזה אינו טמא.
ולמדם והודיעם אסור והתר, שכתו' בהם זאת תורת
הבהמה והעוף. אומת העולם אין להם טמאת לידה, אבל
ישראל נאמר להם: זאת תורת לזכר וגו'. אומות העולם
מלכלכים בנגעים ובזיבות, אבל ישראל נאמר להם:

צריך אתה[19] לשאל מהקב״ה שימסו[ר]את השטן,[20]

כדי שלא ישטין עליך בביאתך למקדש, וחטא

שבא לידך תחלה, התודה עליו ואחר כך הכנס

למקדש, אין לך עון חוץ מדבר אחד, לא נכשלת

אלא בעגל ולא קרוי אלא על שמך שנ' ויגף י״י את

העם וגו' (שמ' ל״ג, ל״ה). ק ח ל ך (וי' ט', ב'), תחלה, עגל בן ב[קר]

לחטאת,

שיתרצה בעדך ויכפר על מעשה עגל, יבוא

עגל וישכח את עגל של זהב. אמ' ל ו: א ה ר ן,[21] שמא

תאמר אין צריך כפרה אלא אני בלבד, והלא כל

(כאן סוף הקטע כ״י אדלר)

[שני דפים של נייר ב־T.-S. Box C 2, מס' 124. העמודים החיצוניים, היינו: א',
ע״א; ב', ע״ב – מטושטשים]

[לפרשת אחרי מות]

(דף א', ע״א)

שלא יתבזו יצאו מבני שם נדב ואביהו שחלק להם הקב״ה

כבוד שלא נשרפו בגדיהם ולא נתבזו. אבל חם שבזה את

אביו, מה כת' ויגד לשני אחיו, גרם לעצמו קללה, שנ' ויאמר ארור

כנען עבד עבדים, וגרם לבניו שגלו ממכונם ונראה קלונם

5   לכל באי העולם, שנ' ויאמר י״י כאשר הלך עבדי ישעיהו וגו',

19 ספרא שמיני, ראש הפרשה (ג) ומקבילות – גינצברג. והוא גם מעיר על שינוי הסגנון.
מצד אחר מעניין לראות שלמרות השינוי בסגנון מעורה הוא מדרשנו במקורו. בספרא אנו
קוראים שמשה אמר לאהרן: ״אעפ״י שנתרצה המקום לכפר עונותיך, צ ר י ך א ת ה ליתן
לתוך פיו של שטן, שלח דורון לפניך וכו'.״ ההתחלה כאן: ״צ ר י ך א ת ה . . .״ בלי
הקדום לו בספרא, מוזרה ואינה הולמת את סגננו השוטף של מדרשנו.
20 אעפ״י שגינצברג ומחברנו לא מצאו לנכון להעיר על הורות שבלשון ״שימסור את
השטן,״ אני מסופק אם הקריאה נכונה, כי צריך היה לומר ״למי,״ או ״בידי מי״ למסור את
השטן. נוטה אני לשער שבמקור היה כתוב ״לאסור״ את השטן. החילוף בין ״א' ל.מ' שכיח.
הלשון המתאימה ביותר כאן היא: ״שיסתום את פי השטן, שלא ישטין, בהקבלה למקור:
״ליתן לתוך פיו של השטן,״ לסותמו.
21 כן הוא בתעתיק מחברנו, דר' מאן, ונמשך אחרי לשון הספרא הנז', במקום ש.ושמא
תאמר . . .״ נסמך ל.שמא ישטינך,״ שהם דברי משה. כשלעצמו הייתי שם כאן את השאלה
בפיו של אהרן, והיית קורא: ״אמר לו אהרן, שמא תאמר וכו',״ – כלום אתה סובר שרק אני
צריך כפרה. אמת, שהלשון ״שמא תאמר״ אינו מתאים כל כך בפיו של אהרן, אבל זה רק מראה
שבעל מדרשנו, למרות השינויים שהכניס, לא יכול היה להשתחרר לגמרי מלשון המקור. וכבר
מצאנו דוגמתו למעלה בהע' 19.

עמ' 83

דבר מצוה או דבר שיש בו תשועה או עצה, אין
מקדים תחלה אלא לזקנים, שכך מצאנו בגאולת
מצרים[14] לא בישר אלא לזקנים שנ' לך ואספת את
זקני יש' (שמ' ג', ט"ז), כשנתנה תורה[15] ל[א נת]נה אלא לזקנים, שנ'
ואל משה אמר עלה אל י"י וגו' (שם, כ"ד, א'), וכשנתנה הכהונה
לאהרן,[16] לא נתנה אלא בפני זקנים שנ' ו י ה י ב י ו ם
ה ש מ י נ י. מלמד שאותן שבעת ימי המלאים
היה משה מקריב קרבנות ואהרן ובניו מקושטים
ככלות ומראה אותם היאך עושה כדי שיתרגלו
בעבודה. שוחט, ואהרן רואה, זורק, ואהרן רואה,
מגיש, מחטא, מכפר, מזה, מניף ומראה את אהרן
ואת בניו, אמ' לו: כסדר הזה שעשיתי לפניך, כך
תהיה רגיל לעשות.[17] ביום השמיני אמ' לו: מה יום[18]
הזה הכהונה נתנה לך מלפני הקב"ה נגד כל זקני
ישראל שנ' ו י ה י ב י ו ם ה ש מ י נ י ק ר א מ ש ה ל א ה ר ן וגו'.

14 בוי"ר הנז': „בהסנה," או „במצרים" (מרגליות, ח"נ: א ב).
15 בכל שאר המקורות: „בסיני."
16 בכל שאר המקורות: „באהל מועד." כדאי להעיר שאם נתבונן בשינויי נוסחה שבשלש
ההערות האחרונות, נמצא שלא מקרה הוא, כי אם כוונת מכוון.
המקור היסודי, המשותף לכולם הוא מאמרו של רשב"י: „לא ב מ ק ו ם א ח ד ... מצינו
שהמקום חלק כבוד לזקנים וכו'," והולך ומונה את הדוגמאות השונות הנז'. רוב המקורות,
ניסוחם מעורה במלת „מקום." ולפיכך הם הולכים ומונים „מקומות" שונים: „סנה או מצרים,
סיני, אוהל מועד." בעל מדרשנו השתחרר מן ה„מקום," והחליפו ב„דבר מצוה או דבר שיש בו
תשועה או עצה." ולפיכך הוא הולך ומונה: גאולת מצרים, מתן תורה, מתן כהונה (דבר שיש
בו תשועה. דבר מצוה).
17 ספרא צו, מכילתא דמילואים, י"ד (ט"ו בגז"ש – טעות הדפוס); ספרא, שמיני, פ"א, י"נ
(נינצבורג); וי"ר י"א, ו'.
מדרשנו מונה שבע עבודות שהראה משה לאהרן: שוחט, זורק, מגיש, מחטא, מכפר, מזה,
מניף. זה מתאים לספרא שמיני הנז' שאומר בפירוש: „שבשעה קלה למדו ש ב ע ע ב ו ד ו ת,"
אלא יש שינוי קל במהותן של העבודות. ואלו הן בספרא שמיני: שחיטה, קבלה, זריקה, הזאה,
חיטוי, יציקה, וכפרה. במקומן של „קבלה" ו„יציקה" יש לנו כאן „הגשה" (מגיש) ו„תנופה"
(מניף). ומעניין לראות שהראב"ד בפירושו „תמה למה הניח תנופה." בספרא צו הנז' יש רק שש
עבודות; חסרה ק ב ל ה.
18 – מ ה י ו ם ה ז ה. אפשר לשמוע הד החתימה בוי"ר הנז': „ר' חלבו אמר כל שבעת
ימי המילואים היה משה משמש בכהונה גדולה וכסבור שלו היא, ובשמיני (מרגליות,
חנ–בט) אמר לו, לא שלך היא אלא של אהרן אחיך היא, ויהי ביום
השמיני קרא."

שאמר נעשה אדם בצלמנו כדמותנו וגו' (בר' א', כ"ו),[6]

מי פתי יסור הנה וגו' (מש' ט', ד'), [וש]התקין גן עדן וגהינם

והזהיר וציוה על האדם ועל זרעו שלא לנטות

מדרכו שנ' ויצו י"י אלהים (בר' ב', ט"ז), אמר להם, אם תשמרו

דרכי, הרי אני מטיב לכם בעולם הזה ולעולם הבא

ואם לאו, הרי גהינם מוכנה להיפרע מכם,[7] לכך

חכמות בנתה ביתה. ד"א[8] חכמות בנתה ביתה,

זה אוהל מועד שלא נבנה אלא בחוכמה שנאמ'

ואמלא אותו רוח אלהים. (שמ' ל"א, ג'), וכן הוא אומ' ואתה

תדבר אל כל חכמי לב אשר מלאתיו רוח וגו' (שם, כ"ח, ג').[9]

חצבה עמודיה שבעה, אלו שבעת ימי

המילואים, טבחה טבחה, אלו הקרבנות שנ' ויגש

את פר החטאת (וי' ח', י"ד), וישחט את העולה (שם, ט', י"ב), ויקרב את

האיל השני [וגו'] (שם, ח', כ"ב),[10] אף ערכה שולחנה (מש' ט', ב'), בהכנת לחם

הפנים בשביל הכהנים. שלחה נערתיה תקרא,

זה משה, שלחו הקב"ה לקראת אהרן ולבניו ולצוותם

על הכהונה,[11] שנ' ויהי ביום השמיני קרא משה לאהרן

וגו' (וי' ט', א'). מה הו[א ו]12ולזקני ישראל (שם),[13] מנהג העולם כשהיה

---

6 גם כאן יש לנו „כויצת הרעיון" במדרשנו. במקור: „שלחה נערותיה, זה אדם וחוה, על נפי מרומי קרת, שהטיסן הקב"ה וקרא אותן אלהות[,], הה"ד (— הוא שאמר) והייתם כאלהים." והנה מדרשנו נועץ תחילתו בסופו ומדלג על החלק האמצעי. קשה להכריע אם יש לנו כאן דילוג מדעת או שלא מדעת. אגב יש כאן סמך להמפרשים (יפ"ת ורש"ש) המחליפים בוי"ר את הפסוק „והייתם כאלהים" בפסוק אחר יותר מתאים. הפסוק של בעל מדרשנו הוא בודאי המתאים ביותר לענייננו.

7 יש לנו כאן הרחבה מצידו של בעל מדרשנו. המקור ממשיך בביאור מדרשי של „חסר לב." ואילו בעל מדרשנו משתחרר ממדרש מילים, ומוסר לנו את הרעיון הכללי של הפרק כולו, כמעט פשוטו כמשמעו, ברמז על: „עזבו פתאים וחיו ואשרו בדרך בינה (6), כי בי ירבו ימיך ויוסיפו לך שנות חיים (11)." ומצד אחר: „ולא ידעו כי רפאים שם בעמקי שאול קראיה." (18).

8 וי"ר שם, ד' (נינצברג) בשם ר' אבא בר כהנא.

9 הפסוק הזה אינו מובא במקור.

10 במקור אין זכר לכל אלה הפסוקים. מצד אחר דילג בעל מדרשנו על: „מסכה יינה, אילו הנסכים" שבמקור.

11 מן „שלחו" והילך הרחבת פירוש היא, ואין לו מקביל במקור.

12 כך הוא בתעתיק מחברנו, דר' מאן.

13 וי"ר שם, ח' (נינצברג). מקבילות אצל ג' ואצל מרגליות. כדאי להעיר שברוב המקורות מכריע הניסוח „חלק כבוד לזקנים." רק במכילתא דרשב"י, הוצ' מק"נ, עמ' 25, נמצא גם: „מלמד שהזקנים [קוד]מין לכל ישראל."

אלא בימי מנשה,[22] כ ה כ נ י ס להיכל צלם שלארבעה
פנים, נסתלקה באותו היום.[23] אבל לעתיד לבוא
עתיד הקב"ה לסבב את ירושלם בחומת אש, שנא'
ואני אהיה לה נאם י"י חומת אש סביב ולכבוד וגו' (זכ' ב', ט').[24]

[לפרשת שמיני]

יט]. ו י ה י ב י ו ם ה ש מ י נ י (וי' ט', א').
כת' חכמות נ ש י ם [1] בנתה ביתה חצבה עמו' שב' (מש' ט', א'),
מלמד שאין הבית נבנה אלא בחכמה שנ' בחכמה
יבנה בית וג' (שם, כ"ד, ג'), וכך הקב"ה לא התקין את עולמו אלא
בחכמה,[2] שנ' י"י בחכמה יסד ארץ כונן שמים וגו' (שם, ג', י"ט)
חצבה עמודיה שבעה (שם, ט', א'), אלו שבעת ימי בראשית,

עמ' 82

שנבראו בהם כל ה[ב ר י ו ת] [3] ונגמרו כל המעשים.[4]
טבחה טבחה (שם, ב'), שהכין הקב"ה וערך וסדר ספוק
לכל יצוריו עד שלא נוצרו, כמות שאמ' תדשא הארץ (בר' א', י"א),
ישרצו המים (שם, ב').[5] שלחה נערותיה תקרא (מש' ט', ג'), הוא

22 ספרא ויקרא, פ"ה, י': "אש שירדה בימי משה לא נסתלקה ממזבח הנחשת עד שבאו
לבית העולמים, אש שירדה בימי שלמה לא נסתלקה ממזבח העולה עד שנסתלקה בימי
מנשה." ועי' סדר עולם רבה, הוצ' ראטנער, פט"ו, הע' י"ג. גינצברג מעיר רק על המקורות
הרחוקים.
23 מן "כהכניס" (כך הוא בכתה"י) עד כאן הוספת ביאור ל"ימי מנשה." ועי' גינצברג
הע' 19.
24 הפסוק הזה משמש חתימה גם בוי"ר ז', סוף.

יט. מקורות: וי"ר י"א, א', ד'; ספרא צו, שמיני.
1 כך הוא גם בכתבי יד אחדים של וי"ר (מרגליות, ח"נ – לפ).
2 וי"ר שם, א' (גינצברג) בשם ר' ירמי' בר' אלעזר. המקבילות אצל מרגליות.
3 כן הוא בתעתיק דר' מאן; גינצברג גורס "ה[ב רו ים]," או "ה[נ ד ב רים]".
4 מן "שנבראו" עד כאן הוספת ביאור של "שבעת ימי בראשית." ואולי יש גם רמז ל"מעשה
בראשית."
5 במקור מובאים הפסוקים מבראשית שלא כסדרם (א', כ"ד; א', ט'; א', י"א), כדי
לשמור את סדר הרמזים במשלי: טבחה – נפש חיה; מסבה – יקוו המים; ערכה שלחנה (פת) –
תדשא הארץ. מדרשנו מוסר רק את הרעיון הכללי של הכנת סעודה, ולא ראה צורך לעזוב
את סדר הפסוקים בבראשית.

[מסלקין] אתן למערכה אחרת, למה, מלמד שארבע מערכות היו שם:
[ואחת למער]כה גדולה, ואחת לקטרת, ואחת לקיום האש, ואחת [לאמורים]
30 [ופדרים] שלא נתאכלו מבערב חוץ משליום כפור שהיו חמשה.18 ו ש מ ו
א צ ל [ה מ ז ב ח] (שם),
[במזרחו שלמזבח]. ו פ ש ט א ת ב ג ד י ו ו ל ב ש ב ג ד י ם א ח ר י ם
(שם, ד'), [יכול כמצות יום]

(כאן סוף העמוד ולא נמצא עוד יותר בתיבות .S-.T הנ"ל. אולם קצת
מן ההמשך הוא בכת"י אדלר, סי' 2597=גנ"ש, א', עמ' 80, שו' 9 והלאה,
והשויתי את הכ"י עם הנדפס שם.)

קטע ז

[גנ"ש 1, עמ' 80]

ה, ב

יכול במצות יום הכיפורים יהיה פושט
בגדיו ולובש בגדים אחרים, ולמה אמ' אחרים,
אחר' שהן פחותין מן הראשונים שפשט. מה
בגדים שלובש תחילה ראויין למלאכתן אף בגדים
האחרונים שלבש ראויין למלאכתן.20 ו ה ו צ י א א ת
ה ד ש ן (שם), כל שהוא למד וכשר לעבודה מרגילין

עמ' 81

אותו לשרת.21 א ש ת מ י ד (שם, ו), אש שירדה
בימי משה לא נסתלקה עד שבאו לבית העולמים
וירדה לחם אש חדשה בימי שלמה ולא נסתלקה

18 ספרא צו, סוף פסוק ב', כדעת ר' מאיר; משנה יומא סוף פ"ה – גינצ'.
19 עפ"י וי' א', ט"ז: „אצל המזבח קדמה אל מקום ה ד ש ן,‟ והכוונה „במזרחו
של מזבח‟ ולא במזרחו של כבש. וזה כדעתו של ר' חנינא בן אנטיגנוס בספרא ויקרא, פ"ט, י"ב:
„שני בתי דשנין היו אחד במזרחו של כבש ו א ח ד ב מ ז ר ח ו ש ל מ ז ב ח ו כ ו'.‟
20 ספרא שם, פרק ב', ו'; יומא כ"ג, ב' (נינצברג). ג. מעיר לנכון שהמאמר כאן מסורס
ומקוטע, ויש לתקנו עפ"י המקורות הנז'. ויש להוסיף שיש לפנינו גם ניסיון של תיקון לשון הספרא
„מה בגדים שלובש . . . אף בגדים שפושט,‟ בניגוד להנוסחא ביומא „מה בגדים שפושט . . .
אף בגדים שלובש,‟ שהיא הנוסחא הנכונה (עי' פי' הראב"ד). בעל מדרשנו מתקן: „מה בגדים
שלובש [תחילה]‟, שהן הן „בגדים שפושט.‟
21 הלכה זו לא נודעה לי ממקום אחר (נינצברג). כנראה שהדברים מכוונים נגד דברי
ר' אליעזר שאומר: „והוציא את הדשן, לימד על ב ע ל י מ ו מ י ן שהם כשרים להוציא
את הדשן‟ (ספרא, שם).

‫[וערכה מבון, הערבים, ומבוא השמש מ]תאכלת והולכת כל ה[לי]לה.‬ 15
‫היא הע על מוקד [ה]‬

‫[כל הלילה,11 לא שהיו מתאכלין והולכין] האימרין כל הלילה, [אי]לא‬
‫שהיה מעלן‬

‫(סוף העמוד שם, ב', ע"א)‬

שעת‬　　　　　‫[מן הארץ לגבי המזבח כל] הל[י]לה12‬

‫[אש תמיד] תוקד על המזבח לא [ת]כבה (וי' ו', ו'),‬
‫ביקש משה‬

‫...... ... ש[ה]יתה האש נר [אית] כשהיא מציתה במזב[ח ולא]‬

‫[היה המזבח מתאכל.13 ולבש הכהן [מדו] בד (שם, ג'), מידה כמדתו, זה‬ 20
‫לכהן‬

‫הדיוט.14 ב ד, שיהיו שלבו[ץ]; ב ד, שיהיו כפולין; ב ד, שיהיו חדש[ני]ם;‬
‫ב ד, ש[לא‬

‫ילבש עמהם בגדים] אחרים.15　　　　מכנסי בד על בשרו (שם),‬
‫ול[א ר]טייה‬

‫[על בשרו; מכנסי בד על בש, שלא יהיה דבר קודם למכנסים.16 והרים‬
‫[את‬

‫הדשן אשר] תאכל האש (שם), וכל(!) (=יכול) עצים, תלמוד‬
‫לומר את העולה (שם), או עולה יכול אברי‬

‫[העולה], תלמוד לומר אשר תאכל האש, יכול בין אמרים שפקעו‬ 25
‫מעל המזבח ובין שעל‬

‫[המזבח] תל מל אש תאכל האש את העולה על המזבח,‬
‫אברים שפקעו מעל המ‬

‫[המזבח קו]דם חצות מעלין17 בהן על המזבח, לאחר חצות מ‬

<hr>

‫11 גז"ש שם, עמ' 79, ממשיך להעתיק דברי הספרא בלשונו; בעל קטענו, כדרכו, מקצר‬
‫ומנסח באופן חפשי. ומאחר ששלש השורות הבאות לקויות ברובן, ההשלמה אינה אלא השערה‬
‫קלושה.‬

‫12 על יסוד גז"ש שם, שו' 12, הייתי מציע להשלים: .[עד שתגיע] שעת / [עולת התמיד‬
‫לשחט]." גינצ' בפתיחתו, עמ' 68—69, האריך בביאור הלכה זאת.‬

‫13 בגז"ש שם ובמקור, וי"ר ז', ה', הדרש הזה נדרש בפסוק .תוקד בו" (וי' ו', ג')‬
‫ולא בפסוק .תוקד על המזבח" (וי' ו', ו'). בגז"ש יש כאן הוספה שאינה אלא המשך‬
‫דברי הספרא.‬

‫14 השווה ספרא צו, פרק ב', א'. זה חסר במקורות, בספרא ומקבילות, – גינצ' שם הע' 22.‬

‫15 ספרא שם ומקבילות – גינצ' שם. ההשלמה עפ"י הספרא.‬

‫16 גז"ש שם. מדברי הספרא (שם, ג') יוצא שמ .ומכנסי בד יהיו על בשרו‬
‫(שמ' כ"ט, ד') נלמד שלא יהא דבר קודם למכנסים, ומפסוקנו .ילבש על בשרו'‬
‫נלמד .ולא רטייה על בשרו," בעל מדרשנו לא דק ומוציא שתי ההלכות מפסוק אחד.‬

‫17 השווה גז"ש שם, עמ' 80 (ה, ב, ג). גינצ' מראה מקום לספרא ומשנה זבחים ט', ו',‬
‫ומציע לקרוא .מועלין בהן ומעלה אותן על המזבח." הניקוד כאן הוא .מעלין", בפתח‬
‫ה.מ'.‬

‹נטטו ⟨היו ישראל משלחין⟩ לשלח› מצורעין. ⁵ גלו מארצם ונסתלקה שכינה
מהן ⟨נפטרו⟩

10 ⟨משלוח מצורעין⟩. ⁶. פרשת תמידין⁷ ⟨מניין⟩, צו את אהרן ואת בניו
לאמר (וי' ו', ב'). ⟨ז⟩את
⟨תורת העולה⟩ (שם), וכ⟨י⟩ על עולת תמיד היא מלמדת, אילא כך
מצוה אתן: מנהג עולה,
⟨על עולת התמיד, ע⟩ל עולת נדבה, ⟨וע⟩ל עולת חובה. ⟨ע⟩ל ⁸ היא העולה
על מוקדה על המזבח
⟨כל הלילה⟩ (שם), שיהא נותנה מבוא⟨ה⟩ השמש והיא מיתאכל⟨ת⟩ והולכת על
גבי המזבח כל הלילה
⟨עד הבקר⟩ (שם), ⁹ מבוא השמש¹⁰ שלבין ה⟨ערבים, שכ כת ⟨ו⟩את הכבש
השני תעשה בין הערב⟨י⟩ם,

5 בגמ"ש שם, עמ' 78, 14—16, יש כאן הוספה: „⟨ו⟩כן מצינו בימי אלישע שהיו / אנשים מצורעים
⟨שלחום מחוץ לשומרון ואפעלפי שהיו / נטים ברעב לא הניחו את המצוה הזאת שנ' / וארבעה /
אנשים היו מצורעים וג',⟨ כיון שגלו . . .".

6 בגמ"ש שם, שו' 18—19, יש כאן הוספה אחרת: „נפטרו מלשלח טמאים ⟨אלא חייבין / לפרוש
מהם ולא לנגוע בהם]." 19 נראה כאילו מפרש את הפיסקה הזאת שאפעלפי ששילוח
מצורע אינו נוהג בזמן הזה אבל טומאת מצורע נוהגת, ולפיכך אסור לנגוע בו.
בפתיחתו, עמ' 71, מאריך גינצ' בהלכה זו שטומאת מצורע נוהגת בזמן הזה, וערכה בשביל
קביעת מקורותיו של בעל המדרש. ואני מפקפק בדבר אם האזהרה „לפרוש מהם ולא לנגוע
בהם" משום טומאה הוא. אני נוטה לראות את אזהרה להתרחק ממצורע מפני הסכנה, אזהרה
המודגשת ביחוד בסוף פ"ז בכתובות. השווה גם וי"ר ט"ז, ג': „אסור להלך למזרחו של מצורע
ד' אמות." ובאמת כל עיקרה של ההוספה לא בא אלא לבאר את המאמר ששילוח מצורע
„קבוע מיד ולדורות." ולפיכך לאחר שנאמר שמשגלו ישראל נפטרו משילוח טמאים מחוץ
לעיר, בכל זאת צריך להתרחק מהם, וזאת היא תמורת שילוח טמאים „לדורות." ממש
כמו שהדלקת נרות בבהכ"נ היא תמורת הדלקת נרות במקדש „לדורות."

7 נ"ש שם, שו' 12 וכו' יש עוד הוספה הבאה לבאר את הקביעות לדורות של
תמידין: „להודיעך זרוז הקרבנות והם מיד ולדורות ואם / בעונות בטלו אילו
שמונה עשרה ברכות שיש' מתפללין ומברכין את השם בכל יום ויום הם / שקולים כקורבנות
לכך נא' צו את אהרן ואת / בניו לאמר . . ." זה מקביל למה שנאמר לפני זה בנוגע לנרות,
ולדעתי גם בנוגע לשילוח מצורע.

קשה להכריע אם ההוספות המעניינות אלו חסרות היו במקור של בעל קטענו, או שהשמיט
אותן מדעת, מפני שלא עמד על משמעותן, או שלא מדעת, מתוך הבלעה.

8 ההשלמה היא עפ"י נו"ש שם, עמ' 78, ה', א', 1—3. לפירוש המאמר, עי' גינצ' שם הע' 3.
השערתו שצ"ל: „אלא כך," מתאשרת מתוך קטענו.

9 לשון ספרא צו א', י"ג.

10 ההשלמה עפ"י נו"ש, עמ' 79. מכאן והילך יש לנו א. פירוש של „מבוא השמש" שבספרא
הנז', שהוא זמן תמיד של בין הערבים, ואחר כך חזר ושנה את המשפט כולו בניסוח שונה,
ובמקום „נותנה" יש לנו „עורכה." כל זאת דוגמא מעניינת של עיבוד המקור ושימושו על ידי בעל
מדרשנו. הרחבת ביאור וניסוח חפשי. אפשר שיש כאן רמז למחלוקת התנאים בפירוש „מבוא
השמש" אם הכוונה היא „ממקום שהשמש זורחת" או „ממקום שהשמש שוקעת" (סוטה ל"ג, ע"ב).
ועי' גינצבורג בפתיחתו, עמ' 69, שהאריך בזה.

יח.

30 [ויעש א]הרן ובניו (שם, ל"ו), 13 לכך נא שינאה תעורר מדנים וגו'. דבר

אח[ר צו, אין]

[צואה אילא] זירוז מיד ולדורות. שלוש פרשיו' נאמרו בצוא[ה, והן]

דף י' ע"ב (שם, ט', ע"א)

[קבו]עות מיד ול[דו]רות, ואלו הן: פרשת נירות, פרשת של [וח טמאין],

[ופרשת תמידין.1 פרש ני]2 כך בין במקדש ובין ב[בתי] כנסיות ובתי [מדרשות],

[לפי שבתי כנ ומד הן כמען] בית המקדש, שכ כת ואיהי להם למקדש [מעט]

[בארצות אשר באו שם] (יח' י"א, ט"ז),3,.. שא[מ] הכת צו את בני ישראל

[ו]יקחו א[ליך]

5 [שמ זית (וי' כ"ד, ב'), היא קבועה מיד ולד]ורות. פרש של טמ מניין, שכ

כת צו את בני ישראל

[וישלחו מ[ן ה]מחנה כל צרוע וכל זב וגו' (במ' ה', ב'), עירות המוקפות

חומה מימות

[יהושע ב]ן נון היו משלחין מצורעין. והיא אחת מעשר קדושות.4 וכשא

[הכת ולא י]טמ[א]ו את מחניהם אש אני שוכן בתוכם (שם, ג'), כל זמן שהיו

בארצם

13 סדר הפסוקים כאן שונה מזה שבגו"ש, עמ' 77.

כאן: וי' ו', ב'; ח', ב'; ו', י"ג; ח', י"ח; ח', ל"א, ל"ו
           6   5   4   3   2   1

גו"ש: וי' ו', ב'; י"ג; ח', ב'; ו', י"ח; ח', ל"א, ל"ו
           6   5   4   3   2   1

בשניהם פסוק א', והוא ח', ב' הוא שלא במקומו. אם נעבירו כאן ממס' 2, ובגו"ש ממס' 3, למספר 4, סדר הפסוקים יהיה ממש כסדרם בתורה. גינצ' מעיר על הפנימה הזאת בסדר, ואין לו טעם' להסבירה. אבל יש טעם לסדר שלנו. בעל מדרשנו מבדיל בין "אהרן ובניו אתו' המדיש ש"אהרן עיקר ובניו טפלין," ובין "אהרן ובניו" או "אל אהרן ואל בניו' סתם בלי "אתו.' 1–2 הן שתי דוגמאות של "אהרן ובניו אתו' כסדרן בתורה; 3–6 הן ארבע דוגמאות של "אהרן ובניו' בלי "אתו' גם כן כסדרן בתורה.

י"ח. מקורות: ספרא, צו. הקבלה: גו"ש שם, עמ' 77 וכו'. כאן המעבר מאגדה להלכה.

1 גינצ' הטיב לסמן בתור מקור ראשי ברייתא דר' ישמעאל בראש ספרא, וגם שאר המקבילות.

2 מכאן והלך הוא פירוש המאמר ששלש הפרשיות הן קבועות מיד ולדורות, ובא ממקור מאוחר.

3 מגילה כ"ט, ע"א – גינצ'. המקורות להדלקת נרות בבתי כנסיות וכו' המסומנים אצל גינצ' אינם ענין לכאן. כאן הנרות בבהכ"נ הם במקום נרות המנורה במקדש; וכל עיקרו של המאמר לא בא אלא לקיים את הכלל שפרשת נירות קבועה לדורות, אפילו לאחר החורבן. אבל במקורות הנזכרים אין זכר לזה, ההדלקה באה שם לרוב להאיר מקומות אפלים. מה שנזכר כאן הוא מנהג שנזכר לגנאי אצל הקראים, ביחוד אצל דניאל אל־קומסי (עי' מאן טקסטס אנד סטדיעס, ח"ב, עמ' 50–51), מפני שראו בו חילול המקדש. ועי' גינצברג, הע' 8.

4 משנה כלים א', ו' – גינצ'.

מספרי. ואתה מוצא[9] שמתחלת הספר ועד הנה לא [נצטווה אהרן]

[ב]קרבנות, אילא כֹת והקריבו בני אהרן (וי' א', ה'), ונתנו [בני אהרן (שם,

ז'), וזרקו]

15 [בנ]י אהרן (שם, י"א), ואהרן ניתר [חק]. מה עשה משה, ב[קש רחמים מלפני]

הקֹבֹה, אֹמֹ לֹפֹ: ר' שֹׁלֹעֹ ב[ואר] שנו [אה ומימיה חביבים ויפים ומתוקים],

[לעצים שלגֹפֹן נֹח]לק להם [כבוד שאינן ניגשין על גבי מערכה, למה, בשביל]

(סוף העמוד שם, ב', ע"ב)

[לנסך מהם][10] יין לנסך, לעצים [של זי]ת נחלק [להם כבוד שאינן ניגשין]

[על גבי מ]ער[כה, ולמה, בשביל שמן להדליק, כי ד]ותנן כל העצים[

20 [כש]ירין למערכה חוץ משל זית ושלגֹפֹן, [ואבל באילן רגילים]

במרביות שלֹתֹא [נֹ]ה [ו]שלֹאֹגֹוֹזֹים ושלֹעֹץ ושל[11 ש]מֹן, לאֹהֹרן אי אתה[

חלק לו כבוד [ב]שביל בניו, לבניו אתה מקרבן ול[ו] אתה מרחק. אֹל הֹקֹבֹה[:]

חייך שבשבילך אני מקרבו, מניין שבשביל מ[שה מחל לו, שכך הוא]

[אומ ובאהֹ]רן התאנף י"י מאֹד להֹשֹ ואתפלל גם בעד אהרן [בעת ההיא]

(דֹב' ט', כ'),

25 ואומֹ וישמע י"י אלי גם בפעם ההיא ולא אבה י"י השחית[ך (שם, י', י'). לכך]

[אמר]

הכֹתֹ ועל כל פשעים תכסה אהבה (מֹשֹׁ י', י"ב), באהבתו של משה כסה

הקֹבֹה [על]

חטא אהרן. ובפרשה ראשונה היקדים בנים לאֹב, ובפרש[ה זו חזר והיקדים]

אֹב לבנים,[12] שֹכֹ כֹתֹ צו את אהֹרן ואת בניו אֹתֹו (וי' ו', ב'),

קח את אהרן [ואת בניו אתו] (שם, ח', ב').

[ז]ה קרבן אהרן ובניו (שם, ו', י"ג), דבר אל אהרן ואל בניו (שם, י"ח), ויאמר

מֹשֹׁ אל א[הרן ואל בניו] (שם, ח', ל"א),

---

9 מכאן והילך בעל מדרשנו, בהתאם כמעט גמור לנֹזֹשֹ, חוזר למקור ראשון, וֹיֹר ז', 8
בסוף, ואין לנו אלא להראות מקום להערתו האחרונה של גינצברנ בנֹזֹשֹ, עמ' 75.

10 משנה תמיד ב', ג' בשינויים – גינצברנ. ההשלמות כמעט כולן עֹפֹי נֹזֹשֹ.

11 כן הוא בתעתיק. בכתהֹ"י האות האמצעית מטושטשת, ספק ש ספק כ. יש לנו כאן
ערבוב שתי נוסחאות: א, וֹשלֹעֹץ שמן' (משנה תמיד'); ב, וֹשל שמן' (נֹזֹשֹ). הסופר התחיל
בֹ.אֹ וגמר בֹ.בֹ.

12 פרפראזה של וֹיֹר שם: ולא עוד אלא שאני עושה אותו עיקר ובניו טפילין.

דף י"ז ע"א (2 Box C, סי' 178, ט', ע"ב)

[בצרעת,³ שכך] כת' וירא משה את העם כי פרוע הוא (שמ' ל"ב, כ"ה), למה
כי פרוע, [אין]

[פרוע אילא] צרעת, מנ', שכ' כת' והצרוע אשר בו הנגע וגו' (וי' י"ג, מ"ה),
[נאמר כן]

[פרוע] ונאמר להלן פרוע, מה פרוע האומר להלן [צרעת, אף פרוע האמור]

[כן צר]עת.⁴ ומהן בחרב, שכ' כת' כה אמר י"י שימו [איש חרבו על ירכו וגו']
(שמ' ל"ב, כ"ז),

5 היכן אמר להרוג איש את חברו, רמז רמז לו בסיני, ש[כ' כת' זבח לאלהים]
יוחרם (שם, כ"ב, י"ט),⁵ כיון שירד ומצא אותם שהשתחוו לעבודה זרה וזבחו
לו [אמר: אילו]

חיבין הריגה, מיד ויפל מן העם ביום ההוא כשלשת אלפי איש (שם, ל"ב, כ"ח).
ומ[הן במגפה],

שכך כת' ויגף י"י את העם על אש א' הע' אש' עשה אה[רן] (שם, ל"ה).
[כיון (ששמע) שידע]

[משה] שניכשלו ישראל מכשול גדול,⁶ עמד ובקש רחמים על [יהם],

10 שכך כת' אנא חטא העם הזה חטאה גדולה, ועתה אם [תשא חטאתם]
וגו' (שם, ל"א, ל"ב).⁷ השיבו: מי אשר חטא לי אמחנו מספרי (שם, ל"ג), היה
ראוי לומר [מי אשר]

חטאו לי, מיד⁸ קפחו על ראש אהרן לומר לו: [אהרן א[שר חטא לי אמחנו]

---

3 אינו בוי"ר, אבל ישנו במה"ג כאן (עמ' 113). המהדיר ראבינאוויץ הטיב להראות מקום
ליומא ס"ו, ע"ב: „שאלה אשה חכמה את ר' אליעזר, מאחר שמעשה העגל שוין מפני מה אי ן
מיתתן שוה," ופיריש": „... שהיו בו שלש מיתות, מיתת סייף ... מית ת
מנפה, ... מיתת הדרוקן." הרי זה כמו מדרשנו, אלא שבמקום „צרעת' יש „הדרוקן."
4 תנ' מצורע, ד' (ח"ב ג') – נינצ' עמ' 75, 11.
5 נינצ' (עמ' 75, 16) הטיב לציין מכילתא יב', י"ב, ילקוט ורש"י. ויש להוסיף תיב"ע
המתרגם שמ' ל"ב, כ"ז: „כדנן אמר י"י אלהא דישראל כל מאן דדבח לטעוות עממיא יתקטל
בסייפא." וזהו ממש תרגומו של הפסוק „זבח לאלהים יחרם' אצל יב"ע. ועי' פי' הרמב"ן על
התורה שדחה פירוש מדרשנו.
6 ההשלמה עפ"י גז"ש, עמ' 75, שו' 18–17. שם נוסף: „עשה בהם דין לפי יכלו ואח"כ עמד
ובקש רחמים ... ." ההוספה באה להסיר סתירה מדומה בין המדרש הבא האומר שמשה ביקש
רחמים על ישראל ובין האמור מקודם, שהביא עליהם ד י נ י ן היינו מכות.
7 הפיסקה הזאת מורחבת בגז"ש על ידי כך שבפיו של משה מושמה תפילה המתחילה
„רבונו שלעולם וכו' ." יש בה סימנים קלושים של תפילות של ימי הבינים. השווה גינצברג בגז"ש,
עמ' 75.
8 נראה שצ"ל: „מ ל מ ד שקפחו ... ." וכן הוא במה"ג, עמ' 113: „מלמד שהיה הקב"ה
קופח על ראשו של אהרן ... ." עפ"י קטענו תיקן המחבר בטופס גז"ש שלו את השורה שלפני
האחרונה בעמ' 75: „חט[או לין קפחו על ראש אה[רן] אומר לו ... ."

[עליו.18 בזמן שהיה בי]ת המקדש קיים. כשאדם מביא את חט[אתו או אשמו]
[והיה סומ]ך ידו עליו [ומתוד]ה, הקב״ה מתרצה לו, אבל עכשו [ו]ידוי הפה
מכ (פר) מני[ן]

[שסל]יחה שלא׳ ‹צע[ק]ה שלו› קרבנו, ווידויו כפרתו, שכך כת על ידי
נביא: קחו עמכם דברים

[וש]ובו אל י״י אמרו אליו בל תשא עון וקח טוב ונשלמה פרים שפתינו (הו׳
י״ד, ג׳),

[לפרשת צו]

25 י[ן].   צו את אהרן ואת בניו (וי׳ ו׳, ב׳). כת שנאה תעורר
מדנים וגו׳ (מש׳ י׳, י״ב), ועל כל פשעי[ם תכסה אהבה], אמרו
[חכמי]ם שנאה מה היא, זו שנאה שנתן אהרן בין ישראל לאביהם
[שב]שמים הין במעשה עגל, ולא לכך היתה כוונתו.1 תעורר מדנים, ש[ה]
[שהע]רה עליהם דיוונין ודיווני דיוונין,2 למה, שהזכה בהן שלש מיתות,
[ואילו] הן שלש מיתות: מהן בצרעת, ומהן בחרב, ומהן במגפה, ומהן

18 ההשלמה עפ״י נז״ש שם, שו׳ 21–18. זה אחד המקומות שמהדורתנו מתרחקת מזו של
נז״ש במידה גדושה. גינצ׳ הראה מקום לספרא. ואם בנז״ש נתקצר הספרא, כמו שהעיר גינצ׳,
הניסוח שלנו הוא קיצור מן הקיצור. ואפשר שיש כאן דילוג מתוך הבלעה בין ״בזמן״
הראשון ו״בזמן״ השני בנז״ש, שו׳ 19. נטייתו של בעל מדרשנו ל״ממש״, והתרחקותו מן
המופשט, משתקפת בזה שתמורת ״חטא שחייבין עליו מיתה״ הוא נותן דוגמה קונקרטית,
״רוצח.״

19 ההשלמה מפוקפקת, והייתי מציע: [ו]ידוי הפה מכ[פר]/ [שצע]ק[ה שלו
ק]רבנו ווידויו כפרתו.... לפי זה יש לתקן גם את הטכסט בנז״ש שם, עמ׳ 74, ו׳, 3–2:
״לו אבל עכשיו [נ]חש[ב לו וידוי הפ]ה ‹כך נתקן ע״י המחבר בגליון טופס נז״ש
שלו› כקרבן [שצעקה]/ לאדם קרבנו ווידויו ‹תיקון המחבר כנ״ל›....״

על המקבילות, השווה גינצ׳ בהע׳ 3 שם. אולם רובן מוסבות על הקריאה בפרשת קרבנות
ומיעוטן על תפילה, אבל לא על וידוי פה. המקור הקרוב ביותר
למדרשנו הוא יומא פ״ו, ע״ב: אמר ר׳ יצחק אמרי במערבא... הקב״ה אדם עובר עבירה
בסתר מתפייס ממנו בדברים שנ׳ קחו עמכם דברים ״וגו׳ ונשלמה פרים שפתינו.״ ומכיון שעוסקים שם בתלמוד בעיקר
בעניין וידוי, מסתבר ש״מתפייס ממנו בדברים,״ רו״ל ״וידוי פה.״

י״ז. מקורות: וי״ר ז׳; מדרש הגדול; הקבלתו – נז״ש שם, עמ׳ 74, ו׳, שו׳ 4 וכו׳.

1 המשפט הזה אינו בוי״ר ולא במה״ג, ואף לא בנז״ש. מפסיק הוא את העניין, ובא ללמד
סנגורייה על אהרן. מעניין לראות שגם בוי״ר נסמך למאמרנו מאמר ר׳ אסי המלמד זכות על
אהרן: ״שהיה אהרן נוטל קורנוס... ואומר להם, דעו שאין בו ממש.״

2 ע״כ בוי״ר ז׳, א׳ (גינצ׳). במקבילות ״דיני דינין,״ דין במובן עונש. אולם בעל מדרשנו
סומכו לשורש ״דוה,״ ומזה דויון או דיוון (עי׳ בן־יהודה, מלון ח״ב, עמ׳ 923), שפירושו צ ר ה
או מ כ ה.

15 [שיהא זכר ולא] טומטום ואנדרוגנס.12 ת מ [ים   (שם), למה, ש]לא יהא
בו מום כל עיקר.]13.

(סוף העמוד ב– 2 C Box, סי' 178, ד', ע"א)

[אל פתח אהל מועד]   (שם), [מל]מד שהוא מיטפל בו ו[מבי]או
אל פתח אהל מו[עד].14.

[יקריב אתו ל]רצנו לפני י'י   (שם), [בצפ]ון,15 למה בצפון,
מלמד [שהעולה נשחטת בצפון]

[אבל שלמים יהיו בדרום(!).16. וסמך ידו, למה ידו, ול[א יד בנו,
שיהא]

[כל אחד ואחד]17 סמך על קרבנו. ונרצה לו   (שם), מ[ל שהק]בה רוצ[ה
לכפר]

20 [עליו (על האדם) בז]מן שהוא חוטא, אבל רו[צח ש]מביא קרבן אינ[ו] מתרצה
[לכפר]

המטרה. מדרשנו בא להגביל את המושג „שנים", ולומר רק „שני שותפים" מתנדבים בקרבן עולה
אחד, אבל לא שנים שאינם שותפים, וזה יוצא מן „עולה קרבנו," ולא „קרבנם." מובן שעל ידי
זה הראייה הראשונה של גינצ' שלפנינו מדרש דבי ר' ישמעאל מוטלת בספק.

12 ההשלמה עפ"י נז"ש שם, ואני מפקפק בדבר, והייתי מציע להשלים: [מן הבקר זכר,
ולא] טמטום . . . השווה מדרש הגדול במקום זה. וגם בנז"ש נראה שהמלה „שיהא" שיגרת העט
היא. בעל מדרשנו, הרודף אחר הפשט, העביר את הדרשה הזאת ממכילתא דפיסחא ד' לכאן,
ואין מן הצורך לומר שמצא אותה בתורת כהנים מבית מדרשו של ר' ישמעאל.

13 ההשלמה עפ"י נז"ש שם. אין מקביל לו לספרא, וגינצ' מייחס זה לבית מדרשו של ר'
ישמעאל (עי' פתיחתו, עמ' 67). ואני מסופק אם יש לפנינו כאן מ ד ר ש ת נ א י ם ו ל א
פ י ר ו ש מ פ ר ש. וגם רש"י וגם הראב"ע מפרשים: „תמים, בלא מום." כלום זה מוכיח
שהשתמשו בתורת כהנים של ר' ישמעאל?

14 ספרא שם (גינצ').

15 גינצ' מעיר „בספרא על פסוק זה הביאו הפסוק צפונה לפני ה' א', י"א לראייה
ש ל פ נ י ה' ה ו א צ פ ו ן." ואגב רהיטא כתב זאת, כי המעיין בספרא יראה ברור
שהספרא מפרש „לפני ה'" בית המקדש, להוציא במה, וכן גם צ פ ו נ ה ל פ נ י ה',
רוצה שרק בבית המקדש – לפני ה' – נוהג דין שחיטת צפון אבל לא בבמה. לפני ה', וסמך
ידו, ואין סמיכה בבמה. צפונה לפני ה', ואין צפונה בבמה. גם כאן קשה להכריע אם מדרש
תנאים לפנינו מבית מדרשו של ר' ישמעאל, או פירוש מפרש הרודף אחרי הפשט.

16 קרי: בדרום. – גז"ש שם, ש' 17. גינצ' מראה מקום לספרא ג', ב' וזבחים נ"ה, א'. ונראה
שבעל מדרשנו מתכוון לא לבד להלכה, כי אם גם להבדיל בין המשמעות של „לפני ה'," האמור
כאן בעולה ו„לפני ה'" האמור בשלמים (וי' ג', א'). כאן, מכיון שנאמר לאחר „פתח אהל
מועד", „לפני ה'," רו"ל יותר פנימה, בצפון; אבל בשלמים „לפני ה'" הוא תיכף כשמגיע
ל„פתח אהל מועד," כלו' בדרום.

17 ההשלמה עפ"י נז"ש שם, שו' 17–18=ספרא שם, פרק ד', ב'. דברי גינצ' בפתיחתו, עמ'
68 שדברי בעל מדרשנו מתאימים למכילתא שמ' כ"א, ו': „אדוניו . . . ולא שלוחו," יהיה מי
שיהיה, זרים בעיני. כי מכיון שבעל מדרשנו כותב: „ולא יד בנו," ממש כמו שמתחיל
הספרא, מסתבר שלקח מן הספרא, אלא שקיצרו. מצד אחר, ההוספה „שיהיה כל אחד ואחד
סומך על קרבנו," הרחבת ביאור של המלקט כדרכו.

(וֹאֶעְפֹּי)]שהם בני מקבלי ברית, תל׳ לו׳ אדם כי] יקריב מכם, עכשו כל
שהוא מכם,7 אבל משומדים

]כתו[ב בהם זבח רשעים תועבה (מש׳ כ״א, כ״ז). קרבן לי׳׳י (וי׳
א׳, ב׳), למה, שתהיה הקדשתו קודמת

]להקרבתו[, שלא יהיה אדם יאמר לי׳י עולה, קרְבָּן,8 לי׳י מנחה, לי׳י
שלמים,]אילא[

10]קרבן לי׳י.9 מן הבה[מה (שם),10 למה, להביא מן שלשה מינים.
אילו הן שלשה מי]נים[

]שור, שה כבשים] ושה עזים (דב׳ י״ד, י״ד). אילו נאמר מן הבהמה מקריב
את קרבן ו]לא נאמר[

]מן הבקר ומן הצאן[(וי׳, שם), הייתי אומר להכליל עימה את
איל וצבי ויחמור (דב׳ י״ד, ה׳). כיון ש]נא[

]מן הבקר ומן ה]צון, יצאו איל וצבי מן הכתוב.10 תקריבו (וי׳, שם),
מלמ]ד[שהי באה נדבת]קרבן[

]שני שותפים] מתנדבים בעלה, שנים אין מת]נדבים בעולה.11 אם עלה
קרבנו (שם, ג׳), מלמד]

---

7 השווה ספרא שם: „ת״ל מכם ועכשו, הא אל תאמר אלא מה ישראל מקבלי ברית
וכו׳.״ בעל מדרשנו מוסר את המלה „ועכשו״ בהרחבת ביאור: „עכשו כל שהוא מכם.״ כל
ההוצאות וכל המפרשים מחברים „ועכשו״ עם הבא אחריו (ועכשו הא אל תאמר) ולא עם
„מכם״ שלפניו.

8 נקוד על „קרבן״ לסימן מחיקה.

9 השווה ספרא שם, ד׳: „שיקדים הקדשו להקרבתה, דברי ר׳ יהודה, אמר ר״ש מנין שלא
יאמר אדם לה׳ עולה וכו׳.״ בעל מדרשנו לא ראה מחלוקת בין ר״י ור״ש (עי׳ הערת וייס),
ואפשר שצריך לקרוא כאן: „וש לא יהיה אדם אומר . . .״.

10 על יסוד קטענו השלים המחבר חמש השורות הראשונות של קטע אדלר, גז׳׳ש, א׳, 72,
באופן זה:

1 . . . . בשלשת המ]נים[

ואילו הן]שור ש]ה[כב]שים ושה עזים אילו נאמר[מן הבהמה
]יקר[יבו את]קרבנם ולא נאמ׳ מן הבקר ומן ה]צאן היינו אומרין
]בא[הכת׳ להכליל עמה את]איל צבי ויחמור[ושאר]שבעת[
]המ[ינים הטהורים]כיון שנאמר מן הבקר[ומן הצאן
5 יצאו שבעת המינים מן הכ]תוב[איל וצבי וג׳ . . .

נינצ׳ כבר הראה על המקבילות „בספרא א׳, ב׳ ובזבחים ל״ד, א׳,״ ועל שנוי הלשון
ונוטה לחשוב שמקור בלתי ידוע לנו לפנינו. אבל אינו מוכרח. קרוב לשער שאין לנו אלא
ניסוח חפשי, בהרחבת ביאור, של אחד המקורות הנזכרים, וביחוד של המקור השני: „איל ו
ואמר קרבן לה׳ בהמה הייתי אומר חיה בכלל בהמה כעניין שנ׳ זאת
הבהמה איל וצבי וכו׳.״

11 ההשלמה עפ״י גז׳׳ש שם, שורה אחרונה מעמ׳ 72 ושורה ראשונה מעמ׳ 73. על יסוד
הספרא הנז׳, משלים נינצ׳ את הסוף: „שנים אין מתנדבים ב]מנחה שנ׳] אם עולה קרבנו,״
ומתקשה „איך נוצא מן עולה קרבנו שאין מנחה באה בשותפות.״ אבל באמת מחברנו קלע אל

היה נפסק,5 וכל כך למה,6 גניי הוא למלך להיות חיילותיו שומעים ד[בריו]
אילא מפי שליח, אם כן לבשר ודם, למלך מלכי המלכים על אח[ת כמה]
30 וכמה.6 לא מ ר, לישראל כל צורכיהן,7 שכך כת̇ ויצא ודבר אל בני
ישראל] (שמ' ל״ד, ל״ד).

דף ט', ע״ב (Box C 1), סי' 45, ד', ע״ב)

[דבר אל בני ישראל] (וי' א', ב'). על הקורבנות. <א ד ם? שמב[יא>...
.. .. .. שכך כת̇ וסמך ידו על וג' (שם, ד'). ו א מ ר ת א ל ה ם,
....
.. .. שי[הא בן שני.2 א ד ם כ י י ק ר י ב (שם), לרבות את
הגירים.3 [מכם],
[להוציא את המשומדים. ומה רא]ית לומר כין, אילא4 אדם לרבות את
הגירים,5 מיכם
5 [להוציא את הגירים, אחר] שריבה הכת̇ מיעט, תלמ̇ ב נ י י ש ר א ל, מה
ישראל [מקבלי]
[ברית, אף הגיר]ים מקבלי ברית, יצאו משומדים שהיו מקבלי ברית ו(הפרו
ברית〉 [ויצאו מן הכלל.6 יכול מפני]

---

5 ספרא שם; במ״ר שם, כ״א.
6 המאמר הזה אינו בספרא ואף לא בבמ״ר, אבל נמצא במדרש הגדול ויקרא, עמ' 6. מי
זקוק למי? המהדיר של מה״ג מציין: „ספרא ובמ״ר.‟ אבל לשוא נבקשנו שם.
7 ניסוח תמציתי של דרשת ר' אלעזר בן אחווי בספרא שם: „יכול היה מדבר עמו לצורך
עצמו, ת״ל לאמר לישראל, בשביל ישראל היה מדבר עמו לא בשביל עצמו.‟ בעל מדרשנו
הרגיש, כנראה, ש„לאמר‟ אינה אלא „אסמכתא‟, ולפיכך הוסיף פסוק אחר שאינו מוציאו מידי
פשוטו.

ט״ז. מקורות: ספרא ויקרא;
1 מכיון שבעל מדרשנו מוסר לנו בפיסקא זו, כמו שנראה להלן, תמצית דברי ספרא
ויקרא, פרש' ב', ושם אנו קוראים: „בני ישראל סומכין ואין בנות ישראל סומכות . . . יכול
לא יסמכו על העולות . . . אבל יסמכו על השלמים . . . ת״ל ו א מ ר ת א ל י ה ם,
לרבות כל האמור בעניין.‟ אני משער שזה היה כלול בשתי השורות הראשונות,
אעפ״י שאינני יודע להשלים את החסר.
2 לא מצאתי הקבלתו בספרא, ואינני יודע משמעותו.
3 ספרא שם, פרשה ב', ג'.
4 א י ל א – או אינו אלא. ואולי היה כתוב „או לא‟ – או אינו, והמעתיק טעה וכתב
„אילא.‟
5 לכאורה שינרת העט היא, וצ״ל: „משומדים,‟ כמו שהוא בספרא,‟ כמו אמור אדם לרבות
ה מ ש ו מ ד י ם, מכם להוציא את הגרים.‟ אבל באמת אפשר לקיים את גירסתנו, וכוונתו של
המדרש היא שאולי „אדם‟ ו„מכם‟ אינם אלא מעין „כלל ופרט.‟ אדם כולל (ריבה) גם את
הגרים ובא „מכם‟ להוציאם מן הכלל, וזהו: „אחר שריבה מיעט.‟ ואולי יש לראות בזה שמבית
מדרשו של ר' ישמעאל יצא מדרשנו.
6 השווה ספרא, שם: „יצאו המשומדים שאינן מקבלי ברית ש ה ר י ה פ ר ו ב ר י ת.‟
ועפ״י זה הייתי נוטה להשלים: „והרי הפרו ברית],‟ במקום „ויצאו מן הכלל]‟ שבתעתיק.

...... ⟨פה א⟩ל פ⟨ה⟩ דיבר אתו, ו⟨על⟩ כל דיבור ודיבור ....

.... אבינו אברהם מלאך דיבר עימו, אבל זה ⟨זכה שהקב״ה דיבר עימו⟩,

טו].

20 ⟨שכך כת פה⟩ אל פה אדבר בו ⟨במ' י״ב, ח'⟩.⁹ מ א ה ל מ ו ע ד ל א מ ר, ⟨יכול מכל הבית⟩,

⟨תלמוד לומר⟩ ודברתי את⟨ך מע⟩ל הכפורת ⟨שמ' כ״ה, כ״ב⟩, אי מעל ה⟨כפורת, יכול מעל⟩

⟨הכפ⟩ כולה, תל לו⟨ ⟩ מבין שני הכרובים ⟨שם⟩,¹ בשעה שהיתה ⟨השכינה מדברת עם⟩

⟨משה⟩ היתה הרו⟨ח נכנ⟩סת בכרובים ומרפרפים בכנ⟨פיהם⟩, והקול ⟨יוצא⟩

עד החצר החיצונה, שכך כת וקול כנפי כרובים עד חצר חיצונה ⟨יח' י', ה'⟩,² ⟨יכול⟩

25 שהיה קול נמך,³ מצינו כל מקום שנאמרה(!) בו קול קול מפי הגבו⟨רה יצא⟩,⁴ שכ כת קול יי על המים אל הכבוד הרעים יי על מים ⟨רבים, קול יי⟩ בכח וג ⟨תה' כ״ט, ג'–ד'⟩,

אם כן למה נאמר עד חצר החיצונה, כיון שהיה מגיע עד חצר ⟨חיצונה⟩

---

9 השרידים של שתי השורות האחרונות בעמוד זה ושל ארבע שורות בראש העמוד הבא הם מעטים וקלושים, וכל נסיון של השלמה הוא לשוא. ובכל זאת ברור למדי שנושא המדרש היא ההשוואה בין „ויקרא אל משה‟ ובין „ויקרא מלאך ה' אל אברהם.‟ ההשוואה הזאת היא גם הנושא של וי״ר א', ט': „ויקרא אל משה, ולא כאברהם, באברהם כתיב ויקרא מלאך ה' אל אברהם ... , המלאך קורא והדיבור מדבר, ברם הכא אמר ר' אבין אמר הקב״ה אני הוא הקורא ואני הוא המדבר.‟ ההדגשה היא איפוא על יתרונו של משה על אברהם. מצד אחר אנו קוראים במ״א: „כיון שראה הקב״ה שהוא (משה) עומד בחוץ, אמר קראו לו ויכנס, כדרך שנא' לאברהם ויקרא אליו מלאך ה'.‟ כאן ההדגשה על הדמיון שביניהם. בעל מדרשנו, כנראה, מרכיב שני המדרשים אעפ״י שנראים מכחישים זה את זה.

טו. מקורות: ספרא ויקרא.

1 ספרא שם, פרק ב', י״ב בשם ר״ע.

2 זה אחד הנסיונות של הסברה „טבעית‟ איך ה' דיבר מבין הכרובים. כבר בספרי נשא, פיס' נ״ח, אנו קוראים: „מגיד הכתוב שהיה משה נכנס ועומד באהל מועד והקול יורד משמי שמים לבין שני הכרובים והוא שומע את הקול מדבר אליו מבין הכרובים.‟ הסברה יתרה אנו מוצאים בבמ״ר י״ד, י״ט: „מלמד שהיה נכנס משה ועומד באהל מועד וקול יורד מן השמים כ מ י ן ס י ל ו ן ש ל א ש לבין הכרובים וכו'.‟ בעל מדרשנו עושה צעד אחד לפנים בהסברה טבעית. הקול אינו יורד מן השמים, כי אם מתהווה מתנועת כנפי הכרובים על ידי הרוח שנכנס ביניהם. ההסברה הזאת מיוסדת על הפסוק ביח' י', ה' הנדרש בספרא שם: „כיוצא בדבר אתה אומר וקול כנפי ... .‟

3 ספרא שם.

4 בכל המקורות: „ת״ל וישמע את הקול ... ומה ת״ל הקול, הקול המתפרש בכתובים ... קול ה' בכח ... .‟ דברי בעל מדרשנו בלתי מובנים. ואולי מתוך אי הבנת הפיס' „ה ק ו ל ה ק ו ל ו כ ו' ‟ בא לידי טעות זו: „כל מקום שנאמרה בו קול קול.‟

[ש]לא נקרא ירד (שם), אילא שירדה שכינה בימיו ממעל [ה3. ......

5 [אי]מתי היה הדבר, בשעה שהעמיד את המשכן.4 כיון ....

[כמו ש]הראהו בחרב, שכך כת' ויאמר כי אהיה עימך [וזה] לך [האות (שמ'
ג', י"ב), זה]

משכן וכל כליו, שכך מצינו שלא עבדו ישראל א[ת י"י עד שהקימו]
את המש'.5 כל דבר ודבר שחיבין בו היה חקוק עליו שם המפו[רש]. ושמונה
עש[פעמ' נזכר]

מתחלת הפרשה ועד סופה,6 שכך כת' כאשר ציוה י"י את מש[ה3. ......

10 .... ה; כ[ן הקב]ה] שכינתו במשכן מעט משה מעט את [עצמו7

[וע]מד לו מן הצד.8 כיון שהביט הקב]ה בכל הכלים שחקק [עליהם שמו,
אמר]

[כל הכ]בוד זה עשה משה, ואני מבפנים והוא מבחוץ, קראו ל[ו ש]יכנס
[אצלו מיד יצא],

[קול] וקרא לו למשה, שכ' כת' ויקרא אל משה וי[דב]ר [יי'
אליו מאהל מועד לאמר [וי' א', א'].

[ויקרא אל משה, ו]ל[ואברהם] ל[א קרא], שכך כת' ויקרא מלאך [יי' אל
אברהם]

15 .... של אברה[ם מ]לאך9. ....

(סוף העמוד ב־2 Box C, סי' 178, ד', ע"ב)

.........הרי או. ....
.... הקב]ה דיבר עימו ויק[ר]א אל משה [וידבר א]לי[ו..........

---

3 השווה וי"ר שם: ד"א ירד, שהוריד את השכינה מלמעלה למטה.' וכאן אני נוטה להשלים:
שירדה . . . ממעלה [על הארץ].'
4 השווה שהש"ר ה', א': ,ואימתי שרת' שכינה עליה (על הארץ), ביום שהוקם המשכן.'
5 הכנסתי את הפיס' בסוגריים, כי לדעתי הרכיב המלקט מדרש אחר כדי להראות
שהשכינה ירדה על הארץ עם הקמת המשכן. המדרש הזה מבאר את הכתוב ,כי אהיה עמך,'
,עמך' – בארץ, מתי? ,בהוציאך העם ממצרים תעבדון את האלהים,' כלו' כשתצאו ממצרים
ותקימו משכן להקריב שם קרבנות (עבודה – קרבנות). ועל פי זה הייתי מציע להשלים: כיון
[שיצאו ממצ' הקים המשכן]/ [ש]הראהו בחרב שכך כת' ויאמר כי אהיה עמך [וזה] לך
[האות וג', זה]/ משכן וכל כליו, שכך מצינו שלא עבדו ישראל א[ת יי' עד שהקימו]/ את
המש'.' מקור המדרש הזה נעלם ממני, אבל רמז לדבר אפשר למצוא בדברי ר' יהושע בן לוי:
,בזכות המשכן שעתידין לעשות ,יצאו ישראל ממצרים)' (מדרש תהילים קי"ד, ה'). ועי' ב"ר
ט"ז, ה': ,אלו הקרבנות שנ' תעבדון את האלהים.'
6 השווה וי"ר א', ז'–ח'. בעל מדרשנו איחד את הנפרדים, כי באמת תחילת ח' אינו אלא
המשכו של ז'.
7 – מיעט משה את עצמו – הקטין את עצמו, על דרך המאמר: ,לכי ומיעטי עצמך'
(חולין ס', ע"ב).
8 הפרט הזה לקוח ממדרש אחר בוי"ר א', ה': ,באהל מועד עמד לו מן הצד.' ועי' תנ'
וי' ג' (ת"ב, ד').

.... בימות הג[שמים, איל]א. ....

.. .. בימות הגשמים, למ[ה, מ]פני שבזכותן [נ]ברא

[לכך נאמר] זית רענן יפה פרי תואר קרא י"י שמ[ך לקול המולה] 5

[גדולה ה]צית אש עליה ורעו דליותיו (יר' י"א, ט"ז).4 שלשה ש[מנים]

[נעשו מ]שלשה זיתים,5 והן שלשה שלשה ש[מנים. הזית הראשון]

[מגרגרו בראש] הזית, וכותש ונותן לתוך [הסל. הזית השני מגרגר]

[בראש הגג וכותש ונותן לתוך הסל. הזית השלישי עוטנו]

(סוף העמוד חסר, וישנו ליקוי בין דף זה ושלאחריו)

דף ט', ע"א (Box C 1), מס' 45, ד', ע"א)

[לפרשת ויקרא]

יד].

.... סל[ח נא לעון העם הזה וג (במ' י"ד, י"ט), ויאמר [י"י סלחתי

כדבריך]1 (שם, כ').

[בני בתיה ב]ת פר[עה] (דה"א, ד', י"ח), וכי בן בתיה היה, והלא בן יוכבד

ה[ויה, ולמה נקרא]

[על ש]מה, משום שנצטערה בו ונתגדל על ידיה, לכך].2 ....

שלכולם שמשה דוגמא המשנה הראשונה מפ"ב דשבת: „וחכמים מתירים ב כ ל השמנים, בשמן
שומשמין, בשמן אגוזים, בשמן צנונות, בשמן דגים, בשמן פקועות." בעל מדרשנו מצטט איפוא
תחילת המשנה „כל השמנים", ואח"כ דוגמא משותפת לכל המקורות, שמן אגוזים, וחותם בדוגמה
האחרונה, שמן פקועות. התבוננות זו והשוואה עם התנ' מרשה לי להציע השלמתן של שתי
השורות הבאות שמחברנו השאיר חלק. בהתאם לתנ' עלינו לבקש בשורות אלו הטעם למה בחר
בשמן זית. ואני משער שבעל מדרשנו השתמש במאמר ר' יהושע בן לוי (מנחות נ"ג, ע"ב): „למה
נמשלו ישראל לזית, לומר לך מה זית אין עליו נושרין לא בימות החמה ולא בימות הגשמים אף
ישראל אין להם בטלה עולמית." על פי זה אני מנסח את כל המאמר: „זית [ולא בכ]ל
השמנים, ... ולא שמן פקועות. ול[מה, לפי שאין/ [אתה מוצא רענן בימות ה]נשמים אילא
[זית שאין עליו נושרין]/ [לא בימות החמה ולא] בימות הגשמים."

4 הפסוק הזה משמש פתיחה לסדרנו בשמ"ר ל"ו, א', ומובא גם כן בקשר עם מאמר ר'
יהושע בן לוי הנז'.

5 השווה מנחות פ"ח, ד'; תנ' הנז' ושמ"ר הנז'. על יסוד המקור הראשון הייתי מציע
להשלים: שלשה ש[מנים הן]/ [שכ' שנינו] שלשה זיתים והן (– ובהן) שלשה שלשה שמנים ...".

6 ההשלמה על יסוד המשנה הנז'.

י"ד.   מקורות: וי"ר א';

1 כפי שיוצא מהמשך הדרש, נושא מדרשנו הוא הפסוק בדה"י, ד', י"ח, המשמש פתיחה
לסדרנו בוי"ר א', ג'. כל השמות שבפסוק מבוארים על משה. השם האחרון „אבי זנוח" נדרש
שם: „שהזניחן מאותה עבירה (– מעשה העגל)". מסתבר שאף בעל מדרשנו ביאר את השם „אבי
זנוח" באופן זה, ולפיכך מובאים אלה הפסוקים כאן.

2 השווה מגילה י"ג, ע"א: „ילדה, והא רבויי רביתיה, לומר לך שכל המגדל יתום או יתומה
בתוך ביתו מעלה עליו הכתוב כאילו ילדו." וגם כאן יש להשלים: „לכן [מעלין עליה כאילו
ילדתו]." ועי' „מדרש חדש עה"ת," סע" ז', הע' 3.

דף ח', ע"א (Box C 2) מס' 178, ג', ע"ב)

[כי דתנן]¹¹ ש[ל]ש [עש]רה השתחואות היו שם, שלבית רב[ן גמליאל]
ושלבית רבי[ ]חנניה בן א[נ]טניס סגן הכהנים היו מש[תחו]ים [ארבע עשר]
[והיכן היתה י]תירה, [כנג]ד דיר העצים [ששם הארון נגנז. מעשה בכהן]
[אחד שהיה מ]תעסק וראה את הרצפה שהיא משונה [מחבירותיה, בא ואמר]
[לחביריו, לא הספיק ל]גמור אוד [אור ?] עומד עליה ואמר לחבירו¹² [לא
הספיק]
[לגמור את הדבר עד שי]צאה נשמתו, וידעו הכל ששם [הארון נגנז ...
.. ת ש .. ישראל וחרבו בעונם ....
... . שב כת]שב כת] והיה כאשר שקדתי [עליהם לנתוש ולנתוץ]
[ולהרוס ולהאביד ולהרע כן אשקוד עליהם לבנות ולנטוע נאם י"י] יר'
ל"א, כ"ח].

(סוף העמוד חסר.)

דף ח', ע"ב (שם, ג', ע"א)

[לפרשת ואתה תצוה]

יג].

[לא אמר]: דבר ויביאו אליך.¹ ולמה בצווי, שהיא ני².............
מ[ותר בכ]ל השמנים, לא שמן אגוז ולא שמן פקעיות,³ ול[א .....]

---

11 שקלים פ"ו, א'. כדאי לציין שלפני „סגן הכהנים" כתוב בכתה"י: „בן אנטיגנוס," עם
נקודות מלמעלה לסימן מחיקה. גם ר' חנינא בן אנטיגנוס הייה בן זמנו של ר' חנינא
סגן הכהנים. להלן קרוב לסוף הקטע נראה שבעל מדרשנו מוסר פירושו של ר' חנינא בן
אנטיגנוס סתם בלי הזכרת שמו.

12 השלמת המחבר אינה מניחה את הדעת, והמאמר נשאר בלתי מובן, כי אנו מוצאים
פעמים „ואמר לחביריו." לדעתי אנו צריכים לשער שכל מה שהיה בטקסט בין „משונה
מחברותיה" ובין „ואמר לחביריו" הרחבת ביאור של מלקטנו הוא, מהו השינוי שראה ברצפה?
ותשובתו היא שראה עמוד אור עומד עליה. ועפ"י זה מציע להשלים: „ראה
את הרצפה שהיא משונ[ה מחברותיה, ראה את]/ [הרצפה שהיה ע]מוד אור עומד עליה,
ואמר לחביריו, ולא הספיק לגמור]/ [את הדבר עד שי]צאה נשמתו ..." מעין הד של אגדה
זו אפשר למצוא בירושלמי שקלים שם: „תני משום ר' הושעי' הקיש עליה בקורנס ויצא
האור ושרפתו." ובשינוי לשון נמצא זה בבבלי ביומא נ"ד, ע"א בשם „תנא דבי ר'
ישמעאל."

י"נ. מקורות: תנ' ות"ב תצוה; ווי"ר ל"א.

1 בהקבלה להתחלת הפרשה הקודמת: דבר ... ... ויקחו לי ...

2 הייתי מציע להשלים: „שהיא נ[ה]נגת מיד ולדורות]." מתאים ל„קבועות מיד ולדורות"
להלן פרשת צו בניסוח ניגנצברג.

3 השווה תנ' תצוה, ו' (ת"ב, ג'): „למה לא שמן אנוזים וכו'." „שמן אנוזים" נזכר בכל
המקורות, ויש הבדל בשאר מיני שמנים. „שמן פקעיות" מיוחד למדרשנו. מתקבל על הדעת

[כל דבר שנע]שה בטיבות עיין לא שלטה בו עיין[5] ושלא שלט[ה, וכל דבר]
[שלא נעשה ב]טיבות עיין שלטא בו עיין. מקדש שב..............
..............למה, שלא נתב[ן]ה.................

15

(סוף העמוד שם, ה', ע"א. אלא ע"י הקרע חסרות שורות אחדות)

.....עי[ין מלפני וסי[6]... כל נדיב לב מישראל הביאו חח [ונזם וטבעת
וג, כל]

[מה שנדב ל]בו. כיון ששמש שלש מאות וששים ותשע [שנים[7] נבלע באדמה]
[שכ]ך כת ויטש משכן שילה אהל שכן באדם (תה' ע"ח, ס'), אל תקרא
[באדם]

[אילא באדמה], להודיעך משכן וכל כליו באדמה.[8] ואתה אומ לא של[טה
בו]

20 [עיין, והלא] כת ויתן לשבי עזו ותפארתו ביד צר (שם, ס"א), זה ארון, זה
ארון

[הברית[9] שלקחוהו פ]לשתים ולבסוף החזירוהו, שהיכה אותם בטחורים
[וישימו אותו בעגלה עם] עכברי זהב, ושלחו אותו לבית שמש. כיון שבנה
[שלמה]

שמש ארבע מאות ועשר שנים

[את בית המקד]ש היכניס את הארון לתוכו. כש[בא טיטוס הרשע והחריב]
[ונחרב בית המק]דש בעונות ישראל, נבלע ארון[10] ב[קרקע הר הבית].....

---

5 עד כמה שאפשר להציל ולקלוט מן השרידים יש לנו כאן מדרש אשר מקורו נעלם ממני.
בא הוא לתת טעם מדוע נחרבו מקדש ראשון ושני, ואילו המשכן נגנז ולא נחרב, "לא שלטה
בו עין האויב." מעלה יתרה למשכן, הוא משיב, שנבנה "בטיבות עיין." מזבדת לבם של ישראל.
מדרשים ידועים מדברים על "ז' מקדשות עתידין ליחרב, אהל מועד וגלגל ושילה ונוב וגבעון
ובנין ראשון ובנין שני (ת"ב תולדות, ח' ומקבילות)." וגם במדרשנו למעלה (קעה) מובא
המדרש שבנימין בכה על צוארו של יוסף, על משכן שילה שעתיד ליחרב.
כנראה שבמדרשים אלה "נחרב" רוצה לומר רק "הפסקת העבודה," אבל לא על ידי אויב,
עי' ב"ר נ"ד, ד', והע' י"א לרד"ל.

מדרשנו מיוסד על התוספתא סוטה פי"ג, א': "משנבנה בית הראשון נגנז אהל מועד קרשיו
קרסיו ועמודיו ואדניו."

6 הייתי מציע להשלים: מאת כל איש אשר ידבנו לבו [הרי טיבות ע]יין מלפני", ומל [אחו'],
כל נדיב לב... . בעל מדרשנו מדיש שבתחילת עבודת המשכן (שמ' כ"ה, ב') ובסופו (שם
ל"ה, כ"ב) נאמר שבא מנדבת הלב.

7 עפ"י סדר עולם רבה פ"ו נבנה המשכן בשנה הראשונה לצאתם ממצרים, ואם כן שימש
ארבע מאות ושמונים שנה (מ"א ו', א'). אולם בעל מדרשנו "כנראה" חושב רק את הזמן שהיה
המשכן בשילה. עי' זבחים קי"ח, ע"ב: "נשתיירו לשילה שלש מאות ושבעים חסר אחד."

8 השווה תוס' סוטה י"ג, א' "הנז' למעלה בהע' 5. ניסוח האגדה על גניזת המשכן וכליו
דומה מעט לזה שבחזון ברוך א', פ"ו, ו'–ז'. שם המלאך לוקח את כל כלי הקודש אשר למשכן
ומוסר אותם לארץ לשמרם עד אחרית הימים. "ותפתח הארץ את פיה ותבלעם."
9 השווה ב"ר נ"ד, ד'.
10 על גניזת הארון השווה תוס' שקלים פ"ב, 18; יומא נ"ב, ע"ב ומקבילות.

דף ז', ע"ב (2 C Box, סי' 178, י', ע"ב)

[את ישראל, שכך] כת' על ידי יחזקאל וארחצך במים ואשטף [דמיך]

[מעליך ואסכך ב]שמן ואלבישך רקמה ואנעלך תחש ואחבשך [בשש].

[ואכסך משי וג'] (יח' ט"ז, ט', י'.)2. [א]י[לו הן. ואילו הן קישוטין שקישטו ישראל את

[המשכן: ז]הב וכסף ונחשת ותכ וארג ותולע שני וש ע ועור אלים

5 [מאד ועור] תחשים ועצי שטים ואבני שהם ואבני מלואים (שמ' כ"ה, ג'–ח', ז'). אמר משה

[לפני הק]בה: כל זה למה, אמר לו: ועשו לי מקדש ושכנתי בתוכם (שם, ח'). נרתע

[מאחוריו ונפ]ל על פניו, אמר לפניו: רב של (=רבונו שלעולם), כת' בכבודך אם יס[תר]

[איש במסתרים ואני] לא אראנו נאם ייי הלא את השמים ואת האר[ץ]

[אני מלא] נאם ייי (יר' כ"ג, כ"ד), היאך יכולין ישראל לבנות לך בית להשרות שכ

10 [שכינתך] בתוכו. אמ לו הקבה: לא כשאתה סבור אני סבור, כך [אני אומר]

[עשרים קרש]ים לצפון ועשרים לדרום ושמונה במערב, והרי [אני]

[מצמצם את] שכיני בין בדי הארון ואדבר עמך.4 ונועד[תי לך ודב אתך וג] (שמ' כ"ה, כ"ב).

לפני זה), ואינו מתקבל על הדעת שסתם מקרה הוא. אני נוטה לחשוב ש,ג' ב,ה' נתחלפה לו
לבעל מלקטנו, ובמקום ,יג' קרא ,יה' ויצא לו ,חמשה עשר' בשתי המקומות.
2 הנוסח כאן קרוב ביותר לזה שבפ"ר, פיס' ל"ג, הוצ' איש־שלום, קנ"ד, ע"א: א"ר
תנחומא ברבי בשעה שיצאו ישראל ממצרים... וקבלו את התורה באותה
שעה קישטם הקב"ה בשלש עשרה תכשיטים ואלו הם יחזקאל
מפרשם, כמ"ש וארחצך במים וכו'. בעל מדרשנו לא גמר את המניין, וכשהוא
מגיע ל,ואכסך משי" הוא אומר לקורא: צא וחשוב. וקשה איפוא לדעת איך השלים את
המספר ט"ו.
3 על דבר מניין התכשיטים במשכן עי' בובר ב,מדרש אגדה" שם, הע' ג'. בעל מדרשנו
מדלג על שמן ובשמים שבאמת אינם ,תכשיטים", ולשוא אנו מבקשים חמשה עשר קישוטים, כי
אפילו אם נחשוב ,תכלת וארגמן ותולעת שני' לג' ואף גם ,אבני שהם ואבני מלואים" לשנים,
לא נקבל יותר מי"ג. וזה מחזק השערתנו שטעות קריאה יה במקום ,יג' לפנינו.
4 השווה שמ"ר ל"ד, א' בסוף ומקבילות. ניסוחנו דומה לזה שבתנ' כי תשא, י': ,שלשה
דברים שמע משה מפי הגבורה ונבהל ונרת ע לאחוריו, בשעה שאמר לו ועשו לי
מקדש ושכנתי בתוכם אמר רבש"ע הנה הנה השמים ושמי השמים לא יכלכלוך. אמר לו, משה, לא
כשם שאתה סבור אלא עשרים קרש בצפון ועשרים לדרום ושמונה במערב ושמונה במזרח
ואצמצם שכינה שלי ואשכון ביניהם וכתיב ונועדתי לך שם ודברתי." עפ"ז נעשו כל ההשלמות.

[וירושלים], קרבנות, ובית דוד, זקנים, מזבח, עצה, תושיה,[7] וכסף [וזהב,
וארץ]

[ישראל] . . . . . . שה . . . . . . הקב̇ה̇ לא הן [היר] אילא בתרומת המ [שכן] . . . .

15 . . . . ̇ה למד ש̇ . . . . . .

(סוף העמוד שם, ה', ע̇ב. אלא ע̇י הקרע חסרות שורות אחדות)

[זהב (שמ̇ כ̇ה, ג̇), למה, לכ]פר על עבדה זרה,[8] ולהסיר את המלכות
שנמש [לה]

[בזהב. עבדה] זרה, שכך כת̇ ויעשו להם אלהי זהב (שם, ל̇ב, ל̇א). למה
[נמשלה]

[מלכות בבל בזהב], לפי שכתוב בה אנת הוא אישא(!) (מ: ראשה) [די
דהבא] (דנ̇ ב̇, ל̇ח).[9]

[כ ס ף] למה, להסיר את המלכו]ת שנמשלה בכסף, אמלכות מדי [ופרס
שנטלה][10]

20 כסף על ישראל, שכך כת̇ ועשרת אלפים ככר כסף אשקל על ידי [עשי
המלאכה]

[אל גנזי המל (אס̇ ג̇, ט̇). נ ח ש ת למה, להסיר מלכות שנמשלה בנחשת,
[זו מלכות]

[יונים שהיה] מצחן עז כנחשת.[11] ת כ ל ת למה, זו מל אדום[12] . . . .

. . . . ת ו ל ע ת ש נ י, לכפר על עון ישראל, ש.

יב].

[אמר] הקב̇ה בחמשה עשר קישוטין[1] קישטתי או [תן כשהוצאתי אותן ממצרים],

25 [ובחמשה עשר] קישוטין אני מחנך את המשכן. ואילו הן [קישוטין שקישט
בהן הקב̇ה]

---

7 שנים אלה לא מצאתי בשום מקור ידוע לי. ואולי הם השנים שהוסיף המלקט על י̇ג
דברים הנזכרים בבמ̇ר הנז̇ כדי להגיע למספר ט̇ו.

8 הטעם הזה ש„זהב בא לכפר על עגל הזהב̇ כאילו שונה מוטיב רווח מעין „יבא עגל
ויכפר על מעשה עגל.̇ ובכל זאת לא מצאתי במקורות ידועים לי, וכנראה שהוספת המלקט
היא. אגב, „ע ב ד ה ז ר ה ̇ היא לדעתי טעות המעתיק. במקור היה כתוב ע̇ז, כלומר
„עגל זהב.̇

9 השווה ת̇ב תרומה, ו̇ ומקבילות אצל בובר.

10 השלמת המחבר. יותר טוב „ששקלה.̇

11 שאר המקורות: „שהיא פחותה מכולם.̇

12 שאר המקורות מוצאים רמז למלכות א ד ו ם ב„עורות אלים מ א ד מ י ם.̇ ואיני
יודע באיזה אופן אפשר למצוא ב„תכלת̇ רמז למלכות אדום. ואני משער שצריך להיות:
„תכלת ו א ר ג מ ן, זו מלכות אדום,̇ כי הארגמן, הפורפירא, היא לבוש מלכות של קיסר
רומי (עי̇ ש. קרויס, פרס ורומי בתלמוד . . . . , תש̇ח, עמ̇ 43).

י̇ב. מקורות: ת̇ב תרומה; שמו̇ר ל̇ד.

1 השווה ת̇ב תרומה, ד̇; מ̇א, ח̇א, עמ̇ 166. מקבילות שם הע̇ ב̇. מעניין לראות שעוד
הפעם למספר „חמשה עשר̇ כאן מקביל בשאר המקורות המספר „שלשה עשר̇ (עי̇ הע̇ 6

דף ז', ע"א (2 Box C, סי' 178, י', ע"א)

[לפרשת תרומה]

[לר]בות את קרבני לחמי לאשי (במ' כ"ח, ב'). אילו שהן ב[צו: ראשונה, צו]
[את] בני ישראל ויקחו אליך, שנייה, צו את בני [ישראל וישלחו]
מן המחנה. צו פרשת קרבן תמיד,[1] צו את בני [ישראל וא' א' את קרבני]
לחמי לאשי (שם, כ"ח, ב'). באמירה למה, שייש בו פורענות וייש [בו אזהרה],
5 ורובו פורענות, דכת' אמר אל בני ישראל אתם עם קשה ע[ורף וגו'] (שמ'
ל"ג, ה'), וייש[

בו אזהרה, אמר אל אהרן נטה את ידך במטך וג' (שם, ח', א'). דבור י[ש]
[ב]לשון בקשה, ובלשון פיים ולשון נחומים.[2] פיי[ס מניין, וינחם אתם וידבר]
על לבם (בר' נ', כ"א), פייס הם נחומים.[3] איזהוא לשון בק[שה, דברו אל כל]
[ע]דת בני ישראל לאמר בעשור לחדש השביעי הזה (שמ' י"ב, ג'), ד ב ר
[א ל ב נ י י ש ר א ל]

10 [ויקחו] ל י ת ר ו מ ה (שם, כ"ה, ב'). למה, כדי שתהיה פרנסתן[4]
מפרשת לשמ[י,[5] לכך נאמ]

[ויהיו לך] לבדיך ואין זרים אתך (מש' ה', י"ז). חמשה עשר דברים[6] [כתובין]
[לשמו ש]להקב"ה, אילו הן: ישראל, בכורות, כהנים, לוים, מקדש, [שמן]
המשחה[,

א. מקורות: תנ' תרומה (ת"ב שם); שמו"ר ל"ה.

1 מקור המאמר המקוטע נעלם ממני, מן החלק הנשאר יוצא שדן הוא בשלשת המונחים
הנרדפים: צו, אמור, דבר. בעוד שנשארו סימני יחוד המבדילים בין שני המונחים האחרונים,
אמירה ודיבור, אין אנו יודעים את הגוון המיוחד שייחס מדרשנו ל,צו'. ודווקא המונח הזה עניין
את בעלי המדרש הקדמונים, השווה ביחוד ספרי במ' פיס' א'. כל שלש הדוגמאות של ,צו'
הנמנות כאן אתה מוצא שם במאמרו של רשב"י ,אין ציווי בכל מקום אלא חסרון כיס.'
2 ההגדרה הזאת של ,אמירה' ו,דיבור' היא בניגוד לכל המדרשים הידועים לי המניחים
לכלל: ,אין ד ב ר בכל מקום אלא ל שו ן ק ש ה . . . ואין א מ י ר ה בכל מקום אלא
ת ח נ ו נ י ם' (ספרי במ', פיס' צ"ט). עי' בר' רבתי, הוצ' אלבק, עמ' 152, שו' 10 ומקבילות
המסומנות ע"י העורך.
3 נראה שבמקור ראשון היה כתוב: ,יש בלשון בקשה ובלשון פיס' בלבד, וכשסמכו על
,וינחם . . . וידבר' הוסיף המלקט לבאר ,פייס הם נחומים.'
כדאי לציין, שבעל הטורים מביא מדרש: ,אמר ר' אבהו ומה לעשות משכן כבוד וכפרה
לישראל אמר דבר אל בני ישראל, לשון פיום.'
4 נראה שט"ס הוא וצ"ל: נדבתן.
5 השווה רש"י: ,לי, לשמי.' וכדאי לציין שרש"י שם גם מבאר ,תרומה, הפרשה יפרישו
לי . . .' וגם בעל מדרשנו משתמש בלשון ,מפרשת לשמי.' מי תלוי במי?
6 השווה ת"ב תרומה, ג' ומקבילות. ברוב המקורות אין אנו מוצאים מספר כי אם ,כל
מקום' (עי' מדרש שמואל, הוצ' בובר, פי"ט, הע' ט'). במקום שנזכר מספר, והוא בבמ"ר ט"ז, י"ז
בסוף, הוא י"ג. ועי' והזהיר לשמות, עמ' ע"ז, הע' ז'.

(סוף העמוד שם, ז', ע"א)

[ש]נקראו על שמו, שכך כתוב כי שחת עמך א' הצ[את וג'] (דב' ט', י"ב),[7]
[וכי]

[ע]מו של משה הם, והלא של הקב"ה, שכך כת' והוצאתי את

20   צבאותי את עמי בני ישראל (שמ' ז', ד'),[8] אילא מתוך שמסר [עצמו עליהם]
נ[ק על ש'. דינין, מניין שנק' על ש', צדקות י"יי עשה [ו]משפ[טיו]

עם ישראל (דב' ל"ג, כ"א),[9] וכי משפטי משה היו, והלא דינין של הקב"ה, שכ'
כ[ת]

כי המשפט לאלהים הוא (דב' א', י"ד), אילא מתך ש[מסר] עצמו על נק[ר]
על שמו,

שכ' כת' וישב משה לשפט (שמ' י"ח, י"ג),[10] לפיכך כל הדינין נמסרו [לו] והוא

25   למדם לישראל, שכ' כתוב ואלה המשפטים. לכך נאמ[ר]
בארח צדקה אהלך (מש' ח', כ'). כי תקנה עבד עברי וש[ו][11]
וג' (שמ' כ"א, ב')

מאחר שכת' והיו בתורתו[12] כי לי בני ישראל עבדים (וי' כ"ה, נ"ה),[13] עבדי
הם, לא ימכר[ו ממכרת]

[עבד] (שם, מ"ב), [מה ס]בה שלזה שהיה כעבד מצרי ולמה, [איל]א מלמד
מתוך שעבר [על]

[מ]צות שביעית, והוא מדלדל וירד עד שמוכר את עצמו לעבד.[14] ולמה,

30   [זה מ]שונה, שהוא עובר על מצ' שביעת גורם לעצמו שימכר [לעבד]

(כאן סוף העמוד, וישנו ליקוי בין דף זה ושלאחריו)

---

[7] כן הוא גם במכילתא שירה פ"א. רוב המקורות מביאים הפסוק מיש' ס"ג, י"א: ויזכר
ימי עולם משה עמו. תנ' בשלח, י' מביא שני הפסוקים.

[8] במכילתא מביא שני פסוקים אחרים לראיה. בעל מדרשנו מבליט שני כתובים המכחישים
זה את זה בקשר עם יציאת מצרים.

[9] רק במדרשים המאוחרים, פס"ר (הוצ' איש־שלום, דף י"ד, ע"ב), ותנ' בשלח, י', מביאים
הפסוק הזה לראייה שהדינין נקראים על שמו של משה. במדרשים הקדומים מהם, מכילתא מס'
דשירה פ"א, מביא את הפסוק שפטים ושוטרים תתן לך (שמו"ר ל', ד' הפסוק ,ואלה המשפטים אשר
תשים לפניהם"), והפסוק ,צדקת ה' עשה ומשפטיו לישראל" ממש'ו ראייה שמשה מסר נפשו
על הדינין. ובאמת ,ומשפטיו" אינו מוסב על משה כי אם על ה', והכוונה צדקת ה' ומשפטי ה'.
אם המדרשים המאוחרים העבירו את הפסוק לכאן מתוך שלא הבינו את המקור או על דעת
עצמם – קשה להכריע.

[10] נראה כאילו הפסוק הזה מורה שמשה מסר נפשו על הדינין. ובאמת זה יוצא מפשוטה
של הפרשה, שכן יתרו אמר לו: ,נבל תבל . . . כי כבד ממך הדבר לא תוכל עשהו" (שם,
י"ח, י"ח). אבל דוקה מפני זה אני חושד את המלקט בהוספת נופך זה. שאר המקורות מביאים
את שמ' ב', י"ב־ט"ו לראייה שמסר נפשו על הדינין.

[11] נקודה על ה,ו' לסימן מחיקה – ש' – שש.

[12] נקודות על שתי מלים לסימן מחיקה.

[13] רמז למאמרו של ר' יוחנן בן זכאי: ,ולא עבדים לעבדים' (קידושין כ"ב, ע"ב).

[14] השווה מאמרו של ר' יוסי בר חנינא בקידושין כ', ע"ב: ,כמה קשה אבקה של שביעית
. . . לא באת לידו עד שמוכר את עצמו," ומקבילות. ניסוח המאמר כאן נראה מאוחר.

אלה המשפטים

דף ו', ע״ב (Box C 2, סי' 178, ח', ע״ב)

י'.

[כת' באורח] צדקה אהלך בתוך נתיבות משפט (מש' ח', כ'), בשבח ת[ורה¹
הכתוב מדבר]

[שלא ניתנה ל]ישראל אילא בתוך הדינין. והיכן ניצטוו י[ש את הדינין],

[קודם ש]נתנה תורה ולאחר שנתנה. ראשונה כת' שם ש[ם] לו חק [ומשפט]
(שמ' ט״ו, כ״ה),

[ולא]חר שנתנה תורה היכן ניצטוו, בזה המקום: ו א ל ה   ה מ ש פ [ט י ם].

5 [א[ש]ר תשים לפניהם,² לפני שמעינו בעינין עשר דברות

[שנא[מרו לו למשה בסיני, יכול דינין נאמרו באותה שעה, ת[למוד]

לומר ו א ל ה, אלה נאמרו בפני עצמן ואלה נאמרו ב[פני עצמן],

[מלמד ש]מאחר שנפסק עינין עשר דברות בא משה [אל תוך]

הערפל ו]נעשתה לו מחצה בערפל ולמד כל הדינין. [וכי בהר]

10 סיני למד] את הדינין בלבד, והלא בשלשה מקומות למד או[נתן],

[והיכ]ן הן שלשה מקומות, במרה, בהר סיני, בע[ר מוא]ב. במרה,

מניין, שם שם לו חק ומשפט ושם נסהו (שמ', שם), בס[יני] מני[ין],

[ו א ל ה   ה מ ש [פ] ט י ם, בע[ר]ב מואב מניין, והיתה לבני ישראל [לחוקת]

[משפ]ט (במ' ל״ו, י״א), אילא רובן שלדינין בהר סיני למד.³ [א ש ר   ת ש י ם

15 ל פ נ י]ה ם, לפני הם ולא לגוים.⁴ שלשה [דברים משה]

[מסר] עצמו עליהם ונקראו על [שמו, ואילו הן: תורה, ישראל ודינין].

[תו]רה, מה כת' זכרו תורת מש[ה עבדי וג'] (מלא' ג', כ״ב) [ישראל מניין],

---

י. מקורות: מכילתא דרשב״י משפטים: שמו״ר ל'.

1 כן הוא בתעתיק. עד כמה שעיני מגעת, השרידים האחרונים הם של ד' ולא של ת',
ולפיכך הייתי קורא „בשבח דין]ין הכ' מדבר שלא] / [ניתנה תורה ל]י[שראל . . .".

2 השווה שמו״ר ל', ג' בסוף: „בתוך נתיבות משפט, התורה באמצע ודינין מלפניה ודינין
מאחריה, מלפניה שנ' שם שם לו חק ומשפט, מאחריה שנ' ואלה המשפטים."

3 מקור המדרש בשלמותו נעלם ממני, ורק יסודות אחדים אפשר לציין. השווה מכילתא
ריש משפטים: „ר' ישמעאל אומר אלו מוסיפין על העליונים, מה עליונים מסיני אף תחתונים
מסיני." תנ[מ]שפטים, ג' ושמו״ר הנז'] : „ואף כאן שמוסיף על הראשונים שנ' שם שם לו חק
ומשפט."

4 השווה גיטין פ״ח, ע״ב: „לפניהם, ולא לפני גוים." ז״א שאסור ללכת לפני ב״ד של גוים.
כאן הכוונה שרק לישראל ניתנו המשפטים ולא לאומות העולם, השווה תנ' משפטים, ה'; שמו״ר
ל', א'. – „לפני הם," מופרד בכתה״י, ואיני יודע אם במקרה או בכוונה.

5 השווה שמו״ר ל', ד', ד', ומקבילות.

6 מתוך הניסוח של שני הדברים האחרים ומתוך ההשוואה עם המקורות יוצא שהסופר
דילג על שורה שלמה, וצריך להשלים: [„וכי שלמשה היא והלא שלהקב״ה שכך כת' תורת ה'
תמימה, אילא מתוך שמסר עצמו עליה נקראה על שמ]ן."

[וא]מ חכמים ג[12 גירים גמורים באו ונתגיירו מאליהן, ומי היו, אברהם תחלה
לג[ירים 13]

20   [יתרו14 ובתיה] בת פר'. ובתיה למה, שזכת במשה רבינו,15 אבל יש גירין
[שמתגיירין]

[מ]יראה, ויש גירין שמתג מאהבה, ויש גירין שמתג מעניות, ויש גירין שמתג
מאליהן. חביב מכולם גר

המתגייר מאליו.16 גר אהבה, כגון נעמן שאהב את הנערה הכתנת(!).17 גרי
יראה, שנתגיירו בימי מרדכי ואס, ורבים מעמי הארץ מתיהדים (אס ח', י"ב),
גר עניות, זה שראה עני בישראל שמתפרנס(!) (– שמתפרנס), והולך ומתגייר
כדי

25   שיתפרס. גר צדק ה ב ה18 מכאליו. ומתוך שחביבין לפני הֹקָֹבָ"ֹה, הזהיר
עליהם

בכמה מקומות:19 ואהבת את הגר (דב' י', י"ט), וגר לא תונה (שמ' כ"ב, כ'),
וגר לא תלחץ (שם, כ"ג, ט'), וכן לעת[יד]
לב הרבה מאומות העולם באים ומתגיירים עם יש, שב ֹכֹֹת כי יר [חם]
"ֹֹ את יעק[ב ובחר] עד (מ: עוד) ביש והניחם על אֹדֹם ונלוה הגר עליהם
ונספחו על בית יעקב (יש' י"ד, א').   ח ז ק20

---

12 מקורו נעלם ממני.

13 ירושלמי בכורים פ"א, ד' (דף ס"ד, ע"א).

14 השווה תנ' יתרו, א': מי הוא זה שבא ונתגייר והיה ג ר ש ל א מ ת, זה יתרו.‏"

15 השווה מגילה י"ג, ע"א; וי"ר א', ג' ומקבילות.

16 השווה בראשית רבתי, הוצ' אלבק, עמ' 149: ,,תני ד' גרים הם, גר אהבה, גר יראה,
גר פרנסה, גר צדק וכו'.‏". המקבילות בהע' 7. בעל מדרשנו מנסח מקור דומה למאד לזה שבבר'
רבתי.

17 נראה שצ"ל: ,,הנערה עם הכתונת.‏" והכוונה לתמר שנ' בה ,,ועליה כתנת פסים‏"
(ש"ב, י"ג, י"ח). מעניין שבעל מדרשנו מכסה את שמה של תמר. וכדאי לציין שאף המקור
היותר קרוב למדרשנו, בר' רבתי, אינו מזכיר כאן אהבה אמנון ותמר, שהיא אמנם דוגמה למופת
של ,,אהבה התלוייה בדבר‏" (אבות פ"ה, י"ו) אבל אינה עניין לכאן, שהרי אמנון לא התגייר
לשמה.

18 בתעתיק: ,,הנה.‏" אבל אין ספק שכתוב ,,הבה‏"=הבא.

19 השווה ת"ב, וי', ג': ,,אתה מוצא מ"ח פעמים הזהירה התורה על הגרים.‏" הניסוח כאן
כאילו רצה להבליט את הניגוד למאמרו של ר"א הגדול: ,,מפני מה הזהירה התורה בל"ו
מקומות . . . בגר, מפני ש ס ו ד ו ר ע (ב"מ נ"ט, ע"ב), ובעל מדרשנו אומר: ,,מתוך
שחביבין לפני הקב"ה.‏" השווה ,,בתי מדרשות‏" לווערטהיימער, בית ד', עמ' ג'–ד'. והשווה
,,משנת דר' אלעזר,‏" הוצ' ענעלאוו, עמ' 305–303.

20 בתעתיק: ,,בית יעק' – נתחיל חלק אלה המשפטים.‏" ואני מפקפק בקריאה זו, כי טרם
מצאתי ,,חלק‏" במובן מן של פרשה. ובאמת המעמיק להתבונן בכתה"י יראה שהמלה השנייה היא
,,יעקב‏", ב,,בית‏" רבתי לסיום סיומה של פרשת יתרו. אחר זה כתב הסופר ,,חסל,‏" והעביר
קולמוס עליה וכתב ,,חזק,‏" שניהם מסמנים סוף פרשה או סוף ספר.

[מנשים יעל א]שת חבר הקני (שו' ה', כ״ד). צדיקים גמורים, זו משפחת יעבץ,
שהיו יושבין בלשכת

[הגמ]ית ומורין הלכה ל[י]שראל, שכך כתוב משפחות סופרים יושבי יעבץ תרעתים
ש[מעתים]

[שוכתים המה הקינים] הבאים מחמת אבי בית רכב (דה״א ב', נ״ה).7. ולמה
זכה לכול הכבוד הזה,

15 [לפי שהניח עבודה זרה ובא להר האלהים] ונתגייר מאליו,8 והודה וברך
למקום, כבו[ד]

[גדול עשה להקב״ה,9 שהרי מ]ס רבוא בני אדם לא היה אי[ש שברכו עד שבא
יתרו, שכך [כת]

[ויאמר יתרו ברוך י]יי אשר הציל וג' (שמ' י״ח, י').10. ולמה נקרא תרעתים,
מלמד שישבו להן על השער11

(סוף העמוד שם, ז', ע״ב)

[ומורין הלכה] לישראל. ומי היו הללו, אילו בניו שליתרו, ש[כך] כת המה
הקינים.

אתכם בלחם ומים, וכי צריכין היו להם לישראל, והלא כל אותן ארבעים שנה שהיו י ש ר א ל
ב מ ד ב ר ה י ה ה מ ן י ו ר ד ל ה ן ו ה ב א ר ע ו ל ה וכו'. ג. מי שעושה חסד עם
מי שחייב לו, יתרו עם משה ויאמר להן קראנה לו ויאכל לחם וכו'. נראה שמי שהוא העביר,
בכוונה או מתוך שיגרת העט, את המשפט המלווה לדוגמה ב', והוא „אשר לא קדמו אתכם
בלחם ומים.” „וכי צריכין וכו'” לדוגמה ג', שהיא „יתרו עם משה,” וע״י כך הכניס
ערבוביה במדרשנו.

כדאי לציין שהמוטיב הזה שה' הספיק לבני ישראל במדבר כל צרכיהם ולא היה מקום
לגמילות חסד ול„צדקה” נמצא גם בספרי דברים פיס' שנ״ה: „צדקת ה' עשה וכו' (דב'
ל״ג, כ״א), וכי מה צדקות עשה בישראל והלא כל מ' שנה שהיו ישראל במדבר באר עולה
להם והמן יורד להם וכו'.”

7 השווה מכילתא יתרו, סוף מסכ' דעמלק (מכדרשב״י, עמ' 135); ספרי במ', פיס' ע״ח;
תנ' יתרו, ד'.

8 השווה תנ' שם, ו' ומקבילות: „זש״ה כ ב ו ד חכמים ינחלו...זה יתרו כשבא
אצל משה...ואף אתה א ד ם ש ב א א צ ל ך ל ה ת נ י י ר ק ר ב ה ו...”.

9 ע ש ה ל ה ק ב ״ ה – השלמת המחבר. אולם על יסוד התנ' הנז' לפני זה, היית מציע
להשלים: „כ ב ו ד [ג ד ו ל ה ו א ל י ת ר ו ש ה ר י מ ש ש י ם ר ב ו א וכו'] הוציא יי״י ממצ'
ולא היה ... עד שבא יתרו ... .” ולא עוד שעל ידי כך אנו מקבלים פרפרזה מעניינת ממדרשו
של ר' פפיס: „ג נ א י ל מ ש ה וסיעתו שהרי ששים רבוא ... ולא היה מהן אחד שפתח
ובירך את המקום עד שבא יתרו ובירך את המקום. (מכדרשב״י, עמ' 131 ומקבילות). כדי שלא
להוציא דברי גנאי על משה, הפך את „הגנאי למשה” ל„כבוד ליתרו.”

10 מן „ולמה זכה” עד „אשר הציל וג' ” היא הוספה המפסיקה את המדרש על משפחת
יעבץ שהמשכו הוא המשפט הבא.

11 השווה תנ' הנז' בהע' 7; ספרי הנז' שב: „על שם שהיו יושבין בפתח שערי ירושלים.”
לפי בעל מדרשנו ותנ' „שערי ירושלים” נרדפים ל„לשכת הגמית.”

[וינשק לו] (שם, כ"ט, י"ג); משה ליתרו בהר האלהים,[2] ו י ש ק ל ו (שמ'
י"ח, ז'). ושל פרישות, [וערפה לנעמי, ותשק]
ערפה [לחמו]תה וג (רות א', י"ד). ושלפרקים, אהרן למשה, וילך ויפגשהו
בהר (שמ' ד', כ"ז). [ושלגדולה],
[שמואל] לשאול, שכך כת ויקח שמואל את פך הש ויצק על ראשו וישקהו
ו[יאמר הלא]

5 [כי] משחך [יי'] למ ע יש (ש"א י', א'). ו י ב א ו ה א ה ל ה (שמ' י"ח, ז'),
מאותה שעה הכניסו לבית המדרש.[3] אמרו [חכמים][4]
[שלש] משפחות יצאו מן יתרו, אילו הן: גוים גמורים, גירים גמורים, צדיקים
גמורים.
[גוים גמו]רים, שבאו עם עמלק להלחם עם ש[אול], שכך כת ויאמר שאול
אל הקיני [לכו]
[סורו רדו] מת עמלק (מ: עמלקי) פן אוסיפך עמו ואתה עשית חסד עם כל
בני ישראל בעלות[ם ממצרים]
[ויסר קיני מ]תוך עמלק (ש"א ט"ו, ו').[5] מה חסד עשה יתרו עם ישראל,
האכילם לחם בצ ממצ [שכך כת ויקח]
10 [יתרו חות]ן מ ש ה וג, (שמ' י"ח, י"ב), ואף על פי שהיה מן ירד
(– יורד) [והבאר עלה (– עולה)], והיו מסתפקין בכל צרכיהן
[מעלה עליו הכת] כשעשה עם כל ישראל[6] גירים גמורים, חבר הַקֵּנִי וחביריו,
שכך כתוב תבר ו[ך]

פרקים, נשיקה של פרישות. נשיקה של גדולה, ויקח שמואל את פך השמן ויצוק על ראשו
וישקהו (ש"א י', א'); נשיקה של פרקים, וילך ויפגשהו בהר האלהים וישק לו (שמ' ד', כ"ז);
נשיקה של פרישות, ותשק ערפה לחמותה (רות א', י"ד)... תנחומא אמר אף נשיקה של
קריבות שנ' וישק יעקב לרחל (בר' כ"ט, י"א)." על יסוד זה נעשתה ההשלמה.
2 טעות סופר, כי זה שייך לשורה שלמטה ממנה: אהרן למשה, וילך ויפגשהו ב ה ר
ה א ל ה י ם וישק לו. "ואילו כאן צ"ל: "וישתחו וישק לו." ובאמת רשמי אותיות ו י ש ת ח ו
ניכרים בין השיטין. אגב יש כאן רמז למכילתא דרשב"י, עמ' 130: אין אנו יודעין מי נשתחוה
למי ומי נישק למי... הא לא נשתחוה ולא נישק אלא מ ש ה ל י ת ר ו.? [הקבלתו במכילתא
דר"י: מ ש ה ל ח מ י ו.
3 מכילתא שם: "זה בית המדרש."
4 מקורו של המאמר נעלם ממני.
5 השווה רד"ק כאן: "ואף שראינו בכיבוש הארץ כי הקינים עלו מעיר התמרים וישבו עם
בני יהודה...הלכו להם כולם או מקצתם לשבת עם העמלקי."
6 המאמר מקוטע ומסורס, ואיני יודע אם ע"י המלקט עצמו או ע"י איזה מעתיק. הקבלתו
אנו מוצאים במדרש שמואל פרשה י"ח, ג' (הוצ' בובר, עמ' נ'): "וכי ע ם כ ל י ש ר א ל
ע ש ה ח ס ד והלא לא עשה חסד אלא עם משה... אלא ללמדך שכל מי שעושה חסד
עם אחד מגדולי ישראל כ א י ל ו ע ש ה ע ם כ ל י ש ר א ל." רק ההתחלה והסוף
מתאימים, אבל כל מה שהוא באמצע במדרשנו סתום. הקבלה עם וי"ר ל"ד, ח' מגלה לנו
שבאמת החלק האמצעי אינו שייך לכאן. המדרש שם מונה ד' מידות (שיטין) בעשיית חסד.
א. מי שעושה חסד עם מי שלא היו צריכין, כגון אברהם עם מלאכי השרת. ב. מי שלא עשה
חסד עם מי שלא היו צריכין לחסד, עמוני ומואבי עם ישראל, דכתיב על דבר אשר לא קדמו

[מים]ינם ואחד משמאלם, אחד למעלה מראשן ואחד מת [קן ומכבד]

5   [להם] את הדרכין, ואחד היה באהל מועד. ³ וחמושים. מה הו[א
    ו]חמושים,

מלמד שט[וכס]ם חמשה מיני זיין, ואילו הן: חרב ותריס ורומח וק[שת]

ואילא.⁴ דבר אחר וחמושים מהו, מלמד שעלו עימן חמשה כיוצא
בהם.⁵   ויקח משה את עצמות יוסף (שם, י״ט). ברוך
הקב׳ה שמ[של]ם שכר

[טוב] לעושה טוב, טובה שא[יראה] חסד⁶ עשה [יוסף ע]ם אבי[ו ו]עי[ם אחיו]

10 [ע]מדה לו ביציאת מצ׳. כי השביע (שם), את יש[ראל קודם מותו, שב
בת וישבע יוסף,] (ברֹ׳ נֹ׳, כ״ה),

[ובשעת יציאה היו כל י]שראל עסוקים [בשאילת כלי כסף וזהב, ומשה
עוסק בעצמות יוסף.]⁷

סוף העמוד חסר. וקרוב לודאי שישנו ליקוי בין דף זה והבא אחריו)

דף ו׳, ע״א (מס׳ 178, ח׳, ע״א)

[לפרשת יתרו ופ׳ משפטים]

[ט].

[ושל גדולה. שלקריבות],¹ יעקב לרחל, שכך כתוב וישק יעקב לרחל (בר׳
כ״ט, י״א); לבן [וליעקב],

³ השווה מכילתא בשלח על פסוק וה׳ הולך לפניהם (י״ג, כ״א): „שבעה עננים, ארבע
מארבע רוחותיהם, אחד למעלה ואחד למטה, ואחד שהיה מהלך לפניהם, כל הנמוך מגביהו
וכו׳.״ לדעת בעל מדרשנו הענן שמלמטה הוא גם המתקן את הדרכים, ונשאר לו ענן אחד
„באהל מועד.״ לא מצאתי חבר לבעל מדרשנו בדבר זה; אפילו בעל מדה״ג מסכים כאן עם
המקורות הידועים המסומנים אצל גינצברג, אגדות היהודים, חלק ה׳, עמ׳ 438, הע׳ 242.
וכדאי לציין, שכל עניין ז׳ ענני הכבוד נזכר כמעט בכל המקומות בקשר עם הפסוק „וה׳
הולך לפניהם יומם בעמוד ענן . . .״, אבל לא בקשר עם „ויסב אלהים.״ והפירוש „שסיבבם
בענני הכבוד״ מוזר הוא לטעמו הפשטני של בעל מדרשנו.
⁴ השווה מדה״ג (מכילתא דרשב״י, עמ׳ 45): „מלמד שעלו מטוכסים בחמשה
מיני זיין, קשת ואלה ותריס ורומח וחרב.״ ועפ״י זה הושלם מאת המחבר.
⁵ השווה מדה״ג (מכילתא דרשב״י, עמ׳ 45): „מלמד שעלו עמהם גרים ועבדים חמשה
כיוצא בהם.״
⁶ נקוד למעלה סימן למחיקה.
⁷ השווה תוספתא סוטה פ״ד, 7: „יוסף זכה לקבור את אביו לפיכך זכה ונתעסק בו משה״
(עי׳ סוטה ט׳, ע״ב; י״ג, ע״א); פסדר״כ, דף פ״ה, ע״ב: „להודיע שבחו של משה, שכל ישראל
עסוקין בביזה, ומשה עסוק בעצמות יוסף.״ המקבילות בהע׳ ק״ה של המו״ל. עפ״י זה נעשתה
ההשלמה.

ט. מקורות: מכילתא יתרו . . .
¹ השווה ב״ר ע׳, י״ב: „כל נשיקה לתפלות בר מן תלת, נשיקה של גדולה, נשיקה של

[תשליכהו] (שמ' א', כ"ב), הושלך ליאור, שכך כתוב מרכבות פרעה (שם,
(ט"ו, ד');[5] פה שאמר מי יה אשר אשמע בקולו (שם, ה', ב')
הצדיק[6]

[הו]דא (– הודה) וא[מ] יי' צבאות ואני ועמי הרשעים (שם, ט', כ"ז); פה
שאמר לא ידעתי את יי' וג (שם, ה', ב'),

[שי]לחם בעל כרחו,[8] [שכך כ]תוב ויהי בשלח פרעה. משל למה
הדבר [דומה, למלך]

10   [שאמר לעבדו: הבא לי דג מן השוק. הלך וה]ביא לו דג מבא[ו]ש. אמר לו:
דג מבאיש]

[אמרתי לך, חייך שלא תזוז מכן עד שתאכל הדג או] תלקה מאה מ[כות , , , ,[9]
....

(סוף העמוד חסר)

דף ה', ע"ב (שם, א', ע"ב)

ח.

[דרך העול]ם(?)[1] תלמיד מרחץ את הרב, כן (– כאן) מה כת ורחצך (יח'
ט"ז, ט'); דרך ה[עולם]

[תל]מיד מלביש את הרב, כן מה כת, ואכסך משי (שם, י'),[2] ויסב אלהים.
[את העם] (שמ' י"ג, י"ח)

[מלמד שס]יבבם בשבעה ענני כבוד: אחד מפניהם, ואחד מאחוריהם, [ואחד]

5 השווה תוספתא שם, פ"ג, י"ג ששם מובאה הדוגמה הזאת של מידה כנגד מידה בסגנון
שונה, ובעל מדרשנו השווה את הסגנון לדוגמאות הבאות.

6 מלת „הצדיק" תלוייה למעלה בין השיטין. הסופר כתב מתחילה: יי'י צ ב א ו ת,
וכשהרגיש טעותו העביר קולמוס על צבאות, והשלים למעלה „הצדיק."

7 יש להשלים [...וגם את ישראל ל א א ש ל ח].

8 השווה מכילתא, ריש פרשת בשלח, ושמו"ר כ', י' בסוף. שתי הדוגמאות האחרונות
מובאות שם בשינוי סגנון.

9 השווה מכילתא, מסכ' בשלח, פרש' א' (הוצ' וייס, עמ' 32); ת"ב בשלח; פסדר"כ,
דף פ"א, ע"ב. אינני יודע על איזה יסוד נעשית ההשלמה ע"י המחבר. על בסיס המקורות הנז'
הייתי מציע להשלים: „דג מבאיש, אמר לו המלך, חייך אין אתה יוצא מאחת משלש אלו, או
תאכל את הדג, און תלקה וכו'."

ח. מקורות: מכילתא בשלח; ת"ב בשלח, י'; פסדר"כ, דף פ"ב, ע"א וכו'.

1 השווה פסדר"כ הנז': „ולא נחם אלהים ... מלמד שלא ניהגן בדרך הארץ ... דרך
הארץ תלמיד מרחיץ וכו'." כל המקורות (המקבילות בהערות בובר לפס"ר)
גורסים „דרך ארץ (או, הארץ)" בהתאם ללשון הפסוק „בדרך ארץ פלשתים." אולם בעל
מדרשנו שאינו נזקק ללשון מקורותיו בחר „דרך העולם," מטבע-לשון עוברת.

2 כל המקורות, לרבות מדה"ג, מביאים את ראש הפסוק „ואלבישך רקמה," שהניגוד
לתלמיד (לעבד) מ ל ב י ש את רבו בולט בו. ואני משער שבעל מדרשנו נמנע מלהשתמש
ב„רקמה," של צבעים, שהוא בטוי ציוריי ופיוטי, ועל כן בחר „ואכסך משי."

10 ....אילו ....ון אתנו וא . ...
....................................שאני

(סוף העמוד חסר)

דף ה', ע"א (Box C 2), מס' 178, א', ע"א)

[סוף הדרשה לפרשת בא, והתחלת הדרשה לפ' בשלח]

[ה]שיר¹² יהיה לכם כליל התקדש חג שמחת החג הולך¹³ בחליל
לב[וא בהר י"י אל]

[צ]ור ישראל (יש' ל', כ"ט).   ז]. ויהי בשלח פרעה. כת
[אלהים מה נורא]

[מעשיך (תה' ס"ו, ג'), אמ]רין¹ לפעולא טאבא יישר פעלך. מה נורא מעשיך,
מא [דחילין מנגיא]

[דידך, הנצלים] צולים צואליהם,² ההורגים(!) (– הנהרגים) הורגים את
הורגיהם, הנש[קעים שוקעים]

5 [את] שוקעיהם, שכך כת³ בסאסאה בשלחה תריבנה לו הגה ברוחו הקשה
[וג'], (יש' כ"ז, ח')

[בסא]תא דאמטו מצראי לישראל בה אתמטי להון.⁴ פה שאמר כ]ל ה[בן
הילוד היא[רה]

12 השווה מכילתא בשלח, התחלת פרשת השירה שדורש הפסוק על „השירה הראשונה
שאמרו ישראל במצרים".
13 נ' המס': „ושמחת לבב כהולך."

ז. מקורות: שמו' כ', י'; פסדר"כ, פיס' י', דף פ', ע"ב וכו' ומקבילות.
1 על הניסוחים השונים של המדרש הזה עי' הערות בובר לפסדר"כ (כ"ו–ל"א), ומאיר עין
לפס"ר, דף צ"ד, ע"א, הע' ח'. הניסוח שלנו מתאים ביותר לזה שבפסדר"כ עפ"י כת"י כרמולי.
2 כל המקורות גורסים: „הנצלבין צולבין את צולביהן." קשה להחליט אם יש לנו שינוי
מדעת, כדי שלא להזכיר עניין ה„צליבה," או שינוי שלא מדעת.
3 מכאן עד „להון" נמצא רק במדרש הגדול שמות, עמ' 130. המוטיב של „מדה כנגד מדה"
בעונש פרעה ומצרים הוא אחד המוטיבים החביבים על בעלי המדרש ועל הפייטנים הקדמונים,
והוא חוזר ונשנה בווריאציות שונות במדרשים וקרובות לפסח. המכילתא בריש בשלח הורה
את הדרך. המלקטים האחרונים ראו לנכון להוסיף את המקור הקדום לביסוסו של הכלל הזה:
„היה ר' מאיר אומר מניין שבמדה שאדם מודד מודדין לו, שנ' בסאסאה בשלחה תריבנה"
(תוספתא סוטה, פ"ג ומקבילות).
4 המשפט הארמי, שכנראה לקוח מאיזה תרגום לישעיה, מלווה במה"ג בפראפראזה עברית:
„במדה שדנו את ישראל בה נידונו."

....שכך כתוב ואברהם בן מאת שנה וגֹ (בר' כ"א, ה'), נשתיירו ת.[7] כשאמר
[לו גר יהיה]

[זרעך בארץ לא להם, לא אמר] לו במצרים, אילא בארץ לא להם.[8] גר
[יהיה זרעך]

... ... 10

(סוף העמוד חסר)

דף ד', ע"ב (שם, ב', ע"ב)

... אחת בימי נח, ואחת במצרים, ואחת בערבות מואב.[9]

[שבק]ש הֹקֹבֹה להכניס את נח אל התבה, אמרו אנשי

[דור ה]מבול:[10] עתיד הֹקֹבֹה להכניס את נח ואת בניו אל התבה

[בשביל] מימי המבול, בשעה שמכניס ואנו נקבצין ואין אנו

5 [מניחי]ן אותן עד שטף כלנו בבת אחת. אמר הֹקֹבֹה: חייכם שאיני מכניסן

[איל]א בעצמו שליום, וראה מי מחא [– מוחה] על ידי, שכך כתוב

[בע]צם היום הזה בא נח וגֹ (בר' י', י"ג). אחת במצרים, נתן להם רשות לצאת

בליל[ה, שכך] כֹתֹ ויקרא למשה ולאהרן לילה וגֹ (שמֹ י"ב, ל"א). אמרו לו משה

[ואהרן: וכי לסט]ים אנחנו, אין אנו יוצאין אילא בעצמו שליום[11]

---

7 השווה מכילתא מסֹ דפסחא, פרשה י"ד: „כתוב אֹ אומר שלשים שנה וארבע מאות שנה
(שמֹ י"ב, מֹ) וכתוב אֹ אומר ועבדום וענו אותם ארבע מאות שנה (בר' ט"ו, י"ג), כיצד
יתקיימו שני מקראות הללו, שלשים שנה עד שלא נולד יצחק נגזרה גזרה בין הבתרים." וביתר
ביאור במכילתא דרשב"י, עמֹ 34: „קֹץ אחד לכולן שלשים שנה וארבע מאות שנה, שלשים שנה
אלו מה טיבן, מיום שנידבר עם אבינו אברהם בין הבתרים ועד שנולד יצחק לֹ שנה, ומשנולד
יצחק ועד שיצאו ישראל ממצרים ארבע מאות שנה." בעוד שבעל מדרשנו מוסר את גוף המדרש
בצמצום קיצוני, הוא מוסיף לבסס את הנאמר שמבין הבתרים עד שנולד יצחק עברו לֹ שנה.
ועי' פרדר"א פמ"ח (קי"ד, ע"א) ובביאור רד"ל שם.

8 כנראה יש לנו כאן התחלה של פרפראזה של המדרש בב"ר מ"ד, י"ח: „א"ר יודן גירות
בארץ לא להם עבדות ענוי לאספטיה שלהם." המאמר הזה בא שם לאחר שנאמר „כי גר יהיה
זרעך בארץ לא להם, משיראה לך זרע," כלומר שחשבון תֹ שנה התחיל מלידת יצחק. עי'
תיאודור במנח"י (עמֹ 440); ובובר בפסדר"כ הנֹ' ומאיר עין לפסֹ"ר הנֹ'. אפשר שהיה כאן
ביאור של המאמר הסתום „מדלנ על הקצין לקצרן ומקפץ על הגֹ' להאריכן." הזמן הקצוב
מכיל גירות וענוי ועינוי עבדות." כדי לקצר את קץ העבדות מאריך הקב"ה את קץ הגירות ומתחילו
מלידת יצחק.

9 השווה ספרי דברים, פיסֹ שלֹ'ז: „בשלשה מקומות נאמר בעצם היום הזה וכו'.".

10 השווה ספרי הנֹ' ובֹ"ר ל"ב, חֹ'. במקורות אלה נאמר רק שאילו לא היה בעצם היום
היו אומרים שלא היו מניחים אותם להכנס. אצל מדרשנו הכל נהפך למציאות. אנשי דור המבול
באמת איימו על נח ובני חברתו שלא יניחום להכנס לתיבה. על ידי כך הכניס בעל מדרשנו
דרמטיות באגדה.

11 השווה מכילתא דרשב"י, עמֹ 29: „ואמר לו בלילה אין אנו יוצאין." ועי' מכילתא דר"י,
מסכת דפסחא, פרשה י"ג. ניסוח בעל מדרשנו קרוב לזה שבפרקי דר' אליעזר פרק מ"ח עם
ביאור רד"ל (דף קט"ו, ע"ב): „עכשיו יאמרו מצרים דרך גנבים עשה מעשיו," ועי' הערת
רד"ל שם.

דף ד, ע"א (Box C 1), מס' 45, ב, ע"א)

[לפרשת בא]

.[]

[זה ב]א (שה"ש ב', ח'), זה משה רבינו שבא ובישר את ישראל.¹ מד' על
הה מקפץ ע[ל הג] (שם),

[מד]לג על הקצין, מק' על השבועות,² מדלג על הקצ' בזכות אבות, מק [על
השבו],

בזכות אמהות³, ולמה, מפני שאבות משולים בהרים, ואמהות משולים [בגבעות],

שכך כתוב   כי מראש צורים אראנו ומגבעות אשורנו⁴ ה[ן עם ו ג, וכת
ה[ן]

5   [עם] כלביא יקום וג (במ' כ"ג, ט' וכ"ד),⁵, מראש צור אראנו מדלג על הקצין
לקוצרין, מק [פץ]

על הגב להארכין,⁶ גזר ת שנה ומשים אתם ת' ול, אילא להודיעך מיום
[שנולד יצחק]

[שכשד]בר ה[ק]ב'ה עם אברהם בין הבתרים בן שבעים שנה היה, ועד שנולד
לו [בן יצאו ל] שנה

ו. מקורות: שמו"ר ט"ו; פסדר"כ, פיס' החודש; פסי"ר, פיס' החודש.

1 השווה שמו"ר ט"ו, ד'; פסדר"כ, מ'ז, ע"א; פסי"ר, הוצ' איש־לשום, ע', ע"א: „זה משה
בשעה שבא ואמר לישראל בחודש הזה נגאלים אתם." כמה מן הצמצום במדרשנו, אבל הוסיף
את התואר „רבינו" למשה. בשאר המקורות אנו מוצאים „משה רבינו" רק כשמדברים אל משה
בגוף שני אבל לא כשמזכירים את משה סתם. אם איני טועה זה סימן לאיחורו של המדרש.
2 במקורות הנז': ומקפץ על החשבונות והעיבורים. משמעותה של „שבועות"
סתום בעיני, ואולי מרמז ל„שבעים (– שבועות) שבעים (בדנ' ט', כ"ד, זמן הקץ.
3 השווה מקורות הנז'. בעל מדרשנו הרכיב שני מדרשים המיוחסים במקורות לאנשים
שונים. עפ"י המקורות ר' יהודה (או ר' יודן) דורש „הרים וגבעות" קצין וחשבונות
(– שבועות) ורבנן דורשים „הרים וגבעות" אבות ואמהות. ובעל מדרשנו דורש מדלג
על הקיצין ומקפץ על השבועות בזכות האבות והאמהות. על
הערבוביה השוררת במקורות שונים בנוגע לניסוחם של מדרשים אלה, עי' מאיר עין לפס"ר
עמ' ע"א, הע' נ"ז.
4 השווה פסדר"כ, פרשת זכור, עמ' כ"א, ע"ב וכו'. על המקבילות במכילתא ובמס' ראש
השנה י"א, ע"א, עי' בובר הע' י"ד, ומאיר עין לפס"ר הנז' סימ' נ"ז.
5 כנראה קושר „הן עם „לבדד וכו' ב„הן עם" כלביא וכו' אבל איני יודע מה זה בא
ללמד.
6 זה אחד מנופכי פירוש של בעל מדרשנו, שאינו ברור לי.

[נתמלא ל]בו מרחמנות בזמן שהוכיח את אחיו וראה אותן שנבהלו [מפניו],
[פי]תה אותן בדברים, אמר להן: ברוך הקֹּבֹּהֹ שיודע אחרית דבר קֹוד[ם]

10 [שנעשה].16 טובה גדולה עשה הקֹּבֹּהֹ שירדתי לכן, ל מ ח [ן י ה ש ל ח נ י,
להיות]
[לכם] שורש בעולם ולא לעשותכם כלאה17 בעולם, שכֹֹּכֹֹ ל מ ח י ה
ש ל ח נ י]
[א ל ה] י ם ל פ נ י כ ם (שם, ה'), אל יחר לכם ואל יהיה הדבר קשה
בעי[ניכם]
. . . . מלפני הקֹּבֹּהֹ והיא . . . .

(סוף העמוד ב–2 Box C, מס' 42, ב', ע"ב. אלא ע"י הקרע חסרות כנראה
שורות אחדות)

[ו י פ ל ע ל צ ו א ר י ב נ י מ י ן (שם, י"ד), וכי שני צוארין היו לבני]מין,
מלמד שצפה
15 [יוסף ברוח הקדש על] שני מקדשים עתידין להבנות בחל[קו]
שלבנימין, [ובעונ]ות הם חרבין, ובנימין צפה ברוח הקדש על
משכן שילה עתיד לבנות בחלקו שליוסף, ובעונות יחרב.
לפיכך זה בכה על חרבניו, וזה בכה על חרבנו.18 ומצינו19 ששֹׁנֹי
שבטים יצאו מן רחל שבאה תשעה (– תשועה) לישראל על ידם.
20 יוסף באה ישועה לישראל על ידו ונתקימו כלם בזכותו,
מנין, שכך כתוב ויכלכל יוסף את אביו וֹא אֹ וֹא כל בֹ אֹ (שם, מ"ז, י"ב).
ובנימין באה
[י]שועה גדולה לישראל על ידו, מצינו שמשעה שפיתה יוסף
[את א]חיו צפה בדבר הזה, ראה מזאל[ו20 של בנימין שע]ל[ה]
(כאן סוף הדף, וישנו ליקוי בין דף זה ושלאחריו.)

16 [שנעשה] – השלמת המחבר. אולם המטיב לעיין ימצא שרשמי הניקוד של חולם ֹ
בסוף המלה החסירה ניכרים למדי. ולפיכך הייתי מציע לקרוא: שיודע אחרית דבר קֹוד[ם]
[ראשיתו], עפ"י הכתוב ,,טוב אחרית דבר מראשיתו' (קֹה' ז', חֹ').
17 כלאה – כלה. כתיב דומה למעלה הע' 11. אמתאי – אימתי.
18 השווה ב"ר שם, י"ב; מגילה ט"ז, ע"ב. החילוף של ,,ראה' (מקורות) ב,,צפה' וההוספה
,,ובעוונות' יחרב סימני אחור הם.
19 מכאן עד סוף העמוד לקוח ממקור בלתי ידוע לי.
20 מזאלו – מזלו. השווה הע' 11, 17.

.... בעצמו, קרא להוציא את השוברים ואת [הפיתק]ין,[10] אמתאי.[11]....
בשעה שביקש להיתודע אל אחיו, קראו והושיבן לפניו כסנדרין.
אמר להם: הלא שנים עשר אתם. אמר: הן הנה אחד עשר. אמר
[לו: א' מ]אחינו מת. אמר: שקר אתם מדברים. אמ להם: הלא אתם מכרתם
20 [אותו] לישמעאלים שירדו למצרים, רצונכם אקראנו ויבא אליכם.
אמרו לו: הין, החזיר את פניו לקיר ואמר: יוסף בן יעקב צא לכן. היו
[מ]סתכלין לארבע פנות הבית לראות מאין יצא.[12] אמר להם: להוה
[ידע לכם ש]אני יוסף אחיכם העוד אבי חי (שם, מ"ה, ג').
לא האמינו לו

דף ג', ע"ב (Box C 1), מס' 45, ג', ע"א)

שפירע את עצמו והראה להן חותם בשרו, מניין, שכך כתוב כ[ון]
ויאמר יוסף אל אחיו גשו נא אלי ויגשו (שם, ד'), בקול קטן, ולמה, [מלמד]
שהראה להן חותם בשרו.[13] באותה שעה תשש כחן כנשים,[14] [ונבהלו]
ולא יכלו לענותו דבר. ולמדנו תוכחת הקבהו לבשר ודם בעול[ם]
5 הזה יוסף הוכיח את אחיו ונבהלו ואחזתם [בו]שה וכלמה, בן אדם כשעמד
(— כשעומד)
בדין לפני הקבהו, על אחת כמה וכמה.[15] אלא הקבהו מרחים בדין. בזמן
שהוכיח (צ"ל: שמוכיח) את אדם בעמדו לפניו בדין, רחמיו מתגלגלין
עליו. כך יוסף

10 הדברים בלתי ברורים לי, ואני משער שרו"ל שטר מכירה ושטר פרעון. בעל מדרשנו
סובר שיוסף העמיד פנים כאילו היה מושב בית־דין, "סנדרין," כדי להאשים את אחיו בעדות
שקר, באמרם שאחיהם מת, כי באמת מכרו אותו. וכדי לבסס את האשמה הכין את ה,שוברים
והפיתקין" המעידים על המכירה. הפרט הזה לא מצאתי במקורות הידועים לי, ואפשר שהמלקט
הוסיף את הנופך הזה.
11 אמתאי – אימתי. הכתיב מעניין.
12 השווה ב"ר שם, ח'; ת"ב ויגש, ח'. בעל מדרשנו, כמנהגו, מרחיב את התמונה ומכניס
מתיחות יתרה בין יוסף ואחיו לפני התוודעותו. מצד אחר נשאר הוא על קרקע המציאות
ומשמיט את התיאורים שבמקורות העוברים את גבול הריאליות, כגון "מיד פרחה נשמתם"
וכדומה.
13 השווה ב"ר שם, י'; מדה"ג בראשית, עמ' 670: "מלמד שהראה להם ברית מילה." כבר
ראינו למעלה שדרכו של בעל מדרשנו להוסיף פירושים למקורותיו. וגם כאן, כנראה, הוא
מוסיף "בקול קטן" כדי לבאר איך יוצא "גשו אלי ויגשו" שהראה להם ברית מילה. האמת
אניד שמשמעות הדברים נעלמה ממני.
14 השווה ברכות ל"ב, ע"א: "מלמד שתשש כחו כנקבה." המליצה הזאת באה כאן במקום
"מיד פרחה נשמתן" שבמקורות, ועי' למעלה בהע' 12.
15 השווה ב"ר שם, י'–י"א; ת"ב שם, ז' בסוף: "אוי לנו מיום הדין אוי לנו מיום התוכחה
וכו'." ועי' קרות יניי, סי' כ"ט, שו' ק"ב (פיוטי יניי, עמ' מ"ז): "אי לנו מיום דין וכו'." אם אינני
טועה כל דברי הפיתוי של יוסף הבאים אחר זה הוא, כנראה, נופך של המלקט בשילוב דברי
הפסוק בר' נ', ה' והרחבתו. ואולי יש כאן הד דברי יוסיפוס ב,קדמוניות היהודים," ספר ב', 9.

[ב]עצמו: גזירת המלך הריגה היא וחמתו מיתה משונה, שנ' חמת מלך מלא[וכי]

[מות] ואיש חכם יכפרנה (מש' ט"ז, י"ד),[3] מה תקנתו, לדבר עמו ולפתותו
בלשון תחנון

[עד] שתגיע חרב על צואר.[4]   כ י   כ מ ו ך   כ',   אמר לו: כשם שפרעה
מלך כן]

[ואת]ה משנהו, כך אבה גדול במקומו, ואני משנהו.[5]   א ד נ י   ש א ל   א] ת
ע ב ד י ו (שם, י"ט), אין אנו]

10   יורדין לסוף] דעתך, בתך אנו מבקשים ליקח, או בתינו אתה
סבור לישא, למה]

[זה שאלת ע]לינו ועל מולדתנו, ולא עוד אילא שלא כיסינו [ממך שום דבר.][6]

[ונאמר א]ל אדני יש ל אב זקן (שם, כ'), תאמר צדיק
כיהודה [יאמר דבר שאינו ברור][7]

[ואחיו מ ת (שם), אילא כך] אמרו חכמים (מותר לשנות מפני היראה).[8]

(סוף העמוד ב–Box C 2, מס' 42, ב', ע"א. חסרות, כנראה, שורות אחדות)

.......[וּהוֹרד]תם את שיבתי ברע[ה שאלה] (שם, כ"ט).......

15 ....[כי עבדך ע' א' הנ' מ' א' לא (שם, ל"ב). כיון ששמע [יוסף][9].......

המבליטות את איומיו של יהודה ומעשה וגבורותיו. בעל מדרשנו נוטה אחרי הפיום, מפני שהוא
קרוב אל הפשט. המקור היותר קרוב למדרשנו הוא ת"ב ויגש, ה' בסוף: "ד"א בי אדני שאל,
ונאמר אל אדני, ועתה ישב נא עבדך וכו', א"ל הקב"ה הרי ריפתה עתה מן הכח הראשון
ודברת תחנונים. וכו'". שניהם מגבבים בטויים בנאומו של יהודה המורים על בקשה ותחנונים:
ת"ב "עבדך – אדני" שחזר ונשנה בנאומו, בעל מדרשנו מדגיש "בי אדני" וגא".

3 השווה תנ' ויגש, ג'. גם שם הפסוק הזה נדרש על יהודה ויוסף, אלא שבהתאם לדעת
הרוב הנז' בהע' הקודמת "חמת המלך" מוסב על יהודה, "ואיש חכם יכפרנה" על יוסף, בעוד
שלפירוש מדרשנו יוסף הוא ה"מלך", ויהודה ה"חכם" המשכך חמתו בדברי תחנונים.

4 הד המאמר הידוע: "אפילו חרב חדה מונחת על צווארו של אדם אל ימנע עצמו מן
הרחמים" (ברכות י', ע"א).

5 השווה ב"ר שם, ו'. ניסוח המאמר בת"ב שם, ו' הוא: "אמר לו כשם שפרעה גדול כאן
ואתה משנהו כך אבא גדול בארץ כנען ואני משנה לו". עפ"י זה השלמתי את החסר בקטע.

6 השווה ב"ר שם, ח'; תנ' שם, ה'. ניסוח מדרשנו קרוב לזה שבמדרש הגדול בראשית,
עמ' 665. שניהם גורסים "אנו מבקשין" במקום "באנו" שבשאר מקורות. בכל המקורות, לרבות
מדה"ג, כתוב "אחותנו" במקום "בתינו" כאן, והדין עמהם, כי לפי גרסתנו צ"ל או "בנותינו" או
"אחת מבנותינו". "בתינו" היא שינגרת העט של "בתך" שלפני זה.

7 השווה ב"ר, הוצ' תיאודור, עמ' 1167: "אדם וודיי כיהודה יאמר דבר שאינו ברור וכו'";
מדרש אגדה ח"א, עמ' ק"ב: "וכי אדם ביהודה...". המלה "וודיי" שלא היתה ברורה לבעל
מ"א (ע"י ביאורו של תיאודור ב"מנחת יהודה") נשמטה על ידו. בעל מדרשנו נותן פרפראזה יפה.

8 במקורות הנז': "אלא אמר יהודה אם קיים יאמר לי לך והבא אותא." רש"י
מקדים לזה: "מפני היראה היה מוציא דבר שקר מפיו." השלמתנו היא בהקבלה למאמר ר'
אלעזר בר' שמעון "מותר לו לאדם לשנות בדבר השלום" (יבמות ס"ה, ע"ב).

9 השווה ת"ב שם; ז'. "כיון ששמע יוסף לא יכול לכבוש רחמיו;" מ"א שם: "כיון שהזכיר
צער אביו לא היה יכול ל ע מ ו ד ע ל ע צ מ ו." על פיהם השלמתי החסר.

[למע]לה מן העניין, ויעקב הלך לדרכו וג׳ (שם, ב׳).6   [ה]לכו ה[מלאכים]
       חן ...

ואמר להן: למי אתם, אמרו לו: שליעקב, כיון שראה עשו כן, אמר לו ליעקב:
       [מי לך]

5   כ ל ה מ ח נ ה ה ז ה א ש ר פ ג ש ת י (שם, ל״ג, ח׳), הוא כסבור על
       דרונו הוא משאל, אמר לו:

ל מ צ א ח ן ב ע י נ י א ד נ י (שם). אמר לו: אחי, יודע אני שהעולם
       הזה לי ניתן, ו[העו]

הבא לך ניתן, בוא ו[נ]תחבר אני ואתה, ונאכל אני ואתה. אמר לו.7 ......
       ....

(סוף העמוד חסר, ויש ליקוי בין דף זה והבא אחריו)

דף ג׳, ע״א – (Box C 1), מס׳ 45, ג׳, ע״ב)

[לפרשת ויגש]

ה.

[אהר]ון אל משה בי אדני (במ׳ י״ב, י״א), ואף יהודה לא דבר אילא בבקשה:
       י ד ב ר [נ א]

[עבדך] ד ב ר ב א ז נ י א ד נ י (בר׳ מ״ד, י״ח), שם בקשה כן (=כאן)
       תחנון. מניין שלשון נא הוא לשון

תחנון,1 שן אל נא אחי תרעו (שם, י״ט, ז׳), אל נא יחר לאדני, ואדברה
       (שם, י״ח, ל׳), הנה נא מצא

[עבד]ך חן בעיניך (שם, י״ט, י״ט), אל נא רפא נא לה (במ׳ י״ב, י״ג), ואף כן
       לשון תחנון, י ד ב ר נ א [ע ב ד]ך

5   ד ב ר ב א ז א ד ו א ל [י ח ר א פ ך ב ע׳], בלשון תחנון.2 נשא
       יהודה קול [וחומר]

---

6 השווה ב״ר ע״ה, י׳: „בא וראה מה כתב למעלה מן העניין וכו׳," ועפ״י זה הייתי מציע
להשלים: „וג׳ (– ויפגעו בו מלאכי אלהים), [במי פגעו, בעשו] ואמר להן וכו׳." השווה גם תנ׳
וישלח, ג׳.

7 השווה סדר אליהו זוטא, י״ט (פרקי ר׳ אליעזר), הוצ׳ איש־שלום, עמ׳ 27: „אמר לו עשו
ליעקב, יעקב אחי בא ונעשה שותפות אני ואתה וכו׳." המקבילות מובאות בהע׳ 18 של המו״ל,
הביטוי „אני ואתה" מיוחד למדרשנו ולסדר א״ז.

ה. מקורות: ב״ר צ״ג; תנ׳ ות״ב ויגש.

1 השווה ספרי במדבר, פיס׳ ק״ג בהתחלה: „אין נא אלא לשון בקשה."

2 עמדתו של יהודה כלפי יוסף שנוי במחלוקת בחוגי בעלי המדרש. יש, והם הרוב, שדרשו
„הגשה למלחמה" (ב״ר שם, ו׳), שכן רגילים היו לראות ביהודה את סמל המלכות והכח, גור
אריה יהודה; ויש, והם המועט, שגרסו „איזה גבור הכובש את יצרו," ייחסו ליהודה עמדה של
הכנעה ופיוס, ודרשו „הגשה לפיוס." הדיעה הראשונה משתקפת ברוב הפתיחות שבב״ר ותנחומא,

25 ביותר, ותלך לדרש את יהוה (שם), להיכן הלכה, ל[בית]
מדרשו [שלשם][9]

(כאן סוף הדף, ויש ליקוי בין דף זה והדף הבא)

דף ב', ע"א (Box C 2), מס' 178, ו', ע"א)

[לפרשת וישלח]

ד[.]

[ו]יהי לי שור וחמור [בר' ל"ב, ו'], [שור] אחד היה לי, [ו]ממנו
קניתי ת זכרים ונ[ת] נק[בות],

[וחמור אחד] היה לי, וממנו קניתי ש זכרים ונקבות, רחלה אחת
[היתה] לי, וממנה קנ[יתי ב] מאות זכרים ונק.[1] ואשלחה להגיד
[לאדו]ני (שם), שלחתי להודיעך בניסין ונפלאות שעשה הקֹב"הֹו, ואין
5 [בן]י צרת עין במ שלקחת מבית [אב]ה.[2] וישובו המלאכים (שם,
ז'), הלכו

[שמי]חים וחזרו עציבים. אמרו לו: א[דו]נינו, לא דייו שלא קיבל
[מאתנו את] השטר,[3] אילא קיבץ עמו ת [אי]ש ובא ללחמך. כיון
[שש]מע כין, ניזדעזעו איבריו ונתחלחלו [ע]יניו ונתעמ[דו]
[שערותיו][4]. . . . .

(סוף העמוד חסר)

דף ב', ע"ב (שם, ו', ע"ב)
. . . . מפרסם, שקע אור שלגדול אורו שלקטן מיתפרסי[ם]
. . . .ה להניצל מיד עשו.[5] שלח הקֹב"הֹ מלאכים לשמרו, מני[ין], ממה שכת[ב]

9 השווה ב"ר ס"ג, ו' ותרגום יב"ע.

ד. מקורות: ב"ר ע"ח, ו' ; ת"ב וישלח, ה'.

1 ב"ר: „ר' יהודה אומר משור אחד יצאו שוורים הרבה וכו' ," ניסוח „קניתי" במדרשנו
תמורת „יצאו" יש לזקוף על נטייתו של בעל מדרשנו לקרב המדרשים אל השכל ואל המציאות,
וכנראה היה חי בחוג שהיה רגיל במסחר בהמות ולא בנידולן. המקור למספרים ת' שוורים וכו'
נעלם ממני. רמז למספר „ב' מאות רחלים" אפשר למצוא במתנת יעקב, „רחלים מאתים."
2 מעין פירוש זה בתרגום יב"ע. מקורו נעלם ממני.
3 השטר – העתקת המחבר. אבל מה עניין שטר לכאן? ועל כן הייתי מציע לקרוא: „לא
דייו שלא קיבל [אותנו] שפיר' – יפה – ," כלו' בסבר פנים יפות אלא שהוא בא להלחם
בך, פראפראזה של המדרש: „את נוהג בו כאה והוא נוהג בך כעשו."
4 השווה ת"ב וישלח, ו': „נעשה גופו כשעוה זו" והערת המו"ל שם. למליצה „נתעמדו
שערותיו" השווה ת"ב שם, ד': „ארצה שעיר, שהוא מעמיד שערות של אדם."
5 כנראה שבא לבאר מדוע פחד יעקב כל כך, והוא מפני שידע שטרם הגיע זמן מלכותו,
ודומה לזה בב"ר ע"ה, ד': „לפניו, לזה שבא שעתו ליטול המלכות לפניו."

[נעקרת] התחיל וביקש רחמים עליה.‏3 לנכח אשתו (שם).‏4 ראוי לומר
[ויעתר]

15 [ויצחק] בעד אשתו, מלמד ששנהן היו מתפללין זה כנגד [זו. היא]
[היתה] אמרת: רבונו שלעול, אם רצונך לתת לי [ולד, אל תתן]
[אילא מן] הצדיק הזה. תו ה[וא היה] אומר: רבונו שלעול [אם]

(סוף העמוד ב־2 Box C, מס' 42, א', ע"ב)

[ורצונך לתת] לי ולד, אל ת[תן] אילא מן הצדקת ה[זאת].‏5
[תו אמרה רב]קה לפני הקְבְּהו: כלום בראת באדם דבר ב[חנם],‏6
20 בר [את] עינים לראות, אזנים לשמוע, פה לדבר, לב להבין, ידים
למשש, רגלים להלך, דדים הללו למה, ה ל ו (=הלא) להניק, מלמד
שעלת [ה]
שנים (=תפלת שנים) לפני מקום) ונתן לה הריון. ו י ע ת ר ל ו י ה ו ה
(שם), בתפלתו,
ו ת ה ר ר ב ק ה א ש ת ו (שם), בתפלתה,‏7 ו י ת ר צ צ ו ה ב נ י ם
ב ק ר ב ה (שם, כ"ב),
היו יורדין ועולין במעיה מגלי (=כגלי) הים.‏8 כיון שהיתה מצטער [ת]

---

3 מקור המאמר נעלם ממני. ביבמות ס"ד, ע"א התלמוד מדניש להיפך שאברהם שהה רק
עשר שנים בלי בנים ויצחק עשרים שנה. לפי תרגום יב"ע היתה יב"ע היתה עקרה עשרים ושתים שנה.
4 השווה יבמות שם: "לנכח אשתו, על אשתו לא נאמר וכו' ". גם מפרש המדרש
רזו'ن כותב: "הוה ליה למימר על אשתו" אולם הדין עם בעל מדרשנו שכך כתוב
"העתירו בעדי" (שמות ח', כ"א).
5 ב"ר ס"ג, ה': "למד שהיה יצחק שטוח כאן והיא שטוחה כאן ואומר רבש"ע כל בנים
שאתה נותן לי יהיו מן הצדקת הזו, אף היא אמרה כן וכו' ". אפיינית היא התמורה "ששניהן היו
מתפללין זה כנגד זו" במקום "שהיה יצחק שטוח כאן והיא שטוחה כאן." – בטויים פשוטים וישרים
לוקחים את מקומם של בטויים ציוריים ומשאלים. פרפראזה אחרת יותר קרובה אל המקור
היא זאת של רש"י: "זה עומד בזוית זו ומתפלל וזו עומדת בזוית זו ומתפללת." התמונה הציורית
בעינה עומדת אלא שנוספה לה משמעותה המפשטת "מתפלל" ו"מתפללת." בעל מדרשנו
הסתפק במסירת המשמעות המפשטת של תפילה.
6 השווה יבמות, שם: ויעתר לו, ויעתר להם מיבעי ליה.". בעל מדרשנו, כנראה, לא קיבל
תשובת התלמוד "שאינו דומה תפילת צדיק בן צדיק," שהרי למעלה מזה חושב למעלתה של
רבקה שאף על פי שבני משפחתה רמאים לא למדה ממעשיהם. וע"כ פותר השאלה באופן אחר,
והוא ש,ותהר רבקה אשתו" אינו אלא הקבלה ל,ויעתר לו," כלו' נתקבלה תפילתה כשם
שנתקבל תפילתו. המדרש הזה נמצא במדה"נ (עמ' 390) בשם ד"א.
7 השווה ברכות ל"א, ע"ב: "והנה היא מדברת על לבה, א"ר אלעזר משום ר' יוסי בן זמרא
על עסקי לבה, אמרה לפניו, רבש"ע כל מה שבראת באשה לא בראת דבר אחד לבטלה,
עינים לראות וכו' "; וע'י' מדרש שמואל הוצ' בובר, עמ' כ', הע' ל"ה. בעל מדרשנו העביר
תפילת־מענה זו מחנה לרבקה.
8 הקבלתו במדה"נ, שם: "מהוא ויתרוצצו, שהיו עולין ויורדין במעיה כגלי הים, זה אומר
אני אצא חחילה וכו' " בעל מדרשנו מביא רק את החלק הראשון שהוא פשוטו של הכתוב,
ומדלג על החלק השני, שכולו דמיון ופיוט.

הכֹּל שׂא אשה בנערותך ושׂא אשה בזקנותך. ילמד כל העולם כלו דרך

25 ארץ מאבינו אברהם שנשׂא אשה בנערותו ונשׂא אשה בזקנותו.

דף א' ע"ב (Box C 1, מס' 45, א', ע"ב)

מא [צ"ל: נשׂא] אשה בנער, שֹנ ויקח אברהם ונחור להם נ (בר' י"א, כ"ט),
ונשׂא אשה בזקנותו [שֹנ ויסף]

אברהם ויקח אשה ושמה קטורא (שם, כ"ה, א'). הוליד בנים בנערותו והוליד
[בנים בזקנותו]

ומכולם לא נתיחס אלא ב א ח א מ ה ם (!) (קרי: באחד מהם), שֹנ כי ביצחק
יקרא לך זרע (שם, כ"א, י"ב). [לפיכך נֹא]

בבקר תזרע את זרע. ן.ג] ו א ל ה ת ו ל ד ו ת י צ ח ק ב א, שׁכן
אשׂ]ריהן של [צדיקים]

5 שמיתחסים על שם אבתם. אף על פי שישמעאל נתיחס בתולדותיו, [ולא
נתיחס]

[א]ילא על שם אמו, שֹנ ואלה תולדות יש[מעאל ב] א אֹש ילדה הגר
[המצרית] (שם, כ"ה, י"ב),

אבל יצחק לא נתיחס אלא על שם אביו, אשר ילדה שרה אֹין]ן כֹת כֹה כאן
[אי]ולא אברהם הוליד את יצחק (שם, כ"ה, י"ט).[1] ויהי יצחק בן [מֹ] שֹנ
(שם, כ'), [למה הזכיר]

הכתוב את ר ב ק ה ב ת ב ת ו א ל (שם), הצדקת מיחסה באב ובאח,
ללמדך [שאף]

10 [על פי ש]הם רמאין היו, ונתגדלה רבקה בינותם, ולא למדה ממע[שיהם]
הרעים.[2] ו י ע ת ר י צ ח ק ל י ה ו ה ל נ כ ח [א] (שם, כ"א), בוא וראה
דרכו שליצחק

לא כדרכו שלאברהם, אברהם נעקרה אֹש כמה שנים ולא ב[קש]
[רח]מים עליה, אבל אבינו יצחק כיון שראה את הדבר [שאשתו]

שבקשתי במדרשים ולא מצאתי מי שיפרש בקר ולילה ביש' כ"א, י"ב על ימי נערות וימי זקנה.
בחוגי המדרש „בקר' ו„לילה' כאן נדרש על עולם הזה ועולם הבא, או על שכרם של הצדיקים
ועונשם של הרשעים לעתיד לבא.

כדאי להעיר שבעל מדרשנו מדלג על הפירושים שבמקבילות המוצאים מידי פשטן גם
את המלים ב ק ר ו ע ר ב גם את המלה ז ר ע, כגון „אם למדת תורה (–זרע) בנערותך
(–בקר) וכו.'

ג. מקורות: ב"ר ס"ג; ת"ב ואלה תולדות.

1 ניסוח מיוחד של המדרש בת"ב, תולדות א' בסוף. במה"ג עמ' 387: „אשריהן של צדיקים
וכו' ' ניסוח קרוב לזה שבמדרשנו.
2 ב"ר ס"ג, ד' ומקבילות.

[ו]שרות מינ אפֿ אך יש ל ועֿ רגֿ ילֿה וידעת כי אני יהוה אשר לא
יבושו קווי (יש׳ מ״ט, כ״ג). אמן כן יהי רצון. ב]. ואלה תולדות
יצחק בן אב[רֿ] (בר׳ כ״ה, י״ט)

10 [כ]תיב בבקר תזרע (במקרא: זרע) את זרעך ולערב אל תנח ידך כי אינך
יודע [אי זה]

י[כשר הזה א]ו זה אם (במקרא: ואם) שניהם כאחד טובים (קה׳ י״א, ו׳).
מדבר הכתוב בצדקה ובזֿ [ע].

[בצדקה, שה]צדקה נקראת זרע, שֿנֿ זרעו לכם לצדקה1 וקצרו (במקרא:
קצרו) לפֿ[י]

[חסד נ]ירו לכם ניר עת (מֿ: ועת) לדרש את יהוה עד יבא ויורה צדק לכם
(הו׳ י׳, י״ב). [אמר]

[הכֿת עשֿה צד]קה] בבקר עשֿ[ה צדקה] בערב, ואם בא לידך עני [בבקר]

15 [עשה עמו] צדקה,2 ואם בא לידך עני בֿ בֿעֿ עשה עימו צדקה [בֿעֿ, כי]
[אין אדם יודע ב]איזה מהם זכה, אם בראשון או באחרון ואם ב[או]
[לידך שניהם ב]בת אחת, הרי מוטב. מדבר בזרע, אמר הכֿת שֿ[א אשה]

(סוף העמוד ב–Box C 2, מס׳ 42, א׳, ע״א)

[בנער]ותיך ושא אשה בזקנותך,3 כי אינך יד[ע אם בנערותך ינתן]
[לך זרע] ואם בזקנותך ינתן לך זרע], ואי את]ה יודע אי זה מהם]
20 טובים, ואם בראֿש ואם באחרון. מה עינין נערות וזקנות אצל בקר
וערב, אלא מלמד שלנערות שלאדם נמשלה בבקר וזקנותו נמש[לה]
בערב, שֿנֿ אמר שומר אתה בקר וגם לילה אם תֿבֿ וגו׳ (יש׳ כ״א, י״ב), אתא
בקר
[אי]ל[ו]ימי נע, וגם לילה, אילו ימי זקנות שדומין לילה.4 לפיכך אמר

ב. מקורות: ב״ר ס״א, נֿ ומקבילות.

1 בבא קמֿא י״ז, ע״א מאמר ר׳ יוחנן בשם ר׳ שמעון בן יוחאי.
2 במקור: "ר׳ יהושע אומר אם בא עני אצלך בשחרית תן לו בערבית תן לו." כמה מן
ההרחבה והביאור בניסוח מדרשנו. מעניין שגם ר׳ דוד לוריא, הגאון שבמפרשי המדרש, מעיר:
"דרש זריעה על צדקה כדאמר זרעו לכם לצדקה וכמ״ש בספֿ׳ק דב״ק."
3 ניסוח הפירוש הזה כאן קרוב ביותר לניסוחו באבות דר׳ נתן, פ׳נ. גם שם שני הפירושים
המובאים כאן מיוחסים לתנא אחד, לר׳ יהושע, בעוד שבשאר המקורות הם נשנים במחלוקת בין
שני תנאים.
4 מן "מה עניין" עד כאן הוספת ביאור של מלקטנו. ההרחבה במקום זה מקבילה לזו
שנרמז עליה בהֿעֿ 2. בפירוש הראשון "בקר" ו"ערב" כמשמען, אבל "זרע" הוצאה מפשוטה,
ובעל מדרשנו ראה לנכון לבסס את משמעותה הסמלית על יסוד הפסוק "זרעו לכם לצדקה."
בפירוש השני "זרע" היא כמשמעה, אבל "בקר" ו"ערב" הוצאו מידי פשטן, ומלקטנו הרגיש את
הצורך לבסס את משמעותן הסמלית על יסוד הפסוק "אתה בקר וגם לילה." אולם מוזר הדבר

[טׄז קטעים מפורדים, ומעורבבים, קרועים ומטושטשים, נמצאים ב־T.-S. Box C 1,
מסׄ 45 (דׄ קטעים); וב־T.-S. Box C 2, מסׄ 42 (בׄ קטעים); ומסׄ 178 (יׄ קטעים).
כתיבה אחת עם נקוד בבלי לכולם. אחרי העיון בצילומים
שהיו לפני, נוכחתי לדעת שהדפים נקרעו באמצע לשני חלקים, באופן שאלו מן
הקטעים הם ראשי הדפים ואלו מהם סופיהם. עׄי הקרע נתקלקלו אילו שורות
באמצע. מדפים אחדים נשארו רק ראשיהם. כאן הם מופיעים כפי סדורם הנכון
(וחבל שיש כמה ליקוים ביניהם), ובתוך תוי ההסגר ניתנים הסימנים כפי הסדר
המעורבב בתיבות של הנׄׄל]

דף אׄ, עׄׄא (Box C 1), מסׄ 45, אׄ, עׄׄא)

[לפרשת חיי שרה ופרשת תולדות]

אׄ. בכל [מ]קום שמזכיר עפרון, עפרון מלא, כיון אהגיע כסף
מה ז כת וישמע אבר אל עפ וישקל אבר לעפ (בר׳ כׄׄג, טׄׄז).[1] ובשכר שׄת
[ה]שתחואות שנשתח׳ אבר לפ ע הא[2] לפני בני חת, פרע לו
הׄקׄבׄה כנגד מדה.[3] היכן נשתח׳ שתי פע׳, ויקם אב ויש לעם הא (שם, ז׳), לפני

5   עם הארץ (שם, יׄׄא),[4] פרע לו הׄקׄבׄהו, שבאו כל האומות והשתחוו לפני בניו שתי
[פע]מים, אחת בימי ש[למה] ואחת לעתיד לב. בימי שלמה מניין, שנ
וישתחוו לו כל מל וגו׳ (תה׳ עׄׄב, יׄׄא) ואחת לעתיד לב מניין, שנ והיו מלכים
אמניׄׄיך

א. מקורות: בׄׄר נׄׄח, ז׳; פסדרׄׄכ צׄׄח, עׄׄב ומקבילות.

[1] המאמר מקוטע ומסורס, ועל פי המקורות נראה לתקנו באופן זה: [את מוצא] בכל
מקום שמזכיר עפרון, עפרון מלא, כיון ש מ ג י ע [לארבע מאות שקל] כסף ... מה ז ה
(קרי: הוא) כתיב וישמע אברהם אל עפרון וישקל אברהם לעפרן, [עפרן תנינא חסר]. ועי׳
״מדרש חסרות ויתרות״, הוצ׳ ורטהימר, ״בתי מדרשות״, חׄׄב, עמ׳ רמ־רמא.

[2] ל פ נ י ע ם ה א ר ץ, לפני בני חת. כנראה הרי זה בא לפרש ששתי ההשתחואות הן
אחת ״לפני עם הארץ״ ואחת ״לפני בני חת,״ כמו שנאמר בבר׳ כׄׄג, ז׳: ״וישתחו לעם הארץ
לבני חת.״

[3] השווה מדרש הגדול, בראשית, עמ׳ 349: בא וראה כנגד שתי השתחויות וכו׳ המהדיר
ציין תופתתא סוטה פׄׄב. שם מונה הרבה דברים שנפרע לאברהם ״מדה כנגד מדה,״ וביניהם
שכנגד ״וישתחו ארצה (בר׳ יׄׄח, ב׳) בישר לבניו לעתיד לבא והיו מלכים אומניׄׄיך ... אפים
ארצה ישתחוו לך,״ אבל לא מצאנו שהשתחוותו לפני עם הארץ, לפני בני חת, תחשב לו לזכות.
העברת המדרש מבר׳ יׄׄח, ב׳ לכׄׄג, ז׳ אפשרית היא רק אם נקבל בפסוק האחרון את הפירוש
המובא בראבׄׄע: ״והאומרים כ י ה ש ת ח ו י ת ו ה י ת ה ל ש ם לא אמרו כלום,״ פירוש,
שכנראה חסר היה מסורת עתיקה.

[4] המשפט המתחיל ״היכן וכו׳ ״ הוא, כנראה, הוספה מאוחרת ממי שלא הבין את הרמז
לשתי ההשתחואות שניתן למעלה (עי׳ הע׳ 2), או שלא הניח את דעתו, מפני ש״עם הארץ״
ו״בני חת״ – היינו הך.

[5] כתובת המזמור: ״לשלמה.״

קסז

שידעו כמה נסים עשיתי עמהם בכל מסע ומסע. הוי אלה מסעי. זש"ה נחית כצאן
עמך...ביד משה ואהרן, מה הצאן הזה אין מכניסין לצל הקורה...מה הצאן
הזה אין מכניסין אותו לאוצרות כך ישראל...עאכ"ו. ילמדנו.

ז א ת ה א ר ץ. מלמד שהראה הב"ה למשה כל מה שהיה ומה שעתיד להיות.
אשר ת פ ל לכם, וכי הארץ נופלת...כעס עליהם משה. מה עשה הב"ה...
שהפיל שרה. לכך נא' זאת הארץ אשר תפל לכם בנחלה, מה לכם, ראויה היא
לכם. למלך שהיו לו עבדים ושפחות, והיה משיא לעבדיו שפחות מן אסיא אחרת,
ולשפחותיו עבדים מן אסיא אחרת, עמד המלך וחשב בדעתו אמ' העבדים שלי
והשפחות שלי. כך הב"ה אמ' הארץ שלי היא, שנ' לי"י הארץ ומלואה וגו', וישראל
שלי, שנ' כי לי בני ישראל, מוטב שאנחיל ארצי שלי לעבדי שלי. הוי א ש ר
תפל ל כ ם. ילמדנו.

איש אשר רוח בו. א"ל הב"ה למשה לפי שאמרת יפקד י"י וגו', שאתה מכיר‬
לרוח כל א' וא', מנה עליהם מי שיודע להוליך כל א' וא' לפי דעתו. וסמכת‬
את ידך עליו, כמדליק מנר לנר. ונתת מהודך עליו. כמערה מכלי אל כלי.‬
ומה שאמ' לי יירשו בני את כבודי, הרי הכבוד אינו זז מבית אביך, שאע"פ יהושע‬
עומד תחתך, ולפני אהרן הכהן יעמוד. ילמדנו.‬

את קרבני לחמי לאשי. א"ר יצחק וכי יש לפני אכילה ושתיה, אם ארעב לא‬
אומ' לך וגו', וא"ת שיש לפני אכילה ושתיה למוד ממשרתי אש להוט ואם יש לפני‬
אכילה ושתיה למוד ממשה, ראה מה כתי' בו... ילמדנו ופסיקתא.‬

כבשים בני שנה. אמ' הב"ה עשר בהמות טהורות בראתי שלש ברשותך ושבע‬
אינן ברשותך, שמא הטרחתיך לצוד בהרים ולהקריב לי, לא אמרתי אלא מאותן‬
שהן ברשותך. הוי כבשים בני כבשים. ילמדנו.‬

ת"ר מעשה בר' מאיר ששאלו זקן א': כתי' לריח ניחח באשה לי"י וכתי' לאשה‬
ריח ניחח לי"י. לא הוה בידיה, נכנס לבית המדרש ושאל, א"ל כאן לעוסקין שלא‬
לשמה וכאן לעוסקין לשמה. גמר' דרך ארץ.‬

א"ר חמא כשם שאדם מברך להב"ה כך הב"ה מברכו, דכתי' אלה תעשו לי"י‬
במועדיכם, אלה עשיתם לא נא' אלא אלה תעשו, תעשו כן לשנה הבאה. ילמדנו‬
פ' בראשית.‬

וכלי הקדש. מהו וכלי הקדש, זה הציץ, דכתי' ביה ופתחת עליו שמות וגו'‬
קדש לי"י. וחצצרות התרועה בידו, כמשמעם. א"ל משה בלעם הרשע מכשף הוא‬
ומלמד להם כשפים, הראו לו את הציץ ששמו של הב"ה גלוף בו והן נופלין עמו,‬
דכתי' ואת מלכי מדין הרגו על חלליהם ואת בלעם בן בעור הרגו החרב. ילמדנו.‬

וכלי הקדש. אלו בגדי כהונה, שנ' ובגדי הקדש אשר לאהרן. תוספתא דסוטה‬
ובילמדנו.‬

וכלי הקדש. א"ר יוחנן אלו בגדי הכהונה שבהן אורים ותומים, כד"א ויקח‬
את כל ארצו מידו. ויצבאו על מדין. הקיפוה מג' רוחותיה וכו'. ספרי.‬

ומקנה רב וגו'. יש מי שנתרבה עשרו לרעתו, כקרח והמן וכיוצא בהן. וכן‬
את מוצא בבני ראובן ובבני גד שהיו עשירים הרבה, והיה להם מקנה רב, והיו‬
מחבבין ממונם וגרמו להם לישב בחוצה לארץ, ולפי' גלו תחלה מכל השבטים,‬
שנ' ויגלם לראובני ולגדי וגו'. מי גרם להם? שהפרישו עצמן מאחיהן בשביל קנינם‬
מנין, ממה שקראנו בענין ומקנה רב וגו'. שאלה מטרונה את ר' שמואל בכמה ימים‬
... א"ל ומאותה שעה מהו עושה, א"ל סולמות, מעלה לזה ומשפיל לזה... הפיל‬
המדינים לפני ישראל כדי שיתעשרו בני ראובן ובני גד, הוי זה משפיל וזה ירים.‬
ולכך נקראים נכסים. שנכסים מזה ונגלים לזה. ולמה נקר' זוזים, שזזים מזה ונתנים‬
לזה; ממון, מה שאתה מונה; מעות, מעט לעת. וכן את דורש כולן. וכן חנה או'‬
י"י מוריש ומעשיר משפיל אף מרומם, אף שהוא מביא על זה מרומם זה. זש"ה‬
לב חכם לימינו ולב כסיל לשמאלו, לב חכם לימינו, זה משה... והטפל עיקר,‬
דכתי' גדרות צאן... לצאנכם. ילמדנו.‬

אלה מסעי. א"ל הב"ה למשה כתוב את המסעות שנסעו ישר' במדבר,‬

פנחס בן אלעזר

פנחס בן אלעזר, בן ששאל עזרו מהאל; בן אהרן הכהן, בן שסלק חרון אף מישראל. ילמדנו.

תחת אשר קנא לאלהיו ויכפר על בני ישראל, ללמדך שכל השופך דמם של רשעי ישר' כאלו הקריב קרבן וכפר על ישראל. ושם איש ישראל המכה אשר הכה. חסרין ואוין: מכה, הכה... ילמדנו.

לפי שהיו אומ' העולם מונין לישר' ואו' שהם בניהם של מצרים: אם בנפשותן של ישר' היו שולטין כ"ש בנשותיהן, א"ר אושעיא באותה שעה אמ' הב"ה למלאך הממונה על ההריון: צייר צורת הולד כדמות האב, הה"ד מ ש פ ח ת הראובני, משפחת השמעוני. א"ר אדי הא ברישא דתיבתא יוד בסופה ־יה מעיד עליהם שהם בניהם של אבתיהם. לאלה תחלק וגו', והלא ליוצאי מצרים נתחלקה וכו'. ילמדנו.

תניא נתן נתן להם, זה חלק אביהן. ב ת ו ך אחי אביהן, זו נחלת אבי אביהן. והעברתם, זו חלק בכורה, ר' אליעזר בן יעקב או' אף חלק אבי אביהן נטלו, דכתי' נתן נתן להם. בתרא פ' יש נוחלין. וספרי ב ל ש ו ן א ח ר.

מה ענין מיתת משה לפ' נחלות, אלא כיון ששמע משה נתן להם אחזת נחלה כסבור שנתרצה לו המקום, אמ' הריני מנחיל לישר' את הארץ, א"ל הב"ה גזרתי במקומה עומדת: עלה על הר העברים הזה. ילמדנו.

ונאספת אל עמך גם אתה כאשר נאסף א ה ר ן אחיך. אין אתה יפה מאחיך. ילמדנו.

ר' שמעון או' למה"ד למלך שהיה מהלך בדרך ובנו עמו על קרובין, כיון שהגיע למקום צר נהפכו קרובין על בנו, נסמית עינו, נקטעה ידו, נשברה רגלו. כל זמן שהיה מגיע לאותו מקום היה או' כאן נסמית עינו שלבני כאן נקטעה ידו כאן נקטעה רגלו. כך הב"ה מזכיר בתורה ג' פעמים מי מריבה, מי מריבה, מי מריבה: כאן הרגתי מרים, כאן הרגתי אהרן, כאן הרגתי משה. הה"ד נשמטו בידי סלע שפטיהם. יפקד י"י וגו'. כל מי שמבקש צרכי צבור כאלו בא בזרוע. מה ראה לבקש הצורך הזה אחר סדר נחלות, אלא כיון שירשו בנות צלפחד את אביהן, אמ' משה הרי שעה שאתבע צרכי, אם הבנות יורשות כבוד אביהן דין הוא שירשו בני את כבודי. א"ל הב"ה למשה נוצר תאנה יאכל פריה, בניך ישבו להם ולא עסקו בתורה, יהושע ששמשך דין הוא שישמש את ישר' שאינו מאבד את שכרו. ילמדנו.

יפקד י"י וגו' איש. א"ל הב"ה איש אתה מבקש, קח לך את יהושע בן נון איש וגו'. א"ל רשל"ע ו א ש ר יוציאם ואשר יביאם, ולא כמני שהוצאתים ממצרים ולא הכנסתים. חופת אליהו.

וסמכת את ידך עליו. משה לא בפיו בלבד היה מלא חכמה אלא אף ידיו מטיפות חכמה, שנ' וסמכת את ידך עליו, וכתי' ויסמך משה את ידיו עליו, וכתי' ויהושע בן נון מלא רוח חכמה וגו'. חופת אליהו.

הלגיסטים ... כבר שלחתי אפסונין לבית ... ולגבריאל והיו מקריבין לפני. ילמדנו פ' צו.

אלו שאין להם חלק לעולם הבא, ג' מלכים וד' הדיוטות. ג' מלכים: ירבעם, אחאב ומנשה; ד' הדיוטות: בלעם, דואג, אחיתופל, גחזי. את מוצא שד' אלו על דבור פיהם נדחפו לגיהנם. בלעם על יד לשונו הרע, שאמ' מן ארם ינחני בלק, מן הרמים הייתי, מן מחיצת האבות, והגחני בלק חרקני לגיהנם, ואין ינחני אלא גיהנם, שנ' בן אדם נחה על המון מצרים. ילמדנו פ' זאת תהיה.

כי לא נחש ביעקב. כשהם צריכין להלחם כהן גדול עומד לבוש אורים ותומים ונשאלין בהב"ה ונוצחין, ולא היו מבדין; וכל הגוים מקסמים ומנחשין והיו מבדין, שנ' ספר אותות בדים וקסמים וגו'. כעת יאמר ליעקב. אותו עת שנ' בו ובעת ההוא יעמד מיכאל וגו', ולישראל מה פעל אל וגו' מה רב טובך וגו' וכתי' כי לויושבים לפני י"י יהיה סחרה, ואין אומה יכולה להכנס במחיצתן. הן עם כלביא יקום. אין אומה בעולם כיוצא בהם. עמדו משינתן שחרית מיד חטופין במצות, בתפילין ובציצית ובק"ש וממליכין להב"ה, ומלחשין ומפליגין לדרך ארץ, ואם נתקל א' מהן ממליך להב"ה. לא ישכב עד יאכל טרף. כשהוא אומ' שמע ישראל וגו' ומלחש אחריו ברוך שם כבוד וכו', המזיקים בורחים ממנו לפי שהוא נמסר ביד המלאכים בזכות ק"ש משומרי יום לשומרי לילה, שנ' נפשי לי"י משומרים וגו', וכשבא לישן מפקיד רוחו ביד הב"ה [ושנ'] בידך אפקיד רוחי. ודם חללים ישתה, בבקר, וי"א נתנבא על משה שלא ישכב עד שיתן נקמה בעמון ומואב ובחמשת מלכי מדין, דכתי' ואת בלעם בן בעור הקסם וגו'. כשראה בלעם הרשע ישר' שמשמרין מצות ואפילו מצוה קלה נזהרין בה, אמ' מי יוכל לקלל את אלה שמשמרין מצות ולא עוד אלא עוד אלא ששמו גלוף בהם: ישראל. ולכך נאמ' י"י אלהיו עמו, לפי' המקללן כאלו מקלל עצמו, וכל המשתתף בהם כאלו משתתף בעצמו, שנ' הנגע בהם כנוגע בבת עינו. ילמדנו.

בלעם הביט בישראל ויצאה עינו כנגדם שלא יכול ליגע בהם, שנ' וישא בלעם את עיניו וירא את ישראל, מה ראה? ראה את הדגלים, התחיל לום' מי יוכל ליגע בבני אדם שהם בכורים לאבותיהם ולמשפחותיהם, שנ' ישכן לשבטיו. ילמדנו פ' במדבר סיני.

משכנתיך, אל תקרי משכנתיך אלא משכונותיך. ילמדנו.

לא היה דבר בעולם שלא גלה הב"ה לבלעם וקלקל בו מיד. ומפני שעתידין כל האומ' לום' לפני הב"ה רשל"ע אלו נתן לנו נביא כמשה קבלנו תורתך, לפי' נתן להם בלעם שהיה חכם כמשה. ומשה היה דבר א' יתר על בלעם, ובלעם היה דבר א' יתר על משה. במשה כתי' ויקרא אל משה ובבלעם כתי' ויקר אלהים אל בלעם; במשה כתי' הודיעני נא את דרכיך ובבלעם כתי' ו י ד ע ד ע ת ע ל י ו ן. סדר אליהו זוטא.

מאי דכתי' כי הנה רחקיך יאבדו וגו' ואני קרבת אלהים לי טוב. בלעם כשראה יום הדין שעתיד לאבד הרשעים עשאו רחוק, שנ' א ר א נ ו ולא עתה אשורנו ולא קרוב, אבל משה כשראה אותו היום והוא מתן שכרן שלצדיקים אמ' כי קרוב יום אידם. ס ד ר א ל י ה ו ר ב ה.

•

עם אלו אלא עם נכבדים מהם, מיד ו י ס ף עוד בלק וגו' ויבאו אל בלעם וגו'
מ א ד, ממה שהיית נוטל לשעבר אני נותן וכל אשר אתה חפץ אני אעשה. א ם
יתן לי בלק וגו'. א"ל אלו היה מבקש לשכור... ספק אין נוצחין... ברכות על
ידו. ויבא אלהים אל בלעם לילה. למה נגלה על בלעם לילה? לפי שלא היה
ראוי לרוח הקדש, שכל נביאי הגוים לילה הוא מדבר עמהם. ילמדנו.
(דף פ"ה, ע"ב)

ואף את הדבר, מלמד שבהתראה הלך. ו י ח ב ש את אתנו. א"ל הב"ה:
רשע כבר קדמך אברהם בעקדת יצחק ויחבש את חמרו, תבא חבישה ותבטל
חבישה. ילמדנו.

וילך עם שרי מואב... כמותם. ויחר אף אלהים כי הולך וגו'. א"ל הב"ה
איני חפץ... לך אתם, מלמד שבדרך שאדם רוצה לילך בה מוליכין אותו.
ויתיצב מלאך... ונעשה לשטן וכן אמ' לבלעם את גרמת לי... שאינה שלי שנ'
הנה אנכי יצאתי לשטן... זה לזה. ילמדנו.

ותרא האתון... האומות בידם וחרב חייהם וישר' בפיהם חייהם, ואתה
מחליף אומנתך ובא עליהם באומנותן, אף אני אבא עליך באומנותך. לפי' וחרבו
שלופה בידו... ספקלוטור להרוג את שונאו... מה ראה לקדמו ג' פעמים...
בראשונה בדרך והיה ריוח מכאן ומכאן לנטות שם... אלא אלו בקש לקלל...
בני עשו. וכשבא לבני יעקב אין דרך לנטות ימין ושמאל שלא היה בהם (דף
פ"ו, ע"א) פסולת... ויפתח י"י את פי האתון, להודיע שהפה והלשון ביד הב"ה,
שהרי פתח פי האתון שהיה סתום, וכך יסתום פי הפתוח, שלא יהיה בו רשות
לקלל את ישר'. זה שלש ר ג ל י ם, למה רגלים ולא פעמים, אלא רמז רמזה
לו אתה מבקש... אע"פ שהגוי מדבר בלשון הקדש לשונו מוסרח הוא... לנשוך
נחש. ראה אנקה... וי"א שאמר להם אינה שלי... גדולה ממנו. ילמדנו.

ה ה ס כ ן וגו'. כיון שדברה מתה... היא ששתקה את בלעם. ואם כן חס
המקום על כבוד רשעים עאכ"ו על כבוד צדיקים. בא וראה כמה חס המקום על
כבוד הבריות וידע צרכן וסתם פיות הבהמות, שאלו היו הבהמות מדברות לא
היו יכולין בני אדם לעמוד כנגדן. ומה האתון הזו שהיא טפשית שבבהמות וזה
חכם שבחכמים כין (–כיון) שדבר לא היה יכול לעמוד בה, שאר בני אדם עאכ"ו.
ויגל... עאכ"ו. ילמדנו.

כי עתה גם אתך הרגתי ואותה החייתי. מכאן אתה למד... חטאתי. אע"פ
שהיה רשע גמור ידע שאין עומד בפני הפורענות... כך אומנתו שכך (דף פ"ו, ע"ב)
אמר לאברהם ויאמר אליו... את שבעת המזבחות וגו'. שבעה כנגד שבעה שבנו
צדיקים ונתקבלו: אדם, הבל, נח, אברהם, יצחק, יעקב, משה. אמ' בלעם הרשע
למה קבלת את אלו? לא בשביל עבודה שעבדו קבלתם, לא נאה לך שתהא נעבד
מע' אומות ולא מאומה א'! השיבתו רוח הקדש טוב ארוחת ירק וגו' מבית מלא
זבחי ריב, שאתה רוצה להכניס מריבה ביני ובין ישר'. בא וראה כמה היה ערום
אותו רשע, התחיל אמ' את שבעת המזבחות ערכתי, לא אמ' מזבחות אלא
ה מ ז ב ח ו ת. אמר משעה שנברא אדם הראשון... (דף פ"ז, ע"א) ועבר

על אומו' העולם נתן עצה רעה והעמיד פרצה לאבד את הבריות מן העולם. ולא
עוד אלא אלא כל הנביאים היו מרחמי' על האומות, שכן ישעיה אומ' לבי למואב יזעק,
וכן יחזקאל נשא על צור קינה, וזה אכזרי עמד לעקור אומה שלמה על לא דבר.
ו י ר א   ב ל ק. מהו וירא, ראה פורענות העתידה לבא עליו על יד ישר' יותר מכל
שונאיו שבעולם. וירא בלק, נח לרשעים...האלהים ויאמ' אמחה וגו'. וירא חם
אבי כנען וגו' ארור כנען, ויראו אותה שרי פרעה וינגע י"י את פרעה; וירא אותה
שכם, ואת שכם ואת חמור אביו הרגו. וכן כולם. ד"א וירא בלק, משל למי
שהושיב שומרים...עבר הגיס והרגו, היה מרתח על עצמו. ואף כאן בלק ראה
מה עשו ישר' בסיחון ועוג שהיה מעלה עליהם שכר לשמרו ונתיירא על עצמו.
ועוד שראה נסי נחל ארנון. ו י ג ר   מואב, מהו ויגר...תצורם וכתי' אל תצר
את מואב ואל (דף פ"ד, ע"ב) תתגר בם מלחמה, מלחמה אין אתה עושה בהם,
ומה אתה עושה בהם? כל מה שאתה יכול...שהיו רואין עצמן גרים בעולם, אמ'
ירדו למצרים ואחזו בה, שנ' וישב ישראל בארץ מצרים והי משכירין להם בתים
...באו ישר' נטלוה משנ·הם גזל שאין בו עולה...לא א"ל הב"ה כי לא אתן
מארץ בני עמון לך ירושה, ואו' כי לא אתן לך מארצו ירושה...לכך היו
מתיראין. ו י א מ ר   מואב אל זקני מדין...כאן אלא מפני שהיו רואין שישר'
מנצחין שלא כדרך כל הארץ, אמ' מנהיג שלהן בישר' נתגדל...אמרו זקני מדין
אין מדתו וכחו אלא בפיו. אמרו אף אנו כנגדן יש לנו איש שכחו בפיו. כ ל ח ך
השור, מה השור...מה השור נוגח בקרניו אף אני כך, שנ' וקרני ראם קרנו.
ו ב ל ק בן צפור מלך למואב בעת ההיא, והלא מתחלתו נסיך...שעה. ילמדנו.

אל בלעם בן בעור פ ת ו ר ה, שם עירו. וי"א כשולחני הזה שכל מלכי
מדין והגוים נמלכין בו...והוא או' לו שסופך למלוך...על עצמי אתה עושה
ואני לבדי מכבדך אלא אם תעקרם...וכנענים כלם משתחוים לך...א"ל ואתה
מאי איכפת לך...מ מ ל י   ממלי כתי', ממלין לי כד"א כי אמלם...לא כך
א"ל הב"ה שאין נוטלים מארצו כלום אלא שבלק ... לאמיתתו. אולי אוכל
נכה בו. כמי שמנכה...ושכר את בלעם לקלל את מואב...תברך מברך.
ילמדנו.

(דף פ"ה, ע"א)

וקסמים בידם...שהיו קוסמין בהם שאם' אם יבא עמנו...אין בו ממש...
שאין בו ממש. ילמדנו.

כל האומות גזרו עצמן (מ)עריות דכתי' ורחל באה עם הצאן וגו', וכתי' ולכהן
מדין שבע בנות וגו', ובלעם הרשע עמד והטעה אותן. וכשם שהטעה את הבריות
באותה עצה כך הטעהו הב"ה, שא"ל מי האנשים האלה עמך, אמ' אותו רשע אינו
יודע בהן, א"כ יש עתים שאינו יודע אף אני אעשה בבניו מה שאני מבקש. ויאמר
בלעם אל האלהים...מוציא שמי בעולם...קבה לי בפירוש. בלק אמ' ואגרשנו
...חפץ בכבודי. ילמדנו ומדרש תלים.

כשחזרו שרי בלק אליו, א"ל כך אמ' בלעם כי מאן י"י וגו'. אין כבודי שאלך

שאלמלא נתנה להם במשובה היה השבט שנתנה להם בתחומו או'... שוין בה.
ר' או' למה נתנה במדבר, לומ' לך מה המדבר הזה לא נזרע ולא נעבד...
דרך ארץ. וכשם שאין המדבר מעלה אריסין (? אולי: ארנון) כך בני תורה בעולם
הזה. וממתנה נחליאל... סנהדרין בצד המזבח... בתחום מי שבאת משדי מואב.
ספרי ובילמדנו.

וממתנה נחליאל וגו'. ממתן תורה נחלו ע"ז ומע"ז בא להם מלאך המות, שנ'
ומנחליאל במות, אל תקרי במות אלא בא מות. סדר אליהו זוטא. (דף פ"ג, ע"א)
אין לך בן חורין אלא ההוגה בתורה חרות על הלוחות, ואו' וממתנה נחליאל, מאי
ואו', וכי תימא בן חורין הוא אגרא לא שקיל ת"ש וממתנה נחליאל, מתן שכר
לעושין עצמן כנחל. וכי תימא נחל זה פעמים פוסק, כד"א באפיק נחלים עברו,
ת"ש ומנחליאל במות, כאותן במות לא פסקי. גמר' דרך ארץ.

זש"ה סור מרע... ורדפהו. לא פקדה תורה... אם באת מצוה לידך אתה
מצוה עליה ולא לרדוף אחריה. והשלום: בקש שלום ורדפהו, בקש שלום
במקומך ורדפהו במקום אחר. וכך עשו ישר' שאעפ"י שא"ל החל רש רדפו אחר
השלום, שנ' וישלח ישר' מלאכים וגו'. כל דבר תורה צריכים זה לזה שמא זה
נוטל מזה. כאן... ושקיל כנגד כולם. א"ל ישר' נעבור (?) בארצך לכבוש את
המלכים (דף פ"ג, ע"ב) א"ל איני יושב... בגבלו וגו'. במחשבה עשה לו הב"ה
למסרו בידם בלא צער, שאלו ישב לו בעירות שלו הוא ואכלוסיו היו ישראל
מתיגעין... אלא מה עשה הב"ה, כנסן לפניהם ומסרם בידם בלא צער, לכך
כת' ו י א ס ו ף סיחון וגו'. רבה פ' אלה הדברים ובילמדנו.

כי חשבון עיר סיחון. אלו היתה חשבון מלאה יתושין אין כל בריה יכולה
לשלוט בה, ואין צריך לומ' שהיה גבור ויושב בעיר מבצר. ילמדנו.

וישב ישראל בארץ האמורי, נשתיירה יעזר, מיד וישלח מלאכים... נאמין
בהב"ה ונעשה מלחמת עמהם... מהו ויפנו ויעלו, מלחמת סיחון עשו... ו י צ א
עוג וגו', מלמד שכנסן הב"ה לפניהם כדי למסרם בידם שלא להטריחם. רבה.
ובילמדנו.

אשרי אדם מפחד תמיד וגו'. כך היא מדת הצדיקים... אינן פורקין יראה
מעליהם. וכן אתה מוצא ביעקב וכו' בפסו' ויירא יעקב. ואף משה תפס את
היראה כדרך (דף פ"ד, ע"א) אביו... או נתלכלכו בעבירה... כפריצי זתים
הפליטין מתוך הגפת... לסיחן. ילמדנו.

ויכו אתו ואת בניו, בנו כתי', שהיה לו בן קשה ממנו. ילמדנו.

וירא בלק

למה נכתבה פרשת בלעם, להודיע למה סלק הב"ה רוח הקדש מאומות
העולם, שכשם שהעמיד נביאים מישר' כך רצה להעמיד מאומות העולם, וראה
שזה הרשע עמד מהן ועשה מה שעשה. שכל הנביאים שהיו מתנבאים לישר' היו
מזהירין את האומות על העבירות, וכה"א בן אדם צופה נתתיך וגו'. וזה שעמד

(דף פ"א, ע"א)

מלך ערד. מי היה מלך ערד...והוא יושב על הפרצה...לאור להם.
ואם עמלק היה למה קראו כנעני, ואם כנעני היה למה קראו עמלק, אלא מפני
שנאסרו...עמלק ונתגרה בישראל' פעם ושתים, א"ל הב"ה...אלא הרי הוא
כנעני שנ' בהם...כנעני. ילמדנו.

ותקצר נפש העם בדרך. והלא כתי' ורוחך הטובה נתת להשכילם, אלא
אותם שנגזרה עליהם גזירה למות במדבר לא היו רואים נחת רוח במדבר ולא
רוח טובה. וג' מתנות נתן הב"ה לישראל וכו' לעיל. וכשנסתלק אהרן מה כתי'
שם: ותקצר נפש העם בדרך, שהיתה השמש זורחת עליהם. ילמדנו פ' במדבר
סיני.

באלהים ובמשה. השוו עבד לקונו...כשהיו מגלין להם סל הבא...שנ' אם
(דף פ"א, ע"ב) יראה...לכך ותקצר נפש העם בדרך, הוא שהתרעמו ונפשנו
קצה בלחם הקלקל. וישלח...בנחשים אלא יבא נחש שהתחיל...לשון הרע
הה"ד ופרוק גדר...ד"א למה נפרע בהם בנחשים, יבא נחש שאוכל מיני הרבה
ואינן נטעמין לו אלא טעם א' שנ' ונחש עפר לחמו, ויפרע מאוכלי המן, שהוא מין
א' וטועמין בו מיני הרבה, דכתי' ויתן להם שאלתם ותאותם יביא להם. את
הנחשים השרפים. ויבא העם אל משה וגו' וישתחוו לפניו ויא' התפלל...נתרצה
להם. מכאן שאין המוחל נעשה אכזרי, וכה"א ויתפלל אברהם אל האלהים וגו',
ואם אינו מוחל נק' חוטא, שנ' גם אני חלילה לי מחטא מחדל להתפלל. ילמדנו.
והיה כל הנשוך. אפי' נשוך מפתן ועקרב וחיה רעה וכלב. ילמדנו.
ויעש משה...שנתרצה להם הב"ה. ילמדנו.

(דף פ"ב, ע"א)

את והב בסופה. שנעשו להם אותות ומופתים בנחלי ארנון כנסים שנעשו
להם...ומה הם הנסים שנעשו להם בנחלי ארנון אדם...חברו בהר הזה...
והדרך יורד לתוך הנחל ועולה. באו אומות העולם וארבו לישר' במערות שבים
ושדים היו לצד ההר הב' כנגד אותן מערות. כשבאו ישר' סמוך להר קפצה הארץ
וקדמה לקבל ישר' כשפחה שראתה בן אדוניה השכן(?) אצלה קפצה לקראתו
וכו' לקמן. והה"ד ומשם בארה, וכי משם היה הבאר, והלא מתחלת ארבעים שנה
היתה עמהם, אלא שירדה לפרסם את הנסים. ילמדנו ורבה פ' אלה הדברים.
היאך היתה הבאר עשויה? כמין סלע והיתה מתגלגלת...והיתה גולה.
ילמדנו פ' במדבר סיני.

(דף פ"ב, ע"ב)

כרוה נדיבי העם וגו', שהיו נשיאים עומדין על גבה...ורווח שהיה בין
הדגלים היה מלא מים וכשהיתה האשה צריכה...חוץ למחנה ומקיפין אותו שנ'
על מי מנוחות ינהלני. וכל הימים שהיו ישר' במדבר כך היו משתמשים. לכך
קלסו עליה באר חפרוה שרים. וממדבר...לשמשון. ד"א למה נתנה במדבר,

הנוראות שאתה מביא עלינו בעלילה אתה מביאן וכו'. בפסוק ביום אכלך. וכן
את מוצא במשה שא"ל אם יראה איש באנשים, איש זה משה המסוי' באנשים, ואו'
עתה תראה אשר אעשה לפרעה, במלחמת פרעה ולא במלחמת ל"א מלכים.
וכיון שא"ל שמעו נא המרים אמר הב"ה לכן לא תביאו וגו'. הוי נורא עלילה על
בני אדם. ילמדנו פ' וישב יעקב.

המה מי מריבה, לבן מלך שנטל אבן וסימא את עינו, היה אביו או' על כל
דבר אבן זו סמאה עינו שלבני. לכך נאמ' המה מי מריבה. ילמדנו. מנהגו שלעולם
אדם עוסק בפרקמטיא...דכתי' וירדו אבותינו מצרים וגו'. משל לב' אחים...
על זקנם...שאותו שטר חוב שפרעתי...וירעו לנו מצרים (דף פ', ע"א)
ולאבותינו. ללמדך שכל זמן שישראל בצרה אף האבות בצרה עמהם. ילמדנו.

נעברה נא בארצך...ולא נשתה מי באר אינו או' אלא מי באר. ללמדך
דרך ארץ... מן החנוני כדי להנאותו...התירו להם כיסכם, שלא יאמרו עבדים
הם, עניים הם, הראו להם עשרכם וידעו שלא הפסדתם כולכם בשעבודכם ואחרי
כן יצאו ברכוש גדול...יש לנו רשות להרוג ולכבוש...לא נטה ימין ושמאל.
זש"ה בהתחברך לרשע פרץ י"י מעשך...בארצו נתפס אותו צדיק. לכך נסמכה
פר' אהרן לפר' מלך אדום. ויסעו מקדש וגו'. מהו כל העדה עדה...מצרים,
והן הן שכחו' בהן חיים כולכם היום. הר ההר...שידעו נסים שעשה...שלא
היה הר במדבר כדי שלא יהיו מתיגעין עולין ויורדין. וג' הרים הניח הענן.
י א ס ף אהרן אל עמיו וגו'. א"ל משה להב"ה: רבוני הניח בני גד ובני ראובן...
לבני ישראל. על אשר מריתם וגו'. זש"ה לא ירעיב... שעמדו ממנו נגזרה
עליהם מיתה ואינן נפטרין...והצדיקים נענשין על עבירות קלות מיתה שלא היה
אדם נתפס עליה. לכך נאמ' על אשר מריתם וגו'. והפשט את אהרן את בגדיו
והלבשתם את אלעזר בנו. א"ל הב"ה הרי אתה מנחמו...מוריש בגדיו לבניו:
והפשט את אהרן את ב ג ד י ו, והלא אם יצא כהן גדול בבגדי כהונה חוץ...
מפני שהיו צמר ופשתים...א"ל הב"ה לעלות להר ההר. ויעש משה כאשר צוה
י"י. ללמדך שאע"פ שא"ל גזרה קשה על אחיו לא עכב. ילמדנו.

ויפשט משה את אהרן. אפשר לומ' כן, כיון שהפשיטו בגדיו מת ערום ונקבר
ערום, אלא כל כהן גדול לובש ח' בגדים וכהן הדיוט ד'. וכך היה אהרן לובש
ח' ואלעזר ד'. נטל משה ד' מאהרן והלבישם לאלעז' ונעשה כהן גדול ונשתיירו
על אהרן ד'. נכנסו (דף פ', ע"ב) למערה וראו מטה מוצעת ומנורה דולקת
ומלאכי השרת עומדין עליה וכו'. באותה שעה נתאוה משה לאותה מיתה. חופת
אליהו.

כשירד משה ואלעזר מהר ההר אמ' להם ישר' היכן היה(!) אהרן? א"ל משה
כבר נפטר לבית עולמו. א"ל אין אנו מניחין אותך עד שתראנו אותו אם חי אם
מת. באותה שעה עמד משה בתפלה. מה עשה הב"ה? קרע את המערה לכאן
ולכאן והראה מטה ואהרן מת מושכב עליה, שנ' ויראו כל העדה כי גוע אהרן.
מיד הפכו פניהם למחנה ישר' וראו ענני כבוד שנסתלקו, שנתן להם הב"ה בזכות
אהרן והם פורחים מטתו באויר. חופת אליהו.

משה כך הגביה ידו והכה בסלע, שנ' ו י ך את הסלע במטהו פעמים. כיון שלקה
הוציא דם, שנ' הכה צור ויזובו, ואין זוב אלא דם, שנ' זוב דמה. בא משה לפני
הב"ה וא"ל הסלע הזה אינו מוציא מים אלא דם נכו'. אמ' הב"ה לסלע: הפוך
דמך למים, שנ' ההופכי הצור אגם מים. חופת אליהו.

ויאמר משה את ידו ויך את הסלע במטהו פ ע מ י ם. הכה פעם א' התחיל
הסלע נוטף מים מועטים, שנ' הן הכה צור ויזובו מים, כזב שהוא נוטף טפים. א"ל:
בן עמרם! אלו ליונקי שדים ולגמולי חלב, מיד הקפיד כנגדו והכהו פעמים, שנ'
במטהו פעמים, יצאו מים ר ב י ם, שטפו כל מי שהיה מרנן כנגדו, שנ' ונחלים
ישטפו. אעפ"כ לא עשה משה אלא מסלע שאמ"ל הב"ה. ומנין שאף אותו הסלע
שאמ' ישר' עליו וכל הצורים שהיו סביבותיו הוציאו מים, שנ' הן הכה צור ויזובו
מים. ילמדנו.

(דף ע"ט, ע"ב)

שאת פני רשע לא טוב, לא טוב להם לרשעים שנושא להם הב"ה פנים בעולם
הזה. לא טוב לו לאחאב הרשע בן עמרי שנשא לו הב"ה פנים בעולם הזה, שנ'
ראית כי נכנע אחאב מלפני וגו'. להטות צדיק במשפט, טוב להם לצדיקים שלא
נשאו להם פנים, טוב להם למשה ואהרן שלא נשא להם הב"ה פנים בעולם הזה,
שנ' יען לא האמנתם וגו', הא האמנתם בי עדין לא הגיע זמנכם ליפטר. לא
האמנתם וגו', וכי לא אמ' משה דבר קשה מזה, והלא קשה מזה אמר: הצאן ובקר
ישחט וגו', אלא הראשונה מפני שלא היתה בפרהסיא אלא לפניו לא נענש עליה,
אבל עכשיו כנגד הרבים. ל כ ן לא תבאו וגו'. זש"ה יש צדיקים שמגיע אליהם
כמעשה הרשעים וגו'. כשקלל הב"ה את הנחש לא הניחו לטעון אלא מיד: כי עשית
זאת ארור וגו'. וכן למשה לא הניחו לטעון אלא מיד: יען לא האמנתם בי לכן
וגו'. משל דמשה ודוד לשתי נשים שלקו בב"ד, אחת קלקלה וא' אכלה פגי שביעית.
אותה שאכלה פגי שביעית א"ל: בבקשה מכם הודיעו לבריות על מה היא לוקה,
שלא יאמרו אף אני קלקלתי. הביאו פגי שביעית ותלו עליה והכריזו ואמ' זו
קלקלה חו אכלה פגי שביעית. אף משה כן אמ': רבוני! הרי גזרת עלי למות
במדבר עם הדור שהכעיסוך, שנ' כמה ימרוהו במדבר וגו'. עכשיו יאמרו הדורות
אני שוה להם, יכתוב על מה נענשתי. הה"ד יען לא האמנתם וגו'. יומא פ' יום
הכפורים. ובילמדנו. א"ל הב"ה למשה באי זה פנים אתה מבקש ליכנס לארץ.
משל לרועה שיצא לרעות צאנו שלמלך ונשבו כל הצאן. בקש הרועה ליכנס
לפלטרין שלמלך, א"ל המלך אם אתה נכנס יאמרו כל הבריות צאן אחר מכניס.
כך אמ' הב"ה למשה דור ההוא שהוצאת ממצרים ששים רבוא וקברתם במדבר
ואתה מכניס דור אחר עכשיו יאמ' אין לדור שבמדבר חלק לעולם הבא, אלא
תהיה בצדן ותבא עמהן, שנ' ויאתה ראשי עם, לכך נא' לכן לא תביאו וגו'. ילמדנו.
לכו חזו מפעלות אלים נורא עלילה על בני אדם. א"ר יהושע בן קרחה אף

מוקדון כד הוה חמי לשמעון הצדיק (דף ע״ד, ע״א) הוה קאים על רגלוי ואו׳ ברוך
אלוהו שלשמעון הצדיק. אשר לא עלה עליה עול. זו אדום הרשעה שלא עלה
עליה עלו של הב״ה... מים טהורים וגו׳. פסיקתא דר׳ כהנא ומדרש תלים
ובילמדנו.

(דף ע״ו, ע״ב)

מאי דכתי׳ לא תמצא בארץ החיים, אין התורה נמצאת אצל מי שמבקש תענוג
תאוה וגדולה בעולם הזה, אלא במי שממית עצמו עמה, שנ׳ זאת התורה אדם כי
ימות באהל. ילמדנו.

א״ר מני כל דבר ודבר שהיה הב״ה או׳ למשה היה או׳ לו טהרתו וטומאתו
ועונשו, קולו וחומרו, וכיון שהגיע לפר׳ אמר אל הכהנים א״ל: רש״ע אם נטמאו
אלה במה טהרתן? ולא השיבו דבר. וכיון שהגיע לפר׳ פרה א״ל הב״ה למשה:
אותה אמירה שאמרתי לך אמור אל הכהנים ואמ׳ לי אם נטמאו אלה במה טהרתן,
זו היא טהרתן: ו ל ק ח ו ל ט מ א וגו׳. א״ל רש״ע וכי טהרה היא? א״ל חקה היא
וגזרה גזרתי, ואין בריה יכולה לעמוד על גזרתי. הה״ד זאת חקת התורה. מדרש
קהלת. ובילמדנו.

(דף ע״ח, ע״ב)

כשיצאו ישר׳ ממצרים והיו מהלכין במדבר הוריד להם הב״ה מן והגיז להם
שלוים והעלה להם הבאר, והיה כל שבט ושבט עושה לו אמת המים ונובעין אצלו,
והיה נוטע תאנים ורמונים וגפנים ועושין פירות בני יומן כשם שהיה בתחלת ברייתו
שלעולם: עץ פרי עושה פרי. חטא אדם, זרע חטים והעלה קוץ ודרדר. משנסתלקה
הבאר מה כתי׳ שם: לא מקום זרע ותאנה וגו׳. וכל כך למה: ו מ י ם אין לשתות.
ילמדנו פרשת קדשים.

והשקית את העדה ואת ב ע י ר ם. מכאן שחס המקום על ממונן של ישראל.
את הקהל אל פ נ י הסלע. מלמד שכל א׳ וא׳ רואה עצמו על פני הסלע, וכיון
שראו נסים שבסלע התחילו לומר יודע משה משה הסלע, אם הוא מבקש יוציא לנו מים
מזה. נמצא משה עומד בספק, אם שומע להם מבטל דברי המקום, והב״ה לוכד
חכמים בערמם, לפי שהיה משה משמר עצמו כל אותן מ׳ שנה שלא להקפיד כנגדן,
שהיה מתירא מן השבועה שנשבע הב״ה אם יראה איש באנשים האלה. אמרו לו:
הרי הסלע, כשם שאתה רוצה להוציא מסלע אחר הוציא לנו מזה, התחיל צווח עליהם:
ש מ ע ו נא המורים, שוטים שכן בכרכי הים קורין לשוטה מורה. ד״א המורים –
מלמדים מלמדיהם. ד״א המורים – מורי חצים. ילמדנו.

(דף ע״ט, ע״א)

לא היה משה יודע איזה, א״ל הב״ה לתת להם ממנו מים, מיד ראו ישראל
סלע א״ל תן לנו מיד מזה. הרים משה מטהו והניחו על גבי הסלע ועשה עצמו
כמדבר עם ישראל, שנ׳ ה מ ן הסלע הזה וגו׳. התחיל מזיע מעצמו. כיון שראה

נכנס משה לאהל מועד לעיני כל ישראל וראה מטה אהרן שפרח, ולא כלו
פרח אלא שעשה הב"ה נס בתוך נס, מקום שהיה בו שם אהרן כתוב הוא שפרח
והוציא פירות, ומקום שהיה בו כתוב שם לוי היה יבש. והה"ד והנה פרח
מטה אהרן ל ב י ת לוי, עד בית לוי ומהו ו י צ ץ ציץ, כשם שהציץ נתון
בראש אהרן כך עשה הב"ה ציץ נזר בראש המטה. ויגמל ש ק ד י ם.
א"ר לוי אותן שהיו שוקדין רעה על אהרן מתו באותו הלילה. ילמדנו.

ג' דברים עתיד אליהו ע"ה להעמיד להם לישר': ארון וצנצנת המן
וצלוחית של שמן המשחה, וי"א אף מקלו שלאהרן בשקדיה ופרחיה, שנ'
ה ש ב את מטה אהרן לפני העדות, ומתרעמין היו על המטה שהיו או' אינו
אלא לפורענות; הוא הביא את המכות על המצרים במצרים ועל הים.
לפי' ידעו שהוא שלנסים. ילמדנו פרשת בא אל פרעה.

זאת חקת התורה

(דף ע"ג, ע"א)

מי יתן טהור מטמא. תמן תנינן כל העוסקין בפרה מתחלתה ועד סופה
מטמאין בגדים. היא עצמה מטהרת הטמאים! אלא אמ' הב"ה חקה חקקתי
וגזרה גזרתי אי אתה רשאי לעבר על גזרתי.

(דף ע"ג, ע"ב)

זאת חקת התורה. אמרות י"י אמרות טהורות וגו'. ר' חנן בר פפי פתר קריא
בפ' פרה שיש... אמר לו משה ואהרן הא בכלל שנ' ו י ד ב ר י"י אל משה
ואל אהרן לאמר. כתי' וידבר שלשת אלפים משל וגו' וכתי' וידבר על העצים
ועל האבנים וגו'. אמ' שלמה על כל עמדתי, ופר' פרה כיון שהייתי מגיע בה
הייתי דורש בה וחוקר בה ושואל בה, אמרתי אחכמה והיא רחוקה ממני. א"ר
יהושע דסכנין בשם ר' לוי ד' דברים יצר הרע מקטרג עליהם ובכולן כתי'
חוקה... וכתיב בה חקת: זאת חקת. דבר אל בני ישראל ו י ק ח ו א ל י ך.
א"ר לוליאני א"ל הב"ה למשה: משה לך אני מלמד טעמי פרה אדומה אבל לא
לאחרים, חוקה היא. גוי אחד שאל את רבן יוחנן בן זכאי... א"ל נכנסה רוח
תזית באותו האיש מעולם? א"ל לאו, א"ל ולא ראית א' שנכנסה בו רוח תזית;
א"ל הן... ישמעו אזניך מה שפיך מדבר... וכתי' ואת רוח הטומאה אעביר מן
הארץ. וכיון שיצא א"ל תלמידיו... לא המת מטמא ולא המים מטהרין אלא
גזרתו של הב"ה היא, אמ' הב"ה חוקה חקקתי. וכו' לעיל. הוי ז א ת חקת התורה.
פסיקתא דרב כהנא ובילמדנו.

ויקחו אליך פרה. מפני מה כל הקרבנות באים זכרים וזו באה נקבה? ר' איבו
לבן שפחה שטנף פלטרין שלמלך, אמ' המלך תבא אמו ותקנח את הצואה. כך
אמ' הב"ה תבא פרה ותכפר על מעשה העגל. ד"א פרה זו מצרים... אלכסנדרוס

(דף ס"ו, ע"ב)

כיון שראה משה המלאך המשחית בעם, אמ' לאהרן מה אתה עומד
קח את המחתה וגו', א"ל אהרן: מרי משה להרגני אתה מבקש, והלא בני
מפני שהקריבו לפניו את הקטרת נשרפו באש, ולי אתה אומר קח את המחתה,
בני הכנסו אש זרה ונשרפו, ואני אוציא אש קודש לחוץ ואיני נשרף! א"ל
משה: מה אתה עומד ומשיח, עד שאתה עומד ומשיח הם מתים, לך ועשה מהרה.
הה"ד והולך מהרה. כיון ששמע אהרן כך, אמ' אם אני מת על ישראל
איני כדאי, מיד ויקח אהרן וגו'. א"ל הב"ה למשה: קח אהרן, גדלהו בלקיחה
כשם שהצל את בני בלקיחה, שנ' קח את המחתה. ילמדנו פ' צו.

בא וראה כמה הקטרת חביבה שעל ידי הקטרת נעצרה המגפה בשעה
שא"ל משה לאהרן קח את המחתה וגו'. ויקח אהרן כאשר וגו' והנה החל
הנגף. מהו החל הנגף, א"ר יהודה בר' סימון היה המלאך נוטל על סדר
מרקחות ולא היה מניח מת בין החיים ולא חי בין המתים אלא על
סדר, כענין שנ' החל הנגף בעד כד"א מהחל חרמש בקמה, כשם שהקוצר קוצר
על סדר. מיד ויקח אהרן וגו'. הלך ומצא המלאך עומד ומחבל, עמד אהרן
כנגדו ולא היה מניחו לחבל, דכתי' ויעמד בין המתים ובין החיים. א"ל לאהרן
הנח אותי ואעשה שליחותי, א"ל אהרן משה שלחני והב"ה שלחך, הרי הב"ה
ומשה באהל מועד נלך אצלם. לא השגיח המלאך עד שעצרו אהרן במתניו והוליכו,
שנ' וישב אהרן אל משה והמגפה נעצרה. מהו והמגפה נעצרה, א"ר
יצחק שנגף למלאך ועצרו. לפי' כשבא משה להפטר מן העולם אמ' ברך י"י
חילו וגו' וכו' התם. ר' יצחק אמר בא וראה כמה הקטרת חביבה שכשבנה
משה את המשכן ואת כליו, ושחט הקרבנות וערך על המזבח, וסדר השלחן
והמנורה – ולא ירדה שכינה עד שהקריבו הקטרת, דכתי' עורי ובאי תימן וגו'.
ילמדנו פ' ואתה תצוה.

אולת קשורה בלב נער וגו'. אולת קשורה בלב נער, אלו ישראל שנ' בו
כי נער ישראל ואהבהו. א"ל הב"ה למשה: טפשים הם ואינם מניחים טפשותם,
ראה כמה מתו מהם במגפה ובשריפה ובליעה, ועד עכשו הם טפשין אין מרחיק
מהם טפשותם אלא המטה, אמו' להם שיביאו איש מטהו והנח אותם באהל
מועד, ואני אברור מהם מי שארצה; מתוך כך הם שותקים. ד"א מטה מטה
לבית אב. אמ' הב"ה מטה הם צריכים שהם עומדים כנגד אהרן, אני נתתי לו
הכהונה והם מתרעמים עליה. איש את שמו תכתוב על מטהו, כל אחד
יכתוב בכתב ידו כדי שיכירו כתב ידן, ואת שם אהרן תכתוב על מטה לוי.
כיון שאמ' הב"ה למשה מיד עשה כן. א"ר חנינא נטל משה קורה ונסרה לשנים
עשר נסרים ואמ' לנשיאים קחו לכם איש מטה א'. לקחו וכתבו להם שמות
השבטים, כל א' שם שבטו, וכתב אהרן שמו בראש המטה ושם לוי למטה
ממנו, ונתן טבעת בין שמו לשם לוי. נטל משה מטה אהרן ונתנה בתוך
המטות ואגדן אגודה א' וחתמן והניחן בבית קדשי הקדשים, שנ' וינח
(דף ס"ז, ע"א) משה את המטת, המטה כתי' מלמד שמטה א' היו. בבקר

יצאו נצבים, לחרף ולגדף, שנ' נצבים, וכי בני אדם היאך יוצאים הלא אין
יוצאין אלא נצבים, אלא מלמד שיצאו כשהם מחרפין ומגדפין, נאמר כאן
יציאה והצבה ונאמר להלן ויצא איש הבינים ויתיצב (דף ס"ה, ע"ב) מה להלן
בחרופין ובגדופין אף כאן בחרופין ובגדופין. א"ר ברכיה בא וראה כמה
קשה המחלקת שב"ד שלמעלה אין קונסין אלא מעשרים שנה ומעלה וב"ד
שלמטה בן י"ג שנה ומעלה, ובזה המחלקת אפי' תינוקות בן יומן נשרפו ונבלעו
בשאול תחתית: נשיהם ובניהם וטפם. ילמדנו.

לא י"י שלחני. משל לשושבין בתו שלמלך שהיו עדותיה בידו, עמד
א' מן המסובין כנגדו וקללו וא"ל לא נמצאו בתולים לבתו שלמלך, עמד
השושבין כנגדו שלמלך וא"ל אם אתה עושה דין בזה ותהרגהו במיתה משונה
לפני הכל מוטב, ואם לאו אף אני או' בודאי שלא נמצאו בתולים לבתו
שלמלך ויתקיים הדבר. אמ' המלך מוטב להרוג את זה ולא יצא שם רע
על בתי. וכן קרח נחלק על משה ואמ' בזאת תדעון כי י"י שלחני, ולא מלבי,
אם כמות כל האדם וגו', אף אני אודה כי לא י"י שלחני אלא מלבי אמרתי.
ילמדנו.

ויהי ככלתו לדבר את כל הדברים האלה ותבקע האדמה אשר תחתיהם.
ללמדך שכל מקום שהוא רוצה הוא מצמיח את הפורענות. ילמדנו.

(דף ס"ו, ע"א)

חיים שאלה, חיים נדונין עד עכשו, ותכס עליהם הארץ. ילמדנו.

א"ר ירמיה בן אלעזר ג' פתחים יש לו לגיהנום . . . זה פתחה שלגהינם.
עירובין פ' עושין פסין. ובחופת אליהו.

וכל ישראל אשר סביבותיהם נסו ל ק ל ם, שהיו צוחין משה הצילנו.
ו א ש יצאה וגו', שאלו נשרף ולא נבלע היו הבלועים מתרעמים ואו' קרח
שגלגל עלינו כל הפורענות הזה הרי נצול ואנו נבלעים; ואלו נבלע ולא נשרף
היו השרופים מתרעמים ואו' קרח שהבביא עלינו כל הפורענות הזה הרי
נצול ואנו נשרפים. לפי' נדון בשני מיתות, להטו האש תחלה לעיני הנשרפים,
למה, שהיתה בידו מחתה, שנ' אתה ואהרן איש מחתתו, וקלעתו האש כדור
והיתה מתגלגלת בו עד שהביאתו לפי הארץ בין הבלועים, שנ' ותבלע הארץ
אותם ואת קרח. ילמדנו.

א"ר יהודה אותה האש שירדה מן השמים במתאוננים שקעה בארץ, ולא
חזרה עוד למקומה בשמים אלא נכנסה ושקעה לה אל אהל מועד וכו' בפסוק
ותצא אש. ואותה האש יצאה ואכלה עדת קרח, שנ' ואש יצאה מאת י"י וגו'.
פרקי רבי אליעזר.

אמ' רב כל המחזיק במחלקת עובר בלאו, שנ' ולא יהיה כקרח.
ר' יוסי או' ראוי להצטרע, כתי' הכא ביד משה לו וכתי' התם הבא נא ידך
בחיקך. סנהדרין פרק חלק. ובילמדנו.

שבניו עושים תשובה, לפי' נשתתף לאותה חזקה. אמ' אני הוא אשר יבחר י"י.
ויאמר משה אל קרח ש מ ע ו נ א בני לוי, יש לך אדם שמדבר עם
ראובן ואו' לשמעון שמע? אלא היה מבקש ממנו שיחזור לו דברים רבים, כיון
שראה שלא שמע לו אמ' עד שלא ישתתפו עמו שבט לוי אחזור להם,
התחיל מזרז בהם: שמעו נא בני לוי. ה מ ע ט מ כ ם, הקטן הכבוד שכבדם,
חזר ואמ' לקרח ו י ק ר ב אתך ואת כל אחיך בני לוי, אתך שהיה גדול
שבשבט שנעשו אחיו טפלים לו. ל כ ן אתה וכל עדתך הנועדים על י"י. כל
המחלקת הזה אשר אתם עושים אינה כנגדנו אלא כנגד הב"ה. א"ל משה אלו
אהרן אחי נטל לעצמו זאת הכהונה יפה עשיתם שנתרעמתם עליו, עכשו
שהב"ה נתן לו – שהמלכות והגדולה שלו – כל מי שעומד על אהרן אחי לא
עליו הוא עומד אלא על הב"ה הוא עומד. לכך כתי' ו א ה ר ן מ ה הוא
כי תלינו עליו. כל הדברים האלה פייס משה לקרח ואין אתה מוצא שהשיבו דבר,
שהיה פקח ברשעו, אמ' אם אני משיב ויודע אני בו שהוא חכם גדול,
עכשו יקפחני בדבריו ויקללני ואני מתרצה לו בעל כרחי, מוטב שלא
אזקק לו. כשראה משה שאין בו תועלת פירש הימנו. ילמדנו.

לא נלך לא נבא לא נאמ' אלא לא נ ע ל ה, פתחו פיהם לפורענות,
לום' שהם מתים בירידה, וכן היה: וירדו הם וכל אשר להם וגו'. אמ'
משה הואיל ולא רצה לבא אצלי אלך אני אצלם אולי יתבישו ויחזרו בהם,
שנ' ויקם משה וילך אל דתן ואבירם וכו' לקמן. ו י ח ר למשה מאד, נטצער
להבא, למה? שאדם הדן עם חברו ומתוכח עמו ומשיבו יש שם נחת רוח,
ואם אינו משיבו הרי הוא מצטער צער גדול. א ל תפן אל מנחתם, אל
תקבלם בתשובה. היה צריך לום' אלא אל תפן אל עבודתם. כך אמ' משה
לפני הב"ה רשל"ע יודע אני שיש לאלה חלק באותה מנחה, דכתי' מלבד עולת
הבקר ומנחתה, והיא שלכל ישראל, ואלו הואיל ופרשו מבניך אל תסתכל
בחלקם, תניחנו האש ולא תאכלנו. ל א חמור אחד מהם נשאתי, מה
שדרכו ליטול לא נטלתי מהם. בנוהג שבעולם אדם שעושה בהקדש נוטל
שכרו מההקדש; בשעה שהייתי עולה ויורד למצרים לא נטלתי משלהם.
ילמדנו.

(דף ס"ה, ע"א)

מה עשה קרח? הלך כל אותו הלילה מפתה ומענה את ישר' ואו' להם
מה אתם סבורים שאני עוסק ליטול הגדולה לעצמי, איני מבקש אלא
שתהא הגדולה חוזרת על כלנו, כי משה נטל המלכות לעצמו ולאחיו
כהונה גדולה. והיה הולך ומפתה כל שבט ושבט עד שנתפתתו עמו. ילמדנו.

ד' נקראו רשעים: המרים יד על חברו להכותו ואע"פ שלא הכהו,
שנ' ויאמ' לרשע למה תכה רעך; והלוה ואינו משלם, שנ' לוה רשע ולא
ישלם; ומי שיש בו עזות, שנ' העז איש רשע; ובעל מחלקת, שנ' סורו נא מעל
אהלי הרשעים. ושתיהן היו בדתן ואבירם: עזות ומחלקת. ו ד ת ן ואבירם

אלא מעולם דברים אלו לא נטמיות מן השמים ומלבך אתה בודאם. ילמדנו ובירושלמי דסנהדרין פרק חלק.

(דף ס"ד, ע"א)

א"ר לוי באותה שעה שבא קרח לחלוק על משה מה עשה, כנס את כל עדתו ואמ' למשה ואהרן: הרביתם עלינו משאוי יותר משיעבוד מצרים, טוב לנו תחת יד מצרים מתחת ידיכם; ועוד שבכל שנה ושנה מתים ממנו ט"ו אלף ומ"ה, עד שבקשו לסקלו. לפי' וישמע משה ויפל על פניו. א"ל משה לא מלאכה אני מבקש ולא אהרן אחי אחי כהונה גדולה, שנ' ואהרן מהו. מיד אמ' משה לפני הב"ה: רשל"ע לא אתה צויתני הקרב אליך את אהרן אחיך? הרי עמדו כנגדנו להורגנו. א"ל הב"ה בקר וידע יי' את אשר לו. מה בקר, א"ר נתן אמ' הב"ה אם יתקבצו כל העולם ויוכלו להפך הבקר לערב כך יוכלו לבטל הפלה (צ"ל: הבדלה) זו; וכשם שהבדלתי בין אור לחשך כך הבדלתי את אהרן מן הכל, שנ' ויבדל אהרן להקדישו קדש קדשים. ד"א בקר, מה ראה לומר להם בקר, אמ' משה שמא מתוך מאכל ומשתה אמ' דבר זה, או' להם ידחה דבר זה למחר, שמא בין כך ובין כך יעשו תשובה. ד"א בקר. א"ל משה הב"ה חלק בין יום ובין לילה, אם אתם יכולים לערבם כך תצליחו בזה, הלא כתי' ויבדל אלהים בין האור ובין החשך, וכתי' ויבדל אהרן וגו', אם תבטלו זה תבטלו זה. ואת הקדוש והקריב אליו, כבר הוא מתוקן. זאת עשו קחו לכם מחתות קרח וכל עדתו, מה ראה לומ' כך, אמ' להם אתם נבדלתם בישר' כמו הגוים, עשו כמו הגוים שיש להם טעיות הרבה וכומרים הרבה, וכולם מתקבצין בבית א', ואנו אין לנו אלא אל אחד ותורה א' ומשפט א' וכהן גדול א', ואתם ר"נ איש מבקשים כולכם להיות כהנים גדולים, כשם שאתם רוצים בכך כך אני רוצה בכך. לכך אמ' אתה וכל עדתך היו לפי יי'. זאת עשו וקחו לכם מחתות, הרי לכם תשמיש היותר חביב, שהיא הקטורת חביבה מכל הקרבנות, וסם המות נתן להם בתוכה, שבה נשרפו נדב ואביהוא. לפי' התרה בהם, שנ' והיה האיש אשר יבחר בו הוא הקדוש, וכי אין אנו יודעין שמי שיבחר בו הוא הקדוש, אלא אמר משה: הריני או' לכם שלא תתחייבו בנפשותיכם כולכם אתם ר"נ, שאע"פ שיבחר מכם לא יבחר מכם אל א', ואותו יבחר יצא חי וכולכם אובדים, הרי אמרתי לכם, ולא טפשים היו שכך התרה בהם וקבלו עליהם לקרב' הם חטאו על נפשותם, שנ' החטאים האלה בנפשותם. וקרח שהיה פקח וחכם גדול מה ראה שלא שב כיון שראה כל כך התראה בו? אלא עינו הטעתו. ראה שלשלת גדולה עומדת הימנו, וזה היה שמואל ששקול כמשה (דף ס"ד, ע"ב) ואהרן, שנ' משה ואהרן בכהניו ושמואל בקראי שמו, וכ"ד משמרות עומדות מבני בניו שכולם מתנבאים ברוח הקדש, שנ' כל אלה בנים להימן וגו'. אמ' קרח אני אצא חי, אפשר הגדולה הזאת עתידה לצאת ממני ואני אובד! והוא לא היה יודע

של יהודה סמוך לדגלו של משה ואהרן, דכתי' והחונים לפני המשכן
קדמה דגל מחנה יהודה, ועמהם יששכר וזבולון, ולפי' זכו כולם להיות
בני תורה, דכתי' יהודה מחקקי, וכתי' ומבני יששכר ידעי בינה לעתים,
וכתי' ומזבולון מושכים בשבט סופר. ילמדנו.

נשיאי עדה קרואי מועד. מי היו? אליצור בן שדיאור וחביריו האנשים
אשר נקבו בשמות. אע״פ שלא פרסמן הכתוב נתן סימניהן ומתוך כך
אתה מכיר אותם. משל לבן טובים שגנב כלים מבית המרחץ ולא היה בעל
הגנבה רוצה לפרסמו, התחיל נותן סימניו. אמרו לו: מי גנב כליך? אמ' להם
אותו בעל קומה, ושניו נאות ושערו שחור וחוטמו נאה. משנתן סימניו
ידעו מי הוא. וכן בכאן אע״פ שסתמן הכתו' ולא פיר' שמותן, כיון שנתן
סימניהם אתה יודע מי הם. נא' כאן נשיאי עדה קרואי מועד ונא' להלן
אלה קריאי העדה נשיאי מטות אבותם. ויקהלו על משה. כשהעביר
משה תער על בשר הלוים עשה (דף ס״ד, ע״א) גם כן לקרח. יצא קרח
והיה מחזר על כל ישר' ולא היו מכירים אותו, אמ' לו מי עשה לך כך? אמ'
להם משה עשה בי כך, ולא עוד אלא שנטלוני בידי וברגלי והיו מניפין אותי
ואו' לי הרי אתה טהור. והביא את אהרן אחיו וקשטו ככלה והושיבו באהל
מועד. מיד התחילו שונאיו שלמשה לגרות בו את ישראל, ואמ' משה מלך וכו'
לעיל, מיד ויקהלו על משה וגו'. אמר להם כל העדה כלם קדושים, כולם
שמעו בסיני אנכי י״י אלהיך. ומדוע תתנשאו על קהל י״י, שאם הייתם שומעים
אתם לבדכם בדין היה שתתנשאו, עכשו שכולנו שמענו מדוע תתנשאו.
מיד נזדעזע משה ולא היה יכולת בידו לבקש רחמים מפני שהיה בידם זה
סרחון רביעי: בעגל, במתאוננים, במרגלים, ובכלם התפלל עליהם. כשהגיע
מחלקתו של קרח נתרשלו ידיו, אמ' כמה אטריח לפייס עליהם. לפי'
וישמע משה ויפל על פניו. ילמדנו.

ויקח קרח. אין ויקח אלא משיכת דברים רכים, שמשך כל גדולי
ישר' והטם אחריו. על ידי מה נחלק, על ידי אלצפן בן עוזיאל בן
אחי אביו שנתמנה נשיא על משפחתו, שנ' ונשיא בית אב למשפחות
אליצפן בן עוזיאל. אמ' קרח ד' בנים היו עם אביו, שנ' ובני קהת עמרם ויצהר
וחברון ועוזיאל. עמרם הבכור זכה למלכות משה ואהרן לכהונה גדולה.
מי ראוי ליטול השניה, לא השני יצהר? אני בנו של יצהר אני ראוי
להיות נשיא על משפחתי, והוא מינה בנו של עוזיא' קטן, בן של אחי אבא
יהי גדול עלי! הריני חולק ומבטל כל מה שעשה. מה כתי' למעלה מן
הענין? פר' ציצית, קפץ קרח ואמ' למשה: טלית שכולה תכלת מה שתהא פטורה
מן הציצית, א״ל חייבת, דכתיב ונתנו על ציצית הכנף פתיל תכלת.
בית מלאה ספרים מהו שתהא פטורה מן המזוזה? א״ל חייבת, דכתי'
וכתבתם על מזוזת ב' פעמים. א״ל קרח: הטלית שכולה תכלת אינה פוטרת
אותה וד' חוטין פוטרין אותה! כל התורה כולה מאתים ושבעים וחמש
פרשיות אין פוטרות את הבית וב' פרשיות שבמזוזה פוטרות את הבית!

כולו ועשרה מתשרי, וירד בעשרה לחדש והיו ישרא' שרויין בתפלה ותענית,
ובו ביום נא' למשה סלחתי כדברך וקבעו הב"ה יום סליחה ומחילה לדורות.
הה"ד כי ביום הזה יכפר עליכם וגו'. ילמדנו פ' כי תשא.

מבן עשרים. בן שהיה פחות מבן עשרים ולא הביא ג' שערות, בין שהיה
עמהם בעצה בין שלא היה עמהם בעצה היה נכנס, דכתי' האנשים העולים
ממצרים, ואם הביא ב' שערות והוא פחות מבן עשרים, אם היה עמהם בעצה
לא היה נכנס, ואעפ"כ לא מת א' מהם פחות מבן ששים. ילמדנו.

(דף ס"א, ע"ב)

והיה לכם לציצית, שתהא נראית. וכמה שיעורה? ב"ש או' ארבע
ובה"ה או' שלש. וראיתם אתו, פרט לכסות לילה, או אינו אלא לכסות סומא,
ת"ל למען תזכרו הרי ראייה וזכירה, זכירה למי שאינו רואה וראיה למי שרואה.
וראיתם אתו, אותו ולא אותה, שאם עשיתם כן כאילו כסא הכבוד אתה רואה,
שהוא דומה לתכלת. וראיתם וזכרתם ועשיתם. הראייה מביאה לידי זכירה
והזכירה לידי עשייה. ילמדנו.

(דף ס"ב, ע"א)

ולא תתורו אחרי לבבכם ואחרי עיניכם. ליבא ועינא סרסורי דחטאה.
ילמדנו.

(דף ס"ב, ע"ב)

למען תזכרו וגו'. משל לאחד שהיה מושלך על המים הושיט לו
הקברניט את החבל א"ל תפוס החבל בידך ולא תניחהו, שאם תניחהו
אין לך חיים. כך אמר הב"ה לישראל כל זמן שאתם מדובקים אתם מקודשים
ואימתכם על הבריות, פרשתם מן המצות הרי אתם מחוללים. ילמדנו.

(דף ס"ג, ע"ב)

קרח חכם גדול היה ומטועני הארון היה, שנ' ולבני קהת לא נתן כי
עבדת הקדש עליהם. מה עצה עשה, קבץ קק"נ ראשי סנדראות ועשה להם
משתה, ועטפם כולם בטליתות שלתכלת. באו בני אהרן ליטול מתנותיהם,
חזה ושוק והזרוע והלחיים והקיבה, עמדו כנגדן אמ' להם: מי צוה
אתכם ליטול כך, משה לא נתן לכם כלום שלא דבר עמו המקום. באו
והודיעו למשה, הלך משה לפייסן, מיד עמדו כנגדו, שנ' ויקמו לפני
משה. ודתן ואבירם ואון בן פלת. מכאן אמ' אוי לרשע ואוי לשכנו, טוב
לצדיק וטוב לשכנו. דתן ואבירם שהיו שכנים לקרח שהיה שרוי בדרום
לקו עמו ואבדו מהעולם, דכתי' משפחות הקהתי יחנו על ירך המשכן
תימנה, ודגלו של ראובן סמוך להם, שנ' דגל מחנה ראובן תימנה. אבל דגלו

ותשא כל העדה ויתנו את קולם ויבכו וגו'. א"ל הב"ה: אתם בכיתם בכיה
שלחנם לפני, אני אקבע עליכם הלילה הזה בכיה לדורות. ומאותה שעה
נגזרה גזרה על בית המקדש שיחרב ושיגלו לבין האומות. וכה"א וישא
ידו להפיל אותם וגו', נשיאות יד כנגד נשיאות קול. ילמדנו.

וילונו על משה וגו' ב מ ד ב ר הזה לו מתנו. משל לא' שעלה
לבימה לידון, הוא דבר בפיו במה שחטא וחייב את עצמו. הניח המלך את
האלוגין שלו ותפש דבריו. א"ל איני דן אותך אלא כמו שאמרת והוצאת
מפיך. אף כאן א"ל הב"ה במדבר הזה יפלו וגו', וכתיב אם לא כאשר
דברתם באזני כך אעשה לכם. ילמדנו.

(דף נ"ג, ע"ב)

ונסו הצללים, אלו המלכיות, ואף משה קראם צל, שנ' סר צ ל ם
מעליהם. ס ד ר אליהו ר ב ה. לרגם אותם. מי הם אותם, משה ואהרן.
וכבוד י"י נראה, מלמד שהיו זורקין אבנים והענן מקבלן. ויאמר י"י אל משה
ע ד א נ ה ינאצני. א"ל הב"ה ב' צווחות צוחתי מפניכם, סופכם לצוח
ד' בד' גליות. הה"ד עד אנה י"י תשכחני נצח, עד אנה תסתיר את פניך ממנו,
עד אנה אשית עצות בנפשי. צוחתי עד מתי לעדה, סופכם לצוח ונפשי נבהלה
מאד ואתה י"י עד מתי. ילמדנו.

(דף נ"ד, ע"א)

כשאמ' הב"ה למשה אכנו בדבר וגו' אמר משה רשל"ע הבט לברית אבותם
שנשבעת להם שתעמיד מהם מלכים ונביאים וכהנים. א"ל הב"ה: ואין
אתה מבניהם? ואעשה אתך לגוי גדול ועצום ממנו. כיון שראה משה
כן עמד ובא במדה אחרת: ויאמר משה ושמעו וגו'. א"ל רשל"ע עשה בשבילך,
שנ' ועתה יגדל נא וגו', תנצח מדת רחמיך למדת הדין... כ א ש ר דברת
לאמר. אני אמרתי לפניך באיזו מדה אתה דן את העולם, דכתיב הודיעני
נא את דרכך, העברת ממני, דכתי' ויעבור י"י על פניו וגו', אותה מדה
שאמרת לי קיים, יגדל נא כח י"י, י"י י"י אל רחום וגו' סלח נא וגו'. קבל
הב"ה את דבריו והודה לו שנ' ויאמר י"י סלחתי כדבריך וכו' לקמן. ילמדנו.

אימתי ירד משה מן ההר? א"ר יהודה בר שלום ק"כ יום עשה משה
אצל הב"ה. כיצד, בחדש השלישי לצאת בני ישראל וגו', בששה לחדש
נתנו להם (דף נ"ד, ע"ב) עשר הדברות לישראל וכתבן, ומשה עלה אל
האלהים ועשה שם ארבעים יום. כיצד הם ארבעים, הרי כ"ד מן סיון וי"ו
מן תמוז, הרי מ'. ירד בי"ז בתמוז, ראה את העגל ושבר את הלוחות
ורידה את הסורחין בי"ח וי"ט, וחזר ועלה בעשרים בתמוז, שנ' ויהי
ממחרת ויאמר משה אל העם וגו' וישב משה וגו', ועשה שם מ' יום,
עשרה מתמוז וכל חדש אב, ועלה בר"ח אלול כשא"ל פסל לך והיה נכון
לבקר וגו' ואיש לא יעלה עמך וגו' ויפסל וישכם ויעל, ועשה שם אלול

ג' פעמים א"ל הארץ: ומה הארץ הטובה, ומה הארץ השמנה. בראשונה
א"ל וראיתם, היו מסתכלין בארץ ישראל, יש ארץ שמגדלת גבורים ויש
ארץ שמגדלת חלשים, ויש שמגדלת אכלוסין ויש שממעטת אכלוסין. ואת ה ע ם
וגו'. מנין אתם יודעין כאן, אם במחנים הם שרויים הם גבורים ובוטחין על
כחן, אם במבצרים הם שרויים הם חלשים, ולבסוף ה ש מ נ ה ה י א, אם
פרותיה קלים הם שמנים, אם חרסים(?) הם רזים. ילמדנו.

והימים ימי בכורי ע נ ב י ם. מכאן אמרו אין תקופת תמוז בלא תאנים
וענבים. ילמדנו. אחימן שהיה או' מאן יבא אלי. ששי שהיה בריא
כשיש. ילמדנו.

(דף נ"ב, ע"ב)

למקום ההוא קרא נחל א ש כ ו ל. זש"ה מגיד מראשית אחרית, אשכול
אוהבו של אברהם היה, ונקרא על אודות האשכול שעתידין ישראל לכרות
ממקומו. ילמדנו.

וישבו מתור הארץ מקץ א ר ב ע י ם י ו ם. אתה מוצא שהלכו מהדרום
לצפון, ובארבעים יום היו מהלכין את כולה, אלא שהיה גלוי לפני
שאמר והיה עולם שהיו עתידין להוציא את דבת הארץ ולגמור עליהם
צרה לחשבון הימים, יום לשנה יום לשנה, שנ', כמספר הימים אשר
תרתם וגו', והקפיץ הב"ה לפניהם את הדרך. ילמדנו.

ו י ל כ ו ו י ב א ו. א"ר יוחנן משום ר' שמעון בן יוחאי מקיש הליכה
לביאה, מה ביאה בעצה רעה אף הליכה בעצה רעה. כל לשון הרע שאין
בו אמת מתחלתו אין מתקיים בסופו. סוטה פ' נאמרין.

ע מ ל ק יושב, מה ראו לפתוח בעמלק, משל לאחד שסרח ולקה
ברצועה; כשמבקשין להפחידו מזכירין לו הרצועה. כך היה עמלק רצועת
מרדות לישראל. ומה ראה לישב לו על הספר תחלת כניסתן לארץ,
כך צוה עשו זקנו לקדם להם, ונעקר ממקומו וישב לו בדרך(?).
ו ה כ נ ע נ י יושב על הים ועל יד הירדן, אלו הגבורים יושבים על
הדרך. לפי' נתכוונו המרגלים לשבור לבם שלישראל, שנ' ויניאו את לב
בני ישראל. ו י ה ס כ ל ב וגו'. לכתחלה אמ"ל אני בעצה עמכם, בעצה
אחת, ובלבבו היה לום' האמת, שנ' ואשים אותו דבר כאשר עם לבבי, וכה"א
ועבדי כלב עקב וגו'. וכשבאו המרגלים אמרו נאמן עלינו כלב. מיד
עלה על הספסל ושיתק ושיתק כל ישראל שהיו מצווחין על משה, שנ' ויהס כלב
וגו'. ילמדנו.

(דף נ"ג, ע"א)

בשעה שאמרו מרגלים וכן היינו בעיניהם נגזרה עליהם, שכשאמרו ונהי
בעינינו כחגבים אמ' הב"ה ויתרתי עליה, אלא וכן היינו בעיניהם, יודעים
הייתם מה עשיתי אתכם בעיניהם, מי יאמר לכם שלא הייתם בעיניהם
כמלאכים. ירושלמי דשלהי תענית. ובילמדנו.

מכל ישר' על פי הב"ה ועל פי משה, שנ' וישלח אותם משה ממדבר
פארן על פי י"י, וכתי' וייטב בעיני הדבר ואקח מכם וגו'. ולא רצה
משה לשלוח מדעת עצמו עד שנמלך בהב"ה ואמ' הם ראוין הם פל' משבט
פל' ופל' משבט פלוני. מכאן אתה למד שהיו צדיקים בפני הב"ה
ובפני משה, ולבסוף נהפכו ועשו כל אותה הצרה, והם גרמו לאותו
הדור שילקו, שנ' כי דור תהפוכות המה, שנתבררו צדיקים ונעשו רשעים.
ד"א שלח לך אנשים. מה כתי' למעלה מן העניין ותדבר מרים ואהרן במשה
וגו', מה ראה לסמוך פרשת מרגלים לפר' מרים, אלא שהיה גלוי
וידוע לפניו שהיו באים ומספרים לשון הרע, לפי' סמך זה לזה. ולפי שדברה
באחיה לקתה בצרעת כדי שידעו הכל ענשו של לשון הרע מהו.
ואעפ"כ לא למדו ממנה. ועליהם הוא או' לא ידעו ולא יבינו כי טח
מראות עיניהם. ד"א שלח לך אנשים. לא היה מן הב"ה שילכו, שכבר אמ'
להם שבחה עד שהיו במצרים, שנ' וארד להצילו מיד (דף נ"א, ע"ב) מצרים וגו',
וכתי' וי"י הולך לפניהם יומם, אלא ישר' הם שבקשו דברים הללו,
וכה"א ותקרבון אלי כולכם ותאמרו נשלחה אנשים וגו', ולא האמינו בתורה.
למה היו דומים? למלך שזימן לבנו אשה יפה ובת טובים ועשירה שאין כמותה
בעולם, א"ל הבן אלך ואראנה, ולא האמין לאביו. מיד הוקשה הדבר
לאביו, אמ' האב מה אעשה לבני, אם או' לו איני מראה אותה לך,
עכשו הוא או' כעורה היא לפי' לא רצה להראותה. א"ל לך ואראה אותה
לך ותדע שלא כזבתי לך, ועל שלא האמנתני קונם אני עליך שאין אתה
רואה אותה בביתך אלא לבנך אני נותנה. כך אמ' הב"ה לישראל:
אני אמרתי לכם טובה הארץ מאד ולא האמנתם בי אלא אמרתם נשלחה
אנשים לפנינו, חי אני אם יראה באנשים האלה וגו'. וכיון שאמ' למשה נשלחה
אנשים לפנינו התחיל משה עומד ותוהה אמ': אפשר לי לעשות דבר
עד שאמלך בהב"ה, הלך משה ונמלך בהב"ה, א"ל הב"ה למשה אין
זה תחלה להם, עד שהם במצרים הלעיגו עלי, שנ' זו לענם גם בארץ
מצרים למודים הם לכך, וידוע אני מי הם, אלא אתה בקשת: שלח לך,
לעצמך. ואלה שמותם. יש אנשים ששמותיהם נאים ומעשיהם כעורים, זה
ישמעאל ועשו: ישמעאל – שומע אל; עשו – עושה רצון עושיו. ויש ששמותיהם
כעורים ומעשיהם נאים, אלו עולי גולה: בני ברקוס בני סיסרא. ויש
ששמותיהם כעורים ומעשיהם כעורים, אלו המרגלים. מה כתי' בהם? סתור
שסתרו מן העולם. ילמדנו.

ויקרא משה וגו'. מה ראה משה להוסיף על שמו של יהושע?
מפני שנטל שכרו מן הארץ ונטל שכר עשרת השבטים: יוד עשרה. ילמדנו.

(דף נ"ב, ע"א)

ויאמר להם עלו זה בנגב, למה בנגב, שכן התגרים עושים מראים
את הפסולת תחלה ואח"כ מראים את המשובח. וראיתם את הארץ.

(מ"ט, ע"ב)

זש"ה חסד ואמת נפגשו וגו'. חסד זה אהרן, שנ' לאיש חסידך.
ואמת זה משה, שנ' בכל ביתו נאמן הוא, וכתי' ויפגשהו בהר האלהים. צדק
ושלום נשקו, זה משה, דכתי' צדקות י"י עשה; ושלום זה אהרן, שנ' בשלום
ובמישור הלך אתי, וכתי' וישק לו. ילמדנו.

והיה ראשיתך מצער וגו', מדבר במשה. א"ר שמואל בר נחמני
שבעה ימים היה הב"ה מפתה למשה בסנה והיה בורח, שנ' שלח נא ביד
תשלח, וכתי' לא איש דברים אנכי וגו', וכתי' ויסתר משה פניו וגו'. ואחריתך
ישגא מאד, פה אל פה אדבר בו וגו'. א"ר שמעון בן יוחאי שהיה
רואה את הדמות. ילמדנו פ' ויהיו חיי שרה.

(דף נ', ע"א)

ויאמר אהרן אל משה בי אדני, מכאן אמ' שיהא כבוד חברך חביב עליך
כרבך, שהרי אהרן אחיו הגדול היה אלא שעשאו כרבו. ילמדנו.

שלח

(דף נ"א, ע"א)

יבש חציר נבל ציץ, למלך שהיה לו אוהב והתנה עמו וא"ל: לך עמי
ואני נותן לך מתנה. הלך עמו ומת. אמ' המלך לבנו של אהובו: אע"פ
שמת אביך איני חוזר בי במתנה שאמרתי ליתן לו, בא אתה וטול אותה.
כך אמ' הב"ה: בא לך עמי שנ' לך לך מארצך וגו', והתנה עמו שיתן לו
מתנה, שנ' קום התהלך בארץ וגו', ומה א"ל הב"ה למשה? אע"פ שמתו האבות
שהתניתי עמהם ליתן להם את הארץ, איני חוזר בי אלא ודבר אלהינו יקום
לעולם. לפ' שלח לך אנשים. השלוחים ששלח
יהושע היו צדיקים שנתנו נפשם להצליח בשליחותם, שנ' חרש לאמ' שלא
יאמ' בני אדם שהם מרגלים, אבל שלוחים ששלח משה היו רשעים.
מנין ממה שקראו בעניין שלח לך. ד"א שלח לך. משל לעשיר שהיה לו
כרם, כשהיה רואה שהיין יפה היה או' הכניסו את היין בביתי, וכשהיה רואה
שהיין חומץ, היה או' הכניסו את היין בבית האריס. אף כאן כשראה שהזקנים
מעשיהם מתוקנים קראם לשמו, שנ' אספה לי שבעים איש וגו'; וכשראה
המרגלים שמעשיהם מקולקלים ועתידין לחטא ולהוציא לשון הרע על הארץ
קראן לשמו של משה, שנ' שלח לך אנשים. ד"א שלח לך אנשים. זש"ה מקצה
רגלים חמס שותה שולח דברים ביד כסיל, אלו המרגלים ששלח משה.
והם כסילים היו, והלא הוא קורא אותם אנשים ואין אנשים בכל מקום אלא
צדיקים, שנ' בחר לנו אנשים זרע אנשים, אלא מלמד שבתחלה היו צדיקים,
ולבסוף נעשו רשעים. ועליהם אמ' משה כי דור תהפוכות המה, שנבחרו

עמי, הריני מביא אחרים שישמרו עמך, והוי יודע שאיני נותן להם
שכר שמירה, אלא מתוך שכר שמירה שנתתי לך הם נוטלין. כך
א"ל הב"ה למשה בשעה שאמ"ל לא אוכל לבדי לשאת, א"ל הב"ה
אני נתתי בך רוח חכמה ודעת לפרנס את בני, ולא היית צריך לבקש
אחרים אלא כדי שיהא בך רוח ודעת ותהיה אתה באותה גדולה,
ועכשו אתה מבקש אחרים עמך, הוי יודע שמשלי אינן נוטלין כלום
אלא ואצלתי מן הרוח וגו'. ואעפ"כ לא חסר משה כלום, תדע שהרי בסוף
מ' שנה א"ל הב"ה: קח לך את יהושע ונתת מהודך עליו, מה כתיב
בתריה ויהושע בן נון מלא רוח חכמה, למה, כי סמך משה את ידיו עליו. ילמדנו.

(דף מ"ז, ע"א)

ר' שמעון או' במחנה נשתיירו... ויהושע מכניס את ישראל לארץ.
סנהדרין פ' דיני ממונות. וסדר אליהו רבה.

מה נבואה נתנבאו? שאמרו אדר מלחמת גוג ומגוג אין פורענות ולא
שעבוד, שנ' ולא יספו. אלדד ומידד על שמעטו עצמן נמצאו יתרים
על הזקנים בחמשה דברים, שהזקנים לא נתנבאו אלא למחר, שנ' ואל
העם תאמרו התקדשו למחר, אבל אלו נתנבאו מיד, ומה שהיה בסוף
ארבעים שנה: יהושע מכניס את ישר' לארץ. הזקנים נפסקה נבואתם
ואלו לא נפסקה נבואתם, דכתי' ויתנבאו ולא יספו. הזקנים נבואתם
משל משה, שנ' ואצלתי מן הרוח אשר עליך וגו', ואלו ותנח עליהם הרוח.
ושמא תאמר הזקנים שהיתה נבואתם משל משה חסר משה כלום, משל
לנר שהיה דלוק והדליקו ממנו כמה נרות והוא לא חסר כלום, כך היה
משה. ילמדנו.

(מ"ח, ע"ב)

וירץ הנער, זה יהושע, כד"א ומשרתו יהושע בן נון נער. ר'
שמעון או' הרי הוא או' ויען יהושע בן נון, הא למדת שלא היה
ראשון יהושע. ספרי. ובילמדנו.

וירץ הנער. מי היה, זה גרשום בן משה. אדני משה כלאם,
מנין שיהא כבוד רבך חביב עליך כמורא שמים, שנ' אדני משה כלאם,
כמו שהב"ה כלאם כך אתה יכול לכלאם. ילמדנו.

(דף מ"ט, ע"א)

והאיש משה ענו מאד, התורה סולּיתה ענוה וכתרה יראה; סולייה
ענוה, דכתי' עקב ענוה יראת י"י, כתרה יראה, דכתי' ראשית חכמה
יראת י"י, ובשניהם זכה משה, דכתי' והאיש משה ענו מאד, וכתי' כי ירא
מהביט אל האלהים. ילמדנו פ' בראשית.

שעל גביהן עומדת. כך הבונה בשמים מעלותיו, אימתי מבוסס למעלה
בזמן שישר' עושין אגודה אחת, הה"ד ואגודתו על ארץ יסדה, וכה"א
ויהי בישרון מלך, אימתי בהתאסף ראשי עם, לכך א"ל הב"ה למשה
א ס פ ה ל י ש ב ע י ם א י ש. אספה לי שבעים איש, אמ' משה
היאך אני עושה להביא אותם מכל השבטים, אם אביא ששה מכל
שבט ושבט הרי הן ע"ב, וכול' לקמן. אספה לי שבעים איש, וכי לא
היה להם משה זקנים לשעבר והלא כבר נאמר במצרים לך ואספת וגו',
אלא אמר משה איני יודע מי ראוי ומי אינו ראוי. א"ל א ש ר י ד ע ת
כי הם זקני העם ושטריו אתם, שנ' בהם ויוכו שוטרי בני ישר' וכו'.
התם. ולפי שמסרו עצמם ללקות על הדבר, לפי' נאמ' ו נ ש א ו אתם
במש' העם, ללמדך שכל מי שמוסר עצמו על הדבר עולה לגדולה
ולרוח הקדש. ד"א אספה לי שבעים איש מזקני ישר', והראשונים היכן
הם, והלא כבר נאמר לך ואספת את זקני ישראל ויצאו ממצרים,
וכשעלה להר עלו עמו, שנ' ואל משה אמר עלה אל י"י וגו' ושבעים
מזקני ישר', וכתי' ואל הזקנים אמ' שבו לנו בזה, אלא כיון שעלה משה
אמר לישראל: לסוף ארבעים יום אני בא, וכשהגיע סוף ארבעים יום
ולא בא, באו ונתקבצו על הזקנים, אמ' להם קומו עשו לנו אלהים כי
זה משה האיש לא ידענו מה היה לו. אמ' להם הזקנים: למה אתם
מכעיסים למי שעשה לנו את כל הנסים הללו. שראו שלא שמעו
להם עמדו עליהם והרגום ולחור עמהם, הה"ד גם בכנפיך נמצאו דם
נפשות צדיקים נקיים. וכשסלח להם הב"ה אמר למשה אספה לי וגו'.
ד"א שבעים מזקני ישר', שבעים זקנים אינו או' אלא שבעים איש,
אותם שדומים לי ולך, י"י איש מלחמה, והאיש משה. ד"א אספה
לי וגו', וכי לא היה להם זקנים וכו' לעיל, הפרשה הזאת אח"כ נאמ' והראשונים
היכן הם, אלא בשעה שבאו ישר' לאותו מעשה ויהי העם כמתאוננים
וגו', ותאכל בקצה המחנה נשרפו כולם באותה שעה, שאף הם הקלו
ראשם בהר סיני כשראו השכינה, שנ' ויחזו את האלהים וגו'; והיו
ראויים לישרף באותו יום אלא מפני שהיה מתן תורה לא רצה לפגוע
בהם דכתי' ואל אצילי בני ישר' לא שלח ידו, מכלל שהיו ראויים להשתלח
בהם יד, ומתי פרע להם, בקברות התאוה. ילמדנו.

(דף מ"ו, ע"ב)

ו י ר ד ת י ודברתי אתך שם, להודיעך שיום מנוי הזקנים היה חביב
לפני הב"ה כיום שנתנה בו תורה, דכתי' וירד י"י על הר סיני. למלך
שהיה לו פרדס ושכר לתוכו שומר, ונתן לו שכר שמירה שישמור
את הפרדס. לאחר זמן א"ל השומר איני יכול לשמרו לבדי אלא הבא לי
שומרים אחרים שישמרו עמי. א"ל המלך לך נתתי את הפרדס כולו
לשמרו וכל השכירות נתתי לך, ועכשו אתה או' הבא לי אחרים שישמרו

(דף מ"ד, ע"א)

א"ר יצחק את מוצא כשירדה אש במתאוננים היה משה עומד ומשקע
ציפי ציפי באותה אש והיא משתקעת, שנ' ותשקע האש, ללמדך שגדולים
צדיקים ממלאכי השרת. ילמדנו פ' וישלח יעקב.

אספה לי שבעים וגו', וכי לא היה להם שבעים זקנים, והלא כבר נא'
עלה אל י"י אתה ואהרן ושבעים מזקני ישר', ופרשה זו אח"כ היתה, והיכן
היו הזקנים, אלא בשעה שעשו ישראל אותו מעשה, דכתי' ויהי העם
כמתאוננים ותבער בם אש י"י ותאכל בקצה המחנה, נשרפו באותה
שעה, שאף הם הקלו ראשם כשראו השכינה, שנ' ויחזו את האלהים.
ילמדנו.

א"ר יודן אותה האש שירדה מן השמים שקעה בארץ ולא חזרה
עוד למקומה אל השמים, אלא נכנסה לה אל אהל מועד, וכל הקרבנות שהיו
ישר' מקריבין במדבר אותה האש היתה יוצאת ואוכלת אותם, שנ' ותצא
אש מלפני י"י וכו'. התם. ואין אדם נפטר מן העולם עד שיעבר עליו
מאותה האש שקעה. ויקרא שם המקום ההוא תבערה, אין תבערה
אלא כאדם שאו' תב איש פלוני למקומו. כך א"ל משה: עשיתם
תשובה ותשקע האש, ואם לאו עדין היא במקומה. כי בערה בם
אש י"י על מה שאירע נקרא ולא היה כן שמו מקדם, אבל אי אתה יודע
מי היו אלה המרגלים? ישר' לעבירה. והאספסוף אשר בקרבו,
אלו הגרים המוספין מכל מקום. ר' שמעון בן מנסיא או' אלו הזקנים
שבהם, שנ' אספה לי וגו', אם כך היו זקנים עושין קל וחומר לשאר
בני אדם. ספרי ובילמדנו.

ומנין שהזקנים נשרפו, שנ' ותבער אש בעדתם ואין עדה אלא סנהדרין,
דכתי' והיה אם מעיני העדה, וכה"א ואף י"י חרה בעם, וכתי' ואף י"י
עלה בהם להרג במשמניהם, אלו סנהדרין ובחורי ישר' הכריע אלו
הבחורים שהיו קרואים זקנים. ויאמרו מי יאכל לנו בשר, וכי
היו מבקשים והלא כל מה שהיו רוצים היה המן נעשה להם תוך פיהם,
שנ' ויתן להם שאלתם וגו', ואם תאמ' שלא היה להם צאן ובקר, והלא
כבר נא' וגם ערב רב עלה וגו', ואם תאמר שכבר אכלום במדבר קודם
כניסתן (דף מ"ד, ע"ב) לארץ והלא כתי' ומקנה רב היה לבני גד וגו',
מכאן א"ר שמואל לא בשר היה שנתאוו אלא עריות, שבו הוא אומר וימטר
עליהם בעפר שאר וגו', ואין שאר אלא עריות, שנ' איש איש אל כל
שאר בשרו וגו', וכן הוא או' וישמע משה את העם בוכה למשפחותיו. לפי'
ויחר אף י"י ובעיני משה רע. ילמדנו ובספרי.

(דף מ"ו, ע"א)

זש"ה הבונה בשמים מעלותיו ואגודתו על ארץ יסדה, לה"ד לפלטרין
שהיתה בנויה על גבי הספינות, כל זמן שהספינות מחוברות פלטרין

או' משום ר' אלעזר אף העקרבנין וחזרתי על כל תלמידיו ובקשתי
לי חסא ולא מצאתי. על מצות ומררים, מצוה לאכול כולו כאחת.
הלל הזקן היה כורכן זה בזה ואוכל', יכול יהו מעכבין זה את זה,
ת"ל יאכלוהו, אפי' זה בפני עצמו וזה בפני עצמו. מכילתא דר'
ש מ ע ו ן ב ן י ו ח א י.

צלי אש ומצות וגו', מגיד שמצות פסח מצה צלי(?) ומרור, ומנין
אתה או' שאם אין להם מצה ומרור שיוצאין ידי חובתן בפסח, ת"ל יאכלוהו.
יכול אף אם אין להם פסח יוצאין ידי חובתן במצה ובמרור, ת"ל יאכלוהו.
ד"א יאכלוהו, הפסח נאכל אכילת שבע ואין מצה ומרור נאכלין אכילת
שבע. מכילתא דר' ישמעאל.

(דף מ', ע"ב)

זש"ה י"י צבאות, הוא מלך הכבוד, שהוא חולק מכבודו ליראיו. נקרא אלהים
וקרא למשה אלהים: ראה נתתיך אלהים לפרעה; מחיה מתים וחלק מכבודו
לאליהו, שנ' ראי חי בנך; לבש הוד והדר דכתי' הוד והדר לבשת, והלביש לבושו
למלך המשיח, שנ' הוד והדר תשוה עליו; הוא מתעלה בתרועה, שנ' עלה אלהים
בתרועה, ואמ' למשה שלך עשיתיך, שנ' ויהי בישרון מלך, מה אני כשאני יוצא
תוקעין לפני, אף אתה ע ש ה ל ך שתי חצוצרת, שבשעה שאתה מכניס לישר' יהו
תוקעין בהן והן מתכנסין אליך. לפי' עשה לך שתי חצוצרות. ד"א
עשה לך, לך אתה עושה ולא לאחר, אתה משתמש בהן ואין אחר משתמש
בהן, תדע שהרי בשעת פטירתו לא תקע בהן, שנ' הקהילו אלי את זקני
שבטיכם, והיכן החצוצרות? אלא מלמד שנגנזו. ילמדנו. ושוחר טוב.

(דף מ"ג, ע"א)

בא וראה כמה היה הארון חביב, שהמשכן כולו לא נעשה אלא
בשביל הארון שהשכינה בתוכו, מה כתי' וארון ברית י"י נוסע וגו',
והיה הורג נחשים ועקרבים ושורפן והורג שונאיהן והיה מקדים ג' ימים
לתור להם מנוחה, וכיון שהיה משה יודע שהיה מקדים ג' ימים היה או'
קומה י"י עמוד המתן להם לישר' עד שתניח אותם, שנ' ויהי בנסע הארן
וגו' ובנחהו יאמר וגו'. ילמדנו פ' ויקהל.

(דף מ"ג, ע"ב)

מאי דכתי' משה איש אלהים, א"ר יוהנן אישה יקימנו וגו', אישה
יקימנו – ויהי בנסע הארון ויאמ' משה קומה י"י. ואישה יפרנו – ובנחה
יאמ' וגו'. אמ' איני זז מכאן עד שתעשה האלפים רבבות. פסיקאתא.

יאירו שבעת הנרות, א"ל לא שאני צריך לכם אלא שתאירו לי כשם שהארתי
לכם, למה, כדי להעלות אתכם לפני האומות, שיהו או' ראו האיך
ישר' מאירין למי שהוא מאיר לכל העולם, לה"ד לפקח וסומא שהיו
מהלכין בדרך, בכל הדרך היה הפקח סומך ונוהג את הסומא, כשנכנסו
לבית אמ' הפקח לסומא: צא והדלק לי נר זה שתאיר, א"ל הסומא: כשהייתי
מהלך בדרך היית סומך אותי, ועכשו אתה אומ' לי צא והדלק לי את
הנר, א"ל הפקח אני רוצה ממך דבר זה שאחזיק לך טובה, כשם שהייתי
אני מוליך אותך בדרך, לפי' אני או' לך שתאיר לי. הפקח זה הב"ה –
עיני י"י משוטטות בכל הארץ; והסומא אלו ישראל, שנ' נגששה כעורים
קיר. והיה הב"ה מנהיגם, שנ' וי"י הולך לפניהם יומם וגו'. כיון שעמד
המשכן קרא הב"ה למשה ואמ"ל: האירו לי כשם שהארתי לכם, לכך
נא' בהעלותך וגו'. הקרבנות כל זמן שהיה המקדש קים הם נוהגין
אבל הנרות לעולם הם נוהגין, הוי אל מול פני המנורה. ד"א אל מול
פני המנורה, שלא יטעך יצרך לומ' שהוא צריך לאורה, ראה מה
כתי' בחלונות „שקופים אטומים", רחבות מבחוץ וצרות מבפנים כדי שיהו
מוציאין האורה לחוץ. הוא מאיר לכל העולם ולאורך הוא צריך?
ולמה אמרתי לך, כדי להעלותך. ש ב ע ת הנרות, כנגד שבעת כוכבים
שמשוטטין בכל הארץ. ד"א בהעלותך וגו', בשר ודם מדליק מנר לנר,
שמא יכול להדליק מתוך החשך? והב"ה האיר מתוך החשך, שנ' וחשך
על פני תהם, מה כתי' בתריה ויאמ' אלהים יהי אור וגו', מתוך החשך
הוצאתי אורה, ולאור שלך אני צריך? ולמה אמרתי לך, כדי להעלותך.
הוי בהעלותך וגו'. ילמדנו.

(דף ל"ז, ע"א)

כשעלה משה להר הראה לו הב"ה מעשה המנורה ונתקשה בה,
א"ל הב"ה הריני עושה אותה לפניך, הראה לו אש לבנה, אש אדומה, אש
שחורה, ירוקה ועשה מהן את המנורה, גביעיה כפתוריה ופרחיה, והוא
או' לו: כך וכך עשה אותה, שנ' וזה מעשה המנורה, שהראה לו באצבעו,
ואעפ"כ נתקשה לעשותה, חקקה על פס ידו וא"ל וראה ועשה כתבניתה,
ואעפ"כ נתקשה בה, אמ' מקשה תיעשה המנורה מקשה היא, מה קשה
היא לעשות. א"ל הב"ה השלך את הזהב באש והיא תיעשה מאליה, שנ'
תיעשה המנורה. ילמדנו.

תיעשה המנורה, מלא ביוד, מלמד שנתקשה בה משה עד שא"ל הב"ה טול
ככר זהב והשלך לאור והיא נעשית מאליה. ילמדנו.

דף ל"ט, ע"ב)

ומררים יאכלוהו, ריבה מרורים הרבה, החזרת והעולשין והתמכה
וההרחבינא והמרור ר' יהודה או' אף הורורין והזרתגלין ר' אלעאי

קרבן בנך. הוי ביום השמיני וגו'. א"ר עזריה א"ל הב"ה ליוסף אתה שמרת
מצות לא תנאף, ושמרת מצות התורה קודם שניתנה, חייך שלא יהא
מפסיק בין שני בניך אלא אפרים מקריב ביום השביעי ומנשה ביום
השמיני. ר' מאיר ור' יהושע היו דורשין את השמות: א ל י ש מ ע –
אלי שמע ולאדונתו לא שמע. ע מ י ה ו ד – עמי היה הודו ולא עם
הרשעה. ג מ ל י א ל בן פדהצור, אמר יוסף גמל אל עמי טובות.
פדהצור – פדה אותי (דף ל"ה, ע"ב) מצרת בית הסוהר. כשירדו אחי
יוסף למצרים צוה יוסף לאשר על ביתו: הבא את האנשים הביתה
וטבוח טבח והכן וגו', והלא אין דרך המלכים לאכל מיום לחבירו,
א"ר יוחנן שבת היתה. א"ל הב"ה אתה שמרת את השבת עד שלא נתנה,
חייך שאני עושה לבן בניך מקריב ביום השבת. ההה"ד ביום השמיני
וגו'. ילמדנו.

(דף ל"ו, ע"א)

בא וראה כמה חיבתן שלישר' לפני המקום, שבזמן שאין עושין
רצונו של מקום הוא מסלק שכינתו מביניהם ומתעלה ויושב בשמי מרום,
והכל צועקין ובוכין, ואין נשמע קולם, וגוזרין צום ומתפלשין באפר
ומתכסין בשקים ואין משגיח בהם. ובזמן שהן עושין רצונו שלמקום אינו מתרחק
מהם כלום, שנ' מבין שני הכרובים וידבר אליו. דרך ארץ רבה.

בהעלותך

דבר אל אהרן ואמרת אליו. מה ראה לצוות אהרן כאן, את
מוצא י"ב שבטים הקריבו לחנכת המזבח ושבט לוי לא הקריב כלום,
והיו מצרים למה דוחפנו מהקרבה לחנכת המזבח. מלה"ד, למלך שעשה
סעודה וזמן כל בני עירו בכל יום ויום, והיה לו אהוב ולא זמנו
עמהם והיה אותו אהוב (דף ל"ו, ע"ב) מיצר לומר שיש לו למלך בלבו
עלי. כשעברה הסעודה זמנו. א"ל לכל בני עירי עשיתי סעודה אחת
ולך אעשה סעודה אחת, למה, שאתה אוהבי. כך א"ל הב"ה לאהרן ולבניו:
כל השבטים עשו חנוכה אחת ואתם לעצמכם עשו חנוכה. לכך נא'
דבר אל אהרן וגו' ואח"כ קח את הלוים וגו'.

בהעלותך את הנרות, בכמה מקומות צוה הב"ה על הנרות להדליק
משמן זית: ואתה תצוה וגו', על המנורה הטהורה יערך אותו אהרן וגו'
בהעלותך וגו', מכאן א"ר טרפון אין מדליקין אלא בשמן זית בלבד.
בהעלותך וגו', אמ' הב"ה לישר' אם זכיתם לפני להדליק נרות אני
משמר נפשותיכם שנמשלו לנר, שנ' נר י"י נשמת אדם וגו'. ד"א בהעלותך
וגו', אמ' ישר' להב"ה רבש"ע כי אתה נרי י"י אל מול פני המנורה

כאחת, היה חוזר ומושח כל אחד ואחד בפני עצמו. ואחרינא אמ' וימשחם,
משיחה בעולם הזה ומשיחה לעולם הבא. פסיקתא דרב כהנא.

הם נשיאי המטות, במצרים, הם העומדים על הפקודים על הדגלים.
פסיקתא דרב כהנא. וברבה.

(דף ל"ג, ע"ב)

קח מאתם וגו', א"ל אהל מועד שאתם עושים פורח באויר ...
ומה אם העגלות שנדבקו באהל מועד ניתן להם הויה שיהו קיימות
לעולם, ישראל שהם דבקים בהב"ה על אחת כמה וכמה, שנ' ואתם
הדבקים בי"י אלהיכם חיים וגו'. פסיקתא דרב כהנא.

(דף ל"ד, ע"ב)

מה ראו נשיאי ישראל להקדים להקדים בקרבנות, את מוצא בשעה שהכריז
משה קחו מאתכם תרומה לי"י וגו', אמ' הנשיאים לא היה משה או' לנו
לעשות משכן מה עשו, לא נתנו בנדבה, אמרו אלו עושין המשכן?
א"ל הב"ה חייכם שיש לכם לדעת שאיני צריך לכם, מה כתי' שם: והם
הביאו אליו עוד נדבה וגו' והמלאכה היתה וגו'. וכיון שראו כן באו והקדימו
בקרבנות. קערת כסף אחת, כף אחת, שעיר עזים א', פר א', איל א',
כבש א'. אמר להם הב"ה: וכן הוא כבודי? אמ' לפניו: רבש"ע במדבר אנו
נתונים, ולפי המדבר הקרבנו לך, כשתכנס לטרקלין שלך כמה קרבנות
כמה פרים נקריב לפניך, שנ' אז תחפוץ זבחי צדק וגו'. למלך שיצא לדרך
והיו מביאין לפניו סעודה לפי הדרך ולפי הפונדק. אמ' להם המלך:
כך אתם מכבדין אותי? א"ל אדוננו! בדרך אנו נותנין לפי הדרך
ולפי הפונדק, לכשתבא לפלטירין שלך תראה כמה נכבד אותך. ילמדנו.

זש"ה שמן וקטרת ישמח לב, אמר הב"ה כל קרבנות שישראל מקריבים
לפני אין חביב עליו כקטרת, שכל הקרבנות לצרכיהם של ישר' הם
באים, והשלמים הם באים על ההרהורי הלב, אבל הקטרת אינה באה
אלא על שמן (דף ל"ה, ע"א) המשחה. הוי שמן וקטרת ישמח לב, וכן
את מוצא שלא נשתבחו קרבנות בעולם כקרבנות הנשיאים. ולמה, שהן
מקריבין קטרת תחלה בקרבנותיהן, וכה"א על כל א' וא' בקרבנו כף
אחת וגו' ואח"ז פר אחד בן וגו'. ולפי' הב"ה משבח קרבן שלכל א'
וא' מהם, זה קרבן פלו', זה קרבן פלוני, לימד שערב לפניו והוא משבחן.
בא וראה כמה הקטרת חביבה לפניו, שלא ירדה שכינה עד שהקריבו
הקטורת, דכתי' עורי צפון ובאי תימן וגו'. ילמדנו.

זש"ה ויהי י"י את יוסף ויהי איש מצליח, איש צדיק היה לו לומ',
ומה מצליח, שווה, א"ל הב"ה שוית אתה מה ששוה אדם הראשון,
ואין מצליח אלא שויה(?), כד"א וצלחו הירדן. א"ל הב"ה בשביל
מצוה שעשית ופירשת מן העבירה אין קרבן יחיד דוחה שבת אלא

ור' שמואל: ר' אלעז' או' ביום כלות להקים, ביום שכלו כל הקמותיו
שלמשכן. תני בכל יום ויום היה משה מעמיד את המשכן ומפרקו.
ובכל בקר ובקר מקריב קרבנותיו עליו, ובשביעי העמידו ולא פרקו.
א"ר זעירא מכאן שהקמת הלילה פסולה לעבודה, דכתי' ביום. ר'
שמואל אמ' אף בשמיני העמידו ופרקו. מנין לפירוקין, א"ר זעירא
ביום כלות משה להקים, ביום שכלו הקמותיו. ר' אלעז' או' ביום
כלות משה, ביום שכלו המזיקין מהעולם. ר' יוחנן או' ביום שכלתה
איבה מן העולם, שעד שלא הוקם המשכן היתה איבה וקנאה ותחרות
מן(?) העולם, ומשהוקם המשכן ניתנה אהבה וחיבה ורעות ושלום וצדק
בעולם. פסיקאתא דרב הונא.

אתה מוצא שהכל נתנו נפשם על המשכן ומשה יותר מכולם, אמר
הב"ה הואיל ומשה נתן נפשו על המשכן איני כותבו אלא על שמו, הה"ד
ויהי ביום כלות משה וגו'. מהו המשכן, א"ל הב"ה אמ' להם שיקימו אותו
שלא יחטאו, שאם יחטאו יהא מתמשכן על ידיהם. הוי להקים את
המשכן. א"ר שמעון כל מקום שנ' ויהי דבר חדש הוא, דבר שנפסק וחזר
לכמות שהיה. א"ר שמואל בשעה שברא הב"ה את העולם נתאוה שיהיה
לו דירה בתחתונים כשם שיש לו בעליונים, ברא אדם וצוהו ועבר
על צוויו, סילק הב"ה שכינתו וכו'. בפ' הוקם המשכן. וכשהוקם המשכן
חזר (דף ל"ב, ע"א) לכמות שהיה, שנ' ויהי ביום כלות משה, ויהי דבר
שהיה נפסק הרבה ימים וחזר לכמות שהיה. א"ר יוחנן מהו ויהי ביום
כלות משה, אל תקרי כלות אלא כלת, שעד שלא הוקם המשכן היו המזיקין
מצויין כל כך, שכשהיה משה עולה למרום היה או' שיר של פגעים: יושב
בסתר עליון וגו' ונגע לא יקרב באהלך עד אהלך אהל מועד. הוי עד
יום שהוקם המשכן היו המזיקין, ביום שהוקם נתכלו. א"ר שמעון בן לקיש
מה לי ללמוד מספר תילים נלמוד ממקומו, דכתי' יברכך י"י וישמרך,
ישמרך מן המזיקין, אימתי, ויהי ביום כלות משה וגו'. א"ר יהודה
יום שהוקם המשכן נתרצה הב"ה לישרא' ונעשה שלום בינו ובין ישר',
שנ' כי ידבר שלום אל עמו, אימתי, ויהי ביום כלות משה להקים את
המשכן. א"ר שמעון בן לקיש מה לי ללמוד מספר תלים, אפי' במקומה
אינה תסרה כלום, דכתי' וישם לך שלום, אימתי, ויהי ביום כלות
משה. א"ר ברכיה הכהן עד שישר' בסיני רמז להם הב"ה כשאבוא
אצליכם אני טעון ברכות. והיכן רמזה, אבא אליך וברכתיך, לכשבא
אצלן ברכן, שנ' יברכך י"י וישמרך, אימתי, ויהי ביום כלות משה.
ילמדנו.

(דף ל"ג, ע"א)

מכיון דכתי' וימשח אותו ויקדש אותו לאיזה דבר נא' וימשחם ויקדש
אתם, ר' איבו א"ר תחליפא וריש לקיש: חד אמ' משה היה מושח כולן

אמ' הב"ה מתחלה הייתי מברך את בני, מכאן ואילך הרי הברכות
מסורות לכם, אתם תברכו את ישרא' שנ' דבר אל אהרן ואל בניו לאמר
כה תברכו את בני ישראל וגו'. אמרה כנסת ישר' לפני הב"ה: רשל"ע
לכהנים אתה או' שיברכו אותנו, אין אנו צריכין להיות מתברכין אלא
מפיך, אמ' להם הב"ה אעפ"י שאמרתי לכהנים שיהיו מברכים אתכם,
עמהם אני (דף ל', ע"ב) עומד ומברך אתכם. לפי' הכהנים פורשים את
כפיהם, לומ' שהב"ה עומד אחריו, וכה"א הנה זה עומד אחר כתלנו
וגו', הוי כה תברכו וגו'. ילמדנו.

בנוהג שבעולם המלך מכבד אוהבו בכסף ובזהב ובגדים ומעשרו,
נכנס לספינה עמד עליו סער הים מאבד נפשו וממונו, לפי שאינו
יכול לשמרו מן הים ומן הליסטים; והב"ה נותן לאוהבו מתנה ומשמרו,
שנ' יברכך י' וישמרך. ילמדנו פ' נח.

יברכך י' וישמרך, עם הברכה שמירה. יברכך י' בעושר. וישמרך
שתהא עושה מצות. ד"א יברכך י' בבנים, וישמרך בבנות, שהבנות
צריכות שמירה. ילמדנו.

יאר י' פניו אליך, יתן לך מאור פנים. ר' נתן או' יתן לך
מאור שכינה, שנ' קומי אורי כי בא אורך וגו', ואו' אל י' ויאר לנו,
ואו' יאר פניו אתנו סלה. ד"א זו מאור תורה, שנ' כי נר מצוה ותורה אור.
ספרי. יאר י' פניו אליך, יעמיד (דף ל"א, ע"א) ממך בנים בני תורה.
ד"א יאר י' פניו, יעמיד ממך כהנים שמאירין את המזבח, שנ' ולא תאיר
מזבחי חנם. ד"א יאר י' פניו אליך, יאר לך מאור פניו, ואין אור
אלא חיים, שנ' באור פני מלך חיים.

ויחנך, ר' חייא הגדול או' יחנה י' אצלך. ר"א ויחנך, יעמיד
ממך נביאים, שנ' ושפכתי על בית דוד רוח חן ותחנונים. ד"א ויחנך, יתן
חנו עליך בכל מקום שאתה הולך. ילמדנו.

ישא י' פניו אליך, בשעה שאתה עושה תשובה, ואם לאו – אשר
לא ישא פנים. ילמדנו.

(דף ל"ב, ע"א)

מתחלה עיקר השכינה בתחתונים היתה, דכתי' וישמעו את קול אל'ים
מתהלך בגן, וכיון שהטא אדם הראשון נסתלקה לרקיע וכו' התם: עד
שעמד משה וזכה והורידה לארץ, שנ' ויהי ביום כלות וגו'. ר'
יהושע דסכנין בשם ר' לוי למה היה אהל מועד דומה, למערה שהיא נתונה
על שפת הים ועלה הים והציף המערה, המערה נתמלאת מן הים
והים אינו חסר כלום, כך אהל מועד נתמלא מזיו השכינה והעולם
לא הסר כלום, לכך נא' ויהי ביום כלות וגו'. עד שלא [הוקם?] המשכן
היה העולם רותת, משהוקם המשכן נתבסס העולם. לכך נא' ויהי ביום
כלות כלת כתיב. א"ר לוי ביומא דעלת כלתא לגנא. ר' אלעז'

(דף י"ט, ע"ב)

אמ' בשם ר' חיננא אביו של ר' חייא הנואף והנואפת עוברין
על עשרת הדברות, כיצד, עובר על אנכי י"י אלהיך, שכל הנואף
באשת רעהו כופר בהב"ה, שנ' כחשו בי"י ויאמרו לא הוא. על לא יהיה
לך אלהים אחרים שכתו' בו אל קנא, ואו' בסוטה ועבר עליו רוח קנאה
וקנא, ב' פעמים למה, א' להב"ה וא' לבעל, וכה"א כי מנחת קנאות הוא,
שתי קנאות. על לא תשא, שהוא נואף ונשבע לשקר שלא נאף. על כבד
את אביך, שהנואף עם האשה מתעברת ממנו ואו' לך(?) ממך אני
מעוברת, והבן גדל ועומד ומכבד את הבעל ובוזה את הבועל שהוא
אביו. על לא תרצח, שהנואף נכנס על מנת שיהרוג או שיהרג. על לא
תנאף, ודאי הוא נואף. על לא תגנוב, שהוא גונב מקור חברו, וכה"א מים
גנובים ימתקו. על לא תענה, שהיא מעידה עדות שקר לבעלה: ממך
אני מעוברת.

(דף כ', ע"א)

על לא תחמוד אשת רעך, שהנואף הוא חומד אשת חברו, וחומד
כל אשר לו, כיון שהבעל בא ליפטר מן העולם סבור שאותו הבן הוא בנו
וכותב לו דיתיקי מכל נכסיו ומורישו כל אשר לו. א"ל ר' חנינא הרי
ט', השבת כיצד עובר עליה? א"ל אם הנואפת אשת כהן, הנואף בא עליה
והיא יולדה ממנו וסבורין שהוא בנו של כהן, ובא ומקריב עולות
בשבת ונמצא מחלל את השבת. ילמדנו.

(דף כ', ע"ב)

שמן לה(?), שהוא אור וקרוי יצהר, וזו אהבה את האפלה, לפי'
לא יהא אור במנחתה. לבונה למה, לפי שהלבונה זכר לאמהות, שנ'
אלך לי אל הר המור ואל גבעת הלבונה, וזו פרשה מדרכיהן לפי' תהא
מנחתה מזכרת עון ולא מזכרת זכות. ילמדנו.

(דף כ"א, ע"א)

למה מים ועפר, מפני שתחלתה מן המים ומן העפר, אדם נוצר
מן העפר והיא מן המים, לפי' תהא נבדקת במים ובעפר, אם טהורה כבריתה,
ואם לא תחזור לעפרה. ד"א למה נבדקת במים ובעפר, לפי שהם
עדיה, שנ' העידותי בכם היום את השמים ואת הארץ. ד"א לפי שאדם זורע
כמה זרעים בעפר ואינו יודע מה הן עד שהמים יורדים עליהם ומודיעים אם
הם שלבעל השדה או מה שזרעו אחרים. ילמדנו.

(דף ל', ע"א) [לבמ' ו', כ"ב]

מנין זכו הכהנים לברך את ישר', א"ר אלע(זר) מיצחק, דכתי'
בו עד כה, ואין כה אלא ברכת כהנים, דכתי' כה תברכו. ורבנן אמרי
ממתן תורה זכו, דכתי' כה תאמר לבית יעקב. ילמדנו פרשת ויחי יעקב.

בכור בבני ישראל וגו', אמ' הב"ה בשביל חבתם של ישראל שניתי
סדרו של עולם. כיצד, כתבתי בתורה שיהא חמור נפדה בשה וכול'.
לעיל.

ואת בהמת הלוים וגו', שכן אתה מוצא שהרג המקום בכורי בהמות
מצרים והציל בהמות ישראל, ולכך הקדיש לשמו בכורי בהמות ישראל,
וכה"א כי לי כל בכור בבני ישראל וגו'. רבה. ילמדנו.

(דף י"ב, ע"א)

זש"ה אל תגזל דל כי דל הוא וגו', מדבר בשבטו של לוי. ולמה
קורא אותו דל? ר' יהודה ור' סימון, חד אמר דלים מן הנחלה, דכתי'
ולבני לוי לא נתן נחלה וגו', לפי' אל תגזל דל מן המתנות; וחד
אמ' דלים במנין. למה, שהיה הארון מכלה בהם, שהיו מסתכלין בשכינה,
לפי' אמ' הב"ה אל תכריתו וגו'. ד"א צפה הב"ה שקרח עתיד לחלוק על
הכהונה, אמ' הב"ה לא בשביל קרח נאבד את הלויים, לפי' אל תכריתו וגו'.
במקום א' הוא או' פקוד את בני לוי, ובמקום א' הוא או' אך
את מטה לוי לא תפקד, אלא שא"ל להוציאן מן הגזרה, שצפה הב"ה שעתידין
ישראל להכעיס והוא אומ' להם במדבר הזה יתמו וגו', ולפי' או'
הב"ה על בני לוי את ראשם לא תשא וגו'. ילמדנו.

(דף י"ג, ע"א) [לבמ' ד', ד']

כך היו בני קהת עושים, ב' כהנים גדולים נושאים להם את הפרוכת
בקונדיסין, והיתה דומה לוילון גדולה ועוביה טפח, ועל ע"ב נימין נארגת,
ועל כל נימה ונימה כ"ד חוטין, וג' מאות כהנים טבילין אותה, וב' כהנים
נושאין אותה בקונדיסין מפני הארון, ואח"כ נותנין כסוי עור תחש שלא
יראה הארון כלום, שנ' ולא יבאו לראות כבלע. א"ר לוי אם רואין בארון
כבלע הזה וכו' לעיל ר' יהודה או' כבלע את הקדש, בשעת הכנסת כלים
לנרתק שלהם. ילמדנו פ' ויקהל.

(דף י"ח, ע"ב) [לבמ' ה', י"ב]

איש איש, ללמדך שהסוטה כופרת בשני אנשים, באיש מלחמה שלמעלה
ובאישה. ילמדנו.

(דף י"ט, ע"א)

ועד אין בה, אע"פ שאין לה עכשיו יש לה לאחר זמן, שנ' והייתי
עד ממהר במכשפים ובמנאפים. כיוצא בדבר ותהי שרה עקרה אין לה
ולד, אע"פ שאין לה עכשיו יש לה לאחר זמן, שנ' ותלד שרה לאברהם
בן. ילמדנו.

(דף ו', ע"ב)

וּבָנִים לֹא הָיוּ לָהֶם וַיְכַהֵן אֶלְעָזָר וְאִיתָמָר. ר' יעקב בר' יוסי
אוֹ' אלו לא היו להם בנים היו קודמין לאלעזר ואיתמר, שכל הקודם בנחלה קודם
בכבוד (ובלבד שיהא נוהג כמנהג אבותיו). פסיקתא. ילמדנו.

וַיְכַהֵן אֶלְעָזָר וְאִיתָמָר עַל פְּנֵי אַהֲרֹן אֲבִיהֶם. ר' יצחק אמ' בחייו,
ר' אחא אמ' במותו. על דעתיה דר' יצחק נא' כאן על פני בחייו ונא' להלן
על פני תרח אביו, מה להלן בחייו אף כאן בחייו. על דעתיה דר'
אחא נא' כאן על פני ונא' להלן ויקם אברהם מעל פני מתו, מה
להלן אחר מיתה אף כאן לאחר מיתה. על דעתיה דר' יצחק דאמ' בחייו
אירעה טומאה באהרן ושימש אלעזר, אירעה טומאה באלעזר ושימש איתמר;
על דעתיה דר' אחא דאמ' במותו מת אהרן ושמש אלעזר, מת אלעזר
ושמש איתמר. פסיקתא. ילמדנו. רבה.

(דף ז', ע"ב) [לבמ' ג', ט"ז]

כתי' פקוד את בני לוי וכתי' את מטה לוי לא תפקד, אמ' הב"ה
כשתפקד אותם אל תפקדם עם ישראל אלא בפני עצמן, לפי שכשעשו
ישראל אותו מעשה לא נשתתפו עמהם, שנ' מי לה' אלי ויאספו אליו כל
בני לוי. פסיקתא. ילמדנו. רבה.

(דף ט', ע"א)

אמ' הב"ה כתבתי בתורה שיהא פטר חמור נפדה בשה, שנ' ופטר
חמור תפדה בשה, אני לא עשיתי כך אלא פדיתי שה בחמור, המצרים
נמשלו לחמור אשר בשר חמורים בשרם, וישראל לשה שה פזורה ישראל,
הרגתי בכורי מצרים והקדשתי בכורי ישראל כי לי כל בכור. לפי'
א"ל הב"ה למשה פְּקֹד כָּל בְּכֹר זָכָר לִבְנֵי יִשְׂרָאֵל. ילמדנו.

הה"ד שִׂים הַמָּה מְלָכוֹת וגו' אַחַת הִיא יוֹנָתִי וגו', משל לאדם
שהיה לו פרגמטוטוס של אבנים של זכוכיות, והיה מוציאן לשוק ולא
היה מניחן במנין, ונכנס להניחן ולא היה מניחן במנין, שלא היה משגיח
בהן, שהיו של זכוכיות. והיה לו פרגמטוטוס אחת שלמרגליות גסות,
והיה נוטלה במנין ומניחה במנין, למה, שהיו לו חשובין ביותר, כך
כביכול הב"ה אמ': לאומות העולם לא נתתי מנין, למה, שאינן חשובין
לפני כלום, שנ' כל הגוים כאין נגדו, אבל בני ישראל, שנ' בהם העמוסים
מני בטן וגו', אני מונה אותם בכל שעה. ולכך נאמ' שְׂאוּ אֶת רֹאשׁ
כָּל עֲדַת בְּנֵי יִשְׂרָ', וכתי' פְּקֹד כָּל בְּכֹר זָכָר וגו'. אמ' רבן גמליאל כל
שאינו חי שלשים יום לא כלו חדשיו והרי הוא כנפל, ומנין אתה אוֹ'
כן, שנ' מבן חדש ומעלה לשא את מספר שמותם. ולקחת את הלוים לי,
שיהיו לקוחים לשמי. אני ה', נאמן אני לשלם שכר טוב על שהם לקוחים
לשמי. תחת כל בכר בבני ישראל, שהבכורות שלי הם, שנ' כי לי כל

מבניכם, מפני שיש בהם מי שנשא אשה מבנות כנען, וכה"א וישאו אותו בניו ולא בני בניו. והאך(?) צוה, אמר להם: יהודה יששכר וזבולון יטענו מטתי מן המזרח; ראובן שמעון וגד מן הדרום; מנשה אפרים ובנימין מן המערב; דן ואשר ונפתלי מן הצפון. ויוסף אל יטעון, לפי שהוא מלך ואתם חייבין לחלוק לו כבוד; לוי אל יטעון, לפי שהוא עתיד לטעון את הארון. וכשאמר הב"ה למשה שיעשו ישראל דגלים התחיל משה מיצר, אמר: עכשיו תהא מחלוקת בין השבטים, שאם אומר ליהודה שישרה במזרח או' אי אפשי אלא בדרום וכן כולם, א"ל הב"ה: משה, מה איכפת לך, הם מכירים דירתם, איש על דגלו באחת לבית אבותם, באותות שמסרו להם אבותם.

וכיצד היו שרויים? משה ואהרן במזרח, שנ' והחונים לפני המשכן קדמה וגו' משה ואהרן וגו'. וסמוכים להם יהודה ויששכר וזבולון, שנ' והחונים קדמה המזרחה דגל מחנה יהודה, והחונים עליו מטה יששכר וגו'. מכאן אמ' אשרי צדיק ואשרי שכניו, אלו ג' שבטים שהיו שכנים למשה ואהרן נעשו גדולים בתורה; יהודה, דכתי' לא יסור שבט מיהודה וגו', ומבני יששכר יודעי בינה לעתים, ומבני זבולון מושכי' בשבט סופר. ובני קהת מן הדרום, וסמוכים להם ראובן ושמעון וגד. מכאן אמ' אוי לרשע אוי לשכנו, אלו הג' שבטים שהיו שכנים לקרח ועדתו בדרום אנדו עמו במחלוקתו וכו'. התם. ולמה צום לעשות דגלים, שהם צבאות י"י. מנגד סביב לאהל מועד יחנו, ומהו מנגד, מרחוק מיל, אמ' הב"ה יהיו ישראל רחוקים מן הא[רו]ן אלפים אמה (שנ' אך) רחוק יהיה ביניכם ובניו כאלפים אמה, ומשה ואהרן היו סמוכים לו, שנ' והחונים לפני המשכן, אמר הב"ה: יהיו אלו חונים לפני המשכן, שאם כעסתי על בני יהיו אלו עושין פשרה ביני וביניכם, לכך היו סמוכים לו. אבל השבטים מנגד סביב לאהל מועד יחנו. ילמדנו.

(דף ו, ע"א) [לבמד' ג', ד']

וימת נדב ואביהוא לפני י"י, א"ר יוחנן וכי לפני י"י מתו, אלא מלמד שקשה לפני הב"ה בשעה שבניהם של צדיקים מסתלקין בחייהן כאביהן. רב נחמן אמ' מהכא, הכא את אמ' לפני י"י לפני י"י ב' פעמים, ולהלן את אמ' על פני אהרן אביהם פעם, אלא מלמד שהוא קשה לפני הב"ה כפלים כאביהם. במדבר סיני, וכי במדבר סיני מתו, אלא שבמדבר סיני נטלו אפופוסין שלהן למיתה. משל למלך שהיה משיא את בתו ונמצא בשושבינון שלה דבר של זמימה, אמ' המלך אם אני הרגו מערבב הריני שמחת בתי, למחר באה שמחתי, מוטב בשמחתי ולא בשמחת בתי. כך אמ' הב"ה אם אני הורג נדב ואביהוא עכשיו הריני מערבב שמחת התורה, למחר שמחתי באה, מוטב בשמחתי ולא בשמחת התורה. רבה. ילמדנו. פסיקתא.

ששה שמות נקראו להר סיני: הר סיני, הר אלהים, הר בשן, הר גבנונים,
ההר חמד אלהים לשבתו, הר חורב. הר סיני, שבו נתנשאו אומות
העולם להב"ה ונתן להם אפופוסין שם. הר אלהים, שישב בו אלהים
בדין, שנ' ואלה המשפטים. הר בשן, הר שבא שם. הר גבנונים, שפסל בו
כל ההרים, כד"א או גבן או דק. ההר חמד, שחמד אלהים לשבתו. הר
חורב, שבו נמשכה חרב מות: ומת הנואף; מות יומת הרוצח; מת
יומתו דמיהם בם. ילמדנו. רבה פ"א.

(מדוע אמרו עמי רדנו, אמרו לו נתת לנו בית המקדש וסלקה
שכינתך ממנו... כאן אני בונה אכסניא שלי ודר בתוכה. הה"ד וידבר
יי' אל משה במדבר סיני, שהיה שם אהל מועד והב"ה דר בתוכו. רבה
פרש' א').

זש"ה בטנך ערמת חטים, למה נמשלו ישר' לערמת חטים? מה החטים
הללו כשהן נכנסות לאוצר במנין הן נכנסות וכשיוצאות במנין הן יוצאות,
אמר הב"ה שיהו ישראל נמנין בכל שעה. אבל התבן והקש אינן נמנין ולא
נמדין, ואומות העולם נמשלין לתבן ולקש: יהיו כקש לפני רוח, ובית
עשיו לקש, וכתי' כל הגוים כאין נגדו. אבל ישראל יש לו הקב"ה הנאה
מהם – קורין קרית שמע ומתפללין ומברכין שמו בכל שעה – לפי' הם נמנין
בכל שעה. הה"ד ש א ו את ראש כל עדת וגו'. ילמדנו, רבה.

(בטנך ערמת חטים, א"ר יצחק למה נמשלו ישר' לחטים... לה"ד?
לאחד שהיה יושב ועושה עטרת למלך וכו'. שמות רבה, פ' כי תשא)

(דף ד, ע"א)

א"ר יהושע דסכנין מאי דכתי' הביאני אל בית היין וגו', אמ'
כנסת ישראל הביאני הב"ה למרתף גדול של יין, זה סיני, שם מיכאל, ודגלו
גבריאל, ודגלו עלי אהבה, הלואי יהא בטקסיס הזה של מעלה, אמ'
הב"ה הואיל ונתאוו בנו להיות בדגלים כן יהיו. הה"ד א י ש על
דגלו באתת.

ד"א הביאני אל בית היין וגו', מלה"ד, לעשיר שהיה לו אוצר
של יין מלא, נכנס לבדק ומצאו כולו חומץ, בא לצאת מהאוצר ומצא שם
חבית יין טוב, אמ' חבית זו חביבה עלי מכל האוצר. כך הב"ה ברא ע'
אומות, ומכולם לא מצא הנאה אלא (דף ד', ע"ב) מישראל, שנ' ודגלו
עלי אהבה. ד"א ודגלו עלי אהבה, אמר הב"ה יש לאומות העולם
דגלים ואין חביב עלי אלא דגלו של יעקב, שנ' איש על דגלו באתת.
מדרש שיר השירים. ילמדנו.

איש על דגלו באתת, מלמד שהיו הדגלים בעלי גדולה וכבוד.
באותות לא היה צריך לומר אלא איש איש על דגלו יחנו בני ישראל, ומה
ת"ל באתת, אלא בשעה שנפטר יעקב אבינו אמר לבנו ליוסף ושכבתי
עם אבתי. חזר על כל שבט וברכן ופקדן, אמר להם: כשתטלו
אותי ביראה וכבוד טלו אותי, ולא יגע אדם במטתי לא מן המצרים ולא

ילקוט תלמוד תורה לבמדבר ודברים

(דף ב, ע"א)

זשה"ה צדקתך כהררי אל וגו'. צדקה שאתה עושה על העולם אתה מביאה מפורסמת כהרים הללו, וכשאתה דן את העולם בתהום רבה, מה תהום זה בסתר אף משפט בסתר. כיצד, כשחרבה ירושלם בט' באב חרבה, וכשהראה ליחזקאל הראהו בעשרים לחדש. למה, כדי שלא לפרסם באיזה יום חרבה; וכשהוא בא לגדל את ישראל הוא מפרסם באיזה מקום, באיזה יום, באיזה חדש, באיזו שנה, באיזו הפרכיא. הוי במדבר סיני וגו'.

ב א ו ה ל מ ו ע ד, עד שלא עמד אוהל מועד דבר עמו בסנה, אח"כ במצרים, אח"כ בסיני. כיון שעמד אוהל מועד אמר: יפה היא הצניעות, התחיל לדבר עמו באהל מועד. ילמדנו.

וידבר י"י אל משה במדבר סיני וגו', וכל כך למה? למלך שנשא אשה ראשונה ולא כתב לה כתובה, גרשה ולא כתב לה גט, וכן לשלישית. לימים ראה עניה אחת בת טובים, בקש לישא אותה אמ' לשושבינו: זו היתומה העניה אני רוצה לישא, ואיני נוהג בה כמנהג הראשונות, שזו בת אבות היא וצנועה במעשיה, אכתוב לה כתובה, באיזה יום ובאיזה שבוע, באיזו שנה באיזה חדש, בכה לחדש, באיזו הפרכיא. כך הב"ה ברא דור המבול, דור הפלגה, סדומים, מצרים, ולא כתב להם מאומה מתי בראם ומתי העבירם. וכיון שעמדו ישראל א"ל הב"ה למשה: איני נוהג בהם כראשונים, שאילו בני אברהם יצחק ויעקב הם, אלא כתוב באיזה יום, באיזה שבוע, באיזו הפרכיא וכו'. לכך וידבר י"י אל משה ב מ ד ב ר ס י נ י – הרי הפרכיא, ב א ה ל מ ו ע ד – הרי המדינה, ב א ח ד לחדש השני–הרי היום, ב ש נ ה ה ש נ י ת – הרי השנה.

ד"א ב מ ד ב ר ס י נ י, בג' דברים ניתנה תורה: באש ובמים ובמדבר. באש, והר סיני עשן כולו וגו'; במים, דכתי' י"י בצאתך משעיר וגו' גם עבים נטפו מים; במדבר, דכת' וידבר י"י אל משה במדבר וגו'. ולמה נתנה תורה בג' דברים אלו? לומר לך מה ג' דברים אלו חנם לכל באי העולם אף התורה חנם לכל באי העולם. ד"א למה במדבר, לומר לך שכל מי שאינו עושה עצמו הפקר כמדבר אינו יכול לקנות את (דף ב, ע"ב) התורה.

וכיון שאתה עושה תשובה, ו ש ב י ' י א ל ה י ך א ת ש ב ו ת ך וגו' (דב'
ל', ג'). אמר הקב"ה: בעולם הזה הייתם קוראים מתוך צרה, והייתי עונה אתכם,
שנ' הוי כי גדול היום ההוא מאין כמוהו ועת צרה היא וגו' (יר' ל', ז').

ש מ ע י ש ר א ל. יתרומם שמו שלהקב"ה לעולם ולעולמי עולמים, שהוא אחד
ושמו אחד, והוא לבדו ואין שני לו, והוא בכבודו ברא את השמים ואת הארץ
והימים והתהומות וכל אשר בים, וכולם משתחוים לפניו, אתה הוא י"י לבדך וגו'
(נחמ' ט', ו'). ואע"פ שיש לפניו כמה שבחות והילולים, חיבב הוא הילולים שלדוד
יותר מכל, מה טעמה, ואלה דברי דוד הראשונים (ש"ב, כ"ג, א'), ואומר ואתה
קדוש יושב תהלות ישראל (תה' כ"ב, ד').

אמר ר' ת נ ח ו מ ה כל מי שהוא עומד ומתפלל לפני הקב"ה באימה
ובידאה, עתיד לשמוח ביום רעה, שנ' עבדו את י"י ביראה (שם, ב', י"א), כדי
שתגילו ברעדה. לפיכך

[כאן נפסק הכ"י, וחסרים כמה דפים בסופו, וחבל על דאבדין.]

חיי וגו' (תה' ל"א, י"א), ואומר מי חכם ויבין אלה וגו' (הו' י"ד, י'), מלמד
שהפשעים שאדם עושה מביאין אותו לידי מכשול. ובמה מתכפר לו, בתשובה.
לכך אמר משה ו ש ב ת ע ד י"י א ל ה י ך, וכתיב שובה ישראל עד י"י
אלהיך.

אמר ר' ת נ ח ו מ ה ד ר ש ו י"י בהמצאו וגו', אלא פעמים שהוא שומע תפלה,
ופעמים אינו שומע, פעמים שהוא עונה, ופעמים שאינו עונה, פעמים שהוא נדרש,
ופעמים שאינו נדרש, פעמים שהוא נמצא, ופעמים שאינו נמצא, פעמים שהוא קרוב,
ופעמים שאינו קרוב, פעמים שהוא נראה, ופעמים שאינו נראה, שנ' והסתרתי פני
מהם (דב' ל"א, י"ז); פעמים שהוא שומע, שנ' וישמע אלהים את נאקתם (שמ'
כ', כ"ד), ופעמים אינו שומע, שנ' ולא שמע י"י בקולכם וגו' (דב' א', מ"ה);
פעמים עונה, שנ' ויענהו באש מן השמים וגו' (דה"א, כ"א, כ"ו), ופעמים שאינו
עונה, שנ' וישאל שאול בי"י וגו' (ש"א, כ"ח, ו'); פעמים שהוא נדרש, שנ' עוד זאת
אדרש לבית ישראל וגו' (יח' ל"ו, ל"ז), ופעמים שאינו נדרש, שנ' הלדרוש אותי
אתם באים וגו' (שם, כ', ג'); פעמים שהוא נמצא, שנ' ונמצאתי לכם וגו' (יר'
כ"ט, י"ד), ופעמים שאינו נמצא, שנ' כצאנם וגו' (הו' ה', ו'); פעמים שהוא קרוב,
שנ' קרוב י"י לכל קוראיו וגו' (תה' קמ"ה, י"ח), ופעמים שהוא רחוק, שנ' רחוק
י"י מרשעים וגו' (מש' ט"ו, כ"ט). לפיכך הוא אומר דרשו י"י בהמצאו וגו'.

אפילו אדם חוטא כמה פעמים והוא חוזר ועושה תשובה, (דף פ"א, ע"ב)
הקב"ה מקבלו, שנ' יעזב רשע דרכו ואיש וגו' (יש' נ"ה, ז'). מהו בהיותו קרוב
(שם, ו'), עד שהוא במ[קומו], עשו תשובה עד שלא יצא ממקומו, שנ' כי י"י יוצא
ממקומו וגו' (מי' א', ג'). ומאי זה מקום הוא יוצא, ולאי זה מקום הוא נכנס, והלא
אין מקום פנוי מכבודו, שנ' כה אמר י"י השמים כסאי והארץ וגו' (יש' ס"ו, א'),
אלא שהוא יוצא משבע מדות שלרחמים, שנ' ויעבור י"י על פניו וגו' (שמ' ל"ד, ו'),
ונכנס לשבע מדות שלפורענות, שנ' אל קנוא ונוקם י"י וגו' (נח' א', ב'), מלמד
שהוא בא על הרשעים באכזריות, וכשהן חוזרין בהן, הוא בא עליהם במדת
רחמים, שנ' יעזב רשע דרכו וגו'.

וכשם שנמשלה תורה כמים, כן נמשל הקב"ה כמים, שנ' כי שתים רעות עשה
עמי וגו' (יר' ב', י"ג). וכיון שעזבו את התורה, כך עזבו אותי, שנ' הוי גוי חוטא
וגו' (יש' א', ד'), ואומר ויעזבו את י"י ולא עבדוהו (שו' י', ו'). ובמים מדד
להם, שהשליכם בהם, כאומות שנמשלו כמים, שנ' מצרים כיאור יעלה וגו' (יר'
מ"ו, ח'). ואילולי רחמיו שלהקב"ה, כבר היו נשטפים בהם, שנ' לולי י"י שהיה
לנו וגו', אזי המים שטפונו וגו', ברוך י"י שלא וגו' (תה'
קכ"ד, ב', ד'—ו'). ומי גרם לישראל כל זאת, אלא שבטלו מן התורה, שהזהירן
משה עליה, שנ' כי ידעתי אחרי מותי וגו' (דב' ל"א, כ"ט). לפיכך הוא אומר
בצר לך ומצאוך וגו' (דב' ד', ל').

אמרו חכמים ז"ל אין ישראל עתידין ליגאל אלא על ידי תשובה, שנ' אל תירא
עבדי יעקב וגו' (יר' ל', י'), ואומר ושב יעקב ושקט ושאנן ואין מחריד (שם),
מלמדך שהתשובה מביאה את הישועה, וכן הוא אומר מי יתן מציון וגו' (תה' נ"ג, ז').

מזבח י״י אלהיך, אלא המקיים דיין על הצבור שלא כראוי, דומה כאילו
עובד ע״ז, מה מזבח מכפר עונותיהן שלישראל, [כך הדיי]נים [מכפרי]ם, ודיין
שאינו הגון, עושה דין שלא כדין ושלא כרצון חכמים, מחייב את ישראל.

הקב״ה יזכה אתכם בדרך ישרה, בדרך שלא תכשלו בה, ויכריע אתכם לכף
זכות, אמן כן יהי רצון.

[לסדר קמ״ה[a] (י״ד[a]): דברים י״ז, י״ד.]

ואמרת אשימה עלי מלך. יתרומם שמו שלמלך מלכי המלכים
הקב״ה שהוא חי וקיים לעולם ולעולמי עולמים, מעביר כל והוא אינו עובר, משנה
את הכל והוא אינו משתנה, ומלכותו קיימת מלכות כל עולמים וגו' (תה' קמ״ה, י״ג),
והוא ממליך כל המלכים, שנ' והוא מהשנה עדניא וגו' (דנ' ב', כ״א), ולב מלכים
בידו, שנ' לב מלך ביד י״י (מש' כ״א, א'), ואומר פלגי מים וגו' (שם).

המלך לא דן ולא דנין אותו, לא מעד ולא מעידין אותו, ולא חולץ ולא
חולצין את אשתו, ולא מיבמין את אשתו, ואין יושבין על כסאו, ואין רוכבים על
סוסו, ואין משתמשין

[בין דף פ' ודף פ״א חסרים כמה דפים.]

[לקריאה בשבת שבין ר״ה ויו״כ: דברים ל', א'.]

[והיה כי יבאו עליך.] ... (דף פ״א, ע״א) אומר כי אתך אני
נאום י״י להצילך (יר' א', י״ט), אלא מנקה לכל בעלי תשובה. ראה כמה גדולה
היא התשובה שהיא מנקה את האדם מעונותיו. לכך נאמר ושבת עד י״י
אלהיך וגו' (דב' ל', ב'). אמר הנביא: אל תבכו למת (שם, כ״ב, י'), זה שהוא
צדיק, למה, שהוא עתיד לחיות, אלא בכו בכה להולך ולא ישוב (שם), לכל
אותן הרשעים שהן הולכים ואינן חוזרין אלא לדין; אל תבכו לאותם שהלכו
בתשובה, אלא לשהלך מן העולם הזה בלא תשובה. שאם אדם מבקש לעשות
תשובה, מכוין את לבו שמא אינו יכול עוד לעשות תשובה ולקבל שכרה,
דכתיב כי החיים יודעים שימותו והמתים (קה' ט', ה'), לפיכך אמר להם משה
ושבת עד י״י אלהיך.

אמר ר' ירמיה כתיב דרשו י״י בהמצאו (יש' נ״ה, ו'), איכן אתה צריך להיות
דורשו, בבתי כנסיות שהוא מצוי שם. אמר ר' לוי בכל מקום שאתה דורש אותו,
הוא מצוי אצלך קרוב, שנ' קרוב י״י לנשברי לב וגו' (תה' ל״ד, י״ט); אם מבקש
אתה לעשות תשובה, ולדרוש את הקב״ה עד שהוא מצוי לך, שנ' שובה ישראל עד
י״י אלהיך וגו' (הו' י״ד, ב'). כי העונות מתיאשים בכשל אדם, שנ' כי כלו ביגון

אוהב משפט וגו' (יש' ס"א, ח'). אמר הקב"ה: אם יעשו, ונתתי פעולתם באמת
(שם), וכן הוא אומר כה אמר י"י שמרו משפט וגו' (שם, נ"ו, א').

ד"א. שופטים ושוטרים. אמר ר' לוי אם שופטים, למה
שוטרים, ואם שוטרים, למה שופטים, אלא שאין מתקיימין אלו
אלא בכוח אילו. וממי אתה למד, מדוד המלך, ויואב בן צרויה על הצבא (ש"ב,
ח', ט"ז), שכל המורד ואינו שומע אל המשפט, מוליכין אותו אצל השוטר ומלקה
אותו. לכך נאמר שופטים ושוטרים.

זש"ה לך אל נמלה עצל וגו', אשר אין לה קצין וגו', תכין בקיץ לחמה וגו'
(מש' ו', ו'–ח'), מה נמלה שאינה גוזלת את חברתה, שהיא מריחה משהו לחברתה,
ומניחה אותו ואינו נוטלת דבר מחברתה, שאין לה קצין שוטר ומושל, ואינן גוזלין
אלו לאלו, ואתם בני אדם, נתן לכם הקב"ה חכמה ובינה ודעת והשכל, על אחת
כמה וכמה שראוי לכם שלא תגזלו איש את רעהו. לכך נאמר לך אל נמלה עצל
וגו'. ומה הנמלה הזו אינה צריכה לדון ולדין, ואתם צריכים לדון ולדין. ד"א,
לך אל נמלה עצל, ומה הנמלה הזו מתקנת מאכלה מקיץ לחורף, אף אתם היכינו
לכם מעשים טובים בעולם הזה, כדי שתאכלו פירותיהם לעולם הבא לעתיד
לבוא.

ד"א. שופטים ושוטרים. זש"ה אשר אין בהם כל מום וגו' (דנ'
א', ד'), מהו ואשר כח בהם וגו' (שם), מה אם יהיה זקן, יש בו כל המדות הללו
ואין בו כח וחיל ומלחמה, יעמוד בהיכל מלך. אמר ר' יודן ביושבים לפני
נבוכדנצר הכתוב מדבר, שהחרטומים האשפים והכשדים, שהיו לפני המלך
נבוכדנצר, היו יוצאים ובאים והיו נצרכים לנקביהן, (דף פ', ע"ב) אבל דניאל
חנניה מישאל ועזריה לא היו נצרכים לנקביהן, ולא לצאת ולבוא, ולא לאכילה
ולא לשתיה. לכך נאמר ילדים אשר אין בהם כל מום וגו'.

ד"א. שופטים ושוטרים. זהו שנאמרה ברוח הקדש על
ידי דוד מלך ישראל צדקתך כהררי אל משפטיך וגו' (תה' ל"ו, ז'). בוא וראה
כשם [שה]הרים כובשים על התהום שלא יעלה ויציף את העולם, כך הצדקה
כובשת את המשפטים, שלא להתחרות בם בבני ישראל. משל לשני חכמים שהיו
עוברים בגשר שלנהר בלילה, אמר להם השומר: הזהרו בכם שלא תטו ימין
ושמאל, שאם תטו ימין ושמאל אבדתם בנהר, כך אמר משה לישראל: הזהרו
בעצמכם שאם תסורו ימין ושמאל מן המצות ומן התורה, נטרדתם מן העולם.
ורוח הקדש אומרת אל תט ימין ושמאל (מש' ד', כ"ז). תמיה אני מן הדיין שיושב
בראש ואומר לא תטה משפט (דב' ט"ז, י"ט), והוא מטה משפט; לא
תכיר פנים (שם), והוא מכיר פנים; לא תקח שחד (שם), והוא
לוקח שחד.

לא תטה. זש"ה גם אלה לחכמים הכר פנים במשפט וגו' (מש' כ"ד, כ"ג).
אמר הקב"ה לישראל: בני, כל מי שהוא מטה משפט, כביכול זעזע כסא הכבוד
שהוא מיוסד על הצדקה ועל המשפט, שנ' צדק ומשפט מכון כסאך וגו' (תה'
פ"ט, ט"ו). לא תטע לך (דב' ט"ז, כ"א), וכי יכול אדם ליטע עץ אצל

אף הנשים לא יהיו חייבות בדינין. ב כ ל ש ע ר י ך (דב' ט"ז, י"ח), בכל עיר
ועיר, שאם עמדה (דף ע"ט, ע"ב) הלכה לפניהן שהיו שואלין לבית דין הגדול
שבירושלים.

ו ש פ ט ו א ת ה ע ם (שם), שיהיו מטים את העם לכף זכות. ד"א,
ו ש פ ט ו א ת ה ע ם מ ש פ ט צ ד ק, שיהיו הדיינים יודעים את מי הם דנין,
ולפני מי הן מעידים, לפני מלך מלכי המלכים הקב"ה, שנ' ושפטו את העם משפט
צדק, וכתיב לא תכירו פנים במשפט וגו' (דב' א', י"ז). הדין המקלקל את הדין
קרוי: עוול, שנוא, משוקץ, חרם, ותועבה. וגורם ה' דברים: מטמא את הארץ,
מחלל את השם, מסלק את השכינה, ומפיל את ישראל בחרב, ומגלה אותם מארצם.

לא תשא פני דל (וי' י"ט, ט"ו), אל תאמר זה עני וזה עשיר, והעשיר חייב
לפרנסו, אזכנו ונמצא מתפרנס [בנ]קיות, לכך נאמר לא תשא פני דל. ולא תהדר
פני גדול בצדק תשפוט עמיתך (שם), שלא יהא הדין מאריך פנים כנגד אחד
ומעיז פנים כנגד אחד, אחד מרבה לדבר כל צרכו, ולאחר אומר תקצר דבריך,
אלא שניהם לפניך בשוה. הוי כקטון כגדול תשמעון (דב' א', י"ז).

אמר ר' יהושע לא היה צריך לומר אלא ל א ת ק ח ש ח ד (דב' ט"ז, י"ט),
שלא תכיר פנים ותטה משפט, אלא אמר ל א ת ט ה מ ש פ ט (שם), מלמד
שכל מי שהוא מטה משפט על מנת שיכיר פנים ועל מנת שיקח שחד, ואפילו שאלת
שלום, אסור. למה, שהשחד דומה לאבן, אם נפל עליה אדם נשבר, ואם נפלה
עליה היא משברת אותו. לפיכך נמשל כאבן, שנ' אבן חן השחד וגו' (מש' י"ז, ח').
לכך הוא אומר כ י ה ש ח ד י ע ו ר ע י נ י ח כ מ י ם וגו' (דב', שם), קל
וחומר עיני טפשים. מעוור עיניו שלחכם מראות אמת, הרי בעולם הזה, יענשו
לעולם הבא עיני מראות השכינה שהכל רואין אותו, שנ' קול צופיך וגו' (יש'
נ"ב, ח'). ו י ס ל ף ד ב ר י צ ד י ק י ם (דב', שם), שהוא מסלף דברי אמת
ומביא תחתיה חובה. לפיכך הוא אומר ל א ת ט ה מ ש פ ט וגו'.

אמר ר' יהודה חביב הוא והמשפט מכל המצות. תדע לך שהוא כן, שהרי
עשרת הדברות כל אחד ואחד אין לו אלא צווי אחד, שנ' לא תשא, לא תרצח,
לא תנאף, לא תגנוב, לא תענה, לא תחמוד (שמ' כ', ז', י"ג–י"ז), אבל המשפטים,
ראה כמה אזהרות עליהם. ונעשו חביבין מן הכל, שנ' עושה צדקה ומשפט וגו'
(מש' כ"א, ג'). ואפילו ביד אדם כמה מעשים טובים אינו משובח בעולם אלא
בצדקה ומשפט. ממי את למד, ממשה איש האלהים, שכל מעשים טובים שהיו
בידו לא נשתבח (דף פ', ע"א) אלא בצדקה ובמשפט, שנ' וירא ראשית (דב'
ל"ג, כ"א). וכן דוד, שנ' ויהי דוד עושה משפט וצדקה וגו' (ש"ב, ח', ט"ו), לכך
הוא אומר עושה צדקה ומשפט. אשרי שומרי משפט וגו' (תה' ק"ו, ג'), אמר ר'
זעירא מי שהוא מגדל יתום בתוך ביתו, עושה צדקה בכל עת (שם). וכל שהוא
עושה משפט וצדקה, גורם לישועה שתבוא על ידו. משה, גדול שבעולם, התחיל
במשפט, שנ' ויצא ביום השני וגו' (שם, ב', י"ג), וכתיב מי שמך וגו' (שם, י"ד).
אמר לו הקב"ה: התחלת לעשות משפט, גרמת לישועה שתבוא על ידך, שנ' ועתה
לכה ואשלחך וגו' (שם, ג', י'). והרבה הקב"ה אוהב את המשפט, שנ' כי אני י"י

מצאנו שצדקה ומעשים טובים וגמילות חסדים חביבין יתר מן הקרבנות, שנ'
עושה צדקה ומשפט נבחר לי"י מזבח (מש' כ"א, ג'). שהצדקה נוהגת בחיים,
וגמילות חסדים נוהגת בעניים בין בעשירים, והצדקה נוהגת בממונו שלאדם,
וגמילות חסדים נוהגת בין בממונו בין בגופו. גדולה היא הצדקה שהיא מלוה
לרשעים ומארכת להם, שכך אמר דניאל לנבוכדנצר להן מלכא מלכי ישפר עלך
וגו' (דנ' ד', כ"ד), ולא כל שכן אף לצדיקים. גדולה היא הצדקה שבה נשתבח
דוד מלך ישראל, שנ' ויהי דוד עושה משפט וצדקה בארץ (ש"ב, ח', ט"ו), ובאי
זה צד היה (דף ע"ט, ע"א) היה עושה, אלא היו שנים נכנסים לפניו בדין, והיה
אחד מהם חייב לחבירו ממון ולא לו ליתן, היה דוד נותן לו משלו, לקיים
מה שנ' עושה משפט וצדקה בארץ וגו'. גדולה היא הצדקה שהיא נתונה בימינו
שלהקב"ה, שנ' כשמך אלהים כן תהלתך וגו' צדק מ[לאה] ימינ[ך] (תה' מ"ח, י"א).
גדולה היא הצדקה שבה ישראל נגאלין, שנ' ציון במשפט תפדה וגו' (יש' א', כ"ז).
אברהם לא נשתבח אלא בצדקה, שנ' כי ידעתיו למען וגו' (בר' י"ח, י"ט). בונה
ירושלם וגו' (תה' קמ"ז, ב').

[לסדר קמ"ה (י"ד): דברים ט"ז, י"ח.]

פ' שופטים. זש"ה מלך במשפט יעמיד ארץ וגו' (מש' כ"ט, ד'), שאין
העולם עומד אלא על הדין; ואיש תרומות יהרסנה (שם), אלא כשהדין נעשה
ובקש הדיין תרומות הוא הורס הדין, והעולם נהרס, לכך נאמר ואיש תרומות
יהרסנו.
ר' שמעון אומר על ג' דברים העולם קיים: על הדין, ועל האמת, ועל השלום,
וכולם בפסוק אחד הן, שנ' אמת ומשפט שלום שפטו וגו' (זכ' ח', ט"ז). נעשה
הדין, נעשה האמת, נעשה השלום, ואין העולם עומד בלא אלו. ובימי ירמיה בטלו
שלשתן: הדין מנין, שנ' ותהי האמת נעדרת (יש' נ"ט, ט"ו); והשלום מנין, שנ' כי
אספתי את שלומי וגו' (יר' ט"ז, ה'). מיד היה העולם מבקש להפך, שנ' ראיתי
את הארץ והנה תהו וגו' (שם, ד', כ"ג), למה, שבטלו חסידות. גרמו הם לעצמם
שיבטל יסודם ויגלו מן הארץ, שנ' וישראל גלה מעל אדמתו (עמ' ז', י"א, י"ג).
הוי מלך במשפט יעמיד וגו', שאין העולם עומד אלא במשפט. לכך אומר
שופטים ושוטרים וגו'.
שיהא שופט ושוטר בעל זרוע, מעשיהם טובים, שנ' ויבחר משה אנשי חיל וגו'
(שמ' י"ח, כ"ה), אנשי חיל, בתורה ובמעשים טובים; שיהא השופט נקי מכל
משפט, שלא יהא לאדם פתחון פה עליו, שנ' ויחר למשה וגו' (במ' ט"ז, ט"ו),
ובשמואל כתיב הנני ענו בי נגד י"י וגו' (ש"א, י"ב, ג').
ר' יהודה אומר יכול אם יהיו הגוים דנין בדינין הללו שאת מותר להיות נדון
בפניהן, כבר אמרו אלה המשפטים וגו' (שמ' כ"א, א'), לפניהם, ולא לפני
גוים, אבה נידון לפני ישראל ואין אתה נידון לפני גוים. ר' אליעזר אומר יכול

בית; כי תראה ערום וכסיתו (שם), אם ראית צדיק צריך להתכסות אל תסתכל
בו, אלא תסתכל בבשרך ותאמר: מה אני ומה הוא, אני והוא בשר ודם, אכסנו
שמא אצטרך ויכסוני אחרים, שנ' ומבשרך לא תתעלם (שם).

אמר רב לוי רש ואיש תככים נפגשו (מש' כ"ט, י"ג), ר ש, זה רש מן הנכסים,
ת כ כ י ם, שהוא אומר לרש: תן לי מצוה ונתן לו זה, מ א י ר ע י נ י ש נ י ה ם
י' י (שם), זה קנה חיי שעה וזה קנה חיי העולם הבא. וכתיב עשיר ורש נפגשו
וגו' (שם, כ"ב, ב'), ע ש י ר, בנכסים, ר ש, זה רש מן הנכסים, אמר רש
לעשיר: תן לי מצוה, ולא נתן לו, ע ו ש ה ש נ י ה ם י' י (שם), מי שעשה לזה
יכול לעשותו עשיר.

לכך הנביא אומר ותפק לרעב לחמך (יש' נ"ח, י'). ואם מבקש עני ממנו
צדקה ואין בידך לתת לו, ענה אותו עניין יפה. ואם יש בידך, אל תאמץ לבבך
ואל תקפוץ את ידך, אלא כי פ ת ו ח ת פ ת ח א ת י ד ך ל ו (דב'
ט"ו, ח'), שאם ידך תהא פתוחה לעניים, הקב"ה מסייע שתהא פתוחה והולכת, אם
פתחת, פותחין לך, היך הוא כתיב יפתח י' י לך וגו' (שם, כ"ח, י"ב). כ י פ ת ו ח
ת פ ת ח, הרי זה פתיחת יד, שאם (דף ע"ה, ע"ב) העני ידו פתוחה לך, אף אתה
פ ת ח י ד ך ל ו. אם עשית כך, אתה זוכה שיפתח לך שערי צדקה, שנ' פתחו
שערים ויבוא גוי צדיק (יש' כ"ו, ב').

ה ש מ ר ל ך פ ן י ה י ה ד ב ר וגו' (דב' ט"ו, ט'), מגיד לך שתהא
באזהרה שלא תהא עיניך רעה, ואם לאו, אתה גורם לנפשך מה שאמר שלמה
ואבד העושר ההוא בעניין רע (קה' ה', י"ג), בשביל ענייה רעה שענית אותו. ולא
עוד אלא ו ק ר א ע ל י ך א ל י' י וגו' (דב', שם), וכתיב הנפש החוטאת
היא תמות (יח' י"ח, ד'), אלא שהוא מבקש ממך, הוי מסתכל בו בעין יפה. היך
דכתיב אשרי משכיל אל דל וגו' (תה' מ"א, ב'), ואין יום רעה אלא יום הדין, הוי
כי גדול היום ההוא וגו' (יר' ל', ז'). ואם אינו עושה כן, כתיב עליו אותם אזנו
מזעקת דל וגו' (מש' ל"א, י"ג).

אמר ר' ירמיה אפילו מי שאינו נותן צדקה, הקב"ה אינו מקפח שכרו על
הדבר שהוציא מפיו, שנ' כ י ב ג ל ל ה ד ב ר ה ז ה (דב' ט"ו, י'), ומהו
ה ד ב ר, אמר הקב"ה נ ת ו ן ת ת ן ל ו (שם), ממ[מ]ונך, ואם לא נתתה, תדבר
בשבילו לאחרים שיתנו לו, אין אתה יוצא חנם לשכר, כ י ב ג ל ל ה ד ב ר.
ומה אם על דבר שאתה מוציא מפיך, אתה זוכה שתבוא עליך ברכה, על אחת
כמה וכמה אם נתת לו מהונך. לכך אמר שלמה מלוה י' י הונן דל וגו' (מש'
י"ט, י"ז), שהוא משלם לך שכר מצוה.

אמר ר' אליעזר מי שעשה מצוה עם מי שאינן צריכים, אלו המלאכים
שנשתלחו אצל אברהם, מהו אמר להם. יוקח נא מעט מים וגו' (בר' י"ח. ד'),
ואקחה פת לחם (שם, ה'), אמרו לו כן תעשה כאשר דברת (שם), כך היא עשיתך
שתהא אוכל, אין אנו אוכלים. אמר לו הקב"ה: אתה אמרת יוקח נא מעט מים,
בחייך אני פורע לבניך במדבר, בישוב ולעתיד לבוא. הרי למדת מה גדול שכרן
שלעושה צדקה, שהיא מנחלת חיים וכבוד לעתיד לבוא.

שפתותיהם מלומר די. ויהי טרף בביתו (שם), מהו טרף, לשון מזונות, מהיכן לך,
הטריפני לחם חוקי (מש' ל"ז ח'), ויהי טרף לכהנים משרתי, כדי שיתן לכם טרף
בעולם הזה ולעולם הבא, טרף נתן ליראיו (תה' קי"א, ה').

[לסדר קמ"ד (י"ג): דברים ט"ו, ז.]

כי יהיה בך אביון. זש"ה פזר נתן לאביונים (תה' קי"ב, ט'),
בעולם הזה, בעולם הזה. יתברך שמו שלמלך מלכי המלכים הקב"ה שהכל
ברשותו, שהוא מעלה לזה, ומוריש לזה, ומוריד לזה, ומרים לזה, ומעשיר לזה,
שנ' כי אלהים שופט וגו' (שם, ע"ה, ח'), וכתיב כי י"י מוריש ומעשיר וגו' (ש"א,
ב', ז'). ומפני מה ברא הקב"ה עניים ועשירים, כדי שיזכו אלו עם אלו, וכדי
שיתפרנסו אלו מאלו, וכדי שיכפרו אלו על אלו, על שום גם את זה לעומת זה
עשה האלהים (קה' ז', י"ד). לפיכך הוא אומר כי יהיה בך אביון וגו'.

היושב בתוך הבית, אתה חייב לתת לו קודם לעניי העיר. באחד שעריך
(דב' ט"ו, ח'), את שהוא עמך, אתה חייב ליתן לו ראשון. למי שהוא בארץ, שנ'
בארצך אשר י"י אלהיך וגו' (שם). מכאן ואילך שאין מוצאין צדקה
מן הארץ לחוצה לארץ. הרי היד פשוטה והלב אינו שפוי, תלמוד לומר לא
תקפוץ את ידך (שם), מגיד שאתה חייב לו משום אחיך, ומשום
אביון. וכתיב וחי אחיך עמך (וי' כ"ה, ל"ו), חייך קודמין לחיי אחיך, ושלאחיך
קודמין לגר, ושלגר קודמין לתושב, ושלתושב באחרונה. וכך הוא אומר פתוח
תפתח את ידך לאחיך (דב' ט"ו, י"א), הרי אחיך, לעניך, הרי
עניי ביתך, ולאביונך, אביוני עירך, בארצך, בארץ ישראל. מגיד
שאתה חייב לו: משום אחיך, משום עניך, משום אביונך, משום לא יצא לחוצה
לארץ. ואם נתתה לו, אתה נושא השכר.

אמר ר' חייא שבעה (דף ע"ח, ע"א) שמות נקראו לעני, ואלו הן: עני, אביון,
מסכן, דך, מך, דל, רש. עני, כמשמעו; אביון, שהוא מתאוה תא[וה] ואין לו;
מסכן, שהוא מסכן בחיו ומסכן למי שיתן לו צדקה; דל, שנדלדל מנכסיו; דך,
שהוא מדוכדך; מך, שהומך עד האסקופה התחתונה וממיך עצמו לפני בני אדם;
רש, שהוא מתרושש ואין לו.

ואוי לאדם שהוא גוזלו, לפיכך אמר שלמה אל תגזל דל וגו' (מש' כ"ב, כ"ב),
ולמה אומר אל תגזל דל וגו', כי י"י יריב ריבם וקבע וגו' (שם, כ"ג), לעולם הבא.
אמר הקב"ה: אפע"פ שגרמו עונותיו וירד מנכסיו, איני שוכחו לעולם, שנ' כי לא
לנצח ישכח אביון (תה' ט', י"ט), שלא לעולם העני עני, והעשיר עשיר, היום
עשיר ולמחר עני. מהו משפיל אף מרומם (ש"א, ב', ז'). לכך ישעיה הנביא מזהיר
למצוה ואומר הלא פרס לרעב לחמך וגו' (יש' נ"ח, ז'), אם ראיתה אכסניים
ואביונים ורעבים לא תהפוך פניך מהם, שמא יצטרף ויאכילנו אחרים; ועניים
מרודים תביא בית כי תראה ערום וכסיתו (שם), אם ראית עני ודאי תן לו מנה
בשוק, ואם בן אבות היה ונעשה עני, אל תתן לו בשוק ותבזהו, אלא מרודים תביא

א ל ה י כ ם. אמר הקב"ה: בעולם הזה בחרתי אתכם ויחדתי שמי עליכם, אבל
לעולם הבא אני משרה שכינתי בתוככם, שנ' והתהלכתי בתוככם וגו' (וי' כ"ו, י"ב).

[לסדר קמ"ג (י"ב) (a): דברים י"ד, כ"ב.]

ע ש ר ת ע ש ר. אמר ר' יצחק בר נחמן למה כותבין עשר בשין וקורין
בסמך, מפני שתעשר, אמר הקב"ה: אם תוציא מעשר בשנה זו, תתעשר לשנה
אחרת. ע ש ו, למה כתיב בשין וקורין אותו בסמך, מפני שעש רע לבגד, אף כן
עשו רע לבריות. י ש ר א ל, למה כתוב בשין וקורין בסמך, ישר לפני אל והוא
שר לפני ישראל. ש ש ו ן ו ש מ ח ה, כותבין בשין וקורין בסמך, אם ששון
ושמחה בסמך, לא ראיתה לאותה השמחה סוף. שלשין חכמתא ולשין טפשותא.
ו י ע ש, ו י ע ש ו (שם, ח' וכו') לכם, כתובין בשין וקורין בסמך, אלא אם היה
מעשה משכן בסמך, לא היה מסתלק לעולם. ו ש כ ו ת י כ פ י (שם, ל"ג, כ"ב),
למה כתוב בשין וקורין בסמך, מפני שהשכינה על תנאי, שאם ישמרו מצותיו
שלהקב"ה השכינה שמורה, ואם לאו, כשם שידותיו שלשין פתוחה, כך השכינה
מסתלקת מבניהם. א ת ה כ ב ש (במ' כ"ח, ד'), למה כתוב בשין וקורין
בסמך, מפני שמכבש עוונותיהן שלישראל. ל ו י ש ט מ נ ו (בר' נ', ט"ו), מה
יש, אמר ר' נתן בשעה שהעלו את יעקב אל ארץ כנען וקברו אותו, כיון שהזרו
בדרך הלך יוסף ונסתכל באותו הבור שהשליכוהו בו אחיו, אמרו אחיו: עד כאן
יש טמון בלבו הדבר. ש ט ן, למה בשין וקורין בסמך, השטן בגימטריא שס"ד,
כנגד ימות השנה כולה חוץ מיום הכפורים, כל השנה כולה הוא אסור, ויום
הכפורים מתירין אותו, יבוא וישוט בעולם ויבוא ויראה את ישראל בבתי כנסיות
בצום ובתפלה והם מתענין יחפי רגל, היה אומר לפני הקב"ה: יש לך אומה
בעולם כמלאכי השרת לא אוכלין ולא שותין ומתפללים כל היום כמותם בעמידה.
התמלא בשוכות עורו (אי' מ', ל"א), למה כתיב בשין וקרי בסמך, שכל הסוכות
כולן בסמך כתובה, וקרא שיהא עליהם זה בעל תנאי, אם זוכה עושין לו סוכה,
ואם לאו, יעשה לו שוכה.

ע ש ר ת ע ש ר (דב' י"ד, כ"ב), למה שתי פעמים, הוציא מעשר כדי
שתתעשר. ולמה פ ת ו ח ת פ ת ח (שם, ט"ו, ח'), שתי פעמים, (דף ע"ז, ע"ב)
פתוח ידך מלמטה, כדי שיפתח לך מלמעלה. ולמה נ ת ו ן ת ת ן (שם, י'),
שתי פעמים, תן לו בעולם הזה, כדי שיתן לך שכרך לעולם הבא. למה ה ע נ ק
ת ע נ י ק (שם, י"ד), שתי פעמים, הענק לו מאוצרותיך שבארץ, כדי שיעניקך
מאוצרות השמים, שנ' יפתח י"י לך את אוצרו (שם, כ"ח, י"ב).

ד"א. ע ש ר ת ע ש ר. הביאו את כל המעשר אל בית האוצר וגו' (מלא'
ג', י'). אמר ר' זעירא היאך אני מקים שני מקראות הללו, לא תנסו את וגו' (דב'
ו', ט"ז), ובחנוני נא בזאת וגו' (מלא', שם), לא תנסו את י"י, בכל, חוץ מזה. ומה
שכרם, אם לא אפתח לכם וגו' (שם). מאי עד בלי די, אמר ר' יודן עד שיכלו

וכן שלמה אמר בני אם תקח אמרי וגו' (מש' ב', א'), אתה נעשה בני. מה
כתיב למעלה מן הענין, כי תעשה הטוב והישר וגו' (דב' י"ב, כ"ח),
מה כתיב אחריו, בנים אתם וגו'.

יש פעמים שהן קרואין עמים, יש פעמים שקרואים עבדים. עבדים, שנ' כי
לי בני ישראל עבדים (וי' כ"ה, כ"ה), עמים, שנ' עמים הר יקראו וגו' (דב'
ל"ג, י"ט). וכשהן חוטאין כבנים, הוא מביא עליהם כבנים יסורין, וכשחוטאין
כעמים, הוא פורע מהם, ואימתי חטאו כעמים, יען שכחת אותי ותשליכו את
תורתי (דף ע"ו, ע"ב) אחרי גוך וגו' (יח' כ"ג, ל"ה), ומה כתיב עליהם, והפיצותי
אותם בגוים וגו' (יח' כ"ב, ט"ו), ועליהם כתיב ויתשם י"י וגו' (דב' כ"ט, כ"ז). ר'
מאיר אומר בנים בין טובים ובין רעים, אין לי אלא אתם.

אל תעשו אגודות אגודות ותהיו חולקין אלו על אלו. ולא תשימו
קרחה (דב' י"ד, א'), כשם שעשה קרח בישראל ונבלעו עמו בני אדם הרבה.
בין עיניכם (שם), אפילו ראש שלסנהדרין, והוא בעל מחלוקת, אין הקב"ה
סולח לו, שאין עיניכם אלא סנהדרין, הרי כתיב והיה אם מעיני העדה וגו'
(במ' ט"ו, כ"ד).

למה, מפני שאומות העולם, כשימות להם מת, משרטין גופן ומצערין עצמן.
למה, מפני שמיתיהן מתים ואינן חיים, שנ' מתים בל יחיו וגו' (יש' כ"ו, י"ד). אבל
אתם אל תעשו כן, מפני מתיכם שאין מתיכם מתים, שסופן חוזרין לחיים. וכן יחזקאל אומר
וידעתם כי אני י"י בפתחי וגו' (יח' ל"ז, י"ג), וכן דניאל אומר ורבים מישיני אדמת
עפר (דנ' י"ב, ב'). הרי אומות העולם שאין להם תקומה, שנ' גערת גוים אבדת
רשע וגו' (תה' ט', ו').

כי עם קדוש אתה (דב' י"ד, ב'), מלמד שאתם מקודשים מכל
העמים. להיות לו לעם סגולה וגו' (שם), מה סגולה חביבה מכל
הנכסים, אף אתם חביבים מכל הנכסים. אמר ר' יהושע ולא עוד אלא שאתה
בן בכור, שנ' ואמרת אל פרעה כה אמר י"י בני בכורי ישראל (שמ' ד', כ"ב),
שאפילו יש לאדם כמה בנים, משנה הוא את הבכור. ולמה קראו בכור, אם בכור
הוא אינו נעבד ואינו נגזז, וכל מי שהוא גחז מועל בקדשים, שנ' לא תעבוד בבכור
שורך וגו' (דב' ט"ו, י"ט), כך הן ישראל, כל מי שהוא גוזלן מתחייב לפני הקב"ה,
שהן קדש, שנ' קדש ישראל לי"י וגו' (יר' ב', ג'), לפיכך, כל אוכליו יאשמו (שם).
אמר ר' ירמיה ולמה נקרא בכור, שאין להם חילופין, שאם מת בכור אין לו
חילופין, כך הוא ישראל, אפילו כל באי העולם מתכנסין אין הקב"ה מחליף אותם
באומה אחרת ולא מואסם, שנ' ואף גם זאת (וי' כ"ו, מ"ד).

אמר ר' ירמיה ומה הזונות שבאו לפני שלמה, שהמו רחמיה על בן שלא היה
מכיר את אביו ואת אמו, שנ' ותאמר האשה אשר בנה החי וגו' תנו לה את הילד
החי וגו' (מ"א, ג', כ"ו), אמר הקב"ה: אם אשה זונה היה לה רחמים על בן שלא
היה מכיר את אביו ואת אמו, על אחת כמה וכמה אני שארחם על בני ישראל שהן
בני, שנ' הבן יקיר לי אפרים וגו' (יר' ל"א, י"ט). כמה חביב לי ישראל, (דף
ע"ז, ע"א) שנ' כי נער ואהבהו וגו' (הו' י"א, א'), וכתיב בנים אתם לי"י

ישמרו ויעבדו וגו' (שם, י"א), שהם משלימין שנותיהן בטובות. אמר ר' ירמיה מפני
עליון לא תצא הרעות (איכה ג', ל"ח), לא רעות לצדיק, ולא טובות לרשע. אף
משה סדר לישראל ר א ֹה א נ ֹכ י וגו', שאם כלתו בטובה היאך עשה לי הקב"ה,
ומשה (דף ע"ו, ע"א) לא ידע כי קרן וגו', ויראו בני ישראל את פני משה וגו'
(שמ' ל"ד, כ"ט, ל"ה).

[לסדר קמ"ב (י"א): דברים י"ב, כ'.]

[כ י י ר ח י ב]. זש"ה אגילה ואשמחה בחסדיך וגו' (תה'
ל"א, ח'), מדבר בישראל, נחית כצאן עמך וגו' (שם, ע"ז, כ"א); א ש ר ר א י ת
א ת ע נ י י (שם, ל"א, ח'), במצרים, שנ' וירא את ענינו וגו' (דב' כ"ו, ז'),
הרבה צרות שהיינו בהם במצרים ובמדבר; ו ל א ה ס ג ר ת נ ו וגו' (תה'
שם, ט'), זה פרעה, שנ' אמר אויב וגו' (שמ' ט"ו, ט'); ה ע מ ד ת ב מ ר ח ב
ר ג ל י (תה', שם), שאמרת למשה וארד להצילו מיד מצרים וגו' אל ארץ טובה
ורחבה (שמ' ג', ח'), זו ארץ ישראל. לכך הוא אומר כ י י ר ח י ב י ' י וגו'.
ע ו ש ה מ ש פ ט ל ע ש ו ק י ם וגו' (תה' קמ"ו, ז'), אלו ישראל, שנ'
עשוקים בני ישראל וגו' (יר' נ', ל"ג); נ ו ת ן ל ח ם ל ר ע ב י ם, שנתן להם
לחם מן השמים (שמ' ט"ז, ד'); י ' י מ ת י ר א ס ו ר י ם, דברים שאסר להם
חזר והתיר להם, זו אכילת בשר שאסר להם מ' שנה שהיו במדבר, היאך יעשה,
מי שנתאווית נפשו לאכול, אמר הקב"ה: הרי שבטו שללוי חונים לפני המשכן, וכל
מי שהוא מבקש לאכול בשר הוא בא אצל הכהן ואצל המשכן אל פתח אהל
מועד, והכהן נוטל סכין בידו, ושחטו לשם שלמים, והזה את הדם על המזבח, ובעל
ובעליו נוטלין ממנו, והוא אוכל ממנו. הרי כתיב איש איש מבית ישראל אשר ישחט
וגו', ואל פתח אהל מועד וגו', למען אשר יביאו בני ישראל וגו' (וי' י"ז, ג'–ה').
וכל הצער הזה למה, שלא יזבחו זבחיהם לשעירים. הרי למד שהיה בשר אסור
להם לישראל, והתירו להם לישראל, שנ' כ י י ר ח י ב י ' י א ל ה י ך וגו'.

[לסדר קמ"ד (י"ג): דברים י"ד, א'.]

ב נ י ם א ת ם. זש"ה אספרה אל חוק י"י וגו' (תה' ב', ז'). כשהיו ישראל
במדבר מעוטפים בעני הכבוד, ועמוד אש מהלך לפניהם, והיו אומות העולם
רואים אותם משתמשים באש היו נבהלים ואומרין: מי הם אילו שכל מעשיהם
באש, שנ' מי זאת עולה מן המדבר וגו' (שה"ש ח', ה'). ובזכות מה להם כל הכבוד
הזה, בזכות התורה, היך כתיב אלה החקים וגו' (וי' כ"ו, מ"ו). לכך אמר אספרה
אל חוק י"י וגו'.

כל מה שצריכה, הוא נותן לה. וכי אינו דורש אלא ארץ ישראל בלבד, הרי הוא
אומר להמטיר על ארץ לא איש וגו' (אי' ל"ח, כ"ו), ומה תלמוד לומר א ר ץ
א ש ר י"י א ל ה י ך ד ו ר ש א ו ת ה וגו', ללמדך שאמר לו הקב"ה: כל
זמן שאני דורש לכל הארצות, ואיני פותח את האוצר אלא בשביל הצדיק בלבד,
שנ' ת מ י ד ע י נ י י"י א ל ה י ך ב ה (דב', שם), שאין הקב"ה מזיז שכינתו
ממנה אפילו שעה אחת. וכל כך למה, מפני הצדיקים והישרים שבתוכה יושבין,
הוא שוכן שכינתו שמה, שנ' עיני י"י אל צדיקים ואזניו אל שועתם (תה' ל"ד, ט"ז).

[לסדר קמ"א (י'): דברים י"א, כ"ו.]

פ' ר א ה א נ כ י. זש"ה ויגל אזנם למוסר, ואומר כי ישיבון מאון, אם
ישמעו ויעבדו וגו', יכלו ימיהם בטוב ושנותיהם בנעימים, ישמעו בשלח (דף ע"ה,
ע"ב) יעברו ויגועו בבלי דעת (אי' ל"ו, י'–י"ב), שאין הקב"ה מביא צרה על
האדם עד שהוא מגלה את אזנו, כדי שיחזור בו; אם חזר בו, הרי יפה, ואם לאו,
מביא עליו מכה. יתברך שמו שלמלך מלכי המלכים הקב"ה שדרכיו לא כדרכי
בשר ודם, כועס על עבדיו ואינו חומל לא על טובים ולא על רעים, והקב"ה אינו
כן, כועס על הרשעים וחומל על הצדיקים. בואו וראו שעשה דין עם אנשי דור
המבול, ומילט את נח ואת בניו, ושפך זעמו על הארץ, שנ' ויגוע כל בשר וגו',
וימח את כל היקום וגו', כל אשר נשמת, ויזכור אלהים את נח וגו' (בר' ז', כ"א,
כ"ג, כ"ב; ח', א'). עשה דין עם דור הפלגה, ומילט את אבר(ה)ם, שנ' ויפץ י"י
אותם וגו', על כן קרא שמה בבל וגו' (שם, י"א, ח'–ט'). עשה דין עם סדומים
ושפך זעמו עליהם, שנ' וי"י המטיר על סדום וגו' (שם, י"ט, כ"ד), ומילט את לוט,
שנ' ויהי בשחת אלהים וגו' (שם, כ"ט). עשה דין עם המצריים והרג מקניהם, ומילט
את מקנה ישראל. עשה דין עם כנענים, שנ' ויהי בנסעם מפני ישראל וי"י השליך
עליהם אבנים וגו' (יה' י', י"א), ומילט את יהושע. לכך אמר אליהוא בן ברכאל
הבוזי ואם אסורים בזקים ילכדו בחבלי עוני, ויגד להם פעלם ופשעיהם כי יתגברו,
ויגל אזנם וגו', אם ישמעו ויעבדו וגו', ואם לא ישמעו בשלח (אי' ל"ו, ח'–י"ב).
מכאן למדנו שלא הביא פורענות על דור המבול, עד שגילה אזנם, שנ' ויאמר
אלהים לנח קץ כל בשר בא לפני וגו' (בר' ו', י"ג). וכן גילה אזנם שלסדומים,
שנ' ויאמר י"י זעקת סדום ועמורה וגו' (שם, כ', כ'), ויאמר אל נא אחי תרעו הנה
נא לי שתי וגו' (שם, כ"א, ז'–ח'). גילה אזנם שלמצריים, שנ' בא אל פרעה וגו'
(שם, ז', כ"ו), כמה פעמים, ואומר כי עתה שלחתי את ידי וגו', ואולם בעבור זאת
וגו' (שם, ט', ט"ו–ט"ז), ושלח אצל פרעה והתרה בו ביד משה, שנ' הנני מביא מחר
וגו' (שם, י"ד), הנה אנכי נגף את כל גבולך וגו' (שם, ז', כ"ז), הנני ממטיר מחר
(שם, ט', י"ח), שהיה מתרה בו. לקיים מה שנ' ויגל אזנם למוסר וגו', למוסר
שלתורה.

ד"א. ישובון מאון (אי' ל"ו, י'), מְלַעֵל בני אדם ומלעול לפני הקב"ה, אם

והארץ לבדה אזכור, שנ' וזכרתי את בריתי יעקב וגו' (וי' כ"ו, מ"ב). אמר ר'
ירמיה חביבה היא ארץ ישראל ששקולה כנגד מעשה בראשית: ביום הראשון כתיב
וירא אלהים את האור כי טוב (בר' א', ד'), ובארץ כתיב כי י"י אלהיך מביאך
וגו' (דב' ח', ז'); ביום שני כתיב יהי רקיע וגו' (בר' א', ו'), ובארץ כתיב ארץ
נחלי מים וגו' (דב', שם); ביום הג' כתיב תדשא הארץ וגו' (בר' א', י"א), ובארץ
כתיב ארץ חטה וגו' (דב' ח', ח'); ביום הד' כתיב יהי מאורות (בר' א', י"ד);
ובארץ כתיב ארץ זית ושמן וגו' (דב', שם); בה' כתיב ישרצו המים וגו' (בר'
א', כ'), ובארץ ישראל כתיב ארץ אשר לא במסכנות תאכל וגו' (דב' ח', ט');
בו' כתיב נעשה אדם בצלמנו (בר' א', כ"ו), בארץ ישראל כתיב לא תשחית את
עצה וגו' (דב' כ', י"ט); בז' כתיב ויברך אלהים וגו' (בר' ב', ג'), ובארץ ישראל
כתיב ואכלת ושבעת וגו' (דב' ח', י'). הרי למדת שארץ ישראל שקולה כנגד
מעשה ברא[שית]. לפיכך משה הזהיר עליה ואומר לישראל: ראו שאתם נכנסים
לארץ חביבה לפני הקב"ה, כמו שאתם חביבים לפני הקב"ה, כמו שאתם חביבים
לפני הקב"ה מכל האומות, שנ' כי עם קדוש וגו' (שם, ז', ו'), והנחילכם ארץ
חביבה לפניו מכל הארצות, תנו דעתכם שלא תחטאו עליה, שאינה כ א ר ץ
מ צ ר י ם.

א ת ה ז ו ר ע לפני הרביעה, וכן על טל ומטר כל הסתיו. מהו ו ה ש ק י ת
ב ר ג ל ך כ ג ן ה י ר ק (שם, י"א, י'), שארץ מצרים אתה שוקע בטיט ומצטער
ונודד שינה מעיניך עד שהיא שותה, ארץ ישראל אינה כן, אלא אתה ישן על
מטתך, והגשמים יורדין, והיא שותה. הוי ל א כ א ר ץ מ צ ר י ם וגו'. וכל
הארצות הקב"ה מכלכלן על ידי אחרים, כגון פרת משקה ארץ בבל, ונילוס משקה
ארץ מצרים, (דף ע"ה, ע"א) אבל ארץ ישראל אין הקב"ה משעינה, לא על נהר,
ולא על ים, אבל הוא משקה אותה מטר מלמעלה, דכתיב הנותן מטר על פני
ארץ וגו' (אי' ה', י'), א ר ץ, זו ארץ ישראל, ע ל פ נ י ח ו צ ו ת, זו ארצות
אחרות שהן שותות על ידי שלוחים.

ו מ ה ת ל מ ו ד ל ו מ ר ל מ ט ר ה ש מ י ם ת ש ת ה מ י ם (דב' י"א, י"א,
אמר להם: במצרים לא הייתם תולים עיניכם לשמים, מכאן ואילך עיניכם לשמים,
אפע"פ שאמרתי לכם שהיא ארץ נחלי מים (שם, ח', ז'), היו יודעין שאם אין
הגשמים יורדין אין הנחלים מושכים, שכך הוא אומר ויהי מקץ ימים ויבש הנחל
(מ"א, י"ז, ז'), מפני מה, מפני שלא היה גשמים וגו' (שם). אמר ר' ת נ ח ו מ ה
ומפני מה לא הבטיח הקב"ה לארץ ישראל שתהא שותה מן הנהר, כשם שארץ
מצרים שותה, מפני ד' דברים: שיהיו הבריות עיניהם תלויים לשמים בכל שעה,
מפני שארץ ישראל הרים ובקעות, אם שותה היא על ידי נהר, אין הרים ובקעות
שותים, ומפני בעלי זרוע שלא יהיו גוזלים את העניים ומשקין לשדותיהן תחלה,
אבל הטללים יורדין מלמעלן, אף הם מפרנסים את הפרות. לכך נאמר ל א
כ א ר ץ מ צ ר י ם ה י א וגו'.

א ר ץ א ש ר י"י א ל ה י ך ד ו ר ש וגו' (דב' י"א, י"ב), היא נדרשת מה
צריכה, אם צריכה חמה, נותן חמה, ואם צריכה גשמים או טללין, או רוחות, או

ל"א, י"ז); אף מילה, לישראל נתנה ולא לעם אחר, וכן הוא אומר ליהושע עשה
לך חרבות צורים ושוב מול (יה' ה', ב'), לך, ולא לעם אחר. לכך הוא אומר
יהיו לך לבדד וגו'.

ד"א. בעת ההיא אמר י"י ליהושע, לקיים מה שנ' כאשר הייתי עם משה אהיה
עמך (שם, א', ה'), למשה אמרתי פסל לך, ואף אתה עשה לך. לא
היה צריך לאמר חרב צור, מה הוא חרבות צורים, אלא אמר לו
הרבה הן החרבות, אלא מול אותם עד שתצילם מהם, ואלו הן: המתהפכת,
והגדולה, והמלאה, והמשתכרת, והאוכלת. המתהפכת, זו גיהנם, שנ' ויגרש את האדם
וגו' (בר' ג', כ"ד); והגדולה, שנ' ביום ההוא יפקוד י"י בחרבו הקשה וגו' (יש'
כ"ז, א'); והמלאה, שנ' חרב י"י מלאה דם וגו' (שם, ל"ד, ו'); להצילם מן הגזרה
אשר גזרתי, שנ' קצף לי"י על כל הגוים וגו' (שם, כ'). לכך נאמר עשה לך
חרבות וגו'. ומהו שנית, מוהל ופורע, לא כבני ישראל וכותיים שמוהלים ולא
פורעים. שנו חכמים המוהל ולא פורע כאילו לא מל, שנ' המול ימול (בר' י"ז, י"ג),
שהוא מוהל ופורע. לכך נאמר שנית.

גדולה המילה שנתנה הקב"ה ברית בינו ובין בני ישראל, שנ' והיתה בריתי
בבשרכם (שם).

[לסדר ק"מ (ט'): דברים י"א, י'.]

כי הארץ אשר אתה בא שמה וגו'. זש"ה בעבור ישמרו חוקיו
וגו' (תה' ק"ה, מ"ה), כדי לשמור התורה בתוכה, ואם אין ארץ ישראל אין תורה
להתקיים, שכך נאמר חטא חטאה ירושלים וגו' (איכה א', ח'), נאמר טבעו בארץ
שעריה וגו' (שם, כ', ט'). אמר ר' יצחק גדולה היא ישיבת ארץ ישראל לפני
הקב"ה, שהיא אדמת קדש ועפר קדש ומרבה בתרומות ומעשרות ובכורים, וכל
מי שהוא מקיים מצותיה כראוי, היא מכפרת עונותיו, היך דכתיב וכפר אדמתו
עמו (דב' ל"ב, מ"ג), ולא לעם אחר, וכן הוא אומר ובל יאמר שכן חליתי וגו'
(יש' ל"ג, כ"ד). לפיכך משה הזהירם ואמר להם: הארץ שאתם נכנסים לתוכה,
לא כארץ מצרים היא וגו', למד שארץ מצרים כולם היו טמאים
ועובדי עבודה זרה, ואפילו שהייתם מעשיכם כמעשיהם, שוקל הקב"ה מעשיכם
ומעשיהם, והיו מעשיכם טובים ממעשיהם, והייתם עומדים, אבל ארץ ישראל,
ושמרתם את כל חקותי וגו' (וי' כ', כ"ב), שאם אין אתם שומרים את התורה ואת
המצוה, היא מקיאה אתכם ואתם גולים ממנה, כמו כשגלה מי שהיה לפניכם,
דכתיב ולא תקיא הארץ אתכם (דף ע"ג, ע"ב) וגו' (שם), וכן הוא אומר לא תעשו
ככל אשר אנחנו וגו' (דב' י"ב, ט'), למה, כי לא באתם עד עתה וגו' (שם, י').
הוי לא כארץ מצרים היא וגו'.

מכאן אמרו חכמים כל היושב בארץ ישראל מקבל עליו עול מלכות שמים
דכתיב אנכי י"י אלהיך וגו' (שמ' כ', כ'). אמר ר' לוי גדולה היא ברית ארץ
ישראל שהיא שקולה כנגד ברית ג' אבות, שבכולם כתיב אזכור, והארץ אזכור,

מסתירין עצמן במערות, דכתיב אין חשך ואין צלמות וגו' (אי' ל"ד, כ"ג), והיתה
נכנסת בהם והורגת אותם. זהו דכתיב עד אבד (דף ע"ב, ע"ב) הנשארים
(דב' ז', כ'). הוי לא תערץ מפניהם וגו' (שם, כ"א).

[לסדר קל"ח (ז'): דברים ח', א'.]

כל המצוה. זש"ה אשרי אדם שומע לי (מש' ח', ל"ד), אשרי אדם מצא
חכמה וגו' (שם, ג', י"ג), כי טוב סחרה מסחר כסף וגו' (שם, י"ד). אמר הקב"ה:
כל מי שהוא אוהב תורה ושומר מצותיה בעולם הזה, זוכה שיהיו פניו מבהיקות
כגלגל החמה, זהו דכתיב ואוהביו כצאת וגו' (שו' ה', ל"א). והיא נותנת חיים
בעולם הזה ולעולם הבא, שנ' שמור מצותי וחיה (מש' ז', ב'), וכתיב כי חיים
הם למוצאיהם ולכל בשרו וגו' (שם, ד', כ"ב), למי שהוא מוצא אותן כראוי תורה.
הוי למען תחיו וטוב לכם (דב' ה', ל'), שכל מי שהוא משמרה, זוכה לחיים, שנ'
עץ חיים היא למחזיקים וגו' (מש' ג', י"ח). וכתיב בני אם תקח אמרי וגו' (שם,
ב', א'), אמר ר' אחא אתה צפון למצות ולמעשים טובים, ואני אצפון לך טובו
שלעולם הבא, שנ' מה רב טובך וגו' (תה' ל"א, כ'). לכך הוא אומר כל
המצוה.

היה ר' יצחק אומר אל תעש דברי תורה עטרה להיות מתגדל בהם, ולא
סחורה להיות מתפרנס בהם, אלא משום יראה; כבלשצר כמה פורענות הביא
הקב"ה עליו, על שנשתמש בכלי בית המקדש, שנ' אדין מלכא זיוההי שנוהי
ורעיונוהי יבהלוניה וקטרי חרציה נשתרין וארכבתיה דא לדא נקשן (דנ' ה', ו'),
כללו שלדבר, ביה בליליא קטיל בלשצר מלכא כשדאה (שם, ל'); ומה מי
שנשתמש בכלי בית המקדש, שיש לו חילופין, כך, המשתמש בדבר שבו נברא
העולם על אחת כמה וכמה שיביא עליו הקב"ה פורענות. לכך הוא אומר
תשמרון לעשות, אם למדתם תורה, היו לומדים על מנת לשמור ולעשות
אותם. אמר ר' אחא כל מי ששומר אותה ועושה, זוכה שתשרה רוח הקדש עליו,
שנ' ושמרתם את דברי הברית הזאת וגו' (דב' כ"ט, ח'), לא ימוש ספר התורה
וגו' (יה' א', ח').

[לסדר ק"מ (ט'): דברים י', א'.]

בעת ההיא אמר י"י אלי פסל לך וגו'. זש"ה יהיו לך לבדך
וגו' (מש' ה', י"ז). לא נתן הקב"ה את התורה, ואת המצות, ואת השבת, ואת
המילה, אלא לישראל בלבד, מנין, שנ' אלה החקים והמשפטים והתורות וגו' (וי'
כ"ו, מ"ו). וכשהוציאם ממצרים בחרם מכל האומות, שנ' כי עם קדוש אתה לי"י
וגו' (דב' ז', ו'), וכן הוא אומר ואתם תהיו לי ממלכת כהנים וגוי קדוש וגו' (שמ'
י"ט, ו'); ואף השבת, שנ' ראו כי י"י נתן לכם השבת וגו' (שם, ט"ז, כ"ט), לכם,
נתנה ולא לעם אחר, וכן הוא (דף ע"ג, ע"א) אומר ביני ובין בני ישראל וגו' (שם,

אחריו, ו ש מ ר וגו', שהוא משמר לך שכר מצות שאתה עושה עם הבריות.
והחכמים שהקדימו אבותיו וגו'. זהו דכתיב כי ההרים ימושו וגו' (יש' נ"ד, י'),
לקיים מה שנ' כל ארחות י"י חסד ואמת וגו' (תה' כ"ה, י'). לכך משה הזהיר
ו ש מ ר ת ם ו ע ש י ת ם א ו ת ם וגו'.

אמר ר' שמעון אם יהא אדם מישראל שיעשה עמו פועל, לא ילין שכרו עד
הבקר. שנו חכמים המלין עובר משום לא תלין פעולת שכיר וגו' (וי' י"ט, י"ג),
ואם לא תבעו השוכר, אינו עובר אלא משום לא תהא אכזרי, אלא יהיו רחמנים
על הבריות ועל חבריו. אמר ר' יוסי הסימן הזה יהיה בידיך: כל זמן שאתה
רחמן, הקב"ה מרחם עליך, שנ' ונתן לך רחמים וגו' (דב' י"ג, י"ח). לפיכך משה
הזהירן ו ש מ ר ת ם ו ע ש י ת ם וגו', מה כתיב אחריו, ו א ה ב ך ו ב ר כ ך
(דב' ז', י"ג), מה ו א ה ב ך, מחב[ב א]תכם לפני הבריות. כך הוא אומר והיה
שארית יעקב בגוים (מי' ה', ז'), כשם שהכל שמחים, כך יהיו שמחים בכם, ועוד
האומות רואים אתכם ומכירים ברכותיהם, שנ' ונודע בגוים זרעם וגו' (יש' ס"א, ט').

ו ה ר ב ך (דב' ז', י"ג), כמו שכתוב והיה זרעך כעפר הארץ וגו' (בר'
כ"ח, י"ד). ו ב ר ך פ ר י ב ט נ ך, שאני מרבה אתכם. ו פ ר י א ד מ ת ך,
שאני מרבה תבואתכם. ומה ראה להקיש פרי הבטן לפרי האדמה, אלא כשם
שפרי האדמה מרובה, כך יהא פרי בטנך מרובים. ו ע ש ת ר ת צ א נ ך, אמר
ר' יהודה שתהא מעשרת לבעלה. ב ר ו ך ת ה י ה מ כ ל ה ע מ י ם וגו'
(דב' ז', י"ד), שיהיו האומות מאשרים, שנ' ואשרו אתכם וגו' (מלא' ג', י"ב). ל א
י ה י ה ב ך ע ק ר ע ק ר ה, (דף ע"ד, ע"ב) לא תהיה תפלתכם עקרה, אלא
כמו שכתוב והיה טרם יקראו וגו' (יש' ס"ה, כ"ד). ו ב ב ה מ ת ך, שתהיו נמשכים
אחרי כצאן שהיא נמשכת אחר הרועה, שנ' אני ארעה צאני וגו' (יח' ל"ד, ט"ו).
אמר ר' לוי אם השלחן מלא, והאוצרות מלאים, ואין אדם יכול לאכול, מה הנאה
יש לו, אלא, ו ה ס י ר י"י מ מ ך כ ל ח ו ל י וגו' (דב' ז', ט"ו), הוי ברכה
שלמה. ומה כתיב אחריו, ו א כ ל ת א ת כ ל ה ע מ י ם וגו' (שם, ט"ז), ומה
עשה להם, שנ' ויתן להם ארצות וגו', בעבור ישמרו חקיו וגו' (תה' ק"ה, מ"ד–מ"ה).

[לסדר קל"ח (ז'): דברים ז', י"ז.]

כ י ת א מ ר ב ל ב ב ך ר ב י ם ה ג ו י ם וגו'. וכתיב כל הגוים כאין
נגדו וגו' (יש' מ', י"ז). אמר הקב"ה: אין הגוים חשובים לפני כלום, אף אתם אל
תתיראו מהם, למה, שאין להם לא ברית, ולא זכות אבותיהם, ולא מצוה. לכך
נאמר ל א ת י ר א מ ה ם (דב' ז', י"ח). ז כ ו ר ת ז כ ו ר וגו' (שם), אמר
הקב"ה: כשאתם בצרה, זכרו שמי ואני אעשה מלחמותכם, שנ' י"י ילחם לכם וגו'
(שמ' י"ד, י"ד), [וכתיב ז כ ו ר ת ז כ ו ר א ת א ש ר ע[ש]ה י"י א ל ה י ך
וגו' (דב' ז', י"ח). וכתיב את אימתי אשלח לפניך וגו' (שמ' כ"ג, כ"ז), הרי אימה,
וכתיב ושלחתי את הצרעה וגו' (שם, כ"ח), וכתיב ושלחתי לפניך מלאך וגו' (שמ'
ל"ג, ב'), הרי מלאך. ואחר כך ו ג ם א ת ה צ ר ע ה וגו' (דב' ז', כ'), שיהיו

[לסדר קל"ח (ז'): דברים ז', י"ב.]

ו ה י ה ע ק ב. זש"ה טוב אחרית דבר מראשיתו טוב ארך רוח מגבה רוח
(קה' ז', ח'). לכך אמר משה: מודיע אני שאין ישראל עושין את אלה, בעקב,
בסוף, כיון שהן מטריחין את פניהן לכל צד וכשיהא צרה להם, באים אצל
הקב"ה, שנ' בצר לך ומצאוך וגו' (דב' ד', ל'), וכן הנביא אומר אומרים לעץ
וגו' (יר' ב', כ"ז), לקיים מה שנ' טוב אחרית דבר מראשיתו. לכך אמר **ו ה י ה**
ע ק ב ת ש מ ע ו ן ו ש מ ר ת ם ו ע ש י ת ם א ו ת ם. אמר להם: שמרו דברי,
ואני משמר אתכם, זכה אדם לשמור מצוה אחת, בזכותה מביאה אותו למצוה
אחרת לעשותה.

זש"ה **ו ש מ ר ת ם ו ע ש י ת ם,** זכה אדם למקצת המצות, סופו לקיים כל
המצות שבתורה. כך שנו חכמים בן עזאי אומר הוי רץ למצוה וכו'. וכן שלמה
אומר צדקה תרומם גוי (מש' י"ד, ל"ד), ואומר צדקה תצר תם דרך וגו' (שם,
י"ג, ו'). כל מי שהוא עושה מצוה אחת, זוכה לעשות צדקה. עושה אדם רשעה,
הוא גורם לעצמו לבוא לידי עון עון אחריו, ונמשכין אחריו עונות הרבה, למה,
שהעונות סומכות זו לזו, שנ' הוי מושכי העון בחבלי השוא (יש' ח', י"ח). הוי
המצוה גוררת מצוה אחרת. לפיכך אמר להם **ו ש מ ר ת ם ו ע ש י ת ם א ו ת ם.**

טעם אחר. **ו ה י ה ע ק ב ת ש מ ע ו ן.** זש"ה כי טוב סחרה מסחר כסף
וגו' (מש' ג', י"ד), אדם שמשתכר למדינת הים גרמימא על ידי הרוח כעסק
בעשרה שנים, והוא בספק שמא ימצא רוח. לכך סוחרה סחרה שלתורה, שיש
רוח בודאי, אין בה ספק.

ו ש מ ר י' י' א ל ה י ך. זש"ה למה אירא בימי רע עון עקבי יסובני (תה'
מ"ט, ו'), אמר דויד לפני הקב"ה: כשיבוא יום הדין איני מתירא ממצות חמורות,
אלא ממצות קלות שבני אדם מעבירים עליהם ואומרין קלות הן. לפיכך נאמר
עון עקבי יסובני.

ד"א. זש"ה גם עבדך נזהר בהם (שם, י"ט, י"ב), אמר דויד: אשמרם בעולם
הזה, כדי שאטול שכרי בעולם הבא. ועליו אמר שלמה בחכמתו נצר תאנה יאכל
פריה (מש' כ"ז, י"ח).

ד"א. (דף ע"ד, ע"א) **ו ה י ה ע ק ב ת ש מ ע ו ן וגו'.** זש"ה על ידי שלמה
אם לא תדעי לך היפה בנשים (שה"ש א', ח'). אמר שלמה בחכמתו על כנסת
ישראל: אם לא תדעי לך וגו', בזמן שתהיו בין האומות ולא תדעו סוד העבור,
צאו וראו הלכות הרועים הרשומים, כיצד שנו חכמים הקדמונים, ועשו כמותן,
שהמקרא מסייע אתכם, שנ' אם לא תדעי לך.

ד"א. **ו ה י ה ע ק ב.** אמר ר' שמואל בר נחמני ראה מה כתיב ל מ ע ל ה
מ ן ה ע נ י ן, לא מרובכם מכל העמים וגו' (דב' ז', ז') ואמר טוב מעט לצדיק
וגו' (תה' ל"ז, ט"ז), ואם תלכו בדרכיו שלהקב"ה, הוא יפנה אליכם והוא מפרה
ומרבה אתכם, שנ' ופניתי אליכם והפריתי אתכם והרביתי (וי' כ"ו, ט'). לפיכך
מזהיר להם על המצות, ואומר **ו ש מ ר ת ם ו ע ש י ת ם א ו ת ם,** מה כתיב

ויצא בה ידי חובתו, משיטהרו הכהנים לאכול בתרומתן, כדברי בית שמאי, ובית
הלל אומרין משתחשך. ועד מתי קורא אדם ערבית ויצא בה ידי חובתו, ר' אלעזר
בן עזריה אומר קורא עד האשמורת [הר]אשונה, ר' אלעזר אומר עד חצות
הלילה, ר' טרפון אומר עד קרות הגבר. מאימתי קורא אדם בשחרית ויצא ידי
חובתו, משיכיר בין תכלת ללבן, ר' אלעזר אומר בין תכלת לכרתן, ועד הנץ
החמה.

ואנו חייבים למהר לבית הכנסת בשעת התפלה. אמר ר' חנינה זה שהוא
הולך לבית הכנסת צריך להקל רגליו, ומאי טעמא, שנ' נדעה נרדפה וגו' (הו'
ו', ג'). ומצאנו שתפלת הצבור חביבה לפני הקב"ה, לפיכך אנו חייבין לשבח
ולברך את שמו ברבים, במקהלות ברכו אלהים וגו' (תה' ס"ח, כ"ז). ובעונותינו
היום אין לנו קרבן ולא מזבח ולא שלמים לכפר על עונותינו, אלא תשובה ותפלה
בלבד, קחו עמכם דברים וגו' (הו' י"ד, ג'), ומי משלם אותם הפרים שהיינו
מקריבים לפניך, שפתותינו, בתפלה שאנו מתפללין לפניך. וכל שהוא מכוין לבו
ומתפלל לפני הקב"ה, הוא שומע תפלתו, שנ' תאות ענוים שמעת י"י וגו' (תה'
י', י"ז), כשתכין את לבם, תקשיב אזניך, לתפלתם.

ותקנו חכמים י"ח ברכות מן המקרא: מגן אברהם, שנ' אנכי מגן לך
וגו' (בר' ט"ו, א'); מחיה המתים, (דף ע"ב, ע"א) שנ' אני אמית ואחיה
(דב' ל"ב, ל"ט); האל הקדוש, שנ' כי בראותו וגו' (יש' כ"ט, כ"ג); חונן
הדעת, שנ' את רוחי אתן בקרבכם (יח' ל"ו, כ"ז); הרוצה בתשובה,
שנ' שובה ישראל וגו' (הו' י"ד, ב'); חנון ומרבה לסלח, שנ' כי אתה
י"י טוב וסלח וגו' (תה' פ"ו, ה'), למען שמך י"י וסלחת וגו' (שם, כ"ד, י"א);
גואל ישראל, שנ' גואלינו י"י צבאות (יש' מ"ז, ד'); רופא חולי עמו
ישראל, שנ' כי אעלה ארוכה לך וגו' (יר' ל', י"ז), הנני מעלה לך ארוכה
וגו' (שם, ל"ג, ו'); מברך השנים, שנ' והשיג לכם וגו' (וי' כ"ו, ה'), ואכלתם
אכול ושבוע (יו' ב', כ"ו); מקבץ נדחי עמו, שנ' אם יהיה נדחך בקצה
וגו' (דב' ל', ד'); מלך אוהב צדקה ומשפט, שנ' ואשיבה שופטיך
וגו' (יש' א', כ"ו); בונה ירושלים, שנ' בונה ירושלים י"י (תה' קמ"ז, ב');
שובר רשעים, שנ' ושבר פושעים וחטאים וגו' (יש' א', כ"ח); משען
ומבטח לצדיקים, שנ' ויבטחו בך כל יודעי שמך וגו' (תה' ט', י"א); מצמיח
קרן ישועה, שנ' שם אצמיח קרן לדוד וגו' (שם, ל"ב, י"ז); בונה
ירושלים י"י, שנ' בונה ירושלים י"י וגו' (שם, קמ"ז, ב'); שומיע
תפלה, שנ' והיה טרם יקראו ואני אענה (יש' ס"ה, כ"ד); שאותך ביראה
נעבוד, שנ' עבדו את י"י ביראה וגו' (תה' ב', י"א); הטוב שמך וגו'
להודות, שנ' בואו שעריו בתודה וגו' (שם, ק', ד'); המברך את עמו
ישראל, דכתיב שאלו שלום ירושלים וגו' (שם, קכ"ב, ו'), וכתיב הנני נוטה
אליה כנהר שלום וגו' (יש' ס"ו, י"ב), וכתיב יהי שלום בחילך וגו' (תה' קכ"ב, ז'),
וכתיב אשמעה מה ידבר האל י"י כי ידבר שלום אל עמו וגו' (שם, כ"ה, ט'),
וכתיב י"י עז לעמו יתן י"י יברך את עמו בשלום (שם, כ"ט, י"א).

כ', ג'), ובקרית שמע כתיב י"י אלהינו וגו' (דב' ז', ד'); בעש' דב' לא תשא את
שם י"י וגו' (שמ' כ', ז'), ובק"ש ואהבת את י"י (דב' ז', ה'), ומאן דרחמיה
למלכיה לא משתבע בשמיה לשקרא; בעש' דב' כתיב זכור את וגו' (שמ' כ', ח'),
ובק"ש כתיב למען תזכרו וגו' (במ' ט"ו, מ'); בעש' הדב' כתיב כבד את אביך
ואת אמך (שמ' כ', י"ב), ובק"ש כתיב למען ירבו ימיכם וגו' (דב' י"א, כ"א;
בעש' דב' כתיב לא תרצח (שמ' כ', י"ג), ובק"ש וחרה אף י"י בכם וגו' (דב'
י"א, י"ז); בעש' הדב' לא תנגוב (שמ' כ', ט"ו), בק"ש כתיב ואספת דגנך (דב'
י"א, י"ד), ולא דגן חבירך; בעש' הדב' כתיב לא תענה ברעך עד וגו' (שמ'
כ', ט"ז), ובק"ש כתיב השמרו לכם וגו' (דב' י"א, ט"ז); בעש' הדב' כתיב לא
תחמוד (שמ' כ', י"ז), ובק"ש וכתבתם על מזוזות וגו' (דב' ז', ט'), ביתך, ולא
הבית החמוד. הוי עשרת הדברות כלולות בקרית שמע. לכך הוא מזהיר את
ישראל ואומר שמע ישראל וגו'.

אמר ר' אליעזר כשאדם קורא קרית שמע צריך להשמיע את אזנו, שנ' והיה
אם שמוע תשמעו וגו' (דב' י"א, י"ג), כדי שתמליכהו עליך בלב אחד.

ואהבת את י"י אלהיך וגו' (דב' ז', ה'). שנו חכמים אהביהו
כנפשך, ותן נפשך עליו. וכן עשו בני ישראל, שנ' אם שכחנו שם אלהינו וגו', הלא
אלהים יחקור זאת וגו', וכתיב כי עליך הרגנו כל היום וגו' (תה' מ"ד, כ"א–כ"ג).

בכל לבבך (דב' ז', ה'), בשני יצריך, ובכל נפשך, כנפשך,
ובכל מאודך, בכל כוחך וכל הונך. מהו היום על לבבך (שם,
ו'), כיום שנצטווית על מתן תורה. ושננתם לבניך (שם, ז'), ר' יהודה
אומר לבניך ולבני בניך, ולא בנותיך. הוי ודברת בם (שם), בבקר ובערב.

ונתתי מטר ארצכם בעתו (דב' י"א, י"ד), וכי אין מטר בקיץ, אי זה הוא
בעתו, אלא זה יורה ומלקוש (שם) : יורה, הראשון, ומלקוש, האחרון, וכן הוא אומר
ונתתי אותם וסביבות גבעתם ברכה וגו' (יח' ל"ד, כ"ו), וכשהן בעתם, הם גשמי
ברכה. ואספת דגנך (דב' י"א, י"ד), דרש שתאסוף את דגנך ותירושך ויצהרך
שיעשו בזמניהם ולא יוצקו. ונתתי (שם, ט"ו), שאין לך ממנה הנאה. השמרו לכם
(שם, ט"ז), הרי אזהרה לכם שלא מתוך שלוה תמרדו כי, כענניין שנ' (דף ע"א, ע"ב)
[פן תאכל] ושבעת וגו', ובקרך וצאנך וגו', ורם לבבך וגו' (שם, ח', י"ב–י"ד),
יכול אף המאורות, ת"ל ולא יהיה מטר וגו' (שם), שאינו מביאה מה שאתה מוביל
לה. ר' יהודה אומר מנין אף ימים לא יגדלו מים והמדברות לא יעשו עשבים,
הוי אומר והאדמה לא תתן את יבולה (שם). יכול אף בעלי אוצרות, ואבדתם
מהרה (שם), מכל צד יבוא הדבר. וכן הוא אומר וחרה אפי והרגתי אתכם וגו'
(שמ' כ"א, כ"ג), וכי אין ידוע כיון שמת האיש תהא אשתו אלמנה ובניו יתומים,
אלא כשיצא למלחמה, יפול בחרב, לא ימלט אחד להעיד על האנשים, ונמצאו
כל הנשים יושבות ומשמרות כשבויים, שמא בעליהן קיימין, ובניהם מתים ברעב
ואינן יכולין למכור בנכסי אביהן, שבני אדם אומרין שמא אביהם בחיים. מה
האלמנה והיתומים נמוכים מכל הבריות.

ושמתם את דברי אלה וגו' (דב' י"א, י"ח). מאימתי אדם קורא קרית שמע

ולמה אין מתפללים שמונה עשרה בשבת, משום שאסור לתבוע צרכיו בשבת,
שלא נתקן אלא בחול בשמונה עשרה. מפני מה תקנו תפלה בלחישה, מפני צרכיו
שלאדם, שנ' והנה היא (דף ע', ע"ב) מדברת על לבה וגו' (ש"א, א', י"ג), בשביל
צרכיה. ואת מוצא תפלת י"ח, ג' ברכות הראשונות וג' אחרונות לשבחו שלהקב"ה,
וי"ב לצרכיו, כנגד י"ב שעות שליום. אמר הקב"ה: התפללו בלחישה, שאני קרוב
לכם, שנ' קרוב יי לכל קוראיו וגו' (תה' קמ"ה, י"ח).

אמר ר' שמואל בר נחמני בוא וראה כמה שמות נקראת: תפלה, צעקה,
זעקה, חינה, פגיעה, עמידה, עתירה, שיחה, חילוי. אמר ר' תנחומה וכי כמה
שמות נקראת תפלה, למה לא נתפלל משה באחת מהם אלא בתחנון, שנ'
ואתחנן אל יי, אלא בשעה שעמד ואמר: רבון העולם, הודיעני באי זו
מדה אתה מנהג את עולמך, שנ' ויאמר אם נא מצאתי חן בעיניך הודיעני נא וגו'
(שמ' ל"ג, י"ג), אמר לו הקב"ה: אני מודיעך, שנ' ויאמר אני אעביר כל טובי וגו'
(שם, י"ט), אמר לו: איני חיב לבריה כלום, וכל מה שאני עושה עם אדם, מצוה
אני עושה עמו וחנם אני נותן לו, שנ' וחנותי את אשר אחון וריחמתי וגו' (שם).
לכך כשנתפלל משה לפניו, אמר לפניו: רבון העולם, אף עמי עשה ותן לי בחנם.
לכך נאמר ואתחנן וגו'.

יי אלהים אתה החלות להראות וגו' (דב' ג', כ"ד). אמר
ר' שמעון בן יוחאי אמר משה לפני הקב"ה: רבון העולם, אתה הוא שפתחת לי
פתח שאתפלל לפניך, בשעה שעשו ישראל לי אותו המעשה, אמר לי הקב"ה
ועתה הניחה וגו' (שמ' ל"ב, י'), ואמר הרף ממני ואשמידם וגו' (דב' ט', י"ד),
באותה שעה ידע משה שפתח לו פתח שיתפלל עליהם, שנ' ויאמר יי סלחתי
כדבריך (במ' י"ד, כ'). לפיכך הוא אומר אתה החלות.

[לסדר קל"ז (ו'): דברים ו', ד'.]

שמע ישראל. אמר ר' אלעזר מפני מה קוראין בקריאת שמע שחרית
וערבית שבכל יום: ברוך שם כבוד מלכותו וגו', אלא אמרו חכמים בשעת פטירתו
שליעקב קרא לבניו ואמר להם: ישמעאל ובני קטורה
הפילגש, אבי יצא ממנו פסולת: עשו ואלופיו, שמה יש בכם פסולת חס ושלום,
אמרו לו: שמע ישראל יי וגו', אף הוא פתח הזקן ואמר: ברוך שם כבוד
מלכותו וגו'.

שמע ישראל. אמר ר' אלעזר וסמיך ליה ואהבת (דב' ז', ד'), (דף
ע"א, ע"א) אנו חייבים ליחד שמו שלהקב"ה בקרית שמע בכל יום פעמים בכל
לב ובכל נפש, דכתיב שמע ישראל וגו', ואהבת וגו'.

אמר ר' לוי לא תהא קרית שמע קלה בעיניך, שעשרת הדברות כלולות בה:
בעשרת הדברות כתיב אנכי יי אלהיך וגו' (שם, כ', ב'), ובקרית שמע כתיב אני
יי אלהיכם וגו' (במ' ט"ו, מ"א); בעש' הדב' כתיב לא יהיה לך אלהים וגו' (שמ'

[לסדר קל"ד (ג'): דברים ב', ל"א.]

ר א ה ה ח ל ו ת י ת ת ל פ נ י ך. זש"ה ואנכי השמדתי את האמורי מפניכם
(עמ' ב', ט'), ובאי זו זכות, בזכות שעמדתם על הר סיני וקבלתם אנכי י"י
אלהיך אשר הוצאתיך מארץ מצרים וגו' (שמ' כ', כ'). בוא וראה מה היו קשים.
אמרו חכמים קשה סיחון מלך האמורי כמגדל חומה, ומה נעשה לו, ואשמיד פריו
ממעל ושרשיו וגו' (עמ' ב', ט'), ומסרו ביד משה רבינו, ואמר לו ר א ה
ה ח ל ו ת י ת ת ל פ נ י ך א ת ס י ח ו ן ו ג ו'. אמר ר' שמעון בן לקיש מה
היתה גבורתן שלסיחון ועוג מלכי האמורי, כשהיה אחד מהם יוצא למלחמה, לא
היה צריך לחבירו שיסיענו, עוג מלך הבשן לא (דף ע', ע"א) היה צריך לסיחון,
שנ' ויצא עוג מלך הבשן לקראתם (במ' כ"א, ל"ג), שלא היה צריך לסיחון,
וסיחון לו היה צריך לעוג שיסיענו. כנס פרעה וחילותיו שנאמרה על מפלתם
שירה, כך על סיחון ועוג, שנ' למכה מצרים בבכוריהם וגו', ויהרוג מלכים אדירים
לסיחון מלך וגו', ולעוג מלך הבשן וגו', ונתן ארצם לנחלה וגו' (תה' קל"ו, י',
י"ח–כ"א). הא למדת שהיו קשים כפרעה וחילותיו. לפיכך כשראה אותם משה,
היה מתירא מהם, עד שאמר לו הקב"ה אל תירא מהם כי בידך נתתי וגו', שנ'
ויאמר י"י אל משה אל תירא אותו כי בידך נתתי וגו' (במ' כ"א, ל"ד). ואילולי
שעזרתי אותם, לא היו יכולים להם, שכן דויד אומר כי לא בחרבם יירשו ארץ
וכו' (תה' מ"ד, ד'), וכן הוא אומר את אימתי אשלח לפניך וגו' (שם, כ"ג, כ"ז),
אמר הקב"ה: אני מפיל אותם בזכותך לפני ישראל.

ומה כתיב ל מ ע ל ה מ ן ה ע נ י ן ו א ש ל ח מ ל א כ י ם מ מ ד ב ר ק ד מ ו ת ו ג ו'
(דב' ב', כ"ו). שנו חכמים על ג' דברים העולם עומד, וכולם כתובים בפסוק
אחד, אלה הדברים אשר תעשו וגו' (זכ' ח', ט"ז). ואין חביב לפני הקב"ה יתר
מן השלום, שכל מי שהוא בשלום הוא עליון והוא נוציח, וכל מי שהוא תופס
מלחמה הוא נופל. שכן אתה מוצא יהואש בן אמציה נתגרה תחלה במלחמה, מה
הוא אומר לא, אמרת הכה הכית את אדום ונשאך לבך וגו' (דה"ב, כ"ח, י"ט).
מי שתופס את השלום נצח, וסיחון תפס את המלחמה ונפל. אמר ר' שמעון בן
לקיש אגרת אחת שלח לו, וכתוב למעלה שלום, ולמטה מלחמה. מיד יצא סיחון
לקראתו. אמרו לו ישראל: אני שלום וכי אדבר (תה' כ"ח, ז'), אמר להם
הקב"ה: אתם יורשים את ארצם, שנ' ועניים יירשו ארץ וגו' (שם, ל"ז, י"א).

[לסדר קל"ה (ד'): דברים ג', כ"ג.]

ו א ת ח נ ן. זש"ה תאות ענוים שמעת י"י תכין לבם תקשיב וגו' (תה' י', י"ז).
אין עומדין להתפלל אלא מתוך כובד ראש וכו', ואפילו נחש כרוך על עקבו לא
יפסוק. ואם כיון לבו הוא נשכר, והקב"ה שומע תפלתו. זהו דכתיב תאות ענוים
שמעת י"י, ואימתי, בזמן שתכין לבם, תקשיב אזניך, לתפלתם.

(דב' ז', י'). לפיכך האריך עם עשו לשלם לו שכר מצות כיבוד אב. אמר
הקב"ה: ממדת הטוב שאני משלם לרשעים בעולם הזה, אתה יודע מה מתוקן
לצדיקים לעתיד לבוא. וכן אתה מוצא בעשו, שלא ירש העולם הזה אלא בשביל
מצוה אחת שהיתה בידו, והיא כיבוד אב, לפיכך הוא אומר ר ב ל כ ם ס ו ב
א ת ה ה ר ה ז ה וגו', ולא עוד אלא שבלשון הזה כיבד אביו, שנ' ויאמר עשו
יש לי רב (בר' ל"ג, ט'), לפיכך פרע הקב"ה לבניו באותו לשון ר ב ל כ ם
(דף ס"ט, ע"ב) ס ו ב וגו'.

וזה שאמר ו י ר א ו מ כ ם ו נ ש מ ר ת ם מ א ו ד (דב' ב', ד'), אמר
ר' שמעון מה אם בשעה שהם יראים ממנו, אמר לנו ו נ ש מ ר ת ם מ א ו ד,
לנפשותיכם, בשעה שאנחנו מובלעים ביניהם זה כמה שנים על אחת כמה וכמה
שאנו צריכים לשמור את נפשינו מהם.

א ל ת ת ג ר ו ב ם כ י ל א א ת ן ל כ ם מ א ר צ ם ע ד מ ד ר ך
כ ף ר ג ל (שם, ה'), עד שיגיע הדבר הזה, לי נקם ושלם לעת תמוט רגלם וגו'
(שם, ל"ב, ל"ה). אמר ר' שמעון עד שיגיע אותו הדבר, חזה הוי עד די התגזרת
אבן לא בידין ומחת לצלמא על רגלוהי (דנ' ב', ל"ד). אמר ר' יוסי בר חנינה
עד שאמר הכתוב אראנו ולא עתה וגו' דרך כוכב מיעקב (במ' כ"ד, י"ז). אמר
ר' אבא עד פורה דרכתי לבדי וגו' (יש' ס"ג, ג'). ר' מאיר אומר עד שיעמדו
רגליו על הר הזיתים, שנ' ועמדו רגליו ביום ההוא על הר הזיתים (זכ' י"ד, ד').

[לסדר קל"ג (ב'): דברים ב', כ"ה.]

ה י ו ם ה ז ה א ח ל ת ת פ ח ד ך. זש"ה תוחלת ממושכה מחלת לב
(מש' י"ג, י"ב), זו היתה מלחמת פרעה, היה משה מביא עליהם מכות, וכל מכה
ומכה היו ישראל סבורין שהוא משלחן, שכך הוא מתנה עמהם ועם משה, ואחר
כך מחזיק לבו. ועץ חיים תאוה באה (שם), זו מלחמת סיחון ועוג, שנ' ראה נתתי
בידך וגו' (דב' ב', כ"ד), לא לשנה, ולא לשלשים יום, אלא ה י ו ם ה ז ה א ח ל
ת ת פ ח ד ך וגו'.

ראה שבחו שלמשה, שהיה פחדו על האומות מסוף העולם ועד סופו, שנ'
ע ל פ נ י ה ע מ י ם ת ח ת כ ל ה ש מ י ם וגו' (שם, כ"ה). וכן בדויד, ויצא
שם דויד בכל הארצות וגו' (דה"א, י"ד, י"ז). אמר הקב"ה לישראל: בעולם הזה
היו שומעים ומתיראים ומפחדים מכם, וכן אני עתיד לעשות לכם לעתיד לבוא,
שנ' וראו כל עמי הארץ כי שם י' נקרא עליך וגו' (דב' כ"ח, י'), ואתם יורשים
אותם, שנ' ובהר ציון תהיה פליטה וגו' (עו' י"ז).

אלה הדברים.

[לסדר קל"ב (א'): דברים א', א'.]

[אלה הדברים.] ... (דף ס"ט, ע"א) אלו שלשה, ובתבערה ובמסה
ובקברות התאוה (דב' ט', כ"ב), הרי שלשה.

ארבעה פעמים ברך משה את ישראל: א' במשכן, ב' באהל, ג' בערבות מואב,
ד' לפני מותו. כשעשו המשכן ברכן, אמר: יהי רצון שתשרה שכינתו במעשה
ידיכם, ואף ישראל הודו לפני הקב"ה, שנ' ויהי נועם י"י אלהינו וגו' (תה' צ', י"ז).
באהל מועד, כשהקריבו את קרבנם, נכנסו משה ואהרן לאהל מועד ויצאו ויברכו
את העם (וי' ט', כ"ג), באותו היום נגלה עליהם השכינה, שנ' כי היום י"י נראה
אליכם (שם, ט', ד'). עוד בערבות מואב, אמר להם י"י אלהיכם וגו'
(דב' א', י'). ולפני מותו בירכן, שנ' וזאת הברכה אשר ברך וגו' (שם, ל"ג, א').
בעולם הזה ברכן, ועתיד לברכם, שנ' הקטן יהיה לאלף וגו' (יש' ס', כ"ב), ואומר
ביום ההוא יהיה ישראל שלישיה וגו', אשר ברכו וגו' (שם, י"ט, כ"ד–כ"ה).

[לסדר קל"ג (ב'): דברים ב', ב'–ג'.]

רב לכם סוב וגו'. זש"ה השבעתי אתכם בנות ירושלים (שה"ש ב', ז'),
כנגד ארבע מלכיות שלא ימרודו באחת מהן, וכשיעלו מן הגולה לא יהיו עולים
המונים המונים שלא ימרודו על המלכיות, ושלא יגלו את הסוד. לפיכך נאמר
השבעתי אתכם בנות ירושלם ד' פעמים, וזו השבועה היא אלה, אמר הקב"ה:
אל תדחקו את הקץ ותמרדו על המלכיות, כצבי, עד שתחפץ (שם), ממה לעתיד
לבוא. אבל למשה אמר רב לכם סוב וגו'.

ואת העם צו לאמר וגו' (דב' ב', ד'), ולמה כך, שכיבד יצחק את
עשו, שנ' ויאהב יצחק את עשו וגו' (בר' כ"ה, כ"ח), אמר הקב"ה: אני פורע לו
שכר כבוד, מאחר שהוא פורע לו שכר שעשה לאביו, הוא פורע ממנו, אבל עכשיו
רב לכם סוב וגו'.

מפני ג' דברים הקב"ה מאריך עם הרשעים: שמא יעשו תשובה, ושמא יולידו
בנים צדיקים, ולשלם להם שכר מצות שעשו בעולם הזה, שנ' ומשלם לשונאיו וגו'

לא היו בני קהת מניחין את הארון ורצין לשלחן ומנורה, אלא אעפ"י שמתמעטין היו נותנין את
נפשם על הארון, וא"כ למה היה מזהיר עליהם אל תכריתו את שבט וגו' אלא מפני שהיו
יודעין שכל מי שטוען בארון שכרו מרובה והיו את השלחן
ואת המנורה וכו'.

לסדר ק"ב

ב. מקורות: ת"ה ות"ב במ' י"ב ומקבילות.

1 ת"ה ות"ב במ' י' וקרוב בניסוחו יותר לת"ב.

2 נראה שצריך להיות: „מה ש[נ]עשית [לנו בשמך]" כפי שהוא בת"ב.

3 נראה שהוספת המסדר הוא בשילוב עם „מה שעשית לנו ב ש מ ך."

4 צ"ל: בשמותינו; אולי יש להשלים החסר: שנ' [אשר שם שמות בארץ] (תה' מ"ו, ט'),
שם שמו בישראל," ברמז לברכות ז', ע"ב: אל תקרי שמות אלא שמות.

5 גם הפסוק הזה משולב לדרשה על ש מ ו של ה' והוספת המסדר היא, ואינה במקורות.

6 יש לנו כאן הרכבה של ת"ב, ו': „חיבה גדולה חיבב הקב"ה את
ישראל כי עשאן דגלים כמלאכי השרת," ובמ"ר פ"ב, י"ט: „להודיעך כמה
היו חביבין לפניו שהם היו צבאותיו..."

7 השווה ת"ב שם, י"ב ומקבילות בהע' ק"נ לבובר.

8 המוסגר על ידי הוספת המסדר שמשלב צוואת יעקב בשעת פטירתו הנזכרת כאן עם
האגדה הידועה תנ' ויחי, ח' (ת"ב, ט') ב"ר צ"ח, ד'; פסחים נ"ו, ע"א: בשעה שהיה יעקב אבינו
נפטר מן העולם קרא לי"ב בניו אמר להם...שמא יש בכם מחלוקת על הקב"ה, אמרו לו
שמע ישראל אבינו...אין בלבנו מחלוקת אלא ה' אלהינו ה' אחד."

9 ט"ס, וצ"ל: ונ ד כמו שהוא במקורות הנז'. דן נזכר אח"כ ביחד עם נפתלי ואשר
במערב.

10 נראה שצ"ל: איני, השווה ת"ב הנז': „אם אני אומר לשבט יהודה שיחנו למזרח, הוא
אומר לי אי אפשי לי אלא בדרום."

11 תמורתו בת"ב: „שצואת אביהם" או „מכסיס אביהן" (ועי' הע' ק"ט לבובר). אולם
במ"א „מסורת אבות" כמו כאן.

12 ו[לבית אבותם].

13 ת"ב שם, י"ג. מקבילות בהע' קי"ב לבובר.

14 המוסגר על ידי. הוספת שילוב של מסדרנו.

סדר ק"ד

ג. מקורות: במ"ר פ"ה, א', ח' ומקבילות.

1 יש להשלים החסר על יסוד במ"ר פ"ה, ח': „הוי נמצאת אומר אפעלפי שהיו (בני קהת)
גדולים מן שאר המשפחות ואין צריך לומר מן ישראל לא היתה רוח גסה נסה
עליהן...לפי שאין גדולה לפני האלהים...כיון שהיו באין לטעון את
הארון היו טוענין בו כעבדים..." קשה לנחש בדיוק.

2 בעל מדרשנו כדרכו משלב מדרש אחר דומה שגם כן בא להבליט את המשפט מיוסד
על שאין גדולה לפני הקב"ה: והוא במ"ר סוף פ"ד: „וכן את מוצא באלעזר הכהן שהיה נוהג
בשפלות לפני המקום. אריב"ל אלעזר היה דוכנין נשיא על הנשיאים שנ' ונשיא
נשיאי הלוי...ואת סבור מפני שהיה אדם גדול היה נותן לאחרים שיטענו את הכלים,
אלא הוא עצמו היה טוען שנ' ופקודת אלעזר בן אהרן הכהן וגו'...להודיעך שאין
גאוה לפני האלהים."

3 שיטתו של מסדרנו בקיצור המקור וצמצומו הגיעה כאן ליד קיצוניות, באופן שבאמת
אין לנו כאן אלא מעין ציונים וסימנים למאמר ארוך בבמ"ר פ"ה, א': „ומנין ש ה י ה ש ב ט
ק ה ת ממעט, אלא אתה מוצא (כאן בא חשבון ארוך ומסובך)...הרי שהיו אפי'
פחות משלישיתן קי"ו. למה כן אלא כשם שאמר ר"א בן פדת...מתוך שהיתה האש יוצאת
ושפה בטועני הארון היו מתמעטין והיו כאו"א רצין זה נוטל את השלחן וזה נוטל את
המנורה וזה נוטל המזבחות ובורחים מן הארון...ר' שמואל בר נחמני אמר ח"ו

הערות לבמדבר

לסדר ק"א

א. מקורות: ת"ב במדבר, ו';

1 ת"ב שם: מכאן שנו רבותינו. הכוונה למכילתא יתרו, סוף פרשה ה' (הוצ' וייס,
עמ' ע"ד[75]), כמו שציין בובר בהע' ס'.

2 וגו' – [מפני אשר ירד עליו ה' באש], כמו שהוא בת"ב.

3 בת"ב מובא הפסוק המקביל משו' ה', ד': ה' בצעדך משעיר ארץ רעשה. גם שמים נטפו
גם עבים נטפו מים. כמובן שבשניהם צריך לצרף ראשית הפסוק הבא: "זה סיני".

4 כנראה יש כאן איזה דילוג, וצריך להשלים עפ"י המקורות הנז' (ת"ב): כך [דברי התורה
חנם הם] (כך בת"ב) החל ב"נאמרו" עד וכדומה. ומן "נאמרו אזהרות" עד "באהל מועד"
מאמר בפני עצמו הבא לפרש "במדבר סיני באהל מועד" (השוה ת"ב שם, ג')
וכנראה יש לנו ניסוח שונה של דברי ר' ישמעאל "כללות (– אזהרות) נאמרו בסיני
ופרטות (– העונשין והמיתות והשריפות והסקילות) נאמרון באהל מעוד" (זבחים קט"ו, ב').

5 בפרהסיא כאן היא שלא במקומה, כי בת"ב שם, ג' ומקבילות מודגש להיפך:
"כיון שעמד אהל מועד, אמר יפה היה הצניעות." וקרוב לודאי שצריך להעביר המלה
"בפרהסיא" למאמר שלפני זה, ובאה לבאר למה ניתנה התורה במדבר. ובאמת במכילתא
יתרו הנז' אנו קוראים לפני המאמר "בשלשה דברים ניתנה תורה": "לפיכך ניתנה במדבר
דימוס פרהסיא במקום הפקר."

6 היינו בפ' פינחס (במ' כ"ו, ב' וכו'). השווה ת"ב פנחס, ו' ומקבילות בהע' ל"נ לבובר.

7 לא מצאתי מקור לזה. בת"ה ויחי, י' וב"ר צ"ט, ח' (הוצ. תו"א עמ' 1279, ע"י מנח"י)
נאמר: כ"ד אלף נפלו משבטו של שמעון בזמרי, והיו אלמנותיו כ"ד אלף ונחלקו שני אלפים
לכל שבט." וכן היא דעת רש"י בם' כ"ו, י"ג לא זכר, כנראה, דברי המדרש, וכותב: "אבל לפי
החסרון...נראה שכל כ"ד אלף נפלו משבטו של שמעון."

8 השווה פדר"א פמ"ז.

9 מדרשנו ל"כי תשא" חסר (עי' ח"א, חלק עברי, עמ' רס"א בראש). השווה ת"ה כי תשא,
ט' (ת"ב, י') ופסדר"כ, פ' שקלים (הוצ' בובר, דף י"ח, ע"א) והע' קכ"ט לבובר.

10 השווה במ"ר פ"ב, י"ט: בא וראה כמה חביבין ישראל לפני המקום... להודיע כמה
היו חביבין לפניו שהם חיי צבאותיו ורוצה למנותן כל שעה.

11 מקור המדרש בלתי ידוע לי. דמיון קלוש למדרשנו במדרש אגדה: "למה סמך אהל מועד
ליציאת מצרים, בזכות אהל מועד יצאו ממצרים."

12 ת"ה ות"ב במ', ד"פ מקבילות בהע' מ"ב לבובר. כרגיל מדרשנו מוסר רק התמצית
ובניסוח שונה המתקרב ביותר לזה שבשהש"ר על פסוק הפתיחה בשם ר' יצחק. מעניינת
ההוספה "יש להן שומרין" שלא מצאתי דוגמתה בשום מקור אחר.

13 השווה "מנחת ש"י שמביא המדרש הזה בשם המסורה והפסיקתא זוטרתא: בני
נפתלי לית בעניין ושאראו לבני דבנים ההו, ליה ובנתא לא הוו ליה ושאראו הוו להון
מסו' וכ"כ ר' טוביה בפסיקתא שלו." במדה"ג, עמ' 159: "שהיה רוב שבטו זכרים" המהדיר מראה
מקום לפסיקתא זוטרתא וילקוט ראובני. ומעניין שבעל הטורים כאן דורש השינוי להיפך:
"בכולן אומר לבני לבד מנפתלי שהוא אומר בני לפי שבשבט נפתלי היו בנות יותר
מבנים."

(מ"א, ב', כ"ח). והיו כל חכמותו שליואב שיברח לאוהל י"י ויחזק בקרני המזבח,
כתיב מעל מזבחי תקחנו וגו', אלא אמר יואב: כל הרוגי בית דין אינן נקברין עם
אבותם, מוטב לי למות כן, לקבר בקברות אבותי, שנ' ויבוא בניהו אל אהל י"י
וגו' (שם, ל'), ויאמר לו שלמה עשה לו כאשר דבר ופגע בו וקברתו (שם, ל"א).
לכך נאמר ל נ ו ס ש מ ה ר ו צ ח וגו', זה שהוא בשגגה.

או בצפון או ב[דרו]ם מניין הוא יודע איכן היא עיר מקל[ט שלו] שיברח
לשם, אמר לו הקב"ה: הכ[ן] לו א[ת] הדרך, והעמיד פטלאות מכוונות כנגד ערי
מקלט, שנ' תכין לו הדרך (דב' י"ט, ג'). לכך דוד מלך ישראל אמר טוב י"י
לכל ורחמיו וגו' (תה' קמ"ה, ט'), ונאמר טוב י"י וישר על כן וגו' (שם, כ"ה, ט'),
אם לרצחנין עשה שיברח[ו] וימלט[ו], לצדיקים על אחת כמה וכמה. זש"ה ידרך
ענוים וגו' (שם).

אמר ר' לוי בכל מקום אתה מוצא ערי מקלט במזרח; אדם הראשון, שנ'
ויגרש את האדם וגו' (בר' ג', כ"ד), הרי מזרח, ולמה נתגרש, אלא שהביא מיתה
לכל הדורות, ונתגרש כדרך הרוצח בשגגה שהוא גולה ממקומו וממשפחתו ויושב
בערי מקלט; וכן קין במזרח, כיון שהרג את הבל, ברח למזרח, שנ' ויצא קין
מלפני י"י (שם, ד', ט"ז).

[בין דף ס"ח ודף ס"ט חסר דף אחד כנראה.]

אמר הקב"ה: ז א ת, התורה הנקראת זאת, שנ' ז א ת ה א ר ץ א ש ר ת פ ל
ל כ ם ב נ ח ל ה וגו' (במ' ל"ד, ב'), כיון שקבלתם את התורה תנחלו את
הארץ. לכך נאמר זאת היתה לי כי פקודיך וגו', למה בעבור ישמרו חוקיו וגו'
(תה' ק"ה, מ"ה).

עד שלא נכנסו ישראל לארץ היו מברכין ברכה אחת: הזן את הכל, וכשנכנסו
לארץ היו מברכין: על הארץ ועל המזון, וכשנבנתה ירושלם הוסיפו: בונה
ירושלם, וכשנהרגו הרוגי ביתתר הוסיפו: הטוב והמטיב. ומכולם אין חביב מברכת
מזון אלא על הארץ ועל המזון, שכך שנו חכמים כל מי שאינו מזכיר על המזון:
ארץ, וברית, ותורה, לא יצא ידי חובתו.

אמר הקב"ה: חביבה עלי ארץ ישראל מהכל, שכן הוא אומר איך אשיתך
בבנים וגו' (יר' ג', י"ט), מה הוא א ר ץ ח מ ד ה (שם), שנתחמדה [מן] אבות
העולם, שכן הוא אומר ארץ אשר י"י אלהיך דורש אותה וגו' (דב' י"א, י"ב).
אמר ר' שמואל לא איש אל ויכזב (במ' כ"ג, י"ט), אלא כשהוא אומר להם:
א[ם חוטאין] הבריות ועושין תשובה, הוא מחזירה, ההוא אמר ולא יעשה וגו' (שם).
תדע לך שהוא כן, אמר הקב"ה לאברהם קום התהלך בארץ וגו' (בר' י"ב, י"ז),
ונתתי לך ולזרעך אחריך וגו' (שם, י"ז, ח'), ואע"פ שהכעיסו אותו בעגל, לא חזר
בו אלא הכניסן לארץ, שנ' כ י א ת ם ב א י ם וגו'. הוי לא איש אל ויכזב,
(דף ס"ח, ע"ב) [זה] בטובה, אבל ברעה מהו אומר, ההוא אמר ולא יעשה וגו'.

[לסדר קל"א (ל"ב): במדבר ל"ה, ט'–י"א.]

ו ה ק ר י ת ם ל כ ם ש ש ע ר י ם. זש"ה אדם עשוק בדם נפש וגו' (מש'
כ"ח, י"ז), זה ההורג בשגגה, למה, ראוי הוא לזה הנהרג שיהרג בתקלה ביד זה
שיהרגנו, זה אדם עשוק בדם נפש. ומה יהיה לו, אמר הקב"ה: עד בור ינוס לא
יתמכו בו (שם), קחו לכם מקום בתחומו, שנ' וישב ראובן אל הבור וגו' (בר'
ל"ז, כ"ט). לכך נאמר עד בור ינוס וגו'.

אמר ר' תנחומא הגוים אין להם מנוס, אבל ישראל יש להם מנוס, שנ'
י"י עוזי ומעוזי ומנוסי וגו' (יר' ט"ז, י"ט). וכן אמר דויד י"י סלעי ומצודתי ומפלטי
וגו' (תה' י"ח, ג'), מ ג נ י, בזכות אברהם, שנאמר לו אנכי מגן לך (בר' ט"ו, א'),
ו ק ר ן י ש ע י, בזכות יצחק, שנ' וישא אברהם את עיניו וגו' (שם, כ"ב, י"ג),
מ ש ג ב י, בזכות יוסף, ויעזוב בגדו אצלה (שם, ל"ט, י"ב). לכך נאמר
ו ה ק ר י ת ם ל כ ם וגו', ת ל ו י, ו נ ס ש מ ה ר ו צ ח וגו' (במ' ל"ה, י"א).

ב ש ג ג ה (שם), ולא בזדון, ואם ילך ויהרוג בזדון, ויאמר: הרגתי בשגגה,
ויברח לערי מקלט, אמר הקב"ה: אפילו ברח ונכנס למזבח, יהרגו אותו, שנ' מעם
מזבחי תקחנו וגו' (שמ' כ"א, י"ד). ומי הוא זה שהרג בזדון וברח אל המזבח
ונהרג, יואב בן צרויה, שנ' והשמועה באה אל יואב כי יואב נטה אחרי אדוניה וגו'

הללו, אלא אמר ר' שמעון כיון שעלה אהרן אל הר ההר וימת שם, שמע הכנעני
כי מת אהרן ובא ונלחם בישראל, ונסעו לאחו[רייהן] ח' מסעות עד שבאו למוסרה,
וראו מטתו שלאהרן באויר בין השמים ובין הארץ, נתקררה דעתם, לפיכך ויבכו
את אהרן וגו' (במ' כ', כ"ט).

וכשעלו ישראל, שבעה ענני כבוד מקיפין אותם: א' מלפניהם, וא' מאחוריהם,
וא' מימינם, וא' משמאלם, וא' על ראשם, שמגין עליהם בקיץ מן החמה ובחורף
מפני הצנה, וא' מפנה להם את הדרך, מגביה את השפל ומשפיל את הגבוה, וא'
שמאיר להם באור יומם ביום ואור לילה בלילה, שנ' לא ימיש עמוד הענן וגו'
(שמ' י"ג, כ"ב).

ומה צורך לכתוב כל המסעות האלו, אמר הקב"ה למשה: מנה להם כל
המסעות, איכן הכעיסוני, ואיכן הביאו נדבות וקרבן, ואיכן קבלו את התורה.
לכך נכתב כל המסעות האילו במדבר.

את מוצא שלעולם הבא עתיד להיות מדבר ישוב, וישוב עתיד להיות מדבר,
מניין, ישושום מדבר וציה וגו' (יש' ל"ה, א'), ואמר ואת עשו שנאתי וגו' (מלא'
א', ג'), ומניין שהמדבר עתיד יהיה ישוב, שנ' אפתח על שפתים נהרות וגו' (יש'
מ"א, י"ח); עכשיו אין דרך במדבר, ועתיד להיות במדבר אילנות, שנ' אתן
במדבר ארז שטה וגו' (שם, י"ט); עכשיו אין דרך במדבר, ועתיד להיות בו דרך,
שנ' אשים במדבר דרך (שם, מ"ג, י"ט). וכל כך למה, בזכות דרך שהלכו בו בני
ישראל, ועתידין להלוך בו, שנ' קול קורא במדבר וגו' (שם, מ', ג'), ואומר סולו
סולו פנו דרך וגו' (שם, נ"ז, י"ד). לכך נאמר נחית עמך כצאן וגו' (תה' ע"ז, כ"א).
כשם שהרועה זהיר בצאן, ביום מפני החמה ובלילה מפני (דף ס"ח, ע"א)
הזאב, כך הקב"ה היה שומר את ישראל ביום ובלילה, שנ' כי שמש וגו' (תה'
פ"ד, י"ב). וכשהיו נוסעים, היו מלאכי השרת וענני כבוד נוסעים לפניהם, שנ'
וי"י הולך לפניהם (שם, י"ג, כ"א). וכי י"י היה מסיעם, הרי הוא אומר ויסע כצאן
עמו וגו' (תה' ע"ח, נ"ב), על פי י"י יסעו בני ישראל וגו' (במ' ט', י"ח). וכן לעתיד
לבוא הקב"ה מסיעם, שנ' לא ירעבו ולא יצמאו וגו' (יש' מ"ט, י'), ל א י ר ע ב ו,
זה המן, ו ל א י צ מ א ו, זה הבאר, ו ל א י כ ם ש ר ב ו ש מ ש, אלו ענני
כבוד, כ י מ ר ח מ ם י נ ה ג ם, זה הקב"ה, שנ' כי אל רחום י"י אלהיך וגו'
(דב' ד', ל"א).

אמר ר' יהודה בעולם הזה היו ישראל נוסעים וחונים ממסע למסע וממקום
למקום, אבל לעתיד לבוא הקב"ה יבנה להם ציון, ונטעים בתוכה, ואינם זזים ממנו
לעולם, שנ' חזה ציון קרית מועדינו וגו' (יש' ל"ג, כ').

[לסדר ק"ל (ל"א): במדבר ל"ד, א'–ב'.]

צ ו א ת ב נ י י ש ר א ל ו א מ ר ת א ל י ה ם כ י א ת ם ב א י ם וגו'.
זש"ה זאת היתה לי כי פקודיך [וגו'], (תה' קי"ט, נ"ו). אמר ר' לוי אימתי זכו
ישראל בחלוק הארץ, בשעה שאמרו וכל אשר דבר י"י נעשה וגו' (שמ' כ"ד, ז').

השלל וגו' (שם, י"א), ויביאו אל משה (שם, י"ב), להודיע שבחן
שלאלו, שלא היו רוצים ליטול את הבזה לעצמן אלא ברשותו שלמשה, שהיו כולם
כשרים ולא נחשדו על הגזל, שנ' ויצאו משה ואלעזר הכהן וגו'
(שם, י"ג), מלמד שמכבדים לעושה מצוה.

ויקצוף משה על פקודי החיל וגו' (שם, י"ד), הקצף הזה
למה, שראה הנשים סוברות שמא יטעו עמהם, ואמר החייתם כל נקבה,
הן הנה היו לבני ישראל וגו' (שם, ט"ו–ט"ז), והרגו מהן אחת ונפלו
בה ד"כ אלף, וקיימתם כל אילו, החייתם כל נקבה. ועתה הרגו
כל זכר בטף וגו' (שם, י"ז). ברוך עושה נקמות ברשעים, אל נקמות
(תה' צ"ד, א').

ד' נקמות האמורות בפרשת האזינו, כנגד ד' מלכיות, ואלו הן: לי נקם ושלם
וגו' (דב' ל"ב, ל"ה), אשיב נקם לצרי וגו' (שם, מ"א), כי דם עבדיו יקום ונקם
וגו' (שם, מ"ג). וכשהקב"ה מתנקם מארבע מלכיות, כל האומות יהיו משועבדים
עם ישראל ויהיו תחתיהם, שנ' ולקחום עמים והביאום וגו' (יש' י"ד, ב'), וכתיב
כי כה אמר י"י רנו ליעקב שמחה וגו' (יר' ל"א, ו').

]לסדר קכ"ט (ל'): במדבר ל"ג, א.[

אלה מסעי. זש"ה נחית כצאן עמך ביד משה ואהרן (תה' ע"ז, כ"א), מהו
נחית, לשון נוטריקון, נחית: נ' נסין שעשית להם, ח' חיים נתתה להם, י' ים
קרעת להם, ת' תורה נתתה להם, על ידי משה ואהרן. ד"א נחית: נ' נשפת, (שמ'
ט"ו, י'), ח' חיל אחז (שם, ט"ו), י' ידמו כאבן (שם, ט"ז), ת' תפול עליהם (שם).
ד"א: נ' נחלת בעזך (שם, י"ג), ח' הסדך וטובך נתת לעמך, י' ידיך כוננו מקדש
(שם, י"ז), ת' תהומות יכסיומו וגו' (שם, ה').

מה הוא כצאן עמך (תה' ע"ז, כ"א), זש"ה ויסע כצאן עמו וגו' (שם,
ע"ח, נ"ב), אלא מה הצאן אין כינוסן לתוך אוצרות, אלא]נ[ועים במדבר, כך
ישראל כל מ' שנה בלא אוצרות, לכך נמשלו כצאן. ד"א, מה הצאן נקבצים
עשתרות עשתרות בלא חומה ובלא דלתים ובריח, כך ישראל כל מ' שנה ישבו
בלא חומה ודלתים ובריח. ד"א, מה הצאן (דף ס"ז, ע"ב) שהרועה מנהיג והן
נמשכין אחריו, כך ישראל נמשכו אחר משה ואהרן, שנהגו אותם בלב טוב ובנפש
חפצה, וכולם אחר השכינה, שנ' אלה מסעי בני ישראל וגו'.

זש"ה שני שדיך כשני עפרים (שה"ש ד', ה'), אילו ש]ני[לוחות הברית. טעם
אחר, בית המקדש ראשון ושני. טעם אחר, בצלאל ואהליאב שעשו את המשכן.
טעם אחר, אילו משה ואהרן.

מ"ב מסעות נסעו ישראל מרעמסס ועד ירדן ירחו. כתוב אחד אומר ויעל
אהרן הכהן אל הר ההר וגו' (במ' ל"ג, ל"ח), וכתוב אחד אומר ובני
ישראל נסעו מבארות בני יעקן וגו' (דב' י', ו'), היאך אני מקים שני מקראות

עתניאל בן קנז וגו' (שם, י"ג). יפתח הגלעדי אמר והיה היוצא מדלתי ביתי
לקראתי וגו' (שם, י"א, ל"א), אמר לו הקב"ה: אפילו חתול, אפילו נמייה, אפילו
כלב, את מעלה אותו לי עולה, מיד נזדמנה לו בתו, ויבא יפתח וגו' ויהי בראותו
אותה וגו' (שם, ל"ד–ל"ה). שאול בן קיש אמר אשר יכה את הפלשתי (ש"א,
י"ז, כ"ו), אמר הקב"ה: אפילו ממזר, תתן לו בתך, נזדמן לו דויד, שנ' ויך את
הפלשתי וימיתה (שם, ג').

אמר ר' שמואל מצאנו בעון ד' דברים גשמים נעצרים: בעון עבודה זרה,
וגילוי עריות, ושפיכת דמים, [והפוסקין צדקה ואינן נותנין]. בעון עבודה זרה,
דכתיב השמרו לכם פן יפתה לבבכם וגו' (דב' י"א, ט"ז), ואחר כך, ועצר את
השמים ולא יהיה מטר וגו' (שם, י"ז); גילוי עריות, דכתיב ותחניפי הארץ וגו'
(יר' ג', ב'), ומה עונשו, וימנעו רביבים וגו' (שם, ג'); ובעון שפיכת דמים, שנ'
ולא תחניפו את הארץ וגו' (במ' ל"ה, ל"ג), כי הדם יחניף את הארץ (שם); בעון
הפוסקין צדקה ואינן נותנין, שנ' נשיאים ורוח וגשם אין וגו' (מש' כ"ה, י"ד).

מצינו עונשו שלנדר יתר קשה מעונש שכתוב, ועונש שבועה קשה כעונש הנדר,
שכל הנודר נדר אסר את נפשו, אפילו בקולר על צוארו. לפיכך היקיש נדר לשבועה
ושבועה לנדר, שנ' איש כי ידור נדר וגו' (במ' ל', ג'), וכתיב וכל
שבועת איסר וגו' (שם, י"ד). אינה יוצאה מבין שניהם לעולם, אם הנשבע
נשבע לשקר, סופה לצאת עליו, שנ' הוצאתיה נאם י"י צבאות וגו' (זכ' ה', ד'). אמר
ר' אבא בר כהנה דרכה שלאש להיות אוכלת עיצים, אבל הכא וכלתה את עציו ואת
אבניו (שם), דברים שאין האש אוכלת אותם, שבועת שוא מכלתן.

[לסדר קכ"ו (כ"ז): במדבר ל"א, א'–ב'.]

[נקם נקמת בני ישראל מאת המדינים.] וצריך אדם
להבין ולראות בעיניו ולחפש את שנקם משונאי י"י, שכך אביגיל אומרת מלחמות
י"י נלחם (ש"א, כ"ה, כ"ח), וכן הוא אומר ונכבשה הארץ לפני י"י ולפני עמו
(דה"א, כ"ב, י"ח). זהו ויאמר משה אל העם החלצו מאתכם וגו'
(במ' ל"א, ג'), אין חילוץ אלא ז[י]ירוח, שנ' חלוצים תעברו וגו' (דב' ג', י"ח).
אמר להם: לא נקמת בשר ודם אתם נוקמים, אלא נקמת הקב"ה אתם נוקמים, שנ'
אל קנא ונוקם י"י וגו' (נח' א', ב').

וישלח אותם משה אלף למטה וגו' (במ' ל"א, ז'), מלמד שהיה
פינחס שקול כנגד כולם. מה ראה משה לשלוח את פינחס, והקב"ה לא אמר לו,
אלא אמר משה: פינחס (דף ס"ז, ע"א) התחיל במצוה הזאת בשטים, הוא יגמור
את המצוה, לכך נאמר ואת פינחס וגו' (שם). וכי בידו היו, אלא
ברשותו הוא, שכך הוא אומר. ואת מלכי מדין הרגו על חלליהם
וגו' (שם, י"ח), מיכאן שאמר מלכי מדין, אלא כדרך שהיו שום בעיצה כך היו
שום בפורענות. וישבו בני ישראל וגו' (שם, ט'), ויקחו את כל

[לסדר קכ"ה (כ"ו): במדבר ל', ב'.]

א ל   ר א ש י   ה מ ט ו ת.   זש"ה נדרו ושלמו לי"י אלהים כל סביביו יובילו
שי למורא (תה' ע"ו, י"ב). אמר ר' תנחומא: בן אדם, ראה דרכך, ודע
לפני מי אתה עומד, ומי הוא בעל מלאכתך, ולפני מי אתה (דף ס"ו, ע"א) מדבר,
ולפני מי אתה נודר ונשבע, לפני מלך מלכי המלכים הקב"ה, מושב יקרו בשמים
ממעל, ושכינת עוזו בגבהי מרומים, ואל תאמר: אינו יודע, כי הכל גלוי וידוע
לפניו, שהוא תוכן לבות, ונוצר נשמות, ומבין, ומשלם לאדם כפעלו וכמעשה ידיו,
שנ' כי תאמר הן לא ידענו הלא תוכן לבות הוא יבין וגו', הוא יודיע, והשיב
לאדם כפעלו (מש' כ"ד, י"ב).

שנו חכמים ז"ל המהרהר בלבו יהא חייב, תלמוד לומר כל נדיב לבו (שמ'
ל"ה, ה'). יכול בשפתיו, לא בלב, או יכול שאינו מוציא את הגומר בלב, הזהר
במוצא שפתיך, תשמור, ושלם נדריך, שנ' מוצא שפתיך תשמור ועשית וגו' (דב'
כ"ג, כ"ד), וכתיב טוב אשר לא תדור משתדור ולא תשלם (קה' ה', ד'), וטוב
משניהם מי שאינו נודר כל עיקר, שנ' וכי תחדל לנדור לא יהיה בך חטא (דב'
כ"ג, כ"ג), שפיו שלאדם הוא מחטי[א] את בשרו, שהוא נודר ואינו משלם, והוא
מכעיס לבוראו ומחבל את מעשה ידיו, שנ' אל תתן את פיך לחטיא את בשרך
וגו' (קה' ה', ה').

אמרו רבותינו מאי דכתיב מוקש אשם ילע קדש וגו' (מש' כ', כ"ד), מה הוא
ואחר נדרים לבקר (שם), אחר אדם נדרו, פנקסו נפתח והקב"ה דורש ממנו, שנ'
כי תדור נדר לי"י אלהיך (דב' כ"ג, י"ב), שתי דרישות: דרישה בעולם הזה,
ודרישה לעולם הבא, ולא עוד אלא שהוא גורם מיתה, דכתיב והיה בך חטא (שם),
וכתיב הנפש החוטאת היא תמות (יח' י"ח, ד'). ולא עוד אלא נקרא כסיל, שנ'
כי אין חפץ בכסיל וגו' (קה' ה', ג').

אמרו חכמים ז"ל בעון איחור נדרים, הבנים מתים, שנ' אל תתן את פיך
לחטי[א] וגו' (שם, ה'), ומעשה ידיך הם הבנים, שנ' והותירך י"י אלהיך לטובה
וגו' (דב' ל', ט'), והרי אומר בפרי בטנך (שם).

אמרו חכמים כל המאחר את נדרו גורם לה' דברים: עבודה זרה, וגילוי
עריות, ושפיכ[ת דמים], ועוצר גשמים מן העולם, וקובר את אשתו. שכן מצינו
בעון שאיחר יעקב נדרו, לקה בה' דברים, ואלו הן: גלוי עריות, שנ' ותצא דינה
(בר' ל"ד, א'), ושפיכת דמים, שנ' ויהי ביום השלישי וגו' (שם, כ"ה); ועבודה
זרה, שנ' ויאמר יעקב אל בניו (שם, ל"ה, ב'); קובר אשתו, ותמת רחל וגו' (שם,
י"ט); ועוצר גשמים, שנ' נשיאים ורוח וגשם וגו' (מש' כ"ה, י"ד).

ד' פתחו בנדרים, ג' השיבו אותם כהוגן, ואחד שלא כהוגן. ואלו הן: אליעזר
עבד אברהם, שנ' והיה הנערה אשר וגו' (בר' כ"ד, י"ד), אמר לו הקב"ה: אפילו
כושית, כנענית, נזדמנה לו רבקה, שנ' ויהי הוא טרם וגו' (שם, ט"ו). כלב בן יפנה
אמר אשר יכה (דף ס"ו, ע"ב) את קרית ספר וגו' (שו' א', י"ב), אמר לו הקב"ה:
אפילו עבד, אפילו ממזר, תתן את בתך לו לאשה, נזדמן לו בן אחיו, שנ' וילכדה

[לסדר קכ"ד (כ"ה): במדבר כ"ח, כ"ו.]

[וביום הבכורים בהקריבכם מנחה חדשה לי'י.]
אמר ר' תנחומא אמרה כנסת ישראל לפני הקב"ה: רבונו שלעולם, זכרנו
קרבנות (דף ס"ה, ע"ב) שהיינו מקריבין לפניך, ובכורים שהיינו מביאים בשמחה,
ושמחה נפשינו כשהיינו עולים לירושלם ומעלים בכורים, כתות כתות כעולי רגלים,
ברינה ותודה ושמחה, שנ' אדדם עד בית אלהים וגו' (תה' מ"ב, ה').

אמר הקב"ה: הביאו שעורים בכורים בפסח, כדי שתתברך לפניך בתבואה
שהיא שעורים; שתי הלחם בעצרת, כדי שיתברכו לפניך בתבואה שהיא חטים;
בכורים בעצרת, כדי שתתברך לפניך פירות האילן; הביאו נסוך המים בחג, כדי
שיתברכו לפניך במים. בוא וראה כמה היתה חביבות המצות לפני הקב"ה ולפני
ישראל.

שנו חכמים כיצד מפריש את הבכורים, יורד אדם לתוך שדהו, ורואה תאינה
שביכרה, אשכול שביכר מן הגפן, רימון שביכר, וקושרן בגמי, ואומר: הרי אלו
בכורים. והיו מעלין אותן לירושלם, ונותנין שבח והודאה לפני הקב"ה בקול:
השקיפה ממעון קדשך מן השמים (דב' כ"ו, ט"ו), עשינו מה שגזרת עלינו, אף אתה
עשה כל מה שהבטחת.

מנחה חדשה, שתהא חדשה, וכן הוא אומר קרבן ראשית וגו' (וי'
ב', י"ב), וכתיב ממושבותיכם וגו' (שם, כ"ג, י"ז). שנו חכמים כל . . . ומשמרם
שלא יחמיצו, ואם החמיצו שיריה עובר בלא תעשה, שנ' כל המנחה אשר תקריבו
וגו' (שם, ב', י"א).

אמר ר' יהודה כשהיה בית המקדש קיים, היה רובן שלמצות הקרבנות שהיו
מקריבין על גבי המזבח, היו יפים לישראל, שכל מי שהיה מתקרב ממנו, היה
מתברך [ממנ]ו; לחם הפנים שהיה על השלחן, בזכותו היה מתברך הלחם; ובזכות
הבכורים שהיו מביאים, היו מתברכין הפירות שבאילן; ובזכות היין שהיה מתנסך,
היה מתברך פרי הגפן; ובזכות התמידין והקרבנות שהיו מתקריבין על גבי המזבח,
היה מתברך שגר בהמה ועשתרות צאן. עכשיו שחרב בית המקדש, ערבה השמחה
ובטלו כל הטובות האלו מן העולם, שנ' ערבה כל (יש' כ"ד, י"א), אימתי, שגלה
משוש הארץ, כשהנביא אומר זרעתם הרבה וגו' (חג' א', ו'). ולעתיד לבוא
מחזיר כל אותן הטובות והברכות לישראל, שנ' ואתם הרי ישראל וגו' (יח' ל"ו, ח'),
ומצמיח קרן לישראל, שנ' שם אצמיח קרן לדויד (תה' קל"ב, י"ז), במהרה בחיינו
ובימינו וגו'.

]לסדר קכ"ג (כ"ד): במדבר כ"ז, ט"ו–ט"ז.[

[**יפקוד י'י אלהי הרוחות לכל בשר.**] ... ‹דף ס"ה, ע"א›
לפיכך הוא אומר אלהי הרוחות וגו'. **איש**, שיהיה בעל כח ובעל חכמה ובעל
גבורה, תמנה על העדה, מי שהוא יודע להלוך עם כל אחד ואחד לפי דעתו,
ויהיה בו כח לסבול; שנ' **אשר יצא לפניהם וגו'** ‹במ' כ"ז, י"ז›, שלא
יעשה כדרך שלמלכי אומות שלעולם, שהם מוציאים העם למלחמה, ויושבים להם
בתוך בתיהם, אלא **אשר יצא לפניהם ואשר יבוא לפניהם**
וגו'; שלא יהא מוציא רבבות ומכנים אלפים, מוציא אלפים ומכנים מאות, **ו ל א**
תהיה עדת י'י וגו' ‹שם›. אמר לו הקב"ה: הרי שבקשת נתון לך, **ק ח**
לך את יהושע בן נון וגו' ‹שם, י"ח›, **והעמדת אותו** ‹שם, י"ט›,
שיהא ממונה מפי אלעזר הכהן על כל העדה; **וצוית אותו לעיניהם**
‹שם›, אמר ר' יהודה אין צווי בכל מקום אלא דברי תורה, שנ' קרא את יהושע
וגו' ‹דב' ל"א, י"ד›; **ונתת מהודך עליו** ‹במ' כ"ז, כ'›, **מהודך**
ולא הודך, כמדליק נר מנר, דומה היה משה לנר שהוא מונח על גבי המנורה,
ידליקו ממנו נרות הרבה, ואורו שלנר לא יחסר כלום, כך היתה חכמתו שלמשה,
והודו לא יחסר כלום; **למען ישמעו כל עדת בני ישראל** ‹שם›,
יהיו נוהגין בו כמ[ו שהיו] נוהג[ין] בך. **ולפני אלעזר יעמוד וגו'**
‹שם, כ"א›, שכשם שאמרתי לך לא תסוב נחלה וגו' ‹במ' ל"ו, ז'›, כך הכבוד הזה
אינו זז מבית אביך, ואין לזה שהוא תחתך רשות לצאת ולבוא אלא על פי בן
אחיך, שנ' **על פיו יצאו ועל פיו יבאו וגו'**. **ושאל לו**
במשפט האורים וגו', יכול שהם נשאלים להדיוט, ת"ל **הוא וכל בני**
ישראל, מה יהושע על הצבור, אף כאן אינן נשאלין אלא למלך, ולבית דין,
ולמי שצורך הצבור בו. ולמה נקרא שמם אורים, שהן מאירים, תומים, שהם
שלמים, כהם ולא מדמם כהם.

ויעש משה כאשר צוה י'י אותו ויקח את יהושע,
ויסמך את ידיו עליו וגו' ‹במ' כ"ז, כ"ב–כ"ג›. ולמה זכה יהושע את
כל הכבוד הזה, בשביל ששמש למשה רבינו, ועסק בתורה בכל כחו, שנ' ומשרתו
יהושע בן נון ‹שמ' ל"ג, י"א›. זש"ה נוצר תאינה יאכל פריה ‹מש' כ"ז, י"ח›, מה
ראה למשול את התורה בתאינה, שרוב האילנות, הגפן והזית והתמרים, נלקטים
כולם כאחד, והתאינה אינה כן, אלא נלקט מעט מעט, כך התורה, נילמדת דבר
דבר, לכך נמשלה כתאינה. הוי נוצר תאינה, זה יהושע, שהגיע לכל השבח והכבוד
הזה בשביל ששמש את משה. הוי נוצר תאינה וגו'.

[לסדר קכ"א (כ"ב): במדבר כ"ה, י'–י"א.]

פינחס. זש"ה טובים השנים מן האחד וגו', ואם יתקפו האחד וגו' (קה'
ד', ט', וי"ב). אמר ר' תנחומא כל ג' צדיקים, שעמדו זה אחר זה, הברית
נכרתה להם ואינה פוסקה לעולם מהם. שכן את מוצא: אברהם, יצחק, ויעקב,
ונכרתה להם ברית, שנ' אשר כרת את אברהם וגו' ויעמידה ליעקב לחוק (תה'
ק"ה, ט'–י'). וכן: בועז, עובד, וישי, ונכרתה להם ברית שאינה פוסקת לעולם,
שנ' הלא לכם לדעת וגו' (דה"ב, י"ג, ה'), ואומר כרתי ברית לבחירי וגו' (תה'
פ"ט, ג'). וכן אהרן, מפני שהעמיד ג' כיוצא בו, זה אחר זה, נכרת ברית לשלישי
שאינה פוסקת לעולם. זהו שאמר הכתוב פינחס בן אלעזר בן אהרן
הכהן, מה כתיב אחריו, לכן אמור הנני וגו' (במ' כ"ה, י"ב),
והיתה לו ולזרעו אחריו וגו' (שם, י"ג). הוי והחוט המשולש לא
במהרה ינתק (קה' ה', י"ב).

אמר ר' אלכסנדרי בוא וראה שכר קנאין לשם הקב"ה. קנא פינחס, וכפר
על בני ישראל, ונתן לו הקב"ה ברית כהונת עולם, לו ולזרעו, שאינה פוסקת
לעולם, שנ' הנני נותן לו את בריתי שלום (במ' כ"ה, י"ב).
אליהו שקנא לשם הקב"ה, שנ' קנא קנאתי וגו' (מ"א, י"ט, י'), ולמה העלהו
בסערה לשמימה, שנ' המה הולכים הלוך ודבר והנה סוסי אש וגו' (מ"ב, ב', י"א).

אמר ר' ירמיה לעולם שבטו שללוי קנאין. במעשה עגל, מה כתיב שם, ויעמוד
משה בשער המחנה וגו' (שמ' ל"ב, כ"ו), והחטא הזה היה גדול ממעשה העגל,
במעשה העגל עמדו בני לוי, וכאן עמדו בני לוי, שכיון שראה פינחס מעשה זמרי,
אמר: זקני וחקנו שלוזה עמדו וגדרו הפרצה הזאת בשכם, וזה עמד ופרץ גדר שגדרו
הזקנים, אין כאן אדם מישראל שיהרגנו, יהרג על ידי, היכן הן האריות, היכן הן
הזאבים. וכיון שראה שאין אדם מישראל עושה כלום, מיד עמד מתוך סנהדרים
שלו, ונטל את הרומח בידו, והלך והרג, והשיב חימה מישראל, שנ' השיב את
חמתי וגו' (במ' כ"ה, י"א).

זו אחת מן העבירות החמורות שהקב"ה מתקנא עליהם: ע"ז, וגלוי עריות, שנ'
ולא כליתי את בני ישראל בקנאתי (שם), ע"ז מניין, שנ' כי
י"י אלהיך אל קנא (דב' ד', כ"ד). מלמד שהיו ראוין לכליה לולי פינחס. אמר
ר' שמעון פינחס, בזכות הזה שעשה, זכה ליטול כהונה

[בין דף ס"ד ודף ס"ה חסר דף אחד כנראה.]

נכנס, היה רואה אותה יושבת מקוש[טת], והיא נותנת לו יין ותירוש, והוא שותה,
והיין מביא לידי זנות, שנ' זנות ויין ותירוש יקח לב (הו' ד', י"א).

ו י צ מ ד י ש ר א ל ל ב ע ל פ ע ו ר (במ' כ"ה, ג'). אמר ר' לוי אחת
היתה בעגל, ועכשיו הרי שנים, כמה דאת אמרת צמד בקר (ש"א, י"א, ז'). ואחר
כך, ו י א כ ל ה ע ם (במ' כ"ה, ב'), מיד, ו י ח ר א ף י ' י ב י ש ר א ל
(שם, ג'), שאין חרון אף בא לעולם ביותר אלא בגלוי עריות. ק ח א ת כ ל
ר א ש י ה ע ם (שם, ד'), ר' יהודה אומר אמר הקב"ה: הרוג את הגדולים שלא
מיחו ביד הקטנים. ור' נחמיה אומר קח את כל ראשי העם ושבו בדינים. וראו
אותם ל ע י נ י מ ש ה ו ל ע י נ י כ ל ע ד ת י ש ר א ל ו ה מ ה ב ו כ י ם
(שם, ו'), שהרי ישראל נלקחים למיתה.

ו י ר א פ י נ ח ס ב ן א ל ע ז ר (שם, ז'), מה הוא ו י ר א, שראה
המגפה בישראל. ו י ק ם, שעמד בזרירות. וכל שבט שמעון מקיפין את אוהל
זמרי, שהיה נשיא שבטו, ואיך היה פנחס יכול להכנס ברומח, אלא מה עשה,
הסתיר את הברזל לתוך אפונדתו, והיה מסתמך על העץ שלרומח. אמרו לו:
להיכן אתה נכנס, אמר להם: אין אתם יודעים שלוי עם שמעון בכל מקום, שנ'
שמעון ולוי אחים וגו' (בר' מ"ט, ה'), וכיון שאמר להם כך, נתנו לו מקום. וכיון
שנכנס, נטל הברזל וחיברו לעץ הרומח. מיד, ו י ב א א ח ר א י ש י ש ר א ל
וגו' (במ' כ"ה, ח').

אמרו רבותינו הרבה נסים נעשו לו באותו היום. נס אחד, שנדבק הברזל לעץ
ולא נפל. ב' שאורך הברזל שמלא שניהם. ג' שסתם המלאך את פיהם ולא יבא
לצווח עד שנטל את שניהם. ד' שהיה כח בידו ליטעון. ה' שהיה הפתח קצור
והגביה עצמו. ו' שלא ירד מהם דם ללכלך את כליו. ז' שנתן כוח בעץ לסבול
ולא ישבר. ח' שדקר האיש למטה והאשה למעלה, ובא המלאך והפכן, האשה
למטה והאיש למעלה, בשביל כבודו שלפנחס. ט' שהיו חיים ולא מתו, שלא יטמא
והוא כהן. י' דבקן המלאך. י"א שעמד הרומח ולא זז לכן ולכן, שלא יצטער
אותו צדיק. י"ב שראו אותן הנשים. ואחר שהפילן מתו, ועצר המגפה, שנ' ויעמוד
פינחס ויפלל ותעצר המגפה (תה' ק"ו, ל'). והיה אוחז הרומח בזרועו על לחיו
ועל קבתו, לכך נתן לו ג' מתנות, שנ' ונתן לכהן הזרוע והלחיים והקבה (דב'
י"ח, ג'), ונתנו לו ד"כ מתנות כהונה ה כ ת ו ב י ם ל מ ט ה.

כיון שיצא, ראה מלאך המות נוגף בעם. הדה הוא דכתיב וחוטא אחד יאבד
וגו' (קה' ט', י"ח), הרי זמרי, שנפלו מישראל ד"כ אלף בשביל [ו]. (דף ס"ד, ע"ב)
וכשעשה פינחס את הדי[ן] נעצרה המגפה, שנ' ויפלל פינחס וגו' (תה' ק"ו, ל'),
ואין ו י פ ל ל אלא דין, שנ' ונתן בפלילים (שמ' כ"א, כ"ב). שכך יבוא מורה
צדק בחינו, ויעשו דין ומשפט באמת בבנין ירושלם, שנ' בונה ירושלם י' וגו'
(תה' קמ"ז, ב').

לקצור, מצותיו עמו, שנ' ובקצרכם את קציר ארצכם וגו' (שם, ט'); יצא לעמר,
מצותיו עמו, שנ' ושכחת עומר בשדה וגו' (דב' כ"ד, י"ט); יצא לדוש, מצותיו עמו,
שנ' לא תחסום שור בדישו (שם, כ"ה, ד'); מאצר את הדגן, מצותיו עמו, מוציא
תרומה, תרומות מעשר, ומעשר שני, לקט שכחה ופאה; בא לאפות, מפריש חלה
ותרומה; בא לאכול, מצותיו עמו, נוטל ידיו, ואחר כך מברך ואוכל, וכן לאחר
סעודה. לכך אמר בלעם מי מנה עפר יעקב.

לכה נא אקחך אל מקום (במ' כ"ג, כ"ז), להיכן לקחו, לראש
הפעור, שראה שבמקום הזה חוטאין ישראל להקב"ה, ומשתחוים לבעל פעור,
והקב"ה חרה אפו בהם, שנ' ויחר אף י"י בישראל (שם, כ"ה, ג'). מיד אמר לו
בנה לי בזה ז' מזבחות (שם, כ"ד, כ"ט), כנגד ז' ימי בראשית. אמר
לו בלק: הרי אני בפה אקללם. התחיל ברכם, שנ' מה טובו אוהליך
יעקב וגו' (שם, כ"ה, ה'). אמר ר' יהודה אוהליך, זה אהל מועד,
משכנותיך, זה בית המקדש, שנ' זאת מנוחתי עדי עד וגו' (תה' קל"ב, י"ד),
וכן הוא אומר לו עמי שומע לי ישראל וגו' (שם, פ"א, י"ד), מה כתיב אחריו,
כמעט אויביהם אכניע וגו' (שם, ט"ו).

[לסדר ק"כ (כ"א): במדבר כ"ה, א'.]

וישב ישראל בשטים. זש"ה טובה חכמה מכלי קרב (קה' ט', י"ח).
אמר ר' תנחומה אמרו חכמים בזכות ד' דברים נגאלו ישראל ממצרים:
שלא שינו את שמותם, ולא החליפו את לשונם, ולא גילו את סודם, ולא נחשדו על
העריות. ומנין שלא שינו את לשונם, שכן יוסף אומר כי פי המדבר אליכם (בר'
מ"ה, י"ג). ומנין שלא חילפו את שמותם, שנ' ראובן שמעון לוי וגו' (שמ' א', ב')
וכל שבטים בירידתם, אף כן בעליתם, שנ' לראובן משפחת הראובני (במ' א', ה';
כ"ו, ז'). ומנין שלא גילו את סודם, שכן את מוצא שאמר להם דבר נא באזני העם
וגו' (שמ' י"א, ג'), והיה הדבר ביום שנים עשר לחדש, ולא גילו הן את הסוד.
ומנין שלא נחשדו על העריות, שנ' גן נעול אחותי כלה וגו' (שה"ש ד', י"ב), תדע
לך שהיה כן, היה איש אחד ופרסמו, שנ' ויצא בן אשה ישראלית וגו' (וי' כ"ד, י').
ולא היו ישראל יודעין כל מ' שנה עד שבאו לשטים מה הן עריות. כשבאו לשטים,
ויחל העם לזנות וגו' (במ' כ"ה, א').

אמרו חכמים ג' עבירות עשו ישראל: בעלו ארמית, ואכלו זבחי מתים,
והשתחוו לבעל פעור. כיצד עשו להם עד שהטעו להם בלק וכל בני מואב, הם
העמידו את בנותיהם מקושטות מבפנים, והזקנות מבחוץ, כמה שיעץ בלעם, שנ'
הן הנה היו לבני ישראל וגו' (שם, ל"א, ט"ז), והיו הנערות מקושטות מבפנים
והזקנות (דף ס"ד, ע"א) מבחוץ עומדות להם, והיה איש מישראל הולך לקנות לו
חפץ, והיתה הזקנה אומרת לו: הכנס לפנים ואני אראך חפצים נאים, וכיון שהוא

ג', י"ז) ; וכן נח ובניו בירכן הקב"ה, שנ' ויברך אלהים את נח וגו' (שם, ט', א').
וחם היה בכלל הברכה, וכיוון שחטא לא היה אביו יכול לקללו, שקדמה אותה
ברכה, שלא אמר ארור חם, אלא ארור כנען (שם, כ"ה). אמר
בלעם: ואם היו יחידים שקדמה אותה ברכה, לא שלטה בהן קללה, ישראל
שבירכן הקב"ה ברכה שלמה, שנ' י"י יברך את עמו בשלום (תה' כ"ט, י"א), כל
שכן. באותה שעה נתקיים על אויביהם המקרא הזה רשע יראה וכעס
שיניו יחרוק וגו' (שם, קי"ב, י'), זה בלק, שהוא רואה דבר הפוך, שנ'
ויהפוך י"י אלהיך לך וגו' (דב' כ"ג, ו') ; שיניו יחרוק ונמס, זה בלעם,
שהיה מבקש לקלל את ישראל, ולא הניחו הקב"ה לקללו, שנ' ולא אבה י"י אלהיך
לשמוע אל בלעם וגו' (שם); תאות רשעים תאבד, אילו זקני מואב
וזקני מדין.

פס'. כי מראש צורים אראנו (במ' כ"ג, ט'), שאין אומה שמחה
לעולם הבא אלא הם, ואינן נידונין עם הגויים, שנ' הן עם לבדד ישכון
(שם), שכתבי והייתם לי קדושים (וי' כ', כ"ו), ואינו מחליף אותם באומה אחרת,
שנ' אני י"י לא שניתי וגו' (מלא' ג', ו').

[לסדר קי"ט (כ): במדבר כ"ג, י'.]

מי מנה. זש"ה מברך רעהו בקול גדול (מש' כ"ז, י"ד), מה הוא בבוקר
השכים (שם), אמר הקב"ה לבלעם: אתה השכמת בבקר על ישראל, אין אתה
מועיל, שהשכמת אברהם קדמה להשכמתך וגו', ואתה עמדת בבקר לקלל את
בניו, קללה תיחשב לו (שם), לאותו האיש, וברכה להם, הה"ד, ולא
אבה (דב' כ"ג, ו').

אמר ר' ברכיה זש"ה אמרו לאלהים מה נורא מעשיך (תה' מ"ו, ג'), כשהרשעים
באים להתגרות בך, יהי פיהם חוזר ומשקרן ומביישן, שכן אתה מוצא בפרעה,
אמר מי י"י אשר אשמע בקולו (שמ' ה', ב'), ואחר כך שקרו פיו ואמר י"י הצדיק
וגו' (שם, ט', כ"ז); נבוכדנצר, בתחלה אמר לחנניה מישאל ועזריה ומן הוא
אלה די ישזבנכון וגו' (דנ' ג', ט"ו), ואחר כך שקר פיו ואמר בריך אלההון וגו'
(שם, כ"ח). ברוב עוזך יכחשו וגו' (תה' שם). וכן בלק שלח אצל בלעם לקלל
את ישראל, בא בלעם לקלל וברכן. אמר לו הקב"ה: אתה סבור שאתה מקללן,
כעפר הארץ ברכתי את יעקב, שנ' והיה זרעך כעפר הארץ (בר' כ"ח, י"ד), מה
עפר הארץ מהם חיים כל העולם, כך בזכות המצות שבניו עושין יחיו כל העולם,
מה עפר הארץ מכלה את הכלים, כך בניו מכלים כל האומות. כיון שהלך ודאג
כך, התחיל אומר מי מנה עפר יעקב וגו'.

אמר בלעם: מי יוכל למנות את המצות שישראל עושין בעפר; (דף ס"ג, ע"ב)
יצא לחרוש, מצותיו עמו, שנ' לא תחרוש בשור ובחמור יחדיו (דב' כ"א, י'); יצא
לזרוע, מצותיו עמו, שנ' שדך לא תזרע כלאים וכרמך וגו' (וי' י"ט, י"ט); בא

ואלו השלשה שראו ויבושו: הנפילים, שנ' ויראו בני האלהים וגו' (בר' ו', ב'),
ולמה נקרא שמם נפילים (שם, ד'), שנפלו ממקום מחצתם; עשו ראה יעקב שקבל
הברכות, הלך אצל ישמעאל לינשא בתו, שנ' וילך עשו אל ישמעאל (שם, כ"ח, ט'),
ולמה בא אצל ישמעאל, אמר לו: בוא אתה הרוג את אחיך, אף אני אהרוג את
אחי, ויהיה העולם כולו לנו; בלק ראה ויבוש, ראה שכל העומד אצל ישראל סוף
הורגין אותו, שלח והביא את בלעם, (דף ס"ב, ע"ב) ראה ויבוש, היה מנחש
בעתים ורואה שעות לקלל את ישראל, ולא מצא זמן, שנ' מה אקוב לא קבה אל
וגו' (במ' כ"ג, ח'), וירא כי טוב בעיני י"י לברך את ישראל וגו' (שם, כ"ד, א');
אחיתופל ראה ויבוש שראו מזלו שנפל מן הרקיע, והיתה מיתתו בחנק כמה שיעץ
לאבשלום, וכל עצה שהיה יועץ מתקיימת, שנ' ועצת אחיתופל וגו' (ש"ב, ט"ז, כ"ג),
וראה כי לא נעשתה עצתו (שם, כ"ג), אמר עתה ישמע דוד ויהרגני, ויצו לביתו
(שם), מה צוה לביתו, אמרו חכמים ז"ל ג' דברים צוה את בניו, אמר להם: אל
תהיו במחלוקת, ואל תמרדו בבית דוד, ואם ראיתם יום טוב שלעצרת ברור,
זרעו חטים לשנה הבאה; המן ראה ויבוש, ראה הכל כורעים ומשתחוים לו, וזהה
דעתו עליו, בקש להשמיד להרוג ולאבד את כל היהודים בשביל איש אחד, שנ'
וירא המן כי אין מרדכי כורע ומשתחוה לו וגו' (אס' ג', ה'), הקב"ה הפר עצתו.

פס'. ויאמר אליו מלאך י"י על מה הכית וגו' (במ'
כ"ב, ל"ב), אלא הודיעו מה האתון שאין לה זכות ולא ברית נצטוות לאמר על
מה הכית, אומה שלימה שאתה מבקש לעקור אל אחת כמה וכמה. שנ' אף בל
נטעו אף בל זורעו וגו' (יש' מ', כ"ד), אילו אומות העולם, שאין להם
נטיעה, דור המבול נעקרה נטיעתן, שנ' וימח את כל היקום וגו' (בר' ו', כ"ג),
אבל ישראל נטועים, שנ' ונטעתים על אדמתם (עמ' ט', ט"ו); אף בל זורעו
(יש' שם), אילו דור המגדל, שנ' ויפץ י"י אותם וגו' (בר' י"א, ח'), אבל ישראל
זרועים, שנ' וזרעתיה לי בארץ וגו' (הו' ב', כ"ה); אף כל שורש בארץ
גזעם, אילו הסדומים, שנ' ויהפוך את הערים האל (בר' י"ט, כ"ה), אבל
ישראל משורשים, שנ' הבאים ישרש ישראל וגו' (יש' כ"ז, ו'); וגם נשף בהם
ויבושו, אילו המצריים, שנ' נשפת ברוחך וגו' (שם, ט"ו, י'); וסערה כקש
תשאם, אילו בלק ובלעם, שנ' ויקם בלק וילך וגו' (במ' כ"ב, כ"א).

וכיון שבא בלעם אצל בלק, אמר לו בנה לי בזה וגו' (שם, כ"ג, א'),
ולמה ז', כנגד ז' מזבחות שנבנו מאדם ועד משה, ונתקבלו לרצון, ואלו הן: אדם,
הבל, נח, אברהם, יצחק, יעקב, משה.

פס'. וישם דבר בפי בלעם (שם, ה'), שלא כטובתו. ויאמר
שוב אל בלק (שם), וישב אליו וגו' (שם, ו'), וכולן מצפין מה יבא
הדבר. וישא משלו ויאמר מן ארם ינחני וגו' (שם, ז'), מן
הרמים הייתי נמנה, והורידני בלק לבאר שחת, הה"ד מן ארם ינחני, מן הרמים
השפילני. מה אקוב וגו' (שם, ח'), אמר בלעם: מן אדם שבירכו הקב"ה,
שנ' ויברך אותם אלהים וגו' (בר' א', כ"ח), לא דבקה בו הקללות, שכן אתה
מוצא כשחטא אדם, מה (דף ס"ג, ע"א) הוא אומר, ארורה האדמה בעבורך (שם,

בגבעון נראה י״י אל שלמה (מ״א, ג׳, ה׳). הוי שהוא רחוק מן הרשעים וקרוב
לצדיקים. לכך נאמר ‏ויבוא אלהים אל בלעם וגו׳. ולא היה לו
לאמר אותה שעה שהנסתרות גלויות לפניך, אלא אמר ‏בלק בן צפור
וגו׳ (במ׳ כ״ב, י׳).

פס׳. ‏ויאמר אלהים אל בלעם לא תלך עמהם וגו׳
(שם, י״ב). אמר לו: ואקללם, אמר לו: לא תאר ‏(שם), אמר בלעם:
ואברכם, אמר לו הקב״ה: ‏כי ברוך הוא ‏(שם), ואינו צריך לברכתך.

פס׳. ‏ויען בלעם ויאמר וגו׳ (שם, י״ח). מיכן אתה אומר שהיה
בו שלשה דברים: עין רעה, ורוח גבוהה, ונפש רחבה. עין רעה, וישא בלעם את
עיניו וגו׳ ‏(שם, כ״ד, כ׳), נסתכל בהם בעין רעה; רוח גבוהה, שנ׳ ‏כי מאן
י״י לתתי וגו׳ (שם, כ״ב, י״ג); נפש רחבה, ‏אם יתן לי בלק מלא
ביתו וגו׳ (שם, י״ח), שהיה מבקש כך. ‏לא אוכל לעבור את פי
י״י ‏אלהי ‏(שם), מתנבא שאינו יכול לבטל את הברכות שיצא מפי הגבורה
לאבות. ‏ועתה שבו נא בזה (שם, י״ט), מתנבא שהוא עתיד להוסיף על
ידו ברכות. ‏ויבוא אלהים אל בלעם וגו׳ (שם, כ׳), ‏(דף ס״ב, ע״א)
ולמה בלילה, שלא היה ראוי לרוח הקדש, שכל הנביאים, שעמדו מן הגוים,
בלילה הוא מדבר עמהם, שנ׳ ויבוא אלהים אל לבן וגו׳. ‏ויתיצב מלאך
י״י בדרך לשטן לו (שם, כ״ב), מלאך שלרחמים היה, אלא לזה היה
שטן.

‏ותרא האתון וגו׳ (שם, כ״ג), ולא היה יכול המלאך לשלוט בו אלא
אם היה ‏חרבו שלופה בידו (שם), והלא הוא שלט בחילו שלסנחריב
ושרפן, שנ׳ ויצא מלאך י״י ויך במחנה אשור וגו׳ (מ״ב, י״ט, ל״ה), וגם נשף בהם
וייבשו (יש׳ מ׳, כ״ד), ולמה, ראה אברהם ושמח; יצחק ראה ושמח, שנ׳ ויצא
יצחק לשוח בשדה וגו׳ (בר׳ כ״ד, ס״ג), וכי כל מי שהוא רואה גמלים הוא שמח,
אלא שראה את אליעזר עבדו, ורבקה ונערותיה, ושמח שאתמול הלך והיום בא;
יעקב ראהו ושמח, שנ׳ וירא יעקב כי יש שבר (שם, מ״ב, א׳), אלא סבר, שראה
ברוח הקודש שיוסף עודנו חי וסברו קיים; משה ראה ושמח, שנ׳ וירא והנה הסנה
בוער באש וגו׳ (שם, ג׳, ב׳), דבר מופלא; יהושע ראה ושמח, שנ׳ וישא עיניו וירא
והנה איש עומד וגו׳ (יה׳ ה׳, י״ג), וכל מי שראה זה הוא שמח, אלא כשראהו הלך
אצלו, אמר לו הלנו אתה אם לצרינו (שם), מיד שמח אותו מלאך, שבא אצל
משה ולא קיבלו כתלמיד, יהושע קיבלו כרב; פינחס ראה ושמח, בשעה שראה
זמרי תפס בבלוריתה שלכזבי ובא אצל משה, אמר לו: זו מותרת או אסורה, אמר
לו משה: אסורה, אמר לו זמרי: זו אסורה ושבביתך מותרת, קצף משה ונתעלמה
ממנו הלכה, והיה לו לומר ולהשיב לו: אני לקחתי זו מבית אביה בביאה בכסף
ובשטר, ואתה שאחות בזנות, אלא נתעלמה ממנו הלכה, וכשראה פינחס כן, אמר
לו: רבינו, והלא כך לימדתני מסיני כל הבועל ארמית קנאין פוגעין בו, אמר לו:
אתה נזכרת הלכה, הדבר תלוי בך, מיד עמד פינחס וקנא, שנ׳ וירא פינחס
(במ׳ כ״ה, ז׳), ראה מעשה ונזכר הלכה.

(במ' כ', י"ח), ומה כתיב שם, וימאן אדום נתון את ישראל וגו'
(שם, כ"א).

ושלחו אל סיחון, שנ' וישלח משה מלאכים אל סיחון וגו'
(שם, כ"א, כ"א). מה הוא בשדה ובכרם (שם, כ"ב), אמרו לו: אין אנו
צריכין לאכל משלך כלום, משלהקב"ה אנו אוכלין, שנ' הנני ממטיר לכם לחם
(שמ' ט"ז, ד'); ולא נשתה מי באר, אין אנו שותין משלך, שעמנו מי
באר, שנ' עלי באר (במ' כ"א, י"ז).

וכיצד היתה הבאר עולה לישראל, היו המים יוצאין ממנו ונעשים נחלים
נחלים, שנ' הן הכה צור ויזובו מים וגו' (תה' ע"ח, כ'). וכיון שהיתה עולה, היו
ישראל אומרין שירה, שנ' לי"י הישועה על עמך ברכתך סלה (שם, ג', ט'). אמרו
ישראל: רבון כל העולמים, בכל נסים שאתה עושה עמנו, עלינו להיות משבחין
אותך ואומרין לפניך שירה, שנ' י"י להושיעני ונגינותי נגנן (יש' ל"ח, כ'), ונ' לי"י
הישועה וגו'; עשיתה לנו נסים במצרים, שלחת עשר מכות, והוצאתנו לחירות,
וטבעת שונאינו בים, ואמרנו שירה; וכן בימי סיסרא שלחצונו בחזקה, ועשית את
מלחמותינו, שנ' מן שמים נלחמו וגו' (שו' ה', כ'), ואף אנו אמרנו שירה לפניך,
שנ' ותשר דבורה וגו' (שם, א'); וכן כשהרגנו סיחון ועוג (דף ס"א, ע"ב) שהיו
אויבינו, והעלית לנו את הבאר, ואמרנו לך שירה, שנ' אז ישיר ישראל
וגו' (במ' כ"א, י"ז). לקיים מה שנ' י"י להושיעני וגו'. וכן לעתיד לבוא כשישראל
רואין נסים ונפלאות שהוא עושה עמם, הן אומרין שירה, שנ' שירו לי"י שיר חדש
כי נפלאות עשה וגו' (תה' צ"ח, א').

[לסדר קי"ח (י"ט): במדבר כ"ב, ב'.]

וירא בלק בן צפור. זש"ה צופה רשע לצדיק ומבקש להמיתו
(תה' ל"ז, ל"ב), זה בלק, שהיה רואה את ישראל יושבין בנחת, וענני כבוד
מקיפין אותן, והמן יורד עליהן, והשלו עולה, והבאר מהלכת, ועמוד האש
לפניהם, והיה רוצה לחבלם, ולא הניחו הקב"ה, לקיים מה שנ' י"י לא יעזבנו
בידו וגו' (שם, ל"ג).

הה"ד רשע יראה וכעס וגו' (שם, קי"ב, י'), זה בלק, שנ' וירא בלק בן
צפור, ומה ראה, ראה אותן נסים שנעשו לישראל, שנפלו לפניהם סיחון ועוג,
נתיירא, שנ' ויגר מואב מפני העם (במ' כ"ב, ג'). מיד וישלח
מלאכים וגו', ועתה לכה נא ארה לי (שם, ה'-ו').

נגלה עליו הקב"ה, שנ' ויבוא אלהים אל בלעם וגו' (שם, ט').
זש"ה רחוק י"י מרשעים וגו' (מש' ט"ו, כ"ט), העולם ומלואו אינו מחזיק כבוד
שלהקב"ה, ואין מקום בעולם פנוי מכבודו, והוא אומר ויבא אלהים אל
בלעם וגו', הרי שהוא רחוק מהם, אבל לצדיקים קרוב הוא, שנ' וירא אליו
י"י וגו' (בר' י"ח, א'), וכן וירא אלהים אל יעקב עוד וגו' (שם, ל"ה, ט'), וכן

אמר להם: אספו הקב"ה. אמרו לו: אתה הוא חלשה דעתך עליו, ולא היו
מאמינין שגוע אהרן, עד שאמר השם לרוח ערסו בין השמים ובין הארץ,
וראו בני ישראל אותו והאמינו, שנ' **ויראו כל העדה כי גוע אהרן**
(במ' כ', כ"ט). ולמה בכו על אהרן **כל בית ישראל** (שם), ועל **משה**
כל בני ישראל (דב' ל"ד, ח'), מפני שהיה אהרן משים שלום בין איש
לאשתו, ומשה היה דן אמת לאמתו, לפיכך בכו על אהרן כל בית ישראל, שכך
שנו חכמים ז"ל הוי מתלמידיו שלאהרן אוהב שלום ורודף שלום, והמקרא מסייעתו
בריתי היתה אתו החיים והשלום, תורת אמת היתה בפיהו וגו' (מלא' ב', ה'-ו').

[לסדר קי"ז (קי"ח): במדבר כ', י"ד.]

פס'. **וישלח משה מלאכים.** זש"ה לא רגל על לשונו וגו' (תה'
ט"ו, ג'), להודיע שבחו וצדקו שלמשה רבינו ע"ה, שאע"פ שנענש מתחת ידי
ישראל, כמה שכתוב **למעלה מן העניין, ויאמר ה' אל משה ואל אהרן**
יען לא האמנתם בי וגו' (במ' כ', י"ב), זש"ה ואכחיד את שלשת הרועים בירח אחד
(זכ' י"א, ח'), אע"פ שמת אהרן באב ומשה באדר, אלא ביום שמתה מרים בניסן
יצאה גזירה על הדור ההוא שהכעיסוהו, כמה ימרוהו במדבר וגו' (תה' ע"ח, מ'),
שלא יהו הדורות אומרין אף משה היה שוה להם, אלא לפיכך נכתב על ידי מה.
על ידי מה אני נענש, אמר הקב"ה: הריני כותבה, יען לא האמנתם וגו', ואומר
ויקציפו על מי מריבה (תה' ק"ו, ל"ב), ובכל כך לא פרק משאו מעליו, אלא עמד
בצדכן, כמו שהיה קודם לכן, כך אחרי ענשו מתחת ידיהם, שלח לבקש את צרכן,
שנ' **וישלח משה מלאכים** וגו'.

מה כתיב (דף ס"א, ע"א) אחריו, **וירדו אבותינו מצרימה** (במ'
כ', ט"ו), ומה היה צריך לומר כך, אלא אמר לו: אני ואתה היינו זקוקין לשעבוד
על אבינו אברהם נגזר מתחלה, שנ' ויאמר לאברהם ידוע תדע וגו' (בר' ט"ו, י"ג),
והרי פרענו אנחנו את השטר, כדי הצער שנצטערנו על ידיהם, שלא תחזירו אותנו
לכך אמר לו **אתה ידעת** וגו' (במ' כ', ט"ו). **ונצעק אל י' וישמע**
את קולינו (שם, ט"ז), שכך אבינו יצחק מתחלה נתן לנו את הקול, ולכם
ידים, שנ' הקול קול יעקב וגו' (בר' כ"ז, כ"ב), לכך נאמר **וישמע קולינו.**
מזכיר לו מה שמור עליהם **בקדש** (במ' כ', ט"ז), **נעברה בארצך** וגו'
(שם י"ז), שלא תרד כן לומר שאמר לנו הקב"ה כל מקום אשר תדרוך כף
רגליכם (דב' י"א, כ"ד), שכבר אמר לנו אל תתגרו בם וגו' (שם, ב', ה').
ויאמר אליו אדום וגו' (במ' ל', י"ח), אלא דע כשאמר לו ישראל
ונצעק אל י' וגו' (שם, ט"ז), אמר לו: כשאנו נופלין בצרה אנו צועקים,
והקב"ה שומע קולינו, ואם היצרתה לנו, יש לנו מי שיעמוד בעדינו. אמר לו: אתם
באתם בשלכם, ואני באתי בשלי, אתם באתם בקול, שנ' הקול קול יעקב וגו'
(בר' כ"ז, כ"ב), ולי נתן את החרב, שנ' **פן בחרב אצא לקראתך**

אם יהיו חטאיכם כשנים כשלג ילבינו וגו' (יש' א', י"ח), אמר הקב"ה:
לשעבר הייתם מטהרין מיד הכהנים, לעתיד אני מטהר אתכם ואין אתם צריכין
לבריה, שנ' וזרקתי עליכם מים טהורים וגו' (יח' ל"ה, כ"ה).

ד"א. פרה אדומה, אמר ר' ינאי משל לעגל שהחריב פלטר
שלמלך, אמר המלך: תבוא אמו ותתקנה, כך הפרה מכפרת על מעשה
העגל. ולמה אדומה כזהב, לכפר על מעשה העגל ודי זהב (דב'
א', א'). ולמה תמימה ואין בה מום, לפי שהיו ישראל
תמימים ונעשו בעלי מומין, לנקותם ממומם ולהחזרן תמימים כשהיו, בזריקת
מי הנדה (במ' י"ט, כ"א). ולמה משליכין לתוכה עץ ארז
ואיזוב (שם, ו'), ללמדך שאם יגביה עצמו כארז, הקב"ה ישפילו
כאיזוב, ואם ישפיל עצמו כאיזוב, הקב"ה יגביהו כארז. ולמה תולעת
שני (שם), שאם יחטא אדם עד שיהיו חטאיו אדומים כתולעת, ויעשה
תשובה, ילבין כשלג, שנ' לכו נא ונוכחה יאמר וגו' (יש' א', י"ח).

עשר פרות נעשו: ט' לשעבר, ואחת לעתיד לבוא.

[לסדר קט"ז (י"ז): במדבר כ', א'.]

פס'. ויבואו בני ישראל כל העדה מדבר סין וגו'.
זש"ה ואכחיד את שלשת הרועים בירח אחד (זכ' י"א, ח'), וכי בירח אחד
מתו, והלא מרים בעשרים בניסן מתה, ואהרן בא' באב מת, ומשה בז' באדר, אלא
כשמתה מרים נסתלקה הבאר, וחזרה בזכות משה ואהרן, מת אהרן נסתלקו ענני
הכבוד, וחזרו בזכות משה, מת משה נסתלקו שלשתן. לכך נאמר ואכחיד וגו'.

פס'. קח את אהרן ואת אלעזר בנו וגו', והפשט את
אהרן את בגדיו, (במ' כ', כ"ה-כ"ו), והיאך עשה משה, פשטן את
בגדיהן והעמידן ערומים, לא נכון לעשות כן, פשט את זה והלביש את זה, לא יהיו
כעניין, אלא שלמעלה מזה יהיה למטה מזה, לא מעשה נס היה, בא ענן וחופה
את שניהן, והפשיט את אהרן את בגדיו.

משה התבייש לאמר לאהרן שהגיעה שעתך להפטר מן העולם, אמר לו
דברי (דף ס', ע"ב) עלילות. אמר לו לאהרן: אם יאמר לך לעשר שנים אתה
מת, מה תאמר. אמר ליה: כל דאי מארי צבי עביד. אמר לו: אם יאמר לשנה
אחת אתה מת. אמר לו: כל דאי מארי צבי עביד. אמר לו: לחודש, אם יאמר
לשעה אתה מת. מיד נפתחו לפניהם שער גן עדן, ונכנסו לתוכה. ראה מטה
מוצעת. אמר לו: עלה על המטה הזו. עלה אהרן, שכב עליה. אמר לו: פשוט
ידיך ורגליך, אמץ עיניך. ועשה כן, ויאסף אל עמיו. מיד אמר משה בלבו: כך
היא המיתה, הלואי בשעת פטירתי אאסוף כן. ובשעת פטירתו, אמר לו הקב"ה:
עלה על הר העברים וגו' (דב' ל"ב, מ"ט).

כיון שירד משה ואלעזר מן ההר, אמרו ישראל למשה: אהרן היכן הוא.

[לקריאה של שבת פרה: במדבר י״ט, א׳–ל׳.]

(דף נ״ט, ע״ב) זאת חוקת התורה. זש״ה מי יתן טהור מטמא לא
אחד (אי׳ י״ד, ד׳). הרי בהרת כגריס טמא, פרחה בכולו טהור, שנ׳ כולו הפך
לבן טהור הוא (וי׳ י״ג, י״ג), מי עשה כן, מי צוה כן, מי גזר, לא אחד, הלא
יחידו שלעולם. כך הפרה טהורה, והשורף אותה טמא, שנ׳ והשורף אותה
וגו׳ (במ׳ י״ט, ח׳), ומי שהוא אוסף את אפר הפרה מטמא, שנ׳ וכבס האוסף
את אפר הפרה וגו׳ (שם, י׳), כל העוסקין בפרה מתחלה ועד סוף מטמאין
בגדים, והיא עצמה מטהרת טמאים, מי גזר כן, הלא יחידו שלעולם.
הוי מי יתן טהור מטמא וגו׳.

זש״ה אמרות י״י אמרות טהורות (תה׳ י״ב, ז׳), אבל שלבשר ודם
אינן אמרות, מה הוא אומר טהורות, אמר ר׳ ברכיה כך מצינו
שעקם הכתוב שתים שלש תיבות בתורה, כדי שלא יחל לדבר על
דבר טמא, שנ׳ מן הבהמה הטהורה ומן הבהמה אשר איננה טהורה
(בר׳ ז׳, ח׳), ומן הבהמה הטמאה אינו אומר כן. הוי אמרות
י״י אמרות טהורות. ואומר ואת הגמל כי מעלה גרה הוא, ואת השפן וגו׳
ואת הארנבת וגו׳ (וי׳ י״א, ד׳–ו׳), שלא להזכיר דבר טומאה, ומתחיל
בטהרה שיש בו. הוי אומר אמרות י״י אמרות טהורות וגו׳.

אמר שלמה כל זו נסיתי בחכמה וגו׳ (קה׳ ז׳, כ״ג), אלא בפרשה זו
שלפרה היה עוסק, והיה תמיה ואומ׳: אין חכמה שלא עמדתי עליה,
ועל הפרשה הזו איני יכול לעמוד, למה, שהיא מטמא את הטהורים
ומטהרת את הטמאים. וידבר על העצים מן הארז אשר בלבנון וגו׳
(מ״א ה׳, י״ג), אמר שלמה: מפני מה מצורע מיטהר בגבוה שבגבוהים
ובנמוך שבנמוכים, על ידי שהאדם הוא מגביה את עצמו כארז, הוא לוקה בצרעת,
וכיון שהוא משפיל עצמו כאיזוב, לכך הוא מתרפא באיזוב.

פס׳. דבר אל בני ישראל ויקחו אליך וגו׳ (במ׳
י״ט, ב׳), משלצבור הפרה באה, ואינה באה משליחיד. אליך פרה
אדומה, אם לומר שתהא תמימה, [הרי נ]אמר אשר אין בה
מום, [ו]מה אני מקיים תמימה, אם אינו עניין למומין, תנהו עניין
לאדמומית. אשר לא עלה עליה עול, שנו חכמים כל המומין
הפוסלין במוקדשין פוסלין בפרה. רכב עליה, נשען עליה, נתלה בזנבה,
עבר בה את הנהר, קיפל עליה את המוסרה, נתן טליתו עליה, פסולה.
אבל קשרה במוסרה, עשה לה סנדל בשביל שלא תחליק, פרס טליתו
עליה מפני (דף ס׳, ע״א) הזבובין. זה הכלל: כל שהוא לצרכה
כשרה, שלא לצרכה פסולה.

ולמה פרה אדומה, לכפר על חטא האדום שעשו עגל שלזהב,
ולא אותו החטא בלבד היה היה אדום, אלא גם כל החטאים אדומים,
לכך תהא הפרה אדומה, וכשהיא נשרפת אפר שלה נעשה לבן, שנ׳

מי שמהלך בענוה ובתמימות לפני הקב"ה, ואשרי בניו אחריו, שנ' מתהלך
בתומו צדיק וגו' (מש' כ', ז').

[לסדר קט"ז (י"ז): במדבר י"ח, כ"ה–כ"ו.]

פס'. ו א ל ה ל ו י ם ת ד ב ר. זש"ה י"י צדיק יבחן וגו' (תה'
י"א, ה'), אבל רשעים, כתיב בהן ורשע ואוהב חמס שנאה נפשו (שם), שאין
הקב"ה מזכה לרשעים שאין עומדין בנסיונו, אמר ר' יוחנן היוצר הזה
אינו (דף נ"ט, ע"א) משגיח להקיש על כלי מרועע, ועל מה הוא מקיש,
על כלי בריא, כך הקב"ה פוסל לרשעים שהן ככלי מרועע. לכן
ורשע ואוהב חמס וגו'.

ראה חיבה שחיבב הקב"ה את הלוים, מתחלה בחר שיהיו משמשין
לפניו, נתן להן את המעשרות, שנ' ולבני לוי הנה נתתי את כל מעשר
בישראל וגו' (במ' י"ח, כ"ו). אמר הקב"ה למשה: שיאמר ללוים שיהיו
מוציאין תרומת מעשר, שנ' ו א ל ה ל ו י ם ת ד ב ר וגו', מגיד כשם
שנכרתה ברית לכהנים על המתנות, כן נכרתה ברית ללוים על המעשרות
שלהן, שנ' ולבני לוי הנה נתתי וגו', ל נ ח ל ה (שם), מה נחלה
שנאמרת בכהנים, מעשר בישראל לנחלה בבני לוי קיימת לעולם. ח ל ף
ע ב ו ד ת ם (שם), כבני לוי שנטלו שכר מה שעשו עמי במדבר באהל
מועד. יכול מפני שבטלה העבודה נבטל המעשר, ת"ל ל נ ח ל ה, מה
נחלה אינה פוסקת, אף המעשר אינו פוסק ולא מתחלף, לא לפי
שבטלה העבודה, הרי הן זוכין בו שכר מה שעשו עמי במדבר. וכשם שאסור
לאכול מן הדמאי, בין קטנית בין יין בין שמן בין שאר פירות, עד
שיפריש תרומה גדולה, כך אסור לבני לוי לאכול מן המעשר כלום עד שיפריש
תרומתו, שנ' ו נ ח ש ב ל כ ם ת ר ו מ ת כ ם כ ד ג ן מ ן ה ג ו ר ן (שם, כ"ז).
לקיים מה שנאמר כבד את י"י מהונך וגו' (מש' ג', ט'), מה הוא כ ב ד א ת י" י
מ ה ו נ ך, מפני שחננך, וממה שנתן לך.

עשר מצות עושה אדם עד שלא יאכל פרוסה: משום לא תחרוש
בשור ובחמור (דב' כ"ב, י'), ומשום לא תזרע כרמך כלאים (שם, ט'),
ומשום לא תחסום שור (שם, כ"ה, ד'), ומפריש לקט שכחה ופאה,
ומפריש תרומה, מעשר, ומעשר שני, וחלה.

תאני ר' נחמיה בנוהג שבעולם אדם לו שדה, הוא נותנה למחצה,
לשליש, לרביע, אבל הקב"ה אינו כן, אלא משיב רוחות, ומעלה נשיאים,
מוריד גשמים, ומפריח טל, ומגדל צמחים, ומדשן פירות, ולא אמר להפריש
אלא אחד מעשרה. בוא וראה מה גדולה היא מצות מעשרות לפני
הקב"ה, שכתיב בתורה לא תנסו את י"י אלהיכם (שם, ו', ט"ז), ומצות מעשר,
הביאו את כל המעשר אל בית האוצר וגו' (מלא' ג', י').

פס'. **והיה האיש אשר אבחר בו מטהו יפרח וגו'**
(שם, כ'), **ועשת פרח מטה אהרן ויגמול שקדים** (שם, כ"ג),
לא רמונים ולא אגוחים, אלא אמר הקב"ה: כל מי שהוא שוקד לעשות לו,
הדה"ד ובית רשעים ישמד (מש' י"ד, י"א), זה קרח ועדתו, הדה"ד
בוטח בעשרו הוא יפול (שם, י"א, כ"ח), ואהל ישרים יפריח (שם, י"ד, י"א),
זה משה ואהרן, לכך נאמר והנה פרח מטה אהרן.

לכך נאמר **וקח מאתם וגו'** (במ' י"ז, י"ז). אמר ר' תנחומא
בשר ודם מכה באזמיל ומרפא ברטייה, הקב"ה אינו כן אלא במה שהוא מכה,
בו מרפא לזה; קרח במקח, שנ' ויקח קרח (שם, ט"ז, א'), ונטל אהרן
כהונה במקח, שנ' קח מאתם מטה מטה וגו'.

ואת שם אהרן (דף נ"ח, ע"ב) **תכתוב על מטה לוי**
וגו' (שם, י"ח). אמר הקב"ה: [ש]תי מטות אני ע[ושה בעולם, מטה] אהרן
ומטה דוד, לזה אני מושח בשמן המשחה, ולזה אני מו[שח בשמן המשחה]; לזה
אני עושה נזר, שנ' ושמת המצנפת על ראשו (שמ' כ"ט, ו'), וכתיב בדוד
ועליו יציץ [נזרו וגו' (תה' קל"ב, י"ח]; לזה] ולבניו אני נותן בכהונה ברית
מלח, שנ' ברית מלח עולם הוא (במ' י"ח, י"ט), ולזה ולבניו אני נ[ותן]
מלכות וברית מלח, שנ' הלא לכם לדעת כי י"י אלהי ישראל וגו' (דה"ב,
י"א, ה'); ושניהם אני מרב[ה] אותם ואת זרעם, שנ' אשר לא יספר צבא
השמים ולא ימד חול הים כן ארבה את זרע דוד עבדי וגו' (יר' ל"ג, כ"ב).

אמר הקב"ה למשה: אמור לישראל אל תהיו רצים אחר השררה,
לבזות אותה למי שאתם מבקשים, אלא למי שאני מבקש אני מעלה,
ואומר י"י מוריש ומעשיר וגו' (ש"א, ב', ז'). שנו חכמים אל תהי רץ אחר
השררה והכבוד שהוא הורג את בעליו. ומניין, שכן מצינו באבימלך בן
ירובשת שבזו את השררה, ולא האריך בה אלא ג' שנים, שנ' וישר אבימלך
על ישראל ג' שנים (שו' ט', כ"ב), ולא עוד אלא שנהרג ביד אשה, שנ' מי
הכה את אבימלך בן ירובעל וגו' (ש"ב, י"א, כ"א); וכן קרח בקש את השררה,
אף הוא מה היה סופו, ותפתח הארץ את פיה (במ' ט"ז, ל"ב). וכל
מי שהוא בורח מן השררה ומהלך בענוה, הקב"ה מעלהו לשררה, שכך
שנו חכמים מפני מה זכה יהודה לשררה, ולהיות מלך, ומלכים ממנו
יצאו, בשביל שהיה עניו, שנ' ועתה ישב נא עבדך וגו' (בר' מ"ד, ל"ג);
וכן שאול לא זכה למלכות אלא שהיה עניו, שכן אמר לשמואל הנביא הלא
בן ימיני אנכי מקטני שבטי ישראל (ש"א ט', כ"א), ומה היה לו, זכה
למלכות, שנ' ושאול לכד המלוכה על ישראל וגו' (שם, י"ד, מ"ז);
וכן משה לא זכה לשררה ולא עשה הקב"ה נסים על ידו, אלא מפני
שהיה עניו, שנ' והאיש משה עניו מאוד (במ' י"ב, י"ג), ועוד אמר מי
אנכי וגו' (שמ' ג', י"א); וכן אהרן מפני שהיה עניו זכה לשררה ולשמש
בכהונה גדולה, שנ' בריתי היתה אתו החיים וגו' (מלא' ב', ה');
וכן אברהם היה עניו, שכתוב בו ואנכי עפר ואפר (בר' י"ח, כ"ז). אשרי

אובד וגו' (תה' קי"ט, קע"ו), מה אבידה האמורה בדוד שעתידה להתבקש,
אף אלו כן. אתה מוצא שחנה מתפללת עליהן, שנ' ממית ומחיה
מוריד וגו' (ש"א, ב', ז'). ד"א. ותפתח הארץ [וגו'], וכי במקום
אחד היו כולם, ר' יהודה אומר הרבה פיות נפתחה הארץ, וכל מקום שהיה
אחד מהם, נבלע. אמר לו ר' ברכיה: והלא פה אחד נפתח לארץ, שנ'
ותפתח הארץ את פיה וגו', אלא שנעשת משפך, וכל מקום שהיה
אחד מהם, היה מתגלגל ויורד, [וא]ם היה לאחד מהם כלי או פקדון בידי
אדם, היה מתגלגל ויורד אחריהן. ואת כל היקום (דב' י"א, ו'),
אמר ר' אלעזר זה הוא ממונו שלאדם שמעמידו על רגליו. ומניין
שנעשת הארץ כמין משפך, והיו מתגלגלין והולכין ויורדין....

[לסדר קט"ו (ט"ז): במדבר י"ז, ט"ז–י"ז.]

פס'. דבר אל בני ישראל וקח מאתם (דף נ"ח, ע"א)
מטה. זש"ה אם תכתוש את האויל במכתש וגו' (מש' כ"ז, כ"ב),
בדור המדבר הוא מדבר, כמה סרפונין [היו, עברו] את הים, מה
כתיב שם, וימרו על ים בים סוף (תה' ק"ו, ז'); באו לרפידים, מריבה,
אומרין היש י"י בקרבנו (שמ' י"ז, ז'); יצאו משם ובאו במעשה העגל, מתו
בשלשה מיתות: מהם נהרגו, ומהם נדקרו במגפה, ומהם בהדר[ר]קון; וכן
במתאוננים, אבדו מהם בשריפה, שנ' ותבער בם אש י"י (במ' י"א, א'); וכן
במרגלים, במדבר הזה יתמו וגו' (שם, י"ד, ל"ה); וכן במחלוקת שלקרח:
מהם הלכו בבליעה, שנ' ותפתח הארץ את פיה (שם, ט"ז, ל"ב), ומהם הלכו בשריפה,
שנ' ואש יצאה מאת י"י (שם, ל"ה). ואחר כל המיתות הללו שראו, לא חזרו בהן, אלא
עומדין ומנאצין כנגד משה ואהרן ומעיזין פניהם כנגדן ואומרין אתם המתם את עם י"י
(שם, י"ז, ו'). הדה"ד כי מרעה אל רעה יצאו וגו' (יר' ט', ב'), וכתיב כי אויל עמי
לא ידעו וגו' (שם, ד', כ"ב), לקיים מה שנ' אם תכתוש את האויל במכתש וגו'.

אמר הקב"ה: מאחר שראו כל המיתות הללו ואינן מתביישין, עכשיו
קח מאתם מטה מטה. מה עשה משה, אמר להם: הביאו מטות,
וכתבו כל אחד ואחד על מקלו ונתנום למשה, שנ' ויתנו אליו
כל נשיאיהם מטה לנשיא אחד וגו' (במ' י"ז, כ"א), הכניסן
לאהל מועד, שנ' וינח משה את המטות לפני י"י (שם, כ"ב).
הדה"ד באור פני מלך חיים (מש' ט"ז, ט"ו).

פס'. ויהי ממחרת וגו' (במ' י"ז, כ"ג). זש"ה וידעו כל עצי
השדה כי אני י"י (יח' י"ז, כ"ד). השפלתי עץ גבוה, זה
קרח, שהיה מגביה עצמו; הגבהתי עץ שפל, זה אהרן; הובשתי
עץ לח, אילו י"א מטות; הפרחתי עץ יבש, זה מקלו שלאהרן,
שנ' ויוצא פרח וגו' (במ' י"ז, כ"ג), אני י"י דברתי ועשיתי.

הלך משה אצל ביתה, ועמד אצל הפתח, וקרא: און בן פלת, און בן
פלת, צא. יצא. אמר לו: המקום ימחול לך.

כיצד עמדו קרח ועדתו כנגדו שלמשה, שנאמר ויקומו לפני
משה וגו׳, ויקהלו על משה ועל אהרן וגו׳ (במ׳ ט״ז,
ב׳–ג׳), הקהילו עליהם כל העדה, ואמרו להם: רב לכם, הרביתם
לכם יותר מדאי, כי כל העדה כולם קדושים וגו׳, כולם
עמדו על הר סיני ושמעו מפי הגבורה אנכי י״י אלהיך וגו׳ (שמ׳ כ׳, ב׳),
ומדוע אתם מתנשאים. באותה שעה שמע משה ונפל על פניו, שנ׳ וישמע
משה ויפול על פניו (במ׳ ט״ז, ד׳), מד[וע נפל], מפני המחלוקת
שראה. וידבר אל קרח (שם, ה׳), אמר: שמא מתוך משחיתם
אמרו כך, ימתינו עד הבקר, שמא יעשו תשובה, והקב״ה מקריב אותם
אליו, לכ[ך נאמר] (דף נ״ז, ע״ב) [בקר וידע י״י], ואת
אשר יבחר בו יקריב אליו. ויאמר משה (שם), קרח...
היא... שנ׳ המעט מכם כי הבדיל אלהי ישראל אתכם,
ובקשתם גם כהונה וגו׳ (שם, ט׳–י׳), לכן אתה וכל עדתך
וגו׳ (שם, י׳), המחלוקת הזו אינה כנגדנו, שאילו אמרו: בזו את הכהונה מעצמו,
יפה הוא [לכם] שנתרעמתם, הקב״ה נתנה לו, מה כנגדו לא נחלק אלא כנגד
מי שנתנה לו.

ויאמר משה בזאת תדעון וגו׳, אם כמות כל האדם
וגו׳, ויהי ככלותו וגו׳, וירדו חיים שאלה וגו׳ (שם,
כ״ח–כ״ט, ל״א, ל״ג). יש אומרים חיים הם נידונים עד עכשיו. ואש
יצאה וגו׳ (שם, ל״ה), היו אלו נבלעין, ואלו נשרפין, וקרח עומד בין השרופין
ובין הבלועין, שאמר לו משה ואתה ואהרן איש מחתתו (שם, י״ג),
והוא לקח יתר מכולם שנשרף ונבלע, שאילו נשרף ולא נבלע, היו
הבלועין אומרין: קרח הביא עלינו הפור [ענות] הזאת וני[צל, ואם היה
נבלע ולא נשרף, היו השרופין אומרין: לא הביא אותנו לצרה זו
אלא קרח, והרי נשרפנו והוא אינו עמנו. לכך עשה הקב״ה בו שתי מכות,
[נ]לכדה בו האש תחלה לעיני כל השרופין שהיה עמהם בקטרת,
והיתה האש מתגלגלת בו עד שהביאתו לפי הארץ בין הבלועין, כענין
שנ׳ ותפתח הארץ את פיה (שם, ל״ב), וצדק[ו] הכל דינו
שלהקב״ה, שהוא גרם לכולם המחלוקת הזאת ולקח עם הבלועים ואם
השרופין. ראה מה גרמו לעצמן, וירדו הם וכל אשר להם
חיים וגו׳ (שם, ל״ג), כמה שנזר ואמר ואם בריאה יברא י״י
וגו׳ (שם, ל׳), והיו צווחים ואומרין, כשהיו יורדין: משה נביא ומלך,
ואהרן כהן גדול, ותורה ניתנה מן השמים. והיה קולם הולך ב[מח]נה
ישראל, וכל ישראל אשר סביבותיהם נסו לקולם וגו׳
(שם, ל״ד), כל כך למה, לפי שחלקו על הקב״ה. אע״פ כן יש להם
רפואה לעתיד לבוא, שנ׳ ויאבדו מתוך הקהל, וכתיב תעיתי כשה

הארץ אשר עברנו בה ארץ אוכלת יושביה וגו' (במ' י"ג, ל"ב); באתם לים
סוף, וקרעתי אותו לפניכם, ושם קלקלתם את העצה ומריתם, שנ' וימרו
על ים בים סוף (תה' ק"ו, ז'); באתם למדבר, והורדתי לכם את המן,
ואתם קלקלתם את העצה ואמרתם: ונפשינו קצה וגו' (במ' כ"א, ה');
באתם לפני הר סיני, וירדתי עליכם בדברים שתחיו בהם, שנ' אני
אמרתי אלהים אתם וגו' (תה' פ"ב, ו'), ואתם קלקלתם את העצה אחר מ'
יום, אכן כאדם תמותון וגו' (שם, ז'). אמר הקב"ה: במה שהטבתי לכם, בו
הכעסתם אותי, אני אמרתי: ונתתי את חן העם הזה בעיני מצרים,
ושאלה אשה וגו' (שמ' ג', כ"א–כ"ב), ובו עשו את המעשה הרע, שנ' מה
לעשות עוד לכרמי וגו' (יש' ה', ד').

בוא וראה כמה טובות עשה להם הקב"ה, סכך עליהם ענני כבוד,
האיר להם בלילה בעמוד אש, שנ' פרש ענן למסך וגו' (תה' ק"ה, ל"ט),
והוריד להם את המן, והגיז להם את ....

[בין דף נ"ו ודף נ"ז חסר דף אחד כנראה.]

[לסדר קי"ד (ט"ז): במדבר ט"ז, א'.]

[ו י ק ח ק ר ח.] .... (דף נ"ז, ע"א) ישראל. יעקב ביקש רחמים על עצמו
שלא יהא ב[סודם], שנ' [בסו]דם אל תב[וא] נפשי (בר' מ"ט, ו'), זה זמרי, ובקהלם
אל תחד כבודי (שם), זה קרח ועדתו, שכפ[רו בכבו]דו שלהקב"ה.
[א ל י א ב], שאיבד ליבו מן התורה; ו א ו ן, שהלך באנינות; ב ן פ ל ת,
שנעשו בימיו פלאים הרבה. אבל און, אשתו פילטתו, הה"ד חכמות נשים
בנתה ביתה (מש' י"ד, א'), זו אשתו שלאון, ואולת בידה [תהרס]נו (שם),
זו אשתו שלקרח. אמרה ליה אתתיה דאון לבעלה: בקש[ת] למהוי
כמשה; אמר לה: לאו; אמרה ליה: אם משה רב, את תלמידיה, ואם קרח
רבא, את תלמידיא, למה לך האי; אמר לה: מאי אעביד, קא מפכרנא בקרח;
אמרה ליה: תיב את בביתא, ואנא מפלטיא לך מקרח. סתרתיה לשערה,
היתה יושבת ושורקת למזייה, ויתבא אבבא, כל דאתא, חזייה, תב.
כיון שפתחה הארץ את פיה והיתה מבקשת לבלוע את און, והיה און יושב
על מטתו, והיתה מבקשת לבלוע אותו, עמדה אשתו ואחזה במטה,
ואמרה: רבון העולמים, כבר נשבע בשמך הגדול שלא יהא במחלוקת
בעולם, מה שמך חי וקיים, אף זה, אם יכפור בשבועה, אתה חי וקיים
שתפרע ממנו. לאחר כך אמרה לו: קום צא; אמר לה: [מ]תבייש
אני ממשה רבינו; אמרה לו: אף אני אעשה זאת עמך. יצאה ועמדה בדרכו
שלמשה, כשעבר משה, היתה צווחת ובוכה. אמר משה: מה טיבה שלאשה [זו],
שמא יש לה דין; אמרו לו: רבינו, אשתו שלאון היא, וכך היה המעשה.

חבל על נשותיהן, עכשיו יהיו אלמנות חיות; אמרה לה מרים: ולמה;
אמרה צפרה: שיפרשו בעליהן מהם; אמרה צפרה: שמיום שדיבר עם
משה בסיני עד היום פירש ממטתו; אמרה לה מרים: וכי משה נדבר בלבד
עם השכינה, והלא אהרן בא אצל אשתו, ואני ובעלי אוכלין על שולחן אחד,
ולמה הוא פירש ממך, שנ' ויאמרו הרק אך במשה דבר י"י וגו' (שם,
י"ג, ב'). ולפי שריגלה בלשונה, לקת בגופה. לכך נסמכה פרשת מרגלים
לפרשת מרים.

ש ל ח ל ך א נ ש י ם. אמר לו הקב"ה: שלח אתה מדעתך, והיכן
פירושו שלדבר, ותקרבון אלי כולכם ותאמרו וגו' (דב' א', כ"ב), אמר
הקב"ה: אני הייתי מהלך לפניכם, שנ' וי"י הולך לפניהם יומם (שמ'
י"ג, כ"א), עכשיו אתם שולחין אנשים לפניכם. לפיכך אמר לו הקב"ה
ש ל ח ל ך א נ ש י ם.

בוא וראה יש בני אדם ששמותם נאים ומעשיהם כעורין, כגון אחאב,
אח לחכמה ואב לע"ז, צדקיה בן כנענה (דף נ"ו, ע"ב), וכיוצא בו. ואילו
הן ששמותם נאים ומעשיהם נ[אים]: אליצור בן שדיאור, שלומיאל בן
צורישדי, נחשון בן עמינדב, ומ[עשיה]ם נאים, שהקריבו חנוכת המזבח, שנ'
ויהי המקריב וגו' (במ' ז', י"ב, ל', ל"ו). ואילו שש[מותם כעורי]ם
ומעשיהן נאים, שבנו בית [מקדש] שני: בני בקבוק, בני חקוקה, בני
[חרחור] (עז' ב', נ"א). ו[אילו ששמותם מכוערין, אלו המרגלים: ג ד י
ב ן ס ו ס י, ב ו ק י ב ן י ג ל י, נ ח ב י ב ן ו פ [ס י] (במ' י"ג,
י"א, י"ד), [ומע]שיהם מכוערים.

א ר ץ א ו כ ל ת י ו ש ב י ה ה י א (שם, ל"ב). והם לא ידעו כי
טובה עשה הקב"ה עמהם, שכל מקום שהיו נכנסין היה ראש העיר מת, מיד
והיו כל בני העיר נטפלין בו ולא היו אלו משגיחין עליהן, וכן בכל
עיר ועיר, מדינה ומדינה. וכן עתיד הקב"ה לעשות באחרית הימים,
שנ' וזאת תהיה המגפה אשר יגוף י"י את כל העמים וגו' (זכ' י"ד, י"ב).

ולמה קרא ליהושע בן נון (במ' י"ג, ט"ז), שהיה שמו הושע, אמר לו:
יה יהושיעך מעצת המרגלים.

[לסדר קי"ב (י"ג): במדבר י"ד, י"א.]

פס'. ע ד א נ ה י נ א צ ו נ י. זש"ה לכן כאכול קש לשון אש
(יש' ה', כ"ד), ולמה כל אילו, כי מאסו את תורת י"י צבאות וגו'
(שם). לכך אמר משה עד אנה ינאצוני, ואומר לא אבו לעצתי וגו' (מש'
א', ל'), אמר הקב"ה לישראל: כל טובה שיעצתי עליכם, קלקלתם אותה
ופרעתם אותה, שנ' ותפרעו כל עצתי וגו' (שם, כ"ה); מתחלה אמרתי למשה:
וארד להצילו מיד מצרים (שמ' ב', ח'), ואתם לא עשיתם כך אלא אמרתם:

מרים ואהרן. במשה מה כתיב, וירד י"י בעמוד ענן וגו' (במ' י"ב, ה'),
ולמה יצאו שניהם והניחו את משה באהל, שאין אומרין שבחו של אדם
בפניו, שנ' בכל ביתי נאמן הוא (שם, ז'), בנחת. אם יהיה נביאכם (שם, ו'),
אמר להם: הנביאים שאמרתם בחלומות וחזונות הייתי מדבר עמהם, ולא
כן נהגתי עם משה, שנ' לא כן עבדי משה (שם, ז'), כי כל מה שלמעלן
ושלמטן גליתי לו, פה אל פה אדבר בו וגו' (שם, ח'). ויחר אף י"י בם
וילך (שם, ט'), וכיון שנסתלקה השכינה, מיד, והנה מרים מצורעת
כשלג (שם, י'). ולפי שאמר אהרן, אל נא תהי כמת (שם, י"ב), מיד
נתפלל משה עליה, שנ' ויצעק משה אל י"י לאמר וגו' (שם, י"ג). ראה
חיבתן שלצדיקים, שמתוך ירידתן, שם היא עלייתן, מרים המתינה שעה
אחת לדעת מה יעשה באחיה, שנ' ותתצב אחותו מרחוק וגו' (שמ' ב', ד'),
ובשביל שנתעכבה על משה [ש]עה אחת, שנ' ותתצב אחותו, אמר הקב"ה:
יהי משה ואהרן וארון וכל ישראל ממתינין לה עד שתטהר, שנ' ואחר נסעו
העם מחצרות וגו' (במ' י"ב, ט"ז). ללמדך שבמדה שאדם מודד, בה
מודדין לו. ומה ראה לומר אחר מעשה מרים שלח לך אנשים,
שהיה צפוי לפני הקב"ה שמרגלים באין ואומרין לשון הרע, לפיכך סמך
הקב"ה העניין זה לזה, כדי שידעו הכל ענשו שללשון הרע, וללמדך
שהנגעין באין על לשון הרע.

פס'. אלה שמות האנשים אשר שלח משה וגו' (שם,
י"ג, ט"ז). מה ראה משה להוסיף על ש[מון] (דף נ"ו, ע"א) שליהושע יוד,
שכלב בן יפונה נטל שכרו מן הארץ, שנ' זולתי כלב בן יפונה הוא
יראה וגו' (דב' א', ל"ו), אבל יהושע נטל שכר עש[רת] המרגלים.

כי חזק הוא ממנו (במ' י"ג, ל"א), ועוד אמרו, ושם ראינו
את הנפילים (שם, ל"ג). אמר ר' יהודה על השנייה לקו, או
על הראשונה לקו, אלא כשאמרו וכן היינו בעיניה[ם] (שם),
כחגב[ים], [ראי]תם מה שעשיתי בפניכם. וגרמו לעצמן כמספר הימים אשר
תרתם את הארץ וגו' (שם, י"ד, י"ד). ולא דיים שלא נכנסו לארץ,
אלא ופגריכם אתם יפלו במדבר הזה (שם, ל"ב). ...שלבשר ודם, גזר עליהם
שלא יכנסו לארץ, אבל לעתיד לבוא הקב"ה הוא משלח, וכל ישראל
מתכנסין לארץ, ורואין בנחמות, שנ' הנה אני שולח לכם את אליה הנביא וגו'
(מלא' ג', כ"ג).

פס'. שלח לך אנשים. אמר ר' יוחנן למה נסמכה פרשת
מרגלים לפרשת מרים, מפני שריגלה בלשונה ודיברה במשה, נביאכם (במ'
י"ב, ו'), כמרים ואהרן כ[הן] גדול, מדברים במשה, שכתוב בו ולא
קם נביא עוד בישראל כמשה (דב' ל"ד, י'), אלא כשאמר הקב"ה למשה
אספה לי ע' איש וגו' (במ' י"א, ט"ז), ובשעה שנאספו היו יוצאין אל אהל
מועד, היתה מרים וצפרה יושבות ומביטות ורואות אותן; התחילה מרים
אומרת: אשריהן שלנשותיהן שלאילו, עכשיו יהיו בעליהן נביאים; אמרה צפרה:

תהי בסובאי יין וגו' (מש' כ"ג, י"ט), כי סובא וזולל יורש וגו' (שם, כ'),
בכל מקום יורש ממון, וכאן יורש מן נפשות.

ר' אומ' לימדתך תורה דרך ארץ, שלא יהא אדם אוכל בשר אלא עד
שיתאוה לו, לכן הוא מזכיר שלש מדות, וכי ירחיב י"י אלהיך את גבולך
ואמרת אוכלה בשר וגו' (דב' י"ב, כ'). אמר ר' שמעון תזבח ואכלת בשר
(שם, ט"ו), הרי ג'. אמר ר' שמעון רק חזק לבלתי אכול הדם (שם, כ"ג),
ומה הדם שנפשו שלא[דם] היתה ממנו, הפורש ממנו מקבל שכר, דברים
שנפשו שלאדם נתאוה להם ומחמדתם, הפורש מהם על אחת כמה וכמה
זוכה לו ולתולדותיו עד סוף כל הדורות. וכל מי שמקיים מצות שחיטה ומצות
הדם, ומשמר פיו מנבלות וטרפות ושקצים ורמשים, זוכה לבהמות וליתן
חיו שדי, ולראות בכל טובות ונחמות שעתיד הקב"ה להראות לצדיקים
ולשמחן בהן לעתיד לבוא, שנ' מה רב טובך אשר צפנת ליריאיך פעלת לחוסים
וגו' (תה' ל"א, ב').

[לסדר קי"א (י"ב): במדבר י"ג, א'–ב'.]

ש ל ח ל ך. זש"ה כחומץ לשנים וכעשן לעינים וגו' (משלי י', כ"ו),
וכתיב מקצה רגלים חמס שותה שולח דברים ביד כסיל (שם, כ"ו, ו'), וכי
כסילים היו, והרי כתיב ש ל ח ל ך א נ ש י ם, ובכל מקום ש[נ']
אנשים בני אדם צדיקים הן, שכן כתיב ויאמר משה אל יהושע בחר לנו
וגו' (שמ' י"ז, ט'), וכן חנה אומרת ונתת לאמתך זרע אנשים (ש"א, א', י"א),
ולמה נקראו אילו כסילים, אלא מפני שהוציאו דבה על הארץ, שנ' ומוציא
(דף נ"ה, ע"ב) דבה הוא כסיל (מש' י', י"ח), וכל מי שהוא מוציא דבה,
הקב"ה מחתם גזר דינו, שנ' וימותו האנשים מוציאי וגו' (במ' י"ד, ל"ז). ואילו
בני אדם גדולים היו, ועשו עצמן כסילים, ועליהם אמר משה כי דור תהפוכות
המה (דב' ל"ב, כ'), ומניין שהיו גדולים, שנבחרו מכל ישראל על צווי
שלהקב"ה, שנ' וישלח אותם משה ממדבר פארן על פי י"י
וגו' (במ' י"ג, ג'), ואחר כך לסוף מ' יום נהפכו ועשו כל אותה הצרה, וגרמו
לדור שילקה אותה המכה. הוי כי דור תהפוכות המה. ומניין שנתבררו
צדיקים מכל שבט ושבט. . . . .

מ ה כתיב למעלה מן הענין, ותדבר מרים ואהרן במשה וגו'
(שם, י"ב, א'), וכי אשה כושית לקח, צפורה מדיינית היית, מה כושי ניכר
במראהו, כך הייתה צפורה ניכרת במראיה ובמעשים הטובים מכל הנשים.
לכך אמר שלמה ברב דברים לא יחדל פשע וגו' (מש' י', י"ט), לא
שהיה יושב ושותק, אלא ח ו ש ך ש פ ת י ו מלהשיח בחבירו, ואומר כי
יש דברים הרבה וגו' (קה' ו', י"א), שלא יושב ומשיח בחבירך, תן דעתך
שלא תהא יושב ומשיח בחבירך, תן דעתך שלא תענש, שאין גדולים

שנ' ותנח עליהם הרוח (שם, כ"ז). ולא עוד אלא שהזקנים לא נתפרשו
שמותן, והללו נתפרשו שמותן. והזקנים לא נתבארה נבואתן, ואילו היו
מתנבאין על גוג ומגוג. בקש הקב"ה לעשות חזקיהו משיח וסנחריב גוג
ומגוג, אלא גרם החטא ונתאחר הקץ עד שילוח אליהו, שנ' הנה אנכי שולח
לכם את אליה הנביא וגו' (מלא' ג', כ"ג).

ולמה ע' איש (במ' י"א, ט"ז), כנגד ע' אומות, שאם יתיעצו על
ישראל, תהא תפלתם של ע' סותרת עצמם. ד"א כנגד שירדו למצרים.

ואם תאמר שנטלו אילו הזקנים מנבואתו שלמשה, יכול שמא חסרה
נבואתו כלום, ולמה היה דומה, לנר שהיה דולק ודולק ממנו נרות ולא חסרה
אורו, כך לא חסרה נבואתו שלמשה, שכתוב ולא קם נביא עוד בישראל וגו'
(דב' ל"ד, י'). אמר הקב"ה: בעולם הזה יחידים נתנבאו, אבל לעולם
הבא כל ישראל יעשו נביאים, שנ' והיה אחרי כן אשפוך את רוחי על
כל בשר וגו' (יו' ג', א').

[לסדר ק"י[a] (י"א): במדבר י"א, כ"ג.]

פס'. ויאמר י"י אל משה היד י"י תקצר וגו'. זש"ה
היד י"י תקצר. מי ימלל גבורות י"י (תה' ק"ו, כ'). מי יוכל למלל גבורתו,
לא מלאך ולא שרף ולא גדול יכולין לתנות כל שבחו של הקב"ה, אלא
מקצת שבחו. החמה הזאת אחת היא מן הבריות שלרקיע, היא נראית קטנה,
וכשהיא עומדת על כחה בתקופת תמוז היא נותנת כל הארץ תחתיה
וממלאה כל העולם כולו. ואם החמה, שהיא אחת מבריות שלהקב"ה, אין אדם
יכול לעמוד כנגד[ה], (דף נ"ה, ע"א) הקב"ה על אחת כמה וכמה.
וכל מה שהצדיקים עתידין לבוא, ממה שהקב"ה נותן להם חכמה, וכל
אחד ואחד מהם פיו נובע שבחות וזמירות להקב"ה, וכל מה שהן עתידין לשבח,
אינן מגיעין לקצת שבחו.

יתרומם שמו של הקב"ה שדבריו הם קיימים לעולם ולעולמי עולמים, שנ'
כן יהיה דברי אשר יצא מפיו וגו' (יש' נ"ה, י"א). לכך הדבר מתמיה
למשה כמה שקראתי לך ולעם הזה, היד י"י תקצר, אלא עתה
תראה וגו', לפי שמשה תמה מן העניין, אמר: מאין לי בשר וגו' (במ' י"א, י"ג),
הצאן ובקר וגו' (שם, כ"ב), לכך הכתוב משיבו: היד י"י תקצר. מיד
ורוח נסע מאת י"י ויגז שלוים וגו' (שם, ל"א). מה
כתיב שם, הבשר עודנו בין שניהם וגו' (שם, ל"ג), כיון
שהיה נותן לתוך פיו, לא ספק לחתכו עד שנפשו יוצאה, שנ' ואף י"י
חרה בעם (שם), מלמד שלא הביא הקב"ה עליהם מכה קשה מזו
שיצאו ממצרים. ויקרא שם המקום ההוא קברות וגו' (שם, ל"ד),
יכול כן היה שמו מקודם, אלא ראה מה העונות גורמין. אמר שלמה אל

[לסדר ק"י (י"א): במדבר י"א, ט"ז.]

פס'. אספה לי שבעים איש. זש"ה טוב י"י למעוז ביום
צרה (נח' א', ז'). כיון שאמר הקב"ה למשה אספה לי וגו', אמר לו: אל
תביאם אלא מאותן שנתנו נפשם על ישראל במצרים, שהיו לוקין בשבילן, שנ'
ויכו שוטרי בני ישראל וגו' (שמ' ה', י"ד). לקיים מה שנ' טוב י"י למעוז
ביום צרה.

כמה אמות צריך אדם לעמוד מפני הזקן. כך שנו חכמים: בתוך
ארבע אמות צריך אדם לעמוד מפני הזקן, שנ' מפני שיבה תקום וגו' (וי'
י"ט, ל"ב), ושואל בשלומו בתוך ד' אמות. ההדור שאמרה תורה, והדרת
(שם), שלא יעמוד במקומו, ולא ישב במקומו, ולא סותר את דבריו,
וקודם לכל ביציאה ובכניסה. ואתן אותם ראשים על העם (שמ' י"ח, כ"ה),
שלא יהי אדם מתעצל מפני הזקן. אמרו רבותינו ז"ל לוקן ד' אמות, עבר,
יושב לו; כהן גדול, מי שהוא רואהו עד שהוא נתכסה, מאי טעמיה, והיה
כצאת משה האהלה יקומו כל העם (שם, ל"ג, ח'); נשיא, כשנכנס, כל העם
עומדין לפניו, ואין רשות לאחד מהן לישב עד שיאמר להן שבו; אב בית
דין, שנכנס, עושין לו שתי שורות, רוצה נכנס בזו, רוצה נכנס בזו;
חכם שנכנס ——— אמרו רבותינו ז"ל כל מי שהוא נתמנה בכסף אין
עומדין מלפניו, ואין קורין אותו רבי, וטלית שעליו כמרדעת שלחמור.

וכיון שנתמנו הזקנים, אלדד ומידד היו שם. ואיך נתמנו הזקנים, כשאמר
הקב"ה למשה אספה לי ע' איש, אמר משה: אם אני לוקח מכל שבט
ה' ה', הרי הן ס', ואם אני לוקח ו' ו', הרי ע"ב. לקח ששה. ר' נחמיה
אומר היאך עשה משה רבינו, נטל ע"ב פתקין, וכתב על ע' מהן זקן,
והניח שנים חלקים, וטרפן בבת אחת. אמר (דף נ"ד, ע"ב) להן: קחו בבת
אחת אחד ואחד. כל שנמצאת פתקו כתוב, אמר לו: נתמנית זקן, עד שנשתיירו
אלדד ומידד, מצאו שנים חלקים. אמר לו ר' ברכיה: ועוד מחלוקת
בדבר, היה להן לומר אם היה פתקי כתוב, היו לוקחין אותו, אלא היאך
עשה משה, לקח שבעים פתקין וכתב זקן, וע"ב חלקין, וטרפן בבת אחת, ואמר
להן: קחו כל אחד ואחד אחת. אם עולה בידו פתק כתוב, אמר לו:
כבר נתמנית זקן. ואם עלה בידו פתק חלק, היה אומר לו: אם היה
עולה בידך כתוב, היית ראוי להתמנות, כבר יש שם פתק כתוב. עד שלקחו
כולן, ונשתיירו אלדד ומידד, שנ' וישארו שני אנשים במחנה וגו'
(במ' י"א, כ"ו).

יהי שמו לעולם מבורך שאינו מקפח שכר כל בריה, על שמיעטו
עצמן ואמרו: אין אנו כדאי להתמנות, נמצאו יתירין על אותם הזקנים,
שהזקנים לא היתה נבואתן אלא משלמשה, דכתיב ואצלתי מן הרוח
אשר עליך וגו' (שם, י"ז). ואלדד ומידד היתה נבואתן [ן משל] הקב"ה,

[לסדר ק"ט (י'): במדבר י', א'–ב'.]

עשה לך שתי חצוצרות כסף. שאלו תלמידיו את רבינו הקדש:
היאך היו תוקעין להכניס את השבת. אמר להם: היה חזן הכנסת בערב שבת
אחר חצות היום עולה לגג גדול או לחומה גבוהה בצורה שבעיר, והיה תוקע
ראשונה, כל שהיו עושין מלאכה בשדות הרחוקי[ם] היו נכנסין; בשנייה, כל
שהיו סמוכים לעיר נכנסין; בשלישית, היו טומנין את החמין, ומדליקין
את הנרות; גמר מלתקוע, אפילו קדירה בידה שלאשה להטמין או נר
להדליק, היתה מנחת אותה לארץ.

פס'. עשה לך שתי חצוצרות כסף. זש"ה ויהי בישורון מלך
וגו' (דב' ל"ג, ה'), מלך, זה משה, אמר לו הקב"ה: משה, עשיתיך מלך,
מה המלך הזה, כשהוא יוצא למלחמה, תוקעין לפניו, כך אתה, כשתהא מבקש
להכניס את ישראל ולצאת למלחמה, תוקעין לפניך.

אמר ר' יהודה עשה לך, משלך, ולך אתה עושה, ולא לאחר,
אתה משתמש בהן, ולא אחר משתמש בהן. תדע לך, שהרי יהושע שהיה תלמידו
לא נשתמש בהן, אלא בשופר, כשבא ליריחו, נתכנסו לשם ז' אומות, שנ' ותעברו
את הירדן ותבאו אל יריחו וגו' (יה' כ"ד, י"א), וכי ז' אומות היו בעלי יריחו, אלא
אם נכבשת יריחו לפני ישראל, כל הארץ נכבשת להם, לפיכך נתכנסו לתוכה, ומה
כתיב, וירייעו כל העם ויתקעו בשופרות וגו' (שם, ו', כ'), מלמד שאפילו יהושע
תלמידו לא נשתמש בהן. לכך כתיב עשה לך, שאין אדם משתמש בהן אלא אתה,
שאתה מלך, ודוד המלך בבית המקדש, שנ' ויעמד הלוים על עמדם, והשיר משורר
וגו' (דה"ב, כ"ט, כ"ה, כ"ח). אמרו רבותינו ז"ל דוד ושלמה העמידו חלוקי
השיר, והיו הלוים עומדין על קרבן ואומרין שיר לפני מי שאמר והיה העולם.

שנו חכמים ז"ל ג' תקיעות היו תוקעין להבטיל את העם מן המלאכה, כיצד,
חזן הכנסת נוטל את החצוצרות ועולה בגג גבוה וכול' לעיל.

השבת בחצוצרות היתה מתקדשת, וכן ראשי חדשים, וכן המועדות, שנ'
וביום שמחתכם ובמועדיכם וגו' (במ' י', י'). (דף נ"ד, ע"א)
וכן כשהיו השונאין באין עליהן, בחצוצרות היו תוקעין, שנ' וכי תבאו
מלחמה וגו' (שם, ט'). ואף כשהלכו להנקם מן המדינים, לא נקמו
מהם אלא בחצוצרות, שנ' וימסרו מאלפי ישראל אלף וגו' (שם, ל"א, ה'–ו').
וכן כשהיו נוסעין, בהן היו תוקעין, שנ' ובהקהיל את הקהל
תתקעו וגו' (שם, י', ז'). וכשעמדו על הר סיני לקבל את התורה, שמעו
קול תקיעת שופר, שנ' ויהי קול השופר וגו' (שמ' י"ט, י"ט). וכן לעתיד,
הגליות מתכנסות לירושלם בשופר, שנ' והיה ביום ההוא יתקע בשופר
גדול ובאו וגו' (יש' כ"ז, י"ג).

וכל כליו, שולחן וכל כליו, מנורה וכל כליה, כיור וכנו, ונמשחו אהרן ובניו
כל שבעת ימי המלואים, וממנו כהנים גדולים ומלכים, וכולו קיים לעולם,
שנ' זה לדורותיכם (שם, ל"א).

[לסדר ק"ח (ט'): במדבר ח', א'–ב'.]

ב ה ע ל ו ת ך. זש"ה פתח דבריך יאיר מבין פתאים (תה' קי"ט, ק"ל).
תתפאר עד לאין חקר, תשתבח עד לאין מספר, תפארתך בפי עליונים,
שבחך בפי תחתונים, העליונים והתחתונים אין יכולין לעמוד על שבחך,
שנ' מי ימלל גבורות י"י ישמיע כל תהלתו (שם, ק"ו, ב'). אמר ר' יהודה
מה פתח דבריך יאיר, אתה סבור שהשמים והארץ נבראו תחלה, כמה
שנ' בראשית ברא אלהים את השמים (בר' א', א'), ואחר כך ויאמר אלהים
יהי אור (שם, ג'). הוי אומר פתח דבריך יאיר. ואף במשכן, כיון שנכנסה
שכינה לתוכה נתמלא אור, שנ' ונהורא עמיה שרי (דנ' ב', כ"ב), וכיון שנגמרה
מלאכת המשכן נתמלא זיו השכינה, שנ' ולא יכול משה לבוא אל אהל מועד
וגו' (שמ' מ', ל"ה). וכשם שבמעשה בראשית דיבור ראשון א̇ו̇ר, כך במעשה
המשכן תחילת דיבור לא דיבר עם משה אלא בא̇ור, שנ' ב ה ע ל ו ת ך
א ת ה נ י ר ו ת. שמא תאמר הקב"ה צריך אור משל בשר ודם, והלא
כתיב ונהורה עמיה שרי, וכתיב עוטה אור כשלמה וגו' (תה' ק"ד, ב'), והרי
השמש שנתן לו הקב"ה מתולדות האש של מעלה, והוא יוצא ומבהיק
כל העולם, ואין כח בעין לראותו, ולאור נירות הוא צריך, ומה הוא ב ה ע ל ו ת ך
א ת ה נ י ר ו ת, בשביל להעלות את ישראל בין האומות.

א ל מ ו ל פ נ י ה מ נ ו ר ה. אמר הקב"ה: מי הקדימני ואשלם וגו'
(אי' מ"א, ג'), הדלקתי לפניכם במדבר, שנ' וי"י הולך לפניכם יומם
(שמ' י"ג, כ"א), והדלקתם לפני במשכן, ואני פורע לכם לעתיד, שנ' כי הנה
החשך יכסה ארץ וגו' (יש' ס', ב'), ואיני מוסר אתכם לאור החמה והלבנה,
שנ' לא יהיה לך עוד השמש לאור יומם ולנוגה הירח לא יאיר לך וגו'
(שם, י"ט).

פס'. ב ה ע ל ו ת ך. ראה מה כתיב למעלה מן העניין, וידבר אליו
(במ' ז', פ"ט), מה דבר אליו, חנוכת לוים, שלמעלה מזו כתיב קרבן נשיאים,
(דף נ"ג, ע"ב) ואין בה ללוים חנוכה. אמר הקב"ה: עתידין הלוים לעשות חנוכה
בפני עצמן, [שנ' ושיציא] בית אלהא דנא וגו', ועבדו כהניא וליואי וגו' (עז'
ו', ט"ו–ט"ז).

ולמה הקריבו אפרים ומנשה ב[חנוכת] המזבח שביעי ושמיני, מפני ששמר
יוסף במצרים שבת ומילה, לפיכך נתן הקב"ה לבניו ז' וח' באמצע נשיאים,
ואומר תן חלק לז' וגם שמונה (קה' י"א, ב').

]לקריאה ביום א' של חנוכה: במדבר ז', א'.[

פס'. ויהי ביום כלות משה. זש"ה היטיבה ברצונך את ציון וגו'
(תה' נ"א, כ'), ומה כתיב שם, אז תחפוץ זבחי צדק עולה וכליל וגו'
(שם, כ"א). אמר ר' יהודה כשנעשה המשכן, הקריבו הנשיאים קימעא,
אמרו לפניו: רבונו שלעולם, לפי שעה ולפי הדרך הקרבנו לפניך, אבל
כשיבנה בית המקדש אנו מקריבין הרבה, שנ' אז יעלו על מזבחך פרים (שם).
וכן הקריב שלמה את זבח השלמים אשר זבח לי"י בקר עשרים ושנים אלף
וצאן ק"כ אלף (מ"א, ח', ס"ג).

אמר ר' ירמיה בששה חדשים נגמרה מלאכת המשכן, ומפרקו ומעמידו,
וסודר עליו קרבנות, שכך שנו חכמים בכל יום ויום היה משה מעמיד את
המשכן וכל בקר ובקר מקריב עליו קרבנות ומפרקו, ובח' העמידו ולא
פרקו, שנ' ויהי ביום כלות משה וגו', שכלו הקימותיו. ולמה היה
אהל מועד דומה, למערה שהיא נתונה על שפת הים, והעלה הים לגליו והציף
את המערה, נתמלאה המערה מהים והם לא חסר כלום, כך אהל מועד משכינה,
היך דכתיב ויכס הענן את אהל מועד וגו' (שמ' מ', ל"ד).

פס'. וביום הקם את המשכן (במ' ט', ט"ו). אותו היום שהקים
משה את המשכן אחד בניסן היה, שנ' בחודש הראשון באחד לחודש הוקם
המשכן (שמ' מ', י"ז). נקרא יום שמיני, שהוא יום ח' לשבעת הנשיאים, היך
דכתיב ויהי ביום השמיני קרא משה (וי' ט', א'). יום ראשון, דכתיב בו
ויהי המקריב ביום הראשון וגו' (במ' ז', י"ב), ונקרא ראשון
לימות שבת, ראשון לחדשים, ראשון לירידת אש, ראשון לחנוכת המזבח,
ראשון לתלמידים, ראשון לקרבן נשיאים דכתיב ויהי המקריב וגו'.

בכל מקום אתה מוצא יהודה תחלה לשבטים: בירידת הים, שנ' היתה
יהודה לקדשו (תה' קי"ד, ב'); בדגלים הוא תחלה, שנ' ונסע דגל מחנה יהודה
(במ' ו', י"ד), ואומר ראשונה יסעו (שם, ב', ט'); במלחמה, ויאמר י"י יהודה
יעלה בתחלה (שו' א', ב'); וכן בקרבנות, ויהי המקריב ביום
הראשון נחשון וגו'. את מוצא עד שלא הוקם המשכן, היה הקול נפסק
ולא היה יוצא חוץ לאהל מועד. יכול מפני שהקול נמוך, ת"ל קול י"י
בכוח וגו' (תה' כ"ט, ד').

ויקדש אותו (במ' ז', א'), ואחר נאמר וימשחם ויקדש
אותם, אלא מה שהיה מושח כל אחד ואחד היה מושח כולן כאחד.
וימשחם, משיחה בעולם הזה ומשיחה לעולם הבא. אמר ר' יהודה
שמן (דף נ"ג, ע"א)]המש[חה שעשה משה במדבר, מעשה נסים נעשה בו
מתחלה ועד סוף, שמתחלה]לא[היה עקר]ון[אלא י"ב לוג, שנ' וקידה חמשה
מאות בשקל הקודש (שמ' ל', כ"ד), ואם לסוך את העצים לא היה מפסיק
שהאור בולע וכן העצים בולעין, וממנו נמשחו משכן וכל כליו, מזבח

מ"ב, י"ח). אמר הקב"ה: אתה לא נתפתה, אע[מיד] לך בנים ומונה אותם
עם השבטים, ואין שבט מפסיק בין קרבן שלשני בניך. והקריבו זה אחר
זה, ביום השביעי נשיא לבני אפרים, ביום השמיני נשיא
לבני (דף נ"ב, ע"א) מנשה.

לקיים מה שנ' מתהלך בתומו צדיק וגו' (מש' כ', ז'), שכיון שעשה מצוה
על מנת ליטול שכרה מיד, כגון אם היה אדם חטא כמה פעמים עד
שלא יעשה מצוה אחת, ואם באה עליו עת צרה הוא מתרעם ואומר: היכן
הוא המצוה שעשיתי שלא עמדה לי, והוא מבקש שכר המצוה ואינו מניח לבניו
כלום. וממי אתה למד מאבותינו, זכור לאברהם ליצחק ולישראל עבדיך
(שמ' ל"ב, י"ג), מה כתיב אחריו, סלחתי כדבריך (במ' י"ד, כ"ז). וכתיב וזרע
צדיקים נמלט (מש' י"א, כ"א), הוי מתהלך בתומו צדיק וגו'. וכן יוסף כמה
יסורין עברו עליו, בתחלה לעבד נמכר יוסף (תה' כ"ה, י"ז), ועל ידי שהשלים
נפשו להקב"ה והלך בדרכיו ושמר מצותיו, הצילו הקב"ה מכל אותן
הצרות וזיכה לבניו אחריו להעמיד שני נשיאים כאחד, לבני יוסף לאפרים
(במ' א', י'). וכן לעתיד לבוא מעמיד ממנו משיח מלחמות, שנ' בכור שורו
הדר לו (דב' ל"ג, י"ז).

וכן מצינו בימי חשמונאי שהיו ישראל בצרות גדולות ממלכות יון,
ועל ידי שהשלימו בני חשמונאי נפשם על ישראל ועל התורה, הצמיח להן הקב"ה
ישועה, ועשה להם נסים, והצילן מיד אויביהן, והפילן לפניהם, ונצחו
אותם. וכיון שחזרו בשלום ובאו לבית המקדש, וגדרו י"ג פרצות שפירצו מלכי
יון, וכנגדן י"ג שמחות, וחינכו את המזבח, ונתנו שבח והודיה להקב"ה,
והדליקו נירות המנורה בשמונת ימי חנוכה ויום טוב שלעצרת, שכך שנו
חכמים ימים שמונה עשר ולילה אחת חיבין לגמור בהן את ההלל בכל שנה,
ואלו הן, ח' ימי החג, וח' ימי חנוכה, ויום שלעצרת, ויום טוב של פסח.

פס'. לשמיע בקול תודה (תה' כ"ו, ז'), אילו הקרבנות. ולספר כל
נפלאותיך (שם), אמר ר' אבון זה ההלל: שיש בו לשעבר, ויש בו לדורות,
ויש בהן לימות המשיח, ויש בו לימות גוג ומגוג, ויש בו לעתיד לבוא.
פס'. בצאת ישראל ממצרים (שם, קי"ד, א'), לשעבר; לא לנו
(שם, קט"ו, א'), לדורות; אהבתי כי ישמע י"י (שם, קט"ז, א'),
לימות המשיח; אסרו חג בעבותים (שם, קי"ח, כ"ז), לימות גוג ומגוג;
אלי אתה ואודך (שם, כ"ח), לעתיד לבוא. כן יאמר הקב"ה,
שעשה נסים לאבותינו בימים האלו, וכשם שזכיתם וקראתם את ההלל
ונתתם שבח והודיה לפני הקב"ה, כך תזכו לעתיד לומר (דף נ"ב, ע"ב) שיר
חדש עם כל ישראל בבנין ביתו, שנ' שירו לי"י שיר חדש וגו' (תה'
צ"ח, א').

ת ב ר כ ו. יכול יהי מברכין אותן בקול נמוך, ת״ל יברכך י׳׳י (במ׳
ה׳, כ״ג). יברכך, בממון, וישמרך, מכל רע, יאר י׳׳י וגו׳
(שם, כ״ה), יעמיד ממך בני תורה שהיא אור, שנ׳ כי נר מצוה ותורה אור
(מש׳ ו׳, כ״ג). ויחנך, בחן, כל מקום שאתה הולך, כמו שנ׳ (דף נ״א, ע״ב)
[ומצא חן ושכל טוב] וגו׳ (שם, ג׳, ד׳). יהיו פני[ך]...........מנין...
הילדים. וישם לך שלום (במ׳ ה׳, כ״ו). אחר כל הברכות הללו
היה מביא שלום, כנגד מגיש שלום, שהשלום שקיל כנגד הכל. חביב הוא
השלום, שכל מעשים וזכיות שעשה אברהם אבינו נתברך בשלום, שנ׳ ואתה
תבוא אל אבותיך בשלום (בר׳ ט״ו, ט״ו). וכן אתה מוצא באבינו יעקב שלא
בקש מן הקב״ה אלא השלום, שנ׳ ושבתי בשלום וגו׳ (שם, כ״ח, כ״א). ובאהרן
כתיב היתה בריתי אתו החיים והשלום וגו׳ (מלא׳ ב׳, ה׳), ונתן לו הקב״ה
השלום שנ׳ הנני נותן לו את בריתי שלום (במ׳ כ״ה, י״ב). ובו נמשלה התורה,
שנ׳ דרכיה דרכי נעם וגו׳ (מש׳ א׳, י״ז), ובו עתיד הקב״ה לנחם את ישראל,
שנ׳ וישב עמי בנוה שלום (יש׳ ל״ב, י״ח).

[לסדר ק״ח (ח׳): במדבר ז׳, מ״ח.]

פס׳. ביום השביעי נשיא לבני אפרים. זש״ה תחת אבותיך
יהיו בניך (תה׳ מ״ה, י״ז). אמר ר׳ שמעון בן לוי הבנים לצדיקים הנאה
להם והנאה לעולם, מה טעם עטרת זקנים בני בנים וגו׳ (מש׳ י״ז, ו׳).
אשרי מי שזכו לו אבותיו, אשרי אדם שיש לו יתד לתלות בה. למה
זכה שבטו שליוסף להיות כשני שבטים, ליטול שני חלקים, להעמיד שני
נשיאים כאחד, ולהקריב שני ימים, אלא על ידי שביררכן יעקב אביהן,
שנ׳ המלאך הגואל אותי וגו׳ (בר׳ מ״ח, ט״ז). אשריהן הצדיקין שהן גוזרין
גזירה, והקב״ה מקים לצדיקים לעולם, שנ׳ ותגזר אומר ויקם לך וגו׳
(אי׳ כ״ב, כ״ח), וכתיב מקים דבר עבדו (יש׳ מ״ד, כ״ו). וכשם שגזר יעקב אבינו
ואמר אפרים ומנשה כראובן ושמעון יהיו לי (בר׳ מ״ח, ה׳), כך הסכים הקב״ה
עמו. לכך כתיב לבני אפרים וגו׳ (במ׳ ז׳, מ״ח), וביום
השמיני נשיא לבני מנשה וגו׳ (שם, נ״ד). וכן לעתיד לבוא,
לי גלעד ולי מנשה ואפרים מעוז ראשי וגו׳ (תה׳ ס׳, ט׳).

יהודה זכה למלוכה, ונתנה ירושה לבניו לדורות, שנ׳ כי יהודה גבר
באחיו (דה״א ה׳, ב׳). לוי זכה לכהונה ולויה. יוסף זכה לבכורה,
לפיכך נטל שני חלקים והקריב שני ימים, ועליו הכתוב אומר מי יתנך כאח
לי וגו׳ (שה״ש ח׳, א׳). כיצד, שאתה מוצא אחר כל הרעות שעשו לו
אחיו, אמר להם ועתה אל תיראו וגו׳ (בר׳ נ׳, כ״א), לפיכך נשתבח מכל
אחיו. ולא עוד אלא שהיה ירא מהקב״ה, שנ׳ את האלהים אני ירא (שם,

[לסדר ק"ד (ד'): במדבר ד', י"ז–י"ח.]

[אל תכריתו את שבט משפחת הקהתי.] ..... (דף נ"א,
ע"א) ...... ואין צריך לומר מישראל. היו טוענין הארון ...... ירמיה.[1]
אל תתמה על הדבר, הרי אלעזר נשיא על הנשיאים, שנ' ונשיאי נשיאי הלוי
[אלעזר בן אהרן הכהן] (במ' ג', ל"ב), והיה טוען משאו, שנ' ופקודת אלעזר בן
אהרן הכהן שמן המאור וגו' (שם, ד', ט"ז). להודיעך שאין גבוה לפני הקב"ה, שנ' אל
תכריתו.[2]

אמר ר' שמואל את מוצא שהיו מתמעטין, ולמה היו מתמעטין, אלא מפני
שהיו יודעין שכל מי שטוען ארון שכרו מרובה, והיו מניחין את השלחן ואת
המנורה.[3]

[בכ"י ישנו פה הפסק של שתי שורות ומחצה חלוקות, וכנראה היו חסרים
למעתיק דפים אחדים, כי השורות הבאות שייכות לדרשה על ברכת כהנים.]

[לסדר ק"ז (ז'): במדבר ו', כ"ב–כ"ג.]

[כה תברכו את בני ישראל.] ..... ומקולליו יכרתו (תה' ל"ז,
כ"ב), הם בלק ובלעם, שנ' ואת מלכי מדין הרגו על חלליהם וגו' (במ' ל"א, ח').
אמר ר' יהודה ובאי זה זכות נטלו ישראל את הברכה, היו רבותינו ז"ל
אומרין בזכותו שלאברהם, שנ' כה יהיה זרעך (בר' ט"ו, ה'), אמר הקב"ה:
חייך שעתידין כהנים לעמוד לברך בניך, הה"ד כה תברכו את בני
ישראל. אמר ר' יהודה בזכות התורה זכו ישראל לברכה הזו, שנ' כה
תאמר לבית יעקב וגו' (שמ' י"ט, ג'), בזכות כה שבסיני זכו ישראל לכה
תברכו.

אמר ר' יהושע בן לוי למה סמך פרשת נזיר לפרשת נשיאות כפים, ללמדך
שכשם שהנזיר אסור ביין, כך נשיאות כפים אסורה ביין, שנ' יין ושכר אל
תשת וגו' (וי' י', ט').

שנו חכמים כהן שהיו ידיו צבועות אסטיס או קוצה או פואה לא ישא
את כפיו, למה, שדרך בני אדם להיות מסתכלין בו. אמר ר' יהושע אם רוב העיר
כך, מותר לישא את כפיו.

שנו חכמים מנין לנשיאות כפים, שנ' וישא אהרן את ידיו אל העם ויברכם
(שם, ט', כ"ב). בעמידה ושלא בעמידה, ת"ל לעמוד לשרת בשם י' וגו'
(דב' י"ח, ה'), וכן הוא אומר ויקומו הכהנים הלויים ויברכו את העם
(דה"ב, ל', כ"ז).

כה תברכו. אמר הקב"ה: היו תולין ופורשין, ופניהם כנגד הקהל,
כדי שתשרה עליהן ברכה. ומניין שהקב"ה מברך את ישראל, ת"ל כה

[לסדר ק"ב (כ'): במדבר ב', א'–ב'.]

פס'. איש על דגלו באותות וגו'. זש"ה נרננה בישועתך
וגו' (תה' כ', ו'),[1] אמרו ישראל לפני הקב"ה: מרננים אנו בישועתך מה עשית,[2]
לכך בשמך נבוס קמינו (שם, מ"ד, ו'), שנ' (דף נ, ע"ב) ויושע י"י ביום ההוא
את וגו' (שמ' י"ד, ל'),[3] ובשם אלהינו נדגול (תה' כ', ו'), שקבע שמו בשמות שנ'
... שם שמו בישראל.[4] וכן אמר יהושע ומה תעשה לשמך הגדול (יה' ז', ט'),
מיד נענה, שנ' ויאמר י"י אל יהושע קום לך וגו' (שם, י').[5]

כמה חיבה גדולה חיבב הקב"ה את ישראל שעשאן דגלים כמלאכי השרת,[6]
שנ' איש על דגלו באותות, שהן צבאותיו שלהקב"ה, וכן הוא
אומר והוצאתי את צבאותי (שמ' ז', ד').[7] ומה ת"ל באותות לבית
אבותם, אלא בשעת פטירתו שליעקב צוה את בניו על דרכיו שלהקב"ה,
וקיבלו עליהם עול מלכות שמים,[8] משגמר חזר וצווה, אמר אליהם: כשתשאו
מטתי, תהיו נושאין אותה ביראה וכבוד, ולא יגע אדם אחר מטתי, לא גוי,
ולא אחד מן המצריים שהם טמאים, וכן עשו, שנ' וישאו אותו (בר' נ', י"ג),
ראובן ושמעון ודן,[9] מן הדרום; אפרים ומנשה ובנימין, מן המערב; דן ונפתלי
ואשר, מן הצפון; יהודה ויששכר וזבולון, מן המזרח; יוסף שהוא מלך, לא יטעון;
לוי שהוא עתיד לטעון ארון הקודש, לא יטעון, רמז זה טוען ארון שלחיים,
לא יטעון ארון שלמת; אם עשיתם כך, הקב"ה משרה אתכם דגלים דגלים.
וכשיצאו ממצרים, באו לשרות ולחנות במדבר. אמר הקב"ה למשה: עשה
אותן דגלים, אמר לפניו משה: ושומעין לי, שמא יאמר יהודה אני[10] מבקש במזרח,
וכן ראובן בדרום, וכן אשר במערב, אמר הקב"ה: אין אתה מחדש עליהן דבר,
כבר מסורת היא בידן מיעקב אביהם, כמו שהקיפו את מטתו, כך יקיפו את משכני.
לכך נאמר איש על דגלו באותות,[11] שמסורת היא בידם מאבותם.[12]

וכיצד היו שרויים, והלוויים יחנו סביב למשכן העדות וגו' (במ' א', נ"ג),
משה ואהרן ובניו מן המזרח, שנ' והחונים לפני המשכן קדמה וגו' (שם, ג', ל"ח),
והסמוכין להן יהודה שהוא מלך, כנגד משה שהוא מלך, ויששכר וזבולון עמו.
מיכן אמרי אשרי הצדיקים ואשרי שכניהם, שהיו כולם שכני תורה, נעשו כולן
בני תורה. ומן הדרום בני קהת, וסמוכין להן ראובן ושמעון וגד, ג' השבטים
שרויין בדרום עם קרח ועדתו, בעסק המחלוקת אבד, ואבדו עמו, ותפתח
הארץ וגו' (שם, ט"ז, ל"ב). ראה מה יצא משמעון במעשה זמרי. ומן המערב
בני גרשון, וסמוכין להן אפרים ומנשה ובנימין. בני מררי מן הצפון, וסמוכין להן
דן ונפתלי ואשר. כאשר הייתה חנייתן, כך הייתה נסיעתן.[13]
וכל שבט ושבט היתה מפה שלדגל ...

[בין דף נ' ודף נ"א חסר דף אחד כנראה.]

[לסדר ק"א (א'): במדבר א', א'.]

[בין דף מ"ט ודף נ' חסרים דפים אחדים.]

ו י ד ב ר   י ' י   א ל   מ ש ה   ב מ ד ב ר   ס י נ י.   [1]שנו חכמים בשלשה
דברים נתנה התורה: באש, ובמים, ובמדבר. באש, מניין, שנ' [2]והר סיני עשן כולו
וגו' (שמ' י"ט, י"ח); במים, מנין, שנ' [3]ארץ רעשה אף שמים נטפו מים (תה' ס"ח,
ט'); במדבר, מנין, שנ' ו י ד ב ר   י ' י   א ל   מ ש ה   וגו'. ולמה ניתנה
בג' דברים הללו, מה אלו חנם לכל באי העו[לם, כך][4] נאמרו אזהרות בהר סיני,
אבל העונשין והמיתות והשריפות והסקילות נאמרו בפרהסיא[5] באהל מועד,
שנ' ו י ד ב ר   י ' י   א ל   מ ש ה   ב מ ד ב ר   ס י נ י   ב א ה ל   מ ו ע ד   וגו'.
אמרו חכמים מפני מה נימנו ישראל בראש חומש הפק[ודים], וחזר ומנאן בסוף
החומש, להודיע מספרן במקום זה ובמקום אחר, שנאמר בראש החומ[ש] מספר
שבטו שלשמעון תשעה וחמשים אלף, שנ' פ ק ו ד י ה ם   ל מ ט ה   ש מ ע ו ן
ט " נ   א ל ף   וגו' (במ' א', כ"ג), ובסוף החומש מספרם כ"ג אלף ומאתים (שם,
כ"ו, י"ד), מפני מה נתמעטו, מפני מעשה זמרי.[6] כתיב ויהיו המתים במגפה כ"ד אלף
(שם, כ"ה, ט'), משבטו שלשמעון כ"ב אלף,[7] ומשאר שבטים שני אלפים.
אמר הקב"ה לזמרי בן סלוא: זקינך קינא על הזנות והרג משכם כ"ב אלף
והסתכנתי לך, ואתה עושה זנות לפני, חייך שאני פורעה לך. לכך מתו משבטו
כ"ב אלף.

פס'.   ש א ו   א ת   ר א ש   (שם, א', ב').   אתה מוצא בי' מקומות נמנו ישראל
כדכתיב ב כ י   ת ש א.[9]   ולמה הוא מונה אותם בכל שעה, שהוא מחבבן.[10]
לכך נאמר למשה שימנה אותם במדבר סיני. מה תלמוד לומר ב מ ד ב ר
ס י נ י   ב א ה ל   מ ו ע ד   (שם. א').   הדבור שקבלתם מהר סיני, עמד
להם לזכ[ות באהל מועד],[11] וכן הוא אומר חזה ציון קרית מועדינו וגו' (יש'
ל"ג, כ').

ש א ו   א ת   ר א ש.   זש"ה שרדך אגן הסהר אל יחסר המזג וגומ' (שה"ש
ז', ג'), ולמה נמשלו ב ח ט י ם,[12]   מה חטים אלו יש להן שומרין, מוציאין אותם
במדה ומכניסין אותם במדה, כך ישראל נמנין בירידתן ונמנין בעלייתן. אבל
התבן אין לו שומר, כך הגויים אין להם שומר, שנ' כל הגוים כאין נגדו וגו'
(יש' מ', י"ז). לכך נאמר ב ט נ ך   ע ר מ ת   ח ט י ם, ואומר מה לתבן את הבר
נאם י"י (יר' כ"ג, כ"ח).

ולמה בכל השבטים כתיב לבני פלוני לבני פלוני, ובנפתלי כתיב בני נפתלי
(במ' א', מ"ב), מלמד שלא היה בו נקיבות.[13]

---

* הערות לספר במדבר נמצאים להלן, דפים קד–קו.

האלהים [וגו'] (קה' ז', י"ד). [וכתיב עשיר ורש נפגשו וגו'] (מש' כ"ב, ב'), [ע ש י ר], שהוא עשיר בנ

כסים, ור [ש], זה רש מן הנכסים. אמר רש לעשיר: תן לי] מצוה, ולא נתן לו,

ע ו ש ה כ ו ל ם י' י, מי שעשה לזה] עני יכול לעשות[ו עשיר, ומי] שעשה לו עשיר

יכול לעשות[ו] עני. הוי עושה כולם י"י. [וכתיב] אשרי משכיל אל דל (תה' מ"א, כ'), נותן אל ד ל אין כתיב,[2]

אלא מ ש כ י ל א ל ד ל, [שהוא מסתכל במ]צוה היך לעשותה.[3] וכן הוא אומר הלא

פרס לרעב לחמך [וגו'] [כי תראה ערום וכסיתו ומבשרך לא תתעלם] (יש' נ"ח, ז'), [הרי] מזהירה אם ראית ערום צריך להתכסות, אל

תסתכל כן [בו], אלא [תסתכל בבשרך ותאמר מה] אני ומה הוא, אני והוא בשר ודם, אכסינו

שמא אצטרך ויכסוני. ואם ראיתה אביונים ורעבים ועניים, אל תהפוך פניך מהם, חשוב שאתה [הוא אחד מהם, שנ' ומ]בשרך לא תתעלם (שם).[4] וכן הוא אומר כל אלמנה ויתום (שמ' כ"ב, כ"א) [ותני בר קפרא אין לך אדם שאינו בא] לידי מדה זו ...... [לא תענון

... אם ענה תענה אתו ... והיו נשיכם אלמנות ובניכם יתמים].

---

2 וי"ר שם, ד'.

3 הניסוח כאן מתאים לזה שבירושלמי פאה פ"ח, הל' ט': ,אשרי משכיל אל דל והוא שמסתכל במצוה איך לעשותה. ועי' מ"ת, מזמור מ"א [נ'], הע' ב' של המו"ל.

4 השווה וי"ר שם, י"ד: ,כי תראה עני וכיסיתו . . . ומבשרך לא תתעלם, בר קפרא אמר הוי רואה בשרו כבשרך, תני בר קפרא אין לך אדם שאינו בא לידי מדה זו."

בחר בדוד עבדו.   ב ר ק י ע י ם: שמים, רקיע, שחקים, זבול, מעון, מכון,
ערבות, ומכולם

בחר בערבות, שֶׁנֶּ סולו לרוכב בערבות (תה' ס"ח, ה').   ב א ר צ ו ת: ארץ,
ארקא, אדמה

פ"ה.

איני שוכח אתכם, היך דכתיב ואף גם זאת בהיותם בארץ אויביהם וגו' (וי'
כ"ו, מ"ד),   ל א   מ א ס ת י ם,

בימי בבל,[1]   ו ל א   ג ע ל ת י ם, בימי מדי, לכלתם, בימי פרס,[2] להפר
ב ר י ת י   א ת ם,   בימי אדום,   כ י   א נ י   י " י   א ל ה י ה ם,   לימ[ות]
המ[שיח.][3]

[לסדר צ"ח (כ"ה): ויקרא כ"ה, ל"ה.]

פ"ו.

ו כ י   י מ ו ך   א ח י ך   ו מ ט ה   י ד ו. וֶשַׁה י"י

מ ו ר י ש   ו מ ע ש י ר   [וגו'] (ש"א ב', ז').   יִתברך שמו שלמלך מל[כי המ]ל[כי]ם
הקב"ה

שהכל [ברשֶׁ]ותו, [מ]וריש לזה ומעשיר לזה, מוריד לזה ומעלה לזה, שכן הוא
אומר כי אלהים

[שופט וגו'] [זה ישפיל וזה ירים] (תה' ע"ה, ח'), [וכתיב י"י מוריש ומעשיר
וגו'. ומ]פני [מ]ה ברא הקב"ה [עניים ועשירים], כדי שיזכו אלו
לאלו,[1] וכדי שית[פרנסו אלו מאלו, כדי שיכפרו אלו על אלו, על שום גם את
זה לעומת זה עשה

פה.   מקורות: ספרא בחקתי, פרק ח'; תרגום יונתן וירושלמי לוי' כ', מ"ד; מ"א ח"ב, עמ' ע"א
ומקבילות: מגילה י"א, ע"א.
[1] הניסוח כאן מתאים עם זה שבתרגום ושבמגילה, והוא גם, כנראה, המתוקן ביותר.
[2] קרוב לשער שיש כאן טעות סופר וצ"ל: בימי   יון, כי מן הנמנע הוא שלא יהיה מזכיר
יון, רמז לנס חנוכה.   פ ר ס   צריך להיות ביחד עם מדי, כי הרמז הוא ל,ימי המן," ל,מלכות
פרס ומדי.'
[3] בברייתא דמגילה: לעתיד לבוא; בתרגום: ביומי גוג.
מכיון שהסעיף שלפני זה נפסק באמצע, מאמרנו מופיע כעין קטע תלוש שאין לו שום קשר
עם מה שקדם לו, ואף שקשה להכריע אם הוא מתייחס לסדרנו או לסדר הבא. אני מציע
השערה קלושה והוא שבסוף הסעיף הקודם נמשך מאמר אחר מאמר ר' לוי בילקוט תה',
רמז תתפ"ח, הנז' בהערתנו לסעיף 83, וגרס: ,בארצות ... ומכולם לא בחר אלא   א ר ץ
י ש ר א ל ...   ברא שבעים אומות,   ו מ כ ו ל ם   ל א   ב ח ר   א ל א   י ש ר א ל ...'.   וזאת
החוליייה המקשרת את הסעיף הקודם עם מאמרנו.

פו.   מקורות: וי"ר פרשה ל"ד ומקבילות.
[1] השווה וי"ר ל"ד, ה': ,גם את זה לעומת זה, עשה הקב"ה עניים ועשירים, כדי שיהיו זכין
אלו לאלו.'

שמו. והיא [וגם הארץ] מתפללת לפני הקב״ה יתיר מכל הבריות [והוא מעברה]
ומוציאה ויוצרת⁴

כל השנה, ומוציאה יבולה לפני הקב״ה. כיון שהבריות עושין מצותו שלמקום, היא
מזמרת לפניו מכנפיה, שנ׳ מכנף הארץ זמירות שמענו וגו׳ (יש׳ כ״ד, ט״ז).
וכשהן חוטאין,

היא לוקה, כמו שמצאנו כשחטא א[דם הראשון], נתקללה] בעבורו, שנ׳ ארורה
האדמה

בעבורך (בר׳ ג׳, י״ז);⁵ חטא דור המבול, לקתה בעבורם, שנ׳ הנני משחיתם
את הארץ (שם, ו׳, י״ג), וכת[יב];

מן האדמה אשר ארֲרה י״י (שם, ה׳, כ״ט); חטאו סדום[יים], לקתה בעבורם,
שנ׳ ויהפוך את ה[ע]רים

האל וגו׳ (שם, י״ט, כ״ה). מוסרו לפחֿ⁶ בשביעית, והיתה שבת הארץ
ל [כם לאכלה] (וי׳ כ״ה, ו׳), שתהא שבת הארץ⁷ (דף מ״ט, ע״ב)
. . . . . . שהיתה בשביתה עדה . . . . והארץ [ע]שתה פירות בשב[י]ל] . . . . . .
ויעשה בו הקב״ה כל, שנ׳ לי״י הארץ ומלואה וגו׳ (תה׳ כ״ד, א׳).

פ״ד.

בוא וראה

שכל השביעיות חביבין לפני הקב״ה: [בדורות, באבות], בבנים, ברקיעים,
בארצות,

בשנים, בחדשים, בימים. ב ד ו ר ו ת: אדם, שת, אנוש, קינן, מהללאל, ירד,
חנוך,¹

שנ׳ ויתהלך חנוך וגו׳ (בר׳ ה׳, כ״ב). ב א ב ו ת: אברהם, יצחק, יעקב, לוי,
קהת, עמרם, משה, ומכולם

בחר במשה,² שנ׳ ומשה עלה אל האלהים (שמ׳ י״ט, ג׳). ב ב נ י ם: אוצם
הששי, דויד השביעי (דה״א ב׳, ט״ו), ומכולם

4 ההשלמה עפ״י מ״א שממשיך את התמונה של עיבור ולידה ומנסח .ויולדֿת כל
השנה" במקום ,ויוצרת."

5 במ״א מוסיֿף: .חטא קין, לקתה בעבורו, שנאמר כי תעבוד את האדמה וגו׳.".

6 צ״ל: לנוח. במ״א: לכך מסר הקב״ה דין לנוח בשביעית.

7 החלק הבא אין בידי להשלימו בכל פרטיו, ולפיכך אני מוסר את הקבלתו במ״א:
.והיתה שבת הארץ וגו׳, שתהא מ ש מ ר ת (צ״ל: מ ש מ ט ה) אחת לשבע, שבשביל השמטה
מוציאה זרעים וכל טוב והיא להקב״ה, שנאמר לה׳ הארץ ומלֿאֿה וגו׳.".

פד. מקורות: מ״א ח״ב, 60—59 ומקבילות (הע׳ ג׳).

1 צ״ל: [ומכלם לא בחר אלא בחנוך] – דילוג מ,חנוך" ל,חנוך."

2 זה מתאים לוי״ר כ״ט, י״א ופסדר״כ קנ״ד, ע״א; במ״א מביא פסוק אחר: ,ומכולם לא
נבחר לדבר עמו פה אל פה כמשה, כמו שנאמר פה אל פה . . .".

3 הע׳ 2. [חרבה יבשה, נשאר תבל, ומכלם לא בחר אלא בתבל, שנ׳ והוא ישפוט תבל
בצדק (תה׳ ט׳, ט׳)].

[פ"ב.]

וכיון שלא קיימו את השביעית,

נשמטה הארץ ובית המקדש [נהר]ס, שנ' כי ארמון נטש¹ המון עיר עזב וג'
(יש' ל"ב, י"ד), וכן הוא

אומר עזבתי את ביתי ונטשתי את נחלתי [וג']¹ (יר' י"ב, ז'), בשביל [שלא
ק]יימו השמטה.¹ אלא

עתיד הקב"ה להחזיר אליה ויטעם עליה נטיעת עולם, שנ' ונטעתם על אדמתכם
וג' [ולא ינתשו עוד מעל אדמתם]² (עמ' ט', ט"ו).

[פ"ג.]

פס'. ש ש ש נ י ם (וי' כ"ה, ג'). יהא מבורך שמו של הקב"ה שרחמיו על כל
מעשיו. והקב"ה [אוהב את ישראל] ולא ביקש להאכילן דבר איסור[] שכך
דר[כה] שלארץ ישר[אל] [להוציא הרבה] פירות בערב [שבתות שביעיות]
ועודם בוסר] בשנה ה[שביעית,

ו ח מ ש י ם ש נ ה י ו ב ל³ ....כשם שצוה הקב"ה
לעשות מלאכה ששת ימים ולנוח ביום שבת, כך צוה על הארץ לעשות שש
שנים ולנוח בז', שהקב"ה חס על בריות[יו] וחביבין ישראל לפני הקדוש יתברך
וישתבח

פב. מקורות: אבות פ"ה, ט' (אדר"נ פל"ח בנו'א); ספרא בחקתי פרק ז'; תנ' בהר, א'
(ת"ב, ב'); שבת ל"ג, ע"א.

1 כמעט בכל המקורות מבוססת הדיעה ש[גלות באה לעולם בעוון שמטה' על וי'
כ"ו, ליד–ל"ה: [אז תרצה . . . כל ימי השמה.' אולם בעל מדרשנו, כנראה, מסמיכה לשמ'
כ"ג, י"א: [והשביעית תשמטנה ונטשתה.' נטש הוא איפוא נרדף ל ש מ ט, ועל כ
הוא מוצא ב[ארמון נוטש' וב[ונטשתי את נחלתי' רמז לשמיטה.

2 [ולא ינתשו עוד מעל אדמתם]. נטש ונתש היינו הך.

פג. מקורות: הסעיף הזה והבא אחריו נמצאים כמעט מלה במלה במ"א ח"ב ע' נ"ט–ס'
והנחתיו יסוד להשלמה.

1 המקום הזה מטושטש לבלי היכר בכתה"י, ופתיחה [יהא מבורך וכו'.' בלתי שכיחה
במדרשנו, ואני נוטה להשלים: [בוא ו ר א ה ט ו ב ו של הקב"ה שרחמיו . . .'. שימוש לשון
חביב על מדרשנו, ומקביל לו במקור מ"א: [בוא וראה ברייותיו(?) של הקב"ה.' ברייותיו
חשודה בעיני.

2 ההשלמה על יסוד מ"א הנז': [והקב"ה אוהב את ישראל ולא ביקש להאכילן דבר
א י ס ו ר (?) שכן דרכה של ארץ ישראל להוציא פירות וזרע הרבה בערבי שבתות ובשביעית
ואינם פירות טובות.' יש כאן הקבלה מילולית חוץ מן הסוף. במקום ואינם פ י ר ו ת
ט ו ב ו ת מדרשנו מתחיל [ועודם' והשאר מטושטש. הצעתי להשלים [ועודם [בוסר] מפני
שמקביל בתוכן ל[ואינם פירוש טובות.'

שמתי סימן השאלה בצידה של [איסור,' מפני שהקשר ההגיוני דורש [ולא ביקש להאכילן
ד ב ר ר ע' ולכן אסר?, ואולי צ"ל: דבר ב ו ס ר.

3 על יסוד מ"א יש להניח שיש לנו כאן דיבר המתחיל של פיסקה חדשה: [ובשנה ה]שביעית
וג' [רמז לשמטה) ו ח מ ש י ם ש נ ה י ו ב ל (ציטוט בלתי מדויק וי' כ"ה, י"א: יובל הוא
שנת החמשים שנה – רמז ליובל), [לקיום חידוש העולם].

[לסדר צ"ו^b (כ"ג^b): ויקרא כ"ה, א.']

[.פ]

[בהר סיני.] ...(דף מ"ט, ע"א) כמה(?) טו[ב]ה בסיני, ונותן את אלו המצות
שבתורה לא (?) בסיני ה[יא שאמרו?] ישראל
נעשה ונשמע, שקטה מיראתה. הוי יראה ושקטה (תה' ע"ו, ט').[1]

[.פ"א]

אמר ר' יהודה כתיב

ו ש ב ת ה   ה א ר ץ   ש ב ת [לי"י.] (וי' כ"ה, ב'). את מוצא שהרבה [וחיבב]
הקב"ה את השביעית,[1] שבשעה ש[קבלו]
ישראל את התורה, הזהירן הקב"ה על השביעית במתן תורה, שהוא[2] מזכיר
בעניינה מהר [בהר?] סיני, שנ' ו י ד ב ר   א ל ה י ם   א ל   מ ש ה   ו ג ו' [בהר
סיני לאמר] (שם, א'), ומה עניין שמטה להר סיני,]ללמ
דך שמשם נצטוו עליה.[3] אמר ר' שמואל> והלא כל המצות נאמרו בסיני, אלא
אף[4] הש[מט]ה

נאמרו כללותיה בהר סיני ודקדוקיה בהר סיני. מה כתיב למעלה מן העניין,
הוצא

את המקלל (שם, כ"ד, י"ד),[5] לפיכך סמך פרשת מקלל לשביעית.

פ. מקורות: פס"ר, פיס' קמייתא י' הדברות, צ"ט, ע"ב וכו' ומקבילות (מאיר עין, הע' י"ז).
[1] הפיסקה מלבד היותה קטועה ראש, היא גם מטושטשת ברובה וקריאתה מחברנו לא
תמיד בטוחה, ולפיכך משכתי את ידי מלהשלימה. ברור, שהכילה את המדרש הידוע שבמקורות
הדורש תה' ע"ו, ט' על מעמד הר סיני, אם כי בניסוח שונה. גם במ"א ח"ב, עמ' 58 משולב
הפסוק הזה בסדרנו.

פא. מקורות: וי"ר כ"ט, י"א; מ"א ח"ב, נ"ט, ע"א ומקבילות (הע' ג'); ספרא ראש פרשת בהר.
[1] ברור שיש כאן רמז למאמר בוי"ר ומקבילות: „כל שביעין חביבין... בשנים
שביעי חביב," אבל רוב המקורות מביאים סמך לדבר הפסוק „והשביעי תשמטנה
ונטשתה." בעל מדרשנו מסמיכו ל„ושבתה הארץ שבת [לה']." זה מתאים לניסוחו של המאמר
בילקוט תה' רמז תתפ"ח: „ברא שנים ובירר לו אחד מהם ושבתה הארץ שבת לה'." עי' פדר"א
סוף פרק י"ח וביאור הרד"ל שם.
[2] אולי צ"ל: שיהא, כלו' שחיבה יתרה נודעת לשביעית שבעניינה נזכר בפירוש שניתנה
מהר סיני. מקורה של התוספת הזאת נעלם ממני.
[3] המוסגר הוא, לדעתי, הוספת ביאור. והוא בלשון שאלה: [תאמר] ללמדך שבסיני נצטוו
וכו'? והלא. כי המקור הם דברי הספרא: „מה עניין שמטה אצל הר סיני" [אם] ללמדך שמשם
נצטוו עליה) „והלא כל המצות וכו'." „אמר ר' שמואל,' אפשר שהוא שם המוסיף והמבאר.
[4] סרוס ודילוג כאן, וצריך לתקן עפ"י המקור: „מה השמטה נאמרה כללותיה בהר
סיני ודידוקיה בהר סיני אף [כולם נאמרו כללותיה ודקדוקיהם בהר סיני]."
[5] עיקר הדרוש חסר, ומקור קדום נעלם ממני, אבל השווה בעל הטורים: „סמך מקלל
להר סיני לפי שבסיני שמעו לא תשא ונדעזע כל העולם וזה שמע ולא נזהר, ועוד כדאיתא
בקדושין שם בן ארבע אותיות חכמים מוסרים אותו לתלמידיהם פעם אחת בשבוע ל כ ך
ס מ ך   ל ו   ש מ י ט ה." אם בעל מדרשנו מתכוין לאחד מן הטעמים של בעל הטורים או
לאיזה מדרש אחר, אי אפשר לדעת.

ימציא את קרבנו אלא שלם, כדי שיתרצה להם,[2] שׁנ' **ל ר צ ו נ כ ם ת מ י ם**
ז כ ר וגו'

(וי' כ"ב, י"ט). וכן מי שהוא מוציא מעשרותיו, לא יאמר: ה ר י נ י מ ו צ י א
מעשר, לא יאמר: שלי

הוא, שׁנ' ונתתם ממנו תרומת י"י (במ' י"ח, כ"ח). פסק ליתן צדקה יתן צדקה,
את שלו הוא,[3]

וכי תדור נדר לי"י אלהיך לא[4] וגו' [תאחר לשלמו כי ד ר ש י ד ר ש נ ו י"י?]
(דב' כ"ג, כ"ב). אמר להם משה: לא תגלגלו [תזלזלו?][7] בדברים הללו,
הסתכלו

באבותיכם, על שאיחר יעקב את נדריו, מה גרם לעצמו, ואחר נדרים לבקר
[איחר אדם את נדרו נתבקרה פנקסו] וגו'

(מש' כ', כ"ה),[5] והיכן נדר יעקב, שׁנ' וידר יעקב נדר לאמר וגו' (בר' כ"ח, כ').

[לסדר צ"ו (כ"ב): ויקרא כ"ג, ט'–י'.]
ע"ט.]

ולא ביקש הקב̇ה̇ מישראל אלא לפי

כוהן, והוא נתן להם כפי כוחו, שׁנ' וי"י הולך לפניהם יומם וגו' (שמ' י"ג, כ"א),
וביקש מהן כפי

כוהן, שׁנ' צו (תצוה – שיגרת העט מויק' כ"ד, ב') את בני ישראל ויקחו אליך
שמן זית זך (שמ' כ"ז, כ"ט);[1] כשנתן להם את המן, לפי

כוחו, שׁנ' הנני ממטיר לכם לחם מן השמים (שם, ט"ז, ד'),[2] וכשביקש מהן,
לפי כוהן ביקש, שׁנ'

ו ה ב א ת ם א ת ע ו מ ר ר א ש י ת ק צ י ר כ ם א ל וגו' (וי' כ"ג, י').
שהוא מכולם יחד.[4] ולא עוד אלא[5]...
[בין דף מ"ח ומ"ט חסרים דפים אחדים.]

[2] פירוש של „לרצונכם'; השווה פירש"י: „הביאו דבר הראוי לרצות אתכם לפני.'
[3] בלתי ברור אם „שלו' רוצה לומר של העני הוא, או, וזה יותר מסתבר, „שלו', רו"ל של
הקב̇ה̇. השווה מאמרו של ר'א איש ברתותא (אבות פ"ג, ח'): „תן לו מ ש ל ו.' ועי' ר"ה דף
ה', ע"ב: „ה' אלהיך, אלו צדקות ומעשרות.'
[4] לא [תאחר לשלמו כי דרוש ידרשנו ח' אלהיך מעמך].
[5] כלו' אל תדחו אל התשלומין מיום ליום, מלשון „מגלגל עמו עד י"ב חודש (יבמות מ"ח, ע"ב),
נעי' בן־יהודה, מלון, כרך ב', עמ' 768.
[6] לבקר [איחר אדם את נדרו נתבקרה פנקסו, יעקב אבינו על ידי שאיחר נדרו נתבקרה
פנקסו] והיכן ... ההשלמה על פי ב"ר פרשה פ"א, ב'.

עט. מקורות: וי"ר כ"ח, ג'; פסדר"כ, פס' העומר, דף ע', ע"א; מ"א ח"ב, 60.
[1] הדוגמה הזאת מובאה רק במ"א.
[2] [ויצא העם ולקטו דבר יום ביומו]. הניסוח כאן דומה לזה שבוי"ר, אלא שבמקום הפסוק
הזה מובא שם הפסוק: „לקטו ממנו ... עמר לגלגלת,' עומר לכל אחד ואחד.
[3] יותר טוב: „אחד.' בוי"ר: עומר אחד מכולם.
[4] ולא עוד אלא [שאינו של חטים אלא של שעורים], השלמה על פי וי"ר.

בכם וגו' [וחייתם] (יח' ל"ז, י"ג–י"ד).8 תחיית המתים מביאה לידי זכר טוב,
מניין, שנ' הנה אנכי שולח לכם את אליה
הנביא וגו' (מלא' ג', כ"ג).

ע"ז.

אמ[רו] ר' [בותינו] ז"ל1 משל לנפש אדם שנמשלה לנר, שנ' נר אלהים נשמת אדם
(מש' כ', כ"ז), מה הנר הזה, כל זמן שיש בו שמן הוא דולק, כלה השמן כלה
אורו, כך האדם,1 כל
זמן שנפשו בו הכל מידבקין בו, יצאת הנפש ברחו ממנו הכל.2 לכך נאמר
ל נ פ ש3
ל א י ט מ א ב ע מ י ו (וי' כ"א, א'). וכשם שהכהנים מזהירין על הטומאה
לפרוש4 ממנה, כך ישראל,
שנ' והזרתם את בני ישראל מטמאתם וגו'3 (שם, ט"ו, ל"א), ש ל א י מ ו ת ו,
לכך הזהירם.3 הרי זה עונש.4
ולא עוד אלא5 שהוא גורם לעצמו מיתה, אלא שהוא מטמא את המקדש, שנ'
ב ט מ א ם
(שם).

[לסדר צ"ד (כ"א): ויקרא כ"ב, י"ז–י"ח.]

ע"ח.

[איש איש מבית ישראל.] בוא וראה היאך הקב"ה מזהיר לישראל עד [על?]
שלא יהשה אדם מהם את נדרו,1 ושלא

8 בירושלמי מובא רק הפסוק האחרון, ,ונתתי ר ו ח י בכם וכו' [וחייתם].'
הפסוק הזה אמנם מתאים לנוסחא שבירושלמי שקלים: ,רוח הקודש מביאה לידי תה"מ,' אבל
אין למצוא כאן רמז לחסידות שמביאה לידי תה"מ, כנראה, שמטעם זה מצטט בעל מדרשנו
את הפסוק ,ו י ד ע ת ם כ י א נ י ה' בפתחי את קברותיכם,' כי ,דעת ה' ' נראה שהוא
נרדף לחסידות אצל בעל מדרשנו (עי' למעלה הע' 7).

עז. מקורות: פסדר"כ (?); ספרא מצורע פרשה ט', ו', ז'.
1 מקורו נעלם ממני. בפסדר"כ, דף קמ"ה, ע"ב אנו מוצאים אמנם את המשל: ,מה דרכו
של שמן להנתן בנר, והן מאירין שניהם כאחת,' אבל הנמשל שם שונה לגמרי.
2 דומה לזה הוא המאמר הידוע: ,תינוק בן יומו חי מחללין עליו את השבת, דוד מלך
ישראל מת אין מחללין עליו את השבת' (שבת קנ"א, ע"ב).
3 השווה ספרא הנז': ,והזרתם את בני ישראל, אין נזירה אלא ה פ ר ש ה.'
4 המשפט כאן מסורס. קרוב לשער שיש לנו כאן הפיסקה השנייה של הספרא: ,והזרתם
את בני ישראל מטמאתם, הרי זו אזהרה, ולא ימותו בטמאתם, זו ענוש.' נראה שחסרה
ההתחלה, וצריך לתקן: [. . . . .] לכך הזהירם, ולא ימותו הרי זה עונש.'
5 מכאן עד הסוף הלשון פגומה והמשמעות בלתי ברור לי.

עח. מקורו נעלם ממני.
1 נראה שבעל מדרשנו מפרש ,ואמרת אליהם איש איש . . . א ש ר י ק ר י ב את
קרבנו לכל נדריהם ולכל נדבותם' לשון צווי, כלו' אמור לכל אחד מהם שיקריב קרבנו אשר
נדר ואשר נדב.

ע"ו.]

מיכן[1] היה ר' פינחס בן יאיר אומר[1] זריזות מביאה לידי נקיות, נקיות מ[ביאה]
לידי טהרה, טהרה מביאה לידי קדושה, קדושה מביאה לידי ענוה, ענוה מביאה
לי[די]

(דף מ"ח, ע"ב) [יראת חטא, יראת חטא] מביאה רוח הקודש, ורוח הקודש
מביאה [לידי חסידות, וחסידות מביאה לידי]

תחיית המתים, ת[חיית] המתים מביאה לידי זכר טוב.[2] שנ[3] וטיהרו וקידשו
מטומאות בני ישראל

(וי' ט"ז, י"ט), וכתיב[4] כי . . הכהן,[5] שנ' כי כה אמר י' רם ונשא שוכן עד
וקדוש

שמו וגו' [ואת דכא ושפל רוח][6] (יש' נ"ז, ט"ו). ענוה מביאה לידי יראת חטא,
מניין, שנ'

עקב ענוה יראת י' וגו' (מש' כ"ב ד'). יראת

חטא מביאה לידי רוח רוח הקודש,[7] לידי חסידות, שנ' אז דברת בחזון לחסידיך
וגו' (תה' פ"ט, כ'). חסידות מביאה

לידי תחיית המתים, מניין, וידעתם כי אני י' בפתחי את קברותיכם וגמ' (sic!),
ונתתי את רוחי

 עו. מקורות: ירושלמי שבת פ"א, ה' ומקבילות.

1 מרובים המקורות למאמרו של ר' פנחס בן יאיר, ומרובים השנויים (עי' מאיר איש שלום
במבואו ל "סדר אליהו רבה . . .", 1904, עמ' 26—27). ניסוח המאמר במדרשנו מתאים כמעט
לגמרי עם ניסוחו בירושלמי שבת הנרשם.

2 כלו' אליהו זכר לטוב (כך הוא בירושלמי שקלים סוף פ"ג; "זכרונו לברכה"
בירושלמי שבת אינו אלא קריאה משובשת של ר"ח ז"ל). וגם בירושלמי אנו מוצאים את אליהו
פעם אחת מסומן בתוארו "זכור לטוב" בלבד. וגם בשביעית, סוף פ"ט: "ר' יהושע בן לוי הוי
מפקד לתלמידיה לא תיזבנון לי ירק אלא מן גינת דסיסרא, קם עמיה זכור לטוב . . .".
וכדאי להעיר שבירושלמי ובמדרשי א"י שמו של אליהו תמיד מלווה בתואר "זכור
לטוב." לא כן בבבלי.

3 מכאן והילך חזרות ושנשות המדרגות הנז' ורמזי פסוק בצדן. מרובים הם הדילוגים בחלק
זה, ואנו משלימים כאן עפ"י המקור הנרשם. ההתחלה חסרה, וצ"ל: [זריזות מביאה לידי
נקיות, ונקלה, וכפר, נקיות מביאה לידי טהרה, וכפר עליה הכהן וטהרה, טהרה מביאה לידי
קדושה] שנ' וטיהרו . . .

4 זה כנראה שריד מן הדילוג שהשלמנו, והוא: "דכתיב [וכיפר עליה] הכהן [וטהרו]
המרמז על "נקיות מביאה לידי טהרה" (עי' ירושלמי הנ"ז).

5 בכתה"י מקום חלק של י"ח אותיות בערך, ויש לשער שצריך להשלים: [קדושה מביאה
לידי ענוה שנ'] כי כה . . .

6 [ואת דכא ושפל רוח].

7 יש כאן דילוג מתוך הבלעה, וצריך להשלים: לידי רוח הקודש [שנ' אז תבין יראת ה'
ודעת אלהים תמצא, רוח הקודש] לידי חסידות . . . בירושלמי שקלים הפסוק הזה
בא שלא במקומו.

[ולסדר צ"ג (כ'): ויקרא כ"א, א'.]

ע"ה].

אמור אל הכהנים.

זשה אימרות י"י אמרות טהורות וגו' (תה' י"ב, ז'). אתה מוצא[1] כל מה שהקב"ה
מזהיר את ישראל,

בשביל קדושתן וטהרתן. הוי אימרות י"י אמרות טהורות. ושתי אמירות נאמרו
בעניין זה: א מ ו ר ו א מ ר ת, שתי אזהרות.[2] ולמה[3] גזר כן הקב"ה על
הכהנים, מפני שהן

נכנסין לבית קוד ש הק דשים, לכך גזר עליהם שלא יטמאו למת, שנ'
אמור אל הכהנים.

כל הפרשיות כתיב[3] בהן אמור לבני אהרן, דבר אל בני ישראל, וכאן כתיב
ואמרת אליהם, ולמה ריב[ה]

אמרות הרבה, שאין חביב לפני הקב"ה יתיר מן הטהרה,[4] שנ' ושמרתם את
משמרת

אהל מועד[5] ואת משמרת המזבח וגו' (במ' י"ח, ה'). ואם לא רצה לטהר
עצמו, הקב"ה מצרפו, שנ'

הנה צרפתיך ולא בכסף וגו' (יש' מ"ח, י'). ואם יטמא באונס, הקב"ה מטהרו,
שנ' והזה הטהור[6] על

הטמא וגו' (במ' י"ט, י"ט).

לזה שבוי"ר, הסיום הוא בפסוק מעמ' ט', ט"ו כבתנ', ולא מיש' ס"א, ט' כבוי"ר. בעל מדרשנו
מכבר, כנראה, חוליה חולייה מקשרת בסדר: ,ונטעתם—ונטעתים,' מאשר חולייה מקשרת ב,הפטרה'.

עה. מקורות: תנ' ות"ב אמור, א'.

1 התחלה זו אינה במקור, וחביבה היא על בעל מדרשנו.

2 הניסוח מתאים לזה שבת"ב. עי' לעיל שם הע' ב'.

3 במקור: ,ל מ ה הדבר דומה, לטבח שהיה נכנס ויוצא לפני המלך, אמר המלך גוזרני
עליך שלא תראה מת כל ימיך, מפני שאתה נכנס ורואה את פני ... כך הקב"ה ג ז ר על
הכהנים הנכנסים לבית המקדש ש ל א י ט מ א ו ל מ ת.' זאת היא דוגמה מאלפת מאופן
הליקוט והקיצור של בעל מדרשנו. הוא משמיט את המשל ומכניס במקומו את השאלה ,ול מָה
גזר ...' המתחילה ממש במלה שבה מתחיל המשל: ,למה הדבר ...' ואף גם מסיים ממש
במלים של המקור: ,שלא יטמאו למת.'

4 כנראה, יש לנו כאן ניסוח אחר של המדרש הקדום והוא שבשביל ,טהרתן' של ישראל
הרבה ,אמרות,' ,אזהרות.' ואפשר שיש לנו כאן רמז וביאור למדרש ר' תנחום (מ"ת י"ב, ד'):
,אמרות ה' אמרות טהורות, אמר ר' תנחום אמר הקב"ה למשה שתי אמירות אמרתי לך והן
טהרות ... ואי זה הוא, זו פרשת אמור אל הכהנים ...' בובר הע' ל"ד מתקן עפ"י וי"ר
פכ"ו, ג', וגורס ,זו פרשת [פרה אדומה ופרשת המת] אמור ...' בעל מדרשנו, כנראה, פירש
מאמרו ,שתי אמירות' אמור ואמרת, והטעם לפי שהן אזהרות על הטהרה (והן טהורות).
ומבאר אח"כ ששתי האמירות נמצאות בפרשת אמור אל הכהנים.

5 בקרא כתיב: ,הקדש.' ,אהל מועד' היא שיגרת העט מפסוק שלפני זה: ,ושמרו את
משמרת א ה ל מ ו ע ד.'

6 השווה פסדר"כ סוף פרשת פרה (דף מ"א, ע"ב): טהור זה הקב"ה שנ' טהור עינים מראות
ברע.

ע"ד.]

אמר ר' יצחק מפני מה האריכו הכנענים בארץ ישראל מאחר שאמר לאברהם

לתת לך (בר' ט"ו, ז'), מפני שחלקו כבוד לאברהם אבינו,

שאמרו לו נשיא אלהים אתה וגו' (שם, כ"ג, ו'), כנגדה פרע להם הקב"ה,

ונתאחרו וישבו בארץ

ת' שנה עד שעלו ישראל ממצרים, שנ' ועבדום וענו אותם ארבע מאות שנה וגו'

(שם, י"ג). ויש אומרים בעבור שנטעו בתוכה נטיעות, האריכו שנים בתוכה, [2]

ומה אם אומות העולם

שנטעו בארץ זכו להאריך שנים עליה, ישראל, אם נוטעין בתוכה ומקיימין מצותן,

על אחת כמה וכמה. בעולם הזה היו ישראל נוטעין ואומות העולם אוכלין, אבל

לעתיד לבוא מה שהן נוטעין זוכין לאכול אותו, שנ' לא יבנו ואחר ישב וגו'

(יש' ס"ה, כ"ב), [3] והקב"ה

נוטען על אדמתן נטיעת עולמים, שנ' ונטעתים על אדמתם וגו' (עמ' ט', ט"ו). [5]

עד. מקורות: ספרא אחרי, פרשה ט', ו'; תנ' קדושים י"א; וי"ר פרשה כ"ו בסוף.

[1] בכתה"י יש כאן מקום חלק, סימן שהעתיק של המעתיק היה פגום ודילג על דבר מה. השוואה עם המקור מראה מראה הטייה גדולה ממנו. בספרא הנז' אנו קוראים: "ר' יוסי הגלילי אומר אחר שהכתוב שוקל מעשה ארץ מצרים כמעשה ארץ כנען ... מפני מה זכו הכנעניים לישב בארצם ארבעים ושבע שנים ... אלא בשביל שכבדו את אברהם אבינו ...". השאלה היא איפוא לא על "ת' שנה" שהיו ישראל במצרים, כי אם על "ארבעים ושבע שנים" שעברו מיציאת מצרים עד כיבוש הארץ.

[2] יש לנו כאן, כנראה, דוגמה מאלפת של חופש השימוש במקורות. השאלה למה נתעכבו בני ישראל מ' שנה במדבר ולא נכנסו תיכף לארץ הטרידה את בעלי המדרש, ותשובות שונות ניתנו לה. אחת מהן היא: "כיון ששמעו הכנעניים שישראל נכנסין עמדו ושרפו כל הזרעים וקצצו כל האילנות וסתרו את הבניינים וסתמו את המעיינות, אמר הקב"ה לא הבטחתים לאבותם שאכניסן לארץ חריבה אלא מלאה כל טוב ... הריני מקיפן במדבר ארבעים שנה עד שיעמדו כנעניים ויתקנו מה שקלקלו" (מכילתא בשלח פ' א'). "אין כאן מעלת נטיעת אילנות ולא "זכות" של הכנעניים, כי אם תיקון אחד בין שאר התיקונים שהוטל עליהם "לתקן מה שקלקלו" בשמ"ר כ', ט"ז הניסוח הוא: "כיון ששמעו הכנעניים שישראל נכנסין לארץ עמדו וקצצו הנטיעות שהיו להן, כיון ששמעו שנתעכבו במדבר מ' שנה ... עמדו ונטעו נטיעות וגדלו אותם." ניסוח דומה הוא בקה"ר ג', ב' בסוף. מכל הדברים שקלקלו נשאר בניסוח זה רק קציצת נטיעות, ומן התיקונים רק נטיעת אילנות. ועדיין לא בשכר הנטיעות שנטעו זכו הכנעניים להשאר בארץ, כי אם "לתקן את הנטיעות שקלקלו." בעל מדרשנו צעד צעד אחר לפנים, ומתוך סבך המוטיבים שבמדרש הנז' הוציא רק את זה שנטיעת אילנות היתה סיבת התעכבותם של הכנעניים בארץ, ודרש את הדבר לשבחה של נטיעת אילנות ול"זכותם" של הכנעניים.

[3] חתימה דומה בתנ' הנז': "היו זורעים ויגיעים ואומות העולם באין ונוטלים ... וכשעושים תשובה ... לא יטעו ואחר יאכל, למה שהן נוטעין ואינן נותשין, שנ' ולא ינתשו עוד וגו' (עמוס ט', ט"ו)." שונה מעט הוא הניסוח בוי"ר: "לפי שבעוה"ז בונה אדם ואחר מכלהו, נוטע נטיעות ואחר אוכל, אבל לעתיד לבוא מה כתיב ... לא יבנו ואחר ישב לא יטעו ואחר יאכל וכתיב ונודע בגוים זרעם."

[4] [ולא ינתשו עוד מעל אדמתם]. אעפ"י שבדרך כלל ניסוח החתימה במדרשנו מתאים

[כסי]תי[3] דברי תורה ולא כסיתי אותם ללמד, אף אתה לא תכלא רחמיך
ממני[2] (שם, י"ב). לפיכך

למדך הכתוב לומר זה הדבר אשר צוה י'י לאמר,[3] ואחר
כך איש איש מבית ישראל וגו'
(וי' י"ז, א'–ב')[5] . . . . .

[בין דף מ"ז, ע"ב, ודף מ"ח, ע"א, חסרים דפים אחדים.]

[לסדר צ"ב (י"ט): ויקרא י"ט, כ"ג.]

ע"ג.

וכי תבאו אל הארץ ונטעתם כל עץ מאכל וערלתם
ערלתו. [. . . . .][1] (דף מ"ח, ע"א) הסמדר. אין לי אלא שלא יאכל,
מניין שלא יצבע   [בו ולא יהנה][2]
ממנו, תלמוד לומר וערלתם ערלתו, ערלתו לרבות את כולן.[2]

פס'. קודש הלולים לי'י (וי' י"ט, כ"ד), מלמד שהוא טעון ברכה
לפניו וברכה אחריו. מיכן היה ר' עקיבא אומר לא יטעום
אדם כלום עד שיברך.[3]

---

[3] השלמת מחברנו. ואולי יותר טוב: „וכשם שלא [מנע]תי ד"ת ולא כסיתי . . .".
[4] השווה תרגום: „בגלל כן את ה' לא תמנע רחם."
[5] הפיס' מקוטעת, ואפשר שהיתה כאן וריאציה של מדרש תנ' אחרי, י' (ת"ב, ט"ז): צפה
הקב"ה שבית המקדש עתיד ליחרב, ואמר הקב"ה כל זמן שבית המקדש קיים ואתם מקריבין
קרבנות לתוכו מתכפר עליכם, אין בית המקדש קיים במה מתכפר עליכם, התעסקו בדברי
תורה, שהן משולין בקרבנות והן מכפרין עליכם, שנאמר זה הדבר. לדעת בעל מדרשנו לא די
עסק בתורה סתם, כי אם צריך ללמד דברי תורה לאחרים כדי להביא כפרה לעולם.

ע"ג.   מקורות: ספרא קדושים, פרשה ג' ומקבילות; ירושלמי ברכות ראש פ"ו ומקבילות.
[1] נראה שצריך להשלים: [לרבות את] הסמדר. השווה ספרא הנרשם נ': „פריו, פרט
לעלים . . . ומי סמדר . . . דברי ר' יוסי הגלילי, ר' עקיבא אמר וערלתם את ערלתו
ערלים לרבות כולם." ועי' משנה ערלה פ"א, ז': ר' יוסי אומר הסמדר אסור.
[2] השווה ספרא שם, ו': „וערלתם ערלים (ערלתו) ערלים לרבות את כולם." בקידושין
נ"ו, ע"ב מובאה הברייתא כמעט בלשון מדרשנו: „ת"ל וערלתם ערלתו, לרבות את כולם." אין
כאן שלש פעמים ערלים לשלשה מיני הנאה, כי אם מלה יתרה ערלתו הבאה לרבות את כולם.
[3] ספרא שם, ט'. הברייתא מובאה כאן בדיוק בלשון הירושלמי, ברכות, ראש פרק ו'.
נוסחת הבבלי (ברכות ל"ה, ע"א): „מכאן אמר ר"ע אסור לאדם שיטעום כלום קודם שיברך."

י"י אלהיך (דב' י"ח, ה'), ועל שהכניסו בניו אש זרה נשרפו. הוי לא נשא
פני שרים.[1] כשהלך משה
אצל אהרן ראה אותו יושב ובוכה, אמר לו משה: עת שהייתי כמה כלי . . . . בן.

ע"א.

. . . [בזאת יבא אהרן אל הקדש, ישראל נקראים קדושים, שנ] קדושים תהיו
(וי' י"ט, ב'), והקב"ה נקרא קדוש, שנ' שוכן עד
מרום וקדוש שמו וגו' (יש' נ"ז, ט"ו), יבוא אהרן שנקרא קדוש, וילבש בגדי קודש,
ויכנס למקדש קודש,
ויכפר על ישראל, שנקראו קדושים, לפני קדוש, היך כתיב כי ביום הזה
יכפר עליכם . . . [לפני י"י תטהרו] (וי' ט"ז, ל').

[לסדר פ"ט (ט"ז): ויקרא י"ז, א'–ב'.]

ע"ב.

פס'. איש איש מבית ישראל וגו'. זשה בני תורתי אל תשכח וגו'
(מש' ג', א'), שמור מצותי וחיה
(שם, ז', ב'), להודיעך שכל דברי תורה חיים, שנ' כי הוא חייכם וגו' (דב'
ל"ב, מ"ז).[1] אמר ר' יצחק אם יהיה אדם יודע דברי תורה אל ימנעם
מישראל, אלא ילמד אותם בסבר פנים יפות,[1] שכן משה
אומר ראה למדתי אתכם חוקים ומשפטים וגו' [כאשר צוני י"י אלהי . . .]
(שם, ד', ה'), מה הוא כאשר צוני י"י (שם), כשלמדני
הוא גם אני מלמד אתכם, וכן תהיו גם אתם מלמדין.[2] אמר דוד צדקתך לא
כסיתי בתוך לבי וגו' (תה' מ', י"א), בשרתי צדק בקהל רב הנה שפתי לא
אכלא (שם, י'), וכשם שלא

---

[1] השווה במ"ר סוף פ' י"ט שדורש הפסוק על מיתת משה.

עא. מקורו נעלם ממני.
[1] כאן, כנראה, מתחילה פיסקא חדשה: [בזאת יבא אהרן אל הקדש (וי' ט"ז, ג'), ישראל
נקראים קדושים שנאמר] קדושים . . . במבנהו דומה הוא מדרשנו למדרשו של ר' עזרא בר
בריה דר' אבטלס במנחות נ"ג, ע"א–ע"ב: "יבוא טוב ויקבל טוב מטוב . . .".

עב. מקורות: ספרא אחרי מות פרשה ו', ב' (?); נדרים ל"ז, ע"א; ל"ח, ע"א.
[1] השווה פסדר"כ פיס' וזאת הברכה, קצ"ו, ע"ב: "ד"א מונע בר, זה שהוא מונע בר של
תורה . . . וברכה לראש משביר, זה שמלמד תורה בעין יפה," נכונה הערת המו"ל (הע' י"ז)
שם: "דרש משביר מן סבר פנים יפות." עי' סא"ר, הוצ' א"ש, עמ' 137: "יש
בו באדם ד"ת יפרנס לאחרים וכו'."
[2] דומה לזה הם דברי ר' חסדא [נדרים ל"ח, ע"א]: ". . . כאשר צוני ה' אלהי, ואני
לכם." והשווה דברי ר' יהודה אמר רב (בכורות כ"ט, ע"א): "ראה למדתי אתכם [כאשר
צוני] . . . מה אני בחנם אף אתם בחנם."

[לקריאה בשחרית של יום הכפורים: ויקרא ט"ז, א'.]

ס"ט.

[אחרי מות.] .... (דף מ"ז, ע"ז) ויאמר צא ועמדת בהר לפני (מ"א,
י"ט, י"א), אבל באהרן נאמר, ונשמע קולו בבואו אל הקודש

וגו' (שמ' כ"ח, ל"ה). וכיון שראו בני אהרן שכך נתברך אביהם, מיד ויקחו
בני אהרן נדב ואביהוא [א]

(וי' י', א'), ולא נטלו עצה לא מאביהם ולא ממשה, מיד פגעה בהן מדת
הדין, שנ' ותצא אש[1]

מלפני י"י ותאכל אותם וגו' (שם, ב'). מניין שכשם שעבודה[2] שלהן שוה, כך
מיתת שניהם

שוה, שנ' אחרי מות שני בני וגו'.

ע'.

זשה מי יודע עוז אפיך וכיראתך

עברתך (תה' צ', י"א), מי יוכל לעמוד במידת הדין. אין הקב"ה נושא פנים
לבריה, שכן הוא

אומר, אשר לא ישא פנים ולא יקח שוחד (דב' י', י"ז), ואומר אשר לא נשא
פני שרים

וגו' (אי' ל"ד, י"ט). תדע לך שהוא כן, שלא היה אדם חשוב מאדם הראשון,
יציר כפיו

שלהקב"ה, ועשאו בגן עדן, שנ' ויניחהו בגן עדן (בר' ב', ט"ו), וכיון שחטא נטרד
משם, שנ'

ויגרש את האדם וגו' (שם, ג', כ"ד). הוי אשר לא נשא פני שרים וגו'. וכן
אהרן, נאמר בו כי בו בחר

הנדה היתה דרכם .... : "לפיכך הקב"ה מדמה טומאת ישראל לטומאת הנדה שנטמאה
ונטהרה, כך עתיד הקב"ה לטהר ישראל וכו'." בקשר עם אי' א', י"ז הובע הרעיון במסכת
תענית כ', ע"א: היתה ירושלים לנדה ביניהם, אמר ר' יהודה אמר רב לברכה, כנדה מה נדה
יש לה היתר אף ירושלים יש לה תקנה.

ס"ט. מקורות: תנ' אחרי מות, ו' (ת"ב, ז'); וי"ר ט"ז, ח' ומקבילות; ספרא, ראש פרשת אחרי
מות.

1 השווה ספרא, מקור המקורות: "בני אהרן, לא נטלו עצה מאהרן, נדב ואביהו, לא נטלו
עצה ממשה, איש מחתתו, איש איש מעצמו עשו, לא נטלו עצה זה מזה." מדרשי אגדה הביאו
רק הפיסקא האחרונה: "לא נטלו עצה זה מזה," "ואת אהרן ומשה לא הזכירו. לא כן בעל
מדרשנו שהרבה להשתמש במדרשי הלכה.
2 נראה שצ"ל: "שעבירת שניהם" כמו שהוא בספרא.

ע. מקורו נעלם ממני. המוטיב העיקרי שאין הקב"ה נושא פנים לשום איש, ומעניש גם את
הצדיקים הולך ומתפתח נ"כ בפדר"כ, פיס' כ"ז (ליוהכ"פ) ומקבילות, אבל אופן ההרצאה שונה
לגמרי, וגם היסוד הוא אחר, והוא קה' ט', ב': "מקרה אחד לצדיק ולרשע."

אמר הקב״ה: כשם שהוא מתאבל ויושב ז׳, בדין הוא שתהא גם היא יושבת ז׳. לכך

נאמר ז׳ ימים (שם, כ״ח).[5]

ס״ח].

שנו חכמים ה׳ דמים מטמאים[1] באשה: האדֹם, והשחֹר,[2]

כמֹמֵי אדמה, וכמֹזג. איזה הוא האדום,[4] כדם המכה; שחור, שחורה;[5] וכקרן

כירקום, כברור שיש בו;[6] כמימי אדמה, כמבקעת[7] בית כרם מיציף (עליהם)[8] מים; וכמזג,

שני חלקים (אחד)[9] מים ואחד יין מן היין השרוני. הרי מן המשנה. מן המקרא

מניין, וטהרה ממקור דמיה (שם, י״ב, ז׳), הרי הם שנים, והיא גלתה את מקור דמיה

(שם, כ׳, י״ח), הרי עוד שנים,[10] ואשה כי יזוב זוב דמה (שם, ט״ו, כ״ה), הרי הכל ה׳ דמים טמאים באשה.

מה נדה דחופה מביתה, טהרה, חזרה לביתה, כך כשחטאו ישראל, נטשו[11] בין האומות

כנדה, שנ׳ היתה ירושלים לנדה ביניהם (איכה א׳, י״ז).[12] . . . . .

---

[5] הקשר בין דם נדה והאשה ,ששפכה דמו של אדם׳ (– ,גרמה מיתה לעולם) מובא במקורות הנרשמים לבאר את המשנה (שבת פ״ב, ו׳) ,על שלש עבירות נשים מתות, על שאינן זהירות בנדה.׳ אופן השימוש במוטיב זה כאשר הוא במדרשנו בלתי ידוע לי ממקור אחר.

סח. מקורות: משנה נדה פרק ב׳, ו׳; ירושלמי, שם (דף נ׳, ע״א).

[1] במש׳: טמאים.

[2] [ובקרן כירכום]. במשנה: וכקרן כרכום.

[3] כן הוא במשנה שבירושלמי; בבבלי: וכמזוג.

[4] כן הוא במשנה שבירושלמי; בבבלי: אדום.

[5] כנראה שיגרת העט, וצ״ל: ,כחרת׳ כמו שהוא במשנה.

[6] כן הוא במשנה שבירושלמי; בבבלי: שבו.

[7] במשנה: מבקעת.

[8] ,מיצף עליו מים׳ (מש׳ ירושלמי); ,ומציף מים׳ (בבלי).

[9] נראה שצריך למחוק המלה הזאת החסרה במקור, כי רחוק מן הדעת לומר שלדעת בעל מדרשנו ,מזג (או מזוג)׳ הוא חלק אחד מים וחלק אחד יין. השווה במ״ר פרשה א׳, ד׳: ,מי שהוא מזוג כראוי מזוג שלישי של כוס יין ושני חלקים מים.׳

[10] השווה ירושלמי הנרשם: ,מניין לחמשה דמים טמאים מן התורה, אמר יהושע בן לוי והיא גילתה את מקור דמיה, וטהר׳ ממקור דמיה, דם יהיה זובה בבשרה, והא ואשה כי יזוב זוב דמה מינהון הוא וכו׳.׳ לעומת זאת השווה דברי ר׳ אבהו בבבלי נדה י״ט, ע״א.

[11] בכתה״י ,נטושה,׳ נרדף לדחופה שמקודם. כוונת המדרש להדניש שאם ישראל וירושלים נמשלו לנדה אין הכוונה שהם טמאים כנדה, כי אם שהם ,נטושים׳, מרוחקים. והשווה איכ״ר, הוצ׳ בובר, עמ׳ מ״ו: ,לנדה ביניהם, לריחוק היתה.׳

[12] מדרש קטוע לפנינו. הרעיון בשלמותו מובא בתנ׳ הנז׳ בסמיכות ליח׳ ל״ו, י״ז, כטמאת

יצא (חב' א', ז') 2.   בוא וראה3 היאך הקב"ה דנו, אין מביא עליו את היסורין
בפעם אחת, אלא קימעא קימעא,

שמא יעשה תשובה. בתחילה הוא מוציא בגופו שאת או ספחת או בהרת (וי'
י"ג, ב'), אם עשה

תשובה, הוא מתרפא, ואם לא, הן נהפכין לצרעת, שנ' והיה בעור בשרו וגו'
(שם). וגוף [ו]

מתקלקל בזיבה, שנ' כי יהיה זב מבשרו (שם, ט"ו, ב'). ואם לא עשה תשובה,
עוד, אשתו נעשית

זבה, והיא פורשת ממנו, והיא מתה בלא בנים. הדדהד ו א ש ה כ י י ז ו ב
ז ו ב ד מ ה י מ י ם.

אבל כל מי שהוא משמר מצותו שלהקב"ה, מצילו מכל צער ויסורין, שנ' שומר
מצוה לא ידע דבר רע וגו' (קה' ח', ה').

ס"ז.

פס'. י מ י ם ר ב י ם (וי' ט"ו, כ"ה), וכמה הם רבים, תני ר חייא
ימים, שנים, רבים, שלשה.1 כל הרואה שלשה כבתחילה תהי זבה, תלמוד
לומר

ע ל נ ד ת ה (שם), אחר נדתה היא מטמאה ואינה מטמאה בתחלה. תני
בר קפרא2

י"א יום שבין נדה לנדה הלכה למשה מסיני, ובלבד אחר נידתה אם ראתה
(דף מ"ז, ע"ב)...3 אין לה אלא יום אחד, זו היא שומרת יום כנגד

יום. אבל אם ראתה ג' ימים בתוך א"י (sic) יום, זה אחר זה, זו זבה גמורה,
ועליה נאמר

ו א ש ה כ י י ז ו ב ז ו ב ד מ ה (שם). אם ראתה בי"ב, הוא דם נדה,
חזרה לנדתה, שנ' ב ל א ע ת

נ ד ת ה4 (שם). ולמה היא נטמאת בנדתה ז' ימים, שהיא גרמה מיתה לעולם,

---

2 אני משער שכאן הוא סוף המדרש לסדר פ"ז, איש איש כי יהיה זב מבשרו, שהכיל קיצור
של תנ' הנ' עם הפתיחה „ממנו משפטו ושאתו . . .".

3 לדעתי, כאן היא ההתחלה לסדר פ"ח. המדרש אינו אלא וריאצייה של סעיף נ"ז וכו'
המדנישים את תפקידם של הנגעים לעורר את האדם לתשובה.

סז. מקרורת: תנ' מצורע ו' (ת"ב, ט"ו); וי"ר י"ט, ה'; ספרא מצורע, פרק ה'.
1 צ"ל: יכול, עי' ספרא מצורע, פרק ח' בראש.
2 נדה דף ע"ב, ע"ב בשם ר' אלעזר בן עזריה.
3 בכתה"י התחלת השורה מטושטשת, ויש להשלים עפ"י המקורות: אם ראתה נדם ב' ימים
בתוך י"א יום] אין לה אלא
4 השווה תנ' מצורע ח' (פי' ר' שרירא גאון), ת"ב מצורע, ח'. עי' בבלי נדה דף ע"ב, ע"ב
וע"ג, ע"א.

נב   קטעי מדרשים מכתבי־יד הגניזה

זוב, וכיון שהוא מוצא טומאה, הבריות מרחיקין ממנו. ה ו י   נ ת ע ב   ו נ א ל ח[2]
(אי' ט"ו, ט"ז). אמר הנביא

תיסרך רעתך ומשובתיך תוכ[יחך] (יר' ב', י"ט), מי מביא עליכם את היסורין,
הרעות שאתם

עושים, ת י י ס ר ך   ר ע ת ך,[3] מן הרעות שבשרו עושה.[4]

ס'ה[.]

אמרו חכמים טומאת האיש

בלובן,[1] וטומאת האשה באודם. כל הנשים מטאות בבית החיצון, שנ' ד ם
י ה י ה

[זו]בה בבשרה (וי' ט"ו, י"ט), אבל הזב ובעל קרי אינן מטמאין
עד שתצא טומאתן לחוץ. . . .*

[לסדר פ"ח (ט"ו): ויקרא ט"ו, כ"ה.]

ס'ו[.]

[ואשה כי יזוב זוב דמה ימים רבים.]. . .הוא צריך, והקב"ה
אינו כן, אלא כשהוא דן לאדם ממנו, שנ' ממנו משפטו ושאתו

מ' ו נ' מתחלפים) לח! ה!. אל הנוטריקון הזה רומז, כנראה, אביי באמרו ש,כל תלמיד חכם
שאין תוכו כברו נקרא נתעב שנאמר אף כי נתעב ונאלח" (יומא ע"ב, ע"ב). לפי פירש"י התלמיד
חכם שאין תוכו כברו נרמז בסוף הפסוק ,איש שותה כמים עולה." אבל באופן זה היה לו
לומר נקרא נתעב ונאלח. ולפיכך מסתבר שגם אביי דרש נאלח ,נאה מבחוץ ומלא ליחה מבפנים,
והוא ,תלמיד חכם שאין תוכו כברו. כדאי להעיר שוי"ר י"ח שהוא הסדר שאנו עוסקים בו
מתחיל במאמרו של עקביה בן מהללאל (אבות פ"ג, א') ,דע מאין באתה, מליחה
סרוחה." ,מלא ליחה סרוחה" שבמדרשנו הוא מעין הד מאמרו של עקביה בן מהללאל.
[2] אפשר שיש כאן רמז לתרגום שמתרגם ,נתעב ונאלח" – ד מ ר ח ק   ו מ ס א ב.
[3] השווה פירש"י במקומו: תיסרך רעתך, סוף שרעתך תביא עליך יסורין. וכדומה לזה
ברד"ק.
[4] כאן הוא חוזר אל הסדר, ודורש, איש כי יהיה זוב – מבשרו, כלו' הזיבה באה מרעות
בשרו.

סה. מקורות: ספרא מצורע פרשה ד', א'; פרק זבים א', ו'; משנה נדה פרק ה', א'.
[1] עי' למעלה סעיף מ"ה שמצטט את המשנה בלשון ,שנו חכמים', וגם כאן ,אמרו חכמים
הכוונה למשנה נדה פ"ה הנז' במקורות. ואמנם מ,כל הנשים' עד הסוף נמצא שם, אבל לא
המאמר הראשון. במשנה ובתוספתא זבים אנו מוצאים את השימוש בשני המונחים ,לובן ואודם',
,בין לובן בין אודם.' והיותר קרוב ללשון מדרשנו היא המשנה בזבים פרק ב', א': ,נותנים עליו
חומרי האיש וחומרי האשה, מטמאים ב ד ם (צ"ל: ב א ו ד ם) כאשה ובלובן כאיש.'
* בכתה"י באים כאן הסעיפים ס"ט–ע"א.

סו. מקורות: תנ' תזריע, ח' (ת"ב, י'); וי"ר י"ח, ב'. תנ' מצורע ד' (ת"ב, י"ב) ומקבילות.
[1] על יסוד התנ' אפשר להשלים להתחלת המשפט: ,אין מדותיו של הקב"ה כמדת בשר
ודם, בשר ודם כשהוא רוצה לרדות את עבדו, לכבלים ומגלבין הוא] צריך.

ס"ב].

.... [ולפי שהגביה את עצמו] כארז.[1] הנגעים באים עליו. וכל זמן שאדם
משפיל עצמו כאזוב, הוא נטהר באזוב, שכן דוד אומר תחטאני
באזוב ואטהר וגו' (שם, נ"א, ט'), לפיכך נטהר בארז ואזוב. אמר ר' אליעזר
לעולם אין יסורין בלא עון,[2] שׁ
בתוכחות [על עון] וגו' (שם, ל"ט, י"ב). ואשרי אדם מוכיחו הקב״ה
בעולם הזה, ממלט אותו מיסורין שנ' [אשרי הגבר אשר תיסרנו וגו']‏[3]
(שם, צ"ד, י"ב)...[3]

[לסדר פ"ז (י"ד): ויקרא ט"ו, א'–ב'.]

ס"ג.

פס'. איש איש כי יהיה זב מבשרו. זשה אין
מתום בבשרי מפני זעמך וגו' (שם, ל"ח, ד'), את מוצא רמ"ח איברים שיש
באדם הזה, וכיון שלוקה
אחד מהם כולן לוקין עמו, הרי הוא אומר אין מתום בבשרי, ואין אדם יכול
לעמוד
לפני זעמו שלהקב״ה.

ס"ד].

ואוי לו לאדם הזה שאינו שוה מאומה, והוא נתעב במיתתו, ואפילו
בחייו נאלח, נאה מבחוץ ומלא ליחה סרוחה מבפנים.[1] זב מבשרו,
שהוא מוציא

סב. מקורות: תנ' מצורע, ג' (ת"ב, ח'); פסדר"כ, דף ל"ה, ע"א: פירש"י במקומו.
1 [ולפי שהגביה את עצמו] כארז. ההשלמה היא עפ"י המקורות הנז'.
2 השווה שבת נ"ה, ע"א: אמר ר' אמי (,ר"א' אפשר לקרוא ר' אמי וגם ר' אליעזר)
אין מיתה בלא חטא ואין יסורין בלא עון... דכתיב ופקדתי בשבט פשעם
ובנגעים עונם (תה' פ"ט, ל"ג). בעל מדרשנו מבכר תה' ל"ט, י"ב: ,בתוכחות על עון יסרת
איש' מפני הסמיכות של עון ליסורין (עון יסרת). אם מדעת עצמו השתמש בפסוק זה או שאב
ממקור בלתי ידוע לי — נעלם ממני.
3 בכתה"י חסר כאן יותר משורה שלמה.

סג. מקורו נעלם ממני. הד קל של המדרש אפשר לקלוט בוי"ר ט"ז, ה'. הפסוק אל תתן את
פיך לחטיא בשרך (קה' ה', ה') נדרש באופנים שונים, ובכולם חזר ונשנה הפתגם: ,אל תתן
לאחד מאבריך להחטיא את כל איבריך."

סד. מקורות: השווה למעלה סעיף ס"ב.
1 נראה שדורש את המלה ,נאלח' נוטריקון בשני פנים: א. נא! ה! לח! וק!. ב. מלא

מרים, שנ' ותדבר מרים וגו' (במ' י"ב, א'), ולקתה בצרעת, שנ' והנה מרים
מצורעת כשלג (שם, י'), עד
שהתפלל עליה משה שנ' [ויצ]עק משה אל [י"י וגו'] (שם, י"ג), ולא ביישה.‎7
.... וידים שופכות דם נקי, זה יואב, שהרג את
חבירו אבנר בן נר ואת עמסה
בן יתרא, ולקה [בצרעת], לא [ואל] יכרת ליואב [מבית יואב]‎8 זב ומצורע
(ש"ב, ג', כ"ט).

ס"א.

והכהן ממתין לו ז' ימים ח' ימים שיעשה תשובה, שנ' והסגירו הכהן שבעת ימים
[שנית]
(וי' י"ג, ה'). אם עשה תשובה, וטיהרו הכהן (שם, ו'), ואם לאו,‎1 ונתץ את
הבית וגו' (שם, י"ד, מ"ה). ראה מה העוונות
גורמין, שבני אדם חוטאין ובתים וכלים לוקין עמהן,‎2 אלא כל זמן שהרשעים
לוקין
בבגדיהן לוקין, שכן אתה מוצא בעדתו שלקרח, שנ' וירדו הם וכל אשר להם
חיים
וגו' (במ' ט"ז, ל"ג),‎3 ואם אינם חוזרין בהן, מה כתיב עליה, תמותת רשע רעה
וגו' (תה' ל"ד, כ"ב). אבל הצדיקים, כשצרה
באה עליהן, הן דורשין את המקום בה, והוא ממלטן מכל צרה, שנ' ותשועת
צדיקים
מי"י מעוזם בעת צרה (שם, ל"ז, ל"ט).

‎7 אולי צ"ל: [רפא נא], ולא [נ]ביישה (כך נראה בכתה"י) ... השווה ספורנו בפירושו:
"בבקשה אני שואל שתרפא ולא נצטרך לביישה להוציאה חוץ למחנה." כל מה
שבין הכוכבים כתוב בכתה"י על הגליון לאורך העמוד. מקצתו נפגם.
‎8 בקרא: ואל יכרת מבית יואב.

ס"א. מקורות: תנ' מצורע ד' (ת"ב, י"ב) ומקבילות.
‎1 כנראה, יש כאן דילוג של הבלעה, וצריך להשלים: "ואם לאו [וטמאו הכהן (שם, ח')]."
זה בנגוד ל"וטהרו הכהן" שבא לפני זה. אחר כך מתחילה פיסקא חדשה: "ונתץ את הבית,
ראה מה העוונות וכו'."
‎2 גם כאן חסר, כנראה, הסוף, וצריך להשלים: "לוקין עמהן, ולמה בתים וכלים לוקין?
כדי שיראו בעליהן ויחזרו בהן]" ... ואם אינם חוזרין ..." השווה ת"נ הנז': "ולמה העצים
והאבנים והכתלים לוקין, כדי שיראו הבעלים ויעשו תשובה."
‎3 כל המוסגר בסוגריים היא הוספת איזה מעתיק. מפסיק את המשכו של המשפט, ואין לו
עניין לכאן. עי' הע' שלפני זו.
‎4 בסנהדרין פ"א, ע"ב ריש לקיש מוצא בפסוק זה רמז ל"מי שלקה ושנה בית דין מכניסין
אותו לכיפה ..." ובעל מדרשנו דורש את הפסוק על מי שלקה ושנה בנגעים.

על האדם, בתחלה מדת הדין נוגעת בביתו. אם חזר בו, טעון חליצה,

שנ' וצוה הכהן וגו' (וי' י"ד, ל"ו), וחלצו את האבנים וגו' (שם, מ'), ואם לא חזר, נתיצה שנ' ונתץ

את הבית (שם, מ"ה). ואחר כך מדת הדין נוגעת בבגדיו. אם חזר בו, טעון קריעה,

שנ' וקרע אותו מן הבגד (שם, י"ג, נ"ו), ואם לאו, טעון שריפה, שנ' ושרף את הבגדים

(שם, נ"ב). ואחר כך מדת הדין נוגעת בגופו, והקב̇ה מפרסמו לכל, והן מכריזין לפניו,

(דף מ"ו, ע"ב) שנ' והצרוע אשר בו הנגע וגו'[4] (שם, מ"ה). ואם חזר בו, הקב̇ה מרפאו ומטהרו מטומאתו,

דכתיב ז א ת ת ה י ה ת ו ר ת ה מ צ ו ר ע וגו' [ביום טהרתו][5] (שם, י"ד, ב'), וכן הוא אומר כי הוא יכאיב ויחבש וגו'

ימחץ וידיו תרפינה (אי' ה', י"ח).

‎ס‎.

ד ב ר א ח ר ז א ת ת ה י ה. וזה שש הנה שנא י"י וגו' (מש' ו', י"ח), ר מאיר אומר ש ש ו ש ב ע ה ר י

י"ג, ורבנן אמרין כ ו ל ה ו ן ש ב ע,[1] אלא ש ה ש ב י ע ה[2] קשה מכולן, וכולן לוקין בסוף בזוב

ובצרעת.[3] ע י נ י ם ר מ ו ת (לשון שקר)[4] (שם, י"ט), אלו בנות ציון, שנ' ויאמר י"י יען כי גבהו

בנות ציון וגו' (יש' ג', ט"ז), וכולן[5] לוקין בצרעת, שנ' וספח י"י קדקד בנות ציון וגו'[6] (שם, י"ז). ל ש ו ן ש ק ר,

‎4‎ [וטמא טמא יקרא]. השווה מועד קטן ה', ע"א ומקבילות: „וטמא טמא יקרא, צריך להודיע צערו לרבים ורבים מבקשים עליו רחמים."

‎5‎ וסמוך לו „ביום טהרתו." ועי' לק"ט ריש מצורע.

‎ס‎. מקורות: וי"ר פט"ז, א' ומקבילות.

‎1‎ נוסחת בעל מדרשנו מתאימה כמעט בכל הפרטים עם נוסחת ק' שב„חילופי נוסחאות" בהוצ' מרגליות.

‎2‎ במקורות: „שביעית." ובהתאם לק' צריך לתקן כאן: „שהשביעי." בכתה"י חלו כאן ידי מקלקל.

‎3‎ במקורות המאמר מיוחס לר' יוחנן.

‎4‎ ל ש ו ן ש ק ר היא שיגרת העט.

‎5‎ ו כ ו ל ן, האם מוסב על בנות ציון? יותר נראה ששיגרת העט היא, או שהוא ציטוט של המאמר הקודם.

‎6‎ כדעת ר' לעזר בוי"ר ובנוסחת ק'.

נ"ח.

פס'. ואיש או אשה כי יהיה בו נגע וגו'. ומה ראה[1]
בו בראש ובזקן, אלא אם גרמו עונותיהן, הצרעת נוגעת בזקנו שלאיש
ובראשה שלאשה, לקיים מה שנ' עונותיו ילכדונו את הרשע ובחבלי חטאתו יתמך
(מש' ה', כ"ב). אם שבין

מתוך הצרה, הקב״ה שומע תפלתן ומרפא אותן, שנ' ויאמר אם שמוע
תשמע לקול יי' אלהיך וגו'... כי אני יי' רפאך (שמ' ט"ו, כ"ו).[2]

[לסדר פ"ה (י"ב): ויקרא י"ד, א'–ב'.]

נ"ט.

זאת תהיה. זה
לכן אנשי לבב שמעו לי וגו' (אי' ל"ד, י'), אמר ר' ירמיה
חס ושלום אין הקב״ה משלם לכל אחד ואחד אלא לפי מעלליו ולפי דרכיו,
היך כתיב, חלילה לאל מרשע ושדי מעול כי פועל אדם ישלם לו וגו'
(שם, י'–י"א). לעולם אין הקב״ה[1] נוגע בנפשות,[1] (בעיתות שאדם חוטא לפניו,
אין

מדת הדין נוגעת בגופו) תחלה, (אלא היא נוגעת בממונו). בוא וראה
מן המצריים, בתחלה נגעה בהן מדת הדין בממונם, שנ' ויך גפנם
ותאנתם וגו' (תה' ק"ה, ל"ג), ויהפוך לדם יאוריהם וגו' (שם, ע"ה, מ"ד), ובסוף
איבד את נפשותם,

שנ' וירא ישראל את מצרים מת על שפת הים (שמ' י"ד, ל'). וכן כשהנגעים
באים

נח. מקורו נעלם ממני.
[1] השווה אבן עזרא על פסוק זה: „והנה פירוש ואיש או אשה כי יהיה בו נגע בראש או
בזקנו של איש.‟
[2] הרי זה מעין חתימה לסעיף הקודם המדניש שהנגעים הם קול ה' הקורא את האדם לשוב
מדרכו הרעה. אם „שמע לקול ה','‟ ועשה תשובה הוא מתרפא מנגעיו.

נט. מקורות: תנ' מצורע, ד' (ת"ב, י"ב); וי"ר פי"ז, ד' ומקבילות; פס"ר, פ"ח, ע"ב, מאיר עין,
הע' נ"ח.

הסעיף הזה ביסודו אינו אלא ניסוח שונה של סעיף נ"ז, אלא שכאן בעל מדרשנו משתמש
במקורות הידועים לנו בשנויים קלים ומעט הרחבה.
[1] במקורות המאמר מיוחס לר' לוי, ולשונו: „אין בעל הרחמים נוגע בנפשות
תחילה.‟ בעל מדרשנו בביאורו מהפך את „בעל הרחמים‟ ל„מדת הדין.‟ כי כל פעם שהקב״ה
„נוגע‟ באדם ומענישו הוא משתמש ב„מדת הדין‟ ולא ב„מדת הרחמים.
[2] הדברים בסוגריים הם תוספת־ביאור ולא מגוף המאמר. בעל מדרשנו הרניש את הצורך
לבאר ש„בנפשות‟ כאן אין משמעה נפש בניגוד לגוף, כי אם גוף בניגוד לממון.
[3] וי"ר מביא את הפסוק: ויך כל בכור במצרים (תה' ק"ה, ל"ו).

על נפשם ועל גופם, ואין לך חביב לאדם מגופו והן חוטאין, אלא שאמר
הכתוב הן כל אלה יפעל אל פעמים שלש עם גבר וגו' (אי' ל"ג, כ"ט).

נ"ז.

פס'. למה נאמר בפרשת

נגעים שאת או ספחת או בהרת (וי' י"ג, ב') ואחר כך והיה בעורו וגו'
(שם), בתחלה

מביא עליו נגעים זכרים[1] שאין מולידין, אם עשה תשובה מתקבל,[2] ואם לאו,
מביא נקבות שהן מולידות, בהרת לבנה (שם, ד'), צרעת נושנת (שם, י"א),
אם פרוח

תפרח הצרעת (שם, י"ב), וכל אחד מהן קשה מחברתה ומצרעת את גופו, שנ'
והיה

(דף מ"ו, ע"א) בעורו בשרו לנגע צרעת (שם, ב'). שאת, אם עשה תשובה,
המקום נושא עונותיו,

שנ' מי אל כמוך נושא עון וגו' (מי' ז', י"ח), וכן הוא אומר הלא אם תטיב שאת
וגו' (בר' ד', ז'),

ל[א] רצה, לפתח חטאת רובץ (שם). מיכן ואילך הרי נגעים באין עליו, שנ'
צרעת

(וי' י"ג, ט"ו), וכת[יב] ובשר כי יהיה בו נגע[2] וגו' (שם, י"ח), לקיים מה
שנ' כי כל ימיו מכאובים וכעס וגו'

(קה' ב', כ"ג). אם עשה תשובה,[3] וטהרו הכהן (וי' י"ג, ו'), ואם
לאו, צרעת נושנת היא וגו' (שם, י"א). ובשר כי

יהיה וגו' [ונרפא] (שם, י"ח), אם שב, אם בעיניו עמד הנתק ושער שחור צמח
בו נרפא וגו' (שם, ל"ז), ואם לאו,

וטמא אותו הכהן נתק הוא (שם, ל').

נז. מקורות: תנ' תזריע, י' (ת"ב, י"ד); מצורע, ד' (ת"ב, י"ב); וי"ר י"ז, ד' בסוף. מקור
המקורות: תוספתא נגעים פ"ו, 7.

הדבר המשותף למקורות ולמדרשנו הוא הרעיון שהנגעים באים על האדם בהדרגה, מן
הקל אל הכבד, ואינם אלא כעין התראה וקריאה לתשובה. אלא שבהתפתחותו של הרעיון בעל
מדרשנו הולך בדרך מיוחדת. המקורות מדגישים שהנגעים מתחילים בבית, הולכים ומתפשטים
לבגדים, ומשם לגוף. ואילו בעל מדרשנו מדגיש את ההדרגה בנגעי הגוף למיניהם, ומבדיל בין
נגעים זכרים ונקבות. אינני יודע את מקורו בפרטים אלה.

[1] משמעותם של ‚נגעים זכרים' ו‚נגעים נקבות' נעלמה ממני.
[2] [המחבר לא זכה למלאות את ההערה הזאת. העורך.]
[3] במקורות: אם ‚חזר בו מוטב.'

נ׳ה].

ב י ו ם ח ',

ביום ולא בלילה.¹ אמרו חכמ[ים]² גדולה מילה שעל כל המצות שעשה אברהם לא

נקרא שלם עד שמל, שנ׳ התהלך לפני והיה תמים (בר׳ י״ז, א׳).

[לסדר פ״ד (י״א): ויקרא י״ג, כ״ט.]

נ׳ו].

פס׳. ו א י ש א ו א ש ה כ י י ה י ה ב ו

נ ג ע צ ר ע ת. זשה כי כל ימיו מכאובים וכעס ענינו (קה׳ ב׳, כ״ג), כל ימי שאדם חי בעולם הזה

מלא מכאובים, ומה הנאה לו בכל ממון שלו כשיסורין באין עליו. ומי גרם לו

שיבואו עליו מכאובים,¹ ו כ ע ס ע נ י נ ו, שהיה מכעיס לפני בוראו בענינו,² ובשביל

כך הוא גורם להביא עליו מכאובים. הוי רבים מכאובים לרשע והבוטיח בי״י וגו'

(תה׳ ל״ב, י׳), אילו הצדיקים שאין צער נוגע בהם, ועלי מי המכאובים, על הרשעים, לפיכך

ר ב י ם מ כ א ו ב י ם ל ר ש ע וגו'. הוי אומר נגע צרעת³ וגו' (וי׳ י״ג, ט'), באותו רשע

שאינו עושה רצון בוראו, לפיכך ר ב י ם מ כ א ו ב י ם. אוי⁴ להם לרשעים שהן חוטאין

נה. מקורות: ספרא תזריע, ריש פרק א' ומקבילות; משנה נדרים פרק ג', י״א.
1 ספרא הנז'.
2 במשנת נדרים הנז' בעל המאמר הוא רבי.

נו. מקורות: וי״ר ט״ו, ד'; מדרש אגדה ח״ב, עמ' ל״ג.
1 השווה תרגום לפסוק שלפני זה: כי מה הווה..., שמתרגם ,ארום מה הנאה אית ליה לנבר וכו'.'
2 השווה קה״ר ב', כ״ג שדורש הכתוב על דור המבול, הסדומיים, המצרים, וכולם מסיים: ,וכעס ענינו, שהכעיסו להקב״ה (ת״ב בראשית ל״ד: לפני הקב״ה) במעשי ידיהם.' וגם תחילת הפסוק כי כל ימיו מכאובים נדרש שם באופן זה: ,שמכאיבין להקב״ה במעשי ידיהם.' אולם בעל מדרשנו מבאר את תחילת הפסוק כפשוטו.
3 [כי תהיה באדם], כנראה שדורש ,באדם,' כלו' באדם הראשון שעבר ,על רצון בוראו.' השווה מ״א ח״ב, עמ' ל״ג: ,ולמה אינו אומר דבר אל בני ישראל ... אלא אדם ... הנגעים אינם באים אלא על אדם שעבר על מצות בוראו.' ועי' וי״ר ט״ז, ד': ,אדם מכם אין כתיב כאן ... אלא אדם ... רבים מכאובים.'
4 מכאן עד סוף הסעיף נראה כאילו יש לנו התחלת מדרש חדש עם פתיחה מאיוב ל״ג, כ״ט, מבוא לסעיף הבא.

יונק חלב טמא, ותינוק² יונק חלב טהור. אמר ר' אלעזר בוא וראה כמה
חביב לפני

הקב"ה יום השמיני. שור או שה שנולד, שנאמר בו ומיום השמיני והלאה

(שם, כ"ב, כ"ז), למה, כדי שיראה שבעת ימים יצירת עולם,³ ואחר כך י ר צ ה
ל ק ר ב ן (שם). וכן נדה

וביולדת יספרו לטומאה, וספרה לה וגו'⁴ (שם, ט"ו, כ"ח). א ש ה כ י
ת ז ר י ע, וסמיך ליה וביום

השמיני ימול וגו'. וכן לחג שבעת ימים לסוכה, ולעצרת כתיב ביום
השמיני עצרת

(במ' כ"ט, ל"ה). וכן בני ישי⁵ בנים, אותם הששי דוד השביעי (דה"א ב', ט"ו)
שמיני היכן הוא,⁶ דכת[יב] ליהודה אליהו
מאחי דוד (שם, כ"ז, י"ח).

נ"ד.

פס'. ו ב מ ל א ת י מ י ט ה ר ה ל ב ן וגו' (וי' י"ב, ו'), ולמה היא מביאה
קרבן, אלא כיון
שהצרות מגיעות אותה,¹ היא נודרת נדרים,² לפיכך היא מביאה קרבן.

² אפשר לראות בזה דמיון קל למאמרו של ר' יהושע דסכנין בשם ר' לוי (פסדר"כ ע"ח,
ע"א): משל למלך שנכנס למדינה והוציא כרוז ואמר כל אכסנאין שיש כאן לא יראו פני עד
שיראו פני המטרונה תחילה, כך אמר הקב"ה בני, לא תביאו לפני קרבן עד שתעבור עליו
השבת. עי' הע' המו"ל סי' פ"ז, פ"ח. יותר קרוב למדרשנו הם דברי בעל הטורים לוי' כ"ב, ז':
ימתין ז' ימים וידע שבראתי העולם בו' ימים ונחתי בז' וישחט לשמי.

³ נשבעת ימים . . . וביום השמיני תקח לה שתי תרים].

⁴ נראה שצריך להשלים: [ולו שמנה] בנים (ש"א, י"ז, י"ב).

⁵ גם כאן יש דילוג, וצ"ל: הוא [אליהו]. עי' רד"ק דה"א, ב', ט"ו שהביא בשם המדרש
.כי הבן השמיני היה שמו אליהוא והוא הנזכר בנגידים שהקים דוד ליהודה מאחי דוד
.ומה שאמר ודוד הוא הקטן על שהיה מקטין עצמו קראו קטן. ואמנם לא למדרשנו הוא מתכוין
אלא למ"ד קי"ט, ע"ב: .צעיר היה דוד והלא אליהוא השמיני, וכן הוא אומר דוד השביעי
(דה"א ב', ט"ו), אליהוא [הוא] השמיני, אליהוא הוא אחריו, אלא שהיה עושה עצמו קטן . . ."
בהוצ' בובר מראה המקום לדה"א בא בטעות לאחר .אליהוא השמיני".

כל המאמר המתחיל .וכן בני ישי וכו' " הוא, כנראה, הוספה מאוחרת, שכן אין כאן
המדובר מ.שמיני" בכלל, כי אם מ.יום שמיני." ולא עוד אלא שקשה לראות איך אפשר להוציא
מכאן ש.ששמיני" חביב, מאחר שדוד .החביב" הוא כאן השביעי. ובאמת הפסוק הזה משמש
ראייה ש.כל השביעין" חביבין (וי"ר, כ"ט, י"א). ואולי בדמיונו של הדרשן-המוסיף אליהו, אחי
דוד, מזדהה עם .אליהו הנביא."

נד. מקורות: תנ' תזריע, ד' (ת"ב, ו') ומקבילות; נדה ל"א, ע"ב.
¹ ת"ב: מניעות אצלה; תנ': מקיפות אותה. בעל מדרשנו מרכיב שתי הנוסחאות.
² תנ': .נודרת שלא תזקק עוד לאישה,* ומתאים כמעט בדיוק לדברי
רשב"י בנדה: .נשבעת שלא תזקק לבעלה." בת"ב יש לראות בלשון נקייה .נודרת
שאינה מכרת אישה עוד." עוד יותר נקייה היא לשונו של בעל מדרשנו.

ובין יולדת בית,[2] או מפלת,[3] חייבות להטמאות בימי לידה. אם זכר[4] (וי'
י"ב, ב'), תשב (שם, ד') לזכר,

ואם נקבה (שם, ה'), תשב לנקבה. והמפלת, ואין ידוע [מה הוא
אם זכר או נקבה],[5] תשב לזכר

ולנקבה,[6] [נותנין עליה חומרי זכר וחומרי נקבה, כיצד, י"ד טמאים ס"ו[7] טהורים].
ילדה זכר ונקבה, או נקבה וזכר, תשב לנקבה.

נ"ב].

האשה מזרעת תחלה,[1]

יולדת בן זכר, שנ' כי תזריע וילדה זכר (שם, ב'). וטמאה
שבעת ימים, וטובלת בליל ח', שהוא יום
המילה, וסופרת ז' נקים (דף מ"ה, ע"ב) ומותרת לבעלה.[2]

נ"ג].

וביום הח' ימול וגו' (שם, ג'), כדי שימול בטהרה,[1] שבשבעת ימים
היה

[2] נרדף ל״שפחה״ שאינה משוחררת (עי' תוס' יבמות הנ"ל), ואינני יודע לשם מה הוא בא.

[3] נראה שהמשנה בכריתות, פרק א', משנה ג': ...המפלת, וכן שפחה
שהפילה ״ הולידה את הצירוף של שפחה ומפלת.

[4] מכאן בעל מדרשנו עובר למשנה נדה פ"ג, ב': ...המפלת (כמין בהמה חיה ועוף בי,
טמאין בין טהורין] אם זכר...".

[5] המוסגר הוא הוספת פירוש ואינו במשנה.

[6] עד כאן דברי המשנה, ומכאן והילך פירוש המאמר ״תשב לזכר ולנקבה.״ השווה פירוש
רש"י: ״לזכר ולנקבה, ל ח ו מ ר א ימי טומאה דנקבה שבועים וימי טוהר כלים לסוף ארבעים
יום כזכר.״

[7] טעות המעתיק, וצ"ל: מ' (ארבעים) כבפרש"י הנ'. כנראה, שני חלקי ה.מ', הימני
והשמאלי, לא היו מעורים, וזה נתן מקום למעתיקים לטעות. כשעיינתי בכתה"י ראיתי שידי
מתקנים(!) עסקו במלה זו.

נב. מקורות: תנ' תזריע, ג' (ת"ב, ד')); וי"ר י"ד, ה'.

[1] בניסוח זה נמצא המאמר בבבלי, נדה דף ל"א, ע"א. במקורות שרשמנו הלשון יותר
נקייה: ״אם קדמה האשה״ או ״הזכר מן האשה.״

[2] השווה ת"ב מצורע בסוף והערת המו"ל שם.

נג. מקורות: מדרש אגדה, ח"ב, עמ' ל"ב; נדה ל"א, ע"ב.

[1] השווה מ"א: מפני מה ... שהתה המילה עד שתצא מ ט ו מ א ה ל ט ה ר ה. המו"ל
הולך בעקבות ה.לקח טוב" ומשלים את החסר כאילו היה לנו כאן ניסוח אחר של טעמו של
ר' שמעון בן יוחאי (נדה הנ'): ״שלא יהיו כולם שמחים ואביו ואמו עצבים.״ אבל מתוך מדרשנו
נראה ש.טומאה וטהרה" מוסב לחלב שהתינוק יונק, ואין לו עניין לדברי ר' שמעון בן יוחאי.
מקור מדרשנו נעלם ממני.

מלא רירין ודם, הכל מנשק[ין] ומחבקין אותו, הוי תועבה יבחר
ב כ ם.

[נ.

לפיכך אליהוא

אומר אשא דעי למרחוק וגו' (אי' ל"ו, ג'), כמה פעולות הוא פועל בי עד שלא
אצא לעולם,

אַף כן צ ד ק הוא עושה עמי, שהוא יודע כמה פעמים אני עתיד לעמוד
ולחטא, והוא משמרני בבטן אמי ובשעת לידתי, הוי ולפועלי אתן צדק.[1]

נ"א].

א ש ה כ י ת ז ר י ע. בין גיורת, בין שפחה, בין משוחררת, ובין בת ישראל,[1]

נ. מקורות: תנ' תזריע, ג' (ת"ב, ד')); וי"ר י"ד, ב'.

[1] המקורות פה אחד שהפסוק באיוב מוסב על יצירת הולד. הדרוש מבוסס בעיקר על
החצי השני של הפסוק "ולפועלי אתן צדק" שנדרש למי שיצר אותי ופעל בי כמה "מעשה
נסים" בלשונו של התנ', או "שבחים" — "פעולות משובחים" בלשונו של ר' לוי בוי"ר. ה"נסים"
ו"השבחים" מתוארים במקורות במשלים שונים, ובעל מדרשנו מרמז עליהם בפתגם קצר:
"כמה פעולות הוא פועל בי עד שלא אצא לעולם." בלתי ברור הוא הקשר עם תחילת הפסוק
"אשא דעי למרחוק" במקורות. בעל מדרשנו הרכיב, כנראה, בדרוש המקורות חלק מדרושו
של ר' מאיר על הפסוק הדורש למרחוק על הרשעים שהם רחוקים מה' (וי"ר, שם בתחילת
הפיסקה). כל הפסוק נדרש איפוא באופן מיוחד: אשא דעי למרחוק כשאני מעלה על דעתי
מעשי רשע המרחיקים אותי מה', "אתן צדק לפועלי" אתנה (אספר) צדקותיו של ה'
ש"אף על פי כן" יצר אותי "ופעל בי כל הפעולות עד שלא אצא לעולם."
ארשה לעצמי להציע השערה בפירוש דברי ר' מאיר הנז': "אמר ר' מאיר הפסוק הזה
משמש שתי לשונות לשון שירה ולשון ז מ ר, לשון שירה על שלותן של צדיקים, ולשון ז מ ר
על מפלתן של רשעים." מתוך חלופי נוסחאות נראה שהמלה ז מ ר היא מפוקפקת. ובאמת
אינה הולמת את העניין הדורש הפיכה של "שירה" ולא זמר שהוא נרדף לה. המפרשים כמעט
כולם מיחסים את דו־המשמעות ל"אשא" דעי; ובאכר מעביר אותה ל"מלים" שבפסוק הקודם.
וכל זה אינו מניח את הדעת. אני משער שר' מאיר מכוון ל"אתן" צדק. כפי שהערנו בעלי
המדרש גזרו "אתן" מ"תנה" ולא מ"נתן", ודרשו "אתנה" "אתנה" צדק. והנה השורש "תנה" נמצא במקרא
שתי פעמים, פעם במובן שיר תהילה (שו' ה', י"א: שם יתנו צדקות ה') ופעם במובן של
קינה (שו' י"א, מ': לתנות לבת יפתח). לשתי הלשונות האלו מתכוון ר' מאיר. בכיוון לצדיקים
הוא לשון שירה, אשורר צדקות (צדק) ה'; בכיוון לרשעים, אקונן מ ש פ ט י ו (צדק). קשה
לחוד איזו מלה היתה במקום ז מ ר או ז כ ר או ד ב ר. ודאי לא ק י נ ה כי אז לא היו
המעתיקים מסרסים אותה כל כך. אפשר שהיה כתוב "יבב" ("יבבה")", מלה בלתי רגילהן
והניעה את המעתיקים לתקנה.

נא. מקורות: ספרא, ריש תזריע; נדה פרק נ', משנה ב' (דף כ"א, ע"א).

[1] השווה ברייתא ביבמות ע"ד, ע"ב: גיורת ושפחה משוחררת. בעל מדרשנו נראה שפירש
הדברים באופן זה: גיורת, שפחה [שאינה משוחררת], משוחררת, באופן שיסכימו לנוסחת
הספרא: "מניין לרבות את הגיורת ואת השפחות, בין משוחררת ובין אין משוחררת." עי' בתוס'
יבמות, שם, ד"ה ושפחה מנין.

חזיר (וי' י"א, ה'–ז').[9] נידמו לנבוכדנצר כחיות השדה: ארי, ודוב, ונמר,
וחזיר יער (דנ' ז', ד' וכו'). וכל אחד
ואחד מן הנביאים נידמו לו כמו דוגמא משאר הדומות.[10] ואחרי כן קץ
המשיח,[8] שנ' ובעת ההיא יעמוד מיכאל השר הגדול העומד וגו' (שם, י"ב, א').

[לסדר פ"ב (ט'): ויקרא י"ב, א'–ב'.]

מ"ח.

א ש ה כ י ת ז ר י ע. זשה אין קדוש כי"י כי
אין בלתך וגו' (ש"א, כ', כ'). בשר ודם צר צורה על הכותל,
אינו יכול לצור על המים,[1] אבל הקב"ה צר את האדם הזה[2] במעי אמו במים,
ו א י ן
צ ו ר כ א ל ה י נ ו[3] (שם).

מ"ט]

אמר הכתוב הן אתם מ א י ן ופעלכם מ א פ ע וגו', מה הוא ה ן א ת ם מ א י ן,
שכל הבריות שנבראו בעולם, מדבר שאינן מאומה נבראו. לכך נאמר ה ן
א ת ם מ א י ן
וגו' (יש' מ"א, כ"ד), מ ל י ח ה ס ר ו ח ה; ו פ ע ל כ ם מ א פ ע, ממאה פעיות
שהאשה פועה, בשעה שהיא
יושבת על המשבר,[1] צ"ט למיתה ואחת לחיים;[2] והתינוק הזה אף על פי שהוא

---

9 מקורות: גמל – בבל, שפן – מדי, ארנבת – יון, חזיר – אדום. עי' הע' צ"ב בת"ב הנז'.
10 נראה שאין זה אלא פרפרזה של התחלת המאמר בוי"ר: כל הנביאים ראו למלכיות
ב ע י ס ו ק ן.

מח. מקורות: תנ' תזריע, ב' (ת"ב, ג'); וי"ר כ"ז, ז' ומקבילות.
1 במק': ש מ א י כ ו ל לצור על המים. כבר מצאנו שדרכו של בעל מדרשנו להפוך
שאלה ריטורית למשפט שלילי.
2 במק': העובר.
3 במק' נוסף: אין צייר כאלהינו.

מט. מקורות: תנ' תזריע, ד' (ת"ב, ו'); וי"ר כ"ז, ז' ומקבילות.
1 ההתחלה הזאת חסרה בתנ' ות"ב, אבל ישנה בשאר מקורות בקיצור: "מאין, מ ל י ח ה
ס ר ו ח ה." יש לשמוע כאן הד מאמרו של עקביא בן מהללאל (אבות פ"ג, א'): מ א י ן
באת, מ ט י פ ה ס ר ו ח ה.
2 עד כאן בתנחומא הנרשם. מכאן והילך הוא מאמר ר' אבהו המובא בתנ' ובת"ב תזריע, א'
בלי קשר עם הפסוק "תועבה יבחר בכם." בשאר המקורות, וביחוד בוי"ר כ"ז, ז' הוא כבמדרשנו.
עי' בובר ח"ב אמור, י"ד, הע' קל"ה.

טמאים שקצים ורמשים, זוכה לזיז שדי.[1] ואין לישראל חיים וגדולה בעולם הזה ובעולם

הבא אלא בתורה,[2] שנ' עץ חיים היא וגו' (מש' ג', י"ח).

מ"ז.

פס'. זאת החיה אשר תאכלו. ולמה ד' אלו פירש שמותם, מפני שיש בהם סימני טהרה. רמז הקב"ה לד' מלכיות, והן מדמות

(דף מ"ה, ע"א) דמיונות:[2] פישון, וגיחון, חדקל, פרת (בר' ב', י"א—י"ד).[3] נידמו לאברהם כעגלה [ועז ואיל ותר]

וגמל (שם, ט"ו, ט').[4] חזר מדמה:[5] חשכה גדולה נופלת עליו (שם, י"ב). נדמו ליעקב כגן [ועד ....].[1]

ובאר.[6] נידמו למשה כזהב וכסף ונחשת ואבנים טובות (שמ' כ"ה, ג', ז'),[7] חזרו ונידמו לו כנחש

שרף ועקרב וצמאון וגו'[8] (דב' ח', ט"ו). ועוד נידמו לו כחיות כבהמה: גמל, שפן, ארנבת,

---

1 פרפרוזה של המאמר במ"ת: אמר ר' ברכיה בשם ר' יעקב לא תאכלו כל נבלה ... טרפה לא תאכלו, וחלב ... ואכול לא תאכלוהו ... ואם לא אכלתם בעולם הזה, חייכם בני שאריסטוון גדול מתוקן לכם לעתיד לבא מסעודת לויתן ומבהמת זיז שדי. מצד אחר, בעל מדרשנו מרמז לוי"ר המאחד בהמות וליותן בקשר להלכות שחיטה. זיז שדי הוא לדעת מדרשנו עוף (עי' וי"ר כ"ב, י' בסוף), ולפיכך זוכה בו „מי ששומר פיו מעופות טמאים."

2 כנראה, בעל מדרשנו דורש זאת תורת הבהמה והעוף, זאת היא התורה המזכה אותנו בבהמה–לויתן–ובעוף–זיז שדי.

מז. מקורות: תנ' שמיני, ח' (ת"ב, י"ד); וי"ר י"ג, ה' ומקבילות.

1 השווה אבן עזרא בפירושו לוי' י"א, ג': והזכיר הגמל והשפן הארנבת והחזיר בעבור שיש לכל אחד מהם סימן אחד של טהרה.

2 =דמיונות, (מתוקן על הגליון בכתה"י, כלומר) המלכיות מתוארות בסמלות (דמיונות) שונים.

3 – בבל, מדי, יון, אדום.

4 השווה ב"ר מ"ד, י"ח. עגלה – בבל, עז – מדי, איל – יון, תור וגול זה אדום.

5 כלו' ועוד ראה אברהם את המלכיות בסמלות אחרים: [אימה], חשכה, גדולה, נופלת עליו – בבל, מדי, יון, אדום (עי' ב"ר הנז', י"ז).

6 צ"ל: נדמו ליעקב בגנ['] עד[רי צאן] ובאר. הכוונה לבר' כ"ט, ב' וכו', ומרמז לב"ר ע', ח': ד"א ... והנה באר זו ציון, והנה שם שלשה עדרי צאן, אלו שלש מלכיות הראשונות ... ונאספו שמה כל העדרים, זו מלכות רומי.

7 השווה תנ' תרומה, ז' (ת"ב, ו'): זהב – בבל, כסף – מדי, נחשת – יון, עורות אילים מאדמים – אדום. אולם כאן נראה כאילו סמל מלכות אדום הן אבנים טובות, ונעלם ממני מקורו. עי' מ"א ח"א, 166–167, הע' ה'.

8 במקורות שונים, וי"ר י"ג, ה' ומקבילות, נרמז שהפסוק הזה מסמל את ארבע מלכיות, אבל הסמלים, חוץ מעקרב, לא נתבארו.

כשרה לשחיטה פסולה.[3] שנו חכמים[4] סימני בהמה וחיה נאמרו מן התורה, וסימני

העוף לא נאמרו.   [אבל] אמרו חכמים כל עוף [ה]דורס טמא, וכל שיש לו אצבע יתירה ועוד[5]

זפק וקרקבן נקלף ביד[6] טהור. ר' אלעזר בר' צדוק[7] אומר ז"ל כל עוף חולק את

רגליו טמא. ובחגבים כל שיש לו ארבע רגלים, וד' כנפים, וקרסולין,[8] וכנפיו חופין את

רובו טהור.[9] ר' יוסי אומר[10] שני קשקשין וסנפיר אחת(ד'), ואלו הן הקשקשין הקבועין בו, והסנפירין

שהוא [ה]פורח בהן.

מ"ו].

פס'. זאת תורת הבהמה והעוף וגו' (וי' י"א, מ"ו). כל מי ששומר הלכות שחיטה,

ושומר פיו מנבלות וטרפות וחלבים ודמים, זוכה לסעודת לויתן. וכל מי ששומר פיו מעופות

3 בצורה יותר מוחשית בספרא: „בין שנשחט רובו של קנה לנשחט חציו."
4 משנה חולין פרק ג', ו'–ז'.
5 ועוד זפק–ווזפק במשנה.
6 בחולין דף ס"ב, ע"ב מונה התלמוד נקלף בסכין ולא ביד בין הספקות. בעל מדרשנו הכניס, כנראה, לתוך משנתנו את מסורת הגאונים, המובאה במשנה תורה, הלכות מאכלות אסורות פרק א' הל' י"ט, שזפק וקורקבן נקלף ביד מוכרח ללוות כל סימן טהרה אחר. ולפיכך כותב: „ועוד זפק . . . נקלף ביד."
7 במשנה: ר' אלעזר בר צדוק אומר. אפשר שבעל מדרשנו קרא ב"ר – בשם ר', ועל כן „ר' אלעזר אמר בשם ר' צדוק ז"ל."
8 כן הוא במשנה שבמשניות; במשנה שבתלמוד: וקרצולין.
9 ליתא במשנה, והיא הוספת־פירוש של בעל מדרשנו. השווה רש"י במשנה, ד"ה ובחגבים: „זהו סימן טהרתם." כשעיינתי בכתה"י ראיתי שהמלה „טהור" כתובה על הגליון.
10 יש כאן דילוג מתוך הבלעה, וצריך להשלים עפ"י המשנה: „ר' יוסי אומר [ושמו חגב, ובדגים כל שיש לו סנפיר וקשקשת, ר' יהודה אומר] שני קשקשין . . .".

מו. מקורות: וי"ר י"ג, ג'; מ"ת י"ח, כ"ה.

איוב אומ[ר] מי יתן טהור מטמא וגו' (אי' י"ד, ד'), התיר הקב"ה את הפרה
ואסר את הגמל, מי

יוכל לטהר או לטמא, הוי מי יתן טהור מטמא, אלא⁵ יחידו שלעולם.

מ"ד.

פס'. זאת הבהמה

אשר תאכלו¹ (וי' י"א, ב'), יכול הבהמה כולה מותרת, ת"ל אך בשר
בנפשו דמו לא תאכלו (בר' ט', ד'), אסר אבר

מן החי, שנ²' על כן לא יאכלו בני ישראל את גיד [הנשה] (שם, ל"ב, ל"ג),
[ללמדך³ על [אבר] מן החי).

פס'.⁴ כל חלב שור וכשב ועז וגו' (וי' ז', כ"ג,⁵) אסר
את החלב ואת הדם. יכול יהו מותרין בזביחה, ת"ל וזבחת ואכלת (דב'
י"ב, ט"ז), מה למדנו הלב[ות] שחיטה

וח"י טריפות [וחלב]⁶ ודם ודקדוקיהן, שכן הוא אומר בסוף הענין.

מ"ה.

ולהבדיל בין הקדש ובין החול וגו'¹

(וי' י', י'), ואין² צריך לאמר בין חמור לפרה וכבר הן מפורשין, אם כן למה
נאמר, להבדיל בין שחי [טה]

---

⁵ בתנ': ל א – בהתאם ללשון הכתוב – "לא אחד," שהתנ' מפרש במשמעות של שאלה
ריטורית.

מד. מקורות: ספרא שמיני, פרשה ב', סימן ד'. הסעיף הזה כולו מקוטע ומסורס, וצריך לתקנו
עפ"י המקור.

1 ההתחלה חסרה, ויש להשלים: [זאת החיה אשר תאכלו מכל הבהמה, משמע מוציא מיד
משמע, מכלל שנאמר כירק עשב נתתי לכם את כל, יכול הכל היה בכלל היתר, ת"ל] זאת
הבהמה ...

2 אני משער שצ"ל: ונאמר על כן ... את גיד הנשה [אסר גיד הנשה], בהתאם
למקור: "וע ל כן לא יאכלו ... גיד הנשה, אסר גיד הנשה."

3 "ללמדך ... החי", אינו אלא ניסוח אחר של "אסר אבר מן החי", וצריך להעבירו
לשם. כשעיינתי בכתה"י מצאתי שהמשפט הזה כתוב על הגליון בדיו שונה.

4 יש למחקו, כי אין כאן פיסקה חדשה כי אם המשך הפיסקא שלמעלה, שבאה להראות
שלא "כל' הבהמה מותרת, כי חלקים ידועים, כגון גיד הנשה, חל ב ו ד ם אסורים.

5 יש להשלים: [וכל דם לא תאכלו (וי', ז', כ"ו)] אסר ...

6 בכתה"י נשלם על הגליון: [ושלא בזביחה], כמו שהוא בספרא.

מה. מקורות: ספרא, סוף שמיני; משנה חולין פ"ג, משנה ו'–ז'.

1 שינרת העט, וצ"ל: בין הטמא ובין הטהור [ובין החיה הנאכלת ובין החיה אשר לא
תאכל] (וי', י"א, מ"ז) שהוא סוף הענין. וי', י', י' אין ענינו לכאן.

2 בספרא: "צריך לאמר" – שאלה ריטורית. השווה למעלה סעיף 44.

[לסדר פ"א (ח'): ויקרא י"א, א'.]

מ"ב.

פס'. ז א ת ה ח י ה א ש ר

ת א כ ל ו. זשה משמים השמעת דין וג' (תה' ע"ו, ט'), אם י ר א ה, למה
שקטה, ואם שקטה

(דף מ"ד, ע"ב) למה י ר א ה, אמר ר' ירמיה[1] כל זמן שהבריאות[2] יראים
מן הקב"ה, יראתו מביאה אותם
לידי שקט,[3] לכך נאמר ארץ יראה ושקטה.

מ"ג.

ז א ת ה ח י ה. ה' דברים[1] נתקשה למשה,
והראה לו הקב"ה, ואלו הן: מנורה, שנ' זה מעשה המנורה וג' (במ' ח', ד');
והירח, שנ' החודש הזה
וג' (שמ' י"ב, ב'); והשרצים,[2] מלמד שהעביר לפני משה בהמה וחיה, ועופות,
ושרצים, והיה מראה
אותו ואומר לו: זה אכול זה לא תאכל, שנ' א ך א ת ז ה וג' (וי' י"א, ד'),[2]
ונאמר כ ל א ש ר ל ו ס נ פ י ר
ו ק ש ק ש ת[3] (שם, ט'), וכן הוא אומר ו א ת א ל ה ת ש ק צ ו מ ן
ה ע ו ף וג' (שם, י"ג),[4] זה טמא וזה אינו טמא. מה

מ"ב. מקורות: תנ' שמיני ו' (ת"ב, י') ומקבילות.

1 השווה פס"ר, פיסקא כ"א (הוצ' איש־שלום, צ"ט, ע"ב־ק', ע"א) במאיר עין הע' י"ז
שמביא את הנוסחאות השונות, ואין שם ר' ירמיה, אבל יש שם ר' יוחנן. ואפשר שהיה כתוב ר"י
ואיזה מעתיק קרא בטעות ר' ירמיה.

2 כנראה שבעל מדרשנו דורש ארץ – יושבי ארץ – הבריות, ומבאר הפסוק כשיושבי ארץ
יראים מה' הם שוקטים, כלו' אינם יראים מבני אדם. ואפשר שמרמז ליראי ה' מן הגוים. המקור
לדרוש זה נעלם ממני.

מ"ג. מקורות: תנ' שמיני, ח' (ת"ב, י"א) ומקבילות; ספרא שמיני, פרשה ב', סי' ב'.

1 ברוב המקורות המובאים בת"ב, הע' ס"ז יש רק "שלשה דברים". במקום א' (שמ"ר
פט"ו) מונה "ארבעה דברים." אבל "חמשה דברים" לא מצאתי בשום מקור אחר. ולכאורה גם
מדרשנו אינו מונה אלא שלשה דברים: מנורה, ירח, שרצים. אך באמת שרצים הם אחד שהם
שלשה: בהמה טמאה, שרץ המים ושקץ העוף. זה יוצא מלשון הספרא: "ז א ת ה ח י ה,
מלמד שהיה משה אוחז ומראה להם לישראל ... א ת ז ה ת א כ ל ו מכל אשר במים – זה
תאכלו וזה לא תאכלו. א ת א ל ה ת ש ק צ ו מן העוף – את אלה תשקצו ואת אלה לא תשקצו."
יש לנו איפוא שלשה דברים בשרצים ("בהמה וחיה, ועופות, ושרצים'). הוסף עליהם "מנורה"
ו"ירח", הרי חמשה.

2 מכאן שהראה לו בהמה וחיה.

3 מכאן שהראה לו שקץ המים.

4 מכאן שהראה לו שרץ העוף.

מ[.

אמר ר' יוסי ב"ר חנינא[1] מן הפסוק הזה את למד ד' דברים.

ו ח נ ה ה י א מ ד ב ר ת ע ל ל ב ה (ש"א, א', י"ג), מיכן שהתפלה צריכה כוונה; ר ק ש פ ת י ה נ ע ו ת, מיכן

שהוא צריך להרחיש בשפתיו; ו ק ו ל ה ל א י ש מ ע, מיכן שלא יהא אדם מגביה קולו

ומתפלל; ו י ח ש ב ה ע ל י ל ש כ ו ר ה, מיכאן שהשכור אסור להתפלל.[2] לכך הוא מצוה

לכהן גדול שלא לשתות יין בשעת העבודה, כדי שלא תטרף דעתו, שהוא משמר את התורה ומשמר את הדעת, שנ' כי שפתי כהן ישמרו דעת וגו' (מלא' ב', ז').[3] לכך

הזהירו י י ן ו ש כ ר א ל ת ש ת, ולא אתה לעצמך, אלא ובניך אתך.

מ"א[.

אשרי אדם שאינו

להוט אחר היין. אתה מוצא בבני יונדב בן רכב שצוה אותם אביהם אל[1] תשתו יין

וגו', ויאמרו לא נשתה יין וגו' (יר' ל"ה, ו'). אמר הקב"ה לירמיהו: אמור להם [חייכם] הואיל ושמרתם

את המצוה הזאת, אין משפחתכם פוסקת מלפני לעולם, שנ' (שכן כתיב) לכן כה אמר י"י לא

יכרת איש ליונדב בן רכב עומד לפני כל הימים (שם, י"ט).

מ. מקורות: ירושלמי ברכות, פ"ד, הלכה א'; תנ' ות"ב הנז'.

1 בבבלי, ברכות דף ל"א, ע"א, המאמר הוא בשם ר' המנונא ובניסוח שונה. בעל מדרשנו מעתיק מן הירושלמי.

2 בתנ' המאמר משולב בדברי ר' יהודה הלוי בר שלום "נכנס היין הדעת יצאה וכו'." בעל מדרשנו תלש סוף הדרוש מן ההתחלה, ומלת "לכך" תלויה באויר. מצד אחר הסמיך מדרשנו עבודה לתפילה, כי תפילה היא כנגד עבודה.

3 בתנ' מביא גם הפסוק הקודם, ת ו ר ת א מ ת וכו' כנגד "משמר התורה". בעל מדרשנו מבכר להוציא הכל מפסוק אחד, ומשתמש בסוף הפסוק ו ת ו ר ה י ב ק ש ו מ פ י ה ו רמז ל"משמר התורה."

מא. מקורות: תנ' שמיני, ה', קרוב לסוף (ת"ב, ט').

1 בפסוק: אבינו צוה עלינו לאמר ל א ת ש ת ו יין; בתנ': שצוה להם ... ש ל א לשתות יין.

ובשעה שאדם מיצר לו, עוסק בתורה והיא משמחתו, שכן דוד אומר לולי
תורתך

שעשועי וגו' (שם, קי"ט, צ"ב). וכת[יב]³ בשיר לא ישתו יין (יש' כ"ד, ט'),
מה הוא יימר שכר לשותיו (שם), שהוא מימר

(דף מ"ד, ע"א) לגוי שהוא עוסק בו. וכל זמן שאדם נכנס אצל מי שהוא גדול
ממנו, אינו צריך

להיות שתוי יין, קל וחומר שהוא נכנס לשרת לפני הקב̇ה̇. לכך הקיש שריפת
בניו שלאהרן לפרשת יין, שאם עבד והוא שתוי יין, עבודתו פסולה.⁴ וכן אתה
מוצא בעשרת השבטים, שנאמר בהן השותין במזרקי יין וגו' (עמ' ו', ו'), מה
כת[יב] אחריו,

לכן עתה יגלו וגו' (שם, ז'). וכן שבט יהודה ובנימין, כתיב בהן וגם אלה ביין
שגו וגו'

(יש' כ"ח, ז'). לכך אמר שלמה אל תרא יין כי יתאדם (מש' כ"ג, ל"א). מה
הוא יתהלך במישרים (שם), שמתוך

שאדם משתכר, הוא רואה הכל לפניו מישור, ומתיר את האיסור⁵ ועשה דבר
שאיפשר לו, ואינו חושש ולא מתבייש. ומה כתיב שם, אחריתו כנחש ישך (שם,
ל"ב), מה הנחש

נושך וממית, כך היין גורם לבעליו לעבור על מה שכתוב בתורה, והוא מתחייב
מיתה וכרת. לכך אמר שלמה אל תהי בסובאי יין (שם, כ'). וכן חבקוק הנביא
אומר

ואף כי היין בוגד גבר יהיר וגו' (חב' ב', ה'), וכל מי שהוא אוהב יין בוגד
באלהים, כיצד, אין השכור יכול לעסק בתורה וניסוח אחר של הדרש
במישרים שהוא מתיר את האיסור,⁶ הרי למדת היין עושה לאדם בוגד באלהים,
לקיים

מה שנ̇ ואף כי היין בוגד.⁷

---

³ מכאן עד .עוסק בו' הוא, כנראה, קטע נתלש מדרוש המדבר בגנות היין, ומקורו נעלם
ממני. נראה כאילו היה דורש יימר כמו ימיר, כלו' שהיין גורם לו להיות לגוי, למומר.
⁴ השווה זבחים י"ז, ע"ב שמוציא מ.יין ושכר אל תשת ... ולהבדיל בין החול .' .. שתוי
יין שעבד חלל, כלו' שעבודתו פסולה.
⁵ השווה תנ' הנז': .סוף שהוא מתיר את העבירות ועושה אותן ה פ ק ר   כ מ י ש ו ר '.
וגם כאן אולי צריך לתקן: ועושה דבר   ש מ י ש ו ר   לו. אולם יותר טוב .ישר לו' בהתאם
לניסוח במ'ר י', ב': ש ע ו ש י ם   כ ל   ה י ש ר בעיניו. השווה ת̇ב̇ הע̇ הטו"ל מס' ל"ז, ל"ח.
⁶ בתנ' לומד מפסוק זה שהיין גורם לד' דברים, עבודה זרה, גלוי עריות, שפיכת דמים
ולשון הרע, וכל זה נלמד מ.זד' ו.יהיר', ולא מ.בוגד.'

בניו ו[ה]צדיק את הדין, שנ' ויאמר משה [אל אהרן] הוא
אשר דבר י׳י לאמר וגו' (וי' י', ג'), והיכן דבר י׳י,
ונועדתי שמה לבני ישראל ונקדש בכבודי (שמ' כ"ט, מ"ג), וקיבל אהרן שכר
על אותה הדמימה.[1]

אמר משה: אמר לי הקב"ה בקרבי אקדש (וי' י', ג'), הייתי סבור
שהדבר תלוי בי או בך, עכשיו
שהדבר בשני בניך, והם חשובים כמותי וכמותך.[2] מיד שתק אהרן וקיבל תנחומ[2]
ים, שנ' וידום אהרן (שם). מיד נתיחד עמו הדיבר וניחמו,[3] לכך
נאמר אחריו וידבר י׳י אל
אהרן לאמר יין ושכר אל תשת וגו' (שם, ט').

[לסדר פ' (ז'): ויקרא י', ח'—ט'.]

ל"ט].

[יין ושכר אל תשת.] זשה פקודי י׳י ישרים משמחי לב וגו' (תה'
י"ט, ט'). אמר
שמואל[1] כל דברי תורה משמחין את הלב, ומצותיה מאירה עינים לאדם
מלחטא,[2]

---

1 בספרא ומקבילות: "השתיקה" או "שתיקתו". נוסחת מדרשנו מעורה במקור "וידם
אהרן". ובכל זאת הד "השתיקה" נשמעת מצורת דמימה. במקרא יש דממה ולא
דמימה, שנעימה פיטנית לה.

2 בוי"ר: "חביבין ממנו, כלו' גדולים ממני וממך" (תנ'). בעל מדרשנו לא יכול היה
לתפוס את הרעיון שמי שהוא יכול היה להיות גדול ממשה, ועל כן תיקן "כמותי וכמותך".

3 מעניינת הטיית המשמעות שהכניס בעל מדרשנו במשפט: "מיד שתק אהרן וקיב ל
תנחומים." לפי פשוטו רוצה לומר שקיבל דברי התנחומים של המובאים מקודם, וזה
יוצא גם מניסוח המדרש בוי"ר: "וידם אהרן, היה לו הדבר לנחמה." אולם לפי ביאורו של בעל
מדרשנו ה"תנחומים" באו לאחר השתיקה, ולא ממש כי אם מה": "מיד נתיחד עמו הדיבור
וניחמו." בוי"ר יחוד הדיבור הוא שכר ולא נחמה, וכך הוא ניסוחו: "מה שכר קיבל על
שתיקתו? זכה שחיבבו הכתוב ונתיחד אליו הדיבר."

לט. מקורות: וי"ר י"ב א', נ' ומקבילות: תנ' שמיני, ה' (ת"ב: ז'), י"א.

1 ברוב המקורות (וי"ר, שו"ט, דב"ר) המאמר נמסר בשם "חזקיה (בר חייא)" או "ר' חייא."
במקורות מפותח הרעיון שהתורה היא תרופה לכל האברים, "מלונמא ללב וקילורית לעינים."
בעירובין נ"ד, ע"א אותו הרעיון בעצמו נמסר בשם ר' יהושע בן לוי, וקדום לו מאמר שמואל
לר' יהודה: שיננא פתח פומיך קרי . . . כי היכי דתתקים ביד ותוריד חיי שנ' כי חיים הם
למצאיהם ולכל בשרו מרפא . . ." אפשר שזה הביא את בעל מדרשנו לייחס גם המאמר הבא
אחר כך גם כן לשמואל.

2 השווה מ"ת קי"ט, סעיף מ"ד: "אפילו אני מתאוה ומבקש לחטוא אין דברי תורה מניחין
אותי." מקבילות בהע' י"ט.

ל"[ז].

ויצאו ויברכו

את [העם] וירא כבוד י'י אל כל העם (שם, ט', כ"ג),
ראה כבוד שהיה שם. וכשראו ישראל

את השכינה, התחילו שמחים ומרננים, שנ' וירא כל העם וירונו
וגו'[1] (שם, כ"ד). ומתוך

כל אותה השמחה נטלו בני אהרן המחתות שלהם, שנ' ויקחו שני בני
אהרן

וגו' (שם, י', א'), מה כת[יב] שם, ותצא אש מלפני י'י וגו' (שם, ב'). אמר
שלמה לצחוק אמרתי מהולל

וגו' (קה' ב', ב'), למה, שמי[2] שהוא שמח היום שמח למחר, וכל מי שמיצר
היום מיצר למחר,

שאין [שמחה] ממתנת לפניו בעולם הזה, שאין את מוצא איש או אשה שהיה
נתון בשם

חה גדולה כאלישבע בת עמינדב אשת אהרן, שהיתה רואה אהרן בעלה
כהן [גדול], ואחיו נביא ומלך,[3] ובניה סיגני כהונה, ואחיה נחשון נשיא, ולא
המתינה בשמחתה,

אלא נכנסו בניה להקריב ויצאה האש ושרפה אותם, שנ' ותצא האש וגו'.
ומה אם

הצדיקים לא ממתינין בשמחתן, הרשעים על אחת כמה וכמה.[4] לכך נאמר
אמרתי להוללים אל תהלו וגו' (תה' ע"ה, ה').

ל"[ח].

אשרי הצדיקים, כשם שמשפט ודין באין

עליהן, הן מצדיקין את הדין, שכך אתה מוצא באהרן שהיה מצטער על
שריפת

לז. מקורות: תנ' שמיני, ב' (ת"ב, ג'); וי"ר י"א, ו'; כ', ב' בסוף, ומקבילות.

[1] עי' וי"ר י"א, ו' מאמר ר' תנחום בר' יודן שהוא מקוטע, וצריך להשלימו עפ"י ירושלמי
יומא פ"א, א' כמו שהעיר לנכון מרגליות בהערותיו לוי"ר הנ'. כמו במדרשנו נסמך הדרש
בוי"ר לפסוק „וירא כל העם וירונו."

[2] ק': לא מי. תיקנתי על־פי תנ' שמיני, ב' (ת"ב, ג'). ובאמת בכת"י כתוב: „למי[=ל[א]] מי.

[3] בתנ': כהן גדול (משמש בכהונה גדולה) ונביא, ומשה ... מלך ונביא. יש בזה משום
נטייה להשוות את אהרן למשה. אבל וי"ר כ', ב' וכן מ"א, ח"ב, עמ' כ' חסרה המלה „ונביא'
אצל אהרן.

[4] החתימה הזאת נוספה במקורות לדוגמאות הבאות לפני זה ולקוחות מן האבות, אברהם
יצחק ויעקב: „ומה אברהם הצדיק כך ... ומה יצחק ... ומה יעקב הצדיק כך ...
הרשעים על אחת כמה וכמה." בעל מדרשנו שדילג על הדוגמאות האלו, כרך את כל החתימות
בחתימה אחת: „ומה אם הצדיקים ... הרשעים עאכ"ו."

לח. מקורות: תנ' שמיני, א' (ת"ב: ב'); וי"ר י"ב, ב' ומקבילות; ספרא שמיני מכילתא
דמילואים, ל"ו (דף מ"ה, ע"ד).

מתרצה להם. לכך נאמר ו י א מ ר א ל א ה ר ן ק ח ל ך ו ג ' (וי' ט', ב'),
שעל יד העגל נתפקקה הכהונה
מידך, ובעגל היא מתבוססת בידך.

ל"ו.

ד"א ו י ה י ב י ו ם ה ש מ י נ י, שמיני למלואים, וראשון
לראשי חדשים, שנ ויהי בחדש הראשון בשנה השנית וגו' (שמ' מ', י"ז). ואותו
היום היה ראש חדש ניסן,

ראש[ון] לראשי חדשים,[1] ראש[ון] לירידת האש, ראש[ון] לשחיטת צאן
בצפון,[2] ראש[ון] לאכילת

קדשים, ראשון לנשיאת כפים, ראש[ון] להקרבת כהנים לעבודה, שנ ויאמר אל
אהרן וגו'

(וי' ט', ב'). ע ג ל, לכפר על מעשה העגל.[2] ו א ל ב נ י י ש ר א ל ת ד ב ר
ל א מ ר ק ח ו ש ע י ר ו ג ' (שם, ג'), ע ז י ם, על שם [וישחטו שעיר
עזים] ויטבלו

את הכתנת בדם (בר' ל"ז, ל"א).[4] באותו היום הקריבו ג' שעירי עזים: אחד
שלישראל, שנ ו א ל ב נ י [י ש ר א ל],

ואחד שלנשיאים, שנ שעיר עזים אחד לחטאת (במ' ז, ט"ז), ואחד שלראש
חדש, שנ ושעיר עזים

(דף מ"ג, ע"ב) אחד לחטאת לי"י וגו' (שם, כ"ח, ט"ו). אי זה מהן דרש משה
(וי' י', ט"ז), אמרו תדיר ושאינו תדיר, תדיר קודם,

ושבראש חדש הוא תדיר, ואותו דרש, ו א ת ש ע י ר ה ח ט א ת ד ר ש
ד ר ש[5] (שם).

פס'.

ו א ל ב נ י י ש ר א ל ת ד ב ר ו ג ', להודיע לכל שנמחל להן על מעשה
העגל.[6]

לו. מקורות: ספרא, מכילתא דמילואים, ריש שמיני; שבת פ"ז, ע"ב ומקבילות.

[1] המקורות מונים „עשר עטרות – עשרה מיני ראשון – שלקח אותו היום. בעל מדרשנו
מונה רק שש.

[2] ראשון זה חסר במקורות שלפנינו, אבל בתוס' (שבת פ"ז, ע"ב) ד"ה ראשון, נאמר
ש„בתורת כהנים (ספרא) במקום אכילת קדשים קתני שחיטתן בצפון." ואילו בעל מדרשנו גורס
שחיטה בצפון בצידה של אכילת קדשים.

[3] ספרא ותנ' הנז'.

[4] עי' ספרא ריש שמיני, וישחטו שעיר עזים; השווה מ"א, ח"ב, עמ'
כ"א: „ואיל (וי' ט', ד'), על שם וישחטו שעיר עזים". נראה שההדרש במ"א הוא שלא במקומו,
וצריך לסמכו ל„שעיר עזים" שבפסוק הקודם כבמדרשנו, וכן הוא בתרגום יונתן.

[5] השווה ספרא שמיני, פרק ב', סעיף ב' (הוצ' וייס, דף מ', ע"ב) וזבחים ק"א, ע"ב. שם
אנו קוראים: איני יודע איזה איזה נשרף, כשהוא אומר ואותה נתן לכם לשאת את עון העדה . . .
איזה שעיר נושא את עון העדה, זה שעיר ראש חודש. טעמו של מדרשנו „תדיר קודם" אינו
מתקבל על הדעת, ואינו במקורות.

[6] תנ' הנז' למעלה סעיף ל"ה. שם פסקתנו הקצרה היא המשך המדרש שבסעיף ל"ה.

[לסדר ע״ט (ו'): ויקרא ט', א'.]

ל״ג.

ויהי ביום השמיני. זשה תן חלק לשבעה
וגו' (קה' י״א, ב'), אם נתתה חלק לנידה ושמרתה אותה
שהיא שבעה, יש לך לראות המילה שהיא לשמונה. ד״א תן חלק לשבעה, זה
אהרן, שקיים
שבעת ימי המלואים, שׂנ ופתח אהל מועד תשבו יומם ולילה [שבעת ימים[2]
(וי' ח', ל״ה). ומפני שנתן (ק: שנתנו) חלק לז',
נטלו כבוד לח', שׂנ ויהי ביום השמיני וגו'.

ל״ד.

אמרו רבותינו כל מקום שכתוב ויהי, משמש
בו צרה ושמחה,[1] שכן אתה מוצא ויהי בשלח פרעה וגו' (שמ' י״ג, י״ז), היה
צרה ושמחה, אלא ולא נחם
אלהים היו[2] שמחה וצרה, אף [כאן] ויהי משמש צרה ושמחה, שמחה שהוקם
המשכן, וצרה
שמתו בני אהרן.

ל״ה.

אשרי ישראל שהקב״ה אינו נוהג עמם כדרך שהוא נוהג עם האומות,
שׂנ כי אעשה כלה בכל הגוים [אך אתך לא אעשה כלה] וגו' (יר' ל', י״א),
אלא כיון שהן חוטאין היו[1] מביאין לפני[ו] קרבן, והוא

לג. מקורות: וי״ר י״ד, ז'; קה״ר י״א, ב' ומקבילות.
[1] בקה״ר מובא בשם ר' הונא. עי' פסדר״כ קצ״ב, ע״ב, הע' נ״ב.
[2] בשם ר' יהודה בקה״ר, ונסמך על ח', ל״ג, ‚ומפתח אהל מועד . . . כי שבעת ימים
ימלא את ידכם." במ״א נסמך הדרש על פסוק ל״ה כבמדרשנו.

לד. מקורות: וי״ר י״א, ז'; במ״ר י״ג, ה'. המקבילות בפס״ר פיס' ה', הוצ' איש־שלום, י״ט, ע״ב,
הע' הׂמׂוׂל, מספר ע״ד.
[1] ברוב המקורות באה אחר כך השלמה: ‚אם צרה אין צרה כיוצא בה אם שמחה אין
שמחה כיוצא בה." ההשלמה הזאת מורה שמשמעות ‚צרה ושמחה" היא לפעמים צרה ולפעמים
שמחה. זה מתאים לדברי ר' אשי במגילה י', ע״ב: ‚כל ויהי איכא הכי ואיכא הכי." בעל
מדרשנו מבאר ‚צרה ושמחה' גם צרה וגם שמחה, כלומר ש‚ויהי" מורה שיש צד של צרה וצד
של שמחה במאורע המסופר.
[2] נראה שיש כאן דילוג של הבלעה, וצ״ל: צרה ושמחה [בשלח פרעה, שמחה] אלא ולא
נחם אלהים, הרי שמחה וצרה.

לה. מקורות: תנ' שמיני, ד' (ת״ב, ו').
[1] בכת״י נראה כאילו היה כתוב: הין=הן.

ל"ב].

ד"א ק ח א ת א ה ר ן וגו', ואין לך שנלקח
לכבוד כאהרן, שלקחו הקב"ה לשרת לפניו, והלביש ח' בגדים שתהא אמתו על
ישראל[1].

[ובאי זה זכות זכה אהרן לכבוד הזה, שהיה מטיל שלום בישראל, שנ' בו בשלום
ובמישור

הלך אתי וגו' (מלא' ב', ו'). אמר הקב"ה: הואיל ונתן נפשו על השלום, ואכל
מפירותיו,[2] שנ' לכן אמור

וגו' (במ' כ"ח, י"ב).][3] לכך נאמר ק ח א ת א ה ר ן. ואחר כך, ו א ת
פ ר ה ח ט א ת ו א ת ש נ י ה א י ל י ם וגו'. ו א ת כ ל
ה ע ד ה ה ק ה ל וגו' (וי' ח', ב'–ג'), וכי מחזיק היה אהל מועד ששים
ריבוא, זה אחד שעשה הקב"ה במעשה

(דף מ"ג, ע"א) נסים שהחזיק מועט את המרובה. ראה היאך הקב"ה כת[יב]
ויאמר אלהים יקוו המים וגו'

(בר' א', ט'), וכל העולם כולו היה מים במים, ולהיכן נקוו אותן המים,
מלמד שהחזיק מועט את

המרובה. אף לעתיד לבוא כך הוא עתיד לעשות לציון, שכל אכלוסי ישראל
מתכנסין

לתוכה והן אומרין: צר לי המקום גשה לי ואשבה (יש' מ"ט, כ'), ומה הוא
עושה, מרחיב

את ירושלים, כמה שנ' הרחיבי מקום אהלך (שם, נ"ד, ב'). וכשם שהלביש
את ישראל בגדים

יפים לשעבר, שנ' ואלביש[ך] רקמה (יח' ט"ז, י') וכל העניינין הזה, ונטלו
(– ונטלן) מהן, שנ' ויתנצלו בני ישראל

(שמ' ל"ג, ו'), ועתיד הקב"ה להחזיר את הבגדים לישראל,[5] שנ' כי הלבישני
בגדי ישע מעיל צדקה וגו'

(יש' ס"א, י').

לב. מקורות: תנ' צו, י"א (ת"ב, ט"ו); וי"ר י', ט' ומקבילות.

1 תנ' הנ"ל: חלוק לו כבוד כנגד כל ישראל וכו'.

2 כל מה שהכנסנו במרובעות מפריד בין הדבקים, שכן ,לכך נאמר קח את אהרן . . .
ו א ת כ ל ה ע ד ה ה ק ה ל" דבוק למאמר ,שתהא אימתו על ישראל," כמו שיוצא מן
המקורות.

עיקר הדרש נדרש על פנחס (עי' מ"א, ח"ב, עמ' קמ"ח) ובעל מדרשנו נתנו ענין לאהרן.

3 השלמתי על-פי מאמרו של ר' אלעזר בוי"ר הנז'. בעל מדרשנו מוסר רק המקום הראשון
,יקוו המים," והאחרון ,אף לעתיד לבוא . . .." הנוסח של הדוגמה האחרונה הוא על-פי התנ'
י"ב ולא עפ"י וי"ר.

4 נקוד לסימן מחיקה.

5 השווה שבת פ"ח, ע"א: אמר ריש לקיש ו ע ת י ד ה ק ב " ה ל ה ח ז י ר ו (שני
הכתרים שנקשרו להם כנגד נעשה ונשמע) ל נ ו.

[ובחר לו] יה וגו' (שם, קל"ה, י'),[2] ומכל ישראל בחר בשתי משפחות הללו:
אהרן ודוד.[3] כשם שבחר באהרן

לו לכהן, שנ' ויבחר אותו מכל שבטי ישראל לי לכהן וגו' (ש"א, ב', כ"ח), וכן
בחר בדוד, שנ' ויבחר

בדוד עבדו (תה' ע"ח, ע'), וכת[יב] ובני דוד כהנים היו (ש"ב, ח', י"ח).
וכשם שנמשח אהרן בשמן המשחה, שנ' זאת

משחת אהרן וגו' (וי' ז', ל"ה), כך נמשח דוד, שנ' ויקח שמואל וגו' (ש"א,
ט"ז, י"ג). וכשם שנ' באהרן מלאך, שנ' כי

מלאך י"י צבאות הוא (מלא' ב', ז'), כך כת[יב] ובית דוד כאלהים כמלאך
י"י צבאות[4] (זכ' י"ב, ח'). כתיב באהרן ונתתה

את נזר הקדש על מצחו[5] (שמ' כ"ט, ו'), וכן כת[יב], ועליו יציץ נזרו (תה'
קל"ב, י"ח). באהרן כת[יב], וילבש אותו את המעיל

(וי' ח', ז'), ובדוד כתיב, ודוד מכרכר (מכרבל)[6] בלבוש בוץ (דה"א,
ט"ו, כ"ז). וכשם שנתנה כהונה לאהרן ולבניו, כך נתנה מלכות

לדוד ולבניו, שנ' לתת לו ניר (ו)לבניו כל הימים (מ"ב, ח', י"ט). וכשם שכרת
השם לאהרן על הכהונה

ברית מלח, שנ' ברית מלח עולם היא וגו' (במ' י"ח, י"ט), כך כרת לדוד
ולבניו ברית

מלח, שנ' הלא לכם לדעת כי י"י אלהי ישראל נתן וגו' (דה"ב, י"ג, ה'). מה
מלח אינה בטלה מן העולם,[7]

כך כהונה ומלכות אין בטילין לעולם. וכן הוא אומר אשר לא יספר צבא
השמים ולא

ימד חול הים (יר' ל"ג, כ"ב). הוי אשרי תבחר ותקרב.

---

[2] בשאר המקורות הפסוק הזה משמש סמך לבחירת יעקב. את בחירת ישראל מבסס ר' יהושע דסכנין בשם ר' לוי (במ"ר הנז') על דב' נ', ו' כך בחר ה' אלהיך להיות לו לעם סגלה.

[3] בניגוד לתנ' שמעמיד את אהרן למעלה מדוד („דוד בחרו אבל לא קרבו . . . אשרי אהרן בכפליים שבחרו וקרבו"), מדגיש בעל מדרשנו שאין בין אהרן ודוד ולא כלום; כל מה שנאמר על אהרן נאמר גם על דוד. גם במדרש שמואל הנז' הושוו אהרן ודוד. כל אחד מהם: „נבחר, נדחה, ונתקרב." גישה דומה לאישיותו של דוד אנו מוצאים במדרש תלים א', ב': „את מוצא כל מה שעשה משה עשה דוד . . . " וגם בעל מדרשנו למעלה סעיף ג' משווה את דוד למשה ששניהם „ברחו מן השררה. כל זה יצא, כנראה, מחוג ידוע שראה בדוד מעין גלגולם של משה ואהרן.

[4] צבאות אין בפסוק זה, ושיגרת העט היא מפסוק שבמלאכי שהובא לפני זה.

[5] במקרא כתוב: „על המצנפת," ויש כאן ערבוביה עם שמ' כ"ח, ל"ו: והיה על מצחו תמיד.

[6] במקרא: „מכרבל." וסופרנו כתב עפ"י ש"א, ו', י"ד.

[7] השווה ספרי במדבר, פיס' קי"ח בסוף (הוצ' איש־שלום, ל"ט, א'), ופירוש רש"י כאן. על המלח בתור סמל לקיום והתמדה, עיין מאמרו של עמנואל לו על המלח (בגרמנית) ב'.

גדול כוחו שלשלום, שכת[וב] בו עושה שלום במרומיו (אי' כ"ה, ב'), כיצד, הרקיע שלמים,

ומלאכי השרת שלאש והן רצין עליו, לא האש שורפת את המים ולא המים מכבין

את האש,[2] ואומר במכת מצרים ויהי ברד ואש מתלקחת בתוך הברד (שמ' ט', כ"ד), לא האש שו

רפת את הברד ולא הברד מכבה את האש. הרי עושה במרומיו שלום. וו[כל] זמן שישראל בעצה אחת, אפע"פ שאין עושין רצונו שלמקום,[3] אין מדת הדין שולטת בהן, שנ' חבור עצבים אפרים הנח לו (הו' ד', י"ז), וכל כך למה, בשביל השלום, ולא כל שכן

אם היו על האמת. ואף לעתיד לבוא, שיחזיר שדי שכינתו לירושלם ויחזיר כל הגליות לתוכה, בתחלה בשלום הוא מבשרן, שנ' הנה על ההרים רגלי מבשר משמיע שלום וגו' (נח' ב', א'), וממלא ירושלם שלום, שנ' כה אמר י"י הנני נוטה אליך כנהר שלום וכנחל שוטף וגו' (יש' ס"ו, י"ב),[4] ומברך את עמו בשלום, שנ' י"י עז לעמו יתן י"י יברך את עמו בשלום (תה' כ"ט, י"א).

[לסדר ע"ח (ה): ויקרא ח', א'—ב'.]

ל"א.

פס'. ק ח א ת א ה ר ן. זשה אשרי תבחר ותקרב וגו' (תה' ס"ה, ה'), אשרי כל מי שבחר

בו הקב"ה. אמר ר' ת נ ח ו מ א[1] מצינו שבחר הקב"ה את ישראל מכל האומות [שבעולם], שנ' כי יעקב

---

[2] השווה פסדר"כ, פיס' א' (הוצ' בובר, דף ג', ע"א וכו'): .והם דרים זה את זה ואינן מזיקין זא"ז." .והן רצין' כאן מרמז, כנראה, על החיות שנאמר עליהן .והחיות רצוא ושב כמראה הבזק." ובאמת בבמ"ר הנז' נאמר: .ה ח י ו ת ש ל א ש והרקיע של שלג . . .".

[3] שאר המקורות: .שאפילו ישראל עובדין עבודה זרה." בכת"י המלים .עושין רצונו של מקום" נוספו אחר כך. הסופר השאיר כאן מקום חלק.

[4] השווה וי"ר ט', ט' בסוף, והערות מרגליות.

* עי' ציון סוף סעיף כ"ג.

ל א.   מקורות: תנ' צו, ח' (ת"ב, י"א); במ"ר ג', ב' ומקבילות.

[1] השווה מדרש שמואל פ"ח, ב' מאמר ר' מ נ ח מ א בשם ר' שמואל בר ר' יצחק בעניין זה.

ידבר שלום וגו' (תה' פ"ה, ט'), ומה דבר, ז ב ח ה ש ל מ י ם, שהיא עושה שלום בין המזבח ובין

הכהנים ובין ישראל, היאך, אתה מוצא שמכל הקרבנות אין ישראל אוכלין אלא התודה, היה דמיה ואמוריה למזבח, והחזה והשוק לכהנים, ועורה ובשרה לישראל,

נמצא בה הנאה ושלום לכל ישראל. לכך נקראת ש ל מ י ם.

כ"ט].

פס'. א ם ע ל ת ו ד ה (וי' ז', י"ב). ראה
היאך הקב"ה מחבב לסלוח עוונותיהן שלישראל. מי שיש לו פר, יקריב פר. ומי שאין

לו פר, יקריב איל. ואם אין לו איל, יקריב שה. ואם אין לו שה, יביא שני תורים או

שני בני יונה. ואם אין לו אחד מכל אלו, יביא סלת, והקב"ה מקבל ממנו ומכפר לו.

והיום שאין הקרבנות, ונשלמה פרים שפתינו (הו' י"ד, ג'), בתחלה (ק': בתפלה) שאנו מתפללים לפניו,

ונחזור בתשובה שאדם עושה לפניו, שאין תשובה שלמה לפני הקב"ה אלא ההודאה.[1]

(דף מ"א, ע"ב) אתה מוצא[2] שכל הקרבנות שהיו באין, היו באין על העבירות, אבל התודה היתה

באה חנם, על ההודאה היתה באה. לכך אמר דוד ז ו ב ח ת ו ד ה י כ ב ד נ י (תה' נ', כ"ג).

ל'.

פס'. ו ז א ת ת ו ר ת ז ב ח ה ש ל מ י ם, שהן עושין שלום, שבכל מקום שאין שם שלום, הקב"ה

ה נוטל מאותו מקום החסד והרחמים, שנ' כי אספתי את שלומי וגו' [נאם ה' את החסד ואת הרחמים][1] (יר' ט"ז, ה'). בוא וראה מה

כט. מקורות: תנ' צו, ו' (ת"ב, צו, ח') ומקבילות; וי"ר ח', ד' מאמר ר' יהושע דסכנין בשם ר' לוי.

[1] מן „והיום שאין קרבנות . . ." עד כאן אינו אלא ניסוח חדש והרחבה של ההוספה שהוסיף תנ' על ת"ב (עי' הע' בובר, סימן מ"ד).

[2] מכאן עד הסוף אינו אלא משנה דברים, — בניסוח כמעט מילולי של התנ' —, של תחילת סעיף כ"ז.

ל. מקורות: ת"ב צו, י'; וי"ר ט', ט' ומקבילות; במ"ר י"ב, ח'.

[1] בתוס' סוף פאה ר' אלעזר ב"ר יוסי מביא את הפסוק הזה להראות „כמה גדול כחן של צדקה וגמילות חסדים שהן פרקליט ושלום בין ישראל לאביהם שבשמים."

ת ש ח ט ה ח ט א ת וגו', שלא לפרסם את החטאים.[1] אף באשם כן, כתיב
במקום

אשר ישחטו את העולה ישחטו את האשם (שם, ז', ב'),
כדי שלא יבייש את החוטאים.

ולמה נאמר בחטאת וכלי חרש אשר תבשל בו תשבר (שם, ו', כ"א), בשביל
שלא להזכיר

עון אותו האיש. אמר שלמה ריבך ריב את רעך וסוד אחר אל תגל (מש'
כ"ה, ט'), כשם שאין

הקב"ה מבקש לגלות סודו שלאדם. עושה אינו יכול להסתירה מלפני הקב"ה,

5   שכן כת[יב] אלהים אתה ידעת לאיולתי וגו' (תה' ס"ט, ו'), שאין הדבר נכחד
מלפני הקב"ה, שכן כת[יב] (דף מ"ב, ע"ב)

[וישראל לא נכחד ממני (הו' ה', ג')......המדה.

כ"ז].

טוב אחרית הדבר מראשיתו (קה' ז', ח').

[הקרבנות הראשונים] היו באין על החטאים, אבל התודה אינו באה על ידי
[שום חטא, לכך הזכיר מע]שה התודה באחרונה שהיא באה על השלום,[1] שנ'
וזאת תורת

[זבח וגו'], אם על תודה וגו'[1] (וי' ז', י"א–י"ב). גדול הוא השלום שהוא חותם
לקרבנות, וחותם לברכות,

שנ' וישם לך שלום[2] (במ' ו', כ"ו), ובשלום עתיד הקב"ה לקבץ ישראל, שנ' כי
בשמחה תצאו ובשלום

[תובלון] וגו' (יש' נ"ה, י"ב).

[לסדר ע"ז (ד'): ויקרא ז', י"א–י"ב.]

כ"ח].

15   פס'. וזאת תורת זבח השלמים. זשה אשמעה מה ידבר האל י"י
וגו' כי

---

1 עי' וי"ר ל"ב, ו'. שם מובא המאמר בשם ריש לקיש; בירושלמי סוטה פ"ח, סוף הל' ט'
(דף כ"ג, ע"א) ר' לוי מוסר המאמר בשם ר"ש בן לקיש. כל מה שבא אחר כך הן ניסוחים
שונים של ההזהרה הזאת: ,שלא לבייש את החטאים', ,שלא להזכיר עון אותו האיש שחטא'.
הסמך למש' כ"ה, ט' אינו ידוע לי, אבל רמז לדבר אפשר למצוא בסנהדרין מ"ד, ע"ב ובסדר
אליהו רבה, פ' י"ח (הוצ' איש-שלום, עמ' 106).

כז. מקורות: תנחומא, וי"ר.
1 השווה תנ' צו, ז' (ת"ב: צו, ט'). ומקבילות.
2 השווה וי"ר ט', ט': מאמר ר' יהושע דסכנין בשם ר' לוי ומקבילות.

כח. מקורות: תנ' צו, ד' (ת"ב, צו ו') ומקבילות. בעל מדרשנו אינו מוסר אלא התמצית.

(דף מ"ב, ע"א) שׁ והכהן המשיח תחתיו מבניו וגו' (וי' ו', ט"ו).
[ואין מושחין מלך בן מלך, <מפני שניתנה]

המלכות בירושה לבניו, שׁ ולמען יאריך ימים [וגו' (דב' ז', כ'), וכתיב גם
בניהם]

עדי עד וגו' (תה' קל"ב, י"ב). <. אם תאמר למה משחו את שלמה, מפני
מח [לוקתו של אדוניה; ואת יהואש],

והוא מפני מחלוקתה שלעתליה; ואת יהואחז, מפני מחל [וקתו שליהויקים]
שהיה גדול ממנו בי"ב שנה. אתה מוצא כל מי שנמשח בקרן, משכה [מלכותו,
אבל]

שאול ויהוא בן נמשי נמשחו בפך, ולא משכה מלכותן, שאול מניין, שׁ [ויקח]
שמואל את פך השמן ויצק על ראשו וישקהו וגו' (ש"א, י', א'), וכן יהוא, שׁ
ולקחת [פך]

השמן ויצקת על ראשו ואמרת כה אמר י"י משחתיך למלך על ישראל (מ"ב,
ט', ג'), [לכך]

לא משכה מלכותן, דוד נמשח בקרן השמן, לכך נמשכה מלכותו, שׁ [ויקח]
שמואל את קרן השמן וימשח אותו בקרב אחיו וגו' (ש"א, ט"ז, י"ג); ושלמה,
ויקח צדוק הכהן

את קרן השמן מן האהל וימשח את שלמה וגו' (מ"א, א', ל"ט), ומשכה מלכותו
עד עולם, שׁ

כה אמר י"י אם תפרו את בריתי וגו', גם בריתי תופר את דוד עבדי וגו'[3]
(יר' ל"א, כ'–כ"א). ואין

מושחין שני כהנים גדולים כאחת.[2] ר' יוחנן אמר מפני איבה, ומה ששנו חכמים
מתקינין לו כהן אחר תחתיו שמא יארע בו פסול ביום הכפורים,
במרובה בבגדים היה, בח' כלים שלכהן גדול, אבל בשמן המשחה לא היו
מושחין שני כהנים גדולים כאחת.[4] אבל אהרן ובניו נמשחו כאחת, שׁ זאת
משחת אהרן וגו' (וי' ז', ל"ה). אבל לדור[ות] לא היו מושחין אלא אחד,
שׁ ביום המשח אותו
(שם, ו', י"ג).

כ"ח.

פס'. זאת תורת החטאת (שם, י"ח). למה הוא אומר במקום
אשר תשחט העולה

---

[3] השווה ספרא שם; ירושלמי הוריות, שם (דף מ"ז, ע"ד, שו' [4]).

וכדאי להעיר שבעל מדרשנו מרחיב ומבאר את החומר הלקוח ממקומות שהם מחוץ
לתחום מדרשי אגדה – חזיון שכבר עמדנו עליו למעלה סעיף ה'.

כו. מקורות: וי"ר. ויש רמז לתלמוד בבלי.

[לסדר ע"ז (ד'): ויקרא ו', י"ב–י"ג.]

כ"ד.

פס'. זה קרבן אהרן ובניו. זהה טוב ינחיל בני בנים וגו' (מש'
י"ג, כ"ב). אמר ר' יהושע שלשה

צדיקים נטלו גדולה, והניחו אותה לבני בניהם, ואלו הן: דוד, ולוי, ואהרן. דוד
זכה ליטול את המלכות, אמר לו הקב"ה, יש לך להנחיל לבני בנים, שנ' אם
ישמרו בניך בריתי וגו' (תה' קל"ב, י"ב), ואומר כי אני י"י אלהי ישראל נתן
ממלכה לדוד לו ולזרעו

ברית מלח (דה"ב, י"ג, ה').[1] ולוי זכה ליטול את הלויה, והנחיל אותה לבני
בנים, שנ' לך

נתתים למשחה ולבניך וגו'[2] (במ' י"ח, ח'). והכהונה זכה בה אהרן, והנחילה
לבני[2] בנים, שנ' ברית

מלח עולם היא וגו' (שם, י"ט). לכך נאמר טוב ינחיל בני בנים.
מה הוא וצפון לצדיק חיל חוטא

(מש', שם); כמה יגעו הכנעניים ליטע נטיעות בארץ ולבנות בתים ולחצוב
בורות, וכו'

ישראל ליטלן, שנ' ובתים מלאים כל טוב (דב' ז', י"א).

כ"ה.

פס'. זה קרבן אהרן ובניו. אין מו
שחין כהן גדול אלא ביום.[1] אמר ר' יהודה[2] אפי' כהן גדול בן כהן גדול טעון
משיחה,

כד. מקור המאמר נעלם ממני. יש בו הד של המאמר הידוע על שלשה כתרים, ביחוד בצורתו
שבספרי במדבר, פיסקא קי"ט (הוצ' איש-שלום, מ', ע"א).

1 במקרא כתוב: "כי ( ) י"י אלהי ישראל נתן ממלכה לדוד [על ישראל לעולם] לו
ו ל ב נ י ו ברית מלח".

2 קשה לראות איך אפשר להסב הפסוק הזה על לוי, מכיון שמתחיל "וידבר ה' אל
אהרן. כנראה יש כאן סירוס פסוקים וצריך לתקן: "והכהונה זכה בה אהרן והנחילה . . . שנ'
לך נתתי . . . לחק עולם . . . ולוי זכה ליטול את הלויה והנחילה . . . שנ' ברית מלח עולם היא
[וגו' ולבני לוי (שם, כ"א)]." ובאמת לפי הספרי הנז' פסוק אהרון זה "מגיד שכשם שהברית
כרותה לכהונה כך ברית כרותה ללוים." ועיין מאיר עין, הע' כ"ג שם.

כה. מקורות: ספרא צו; הוריות דף י"א–י"ב.
1 ספרא צו, פרשה ג', ד' (הוצ' וייס, ל"א, ע"ב).
2 מכאן עד סוף הסעיף שקוע תוכן שאפשר למצוא במקורות ארצישראליים, בתוס'
סנהדרין פ"ד, י'; ירושלמי הוריות פ"ג (דף מ"ז, ע"ג); וי"ר י', ח' ועוד – וגם בתלמוד בבלי,
הוריות דף י"א, ע"ב–דף י"ב, ע"א ומקבילות. בעל מדרשנו השתמש בעיקר בתלמוד בבלי. הוא
שילב את טעמי התלמוד לתוך גוף הברייתא. ובסגנון הברייתא גופה משתקף יסוד הבבלי.
ביטויים מעין "אם תאמר", "משכה מלכותו", "לא משכה מלכותו" וכדומה נמצאים רק בבבלי
ולא בשאר המקורות.

בנסיעתן. וכשהיו חונין, היו מניחין אותה על גבי המזבח. לקיים מה שכתוב
ו ה א ש
ע ל ה מ ז ב ח ת ו ק ד ב ו ו ג׳[1] (שם, ה׳).

כ"ג.

ולמה פותחין לתינוקות בתורת כהנים ובסדר קרבנות

תחלה, שמעת שבטל התמיד ובטלו קרבנות מן המזבח, תיקנו חכמ[ים] שיהיו
מחנכין לתינוקות בתורת כהנים ובסדר הקרבנות, שכל שעה שנכנס מיכאל
10 ושומע תינוקות שלבית רבן בסדר קרבנות, עולה לפני הקב"ה ומלמד זכות על
ישראל,
והקב"ה מעלה עליהם כאילו מזבח בנוי וכהן גדול עומד ומעלה עליו כל
הקרבנות
שבתורה ומכפר על עונותיהן שלישראל,[1] ואין העולם מתקיים אלא בהבל פיהם
שלתינוקות שלבית רבן,[2] מאי דכתיב הקול קול יעקב וגו׳ (בר׳ כ"ז, כ"ב),
אמר ר׳ יוסי כל זמן
15 שקולו שליעקב נשמע בבתי כנסיות ובבתי מדרשות, אין האומות שולטין בהן.[3]

1 כל הסעיף אינו אלא פאראפראזה של מאמר ספרא, צו, פ׳ ב׳ (הוצ׳ וויס, ל׳, ראש עמ׳
ג׳): לא תכבה, אף במסעות, מה עושים לה, כופים עליה פסכתר, דברי ר׳ יהודה, ר׳ שמעון
(— ר׳ נחמיה במדרשנו) אומר אף בשבת, ומסעות מדשים אותה שנ׳ ודשנו את המזבח ופרשו
עליו בגד ארגמן. השווה ירושלמי יומא סוף פרק ד׳. לדעת בעל מדרשנו כולם מודים שאף
בשעת המסעות היתה אש על המזבח, ועל מה נחלקו? באופן הנחתה. לדעת ר׳ יהודה נשארה
האש על המזבח ממש מכוסה בפסכתר, ובגד ארגמן פרוש מלמעלה; ולדעת ר׳ נחמיה
(— שמעון) העבירו מקודם את האש מן המזבח אל מחתה, פרשו בגד ארגמן על המזבח ממש,
ועל הבגד שמו את המחתה עם האש. . .".

כג. מקורות: תנח׳ צו, י"ד; וי"ר ז׳, ג׳ בסוף.
1 השווה מעשיות (חיבור יפה מהישועה) לר׳ נסים בר׳ יעקב (הוצ׳ ווארשא תרמ"א, עמ׳
כ"ו): "ואני נסים שאלתי בילדותי את אבא מרי . . . מפני מה מתחילים את התינוקות לקרות
תחילה בספר ויקרא . . . ויאמר לי הקרבנות הם היו כפרה לחטאת ישראל ולסליחה
לעונותם, וכשחרב בית המקדש . . . תקנו רז"ל ללמוד את בנינו תחילה בספר ויקרא שתחשב
קריאתם בקרבנות כאילו קרבנו . . . ועלות לפני הקב"ה ויכפר לנו על חטאתנו." אין להחליט
מכאן שבעל מדרשנו השתמש במקור זה, כי, כנראה, השתמש אבי ר׳ נסים באיזה מדרש, ולא
מדעתו הגה את הפתרון הזה. ר׳ נסים מביא שם טעם אחר בשם חכמים המתאים לדברי ר׳
איסי בוי"ר ז׳, ג׳. בתנח׳ צו י"ד יש מעין הרכבה של שני הטעמים.
2 שבת קי"ט, ע"ב מאמר ר"ל בשם ר׳ יהודה נשיאה.
3 השווה ב"ר ס"ה, ב׳ בשם ר׳ אבא בר כהנא. בכתי"ב באים במקום זה הסעיפים כח–ל,
היינו מדרש לסדר ע"ז[א] מחברנו העבירם למקומם.

גנאי[2] הוא לו, אבל כלי תשמישין שלהקב̇ה̇ כולן שבורין, שנ̇ זיבחי אלהים רוח
נשברה[3] (תה' נ"א, י"ט), ואומ̇[ר]

קרוב י"י לנשברי לב (שם, ל"ד, י"ט). לכך נאמר כי חסד חפצתי וגו'.

כ"א.

זאת תורת העולה (וי' ו', ב'), וזאת
תורת המנחה וגו' (שם, ז'). הוא[1] היה אומר[2] דכת̇[יב] ובוחן כליות
(תה' ז', י'), עני שמביא מנחה בלב טוב

ובנפש חפיצה, גדולה היא לפני הקב̇ה יתר מהשור שהביא העשיר בגסות
ובגאוה,

אלא אם היו טהורי לב, ומביא כל אחד ואחד כמתנת ידו, חביבין לפני כולן
כאחד,[4]

(דף מ"א, ע"א) שנ̇ ולחץ יחלק(!) עני בעניו וגו' (אי' ל"ו, ט"ו).[5]

כ"ב.

פס'. כתיב ודשנו את המזבח (במ' ד', י"ג), וכתיב תוקד על המזבח
ל א ת כ ב ה (וי' ו', ו'), היאך אני מקיים שני מקראות הללו, אמר ר יהודה
היו כופין עליו פסכתר,

ור̇ נחמיה אמר היו מדשנין את המזבח, ומניחין את האש במחתה, והיו מכסין
5   את המזבח בבגדי ארגמן, והיו מניחין את המחתה ממעל לבגדים. כך היו עושין

---

2 בוי"ר הוצ̇ מ̇. עמ̇ קנ"ב: גניי – צורה ארצישראלית –. ועי̇ חלופי נוסחאות שם.
3 הפסוק הזה, תה' נ"א, י"ט, משמש פתיחה בוי"ר ז', ראש סעיף ב' ותופס מקומו של
הפסוק כי חסד חפצתי (הו' ו', ו') כאן.

כא. מקורות: וי"ר ג', א' וה'; מנחות, עמ' אחרון.
1 אפשר שמוסב על ר' אלכסנדרי הנזכר לפני זה.
2 צריך להשלים: [מהו] דכתיב. מכיון שהפתגם „הוא היה אומר" יחיד במינו במדרשנו,
אני נוטה לחשוב שמתחילה היה כתוב: ה ד א ד כ ת י ב, ואיזה מעתיק, מתוך שיגרת העט,
כתב „ה ה א ד כ ת י ב", ובא מעתיק אחר ופתר ה ה א = ה ו א ה י ה א ו מ ר.
3 בקרא כתוב: ובוחן [לבות ו]כליות.
4 השוה סוף מנחות המאמר בשם ר' שמעון בן עזאי: „ונאמר בשור הנס אשה ריח נחוח
... ובמנחה אשה ריח נחוח, לומר לך אחד המרבה ואחד הממעיט ובלבד שיכוין את לבו
לשמים." מדרשנו מוציא את זאת מ„זאת תורת" המשותף לעולה ולמנחה, ואפשר לנסח את
מדרשנו בלשון הברייתא: „נאמר בשור הנס זאת תורת . . . ובמנחה וזאת תורת המנחה, לומר
לך שאם יהיו טהורי לב (– שיכוין לבו לשמים) ומביא כל אחד ואחד כמתנת ידו (– אחד
המרבה ואחד הממעיט) חביבין לפני כולן כאחד.
5 ע"ש יבמות ק"ב, ב': „בשכר עניו יחלצו מדינה של גהנים." ובעל מדרשנו מבאר „בקרבן
עני שלו יחלצו מדינה של גהנים."

כב. מקורות: ספרא.

י"ט].

פס'. **ואש המזבח תוקד בו.** אמר
הקב"ה: אדום החריבה את הבית, ובטלה את האש שהיתה על המזבח תמיד,
אף אני מדליק בה אש תמיד, שנ' **לילה ויומם לא תכבה** (יש'
ל"ד, י')[1]; היא ביטלה הקטרת, אף
אני מקיים בה, **לעולם יעלה עשנה** (שם); היא אומרת שכח אל
הסתיר וגו' (תה' י', י"א), ואני אומר **לנצח**
נצחים אין עובר בה (שם), ולא יהיה ממנו זכרון, שנ' ולא יהיה
שריד לבית עשו (עו' י"ח); ובמדה
שאדם מודד, בה מודדין לו; היא שרפה את הבית, שנ' שלחו באש מקדשיך
(תה' ע"ד, ז'), אף
אני שורף אותה, שנ' הנני אליך והבערתי בעשן רכבה (נח' ב', י"ד), ונוקם
ממנה שעשת בהי
כל, שנ' כי נקמת יי' היא וגו' **[היא נקמת היכלו]** (יר' נ"א, י"א,
ומוסרן ביד עמי ועושין בהן **נקמה** (נקמתי), שנ'[4] ונתתי
את נקמתי באד[ום] ביד עמי ישראל (יח' כ"ה, י"ד).

כ'].

ד"א **צו את אהרן. זשה כי חסד חפצתי**
ולא זבח (הו' ו', ו'). אמר ר' יהודה[1] ראה מה שפסל הקב"ה, כך הכשיר.
הכשיר באדם, לב נשבר
(תה' נ"א, י"ט), פסל בבהמה, או שבור (וי' כ"ב, כ"ב). אמר ר' אלכסנדרי
ההדיוט הזה אם משתמש בכלי שבור,

יט. מקורות: תנחומא; פסיקתא דר' כהנא.

1 השווה תנ' תרומה, בסוף: בזכות המזבח שהאש בוערת בו ביום ובלילה אני נפרע
ממלכות אדום באש ותהא נשרפת ביום ובלילה שנאמר לילה ויומם ...'.

2 השווה תנח' וארא, י"נ: ולפי ששרפה ביתי שהעשן היה יוצא ממנו ... לפיכך תעלה
עשנה.

3 מאמר ר' מאיר בתוספתא מסכת סוטה פרק ג', א', ומקבילות. הכלל הזה הוא היסוד
לכל הפיסקה, למה שנאמר לפני זה ולמה שבא אחר כך, שבאמת אינו אלא ניסוח שונה של
האמור מקודם.

4 השווה פסדר"כ, הוצ' בובר, עמ' קפ"ז, א': ומה אני עושה להן? מוסרם בידכם ואתם
גובים נקמתי מהם ... בכת"י כתוב: נקם, והייתי קורא: נקמ[תי] בהקבלה
למקור.

כ. מקורות: וי"ר ז', ב'.

1 שם האומר בוי"ר הוא ר' ,ר' אבא בר יודן.'

...ושבה [בעולה] נתרצה הקב"ה לעולם אחר המבול, שנ' ויבן שם[8] מזבח
ליי,[9] וירח יי
(בר' ח', כ'–כ"א), (דף מ', ע"ב), שהקב"ה נתרצה[10] לעולם אחר המבול.

י"ח.

וכל מי שהוא מעלה עצמו, סופו ליפול,[1] שעשה
הקב"ה סימן,[2] שנ' היא העולה.[3] פרעה עילה עצמו, שנ'[4] מי י"י אשר
אשמע בקולו (שמ' ה', כ'), ומפני
שעילה עצמו ואמר אני [פרעה] (בר' מ"א, מ"ד),[5] ואמר עוד לי יאורי וגו'
(יח' כ"ט, ג'), לכך על מוקדה על המזבח, וכן היה
לו, ואש מתלקחת וגו' (שמ' ט', כ"ד). הוי היא העולה. אף סנחריב
עילה עצמו, שנ' אני עליתי מרום
הרים ירכתי לבנון וגו' (מ"ב, י"ט, כ"ג), אמר לו הקב"ה: ביד מלאכיך חרפת
י"י (שם, כ"ב), ומה היה לו, ויצא
מלאך י"י ויך במחנה אשור מאה ושמונים וחמשה אלף וגו' (שם, ל"ה), ואתה
ביד מלאכיך,
ואני [ביד] מלאך.[7] ומה היה לו, ותחת כבודו יקד יקוד כיקוד אש (יש'
י', ט"ז). הוי היא העולה. וכן
נבוכדנצר עילה עצמו, שנ' אעלה על במתי עב אדמה לעליון (שם, י"ד, י"ד),[8]
ואני עושה לך,
ולך טרדין מן אנשא וגו'[9] (דנ' ד', כ"ב). הוי היא העולה.

8 שינרת הקולמוס מבר' י"ב, ז', ח' ועוד, אבל צ"ל: נח.
9 [. . . ויעל עלות במזבח].
10 וזהו פירוש של „וירח ה'," כדי להרחיק הגשמות; השווה תרגום אונקלוס: וקביל יי
בר ע ו ו א ית קרבניה." ועי' ראב"ע על הפסוק: „חלילה להיות ה' מריח . . . רק הטעם
שקיבל העולה וישרה לפניו."

יח. מקורות: ת"ב צו, ג' ; וי"ר ז', ו'.
1 ליפול [נאבש] – לילך ב א ש (ת"ב) – נידון ב א ש (וי"ר).
2 = סימן לדבר. פארפרזה או ביאור של „נומוס הוא וקילוסין הוא" שבוי"ר, ועי' ת"ב
הערת בובר (י"ב).
3 יש להשלים: [על מוקדה] עפ"י ת"ב.
4 צ"ל: ש א מ ר כמו שהוא בת"ב.
5 הפסוק הזה אינו מובא בת"ב.
6 כך הוא גם בוי"ר, אבל בת"ב מובא הפסוק „ברד ונחלי אש" (תה' י"ח, י"ד).
7 נראה שצ"ל: [ביד] מלאך.
8 בת"ב: ומה ע ש ה לו, כלו' המלאך.
9 המאמר מקוטע, שכן חסר העיקר שנידון באש, ועי' בת"ב ובוי"ר.

[לסדר ע"ו (ג[ª]ª): ויקרא ו', א'–ב'.]

[י"ז].

צ ו א ת א ה ר ן. מה כתיב למעלה מן הענין, והיה כי יחטא ואשם
וגו'[1] (וי' ה', כ"ג), ואחר כך זאת תורת העולה (שם, ו', ב'). אם בקשת להקריב
קרבן, לא תגזול, שנֵ כי

אני י"י אוהב משפט שונא גזל בעולה וגו' (יש' ס"א, ח'). ואימתי אתה מעלה
עולה ואני מקבלה,

בשעה שכפיך נקיים מן הגזל, שכן דוד אומר מי יעלה בהר י"י ומי יקום וגו', נקי

כפים וגו' (תה' כ"ד, ג'–ד'). אמר ר' אלעזר[2] מתחלת הקרבנות אתה למד,
שנֵ אדם כי יקריב מכם קרבן

וגו' (וי' א', ב'), ואינו אומר א נ ו ש[3] אלא א ד ם, ולמה א ד ם, אמר
הקב"ה: כשתהא מקריב לפני,

תהא כאדם הראשון שלא היה בידו גזל אפילו בעולה. לפיכך נאמר אחריו
ז א ת ת ו ר ת

ה ע ו ל ה. ולמה נקראת ע ו ל ה,[4] שהיא עליונה מכל הקרבנות. רצונך
לידע[5] של כל מי שהוא

מביא חטאת, הכהן נוטל ואוכלת, מן האשם ומן המנחה, כהן נוטלה ואוכלה,
וזבח השלמים לבעלים, אבל העולה אין אדם[6] טועם ממנו כלום, אלא הכל
עולה למזבח. לכך נאמר ה י א ה ע ו ל ה. מי שהוא מביא חטאת מפני
שחטא,
ומביא אשם[7]

י"ז. מקורות: ת"ב, צו, ב'.

1 [והשיב את הגזלה אשר גזל] עפ"י ת"ב הנ"ל.

2 שם האומר חסר בת"ב. הניסוח שם: „ומתחילת הקרבנות אתה למד", כאילו אינו
אלא המשך הדרש הקודם.

3 יותר טוב: איש.

4 בת"ב: דבר אחר זאת תורת העולה, למה נקרא . . .

5 בת"ב: תדע.

6 בכתה"י על הגליון מתוקן: ב ר י ה; וכן הוא בת"ב.

7 המאמר קטוע, ובאמת בכתה"י יש כאן מקום חלק יותר מחצי שורה. סימן שכתה"י
שהשתמש בו המעתיק האחרון היה פגום במקום זה. כנראה יש כאן טעם אחר שהעולה עליונה
על שאר הקרבנות לפי שאינה באה על חטא ממש כי אם על הרהור הלב, השווה תנ' צו, ין:
כך שנו רבותינו היתה עולה כולה קדושה מפני שלא היתה באה על עונות, אשם היתה באה על
הגזלות, אבל העולה לא היתה באה לא על חטא ולא על גזל אלא על הרהור הלב היא באה.
ועי' וי"ר ז', ג' ומקבילות.

ט״ז.

אמרו חכמים מי שהוא מגיד עדות שקר, מביא

ג' רעות לעולם: גלות, וחרב, ורעב, שנ' מ פ י ץ ו ח ר ב ו ח ץ ש נ ו ן וגו'
(מש' כ״ה, י״ח). מפיץ, זה גלות שנ'

ויפץ י״י אותם משם (בר' י״א, ח'). ו ח ר ב, כמשמעו. ו ח ץ ש נ ו ן, זה
רעב, שנ' חצי אכלה בם (דב' ל״ב, כ״ג), ומה
(דף מ', ע״א) כתיב אחריו, מזי רעב וגו' (שם, כ״ד). ומי גרם לשלש רעות
הללו לבוא בעולם, א י ש ע ו נ ה ב ר ע ה ו
ע ד ש ק ר (מש' כ״ה, י״ח).1 אבל מי שהוא יודע עדות שלאמת על מי
שמגדף שמו שלהקב״ה ואינו מעיד,
מתחייב עמו.2 וכן כל עדות שהוא יודע, א ם ל א י ג י ד ו נ ש א ע ו נ ו (וי'
ה', א'). אמר משה לישר[אל]:3

תהיו סבורין שהזהרתי אתכם להיות נשבעין בשם אלוהיכם אלא אם כן יהיו
בכם

שלש מדות הללו, שנ' את י״י אלהיך תירא וגו'4 (דב' י', כ'). וכיון5 שנתן לכם
הקב״ה את האמת,

שנ' תתן אמת ליעקב חסד לאברהם (מי' ז', כ'), לכך היו [תהיו?] ישראל זהירין
שלא להשבע ושלא

להעיד אלא באמת, שקרא אתכם זרע אמת, שנ' ואנכי נטעתיך שורק כולו
זרע אמת וגו' (יר' ב', כ״א), ותהיו אוהבים את האמת, שנ' והאמת והשלום אהבו
(זכ' ח', י״ט), וכתיב

אלה הדברים אשר תעשו, אמת ומשפט שפטו בשעריכם (שם, ט״ז), והקב״ה אמת,
שנ' וי״י אלהים אמת הוא אלהים חיים ומלך עולם (יר' י', י').

טז. מקורות: פתיחתא דאיכה רבתי; ת״ב.

1 השווה פתיחתא דאיכ״ר, י״ג, פירוש המלים במובן גלות, חרב ורעב בשם ר' חנינא בר
פפא, אבל מביא סמוכים לדבריו מפסוקים אחרים. לדעת רבא (סנהדרין כ״ט, ע״א) השתמש
בית הדין בפסוק זה (מש' כ״ה, י״ח) לאיים על העדים שלא יעידו עדות שקר.

2 ת״ב וי' י״ד: „מי ששומע גידופו של הקב״ה ואינו מגיד מתחייב עמו."

3 השווה ת״ב וי' ט״ו בסוף הפרשה, וצ״ל: „[לא] תהיו . . ." בכתה״י נראה כאילו כתוב:
אמ' משה ל י ש ר א ל. ממעל לריש סימן של הקצרה . . . וצריך איפוא לקרוא: „לישר[אל]:
אל תהיו."

4 [ואותו תעבוד ובו תדבק ואח״כ ובשמו תשבע] עפ״י ת״ב הנ״ל.

5 מקורו של החלק האחרון של מדרשנו בלתי ידוע לי.

נאמ[ר] הוצאתיה וגו'. מלמד⁶ ששבועת שוא חלול השם, שנ' וחללת את שם
אלהיך וגו'
(וי' י"ט, י"ב), אם⁷ חללת את השם, את נעשה חולין לחיה ולבהמה.

ט"[ז].

פס'. וְשָׁמְעָה קוֹל אָלָה
(וי' ה', א'), שבשעה שהנפש חוטאת, באות עליה כל אלות שבתורה.¹ וְהוּא
עֵד. אַתָּה מוֹצֵא
שלשה דברים ברשותו שלאדם, וג' אינן ברשותו וכול'.² וְהוּא עֵד אוֹ
רָאָה אוֹ יָדָע. אמר
ר' לוי³ באותה שעה שקיבלו ישראל את התורה, הודיען הקב̇ה שאין כמותן⁴
בעולם,
שנ' הבו לל̇י בני אלים הבו לל̇י כבוד ועז וגו' (תה' כ"ט, א'), הבו, הביטו⁵
בעליונים, הבו, הביטו⁵
בתחתונים, וראו שאין אלוה חוץ ממני. לכך הוא אומר וְהוּא עֵד וגו'
שמעידין עלי
שאני יחיד [בעולמי],⁶ שנ' אתה הראית לדעת וגו' (דב' ד', ל"ה). אוֹ יָדָע,
וידעת היום וגו' (שם, ל"ט). אִם לֹא יַגִּיד,
אם ישראל מגידין⁷ את התורה, נושא עונו.

6 ספרא קדושים, פרשה ב' (הוצ' וייס, פ"ח, עמ' ג'). אולם שם הפסוק בא קודם, וכאן
אולי יותר טוב היה היה לתקן: "מניין".
7 צ"ל: [ד"א] אם . . . כמו שהוא בספרא הנז'. השווה למעלה ח"א, הע' 558.

טז. מקורות: ת"ב; וי"ר.
1 מקורו של הדרש נעלם ממני. לכאורה נראה כאילו היה דורש את הפסוק: ונפש כי
תחטא ושמעה כל (במקום קול) אלה. אבל מסתבר שהדרש מבוסס על הגזרה השווה שבין
"ושמעה קול אלה" והכתוב "והיה בשמעו את דברי האלה הזאת" (דב' כ"ט, י"ח).
השווה ת"ב וי"ח, בובר, הע' פ"ז; מ"א, ח"ב, עמ' 10, הע' ב'.
3 פשר הפסוק על מתן תורה, מעמד הר סיני שבו שבו כביכול החמן ישראל לעד על אחדותו
של אלהים, נמצא בשינוי צורה בוי"ר ו', ה' (הוצ' מ. קל"ז וכו') בשם ר' פנחס. הסוף (שם, עמ'
קמ"ב) מתאים כמעט כולו למדרשנו.
4 בכתה"י נראים רשמי מחיקה ותיקון. ועד כמה שיכולתי לראות נראה כאילו היה כתוב
שם מתחילתה "כמותן", מוסב על ישראל, ותיקנו "כמותו", מוסב על ה'.
5 הדרש הבו – הביטו הוא מחר, ומקורו נעלם ממני.
6 בכתה"י יש כאן מקום חלק שמחברנו מילא במלת [בעולמי], אבל מסתבר שצ"ל: [או
ראה] שנ' אתה הראית כמו בוי"ר הנז'.
7 צריך לתקן עפ"י וי"ר: אם [אין] ישראל מגידין (במקום מעידין) את התורה.

מוצא בעכן, כיון שחטא, היה קצף על ישראל כולם, שׁנ׳ הלא עכן בן זרח וגו׳ [5]
(יהו׳ כ״ב, כ׳). אלא אשרי

ישראל בכפרות שנתן להם הקב״ה, שהיה אדם חוטא, הוא מביא קרבן, ומתכפר
עליו

על ידי תשובה גמורה, שנ׳ יעזוב רשע דרכו וגו׳ (יש׳ נ״ה, ז׳), ומה כת[וב] שם,
כי ביום הזה יכפר

עליכם וגו׳ (וי׳ ט״ז, ל׳),[6] אמר הקב״ה: בעולם [הזה], על ידי שהיה יצר הרע
שׁולט בכם, הייתם חוטא[ין],

אבל לעתיד לבוא אני עוקרו מכם, שׁנ׳ והסירותי את לב האבן מבשרכם
(יח׳ ל״ו, כ״ו).[7]

[לסדר ע״ו (ג׳): ויקרא ה׳, א׳.]

י״ד].

פס׳. ונפש כי תחטא ושמעה קול אלה וגו׳. שׁנו חכמים אין
אלה אלא שבועה, שׁנ׳

והשביע הכהן וגו׳ [1] (במ׳ ה׳, כ״א). בוא וראה דברים שאין האש שורפתן,
והן שבועות שקר מכלתן,

מאי טעמ[יה], הוצאתיה נאם י״י אלהים וגו׳ [2] (זכ׳ ה׳, ד׳). אמר ר׳ אבא
בר כהנא דרכה שלאש אוכלת עצים,

ומשארת אבנים, ברם הכא „וכלתו את עציו ואת אבניו״ (שם). וכת[יב]
שבועת י״י תהיה בין שנ[י הם]

(שמ׳ כ״ב, י׳),[4] לעולם, או הנשבע, אם נשבע, לשקר, או המשביע משביעו על
השם,[5] לכך

5 – [ועל כל עדת ישראל היה קצף].
6 אלא אשרי... וגו׳. המאמר מקוטע, ויש בו מעין הד של המשנה האחרונה
ביומא ושל ארבעה חלוקי כפרה של ר׳ ישמעאל (יומא פ״ו, ע״א).
7 לקוח מת״ב, וי׳, י״ב בסוף.

יד. מקורות: ספרא; וי״ר.
1 [את האשה בשבועת ה אל ה]. השווה ספרא ויקרא, פרק י״א (הוצ׳ וייס כ״ב, עמ׳ ג׳
ומסורת התלמוד שם); וי״ר ו׳, ה׳ (הוצ׳ מ. עמ׳ קל״ט והע׳ המו״ל).
2 [ובאה אל בית הגנב ואל בית הנשבע בשמי לשקר]. השווה למעלה, ח״א, עמ׳ ר״י.
מקבילות בהע׳ 559, וביחוד פ״ר (הוצ׳ איש־שלום, קי״ג וכו׳). עי׳ גם וי״ר ו׳, ג׳ (הוצ׳ מ. עמ׳
קל״ה, קל״ו).
3 למעלה בח״א הנז׳ הדרש הבא קודם למאמרו של ר׳ אבא בר כהנא.
4 מן המקבילות יוצא שההבלעה יש כאן, וצ״ל: ... שׁנ[יהם [אינה יוצאת מבין שניהם]
לעולם ...
5 נראה שצ״ל: „[אם] משביעו על ה ש ק ר ״ בהתאם למקבילות.

י"ב].

כמה

פעמים נ פ ש. תן דעתך שלא תחטא ראשונה, שלא תבוא לידי שנייה. ושמא
תאמר: הרי אני חוטא בסתר, מי יודע בי שאני חוטא, שנ׳ הנסתרות לי״י אלהינו
(דב׳ כ״ט, כ״ח), וכל החטאים שאתה עושה בסתר, גלוי וידוע לפני הקב״ה,
אין צריך לאמר מה

שאתה עושה בגלוי, אעפ״פ שאין אדם יודע שאת חוטא, הקב״ה יודע, שנ׳
אם יסתר איש במסתרים ואני לא אראנו וגו׳ (יר׳ כ״ג, כ״ד), וכתיב אין חושך
ואין צלמות

להסתיר שם וגו׳ (אי׳ ל״ד, כ״ב). ובשעה שאדם הולך לעשות עבירה, הוא
מתכון לעשות

בערב ואומר: אסתיר את עצמי שלא יראה אותי שום בריא [– בְּרִיָּה], שנ׳
בנשף בערב יום

באישון וגו׳ (מש׳ ז׳, ט׳), שמא מן הקב״ה יכול להסתר, שנ׳ בו ידע מה בחשוכה
וגו׳ (דנ׳ ב׳, כ״ב).[1]

י"ג].

אמרו

רבותינו ששה פעמים כת[ו]יב] בו נ פ ש כי תחטא, אמר ר׳ לוי[1] כנגד
ששת ימי

בראשית. אמר הקב״ה לנפש: לא הספיק לך כל מה שבראתי בששת ימי
(דף ל״ט, ע״ב) בראשית, אלא את שוגגת והולכת וחוטאת וגונבת וגוחלת בשביל
לאכל. הזהיר לנפש

שלא תחטא. אמר הקב״ה: שאמרתי לנפש, לכל ישראל אמרתי,[2] שאם חטא
אדם אחד

חטאו כולם, שנ׳ האיש אחד יחטא וגו׳[3] (במ׳ ט״ז, כ״ב), ללמדך שכל ישראל
ערבין זה[4] לזה, שכן אתה

יב. מקורות: מסופקני אם הפיסקה החדשה מתחילה כאן. נוטה אני לראות במשפט המסיים:
„עד שלא תבוא לידי שנייה" חתימתה של הפיסקה הקודמת שנושאה הוא „עברה גוררת עברה."
אולם נושא פיסקתנו הוא שאי אפשר לו לאדם להסתיר את עוונותיו. קשה לראות מה עניינו של
הנושא הזה לכאן, ובאמת אין למדרשנו מקביל לא בתנ׳ כאן ולא בוי״ר, אבל יש דוגמתו בת״ב
נשא ו׳, ח׳ ומקבילות. השווה גם ת״ב בשלח קרוב לסוף הפרשה.
1 רמז לב״ר א׳, ו׳: ידע מה בחשוכא, אלו מעשיהם של רשעים.

יג. מקורותיו: וי״ר ד׳, ב׳ (הוצ׳ מ. עמ׳ פ״ד); ות״ב וי׳ י״ב (הוצ׳ מ. עמ׳ צ״א).
1 בוי״ר: ר׳ יהושע דסכנין בשם ר׳ לוי. ועי׳ ח״נ והע׳ מרגליות.
2 כלומר, כל ישראל בכלל נפש. פרפרוה וביאור מאמרו של חזקיה בוי״ר ד׳, ו׳ בהתחלה.
3 [ועל כל העדה תקצף].
4 השווה סנה׳ כ״ז, ב׳ ושבועות ל״ט, א׳.

ביוד ואחד בהא, מה טעם כי ביה י"י צור עולמים (יש' כ"ו, ד'), אל תקרא
צור אלא צייר (דף ל"ט, ע"א)

ולא ידעינן איזה ביוד, ואי זה בהא, מה טעם כי ביה י"י צור העולמים,[3]
מה דכתיב אלה תולדות השמים והארץ בהבראם (בר' ב', ד'), בהא בראם,
העולם הזה בהא,

והעולם הבא ביוד,[4] מה כל האותיות תופסין את הלשון, והא אינו
תופס את הלשון, כך לא בעמל ולא ביגיעה ברא הקב"ה עולמו אלא
בדבר, שנ' בדבר י"י שמים נעשו וברוח וגו' (תה' ל"ג, ו'), לכך[5] דוד משבח
בשתיהן, הללויה,

ואוי להם לרשעים שמגדפין את השם, שכל מי שהוא מגדף את השם חייב
מיתה,[6] שנ' ונוקב שם י"י מות יומת (וי' כ"ד, ט"ז).

י"א].

ד"א נפש כי תחטא בשגגה. וזה גם בלא
דעת נפש לא טוב ואץ ברגלים חוטא. כך שנו חכמ'[1] שמצוה גוררת מצוה,
ועבירה גוררת עבירה. כך אמר שלמה צדקה תצור תם דרך וגו' (שם, י"ג, ו'),
כל מי
שהוא עושה צדקה אחת, זוכה לעשות צדקה הרבה, ורשעה תסלף [חטאת]
(שם), כיון שאדם
עושה רשעה אחת, גורם לעצמו לבוא לידי רשע אחר,[2] למה, שהעונות סמוכות
זו לזו, שנ' הוי מושכי העון בחבלי השוא וגו'[3] (יש' ה', י"ח), וכיון שאדם עושה
עון מושכין אחריו
עונות הרבה, עשויות כשלשלת שלמרגליות כיון שאדם נוטל אחד מהן נוטל
את כולן, למה, שהן [ובכת"י: שאין] חרוזות זו בזו. לפיכך כתיב כן (– כאן)
נפש כי תחטא וגו'.[4]

---

[3] שיגרת הקולמוס מן השורה שלמעלה, וצריך למחוק.

[4] עד כאן לקוח מירושלמי הנרשם; מכאן עד "בדבר ה' שמים נעשו," נמצא בב"ר הנ',
אלא שיש לנו כאן דילוג מתוך הבלעה בראש, וצריך להשלים: [ולמה נברא העוה"ז בה"א
והעוה"ב ביוד], מה כל האותיות וכו'.

[5] חזר להעתיק מן הירושלמי.

[6] ת"ב וי' ט"ו: אבל המגדף נוטל אפופסין, שנ' ונוקב ... עי' בובר, הע' ס"ח.

יא. מקורות: אבות פ"ד, ב'; ת"ב וי', י'; תצא, א' ומקבילות; ירושלמי קידושין, סוף פ' א';
ספרי במדבר, פיס' קי"ב (הוצ' איש־שלום, ל"ג, ע"א, ד"ה והנפש).

[1] ת"ב: שנו רבותינו.

[2] השווה מאמר ר' ירמיה בשם שמואל בר רב יצחק, בירושלמי קידושין הנז': "שמר אדם
את עצמו מן העבירה פעם ראשונה ושנייה מכן ואילך הקב"ה משמרו."

[3] ספרי הנז'. גם שם נסמך המאמר מצוה גוררת מצוה לפש' ה', י"ח. וע" "מאיר עין" שם.

[4] [בשגגה מכל מצות ה'... ועשה אחת מהנה]. וכנראה שדרש כי אם עשתה "אחת
מהנה", סופה של הנפש לחטוא בכל מצות ה'.

וידוע לפני הקב̇ה שהמלח, שהביאה אותה אלמנה, חביב עליו יותר מן השור
שהבי

א עשיר, הקב̇ה בוחן לבבות וכליות, אמר להן: ו כ ל ק ר ב ן מ נ ח ת ך
ב מ ל ח ת מ ל ח ו ג ו'
(שם, ב', י̇ג), ולא הביאו עמם מלח, כלום אמרו: יש אדם שעמו מלח, באותה
שעה שמחה

אותה אלמנה ונתנה הודאה לפני השם, והועלה שורו שלעשיר במלח שהביאה
אותה האלמנה, ונתרצו שניהן.[6] כך הקב̇ה עתיד לרצות מנחת יהודה וירשלם,
שנ̇ וערבה לי̇י מנחת יהודה וגו' (מלא' ג', ד').

[לסדר ע̇ה (ב'): ויקרא ד', א'–ב'.]

[י'.]

פס'. נ פ ש כ י ת ח ט א ב ש ג ג ה. זש̇ה א ל ת ב ה ל
ע ל פ י ך ו ל ב ך א ל י מ ה ר ו ג ו' (קה' ה', א'). אמר ר יהושע אוי לו[1] לאדם שהוא
מגדף לפני הקב̇ה,

בוא וראה,[2] כשנבראו העליונים והתחתונים, בחצי השם נבראו שני עולמות, אחד

6 השווה וי̇ר ג', ה' (הוצ' מ. עמ' ס̇ו–ס̇ח. מקבילות בהע'). כמעט כל הפיסקה באה
להבליט חשיבותו של קרבן עני על ידי ספורים שונים. בשנים מהם באים לידי ביטוי מוטיבים
המשמשים יסוד למדרשנו. א', ספור על שור, קרבן עשיר, שאי אפשר היה למשכו למקום
הקרבתו עד שבא עני ואגודת ירק בידו ,ונמשך השור לקרבן.' אותו המוטיב חוזר במדרשנו. אי
אפשר היה להקריב את השור, קרבנו של העשיר, אלא על ידי המלח של האלמנה העניה.
ב', אשה אחת שהביאה קומץ אחד של סולת' והייה ,הכהן מבזה אותה עליה.' יחס הבוז של
הכהן לקרבן של אשה ענייה בא לידי ביטוי גם במדרשנו: ,והיתה מתביישת לומר
לכהן קח נא את ברכתי מידי . . .' אבל עניין המלח חסר בוי̇ר. ואולי נוסחת בעל
מדרשנו בוי̇ר היתה: מעשה באשה אחת שהביאה קומץ אחד של מ ל ח במקום ש ל ס ו ל ת,
ועל ידי כך ניתנה לו ההזדמנות לשלב שני המוטיבים בסיפור אחד.
אם נקבל נוסחא זאת תסתלק תמיהתו של מרגליות: ,והרי אין מנחה באה פחות מעשרון,'
כי אין כאן המדובר במנחה. אולם בשו̇ט כ̇ב, ל̇א הנוסחה: ,קומץ אחד של סולת ל ה ק ר י ב
מ נ ח ה.'

י. מקורות: ת̇ב וי̇, י̇ג (עמ' 3), תנ' ז'; ירושלמי חגיגה פ̇ב, א' (דף ע̇ז, 3), ב̇ר פי̇ב, י'.
1 תנ': ,א ל ו בני אדם שמחרפין שמו של הקב̇ה', בלי שם הדרשן. בעל מדרשנו מסר
כאן, כנראה, שמו של בעל המאמר הבא אחר כך. עי' בהע' הבאה.
2 בניגוד לדרכו של בעל מדרשנו לקצר, כאן להיפך הוא משלים את הרמז שבתל̇ על
יצירת העולם בחצי השם. מביא הוא את המאמר בשלימותו בעיקר מן הירושלמי הנז', ואף גם
משלימו מב̇ר הנז'. הדרש הזה מובא בירושלמי בשם ,ר' אבהו אמר ר' יוחנן,' ובבבלי
מנחות כ̇ט, ע̇ב בשם ר' יהודה בר ר' אילעאי. כנראה שהמאמר נמסר בשם ר' י,
ובעל מדרשנו שחיבה יתרה נודעה לו לשמו של ר' יהושע (עי' הע' 100), פתר את ראשי
התבות: ר' יהושע. מכאן השם שבראש הסעיף.

בת פרעה, לפיכך ותקרא שמו משה (שמ' ב', י'), לפיכך ויקרא אל
מ ש ה. אשרי משה שכל
ישראל עומדין, וכהנים ולוים עומדין, ולא נדבר עם אחר אלא עם משה, שנ׳
ו י ד ב ר י׳ י א ל י ו.

ט׳[.]

מאי דכתי[ב] כי אני י׳י אוהב משפט שונא גזל בעולה וגו׳ (יש׳ ס״א, ח'). למה
קרבן בה[1]
בהמה נאמר בו קרבו וכרעיו (וי׳ א', ט'),[2] ובעוף והסיר את מראתו
(שם, ט״ז). לפי שהבהמה בעלה מב
מביא לה מי מאכל והיא אוכלת, והעוף פורח ואוכל מזה ומזה, גזל, לפיכך משליך
קרקבן[3] שלה. אמרו חכמים[4] העשיר בשורו, עני בתורו, יתום בביצתו, אלמנה
בתרנגלתה.[4]
אמר ר׳ יצחק בו (=בוא) וראה מעכשיו שהקב׳ה אינו מקפיח שכר בריה,[5]
כשצוה על הקרבנות,
הלך כל אחד והביא קרבנו, היתה אלמנה אחת, לא היה אצלה אלא [בכת״י
אלה] רובע מלח, נטלתו
בבגדה והביאתו, והיתה מתביישת לומר לכהן: קח נא את ברכתי מידי, גלוי

כדאי להעיר שגם ביחסו השלילי לשאול (עי׳ למעלה סעיף ג', הע' 2) בעל מדרשנו הולך
בעקבותיו של המיוחס לידידיה האלכסנדרוני. עי׳ מאמרו המעניין של א. שפירא: „שאול
שבמיוחס לידידיה ומשיח בן אפרים בספרות הרבנית", ‏*Proceedings of the American*
Academy for Jewish Research, vol. XXI (1952), 119 ff.

ט. מקורות: וי״ר ג', ד'; ג', ה' (הוצ׳ מ. עמ' 64—68). המקבילות בהערות המו״ל.

1 בוי״ר ג', ד' הובא המאמר בשינוי לשון בשם ר' תנחום בר חנילאי ובלי קשר עם יש׳
ס״א, ח'; בלק״ט משולב הפסוק במאמרו של ר' תנחום, וכמו כן במדרש אגדה במקומו (ח״ב,
עמ' ו').

2 הכוונה לסוף הפסוק: והקטיר הכהן את הכל המזבחה. בוי״ר מובא: והקריב הכהן את
הכל המזבחה, וכל המפרשים מראים מקום לוי׳ א', י״ג ומוכרחים הם להוסיף בסוגריים
„והקטיר" לפני „המזבחה". יותר נראה שגם בוי״ר הכוונה לפסוק ט', אלא שאיזה מעתיק טעה
וכתב והקריב במקום והקטיר.

3 זפק בוי״ר.

4 השווה פסחים קי״ח, ע״א: „א׳ר חסדא (קרי: ר' יהושע בן לוי) מאי דכתיב הודו לה'
כי טוב, הודו לו׳ למי שגובה חובתו של אדם בטובתו, עשיר בשורו, ע נ י ב ש י ו, יתום בביצתו,
אלמנה בתרנגלתה." עי׳ מ׳ט קל״ו, א' הערת בובר. בעל מדרשנו רואה בזה מעין ניסוח מיוחד
של מאמר המשנה האחרונה במנחות: „נאמר ב ע ו ל ת ב ה מ ה...ו ב ע ו ל ת ע ו ף...
ללמד שאחד המרבה ואחד הממעיט וכו'." „עשיר בשורו" – עולת בהמה; „עני בתורו" –
עולת העוף, ת ו ר י ם ובני יונה. נכונה הערתו של מחברנו שכאן מתחילה פיסקה חדשה הדנה
בחשיבותו של קרבן עני, שהיא גם הנושא של וי״ר ג', ה'.

5 השווה ב״ק ל״ח, ע״ב מאמר ר' חייא בר אבא בשם ר' יוחנן.

ביותר, אמר: זה לא יגעתי בו מקטנותו, בא אלי להיות עם צאני, אף אני
אהבבהו.[2] כך גירי הצדק, אמר הקב״ה: בשביל שחסה בצלי, כאזרח מכם יהיה
לכם וגו׳ (וי׳ י״ט, ל״ד). צא ולמד מבתיה בת פרעה שגדלה את משה, ונקרא
על שמה,

שנ׳ ואשתו היהודית ילדה את ירד אבי גדור ואת חבר אביסוכו ואת יקותיאל
(דף ל״ח, ע״ב) אבי זנוח א ל ה בני בתיה בת פרעה (דה״א, ד׳, י״ח), והלא
יוכבד ילדה אותו, ללמדך שכל מי

שמכניס תלמיד ח כ ם (יה) לתוך ביתו, ומאכילו ומשקהו, מעלה עליו הכתוב
כאלו ילדו,[3]

שנ׳ א ל ה תולדות אהרן ומשה (במ׳ ג׳, א׳), וסמיך ליה ואלה שמות בני
אהרן (שם, כ׳), אהרן ילד,[4]

ומשה גדל, לפיכ[ך] נקראו על שמו, וכיוצא בדבר בתיה בת פרעה, שנ׳ ויגדל
הילד

ותביאהו לבת פרעה (שמ׳ ב׳, י׳).

ח.[׳]

עשר שמות נקראו לו: ירד, אבי גדור, חבר, אבי סוכו, מלכיה[5] בן נתנאל,
טוב, עניו, משה, וכולם לא קרא אותו אלא בשם שקראה אותו בתיה

2 המשל הזה נמצא, בשינוי לשון ובהרחבת דברים, בבמ״ר פרשה ח׳, ב׳ ובמ״ת קמ״ו, ח׳.
במקבילות: ה צ א ן כ ך ה י א ד ר כ ה . . . . אבל הצבי . . . אין דרכו ליכנס לישוב . . .
וזה הצבי נכנס וישב אצלנו . . . משנת ר״א.
3 השווה מגילה י״ג, א׳ וסנהדרין י״ט, ב׳. ר׳ יוחנן מוציא מכאן ש.כל ה מ ג ד ל ל י ת ו ם
ב ת ו ך ב י ת ו כאילו ילדו."
4 השווה סנהדרין, שם. ר׳ שמואל בר נחמני בשם ר׳ יונתן מוציא מכתוב זה שכל המלמד
בן חברו תורה כאילו ילדו, ונוסחו: .אהרן ילד ומשה ל י מ ד."

ח. מקורות: וי״ר א׳, ג׳ (הוצ׳ מ. עמ׳ ז׳ וכו׳, המקבילות בהערות).
המאמר כאן יש לו שנויים חשובים, אבל קודם כל צריך תיקון. קרוב לשער שיש כאן
דילוג, כי כשאתה מונה את השמות אין אתה מוצא אלא שמונה. ובאמת חסרים שני שמות
שנמצאים ברוב המקורות, והם יקותיאל ואבי זנוח. שניהם מפורשים בדה״י א, ד׳, י״ח שהוא היסוד
לכל המאמר. מצד אחר הכניס בעל מדרשנו שני שמות החסרים בשאר מקורות עבריים
הידועים לי, והם מלכיה וטוב, ועו. אני משער שבהתאם עם מקורות אחדים, הנזכרים בהע׳ מרליות
הנ״ל, היסס מחברנו למנות אבי זנוח בין שמותיו של משה, ומנה את .יקותיאל אבי זנוח" לשם
אחד. באופן זה מצא מקום בפסוק הנ׳ רק חמשה שמות: ירד, אבי גדור, חבר, אבי סוכו ניקותיאל
אבי זנוח]. צירף להם: מלכיה, [שמעיה] בן נתנאל, טוב, עניו, משה. שמעיה בן נתנאל נמצא
גם בשאר המקורות; טוב אינו אלא .טוביה." .טוביה" הנז׳ בוי״ר אלא שמדרשנו הולך בשיטתו של ר׳ מאיר
(השווה סוטה י״ב, א׳). כדי להשלים את המספר הוסיף ר׳ יהושע בן לוי את השם .לוי.׳ בעל
מדרשנו הטיב לראות בזה מעין .לוי מסייע לוי," ועל כן הכניס במקומו .ענו׳ עפ״י בם׳ י״ב, ג׳.
עדיין נשאר לו למלאות את השם .אבי זנוח" שהוציא מן המנין, הלך והכניס במקומו .מלכיה׳
שאמנם חדש הוא במסורת העברית, אבל אנו מוצאים דוגמתו, מ ל כ י א ל, אצל המיוחס
לידידיה האלכסנדרוני ואצל קלמנס האלכסנדרוני. עי׳ אגדות היהודים לר״ל גינצברג, חלק ה׳,
עמ׳ 400 ודר׳ שאול ליברמן במאמרו .חזנות יניי,״ ס י נ י כרך ד׳, עמ׳ רל״ב.

ה'.

ד"א ויקרא אל משה. ולמה קרא אותו ואחר כך דבר אליו, ללמדך
דרך ארץ, מלמד שכל מי שהוא מבקש לדבר עם חבירו דבר, לא דרך ארץ
היא

להרים קולו, אלא יקראהו ואחר כך ידבר אליו בצנעה, כך עשה הקב"ה, קרא
למשה תחלה ואחר כל דבר אליו, שנ' ויקרא אל משה וידבר.

ו'.

אמר ר' שמואל

בן נחמן[1] בוא וראה כמה בין קריאת נביאי ישראל לקריאת נביאי אומות העו
[לם]. במשה כת[י]ב[2] ויקרא אל משה, קריאה שלמה. בבלעם כתיב ויקר
אלהים אל בלעם (במ' כ"ג, ד')[2],

קריאה כפולה. בשעה שהתחיל משה את המשכן והקימו על כנו, פרס עליו
כרים וכסתות, ואמר משה: עכשו נחתי, ששלמתי מעשה משכן. עתה היא
תחלת מעשה משכן, לפיכך קרא לו, שנ' כי ענן י"י על המשכן יומם (שמ'
מ', ל"ח),[3] וסמיך

ליה ויקרא אל משה.

ז'.

אמר ר' אלכסנדרי[1] כמה חביבין הגרים לפני הקב"ה שצוה
עליהם במ"ח מקומות. משל לצבי שנכנס לתוך עדרו שלרועה, כמה חיבבו

ה. מקורות: יומא ד', ע"ב: "הקדים קריאה לדיבור, ללמדך דרך ארץ שלא ידבר אדם
לחברו אלא אם כן קורהו," ומובא בילקוט סימן תכ"ט. בניגוד לדרכו לקצר ולמסור רק ראשי
פרקים של המדרשים, הדרשן כאן מרחיב ומבאר את המקור. נראה שהמאמר הלקוח מתלמוד
בבלי היה בלתי ידוע בחוג המאסף, שהוא בעיקר ממדרשי א"י, וראה צורך לבארו.

ו. מקורות: וי"ר א', י"ג (הוצ' מ. עמ' כ"ח. המקבילות שם בהערות). הסעיף הוא, כנראה,
מקוטע ומסורס.

1 בוי"ר הוא בשם ר' חמא בר חנינא.

2 כנראה יש כאן דילוג של שתי תיבות. בהתאם למקור הנז' צריך להיות: "בבלעם כתיב
ויקר אלהים אל בלעם [חצי קריאה]" מתאים ל"חצי דיבור' במקור. אחר כך מתחיל דרש
חדש: "קריאה כפולה," כלומר מה טעמו של כפל לשון ויקרא . . . וידבר וכו'. התשובה
מכילה מעין ניסוח חדש של המדרש שבסעיף ג' (ת"ב א', ד'), והוא שלאחר שנגמר משה את
מלאכת המשכן אמר "עכשיו נחתי" (– מה יש לי לעשות), וה' "זרזו ואמר לו: עכשיו היא
תחילת מעשה [עבודת] המשכן, כלומר "סדר הקרבנות."

3 גם כאן יש לנו כנראה דרש נפרד שאינו אלא כפל עניין של סוף עניין ב', הבא לקשור
את סדרנו עם ה"כתוב למעלה מן העניין". השווה תרגום יונתן ותרגום ירושלמי.

ז. מקורותיו: תנ' וי' א', ב' (ת"ב א', ג'); וי"ר א', ג' (הוצ' מ. עמ' ז'–י"ג).

1 בת"ב בשם ר' יהודה בר שלום. המקבילות, ת"ב ג', הע' כ"ז. השווה מכילתא משפטים
פי"ח: "חביבין הגרים שבכל מקום הוא מזהיר עליהם."

(שמ׳ ל״ד, כ״ט). בעולם הזה עילהו הקב״ה, שנ׳ ולא קם נביא עוד בישראל
כמשה וגו׳ (דב׳ ל״ד, י׳), אף לעולם הבא
הוא בראש כל הצדיקים והנביאים, שנ׳ ויתא ראשי עם (שם, ל״ג, כ״א).

ד׳.

פס. ויקרא אל

מ ש ה. זשה׳ מקים דבר עבדו ועצת מלאכיו וגו׳ (יש׳ מ״ד, כ״ז). אמר ר׳
יהושע בן לוי[1]
בשעה שאמר הקב״ה למשה סדר הקרבנות שיהו ישראל מקריבין ויכפר להם,
והיה משה מצטער על הדבר שנ׳ איכה אשא לבדי (דב׳ א׳, י״ב), אמר לפני
הקב״ה: מדוע לא
מצאתי חן בעיניך[2] (במ׳ י״א, י״א), אמר לו: אספה לי שבעים איש מזקני וגו׳
(שם, ט״ז), ואומר ואצלתי מן
הרוח וגו׳ (שם, י״ז), תאמר חסרה נבואתו שלמשה כלום, לא, משל לנר ערוך
והדליקו ממנו
ע׳ נירות.[3] ספרי במדבר, בהעלותך, צ״ג (הוצ׳ איש שלום, כ״ה, ע״ב).

ד. הסעיף הזה נראה כאילו הוא מקוטע וחוץ למקומו. יש׳ מ״ד, כ״ז אמנם נדרש על משה
ומשמש פתיחה לסדר נ״ד במדרשנו (עי׳ ח״א, עמ׳ רכ״א, הע׳ 675), אבל בלי שום קשר עם
סדר קרבנות. לדעת המחבר (למעלה עמ׳ 8) עיקר הדרש חסר, וכנראה שסוֹבר שמאמר
ריב״ל הבא אחר הפתיחה אין לו שייכות לה.
אני משער שיש כאן הרחבה מלאכותית של הדרש שלפני זה. שם מובע הרעיון כי כשנגמרה
מלאכת המשכן חשב משה שהוא יכול "לעמוד" ולנוח, אבל ה׳ זירזו כי עדיין תפקיד גדול מוטל
עליו "ללמד לישראל סדר הקרבנות היאך יהיו מקריבים." הדרשן הוסיף נופך: "ויכפר להם,"
ועל ידי כך קבע קשר עם דב׳ א׳, י״ב: "איכה א ש א לבדי טרחכם ו מ ש א כ ם ... כאילו
סירב משה להיות הוא לבדו מלמד את ישראל סדר קרבנות "לכפר עליהם" (לשאת טרחם).
וכמו כן הסב את תלונתו של משה בבמ׳ י״א, י״א: "לשום את מ ש א כל העם עלי" על
לימוד סדר הקרבנות עם העם. לפי זה דרש מאת ה׳ להעמיד מורים אחרים, זקנים ללמד לעם
סדר הקרבנות. ה׳ אמנם תיכף נאות לשאלתו ואמר לו "אספה לי שבעים איש." הדרשן ביאר
"ועצת מלאכיו ישלים," זה משה, שנ׳ אספה לי וכו׳. אולם בכל זאת הדיבור בא רק למשה
וכולם ניהנו מאורו, וזהו "מקים דבר עבדו," זה משה. ויקרא אל משה וידבר ה׳ אליו.
וכדאי להעיר לפירושו של הרמב״ן על הפסוק דב׳ א׳, י״ב לא רחוק הוא מפי׳ מדרשנו
ז״ל: "... אמר טרחכם כנגד והודעת את חוקי האלהים ... כי טורח גדול היה ללמד
ליוצאי מצרים החוקים והתורות."

1 שמו של ר׳ יהושע בן לוי חשוד בעיני, השווה הסעי׳ הקודם.
2 בכתוב: ולמה לא מצאתי ... לשום את משא כל העם עלי.
3 השווה ספרי במדבר, פיס׳ צ״ג (הוצ׳ איש־שלום, דף כ״ה, ב׳) ומ״א, ח״ב, עמ׳ ק״א.
מקבילות, בובר, הע׳ כ״ו. ויש להוסיף ראב״ע בפירושו: "והמשל בנר."

.['ג]

זשה גאות אדם תשפילנו (מש' כ"ט, כ"ג). אמר ר' שמואל[1] כל מי
שהוא רודף אחר השררה, השררה בורחת ממנו. דוד ברח מן השררה, שנ'
מי אנכי י"י

אלהים וגו' (ש"ב, ז', י"ח), והיתה השררה רודפת אחריו, שנ' ועש לך שם
גדול כשם הגדולים

אשר בארץ (שם, ט').[2] אבל אבימלך בן ירובעל, על שרדף אחר השררה,
ברחה ממנו, שנ'

וישלח אלהים רוח רעה בין אבימלך ובין בעלי שכם וגו' (שו' ט', כ"ג).
ומשה ברח מן השררה,

שנ' שלח נא ביד תשלח (שמ' ד', י"ג), ולבסוף הלך למצרים, ועשה אותות
בה, והוציא את ישראל,

וקרע להם את הים, והוריד להם את המן, והגיז להם את השליו, והוציא
להם מים

מן הסלע. אמר: מיכן ואילך מה יש לי לעשות. אמר לו הקב"ה: עוד יש
ל ך מלאכה ללמד

לישראל טומאה וטהרה, וללמדם סדר הקרבנות היאך יהיו מקריבין, שנ'
אדם כי יקריב

מכם קרבן וגו', פס'[3] ואם מן הצאן קרבנו וגו', ואם מן העוף, וכי תקריב קרבן
מנחה

לי"י (דף ל"ח, ע"א) וגו' וזאת תורת זבח השלמים וגו' (וי' א', ב', י', י"ד;
ב', א'; ז', י"א). ברח מן השררה, והיא רדפה אחריו, לקיים

מה שנ' ושפל רוח יתמוך כבוד (מש' כ"ט, כ"ג), זה משה, ומשה לא ידע כי
קרן עור פניו וגו'[4]

ג. הקבלתו: ת"ה וי' א', ג'; ת"ב א', ד'. בדרך כלל מתאים מדרשנו עם נוסחת ת"ה.
1 קרוב לשער שהכוונה לר' שמואל בר' נחמן, הדרשן הידוע. השם חסר בשאר המקורות,
ושמותיו של בעל מדרשנו חשודים קצת (עי' הערתנו לסעיף הקודם). אולם כדאי לציין שדברי
ר' לוי המובאים באמצע הפיסקה בשאר המקורות מיוחסים באמצע במדרש חזית לר'
ש מ ו א ל ב ר נ ח מ ן (עי' בובר הע' ל"ה).
2 במקבילות: „שאול ברח מן השררה . . .". חלופי־גברא של דוד במקום שאול מעניינים
למדי. בחוני האמוראים התהלכו, דיעות מתנגדות בנוגע לשאול. יש שהדגישו את חסרונותיו,
ותלו את עלייתו לגדולה בזכות זקנו (וי"ר ט', ג' ומקבילות), ויש שהדגישו את מעלותיו, וביחוד
מדת הענוויות וההצניעות שהיתה בו (יומא כ"ב, ב'). עי' „אגדות היהודים" לר"ל גינצברג, כרך
ו', הע' 79–80, עמ' 238. בעל מדרשנו, או המקור שממנו שאב, שייך היה כנראה לחוג הראשון,
ואי אפשר היה לו להעמיד את שאול במחיצתו של משה. הוציא את שאול והכניס את דוד
במקומו.
3 כנראה ט"ס וצריך למוחקה.
4 אינני יודע מה עניינו של הפסוק הזה לכאן. במקבילות מובא הפסוק „ותחסרהו מעט
מאלהים ו כ ב ו ד והדר תעטרהו (תה' ח', ו')" הקבלה ל„יתמוך כבוד".

תאמר שהיו ישראל שומעין הקול, ת״ל ו י ש מ ע, הוא היה שומע את הקול
לעצמו וכן נאמ

מאוהל מועד לאמר (וי׳ א׳, א׳) מלמד שהקול נפסק ולא היה יוצא חוץ
לאוהל.6 אמר ר׳ יהודה7

גזר הקב״ה לקול שהוא יוצא והולך אל משה בלבד, והוא היה שומע לעצמו.
אמר ר׳ ברכיה

הכהן8 ראה מה כתיב לעשות לרוח משקל וגו׳ (אי׳ כ״ח, כ״ה), על כל דבר
ודבר עושה הקב״ה משקל,

ומים תיכן במדה (שם), וכן הוא אומר הנותן מטר על פני [ה]ארץ וגו׳ (שם,
ה׳, י׳),9 מלמד שעשה הקב״ה דרך לקול

שיהא הולך אצל משה בלבד. לכך נאמ ו י ק ר א א ל מ ש ה, למשה
היה מדבר,

ולא היה אחר שומע.

ב׳.

אמר ר׳ יהושע ומה היה צריך לקרות אותו,1 אלא תסתכל מה למעלה ממנו,
ואתה יודע על מה קראו, [שהכתוב אומר דרשו מעל ספר י׳י וקראו וגו׳
(יש׳ ל״ד, ט״ז), כשם שההרים

מיוסדים זה על זה, כן הפרשיות שבתורה מיוסדות זו למעלה מזו,[2 ומה
למעלה מן

הספר הזה, ולא יכול משה לבוא אל אוהל מועד וגו׳ (שמ׳ מ׳, ל״ח), וכיון
שראה הקב״ה שאינו יכול לבוא, קרא אותו דכת ו י ק ר א א ל מ ש ה.

<hr>

6 זה נוסף מספרא, פ״ב, י׳ בסוף.
7 שם הדרשן חסר בשאר המקורות.
8 גם כאן חסר השם בשאר המקורות.
9 יש להוסיף: ודרך לחזיז קולות כמו שהוא בשאר המקורות.

ב. הקבלת הסעיף בת״ה. בשתי ההוצאות הראשונות בהתחלה, ובמאוחרות בתחילת סימן ח׳.
כידוע כל הסימן הוא מאיזה דרשן מאוחר שהשתמש בדברי הרמב״ם ורבינו סעדיה גאון
(עי׳ בובר, מבוא, עמ׳ ס״ב, רייפמאן, בית תלמוד, ג׳, 183). מקורו של הדרש שלנו הוא כנראה
הרעב״ע בפירושו: הטעם ויקרא אל משה אחר ולא יכול משה.״ ועי׳ גם פירושו לש׳ מ׳, ל״ה.
גם הרמב״ן בפירושו לשני הפסוקים מדניש את הקשר שביניהם מבלי להזכיר שום מדרש.
1 שם הדרשן נפקד במקביל, וספק גדול הוא אם זהו שם בדוי.
2 הכנסתי את המאמר הזה בסוגריים, כי הוא בא רק לבסס את דרך הדרש הידוע בשם
מה כתוב למעלה מן העניין,״ ומפסיק בין השאלה והתשובה. דרש דומה לזה נמצא בוי״ר
כ״ה, ח׳, ועי׳ למעלה בגוף הספר עמ׳ 234.

ויקרא

[לסדר ע״ד (א׳): ויקרא א׳, א׳.]

א׳.

פ' ו י ק ר א.   זש״ה ברכו י״י מלאכיו
גבורי כח עושי דברו וגו' (תה' ק״ג, כ׳).   אשרי הצדיקים שהקֹבֹה
הקריבן ונתן להם כח לעמוד בדרכיו,[1]
שכן אתה מוצא כיון שעמדו ישראל על
הר סיני ושמעו קול הדיבור הראשון, נתיראו והרתיעו לאחוריהֹם י״ב מיל,
שֹ וירא העם וינעו ויעמדו וגו' (שמ' כ', י״ח),[2] ואמרו למשה דבר אתה עמנו
ונשמעה וגו'
(שם, י״ט), (דף ל״ז, ע״ב) וכן עשה משה, ויעמד העם מרחוק (שם, כ״א),
לפיכך כיון שעמד משה,[3] לא קראֹ אלא למשה שהוא
יכול לעמוד, לקיים מה שֹ גבורי כח עושי דברו וגו'. תאמר שהיה מדבר
בקול נמוך,
בשביל כך משה ע מ ד,[4] ת״ל וישמע את הקול מדבר אליו (במ' ז', פ״ט),
אי זה קול, אותו הקול שֹ במתן
תורה, קול י״י בכח וגו' (תה' כ״ט, ד'), אשר   ב ו   היה מדבר עם משה על
כל דיבור ודיבור ואמירה   ו צ י ו ו י,[5]

א. הפתיחה משותפת לוי״ר (א׳, א׳) ולתנחומא (א׳, א׳).   בשניהם נזכר ר' תנחום בן חנילאי
בקשר עם הדרש שבסעיף זה.   מדרשנו הוא בעיקר קיצור מן התנחומא – שבה פתיחתנו באה
בהרחבת עניין – בהוספת נופכים מן המכילתא והספרא.   המקבילות אצל בובר ומרגליות.
[1] יש כאן מעין הד הפתיחה לסדר ע״ח (להלן עמ' כט): "אשרי כל מי שבחר בו
הקב״ה . . .," המוסב על אהרן, וכאן על משה.
[2] מכילתא יתרו פ״ט (הוצ' וייס, עמ' 79), שבת פ״ח, ע״ב.   בהתאם לדרש זה מדרשנו חזר
ושונה שבחו וגבורתו של משה בא לידי ביטוי   ב ע מ י ד ה, לא הרתיע לאחוריו כי אם   ע מ ד
ב מ ק ו מ ו.   שאר המקורות מבססים את גבורתו של משה בניגוד לחולשתם של ישראל על
הפסוק "אם יוספים אנחנו   ל ש מ ו ע . . ." ומתנו' (דב' ה', כ״ב), ולפיכך מעמידים את כחו
של משה על   ה ש מ י ע ה.
[3] מקבילו במ״א (ח״ב, עמ' ד'): "כיון שעמד   ה מ ש כ ן' נראה יותר נכון.
[4] שאר המקורות: לפיכך היה יכול   ל ש מ ו ע.
[5] "בו' . . . , "וצווי".   מתאים לנוסחת תנחומא הנד'.   השווה בובר, העֹ י״ב, י״ג.

המספרים של העמודים בחלק העברי הם באותיות עבריות, ושל גוף הספר בסימנים הרגילים.

תודתנו נתונה בזה להרב ישכר דוב קאלכמאן מסינסינטי שעבר על החלקים העבריים בעיון רב ותיקן כמה שגיאות ושבושים בהעתקות מכתבי היד ובעלי ההגהה.

וגם למר דוד סקאראטון, עמוד הימיני של דר. י'עקב'ס, ולדר. מנחם ג. גלען ולמר יצחק הופמאן אנחנו מביעים את תודתנו בעד עבודתם המסורה והחרוצה בקשר עם הוצאת הספר הזה.

לוח הקיצורים

בציטטים מתנ״ך השתמשתי בקיצורים אלה:

שה״ש=שיר השירים	מי׳=מיכה	מ״א=מלכים א׳	בר׳=בראשית
קה׳=קהלת	נח׳=נחום	מ״ב=מלכים ב׳	שמ׳=שמות
אס׳=אסתר	חב׳=חבקוק	יש׳=ישעיה	וי׳=ויקרא
דנ׳=דניאל	צפ׳=צפניה	יר׳=ירמיה	במ׳=במדבר
עז׳=עזרא	זכ׳=זכריה	יח׳=יחזקאל	דב׳=דברים
נחמ׳=נחמיה	מלא׳=מלאכי	הו׳=הושע	יה׳=יהושע
דה״א=דברי הימים א׳	תה׳=תהלים	יו׳=יואל	שו׳=שופטים
דה״ב=דברי הימים ב׳	מש׳=משלי	עמ׳=עמוס	ש״א=שמואל א׳
	אי׳=איוב	עו׳=עובדיה	ש״ב=שמואל ב׳

אין קיצורים בציטטים מיונה, חגי, רות, ואיכה.

ואלה הם ראשי תיבות כפי הא״ב, וגם קיצורים אחרים:

ילה״מ=ילקוט המכירי.	אג״ב=אגדת בראשית, הוצ׳ באבער.
יל״ש=ילקוט שמעוני.	אדר׳״נ=אבות דרבי נתן, הוצ׳ שעכטער.
ילת״ת=ילקוט תלמוד תורה.	אהצ״ו=אהבת ציון וירושלים.
ל״י=לשון יחיד.	או״מ=אוצר מדרשים, הוצ׳ ווערטהיימער.
למ״א=לקוטים ממדרש אבכיר, הוצ׳	אי״ר=איכה רבתי.
באבער,	ב״מ=בתי מדרשות, הוצ׳ הנ״ל.
לק״ט=לקח טוב.	בה״מ=בית המדרש, הוצ׳ יעלינעק.
ל״ר=לשון רבים.	במ״ר=במדבר רבא.
מ׳=משנה.	ב״ר=בראשית רבא.
מ״א=מדרש אגדה, הוצ׳ הנ״ל.	גז״ש=גנזי שעכטער.
מא״ש=מאיר איש שלום.	ד״ס=דקדוקי סופרים.
מה״ג=מדרש הגדול; א׳ =לבראשית, הוצ׳	ד״ר=דברים רבא.
שעכטער; ב׳ =לשמות, הוצ׳ האפפמאנן	הו״ב=הוצ׳ באבער.
(עד פ׳ יתרו, והנשאר מכ״י בספריה	הו״ה=הוצ׳ הארואוויטץ (של ספרי,
של הסמינריון בניו־יורק); ג׳ =לויקרא,	במדבר).
הוצ׳ ראבינאוויץ; ד׳ =לבמדבר (מכ״י	הוה״ר=הוצ׳ הארואוויטץ־רבין (של
בספריה הנ״ל); ה׳ =לדברים (מכ״י	מכילתא).
בספריה הנ״ל).	הות״א=הוצ׳ תיאודור־אלבעק (של ב״ר).
מכדרשב״י=מכילתא דרבי שמעון בן יוחאי	וי״ר=ויקרא רבא.
(הוצ׳ האפפמאנן).	וש״נ=ושם נסמן.
מ״ת=מדרש תהלים, הוצ׳ באבער.	הע׳ =הערה.